INTERNATIONAL BUSINESS
AN ASIA PACIFIC PERSPECTIVE

Andrew Delios
and
Paul W. Beamish

PEARSON
Prentice
Hall

Singapore   London   New York   Toronto   Sydney   Tokyo   Madrid
Mexico City   Munich   Paris   Capetown   Hong Kong   Montreal

Published in 2004 by
Prentice Hall
Pearson Education South Asia Pte Ltd
23/25 First Lok Yang Road, Jurong
Singapore 629733

Pearson Education offices in Asia: *Bangkok, Beijing, Hong Kong, Jakarta, Kuala Lumpur, Manila, New Delhi, Seoul, Singapore, Shanghai, Taipei, Tokyo*

Printed in Singapore

4   3   2
07   06   05   04

ISBN 013-127-533-X

table of contents

about the authors

Andrew Delios is an Associate Professor in the Department of Business Policy, NUS Business School, National University of Singapore. Andrew Delios is the chief editor of *Asia Pacific Journal of Management*. He is an author or co-author of five books and more than 40 published journal articles, case studies and book chapters. His articles have appeared in *Academy of Management Journal*, *Administrative Science Quarterly*, *Asia Pacific Journal of Management*, *Strategic Management Journal*, *Journal of International Business Studies*, *Journal of World Business* and *Asian Case Research Journal*. His research has received awards from the *Administrative Science Association of Canada* and the *Academy of International Business*. Aside from his current residence in Singapore, he lived and worked in Hong Kong for several years and Japan for two years. As well, he has worked in Canada, India, China, Australia, Sweden, New Zealand, Finland and the United States. He has written case studies and conducted research on companies situated in Canada, China, India, Italy, Hong Kong, Sweden, Japan and Vietnam. His research looks at foreign direct investment and global competition issues in emerging economies, and the international strategies of Japanese multinational corporations.

Paul W. Beamish is Associate Dean of Research and Development and professor of International Strategy at the Richard Ivey School of Business, University of Western Ontario. He is the author or co-author of over 30 books, 75 articles or contributed chapters, and 75 case studies. His articles have appeared in *Strategic Management Journal*, *Journal of International Business Studies*, the three *Academy of Management* journals and elsewhere. His consulting and management training activities have been in both the public and the private sector for such organizations as Boeing, Labatt/Interbrew, The World Bank, the Canadian Foreign Service Institute, and the Harvard Institute for International Development. He has received case writing awards from the European Foundation for Management Development, The Management Development Centre of Hong Kong, and the Administrative Sciences Association of Canada. He worked for the Procter & Gamble Company of Canada and Wilfrid Laurier University before joining Ivey's faculty in 1987. As founding Director of Ivey's Asian Management Institute he is overseeing a process for the writing of over 200 new Asian cases over a five-year period. He teaches on Ivey's executive MBA program in Hong Kong.

list of abbreviations

CARICOM	Caribbean Community and Common Market
COMESA	Common Market for East and South Africa
ECOWAS	Economic Community of West African States
EU	European Union
GCC	Gulf Cooperation Council
NAFTA	North America Free Trade Agreement
OAPEC	Organization of Arab Petroleum Exporting Countries
SADC	Southern African Development Community
MERCOSUR	Southern Common Market
GNP	Gross National Product
TNI	Transnationality Index
DOI	Degree of Internationalization
SEZ	Special Economic Zone
OCC	Opening Coastal Cities
NTZ	New and High Technology Industrial Zones
ETDZ	Economic and Technology Development Zones
FTZ	Free Trade Zones
GDP	Gross Domestic Product
HRM	Human Resource Management
ILO	International Labour Organization
JIC	Japan Intercultural Consulting
APEC	Asia Pacific Economic Cooperation
CPI	Corruptions Perceptions Index

preface

Conversations about international business and globalization tend to be peppered with phrases like 'ongoing growth', 'continued rapid advance', 'spectacular increases' and 'worldwide integration', to identify a few. These phrases reflect the reality of the business environment in the Asia Pacific in the first few years of the 21st century.

These trends in the international business environment are unmistakably clear. Even in the post-1997 world in Asia, where many economies are just beginning to emerge from the ravages of the Asian Financial Crisis, international business remains an indelible part of the economic landscape. International business is a reality in two parts of the business world in the Asia Pacific. First, the pursuit of international business opportunities by companies in the region has never been so vibrant and important as when domestic economies have been in a period of slowdown or decline. Second, trading and foreign direct investment from countries inside and outside the region continued to sculpt domestic business landscapes, creating new competitive contours for firms indigenous to the host economies of the Asia Pacific.

We wrote *International Business: An Asia Pacific Perspective* with these trends in mind. The text and cases in this book apply the most recent thinking on international business and international management to understand the competitive environment that underlies international strategy issues relevant to a firm competing in the Asia Pacific region. To develop this understanding, we have organized the materials in the text portion of this book into three sections: (1) the international business environment; (2) managing international growth; and (3) multinational management.

In the first section, we present ideas and concepts about approaches to analyzing and understanding the international business environment. We focus on issues of measurement of various dimensions of national institutional environments. These dimensions include the economic environment, the cultural environment and the political environment. Beyond the measurement issue, we are also concerned with the management of these dimensions for a newly-internationalizing firm and for a well-established multinational firm.

There are several strategic decisions that are critical to the success of international growth initiatives. These decisions form the backdrop for the second section, in which we identify the options available to a manager of an internationalizing firm, when considering expansion into a new country. In addition to the need to be cognizant of the various strategic options available for international expansion, a manager must contend with several unique management issues, such as strategic alliances, entry mode choices, geographic market choices and timing of entry, that arise in an internationalizing firm. We put forward several viewpoints on how one can manage these issues. Along with this, we discuss two important forms of business organization – multinational firms and business groups – that need to be considered when making international expansion decisions in the Asia Pacific region.

In the third section, we move to the case of the on-going management of a multinational firm. We look at four major issues that arise in multinational management: strategy and structure of a multinational firm, subsidiary-level strategy issues, human resource management practices, and the management of ethical and social responsibilities. This section develops the theme that a multinational manager must contend with on-going globalization pressures, but a manager does so in the context of trying to maximize gains from integrating activities across countries, while not losing sight of the unique competitive demands of each host country market.

In developing the materials in this text, we highlight conceptual and strategic issues that underlie international business, but are particularly prominent in the Asia Pacific region. In doing so, we discuss ideas, concepts and the application of international business theories in a general way, but we make specific reference to the Asia Pacific using a plethora of examples. We have integrated some of these examples into the main text, while others we have highlighted by placing them in figures, tables and textboxes.

When developing these examples, we worked with a wide definition of the Asia Pacific. We defined the Asia Pacific as the countries that range from the Indian subcontinent in the west to Japan in the east, and from Mongolia in the north to the southern tip of Stewart Island in New Zealand. Our wide perspective on the geography of the Asia Pacific matches the text's wide perspective on the topics that are most relevant to individuals contemplating, or engaging in, a career in international management.

The overarching perspective taken in our writing of this book is unmistakably managerial. We see international business as an applied business topic. We hope that our book can help prepare an individual for the kinds of situations and decisions that will be encountered when operating in international markets and when formulating and implementing international strategy. To help meet that objective, we include 15 business cases that illustrate genuine decisions and situations faced by a variety of firms operating in numerous Asia Pacific contexts. These decisions and situations mirror many of the issues covered in the 13 chapters that form the core textual material of this book.

With its managerial focus, this book is intended for use by undergraduate, graduate and executive level international business and international management courses. The book is particularly relevant to courses that focus on international business and international management issues in the Asia Pacific region. We provide references to readings that can be used to supplement any of the topics covered in the text. The fifteen cases in this book can also be supplemented by accessing any of the other more than 300 cases Ivey Publishing has on international business and other management issues for companies operating in the Asia Pacific.

acknowledgments

Many people have helped make this book possible. Our thanks go to Daniel Lim, Acquisitions Editor at Pearson Education South Asia, who encouraged us to write this book, and its predecessor, *International Business in the Asia Pacific*. We would like to thank the numerous research associates and assistants involved in the development of the text. Ajai Singh Gaur, Le Thi Thu Huong, Nguyen Hoang Phi, Qian Lihong, Billy Pang and Wu Zhijian each worked exceptionally hard and well to help to develop various parts of the text. Jennifer Ilkiw was responsible for combing through hundreds of media reports in writing many of the examples we hope provide a unique Asia Pacific flavour to this book.

Numerous colleagues provided support and valuable feedback on this text. We received a great deal of intellectual and collegial support from our colleagues at the NUS Business School, the University of Auckland Business School and the Richard Ivey School of Business, as we developed the text and cases for this book. We would like to thank Julian Birkinshaw, Witold J. Henisz, Jane W. Lu, Ishtiaq P. Mahmood and Andre Perketi for previewing various chapters, and offering insightful comments.

Andrew Delios
Paul W. Beamish

SECTION I

The International Business Environment

1 INTERNATIONAL BUSINESS

Companies have been becoming increasingly international in the scope of their operations. Companies both large and small have internationalized activities in an attempt to improve competitiveness and capture greater shares in more geographic markets worldwide. Since the 1950s, this internationalization trend has been prominent among companies from North America and Western Europe. But beginning in the 1980s, companies from the Asia Pacific region have become progressively more active as participants in the global economy.

Up until the 1980s, the involvement of many countries in the Asia Pacific region in the global economy had been as recipients of foreign direct investment (FDI). Firms from North America and Europe perceived advantages to moving productive activities to countries in the Asia Pacific region and undertook a substantial amount of FDI in countries in the Asia Pacific.

This pattern of FDI in the Asia Pacific has continued up until the 2000s. It has been accompanied by more and more firms based in the Asia Pacific moving into foreign markets by exporting, by licensing and by foreign direct investment.

The international business environment for a company operating in the Asia Pacific region encompasses both of these trends. An Asian Pacific company faces a substantial amount of competition in its home markets from foreign firms, but it also faces substantial opportunities in foreign markets. A good understanding of both of these features of the international business environment is necessary for a company to compete successfully in its domestic and foreign markets, just like Tata Consulting Services (see Box 1-1).

To help develop this type of understanding, this book introduces the topic of international business from several vantage points. One perspective concerns the process of becoming an international company. Another involves consideration of the management complexities of operating a multinational company. A third deals with the difficulties and challenges or managing and working as an expatriate manager. Finally, one must also consider the competitive implications of facing strong foreign competitors in a home market.

This book provides these perspectives from the standpoint of a firm that has its primary source of business activities in the Asia Pacific region. Although many international business concepts and ideas are the same across the world, certain features of the Asia Pacific region, such

Box 1-1   Tata Consultancy Services

Companies in the Asia Pacific have long faced the daunting specter of competition in their home market from multinational firms. Declining barriers to international business does not only mean new competition; however, it can also mean new opportunities. Mumbai-based Tata Consultancy Services (TCS) has taken such a perspective to seize opportunities in international markets to support its product and geographic expansion strategies.

TCS (*www.tcs.com*) is a member firm in the Tata Group (*www.tata.com*), India's largest industrial business group. TCS was established in 1968, under the idea that a thorough understanding of management problems in Indian industry could be resolved through the effective use of information technology. By 2003, TCS was India's largest software developer, with clients in over 55 countries around the world, over 100 branches globally and 24,000 consultants on its payroll.

To achieve this impressive growth and size, TCS focused part of its geographic expansion efforts in Asia. It built up its presence in the Asia Pacific region by being the first Indian IT consulting company to set up a wholly owned subsidiary for software development in China. China is an important strategic region for TCS as it is often seen as one of the largest, untapped markets in the world with an installed base of approximately 17 million computers in 2001. In commenting on TCS' growth into China, Girija Pande, Regional Director for TCS in the Asia Pacific, stated that 'TCS has made inroads into various market segments, including manufacturing, telecommunications and the financial services industries. We will continue to expand our workforce substantially by the end of 2003 to support our continued growth.'

TCS has undertaken product expansion along with its geographic expansion. In 2002, in North America, the company launched a new business that services lifestyle and health care practices. At the same time, TCS targeted and entered media and entertainment technology services in the United States. More recently, through the acquisition of accounting services firm Airline Financial Support Services (*www.airlinefinancial.com*), in India in mid-2003, TCS entered the call centre business. These activities have contributed to TCS making substantial inroads into a number of major business areas in various regions of the world. In the United States, for example, TCS provided satellite and TV services for major companies such as Comcast (*www.comcast.com*), CNBC (*www.moneycentral.msn.com*) and NBC (*www.nbc.com*) and information technology services in Australia, where it butts heads with other multinational Indian IT firms such as Infosys (*www.infosys.com*) and Satyam (*www.satyam.com*).

Sources:

"India: Tata Consultancy Services Plans to Sep up Software Development Centre in Uruguay," *IPR Strategic Business Information Database*, 8 May 2002.

"China Figures High on India's IT Plans," *Asia Africa Intelligence Wire*, 2 September 2002, accessed from *http://www.financialexpress.com/fearchive_frame.php*, 26 December 2003.

"Tata Names Altman to Head Consulting Practice," *Communications Today*, 6 November 2002, vol. 8, no. 212.

"TCS Enters Call Center Biz," *Asia Pacific Telecom*, May 2003, Vol. 7, No. 5, pp. 4–5.

as the spectacular growth and then decline of many of the Asian Pacific economies from the 1980s to the 2000s, and the staging ground Asia Pacific countries have been for competition between multinational firms, mean that international business does acquire unique aspects in the region.

Aside from these contextual features, it is important to remember that international business is about the management of a firm as it becomes international or as it operates as a multinational firm. As a management topic, it is necessarily an applied topic. This book stresses the application of ideas, concepts and theories in international business to the practice of managing a multinational company that operates in the Asia Pacific and elsewhere in the world.

The Multinational Company

What is a multinational company? Is it the same as a transnational corporation? Is it the same as a multinational corporation (MNC)? Is it the same as an international firm? Is it the same as a multinational enterprise (MNE)? The answer to all of these questions is 'Yes'.

A multinational company (or firm) can be identified by any of the above names. Differences can exist among types of multinational firms, and these differences can be reflected in these various names. Ultimately, all multinational firms share the same common characteristic. A multinational firm is one that has productive operations in more than one country. It engages in business activities in its domestic market, sometimes called its home country. It also engages in business activities in foreign markets, which are sometimes called host countries.

A multinational firm becomes multinational by undertaking a foreign direct investment (FDI). An FDI is the purchase of assets in a foreign country by a firm, where that purchase provides control over the use of those assets. The assets can be another company, which in this case would be an FDI by acquisition. The assets can also be items such as land, equipment and buildings that are then used to construct and operate a foreign subsidiary.

A foreign subsidiary is an organization in the host country that is an extension of a firm's operations into a host country for the purpose of conducting its business activities. A foreign subsidiary is the consequence of a foreign direct investment. A foreign subsidiary can be owned in whole or in part by a foreign firm.

If a foreign firm has a partial ownership of a foreign subsidiary, the portion of its ownership must be large enough to confer some control over the operations of the foreign subsidiary. Typically, a 10 to 20 per cent ownership is the minimum amount of ownership necessary to confer some control. If a firm's ownership is less than 10 per cent, its investment can be considered to be a foreign portfolio investment. A foreign portfolio investment is the purchase of partial ownership of assets in a host country that confers rights to the returns from the use of those assets, but provides no effective control over the use of those assets.

The definitions and descriptions of a multinational firm, foreign direct investment and foreign subsidiary are a key to understanding the material in this book. International business centers around multinational firms. A firm becomes a multinational firm by undertaking foreign direct investment. When it undertakes a foreign direct investment, it has a foreign subsidiary operation.

Equity and Non-Equity Modes of International Participation

Foreign direct investment is typically called an equity mode of investment. Within the equity mode of investment, there can be several types. One of these is the previously mentioned entry by acquisition. Another equity mode is a wholly owned greenfield subsidiary. Yet another is a joint venture operation. Joint ventures, and their non-equity counterparts in strategic alliances, exploded in popularity in the 1990s.

Aside from foreign direct investment, a firm can participate in international markets by several other means. A firm's managers can export its products to foreign markets, its products can be licensed for use by firms in its international markets; a firm can engage in franchising; it can negotiate turn-key contract operations; and it can negotiate international subcontracting agreements. These are just a few of the many types of non-equity modes of international participation.

Non-equity modes and equity modes of international participation are differentiated from one another by identifying whether a firm has ownership of assets in its foreign markets. If there is ownership, as in a foreign direct investment, then that mode of international participation is called an equity mode. If these is no ownership, then that mode is called a non-equity mode.

Non-equity and equity modes have these difference in definitions, but both are means by which a firm can compete in international markets. These methods of foreign market entry involve extending a firm's sales and production into international markets, through a variety of arrangements. Although there is this multitude of foreign market entry modes, the most commonly used modes are wholly-owned greenfield subsidiary, acquisition, joint venture, exporting, licensing, technology transfer and strategic alliances.

These modes are commonly referred to as entry modes. In this case, entry means that a firm is moving into an international market. A firm's movement into international markets involves choices about the timing of entry, when should it go international and when should it move into a particular market. It involves choices about which mode to use when entering a foreign market. It also involves choices about which foreign markets to enter. These choices are all important parts of a firm's internationalization process.

One of the consequences of large numbers of internationalizing firms is that the world's economy becomes more globalized. Without the international activities of firms and without multinational firms, there would not be a globalizing economy. Environmental factors are part of the reason why firms are becoming more internationalized and economies more globalized. We consider these forces for internationalization and globalization next.

The Globalizing Economy

A number of trends push economies to become more integrated and globalized. As economies become more integrated, the barriers to international participation by firms become lower.

Consequently, a firm can move into foreign markets with greater ease, lower costs, and with better prospects for doing so profitably.

Trends that are driving globalization and economic integration include reductions in the importance of national borders, increases in similarities in consumer tastes across world regions, changes in technology and communication that make distances seem less, the transition of command economies to market economies, the rise of global standards for production and product quality, and a general reduction in governmental policies that regulate the flows of people, products and capital across national borders.

One standard that drives the globalization and harmonization of product markets is one we see everyday. It is the successful and well-known global standard known as the Universal Product Code (UPC). First scanned on 3 April 1974, by 2003 the UPC was used by more than one million companies doing business in more than 140 countries across 23 industries.[1] The UPC can be scanned up to 5 billion times per day.[2]

Standards can also emerge at the business-to-business side of a company's operations. For example, supply chain management is an area in which a number of organizations are collaborating efforts to achieve global standards.[3] The US-based Uniform Code Council (UCC) (*www.uc-council.org*) has a mission to enhance supply chain management and establish globally related standards. To meet this mission, the UCC has placed subsidiaries across the global marketplace. The UCC develops, promotes, maintains and expands global supply chain standards. One such initiative is the Global Commerce Initiative (GCI) (*www.globalcommerceinitiative.org*). Global retailers and manufacturers are undertaking GCI to develop and promote the use of global standards, particularly in the area of data synchronization and supply chain technologies. GCI represents efforts by nearly 850,000 companies of various sizes around the world whose product offerings span the entire supply chain for consumer goods.[4]

Globalization trends, as reinforced by the emergence of global standards such as the UPC and initiatives such as the GCI, operate together to shorten physical and perceptual differences to, and to reduce the costs of, a firm's activities that cross borders. These reductions facilitate the conduct of international business, and hence its growth.

Although the consequence of these trends is generally referred to as globalization, it might be more correctly thought of as the internationalization of a firm's business strategies. A firm's internationalization proceeds first through a regionalization, in which it builds up a concentrated set of overseas activities in countries in the same region – Asia, North America, South America, Europe, for example – of the world. Beyond that, when several regions of the world eventually become the staging points for a firm's international activities, it is only then a truly global firm. Few firms are yet beyond the regional expansion point in their international activities,[5] but others such as Haier are moving aggressively into many world regions (see Box 1-2).

For most firms, the majority of their international activities are concentrated in one of the three Triad regions of the world. A firm based in the United Kingdom, France or the Netherlands

Box 1-2 Haier's International Expansion

China's Haier Group was a small refrigerator manufacturer which turned into a multinational company by leveraging the trends driving the globalizing economy. Haier, founded in 1984, was one of China's top electronic and information appliance makers, and the number two refrigerator manufacturer in the world in 2003.

For the Haier Group (*www.haier.com*), a successful globalization strategy included developing and establishing a brand name. Believing that its products would attract consumers at home and abroad, Haier developed its brand by focusing on improving quality, meeting the customer's needs, and diversifying into other appliances, such as electronics, wine-chillers, and air-conditioners. The branding initiative was successful, making Haier an international brand name and a well-established company in the United States and Germany. By 2003, Haier had 13,000 products in 89 product lines and held 30 per cent of domestic market share in China in refrigerators, freezers, air-conditioners and washing machines.

In implementing its globalization strategy, Haier found it necessary to localize its networks for design, production, distribution, after-sales services and its sales centers. To accomplish this, the company established 18 design institutes, 10 industrial complexes, 13 overseas production factories. It employed local workforce for design and production, and opened regional head offices in New York, USA, Varese, Italy, and Qingdao, China. To reach the consumer, Haier had 58,800 sales agents in its localized sales offices, and had its products in 12 of the top 15 European, and 9 of the top 10 American, chain supermarkets.

Haier's global development strategy included entries by joint ventures, acquisitions and direct establishments of its presence in new markets. In 1999, Haier entered the US market by establishing a regional sales and marketing division (*www.haieramerica.com*). By 2001, Haier had established manufacturing facilities in the Haier American Industrial Park in South Carolina, while placing its head office, the Haier Building, in New York City.

Meanwhile on the other side of the world, to enter Pakistan, in February 2001 Haier, jointly established a facility with Pakistan-based Panapak Electronic Company to produce Haier air-conditioners. Once the market was firmly established, the Group opened the Haier (Pakistan) Industrial Park in Lahore in April 2001.

Haier entered the European market (*www.haiereupore.com*) by acquiring 100 per cent of an Italian refrigerator plant belonging to Meneghetti Equipment in 2001. As a result of that transaction, Italy housed the head office and production facilities for Haier Europe. Haier had warehouses in four European countries and sales offices in twelve.

In early 2002, Haier entered the Middle-East in a joint venture with South Electronics Company, and Syrian and Lebanese partners to establish the Haier Middle East Trading Co. (*www.haiermideast.com*) This division worked to expand Haier's market share and raise the brand's reputability in Jordan, Lebanon, Syria, Palestine, Iraq, Egypt and Kuwait.

Sources:

http://www.haier.com/english/about/index.html, 12 November 2003.

"Can Haier Freeze Out Whirlpool and GE?," *BusinessWeek Online*, *http://www.businessweek.com/*, 11 April 2002.

"Haier Facility Opens in Pakistan," *Appliance*, June 2001, Vol. 58, No. 6, p. 16.

"Haier Buys in Europe," *Appliance*, August 2001, Vol. 58, No. 8, p. 15.

http://www.rhvacnet.com/english/news/view.asp?newsid=10149, 17 November 2003.

generally has most of its international activities in Europe. A representative firm based in Thailand, Japan or Singapore would tend to have the majority of its international activities concentrated in Asia. Similarly, a firm based in the United States would have much of its operations based in North and Central America.

The concentration of a firm's international activities in one of the three Triad regions is the most pervasive pattern in the internationalization of firms in the early 2000s. It does not mean that some firms do not have an even spread of operations around the world, but it does mean that for most firms the reality of being a multinational firm is one in which sales and production tend to be centered in one of the three Triad regions.

Not surprisingly, in this globalizing world, the most relevant realm for a company operating in the Asia Pacific region, is other countries in the Asia Pacific. A typical multinational firm in the Asia Pacific might have operations in all Triad regions, but it is likely to have the majority of activities concentrated in other countries in the Asia Pacific. Likewise, its competitors, suppliers and buyers will each have a strong focus on the Asia Pacific region. This creates a regionalization to international competition that reinforces the importance of understanding how international business unfolds in the Asia Pacific.

Trade Agreements and Disappearing Borders

In the mid-1940s, the world was one in which tariffs averaged 45 per cent. This level of tariffs, which are taxes on imported goods and services, acted as a significant barrier to trade. Although tariffs can raise money for a government, this comes at the cost of raising the cost of imported goods to a nation's consumers.

In the second half of the 20th century, policy makers responded to high levels of tariffs, and its trade distorting implications, by instituting rounds of negotiations aimed at reducing worldwide levels of tariffs. These negotiations first took place in 1947, and became known as the GATT, or General Agreement on Tariffs and Trade, once completed.

The result of GATT was a substantial reduction on tariffs in several important trading nations in the world. The tariff reductions were prominent across a wide range of manufactured products such as wood, pulp and paper, furniture, metals, and non-electrical machinery. However, other areas such as agriculture, textiles and telecommunications, which are three of the most heavily subsidized sectors, were still protected by tariff barriers.[6]

Subsequent rounds of talks, including those in Uruguay and Doha, continued to work to reduce tariff barriers and liberalize trade in other important areas of the economy such as agriculture and services, including banking. Trade agreements for services were eventually extended to provide enhanced protection for intellectual property (patents, copyrights and trademarks), which has been a long-standing source of trade friction among nations. Issues concerning non-tariff measures, trade remedies (anti-dumping, countervailing measures and safeguards) and dispute settlements were also brought into international trade rules, through these most recent rounds of trade talks.

The GATT, which concentrated on tariff reduction, gave way to the creation of what is the now well-known as WTO, the World Trade Organization (*www.wto.org*). The WTO is a permanent multilateral trading system that oversees trade development issues and deals with the rules of trade between nations. The trade deals from WTO represent the most comprehensive and complex package of trade liberalization to date. Unlike previous agreements, in which trade clauses applied provisionally to a participating nation's favour, membership in the WTO means that a nation is party to all its multilateral agreements. In addition, the scope for discriminatory, unilateral policy actions becomes much more limited under WTO as each member is committed to imposing tariffs on a Normal-Trading-Relations (NTR) basis.

The coverage of the WTO is impressive. In 2003, 146 nations were in the WTO. The admission of the People's Republic of China (China) to the WTO in 2003 remains one of the most high profile admissions in recent years.

Despite accelerated development in the liberalization of world trade through GATT and WTO, many issues remain unresolved on the international trade front. One of these issues concerns the on-going negotiation among nations on agriculture which brought the current Doha round to the brink of collapse on many occasions. Substantial trade barriers also continue to remain in other areas such as textiles which has been the focal point of dispute between developed and developing nations. Another issue ranking high on the WTO's agenda is investment liberalization which was not on its development agenda until recent years when investment flows began to surge following the globalization of production. Other issues of increasing concern include the emergence of electronic commerce, the resurgence of non-tariff barriers, environmentalism, technology transfer, trade policy harmonization and national development policy. Each of these occupied a spot on the agenda in the most current trade talks.[7]

In essence, these rounds of talks have laid the building blocks for a freer, more transparent and more predictable international trading system. Clearly, work remains to be done to further liberalize trade. However, one result is quite clear – since the onset of GATT and WTO, tariffs on manufactured products have continued to fall to the point where they reached an average of less than four per cent in 2003.

A related consequence of these talks is that nations that are participants in the talks, and parties to the resultant agreements, lose some degree of independence in policy setting. If a nation adheres to a trade agreement, it loses autonomy to set tariff and non-tariff barriers as a means to control trade, and influence the development of domestic industries. This loss of independence and autonomy can be particularly profound when nations begin to form tighter forms of union in regional trading blocks or in economic unions.

Forms of Economic Integration

Economic integration can take various forms that vary from weak to tight levels of economic union. A weak form is one in which a nation holds substantial autonomy and discretion in setting the terms of trade and investment with other nations. The tools a nation has at its disposal for doing this include tariffs, restrictions on the flows of capital and people and non-tariff barriers, such as product standards and certifications required for the sale of a product in a nation. A strong form of integration is one in which this autonomy and discretion is removed in favour of a free flow of products, capital and labour across borders.

The trend in the 1990s and the early part of the 2000s has been towards the latter. Economies have become increasingly integrated through a variety of trading and regional agreements (see Table 1-1). These agreements have encompassed most nations in the world such that there are few nations that do not participate in any agreement. The transition of the former command economies of China, Vietnam and Eastern Europe to market economies has led to a widening of the scope of nations included in such agreements.

Table 1-1 illustrates how these types of economic integration vary by four features of the economy. The four types of economic integration range from the least integrated, a free trade area, to the most integrated, an economic union. A fifth form of integration extends economic union to political union.

In all types of economic integration, nations agree to remove tariffs and quotas. This removal effectively permits goods and services to flow freely among member nations just as goods and services flow freely within a nation. The scope of free trade can be limited to certain specific sectors of the economy, but as nations increase the level of economic integration, more and more sectors become tariff and quota free. Importantly, in a free trade area, a nation still retains autonomy to set tariffs and quotas for trade with nations outside the free trade area.

After forming a free trade area, the next step is to form a customs union. In a customs union, members establish a common trade policy, that is, a common set of tariffs and quotas with non-members.

Table 1-1:   Types of Economic Integration

Type	Removal of tariffs and quotas among members	Common tariff and quota system	Removal of restrictions on factor movements	Unification of economic policies and institutions
Free trade area	Yes	No	No	No
Customs union	Yes	Yes	No	No
Common market	Yes	Yes	Yes	No
Economic union	Yes	Yes	Yes	Yes
Political union	Yes	Yes	Yes	Yes

Source: Adapted from Franklin R. Root, *International Trade and Investment* (Cincinnati, Ohio: South-Western Publishing Company, 1992), p. 254; Sourced from Michael R. Czinkota, Ilkka A. Ronkainen, and Michael H. Moffet, *International Business* (South-Western: Australia, 2002), p. 196.

The next step is to form a common market. Unlike a free trade area and a customs union, member states in a common market permit factors of production such as capital and labor to move freely within the states that comprise the common market. This freedom means that capital can flow to the regions and industries where there might be the highest returns, while people can move across nations within the common market to find the best employment and living opportunities. This freedom of movement should promote economic growth through a more productive use of factors of production.

The final step is to form an economic union. Members in an economic union yield autonomy and independence to set national level monetary and fiscal policies to a union-wide policy making body. An economic union may involve the institution of a common currency, just as with the establishment of the Euro in the European Union.

Examples of Economic Integration

With the growth in initiatives in economic integration since the 1980s, the number of free trade agreements and other types of economic union have grown correspondingly. The imperatives to form such unions have been strong enough that it is difficult to identify a country that is not at least a party to one bilateral or multilateral trading agreement.

One common characteristic of major trading agreements is that they tend to be geographically focused. A nation is much more likely to be in a trading agreement with a nation that is geographically proximate to it, than with one that is geographically distant. As a result, we tend to think of trade agreements on a region-by-region basis.

For example, we have already made reference to the European Union. Fifteen European countries are members of the union in 2003, with another 13 countries either engaged in negotiations to join the European Union, or interested in joining the union (see Table 1-2).

Numerous free trade agreements exist in Africa (see Table 1-3). These include the Southern African Development Community (SADC), the Common Market for East and South Africa (COMESA) and the Economic Community of West African States (ECOWAS). As noted in the names of these examples, the agreements tend to involve states that are located in similar locations in the African continent, such as the southern, eastern or western portions of continent.

Moving to the northern part of Africa, plus to the Arab nations to the east of Africa, brings us to several other areas of economic integration. There is the Gulf Cooperation Council and the Arab League, which includes both Northern African and Middle Eastern countries. We also have the Organization of Arab Petroleum Exporting Countries (OAPEC). OAPEC, which was established in 1968, is an inter-governmental organization that fosters cooperation among its members to help develop the petroleum industry. OAPEC is not to be confused with OPEC (*www.opec.org*, founded in 1960), which is an organization involving member countries from Africa, Asia, the Middle East, and Latin America, that has the purpose of supporting market stability for oil, and ensuring a fair price for oil.

Table 1-2: **Members of the European Union (2003)**

EU Member States (year of entry)	Candidate Countries
Belgium (1950)	Bulgaria
Denmark (1973)	Czech Republic
Germany (1950)	Estonia
Greece (1981)	Cyprus
Spain (1986)	Latvia
France (1950)	Lithuania
Ireland (1973)	Hungary
Italy (1950)	Malta
Luxembourg (1950)	Poland
Netherlands (1950)	Romania
Austria (1995)	Slovenia
Portugal (1986)	Slovakia
Finland (1995)	Turkey
Sweden (1995)	
United Kingdom (1973)	

Source: http://www.europa.eu.int/index_en.htm, 14 March 2003.
Note: 1950 refers to the date at which the nations subscribed to the Schuman declaration. The Treaties of Rome, which established the European Economic Community, were signed in 1957.

Table 1-3: **Areas of Economic Integration**

Name	Acronym	Members	Website
Association of South East Asian Nations	ASEAN	Brunei Darussalam, Cambodia, Indonesia, Laos, Malaysia, Myanmar, Philippines, Singapore, Thailand, Viet Nam	*www.aseansec.org*
Andean Common Market	ANCOM	Bolivia, Colombia, Ecuador, Peru, Venezuela	*www.comunidadandina.org*
Arab League	–	Jordan, United Arab Emirates, Bahrain, Tunisia, Algeria, Djibouti, Saudi Arabia, Sudan, Syria, Somalia	*www.arableagueonline.org*
Central American Common Market	CACM	Costa Rica, El Salvador, Guatemala, Honduras, Nicaragua	*www.sieca.org.gt*
Caribbean Community and Common Market	CARICOM	Antigua and Barbuda, The Bahamas, Barbados, Belize, Dominica, Grenada, Guyana, Haiti, Jamaica, Montserrat, St. Kitts and Nevis, St. Lucia, Suriname, St. Vincent & the Grenadines, Trinidad and Tobago	*www.caricom.org*

Table 1-3: continued

Name	Acronym	Members	Website
Common Market for East and South Africa	COMESA	Angola, Burundi, Comoros, Congo, Djibouti, Egypt, Eritrea, Ethiopia, Kenya, Madagascar, Malawi, Mauritius, Namibia, Rwanda, Seychelles, Sudan, Swaziland, Uganda, Zambia, Zimbabwe	*www.comesa.int*
Economic Community of West African States	ECOWAS	Benin, Burkina Faso, Cabo Verde, Cote D'Ivoire, Gambia, Ghana, Guinea, Guinea Bissau, Liberia, Mali, Niger, Nigeria, Senegal, Sierra Leone, Togolese	*www.ecowas.int*
European Union	EU	Austria, Belgium, Denmark, France, Finland, Germany, Greece, Ireland, Italy, Luxembourg, Portugal, Spain, Sweden, The Netherlands, United Kingdom,	*europa.eu.int*
Gulf Cooperation Council	GCC	Kuwait, Qatar, Oman, Saudi Arabia, Bahrain, United Arab Emirates	*www.gcc-sg.org*
North America Free Trade Agreement	NAFTA	Canada, United States, Mexico	*www.nafta-sec-alena.org*
Organization of Arab Petroleum Exporting Countries	OAPEC	Algeria, Bahrain, Egypt, Iraq, Kuwait, Libya, Qatar, Saudi Arabia, Syria, Tunisia, United Arab Emirates	*www.oapec.org*
Southern African Development Community	SADC	Angola, Botswana, Congo, Lesotho, Malawi, Mauritius, Mozambique, Namibia, Seychelles, South Africa, Swaziland, Tanzania, Zambia, Zimbabwe	*www.sadc.int*
Southern Common Market	MERCOSUR	Argentina, Brazil, Paraguay, Uruguay	*www.mercosur.org.uy*

Sources: www.aseansec.org, 19 March 2003; *www.comunidadandina.org*, 19 March 2003; *www.arableagueonline.org*, 19 March 2003; *www.sieca.org.gt*, 19 March 2003; *www.caricom.org*, 19 March 2003; *www.comesa.int*, 19 March 2003; *www.ecowas.int*, 19 March 2003; *www.europa.eu.int*, 14 March 2003; *www.gcc-sg.org*, 19 March 2003; *www.nafta-sec-alena.org*, 19 March 2003; *www.oapec.org*, 19 March 2003; *www.sadc.int*, 19 March 2003; *www.mercosur.org.uy*, 19 March 2003.

Moving across the Atlantic Ocean to North and South America brings us to several other free trading areas. The North America Free Trade Agreement (NAFTA) includes just three countries – Canada, the United States and Mexico – but it has the largest GNP, greater than USD 11 trillion, among all trading areas. Other trading areas include the Southern Common Market (MERCOSUR), the Caribbean Community and Common Market (CARICOM), the Andean Common Market (ANCOM) and the Central American Common Market (CACM).

As indicated in the names for the trading areas in Central and South America, the degree of economic integration is quite tight, compared to the NAFTA agreement.

Moving west again, but this time across the Pacific Ocean, we encounter one other trading area. This is the Association of South East Asian Nations (ASEAN). The ASEAN free trade area (AFTA) includes Brunei, Indonesia, Laos, Malaysia, Myanmar, Philippines, Singapore and Thailand.

Size and Prevalence of Multinational Companies

Firms have responded to the liberalization of trade and investment regimes by locating larger and larger portions of productive activities in overseas markets. This response has not only increased the number of multinational firms, but it has also increased the degree of multinationality of many of these firms. Finally, it has led to firms from a larger number of nations pursuing a strategy of growth in international markets.

Number of Multinational Companies

There is no precise way to count the number of multinational companies. Estimates of the number of multinational companies in the world must be taken as exactly that – an estimate. One agency that produces annual, rigorously compiled numbers on multinational companies is the United Nations Conference on Trade and Development (UNCTAD) (*www.unctad.org*).

Each year, UNCTAD produces a World Investment Report (*http://r0.unctad.org/wir/*) that has the general goal of outlining the current state of international trade and investment. In 2002, UNCTAD's World Investment Report identified that there were more than 500,000 multinational companies operating worldwide. The nation with the most multinational companies is the United States. Other leading nations, in terms of the number of companies, included Japan, the United Kingdom, France and Germany. These same countries housed the largest percentage of the world's largest multinational firms (see Table 1-4). The United States alone was the home country to 23 of the top 100 multinational firms.

Although the United States had the most companies among the top 100, its dominance as the home to the world's largest multinational firms has declined over time. In 1976, it was home to almost 50 per cent of the world's largest multinational firms. By 1997, it had just over 30 per cent of the world's 500 largest multinational firms. The United Kingdom has experienced a similar decline from 19 per cent to 12 per cent, while Japan's share rose from four percent to 25 per cent. Germany and France have been consistent, with each being the home for about eight percent of the world's 500 largest multinational firms.

The industrial distribution of the world's largest multinational firms has shown some change over the past decade. The world's 100 largest multinational firms could be found in the electronics, motor vehicles, petroleum, foods and chemicals industries at the start of the 1990s. By the end

Table 1-4:   Top 100 Multinational Companies by Home Country (2002)

Country	Number of Multinational Companies	Country	Number of Multinational Companies
United States	23	Spain	2
Japan	16	Finland	1
United Kingdom	14	Belgium	1
France	13	Australia	1
Germany	10	Venezuela	1
The Netherlands	3	Korea	1
Sweden	3	Norway	1
Switzerland	3	Malaysia	1
Italy	2	Mexico	1
Canada	2	Hong Kong	1

Source: UNCTAD, *World Investment Report 2003* (New York: United Nations, 2003), Annex Table A.I.1, pp. 187–188.

of the 1990s, firms in the pharmaceuticals industry making it to the top 100 had quadrupled from two to eight. This multinational growth within the pharmaceutical sector was part of a trend towards the globalization of research and development, and the distribution of ethical pharmaceutical products. Several companies engaged in trading and retailing also cracked the top 100. In the retail industry, emerging giants such as Wal-Mart and Carrefour began to internationalize their operations on a wide scale.

Table 1-5 provides more insights into these trends by listing the total assets, foreign assets, total sales, foreign sales and TNI (Transnationality Index) for large multinational firms. It identifies the 50 largest multinational companies as of 2002, where the largest multinational company is the one with the largest figure for foreign assets. This criterion places Vodafone at the top of the charts, although General Electric and General Motors would be at the top, if we looked at total assets instead of foreign assets.

Among the 20 largest multinational companies, there are ten different countries represented. This distribution reflects the 1980s to 2000s trend, as discussed earlier, to a more widespread distribution of multinational firms across countries of the world. Even with this trend, a few firms from Asia manage to top this list. Toyota Motors, Nissan Motors, Honda Motors, Sony and Mitsui & Co from Japan can be found on this list. Just a few years ago, this same list of the largest multinational companies included many other Japanese general trading companies (sometimes called sogo shosha), such as Marubeni, Sumitomo and Mitsubishi. These companies have faced quite severe pressure on their operations since the close of the 1980s, resulting in a substantial reduction in their domestic and foreign assets and revenues.

Hutchinson Whampoa at number 17 is the largest Asian-based company to be found on the list of the world's top 50 multinational companies. Once we exclude Japan, we can see in Table

Table 1-5: The World's 50 Largest Multinational Companies (2002)

Rank	Name	Home Country	Foreign Assets	Total Assets	Foreign Sales	Total Sales	TNI (%)
1	Vodafone	UK	187,792	207,458	24,602	32,744	83.2
2	General Electric	US	180,031	495,210	39,914	125,913	39.0
3	BP	UK	111,207	141,158	141,225	175,389	80.5
4	Vivendi Universal	France	91,120	123,156	29,652	51,423	66.3
5	Deutsche Telekom AG	Germany	90,657	145,802	11,836	43,309	40.0
6	Exxonmobil Corporation	US	89,426	143,174	145,814	209,417	64.8
7	Ford Motor Company	US	81,169	276,543	52,983	162,412	38.4
8	General Motors	US	75,379	323,969	45,256	177,260	29.8
9	Royal Dutch/Shell Group	Netherlands	73,492	111,534	72,952	135,211	59.3
10	TotalFinaElf	France	70,030	78,500	74,647	94,418	74.9
11	Suez	France	69,345	79,280	29,919	37,975	78.2
12	Toyota Motor Corporation	Japan	68,400	144,793	59,880	108,808	59.3
13	Fiat Spa	Italy	48,749	89,264	24,860	52,002	51.5
14	Telefonica SA	Spain	48,122	77,011	14,303	27,775	57.3
15	Volkswagen Group	Germany	47,480	92,520	57,426	79,376	57.4
16	ChevronTexaco Corp.	US	44,943	77,572	57,673	104,409	55.3
17	Hutchison Whampoa Ltd.	Hong Kong	40,989	55,281	6,092	11,415	65.6
18	News Corporation	Australia	35,650	40,007	13,880	15,087	84.7
19	Honda Motor Co Ltd.	Japan	35,257	52,056	40,088	55,955	62.8
20	E.On	Germany	33,990	87,755	22,744	71,419	37.6
21	Nestlé SA	Switzerland	33,065	55,821	34,704	50,717	75.0
22	RWE Group	Germany	32,809	81,024	23,151	58,039	40.8
23	IBM	US	32,800	88,313	50,651	85,866	50.2
24	ABB	Switzerland	30,586	32,305	18,876	19,382	95.6
25	Unilever	UK	30,529	46,922	28,675	46,803	66.5
26	ENI Group	Italy	29,935	55,584	19,437	43,861	43.8
27	BMW AG	Germany	29,901	45,415	25,304	34,482	54.4
28	Philips Electronics	Netherlands	29,416	34,070	27,598	28,992	88.4
29	Carrefour SA	France	29,342	41,172	31,513	62,294	62.6
30	Electricité De France	France	28,141	120,124	12,468	36,502	27.0
31	Repsol YPF SA	Spain	27,028	45,575	13,752	39,135	47.0
32	Sony Corporation	Japan	26,930	61,393	38,605	57,595	56.7
33	Aventis SA	France	26,368	34,761	13,377	20,567	64.4
34	Wal-Mart Stores	US	26,324	83,451	35,485	217,799	23.2
35	DaimlerChrysler AG	Germany	25,795	183,765	43,556	137,051	22.1

Table 1-5:   continued

Rank	Name	Home Country	Foreign Assets	Total Assets	Foreign Sales	Total Sales	TNI (%)
36	Lafarge SA	France	24,906	26,493	10,537	12,280	89.7
37	Nissan Motor Co Ltd.	Japan	24,382	54,113	29,078	47,091	45.6
38	AES Corporation	US	23,902	36,736	5,809	9,327	73.2
39	Roche Group	Switzerland	22,794	25,289	17,156	17,463	91.8
40	BASF AG	Germany	20,872	32,671	17,108	29,136	55.9
41	Deutsche Post AG	Germany	20,840	138,837	9,844	29,924	22.3
42	Bayer AG	Germany	20,297	32,817	15,778	27,142	54.9
43	GlaxoSmithkline Plc	UK	20,295	31,758	27,319	29,689	70.9
44	Royal Ahold NV	Netherlands	19,967	28,562	40,150	59,701	68.4
45	Compagnie De Saint-Gobain SA	France	19,961	28,478	19,091	27,245	71.7
46	BHP Billiton Group	Australia	19,898	29,552	14,821	17,778	71.8
47	Diageo Plc	UK	19,731	26,260	13,747	16,020	85.8
48	Conoco Inc.	US	19,383	27,904	17,530	38,737	55.5
49	Philip Morris Companies Inc.	US	19,339	84,968	33,944	89,924	27.8
50	National Grid Transco	UK	19,080	24,839	3,829	6,308	71.4

Source: UNCTAD, *World Investment Report 2003* (New York: United Nations, 2003), Annex Table A.I.1., pp. 187–188.
Note: All figures are in USD millions.

1-6 that other large companies in Asia require substantial growth in their foreign assets before moving up the ranks of the world's top 50 list.

National Grid Transco, at number 50, had USD 19.1 billion in foreign assets in 2002. The number two company in the top 25 multinational companies in Asia list, Singtel Ltd, had about 80 per cent of that at USD 15.6 billion. Singtel Ltd had foreign assets that were twice as large as Malaysia's Petronas, the number four company in the Asia list.

Several companies from South Korea were part of the list of Asia's largest multinational companies. These companies, such as Samsung Corporation and Samsung Electronics, were largely affiliated with a business group structure called 'chaebol'. Several Hong Kong companies made the list. Some, such as First Pacific, had a very low percentage of revenues and assets attributable to operations in their Hong Kong base, but had substantial operations in other countries in Asia, such as Indonesia and the Philippines. Other large companies such as Jardine Matheson in Hong Kong had a long history and a strong connection to the British colonial heritage of Hong Kong. Companies from Taiwan, Singapore, Malaysia and China completed the list of the top 25, marking a widening distribution of large multinational firms across different Asian countries.

In this context of growing multinational firms from Asia, the evolution of Taiwan-based

Table 1-6:   Asia's 25 Largest Multinational Companies (2002, excluding Japan)

Rank	Name	Home Country	Foreign Assets	Total Assets	Foreign Sales	Total Sales	TNI (%)
1	Hutchison Whampoa Ltd.	Hong Kong	40,989	55,281	6,092	11,415	65.6
2	Singtel Ltd.	Singapore	15,594	19,108	1,362	4,054	65.6
3	LG Electronics Inc.	South Korea	11,561	20,304	10,009	22,528	50.3
4	Petronas - Petroliam Nasional Berhad	Malaysia	7,877	37,933	5,359	17,681	22.2
5	New World Development Co., Ltd.	Hong Kong	4,715	16,253	565	2,933	17.1
6	Neptune Orient Lines Ltd.	Singapore	4,674	4,951	2,970	4,737	81.8
7	Citic Pacific Ltd.	Hong Kong	4,184	7,798	1,109	2,212	55.5
8	Jardine Matheson Holdings Ltd.	Hong Kong	4,080	7,166	6,297	9,413	60.3
9	Samsung Electronics Co., Ltd.	South Korea	3,840	41,692	25,112	37,155	36.4
10	Guangdong Investment Ltd.	Hong Kong	3,694	4,042	854	932	91.0
11	Shangri-La Asia Ltd.	Hong Kong	3,606	4,565	458	560	79.9
12	Hyundai Motor Company	South Korea	3,210	33,216	6,943	33,199	12.2
13	Flextronics International Ltd.	Singapore	2,983	4,115	5,363	6,691	75.0
14	City Developments Ltd.	Singapore	2,870	6,454	857	1,302	63.4
15	Samsung Corporation	South Korea	2,800	9,400	5,800	32,300	17.4
16	China National Chemicals, Imp. & Exp. Corp.	China	2,788	4,928	9,145	16,165	39.2
17	Guangzhou Investment Company Ltd.	Hong Kong	2,129	2,559	362	433	88.4
18	Taiwan Semiconductor Manufacturing Co., Ltd.	Taiwan	2,033	10,446	..	3,751	7.0
19	First Pacific Company Ltd.	Hong Kong	2,007	2,046	1,852	1,852	99.3
20	Acer Inc.	Taiwan	1,686	3,344	2,198	3,754	53.1
21	Posco	South Korea	1,589	18,164	1,378	10,497	9.6
22	San Miguel Corporation	Philippines	1,584	3,203	743	2,384	31.2
23	CLP Holdings	Hong Kong	1,559	6,798	93	3,205	8.9
24	United Microelectronics Corporation	Taiwan	1,462	9,140	966	2,081	24.7
25	Keppel Corporation Ltd.	Singapore	1,422	6,332	661	3,283	23.5

Source: UNCTAD, *World Investment Report 2003* (New York: United Nations, 2003), Annex Table A.I.2., p. 189.
Note: All figures are in USD millions.

Acer, number 20 in Table 1-6, is worth reviewing. Acer (*www.global.acer.com*) emerged in 1976 as it began to commercialize microprocessor technology. The company grew and expanded its scope in the next 25 years in an effort to become a diversified, global conglomerate and 'Taiwan's answer to Japan's Hitachi Ltd. and South Korea's Samsung Group'.[8] In 1981, Acer opened its first manufacturing plant in Hsin Chu, Taiwan. Eight years later, Acer initiated its globalization strategy, forming a joint venture with Texas Instruments to enter the Japanese firm dominated computer chip industry. Acer then expanded its product line in the early 1990s by entering the personal computer (PC) market, producing, among other products, one of the first stripped-down, under-$1000, user-friendly PCs.

At the turn of the century, losses in the US market and the erratic chip-market led Acer to restructure. In 2000, Acer divested parts of several of its businesses, to refocus the parent company on selling and branding its IT products and services. Three independent affiliates emerged from the restructuring: Wistron (*www.wistron.com*), an OEM manufacturer of computer electronics; BenQ (*www.benq.com*), a developer of communications and media solutions; and ALi Corp. (*www.ali.com.tw*), a chip manufacturer. Other divisions that were spun-off included Au Optronics, formally Acer Display, which went public in 2000 (*www.auo.com*) and Ambit (*www.ambit.com.tw*), a communications equipment designer and manufacturer. In 2003, Acer was no longer a single multinational company. Instead, it was the pan Acer Group of companies, which were separate businesses held under the pan Acer Group umbrella.

How Multinational is Multinational?

Tables 1-5 and 1-6 show the readily recognizable numbers of assets and sales, along with the less recognizable TNI. The TNI is included in these tables to show just how multinational each multinational company is. TNI is simply a measure of what proportion of a firm's activities fall outside of its home country.

The TNI helps with our understanding about trends in multinational expansion among the world's largest firms. It provides more information than just identifying if a firm is multinational. The definition of a multinational firm is clear – it is a company that has operations in more than one country of the world. But are all multinational firms equally multinational? When scanning the TNIs in Tables 1-5 and 1-6, the answer is 'No'.

As just mentioned, the TNI defines multinationality by looking at what proportion of a firm's activities fall outside of its home country. One way to define a TNI is to look at how many countries in which a firm has made foreign investments, or to how many countries it exports. Another way is to count how many foreign subsidiaries it has. For each of these, the greater the count, the higher a company's index of multinationality.

A second way to define a firm's degree of multinationality is to look at the international dispersion of its employment, sales and assets. By doing this we can construct indexes such as a firm's degree of internationalization (DOI), or its TNI. The TNI is a ratio that represents the average of the values of the percentage of a firm's sales, a firm's assets and a firm's employment in its international markets.

$$TNI = (Si + Ei + Ai)/3$$

where: S = total sales, Sf = foreign sales
Si = foreign sales index (Sf / S*100)

E = total employment, Ef = foreign employment
Ei = foreign employment index (Ef / E*100)

A = total assets, Af = foreign assets
Ai = foreign asset index (Af / A*100)

Whichever of these indexes is used, the same conclusion is reached. Companies are becoming increasingly international (see Figure 1-1). As an example, the TNI of the world's largest multinational companies shows a general upwards progression. This increase in TNI is even greater for small companies that have a higher percentage growth rate than the world's largest multinationals.

For the companies listed in Tables 1-5 and 1-6, we notice an interesting cross-national trend. The companies from large economies like Japan and the United States have, on average, lower TNIs, than multinational companies from smaller economies. This discrepancy should not be that surprising. A large home economy should be home to a larger percentage of a firm's sales than a small home economy. Eventually, multinational companies based in small economies

Figure 1-1:   Transnationality of Top 100 TNCs (1990-2000)

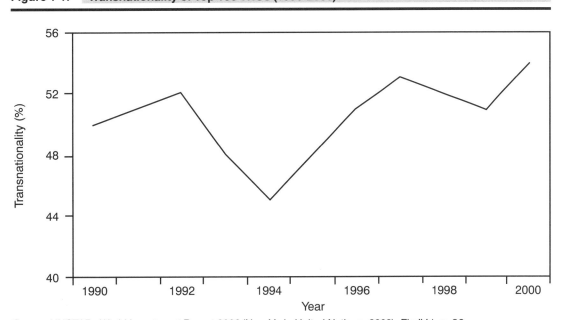

Source: UNCTAD, *World Investment Report 2002* (New York: United Nations, 2002), Fig IV.1, p. 96.

such as Singapore and Hong Kong could approach the TNIs of large, well-established Swedish multinational firms such as Electrolux, Alfa Laval and Ericsson, each of which has a TNI greater than 90 per cent. Indeed, some large multinational companies in Asia already do. Want Want Holdings of Singapore had a TNI of 97.9 per cent in 2001. Other companies such as Hong Kong's Orient Overseas International Ltd and Guangdong Investment Ltd, or Singapore's WBL Corporation Ltd and Asia Pacific Breweries Ltd, had TNIs that exceeded 75 per cent.

Trends in Foreign Direct Investment

In becoming increasingly international, firms worldwide are undertaking larger amounts of foreign direct investment. The growth in foreign investment has been very consistent in the past three decades. With but a few years as exceptions, including the years 2001 and 2002, versus the years 2000 and 2001, the volume of FDI in one year has exceeded that in the preceding year (see Figure 1-2). The result is that by the year 2000, more than USD1.5 trillion flowed from one country to another in the form of foreign direct investment.

FDI growth has been consistent, but the destination and origin of FDI flows has been undergoing change, especially since the onset of the 1990s. The principal change has been a growth in the participation of developing nations in the world as both sources and recipients of FDI flows (see Figures 1-3 and 1-4).

Figure 1-2: **FDI Worldwide (1970-2002)**

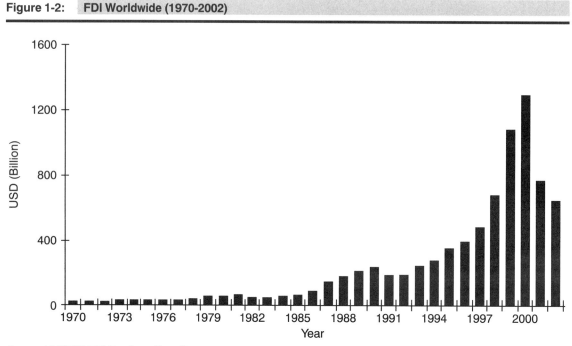

Source: UNCTAD FDI Database (*http://stats.unctad.org/fdi/*), 3 December 2003.

Figure 1-3: **FDI Outflows (1970-2002)**

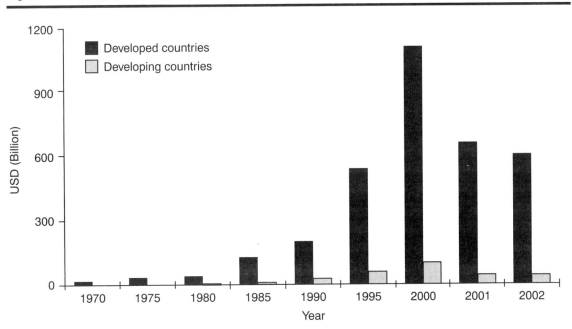

Source: UNCTAD FDI Database (*http://stats.unctad.org/fdi/*), 9 April 2003.

Figure 1-4: **FDI Inflows (1970-2002)**

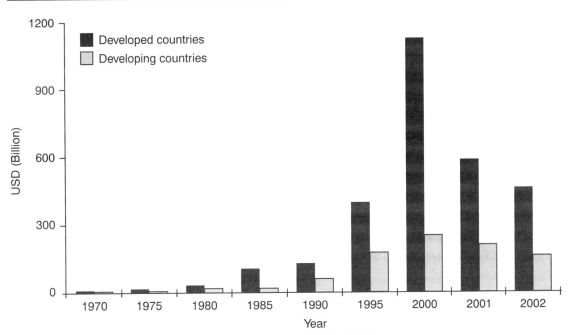

Source: UNCTAD FDI Database (*http://stats.unctad.org/fdi/*), 3 December 2003.

Although there has been this change, developing countries have had a considerable gap to overcome in being sources and recipients of FDI flows. Even with a growing volume in FDI outflows that outpaced growth from developed countries in percentage terms in the 1990s, developing countries still lagged developed countries in 2002 in aggregate FDI outflows.

The flipside is FDI inflows. In this case, the gains made by developing countries have been much more rapid. The gap between inflows received by developed and developing countries has narrowed considerably from 1970 to 2002 (Figure 1-4). As we move into the mid-2000s, this trend shows no signs of abating.

As suggested within these trends, by the onset of the 2000s, we still had the same base situation as in the 1970s, but with some shifts in the net positions of developed and developing countries. Developed countries were the major sources of FDI outflows and by and large the largest recipients of FDI inflows. A considerable portion of developed countries' FDI outflows went to developing countries as well. This meant that developing countries still received more inward FDI than they expended on outward FDI. In this way, developing countries were net recipients of FDI (Figure 1-5).

Interestingly, in 2002, North America was a net recipient of FDI for the second consecutive year. Only the countries of Europe were in a net contributor position. In much of the preceding two decades, the United States (but not Canada) had produced more FDI outflows than it had received FDI inflows. Part of the emerging popularity of the United States as a destination for FDI inflows relates to changing motives for FDI, in which a technology sourcing motive has

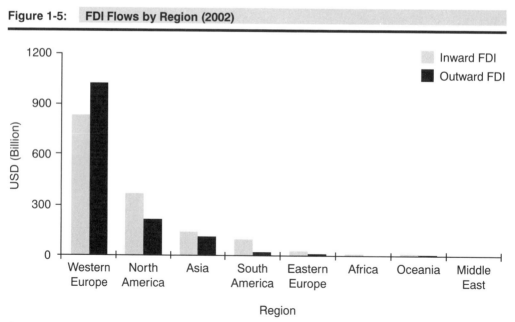

Figure 1-5:   FDI Flows by Region (2002)

Source: UNCTAD FDI Database (*http://stats.unctad.org/fdi/*), 3 December 2003.

become more prominent in recent years. For now, however, it is important to note that FDI inflows into Asia exceeded outflows, reinforcing the idea that foreign competition is a significant management challenge for managers in firms based in the Asia Pacific.

International Management Issues

Understanding how to compete against foreign firms is just one of the major management issues faced by managers in firms based in the Asia Pacific region. Managers must also contend with a host of other issues. Some of these relate to the practice of international business in general, while others concern the management of firms based in the Asia Pacific in specific.

A manager in a firm that is active internationally faces a much more complex external environment than does a manager in a firm that competes solely in its home market. The internal management of a multinational firm can also be more complex than for the case of a primarily domestic one, as can be many of the management tasks.

The complexity in the external environment comes from the variety of cultural, economic, legal and social conditions encountered when a firm has operations in many countries. Across countries, cultures are diverse, economic and political systems vary in noticeable and important ways, and values and languages can have few similarities across nations. Each of these make management tasks either more complex or unique, and can raise the costs of a firm's operations.

The complexity in the internal firm environment can come from managing globally diversified operations. Issues of organizational design and organizational structure increase in importance as a firm's internationalization process matures. As a firm internationalizes, questions can arise about how to compete against locally-based firms, or against foreign competitors that have set up operations in a firm's home country. The management of subsidiary operations, along such dimensions as autonomy, control and types of value-added activities in a subsidiary, compounds in complexity, such as those that Carrefour has experienced in expanding its retail operations in Asia (see Box 1-3).

Complexity in internal operations can come from a variety of other areas. A firm operating internationally is likely to have a greater diversity among its employees than a domestic firm. This diversity can be reflected in native languages, tastes, background education and expectations about relationships to supervisors and subordinates. This diversity means that it can be more challenging and expensive to develop human resource management systems for selection, recruitment, training, promotion and compensation of employees. Expatriate management can be a Byzantine task. Typically, expatriates struggle to cope with the singular demands of an overseas assignment in which culture, business relationships and ethical standards can vary from the norms in the home country.

These issues can each assume a heightened prominence as a firm increasingly expands its range of international operations. Navigating successfully through this sea of challenges is not beyond the scope of an effective manager. Furthermore, the costs encountered by a firm in meeting these challenges can be more than offset by the gains from the effective and successful management of a firm's internationalization. This idea is echoed in the on-going internationalization trend. In increasing numbers, firms from all regions of the world continue to assume the challenge of moving into international markets. This idea is also reflected in the performance of international firms.

Box 1-3   Carrefour's International Expansion in Asia

France-based Carrefour (*www.carrefour.com*) is the second largest retailer worldwide, with 9,632 stores in 30 countries. Carrefour focuses its stores in three retail formats, hypermarket, supermarket and hard discount. The retail giant first entered the Asian market in 1989 when it opened a hypermarket in Taiwan. Since then, it has continued to expand in Asia with subsequent entries made into Malaysia, China, South Korea, Thailand, Singapore, Japan, Indonesia, and the United Arab Emirates. It currently operates 137 hypermarkets in the Asia Pacific.

Carrefour grows in the Asia Pacific by successfully determining the proper approach for each new market, and then matching its commitment level to the country's potential. Joel Saveuse, Carrefour's chief operating officer (COO) states that 'The best way to learn about a new country whose potential for growth you're not sure of is to test it with a local partner.' In cities such as the Arab Emirate of Dubai, where potential in uncertain, Carrefour entered the market as a minority partner, and provided only the Carrefour name and a financial investment to the hypermarkets (*www.carrefouruae.com*). In markets such as China, where the perceived opportunity is great, Carrefour enters aggressively. In China in 2003, Carrefour was among the top three retailers and it was the leading hypermarket operator. By the end of 2004, Carrefour expects to operate 65 to 70 hypermarkets in China, as well as 500 to 600 discount stores by the end of 2007. Carrefour's entry strategies have not always been successful. The company was unable to establish itself in Hong Kong, and pulled out after four years, with losses of US$400 million.

Carrefour's success in new markets is partly derived from its willingness to learn about a host country's local culture and customs and plan accordingly. One of the retailer's core values is to 'respect our staff, suppliers and customers. Listen to them and accept their differences. Understand and respect the lifestyles, customs, cultures and individual interests in all countries and religions where we do business.' Carrefour adheres to these values when planning new stores in different markets. For instance, in Japan, where France and the French culture are popular, Carrefour adapted its stores to meet the desires of Japanese customers by doubling the number of French products (*www.carrefour.co.jp*). In China, the bicycle department was a major department and, given the size and diversity of the country, the Beijing and Shanghai stores do not offer the same local products. In Malaysia, the meat department is designed to respect Muslim religious practices.

Sources:
http://www.carrefour.com, 12 November 2003.
"Where Carrefour has a presence that presence is growing," *MMR*, 10 March 2003, Vol. 20, No. 5, p. 38.
"Global ambitions," *European Cosmetic Markets*, July 2003, Vol. 20, No. 7, pp. 265–268.
Robert Murphy, "Carrefour Net up 10% in Half," *WWD*, 29 August 2003, p. 2.
www.amrc.org.hk/alu/ALU36/003615.htm, 15 November 2003.
"Asia is promising for the long term," *MMR*, 10 March 2003, Vol. 20, No. 5, p. 40.

Consistently, whether it is a large European, American or Japanese multinational firm, the greater the degree of a firm's multinationality, the greater its performance. There is some limit to the performance gains from international expansion (Figure 1-6). A firm should not forego all domestic activities to pursue 100 per cent of its sales from foreign operations. However, a substantial movement of a firm's activities into international markets can be met with positive growth in sales and financial performance.

Although there are gains attributable to the international growth of a firm, the gains will not always be immediate. When we consider the performance of small internationalizing firms alongside that of the large multinational firms depicted in Figure 1-6, we find that small internationalizing firms must pay an initiation fee to join the ranks of well-established multinational firms. This initiation fee covers the costs of a substantial number of management challenges to be met when a firm is becoming a multinational firm.

We have identified some of the challenges in our earlier discussion in this chapter. Several of these challenges can be at their greatest during the early internationalization stage, during which a firm's managers must learn how to operate in international markets. Effectively managing the obstacles to early growth into international markets can shorten the time from the first performance decreasing steps in internationalization to achieve the heightened economic performance that comes later in the internationalization process. Other challenges increase in prominence once a firm's operations have a substantial multinational content. Effective management of the barriers to continued expansion into international markets can widen the positive performance scope of a firm's geographic expansion (see Figure 1-7).

Figure 1-6:   Multinationality and Performance: Large Multinational Firms[9]

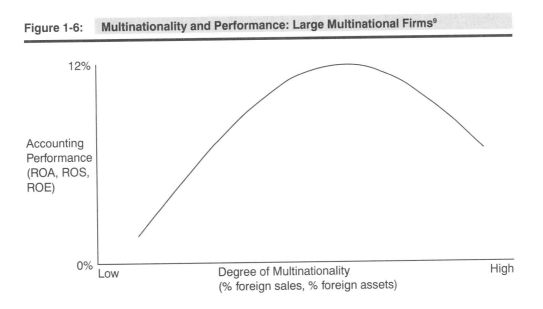

Figure 1-7:   Multinationality and Performance: Large and Small Firms

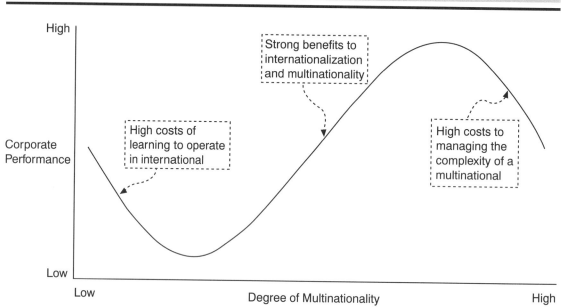

Source: Adapted from Jane W. Lu and Paul Beamish, "International Diversification and Performance: The S Curve Hypothesis," *Academy of Management Journal* (2004, Forthcoming).

We take into account the management challenges to internationalization and those encountered in the management of a multinational firm in the subsequent chapters of the book. The management mission in international business is one of the management of the internationalization process of a firm, and once internationalized, the management of a multinational firm.

For managing internationalization, a manager should understand the drivers of internationalization (see Chapter 2), the cultural and political sources of uncertainty and complexity in the international environment (see Chapters 3 and 4), and the major decisions encountered when expanding in international markets (see Chapters 5, 6 and 7).

For managing a multinational firm, a manager should understand the essential competitive issues underlying a multinational firm's expansion (see Chapter 8) and the competitive challenge posed by strong groups of domestic firms (see Chapter 9). Management issues in a multinational firm also involve understanding the sources of tension, conflicting demands and trade-offs in a multinational firm's operations (see Chapter 10), the exceptional circumstances encountered when managing a subsidiary operation of a multinational corporation (see Chapter 11), the dilemmas in human resource management created by international operations (see Chapter 12), and the ethical responsibilities of managing a multinational firm (see Chapter 13).[10]

By any stretch of the imagination, these issues are not exhaustive of those that underlie the international business and international management fields. However, in many ways, these are the ones that are truly unique to a manager in a firm competing in international markets. By mastering the issues covered in this and the next 12 chapters, a prospective international manager can acquire a thorough grounding in international business that can be used to support the development of multinational management skills and expertise in operating in a particular area of international business – be it international marketing, international corporate finance, international accounting, or international strategy. We begin that development in Chapter 2 with an exploration into the environment of international business.

Notes

[1] *http://www.uc-council.org/ean_ucc_system/*, 15 November 2003.

[2] "Barred for Life: UPCs at 25," *Chain Store Age*, December 1999, Vol. 75, No. 12, p. 146.

[3] Kathleen Hickey, "Getting in Tune: Standards Organizations See Wider Embrace of Supply-chain Standards, Greater Collaboration," *Traffic World*, 21 July 2003, Vol. 267, No. 29, pp. 17–18.

[4] "GCI Plans Strategy for Global Standards," *MMR*, 17 December 2001, Vol. 18, No. 18, p. 48.

[5] Alan M. Rugman, *End of Globalization* (London: Random House, 2001).

[6] *http://www.wto.org/english/docs_e/legal_e/ursum_wp.htm*, 18 November 2003. *http://www.wto.org/english/docs_e/legal_e/ldc2_512.htm*, 9 April 2003.

[7] *http://www.wto.org/english/tratop_e/dda_e/dda_e.htm*, 4 April 2003.

[8] Bruce Einhorn, "A Proud Papa Called Acer," *BusinessWeek*, 9 September 2002, No. 3798, p. 24.

[9] Several researchers find this result, including J. Michael Geringer, Paul W. Beamish and Richard C. daCosta, "Diversification Strategy and Internationalization: Implications for MNE Performance," *Strategic Management Journal*, 1987, vol. 10, no. 2, pp. 109–119; M. A., Hitt, R. E.Hoskisson and H. Kim, "International Diversification: Effects on Innovation and Firm Performance in Product-diversified Firm," *Academy of Management Journal*, 1997, Vol. 40, No. 4, pp. 767–798. Other research has found a positive relationship between a firm's degree of internationalization and performance including Andrew Delios and Paul W. Beamish, "Geographic Scope, Product Diversification and the Corporate Performance of Japanese Firms," *Strategic Management Journal*, 1999, Vol. 20, No. 8, pp. 711–727; Jiatao Li and Stephen Tallman, "Effects of International Diversity and Product Diversity on the Performance of Multinational Firms," *Academy of Management Journal,* 1996, Vol. 39, No.1, pp. 179–196.

[10] In our discussion of the topics covered in this book, we make reference to numerous articles and studies in the international business and international management journals. Our referencing is not exhaustive of all possible studies in the various areas. A more complete list of studies can be found in reviews published by Steve Werner, "Recent Developments in International Management Research: A Review of 20 Top Management Journals," *Journal of Management*, 2002, Vol. 28, Issue 3, pp. 277–297, and Jane W. Lu, "The Evolving Contributions in International Management Research," *Journal of International Management*, 2003, Vol. 9, Issue 2, pp. 193–213.

2 THE INTERNATIONAL BUSINESS ENVIRONMENT

When a firm crosses national borders, the managers in the company are faced with potentially dramatic differences in the environment in which the company operates. Changes can come along in a number of dimensions. Culture, language and social customs can differ from one country to another. The political system and rule of law can, likewise, vary. The economic system including the currency used for exchange, the banking system and the degree of central planning can also be quite different. Differences along each of these dimensions can have a substantial influence on the types of practices utilized by a company in its operations, as well as the strategies adopted by an international company in its multiple host country markets.

In this sense, the environment of international business is a multi-faceted and fascinating one. It is multi-faceted in the tremendous range of economic conditions, national political systems, cultures and value systems, and legal and social conditions encountered in the countries in which a multinational firm can operate. Each of these facets of a country can be thought of as a piece of a national institutional environment.

A variety of host country characteristics – political and legal rules, the economic environment and the social and cultural norms for business transactions – constitute a nation's institutional environment.[1] These variables define the conditions under which business occurs. National institutional environments can be characterized in a number of ways. We can identify specific dimensions of a country to identify how variance in that dimension will influence international business. Alternatively, we can cast a general characterization of a country, based on the general tenor of the dimensions comprising its institutional environment.

In describing an institutional environment in general, we can identify it as strong or weak, or somewhere in between. When an institutional environment is weak, it means that hazards can accompany business transactions in that country.[2] Weaknesses in the institutional environment refer to conditions that undermine property rights, and other national level characteristics that help to govern business exchanges, and increase risks in exchange. For example, where property rights are weak and environmental risks are greater, returns from any investment are less predictable. The uncertain shadow cast over the business environment, palls incentives to undertake transactions in that environment because property rights are not protected, and it is difficult to project reasonable expectations about returns from a business activity. Accordingly, when such uncertainty emerges, trading and investment transactions are likely to be fewer in number, and less in magnitude.

The uncertainty that extends from a nation's institutional environment can emerge from dimensions such as culture, politics and law. In Indonesia, business law relies heavily on laws and regulations that were issued during the Dutch colonial era. The process of replacing the old colonial laws and creating new ones that are adaptive to the changing economy and to the transitioning political system has been slow.

For example, the Indonesian government has made moves to address the current employment laws known as the Manpower Affairs Legislation. The new laws were first passed by Parliament in 1997 and due to come into effect in October 1998. However, a law was passed in 1998 to delay its implementation until October 2002. Just before the new laws were to take effect in 2002, Parliament agreed to scrap the existing legislation and perform a rewrite. This meant that foreign and domestic companies had to continue to subject their employment matters to disconnected government and ministerial decrees while the legislature was still trying to reach a consensus on the legislation.[3] Uncertainty about employment laws can, among other things, increase administrative costs. It can also alter the risk and return ratio for foreign companies doing business in Indonesia.

A nation's political and governance systems can likewise inject uncertainty that deter foreign and domestic investment. When the People's Republic of Bangladesh became a democratic nation in 1991, there were hopes that weaknesses in its governance system would be reformed. However, a weak institutional environment remains and the current government has been slow to undertake changes. As a result, the Bangladeshi government and economy continue to be characterized by poor governance and the weak performance of public institutions in the areas of the rule of law and order, corruption, and arbitrary decision-making.

These inefficiencies can hamper the development of business and the economy. Bangladesh, the eighth most populated and among the world's poorest countries, has vast natural gas supplies that could help the country deal with its economic problems. Farooq Sobhan, President of the Bangladesh Enterprise Institute, feels that if Bangladesh exploits its natural resources appropriately, 'it can emerge as an Asian tiger economy that will one day rival Malaysia or Thailand … If it is done properly the entire economy will be transformed, benefiting everyone from the humblest rickshaw puller to the wealthiest industrialist.'[4] Decisions on how to best exploit the gas supplies are entangled with the country's politics. Companies such as Shell (*www.shell.com*) and Unocal (*www.unocal.com*) vie for the chance to develop the fields, but they must continually work to negotiate proposed projects with the government and other officials.

In this sense, national institutional environments are an inescapable part of international business as they influence the costs and returns of operating in a particular country. Yet, at the same time, an understanding of national institutional environments is an indispensable part of the knowledge that an international manager must develop. Knowledge of the key facets of national institutional environments permits an international manager to identify the dimensions of a country that can create uncertainty in a business transaction. The same knowledge allows a strategy to be formulated that can help to mitigate risks by aiming that strategy at the areas of uncertainty and weakness in an international business environment. This general theme – understanding dimensions of institutional environments, projecting the likely impact of a particular dimension on the trading, foreign direct investment, manufacturing and sales activities of a firm, and developing strategies for coping with that expected impact – underscores the material we will discuss in Chapters 2, 3 and 4.

Managing International Business

Tremendous range in national institutional environments can create heightened uncertainty in a manager about how to operate in any one country. The first step to the successful management of a firm's diverse range of international operations is to understand this diversity in national institutional environments.

This understanding begins by first developing knowledge about the basic facts of the different countries and regions in the world. It is important to know which countries are among the fastest growing in the world and which are the largest markets in terms of gross domestic product (GDP) or population, or GDP per person.

Next, the knowledge can be extended to a country's level of integration in the global economy. What is the level of involvement in international trade? Is a country a net exporter, or a net importer? Has it been a source of foreign direct investment (FDI)? Is it a popular destination for FDI?

This knowledge can then be extended to include features of the host country that affect the costs of doing business. What are the comparative labour costs? What are the costs of other factors of production? What are the tax levels? Are there special areas or zones in a country that offer reduced tax and tariff rates for foreign firms?

This knowledge can also be developed while managers in a firm consider non-financial elements of national institutional environments. Two of the most prominent among these are the cultural and political environments. Both of these can inject a substantial amount of uncertainty in a firm's international operations. Consequently, we will cover the cultural environment in Chapter 3 and the political environment in Chapter 4.

In this chapter, we will consider the analysis of basic economic and financial data with a specific focus on trends in the Asia Pacific region. This chapter has several tables that present basic data on GDP, population, trade and investment as a starting point for understanding cross-country differences. This chapter then moves on to discuss the means of analyzing these data in the context of an international business decision.

It is important to emphasize that this is only a starting point. For any investment or trade decision, in-depth information on other features of a country, such as its relative cost levels, or its political and cultural environments, should also be gathered and analyzed. Only then, can an effective international business decision be reached.

Country Competitiveness

The potential range of variables that can be compared across countries shows up in the World Competitiveness Report compiled by IMD (*www.imd.ch/wcy*) and the World Economic Forum's Global Competitiveness Report (*www.weforum.org*).[5] These two bodies publish competitive reports on an annual basis, as drawn from data compiled from a survey of thousands of executives worldwide.

The individual items in these reports can be useful for analyzing facets of a country's economy such as the cost of doing business, the state of intellectual property protection, country risk, level of acceptance of foreign businesses, and at least 300 other indicators. The reports provide detailed and comprehensive data on the strengths and weaknesses of major economies in the world. The rankings by country consider how a firm can gain competitiveness from being situated in a particular economy.

To develop the overall competitiveness rankings of different countries, IMD and the World Competitiveness Forum collapse all the data they compile into one indicator (as in the case of IMD), or two indicators (as in the case of the World Economic Forum) (see Table 2-1). Since the first reports, the number of economies covered has increased to 60 by the IMD and 80 by the World Economic Forum. These countries have been the major contributors to the world economy.

Several economies in Asia Pacific have been historically placed at or near the top of the World Competitiveness rankings. Singapore, Hong Kong and Taiwan have been among the leaders. Other countries such as Thailand, China, Malaysia and the Philippines rank highly on some of the economic dimensions, but have a lower overall ranking because of difficulties encountered in the social and political dimensions of their national institutional environments.

In the 2002-03 rankings, Taiwan was placed at number three in the World Economic Forum's growth competitiveness ranking, just ahead of Singapore at number four. These countries each scored lower on the World Economic Forum's microeconomic competitiveness ranking and IMD's ranking. Reflecting the difficult conditions in the Asian business environment with the continued recession in Japan, and the after effects of the Asian financial crisis, few Asian countries were in the top 20 of either of the three competitiveness rankings.

Another notable feature of these rankings is that countries vary considerably from one ranking to the other. This difference emphasizes the need to consider multiple features of national institutional environments, when analyzing a country.

Table 2-1:   World Competitiveness Rankings (2002/03)

Country/ Region	World Economic Forum Growth Competitiveness Ranking	World Economic Forum Microeconomic Competitiveness Ranking	IMD Ranking
United States	1	1	1
Finland	2	2	2
Taiwan	3	16	24
Singapore	4	9	5
Sweden	5	6	11
Switzerland	6	5	7
Australia	7	14	14
Canada	8	10	8
Norway	9	21	17
Denmark	10	8	6
United Kingdom	11	3	16
Iceland	12	17	12
Japan	13	11	30
Germany	14	4	15
Netherlands	15	7	4
New Zealand	16	22	19
Hong Kong SAR	17	19	9
Austria	18	12	13
Israel	19	18	25
Chile	20	31	20
South Korea	21	23	27
Spain	22	25	23
Portugal	23	36	33
Ireland	24	20	10
Belgium	25	13	18
Estonia	26	30	21
Malaysia	27	26	26
Slovenia	28	27	38
Hungary	29	28	28
France	30	15	22
Thailand	31	35	34
South Africa	32	29	39
China	33	38	31
Greece	38	43	36
Italy	39	24	32

Table 2-1: continued

Country/ Region	World Economic Forum Growth Competitiveness Ranking	World Economic Forum Microeconomic Competitiveness Ranking	IMD Ranking
Czech Republic	40	34	29
Brazil	46	33	35
India	48	37	42
Slovak Republic	49	42	37

Sources: The Global Competitiveness Report (2002-3) (Geneva: World Economic Forum, 2002); International Institute for Management Development; *The World Competitiveness Yearbook (2003)* (Lausanne: International Institute for Management Development, 2003).

The Economic Environment

Economic environments can be characterized in a number of ways. General indicators reported daily and weekly in the business press and other media provide information on economic growth rates, expected growth rates, inflation rates, exchange rates and other aspects of the macroeconomic environment.

Precise indicators of various facets of the economy, that can be industry specific, are likewise widely available in many countries of the world. Housing starts, inventories, unemployment or employment rates, labour force participation, consumer confidence indices and a host of others can each be used to shine projections of the future performance of the economy.

Jointly comparing such a potentially large number of indicators in each country of the world is likely a task best left to statistical analyses on a desktop computer. Even with the help of technology in understanding macroeconomic trends, a good knowledge of basic features of national economic performance can be essential material to an international manager. These data can be used to gauge market size, market growth and the market potential of an economy for trade and investment. A set of numbers such as these can be found in Table 2-2.

Table 2-2: Worldwide Population and GDP Statistics by Economy (2002)

Country/Region	Population ('000s)	GDP (USD billion)	GDP per capita (USD)	GDP growth rate	GDP per capita growth rate
Albania	3,164.4	4.11	1,300	6.48	5.46
Algeria	30,835.0	54.68	1,773	2.10	0.61
Angola	13,512.0	9.47	701	3.17	0.28
Antigua and Barbuda	68.5	0.68	9,961	0.20	−0.52
Argentina	37,488.0	268.64	7,166	−4.45	−5.62
Armenia	3,088.0	2.12	686	9.58	9.40
Australia	19,387.0	368.73	19,019	3.90	2.80

Table 2-2:   continued

Country/Region	Population ('000s)	GDP (USD billion)	GDP per capita (USD)	GDP growth rate	GDP per capita growth rate
Austria	8,132.0	188.55	23,186	1.02	0.75
Azerbaijan	8,116.1	5.59	688	9.88	8.97
Bahrain	651.0	7.94	12,189	0.00	−0.41
Bangladesh	133,350.0	46.71	350	5.27	3.46
Barbados	268.2	2.76	10,282	1.48	1.03
Belarus	9,970.3	12.22	1,226	4.10	4.46
Belgium	10,286.0	229.61	22,323	0.99	0.66
Belize	247.1	0.81	3,258	5.08	2.05
Benin	6,436.7	2.37	368	5.00	2.31
Bhutan	828.0	0.53	644	7.00	4.02
Bolivia	8,515.2	7.97	936	1.23	−0.99
Bosnia and Herzegovina	4,060.0	4.77	1,175	6.00	3.83
Botswana	1,695.0	5.20	3,066	6.31	5.05
Brazil	172,390.0	502.51	2,915	1.50	0.15
Bulgaria	7,913.0	13.55	1,713	4.00	5.95
Burkina Faso	11,553.0	2.49	215	5.64	3.09
Burundi	6,938.0	0.69	99	3.20	1.25
Cambodia	12,265.0	3.40	278	6.30	4.19
Cameroon	15,197.0	8.50	559	5.30	3.07
Canada	31,082.0	694.48	22,343	1.45	0.43
Cape Verde	446.4	0.59	1,317	3.30	0.62
Central African Republic	3,770.8	0.97	257	1.50	0.05
Chad	7,916.0	1.60	202	8.50	5.46
Chile	15,402.0	66.45	4,314	2.80	1.53
China	1,271,900.0	1,159.00	911	7.30	6.51
Colombia	43,035.0	82.41	1,915	1.40	−0.34
Comoros	571.9	0.22	386	1.95	−0.53
Congo, Dem. Rep.	52,354.0	5.19	99	−4.52	−7.09
Congo, Rep.	3,103.4	2.75	886	2.90	0.07
Costa Rica	3,873.0	16.11	4,159	0.92	−0.72
Cote d'Ivoire	16,410.0	10.41	634	−0.90	−3.30
Croatia	4,380.8	20.26	4,625	4.08	4.06
Cyprus	760.7	9.13	12,004	4.00	3.50
Czech Republic	10,224.0	56.78	5,554	3.26	3.76

Table 2-2: continued

Country/Region	Population ('000s)	GDP (USD billion)	GDP per capita (USD)	GDP growth rate	GDP per capita growth rate
Denmark	5,359.0	161.54	30,144	0.95	0.59
Djibouti	644.3	0.58	894	1.59	−0.35
Dominica	71.9	0.26	3,661	−4.28	−4.11
Dominican Republic	8,505.2	21.21	2,494	2.72	1.12
Ecuador	12,879.0	17.98	1,396	5.60	3.69
Egypt, Arab Rep.	65,177.0	98.48	1,511	2.90	1.00
El Salvador	6,400.0	13.74	2,147	1.83	−0.14
Equatorial Guinea	469.1	1.85	3,935	1.35	−1.27
Eritrea	4,203.0	0.69	164	9.71	6.95
Estonia	1,364.0	5.53	4,051	5.04	5.46
Ethiopia	65,816.0	6.23	95	7.72	5.24
Fiji	817.0	1.68	2,061	2.59	1.95
Finland	5,188.0	120.86	23,296	0.74	0.43
France	59,191.0	1,309.80	22,128	1.83	1.32
Gabon	1,260.8	4.33	3,437	2.50	0.00
Gambia, The	1,340.8	0.39	291	6.00	3.01
Georgia	5,224.0	3.14	601	4.50	6.20
Germany	82,333.0	1,846.10	22,422	0.56	0.41
Ghana	19,708.0	5.30	269	4.00	1.88
Greece	10,591.0	117.17	11,063	4.10	3.80
Grenada	100.4	0.40	3,965	−4.70	−6.04
Guatemala	11,683.0	20.50	1,754	2.10	−0.50
Guinea	7,579.7	2.99	394	3.56	1.31
Guinea-Bissau	1,225.6	0.20	162	0.20	−1.98
Guyana	766.3	0.70	912	1.46	0.76
Haiti	8,132.0	3.74	460	−1.70	−3.79
Honduras	6,584.7	6.39	970	2.58	−0.03
Hong Kong, China	6,725.0	161.90	24,074	0.15	−0.75
Hungary	10,187.0	51.93	5,097	3.80	3.14
Iceland	282.0	7.70	27,312	3.02	2.29
India	1,032,400.0	477.34	462	5.40	3.72
Indonesia	208,980.0	145.31	695	3.32	1.97
Iran, Islamic Rep.	64,528.0	114.05	1,767	4.81	3.40
Ireland	3,839.0	103.30	26,908	5.85	4.61

Table 2-2: continued

Country/Region	Population ('000s)	GDP (USD billion)	GDP per capita (USD)	GDP growth rate	GDP per capita growth rate
Israel	6,363.0	108.32	17,023	−0.85	−2.88
Italy	57,948.0	1,088.80	18,789	1.78	1.32
Jamaica	2,590.0	7.78	3,005	1.73	1.06
Japan	127,030.0	4,141.40	32,602	−0.58	−0.71
Jordan	5,030.8	8.83	1,755	4.20	1.22
Kazakhstan	14,895.0	22.39	1,503	13.20	14.45
Kenya	30,736.0	11.40	371	1.10	−1.02
Kiribati	92.8	0.04	430	1.56	−0.74
Korea, Rep.	47,343.0	422.17	8,917	3.03	2.30
Kuwait	2,044.3	32.81	16,048	−1.03	−3.92
Kyrgyz Republic	4,955.0	1.53	308	5.31	4.46
Lao PDR	5,403.2	1.76	326	5.68	3.25
Latvia	2,359.0	7.55	3,200	7.56	8.15
Lebanon	4,384.7	16.71	3,811	1.30	−0.01
Lesotho	2,061.7	0.80	386	4.00	2.65
Liberia	3,213.8	0.52	163	5.30	2.56
Lithuania	3,482.0	11.99	3,444	5.86	6.59
Luxembourg	441.0	18.54	42,041	1.00	0.31
Macao, China	440.0	6.20	14,089	2.13	1.67
Macedonia, FYR	2,035.0	3.43	1,683	−4.06	−4.66
Madagascar	15,976.0	4.60	288	6.00	3.00
Malawi	10,526.0	1.75	166	−1.47	−3.48
Malaysia	23,802.0	88.04	3,699	0.39	−1.85
Maldives	280.3	0.58	2,082	2.08	−0.23
Mali	11,094.0	2.65	239	1.44	−0.88
Malta	395.0	3.62	9,172	−0.73	−1.99
Marshall Islands	52.5	0.10	1,830	0.60	−0.74
Mauritania	2,749.2	1.01	366	4.64	1.44
Mauritius	1,200.0	4.50	3,750	7.20	6.04
Mexico	99,420.0	617.82	6,214	−0.31	−1.76
Micronesia, Fed. Sts.	120.2	0.24	1,973	0.90	−0.89
Moldova	4,270.0	1.48	346	6.07	6.27
Mongolia	2,421.4	1.05	433	1.40	0.42
Morocco	29,170.0	34.22	1,173	6.50	4.80
Mozambique	18,071.0	3.61	200	13.90	11.50

Table 2-2: continued

Country/Region	Population ('000s)	GDP (USD billion)	GDP per capita (USD)	GDP growth rate	GDP per capita growth rate
Namibia	1,792.1	3.10	1,730	2.75	0.74
Nepal	23,585.0	5.56	236	4.82	2.41
Netherlands	16,039.0	380.14	23,701	1.13	0.37
New Zealand	3,849.0	50.43	13,101	3.20	2.71
Niger	11,184.0	1.95	175	7.57	4.19
Nigeria	129,870.0	41.37	319	3.90	1.53
Norway	4,513.0	166.15	36,816	1.40	0.91
Pakistan	141,450.0	58.67	415	2.74	0.29
Palau	19.5	0.12	6,280	1.00	−1.07
Panama	2,897.0	10.17	3,511	0.27	−1.22
Papua New Guinea	5,252.5	2.96	563	−3.53	−5.78
Paraguay	5,390.0	7.21	1,337	2.70	0.16
Peru	26,347.0	54.05	2,051	0.20	−1.35
Philippines	78,317.0	71.44	912	3.40	1.17
Poland	38,641.0	176.26	4,561	1.00	1.02
Portugal	10,024.0	109.80	10,954	1.65	1.49
Puerto Rico	3,840.0	67.90	17,682	5.58	4.92
Romania	22,408.0	38.72	1,728	5.30	5.43
Russian Federation	144,750.0	309.95	2,141	5.00	5.58
Rwanda	7,933.0	1.70	215	6.72	4.48
Samoa	174.0	0.25	1,465	10.00	8.74
Sao Tome and Principe	151.1	0.05	311	3.00	0.89
Saudi Arabia	21,408.0	186.49	8,711	1.20	−2.04
Senegal	9,767.8	4.65	476	5.75	3.17
Seychelles	82.4	0.57	6,912	−8.10	−9.43
Sierra Leone	5,133.4	0.75	146	5.40	3.30
Singapore	4,131.0	85.65	20,733	−2.04	−4.72
Slovak Republic	5,404.0	20.46	3,786	3.29	3.23
Slovenia	1,992.0	18.81	9,443	3.00	2.84
Solomon Islands	430.8	0.26	614	−9.00	−11.48
South Africa	43,240.0	113.27	2,620	2.22	1.19
Spain	41,117.0	581.82	14,150	2.76	1.22
Sri Lanka	18,732.0	15.91	849	−1.45	−2.84
St. Kitts and Nevis	45.1	0.34	7,609	1.69	−0.68
St. Lucia	156.7	0.66	4,222	−3.69	−4.55

Table 2-2: continued

Country/Region	Population ('000s)	GDP (USD billion)	GDP per capita (USD)	GDP growth rate	GDP per capita growth rate
St. Vincent and the Grenadines	115.9	0.35	3,047	−0.58	−1.34
Sudan	31,695.0	12.53	395	6.88	4.86
Suriname	419.7	0.76	1,803	5.87	5.20
Swaziland	1,067.9	1.25	1,175	1.60	−0.58
Sweden	8,894.0	209.81	23,590	1.21	0.92
Switzerland	7,231.0	247.09	34,171	1.33	0.62
Syrian Arab Republic	16,593.0	19.50	1,175	2.80	0.30
Tajikistan	6,244.7	1.06	169	10.20	9.29
Tanzania	34,450.0	9.34	271	5.69	3.38
Thailand	61,184.0	114.68	1,874	1.80	1.04
Timor-Leste	753.0	0.39	517	18.24	15.73
Togo	4,653.4	1.26	270	2.70	−0.09
Tonga	100.7	0.14	1,406	3.08	2.55
Trinidad and Tobago	1,309.6	8.84	6,752	5.00	4.31
Tunisia	9,673.6	19.99	2,066	4.91	3.72
Turkey	68,529.0	147.68	2,155	−7.39	−8.70
Turkmenistan	5,435.0	5.96	1,097	20.50	17.17
Uganda	22,788.0	5.68	249	4.63	1.97
Ukraine	49,093.0	37.59	766	9.10	10.01
United Kingdom	58,800.0	1,424.10	24,219	2.21	2.07
United States	285,320.0	10,065.00	35,276	0.30	−0.79
Uruguay	3,361.0	18.67	5,554	−3.14	−3.84
Uzbekistan	25,068.0	11.27	450	4.50	3.16
Vanuatu	201.2	0.21	1,058	−3.96	−5.96
Venezuela, RB	24,632.0	124.95	5,073	2.67	0.74
Vietnam	79,526.0	32.72	411	6.84	5.49
West Bank and Gaza	3,089.5	3.97	1,286	−11.90	−15.42
Yemen, Rep.	18,046.0	9.28	514	3.10	0.02
Yugoslavia, Fed. Rep.	10,651.0	10.86	1,020	5.50	5.36
Zambia	10,283.0	3.64	354	4.92	2.94
Zimbabwe	12,821.0	9.06	706	−8.42	−9.80

Source: World Development Indicators CD (The World Bank, 2003).

Table 2-2 provides data on population, GDP, GDP per capita, GDP growth rates and GDP per capita growth rates. Aggregate statistics on GDP and population provide a good summary of market potential. GDP per capita identifies the average wealth of an individual in a country. Per capita GDP growth and GDP growth detail the direction in which an economy has been moving.

In several countries in Asia, GDP growth and GDP per capita growth rates were spectacular and in many ways unprecedented during the 1950s to the 2000s. Japan led the way with 20 to 30 years of strong growth, moving from per capita GDP levels not much different from India in the 1940s, to a level exceeding the United States in the 1990s.

Japan's spectacular growth was followed by the five to seven per cent annual GDP growth rates in Singapore, Hong Kong, South Korea and Taiwan, starting from the 1960s and 1970s. Other countries in Asia, such as the Philippines, Thailand and Indonesia, likewise experienced strong growth, up until 1997.

India and China, the two largest countries in the region, dropped behind each of these countries during the 1950 to 1990 period. Economic reforms aimed at the liberalization of China's and India's economies, with a goal of increased integration with the rest of the world's economies, stimulated strong growth in China from the 1980s and good growth in India in the 1990s. In the 1980 to 2000 period, the southern province of Guangdong saw economic growth rates rivaling those of Singapore, Hong Kong, South Korea and Taiwan. Eastern provinces in China followed suit, growing at a rate of more than six per cent per year.

The result was that in 2002, China was the largest market in the world by population, with a GDP exceeding that of Italy's. Singapore and Hong Kong had per capita GDP levels easily comparable to that in other former Commonwealth countries such as Canada, Australia, New Zealand and South Africa.

Although many economies in Asia are still called developing or newly-emerging industrialized economies, the reality of the numbers indicates that the market potential in these economies, either on an aggregate level or on a per capita level, matches or exceeds that in many so-called developed economies. This trend has not been missed by international managers. Without a doubt, foreign direct investment and trade was instrumental in the development of many of these economies. Singapore, as an example, had inward foreign direct investment levels of about 15 per cent of national GDP in the 1990s. Foreign direct investment and trade can both follow and stimulate economic growth.

Given the prominence of foreign investment and trade as a component in any economy, it is useful to understand the trends and standings of a particular economy. Table 2-3 provides information on manufactured imports and exports, and net FDI (inflows of FDI less outflows of FDI) for a collection of countries largely similar to that in Table 2-2.

Table 2-3 reveals the considerable variance in the integration of numerous economies in the world's economy via trade. The United States has a clear dominance in world international trade, importing goods and services to a value of almost USD 1.4 trillion in 2001, while exporting nearly USD 1 trillion in the same year. The trading account deficit of nearly USD 400 billion, stood in contrast to the near balance in inward and outward FDI in the U.S. in 2001.

Table 2-3:   Worldwide International Trade and FDI Statistics (2001)

Country/Region	Exports (USD billion)	Imports (USD billion)	Net FDI (inflows less outflows) (USD billion)
Albania	0.79	1.71	0.21
Algeria	20.33	11.70	1.18
Angola	7.01	5.90	1.12
Antigua and Barbuda	0.47	0.54	0.04
Argentina	30.68	27.30	3.34
Armenia	0.54	0.97	0.07
Australia	80.03	78.52	−7.22
Azerbaijan	2.37	2.13	0.23
Bahrain	6.40	4.69	−0.14
Bangladesh	7.20	10.42	0.17
Barbados	1.31	1.45	0.02
Belarus	8.29	8.72	0.10
Belgium	193.83	186.18	−12.46
Belize	0.44	0.60	0.03
Benin	0.36	0.66	0.13
Bolivia	1.46	1.95	0.66
Bosnia and Herzegovina	1.27	2.57	0.20
Botswana	2.64	1.80	..
Brazil	67.14	72.34	24.89
Bulgaria	7.55	8.56	0.68
Burkina Faso	0.25	0.64	0.03
Burundi	0.04	0.13	..
Cambodia	1.81	2.09	0.11
Cameroon	2.71	2.48	0.17
Canada	304.28	268.35	−8.13
Cape Verde	0.15	0.34	0.00
Central African Republic	0.12	0.14	0.01
Chad	0.23	0.84	0.08
Chile	23.04	21.70	3.04
China	299.41	271.32	37.36
Colombia	15.98	15.69	2.29
Comoros	0.03	0.06	0.00
Congo, Dem. Rep.	0.92	0.87	0.03
Congo, Rep.	2.32	1.38	0.06
Costa Rica	6.88	7.24	0.45

Table 2-3: **continued**

Country/Region	Exports (USD billion)	Imports (USD billion)	Net FDI (inflows less outflows) (USD billion)
Cote d'Ivoire	4.10	3.36	0.14
Croatia	9.47	10.69	1.37
Cyprus	4.33	4.71	−0.05
Czech Republic	40.34	41.90	4.83
Denmark	73.65	63.29	−2.39
Dominica	0.13	0.17	0.01
Dominican Republic	5.07	6.80	1.20
Ecuador	5.60	6.15	1.13
Egypt, Arab Rep.	17.32	22.33	0.51
El Salvador	3.98	5.89	0.28
Eritrea	0.15	0.52	0.01
Estonia	5.01	5.22	0.34
Ethiopia	0.96	1.95	0.05
Finland	48.80	38.16	−4.72
France	365.63	345.07	−30.69
Gabon	2.62	1.76	0.20
Gambia, The	0.21	0.28	0.04
Georgia	0.69	1.20	0.16
Germany	645.54	610.57	−11.22
Ghana	2.77	3.74	0.09
Greece	30.07	41.29	0.97
Grenada	0.23	0.28	0.03
Guatemala	3.81	5.73	0.46
Guinea	0.83	0.88	0.09
Guinea-Bissau	0.08	0.15	0.03
Guyana	0.66	0.78	0.06
Haiti	0.47	1.25	0.002
Honduras	2.45	3.51	0.20
Hong Kong, China	232.96	224.36	13.86
Hungary	31.40	32.51	2.10
Iceland	3.12	3.15	0.00
India	65.16	73.66	3.30
Indonesia	59.69	47.33	−3.28
Iran, Islamic Rep.	32.04	24.51	0.40
Ireland	98.54	83.14	4.46

Table 2-3: continued

Country/Region	Exports (USD billion)	Imports (USD billion)	Net FDI (inflows less outflows) (USD billion)
Israel	39.67	43.51	2.09
Italy	307.80	290.36	−6.88
Jamaica	3.23	4.34	0.52
Japan	432.55	406.43	−32.31
Jordan	3.90	6.09	0.09
Kazakhstan	10.37	10.90	2.75
Kenya	2.97	3.94	0.01
Korea, Rep.	181.15	171.23	0.60
Kuwait	17.96	12.27	−0.36
Kyrgyz Republic	0.56	0.56	0.00
Lao PDR	0.54	0.60	0.02
Latvia	3.44	4.09	0.17
Lebanon	1.92	7.03	0.88
Lesotho	0.27	0.68	..
Lithuania	6.05	6.70	0.44
Macao, China	6.06	3.84	..
Macedonia, FYR	1.39	1.91	0.44
Madagascar	1.32	1.46	0.01
Malawi	0.46	0.66	0.03
Malaysia	102.43	86.25	0.29
Maldives	0.55	0.44	0.01
Mali	0.83	1.12	..
Malta	3.18	3.34	0.29
Mauritania	0.38	0.51	0.03
Mauritius	2.87	2.83	−0.05
Mexico	170.59	185.16	21.02
Moldova	0.74	1.10	0.15
Mongolia	0.67	0.84	0.06
Morocco	10.40	12.22	2.73
Mozambique	0.78	1.59	0.48
Namibia	1.66	2.05	..
Nepal	1.25	1.78	0.01
Netherlands	247.33	227.05	11.58
New Zealand	18.26	16.66	1.43
Niger	0.33	0.49	0.01

Table 2-3:   continued

Country/Region	Exports (USD billion)	Imports (USD billion)	Net FDI (inflows less outflows) (USD billion)
Nigeria	19.97	20.26	1.80
Norway	77.52	48.34	3.25
Oman	11.42	6.99	0.04
Pakistan	10.57	11.35	0.29
Palau	0.02	0.10	..
Panama	3.39	3.55	0.51
Paraguay	1.68	2.75	0.07
Peru	8.55	9.34	1.06
Philippines	35.20	33.88	1.95
Poland	51.33	58.19	5.80
Portugal	34.73	45.29	−1.93
Puerto Rico	54.84	68.20	..
Romania	12.98	16.12	1.17
Russian Federation	114.09	74.84	−0.06
Rwanda	0.16	0.44	0.01
Sao Tome and Principe	0.02	0.04	0.01
Saudi Arabia	78.21	45.59	0.02
Senegal	1.37	1.75	..
Seychelles	0.48	0.65	0.05
Sierra Leone	0.13	0.28	0.00
Singapore	148.65	130.05	−1.61
Slovak Republic	15.14	16.88	1.46
Slovenia	11.30	11.42	0.37
South Africa	31.50	28.65	10.85
Spain	174.08	182.68	−6.16
Sri Lanka	5.88	6.95	0.17
St. Kitts and Nevis	0.15	0.25	0.08
St. Lucia	0.32	0.40	0.05
St. Vincent and the Grenadines	0.16	0.22	0.04
Sudan	1.65	2.02	0.57
Suriname	0.52	0.64	..
Swaziland	0.86	1.02	0.03
Sweden	97.46	85.11	6.13
Switzerland	112.36	101.62	−2.42
Syrian Arab Republic	7.45	6.00	0.21

Table 2-3:   continued

Country/Region	Exports (USD billion)	Imports (USD billion)	Net FDI (inflows less outflows) (USD billion)
Taiwan	143.20	127.31	−0.10
Tajikistan	0.67	0.80	0.01
Tanzania	1.46	2.27	0.22
Thailand	75.98	69.04	3.66
Timor-Leste	0.04	0.20	..
Togo	0.41	0.63	0.07
Trinidad and Tobago	4.84	3.80	0.84
Tunisia	9.51	10.32	0.46
Turkey	49.76	45.85	2.77
Turkmenistan	2.78	2.81	0.13
Uganda	0.66	1.45	0.14
Ukraine	21.09	20.47	0.77
United Kingdom	386.22	416.94	28.87
United States	998.03	1,365.32	2.96
Uruguay	3.48	3.71	0.32
Uzbekistan	3.20	3.15	0.08
Venezuela, RB	28.32	21.94	3.30
Vietnam	17.91	18.57	1.30
Yemen, Rep.	3.52	3.46	−0.21
Yugoslavia, Fed. Rep.	2.76	5.16	0.17
Zambia	0.99	1.36	0.07
Zimbabwe	1.98	1.87	0.01

Source: World Development Indicators CD (The World Bank, 2003) & The World Bank Group: (*http://www.worldbank.org/data/*), 8 November 2003; *http://2k3dmz2.moea.gov.tw/gnweb/english/e_main.aspx?Page=E*, 20 November 2003.

Japan, traditionally thought to be the prime source of trading deficits in the United States, had total exports about equal to the value of the USD deficit in trade. Japan showed a modest surplus of USD 26 billion in its trading accounts.

Other nations in Asia similarly showed a surplus in trade accounts. Indonesia, had a surplus of USD 12 billion. China and Thailand had a value of exports about 8 per cent greater than imports. Australia, Singapore, the Philippines, and New Zealand had modest surpluses, while India and Bangladesh had modest deficits. Viet Nam imported as much as it exported. Nepal had extremely low levels of exports and imports, by the standards of other countries in the Asia Pacific.

The general trend in the balance of FDI flows reflects the discussion in Chapter 1 that compared the flows of FDI to and from developing countries and to and from Asia. Countries in Asia tend to be net recipients of FDI, with much of the surplus emerging from the net inflows of FDI into Asia from Europe and North America. China was the largest net recipient, having a surplus of nearly USD 40 billion. With FDI inflows of about USD 50 billion, the net surplus in China comes from China's established importance as a source for FDI inflows, as well as the early stage of its companies' international expansion, with a yet modest FDI outflow of about USD 5 to 10 billion in the latter half of the 1990s.

The FDI surplus of China and the USD 14 billion FDI deficit of Hong Kong might become less extreme, if Hong Kong's capital outflows to China were not considered to be FDI. Hong Kong is China's largest source of FDI, and its major trading partner. As China moves towards a greater degree of political union with Hong Kong, its foreign trading and FDI accounts will be folded in with China's, thereby reducing aggregate volumes of reported FDI, and their respective surpluses and deficits.

Aside from Hong Kong, Japan was the only other country in Asia with a large deficit in its FDI flows. Japan directed USD 32 billion more as investment in foreign countries, than it received in FDI inflows. More than 40 per cent of Japan's FDI outflows went to countries of Asia, helping to lead to surpluses in the FDI accounts of countries like Thailand, Singapore, Viet Nam and Indonesia.

International Trade and FDI

The trends outlined in Table 2-3 identify the state of the world at the break of a new century, following a century that saw consistent growth in international trade and foreign direct investment. The growth in trade and FDI reflects the simple fact that there are gains for a firm that engages in trade. Policy makers and economists alike identify that there can be gains to an economy from growth in trade and FDI.

Economic growth does not come with equal opportunities for growth for all firms. Increased foreign trade and FDI can place domestic firms at risk. Competition in the domestic market is heightened when a foreign firm enters the market. Local firms in a host country face an imperative to improve operations and competitiveness, or risk falling profit levels or even organizational failure. As a consequence of increased trade and FDI, local firms often increase productivity levels, enhancing the host country economy as a whole.[6] There are competitive implications for a local firm by the increased involvement of foreign firms.

International trade and FDI are becoming an increasingly relevant part of the competitive environment for all firms. For an international manager, it is vital to understand the impetuses to international trade and FDI. We deal with the first of these, international trade, while reserving the discussion of the forces that drive the development of multinational firms to Chapter 8.

An Historical Perspective on International Trade[7]

International trade is not a recent phenomenon. Firms had been trading across borders long before the emergence of the modern nation. Although international business on a significant scale began in the middle of the 19th century, individuals, merchants and bankers had exchanged goods and services over borders for centuries (see Figure 2-1).

In Asia, some of the earliest trading activities were done in what is current day China. Indirect trading contact between China and Southeast Asia can be traced back as far as the Shang Dynasty (1600 BC to 1100 BC). By the beginning of the first century BC, several important maritime trade routes provided links between the Indian subcontinent and Southeast Asia. These routes converged on the Kra Isthmus in Thailand. Traders moved goods from as far away as the eastern Mediterranean to the Gulf of Thailand. From the gulf, trade routes ran to Guangdong, to the Straits of Malacca and to southern Sumatra and northern Java.

The best known trade route in these times is perhaps the fabled Silk Road. With a route cutting across northern and western China, it bridged ancient Chinese and Western civilizations. During the Tang Dynasty (200 BC to 400 AD), this 11,000 kilometer route snaked through China, Central Asia, Northern India, and the Parthian and Roman Empires. It connected the Bohai Bay region of the Yellow River Valley to the Roman Empire's heart in the Mediterranean Sea. Even 1000 years later, the Silk Road still captured the imaginations of adventurers and traders such as the Venetian merchant Marco Polo who followed it into China in the middle of the 13th century.

In the 15th century, traders from China made seven great maritime expeditions, as guided by the orders of the Ming Emperor Yongle. Admiral Zheng He commanded these expeditions, which had 37 countries as the destinations for the admiral's fleets. Admiral Zheng He's trading

Figure 2-1:   Periods of Trade in Asia

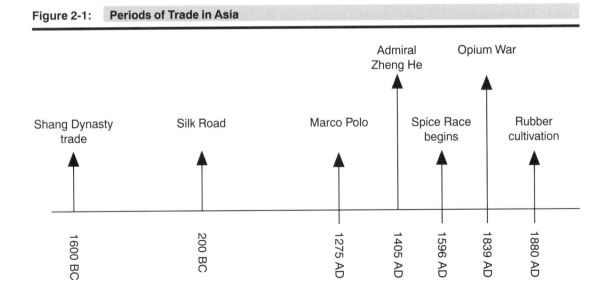

expeditions brought in a new era of maritime trade. China developed a substantial trading influence in Southeast Asia during a time of expanded international commerce that spanned 200 years.

By the early 16th century, Europeans began to enter Asian trade in greater numbers. The Portuguese seized Malacca in 1511 to mark the start of this era in European colonial trade in Asia. The Portuguese expedition to Malacca also initiated the race for the lucrative spice trade. The intensity of the battle for trade was only heightened by the concentration of spices on a few islands. The Dutch arrived in Southeast Asia in 1596, and soon seized the spice trade by moving into the former Portuguese holdings of the Maluku islands, Sri Lanka and Malacca. The Dutch successfully battled the British for the Bandar Islands. Soon, the Dutch East India Company had control of the principal spice producing regions.

Trade extended from the Spice Islands to the west. This trade grew in response to growing demand for rubber as sparked by the emergence of consumer demand for automobiles in the 1880s. Malaya proved to be a promising site for the production of rubber once Sir Ridley Scott exported rubber seeds from Brazil to Malaya. Large plantations quickly sprouted on the Malay Peninsula. Soon, Malayan tin and Malayan rubber dominated world markets.

In the same era, the British were engaged with trade with merchants from China for Chinese tea, silk and porcelain. The difficulty with this trade was that Western goods were in low demand in China. To ameliorate this problem, the British implemented a third-party trading system in which British merchants exchanged their merchandise in India and Southeast Asia for raw materials and semi-processed goods. These goods were in demand by merchants and consumers in Guangzhou. In the early nineteenth century, raw cotton and opium from British plantations in India were staple British imports into China. Opium was an illegal import into China because of the widespread addiction in China in the mid-1830s. The Qing government reacted to the continued trade of the British by confiscating and destroying nearly 20,000 chests of British opium. This action initiated the First Opium War, which concluded with the Chinese government signing the Treaty of Nanking in 1842. This Treaty ceded the island of Hong Kong to the British, and accorded Britain most-favoured nation trading privileges, paving the way for Hong Kong's 1960s emergence as a leading centre of international trade in the latter decades of the 20th century.

The ubiquity of international trade across nations and centuries, and its growth, sparked many economists to develop explanations about why firms engage in trade across national borders. These explanations are commonly called trade theory.

International Financial Markets

Before moving to trade theories, it is important to develop an understanding of international financial markets. International financial markets facilitate exchange when the home currencies of two firms differ. Hence, international financial markets are the means by which firms in different nations mediate their trading transactions.

We encounter one essential element of international financial markets almost daily. This element is the exchange rate. We see the exchange rate displayed in shop windows and banks in major tourist areas. It can be found quoted daily in newspapers, and a simple search of the internet will reveal an abundance of sites providing current and past exchange rates, and even exchange rate calculators.

An individual can arrange to exchange a currency at the present time, or at some time in the future. When the transaction is immediate the spot rate is used for conducting the transaction. When the transaction is sometime in the future, the forward rate can be used. The forward rate is the exchange rate that will be used when the currencies are exchanged in the future, whether the exchange occurs one month or even one year into the future.

In some cases, the forward and spot rates will be very close. At other times, the forward and spot rates can differ considerably, such as when there is considerable uncertainty in international markets. Forward and spot rates can show some variance as well depending on whether a currency has a fixed or floating exchange rate. A fixed exchange rate system is one in which the exchange rate for trading one currency for another is set by an international agreement. A floating exchange rate is one in which the demand and supply for a currency determines its exchange rate against other currencies.

Fixed exchange rates were common from the 1940s to the early 1970s. The fixed exchange rates adopted in the Bretton Woods Agreement established a small range in which currencies could float against the US dollar. The creation of the International Monetary Fund (IMF) and the World Bank provided institutions that could support fixed exchange rates. The IMF holds stocks of gold and currencies to support individual currencies. The World Bank is an international lending body.

In the early 1970s, many currencies were no longer pegged against the US dollar. Instead, the currencies were allowed to float against one another. A national government could intervene to influence the value of its currency in international markets. Such intervention, however, becomes more difficult as the volume of international financial transactions continues to increase through the 1990s and 2000s.

Nominal and Real Exchange Rates

An important concept to understand when looking at patterns in exchange rates is the difference between nominal and fixed exchange rates. A nominal exchange rate is the quoted rate of one currency versus another, whether that quote is the spot rate or the future rate. A nominal exchange rate is the relative price between currencies.

The real exchange rate is the quoted exchange rate, but with consideration given to differences in inflation rates for each currency. The real exchange rate provides the relative price between goods and services in two countries, not just the relative price between currencies, as in the nominal exchange rate. We can think of the real exchange rate as the the an index of foreign exchange in which we adjust the nominal exchange rate for relative price level changes (essentially inflation rates) across countries, since a base time period.

In one isolated exchange transaction at one point in time, the nominal and real exchange rate are effectively the same. Over time, however, the two can differ quite dramatically. The difference between the real and nominal exchange rate becomes great when inflationary forces in one country are much greater than in another country.

Changes in the real exchange rate help define situations in which there are winners and losers in exporting, importing and foreign direct investment transactions. We can consider winners to be firms in the countries in which changes in real exchange rates have increased the profitability of a trading or investment transaction, while losers are the firms that saw the profitability of a transaction decline.

Nominal Exchange Rates in the Asia Pacific

Table 2-4 identifies the nominal exchange rates of the US dollar and numerous Asian currencies against the Chinese Yuan. It marks the changing value of the Yuan against these currencies in the 1990 to 2003 period. Although the exchange rates of the Chinese Yuan (and Hong Kong dollar) have been more or less fixed by pegging the value of these currencies against the US dollar, other currencies in Asia float against the US dollar. The other currencies moved up and down in broad bands against the US dollar in the 1990 to 2003 period. In the first half of the 1990s, there was a period of sharp evaluation in the value of most Asian currencies against the US dollar. Meanwhile, the Chinese Yuan moved in the opposite direction. The devaluation of the Yuan in 1994 against the US dollar decreased the value of the Yuan against that of other currencies in the region.

If we take 1990 as the baseline exchange rate across all currencies listed in Table 2-4, changes in nominal exchange rates have been quite dramatic, and moving in two opposing directions, over the next decade. The first direction was towards the increased value of other currencies against the Chinese Yuan. By 1994, the Indonesian Rupiah stood at more than 1.5 times its 1990 nominal value of the Yuan. The Japanese Yen had increased in value by almost 2.5 times, with the Thai Baht and the Taiwanese new dollar appreciating by almost two times.

This change in exchange rates was a consequence of the change in the peg of the Chinese Yuan against the US dollar. In 1993, it cost about 5.8 RMB to buy one US dollar. In 1994, it required 8.7 RMB to buy one US dollar. With this devaluation in the Yuan, it was not surprising to see an explosion in FDI inflows into China, as it became a substantially more cost competitive environment.

The growing cost attractiveness of China, based on its nominal exchange rate, continued through 1997, until the onset of the Asian Financial Crisis. China was largely immune to the destructive forces of the Asian Financial Crisis. Its currency, along with Hong Kong's, after the authorities in Hong Kong battened down the hatches against the incursions of speculators into

Hong Kong's foreign currency and stock markets, remained stable against the dollar. Other Asian currencies fell, with severe drops for currencies such as the Rupiah.

Table 2-4: Nominal Exchange Rates against China's Yuan (RMB)

Year	US Dollar	Japanese Yen	Thai Baht	Hong Kong Dollar	Singapore Dollar	Malaysian Ringgit
1990	4.72	0.032	0.18	0.60	2.50	1.75
1991	5.23	0.039	0.21	0.67	2.98	1.92
1992	5.40	0.043	0.21	0.70	3.30	1.99
1993	5.84	0.046	0.23	0.75	3.52	2.25
1994	8.70	0.078	0.34	1.13	5.41	3.18
1995	8.44	0.086	0.34	1.09	5.80	3.30
1996	8.29	0.079	0.33	1.07	5.83	3.23
1997	8.33	0.071	0.32	1.08	5.93	3.37
1998	8.31	0.063	0.15	1.07	4.69	1.81
1999	8.28	0.073	0.22	1.07	4.91	2.17
2000	8.28	0.078	0.22	1.06	4.96	2.18
2001	8.28	0.070	0.19	1.06	4.78	2.18
2002	8.29	0.067	0.19	1.06	4.65	2.18
2003	8.28	0.077	0.21	1.07	4.82	2.18

Year	Philippines Peso	Taiwan New $	South Korean Won	Indonesian Rupiah	Vietnamese Dong
1990	0.22	0.18	0.0070	0.0026	—
1991	0.19	0.20	0.0073	0.0028	—
1992	0.21	0.21	0.0071	0.0027	—
1993	0.24	0.23	0.0074	0.0028	—
1994	0.32	0.33	0.0107	0.0041	—
1995	0.34	0.32	0.0106	0.0038	—
1996	0.32	0.30	0.0105	0.0036	—
1997	0.32	0.30	0.0098	0.0035	—
1998	0.19	0.24	0.0047	0.0010	—
1999	0.21	0.26	0.0071	0.0010	0.00060
2000	0.20	0.27	0.0073	0.0011	0.00059
2001	0.16	0.25	0.0065	0.0009	0.00057
2002	0.16	0.24	0.0067	0.0009	0.00057
2003	0.15	0.24	0.0069	0.0010	0.00055

Source: Datastream.

The result was that in 2003, the Indonesian Rupiah had less than half its 1990 value against the Yuan and less than 30 per cent of its 1994 value. The Philippine Peso was also below its 1990 nominal value against the RMB, while the Thai Baht was at about the same value. As a consequence, China had become a much less attractive place for cost-oriented foreign investment because of the Yuan's climb against other Asian currencies in the year following 1997.

If we begin to consider the different inflationary forces inside each country in the same period, we can have a more accurate picture of the real exchange rate. If we take two simple facts about consumer price index (CPI) increases, where the US has seen a growth rate of CPI of about 1.3 in the 1990s, while China has experienced CPI growth of more than two times in several of its cities, we can see that the real exchange rate in China is not moving in a favourable direction. Favourable in this sense, means in a direction that supports the cost competitiveness of China. If one is a foreign investor from China, then these trends in nominal and real exchange rates would be favourable.

Trade Theory

Trades theories help identify the reasons behind international trade. Firms engage in exports and imports because there are certain advantages that can be gained and exploited through international market participation. A firm's advantages in international trade can be a consequence of it being situated in a particular country. Trade theory considers a firm's home country explicitly in explaining patterns of international trade.

The home country can provide advantages to a firm through the factors of production that are available, through the relative price levels of factors of production, through the availability of skilled labor and technology and through the industrial environment in terms of competitive conditions that exist in the home country for the production of a particular good or service. Trade theories deal with each of these advantages.

The advantage to an international manager in understanding these sources of trading advantages is that it provides a means of diagnosing the sources of competitiveness of an industry rival. It also provides a means of analyzing the advantages that could come from locating production in a particular country. Finally, it could help a manager forecast and plan for future trends in trading patterns in international markets.

Classic Trade Theories[8]

Adam Smith published one of the first explanations of trade in his famous book, *The Wealth of Nations*. His trade theory can be called the theory of absolute advantage. This theory extended from his observation that firms in one nation, perhaps owing to the plentiful supply of a factor of production or a particular skill of a nation's workers, could always produce a product more efficiently than the firms in other nations. This efficiency meant that a nation had an absolute advantage in the production of a product.

International trade is a consequence of two or more nations having absolute advantages in different products. Each nation can specialize in the products in which it has an absolute advantage. Specialization means that each nation can produce more than it would otherwise. These products could then be traded across borders. Trade ensures that no nation is lacking in a particular product, and specialization means that more is available for all.

David Ricardo extended the ideas of Adam Smith by asking the basic question, 'Could a nation trade if it did not have absolute advantage in anything?'. The answer to this question is 'Yes', if one considers the idea of comparative advantage. Comparative advantage refers to the superior efficiency, that arises because of technology differences, a nation has of producing one product over another product. Even if a country does not possess an absolute advantage in the production of a product, it can specialize in the production of the product in which it has comparative advantage, and then engage in trade.

The main point we can derive from these two classical theories of trade is that there can be gains to a nation from engaging in international trade. These gains come from product specialization in firms that have an absolute or comparative advantage in their production of a particular good or service. The real world of international business is much more complex than the two country, two product models that help explain these trade theories. That said, the basic insight that material gains can be made to a nation's consumers from improved international trade is an essential motivation of the continued liberalization of world trade.

Factor Proportions Theory

The classic trade theories of Ricardo and Smith provided good explanations as to why there is international trade. Yet, the explanation was incomplete, particularly with respect to the issue of factor endowment differences. The work of Heckscher and Ohlin in the early parts of the 20th century addressed this issue of factor endowments and changed trade theory considerably.

The factor proportions theory of Heckscher and Ohlin considers that two factors of production, labour and capital, are required to produce a good. Countries differ in their endowments of each factor. Goods also require different amounts of each factor in their production.

As an example, to produce one unit of one good, such as textiles, it might require four units of labour and one unit of capital. To produce one unit of another good, such as computer chips, it might require four units of capital and one unit of labour for its production. In this sense, the proportions of the factors of production that are required to produce each good are different.

Next, we move to a consideration of the differences in factor endowments across countries. Factor endowments can differ across countries. These factor endowment differences can be persistent because factors of production are assumed to be immobile between countries.

Differences in levels of factor endowments coupled with cross-country immobility mean that factor prices across countries vary. A country with a relative abundance of a factor will have a lower price for that factor than a country without an abundance of that factor. The lower the factor prices in a country or the more abundant a particular factor, the lower the costs of goods produced with that factor.

Note that the differences in the cost of producing one good or another in one country or another does not depend on technology differences or other factors that might influence the efficiency of production. Instead it comes from a comparison in the availability and price of labour, capital and other factors of production across countries.

Building on these key ideas, factor proportions theory states that the firms in a country should focus on the production of a good that uses factors that are in abundant supply. Labour intensive products should be produced in countries with an abundant labour supply. Capital intensive products should be produced in countries with an abundant supply of capital.

The concentration of production in labour or capital intensive products should be accompanied by the export of those products. Countries should import products that use a factor of production in which the country does not have a high endowment.

Product Cycle Theory

The factor proportions theory helps move our understanding of international trade beyond the ideas of comparative and absolute advantage. It raises the issue of considering the inputs into the production of a good when analyzing international trade patterns.[9]

Later developments in trade theory continued to expand the world beyond the two country, two product and two factors of early trade theories. Researchers in international business began to address trade theory questions in the early 1960s. Vernon's Product Cycle theory,[10] as the name suggests, moved the focus of trade analysis to the level of the product. Vernon's basic contention was that the stage of product production determines which countries import and export a particular product.

Vernon identified that all products go through the new product, maturing product and standardized product stages. At the new product stage, high investment in research and development is required as the product tends to be at the forefront of the innovation and technological curve. At the maturing product stage, production is less innovative and more standardized. Success in production moves more towards a cost reduction focus, which can reduce the advantages domestic firms in developed economies have in the production of a product. In the standardized product stage, competition is cost-based. Advantages to production are confined to areas where labour and other factor costs are lowest.

The loci of production, exporting and importing, changes with these stages. At the new product stage, developed countries tend to be exporters because a key success factor in production is access to leading-edge technology and highly skilled labour. Developing countries tend to be importers.

At the maturing product stage, production levels in developed countries begin to decline, as key success factors move from innovation and product differentiation to cost-based considerations. Developing countries with abundances in low cost factors of production, such as a low cost labour force, become increasingly attractive as sites of production. Developed countries consequently see export levels fall, and import levels rise. Developing countries experience the opposite – a decline in imports and a rise in exports.

In the standardized product stage, this transition is completed. Production is almost completely concentrated in developing countries. Developing countries produce more than they consume, and developing countries' exports exceed imports. Meanwhile in developed countries, production levels have dropped to the point where domestic demand cannot be satisfied by domestic production. Consequently, the value of imports increases.

Theory of National Competitiveness

The book, *The Competitive Advantage of Nations*, outlines one of the most recently formulated theories of international trade.[11] Two ideas are intertwined in this book which presents theory, examples, and advice about international and national competition. The first idea is that international competition is not for the weak. The second is that innovation is the key to survival in internationally competitive markets (see Box 2-1).

Box 2-1   Australia's Wine Industry

Australian wine makers have been innovating continuously to remain competitive in an industry that includes masters such as Italy, France and Spain, and new entrants such as the United States, Canada and Chile.

Although the Australian wine industry has existed for nearly 200 years, it has had its most significant period of expansion in the past 15 years. Most of this growth has been driven by expansion into international markets. From 1990 to 2002, wine production increased from 383 million litres to 806 million litres, grape plantings grew from 60,000 hectares to more than 139,000 hectares, and annual exports expanded from 38 million litres (AUS$121 million) to 354 million litres (AUS$1.7 billion). Outside of Europe, Australia is now the world's largest exporter of wine, as given in statistics published in *www.wineaustralia.com.au*.

Apart from a united industry and a shared strategy, Australia's success as a wine exporter can be attributed to its participant firms' abilities to innovate. Australian wine personal have technical expertise, and the country has high-quality viticulture and oenology educational and training facilities. Most importantly, the business culture in the Australian wine industry is one that promotes and encourages innovation. The Australian government encourages the wine industry to study and analyze all forms of success, even those that do not fit with traditional approaches. This includes applications of new technology, and new or different approaches to marketing and distribution.

Australia is not the only Asia Pacific country to be noted for its innovation in wine. The New Zealand wine industry (*www.nzwine.com*) was recently selected as the Wine Region of the Year for 2002 by the US wine publication, *Wine Enthusiast Magazine*. The award highlighted the industry's innovation, consistency, diversity and value. The growing sales of New Zealand wines reflect its improvement. In the 1990s, New Zealand wine trade grew by 300 per cent, with exports reaching $246 million for the year ended June 2002.

Sources:

http://www.dfat.gov.au/media/speeches/foreign/2001/131101_fa_wine.html, 14 November 2003.

http://biz.tizwine.com/stories/storyReader$2873, 17 November 2003.

http://www.marketnewzealand.com/home/index/, 20 November 2003.

The theory of national competitiveness sees the world as becoming an increasingly competitive place. A nation's industries must compete in those sectors in which they possess national advantage. To do otherwise is to fight a losing war, one in which battles cannot be consistently won because the precursors for success do not exist in the home industrial environment.

To win battles, a company must invent and innovate relentlessly. Competitive advantage is fleeting and there must be pressures on the company to continually change and grow. Domestic, or home country, pressures for change and innovation lead a company to create competitive advantage and become successful in a market. Productivity increases, the only real measure of growth and improvement, increases and the attending competitive advantage lead to overall increases in national and international standards of living. Competition is a beneficial force to society as it sparks increases in material standards of living by preventing managers in companies from becoming complacent. Private companies are the focal point for national competitiveness. Where the right conditions are in place, companies must respond to the demands of the market by innovating and increasing productivity. Owners and managers in companies must avoid a short-term perspective. Harvesting strategies lead to failure. A focused strategy concentrating on continued long-term innovation and productivity gains is a must for international competitiveness.

The home government has a role in helping with the development of competitive companies. Education, research and development, and infrastructure can be government sponsored areas of investment that spur the creation of the national advantage. Governments must also ensure that a nation's markets are internationally contestable. Protected markets lead to stagnation, complacency, and the removal of the impetus to innovate. Open, vigorous international competition is required for the creation of international competitive advantage.

The Diamond

The core of the theory of national competitiveness centres on the framework of the Diamond. In the Diamond, the intensity of competition in an industry in a nation is influenced by four mutually reinforcing determinants. These four determinants form a dynamic system that supports companies in their endeavours to compete in world markets (see Figure 2-2). The Diamond of determinants is further supported by chance events and government actions and policies. Government and businesses can work to intensify the determinants and strengthen the Diamond.

Company Strategy

An important development in the theory of national competitiveness is the role ascribed to individual companies. Firms are at the forefront of international competition. Managers in a firm should have the goal of actively seeking and exploiting important sources of national advantage. A company must set its sights on creating and sustaining internationally measured competitive advantage (see Figure 2-3). A global strategy and a home base in the right nation helps develop international competitive advantage.

Figure 2-2:   The Four Corners of the Diamond

Factor Conditions: A nation's position in resources such as labour, infrastructure and natural resources. More important than a nation's advantageous position in these factors is its disadvantages in certain factors. Select disadvantages lead companies to innovate and upgrade and create competitive advantage.

Demand Conditions: The nature and extent of home demand for an industry's products. Sophisticated home buyers lead companies to create competitive advantage.

Related and Supporting Industries: The presence or absence of internationally competitive supplier and related industries supports innovation and upgrading.

Firm Strategy, Structure and Rivalry: The conditions in a nation governing how companies are created, how companies are organized and how competition unfolds. The vigour of domestic competition is particularly important as it serves as a training ground for competition on an international scale.

Figure 2-3:   Principles of Firm Behaviour

1.   Competitive advantage grows out of improvement, innovation and change.
2.   Competitive advantage involves the entire value system.
3.   Competitive advantage is sustained through relentless improvement.
4.   Sustaining competitive advantage demands that sources of advantage be upgraded.
5.   Sustaining competitive advantage requires a global approach to strategy.

Following the recurring theme of change, competition and the importance of innovation and investment, five principles of international competition that define successful strategy underscore the dictates for firm behaviour. Critical to the development of competitive advantage is innovation. The five principles relate broadly to a competitive environment in which a company should be directed to stimulate its investments and innovation. Managers in a firm must work actively to improve the conditions of competition in their home base. As some managers are too quick to conclude, global competition does not eliminate the importance of the home nation's contribution to the development of competitive advantage. Companies must not leave the management of the Diamond solely to external bodies like the government – they must work actively to ensure high quality human resources, infrastructure and scientific knowledge.

In implementing these ideas, managers can analyze the home base to discover the industries and segments in which the home base is favourable. Using the corners of the diamond as guidelines, a manager can evaluate the potential of an industry by asking such questions as: Are there capable domestic rivals? Does the industry attract outstanding talent? Are selective factor disadvantages in the nation leading indicators of foreign circumstances? Do the buyers' needs anticipate those of other nations? Are there strong positions in related and supporting industries? In areas where the home base is deficient, a company can work to improve that corner of the diamond or implement a global strategy that off-sets some of the disadvantages associated with that deficiency. An effective strategy is built on an understanding of the diamond and its implications for a company.

Synopsis

The theory of national competitiveness is one that unequivocally advocates competition. It sees the home environment as providing conditions that support a company's competitiveness. The Diamond of national competitiveness, or the Double-Diamond,[12] provide a means by which to analyze a nation to understand why collections of firms from one industry in one nation do particularly well. The idea of the Diamond, and its explicit focus on location as a source of advantage, links well to core theories of multinational enterprise that we will discuss in Chapter 8. For now, it encapsulates some of the most recent advances in theories on international trade, investment and competitiveness.

Summary

This chapter outlines several of the mainstays of economic, trade and foreign direct investment analysis that are useful for decision-making in international business. The analytical frameworks reviewed in this chapter shows how some of these bastions of data relate to the attractiveness of individual nations for a firm's operations.

In this sense, the facts and frameworks in this chapter provide a first and important step in developing knowledge about national institutional environments. Overall economic growth rates, country competitiveness and trade and investment trends define the general environment for a firm's operations. More specific information can, and should, be obtained by looking at these same trends in individual product sectors. Product specific information relates particularly to how one country or another can be an advantageous site for the production or sale of a particular product, such as steel, textiles, automobiles, consulting services, consumer banking and so forth.

Knowledge about the economic environment is just one of the aspects of national institutional environments that is relevant to an international manager. It is perhaps the easiest facet of the national institutional environment about which to gather information because data are readily available from a variety of sources, with very specific information provided by government sponsored investment agencies.

As we move into the next two areas of national institutional environments, namely the cultural and political environments, it should become clear that these areas are less well-defined and measured. It is fairly easy to measure exports in a given year, but how does one measure culture? How does one measure politics? We can come up with categories for cultural and political systems but it is necessary to think of how and if these categorizations help with decision-making by an international manager.

These challenges are just part of the added complications that create the heightened levels of uncertainty that accompany international business. Developing a thorough knowledge of economic factors provides a good foundation to interpreting opportunities and threats in a firm's international markets. This knowledge provides the foundation for making effective decisions, with a strong economic rationale, that can support the performance of a firm in its domestic and international markets.

Notes

[1] Douglas North, *Institutions, Institutional Change, and Economic Performance* (Cambridge: Cambridge University Press, 1990).

[2] D. North and B. Weingast, "Constitutions and Commitment: The Evolution of Institutions Governing Public Choice in 17th Century England," *Journal of Economic History*, 1989, Vol. 49, pp. 803–832.

[3] Baker and McKenzie, *Employment Law*, Asia Pacific Law at Work, *http://www.bakerinfo.com/NR/*, January 2003.

[4] "Pipe dreams; Bangladesh's natural gas," *The Economist* (US), 9 February, 2002, Vol. 362, Issue 8259, p. 55.

[5] World Economic Forum, *The Global Competitiveness Report (2002-3)* (Geneva, Switzerland: World Economic Forum, 2002), International Institute for Management Development; *The World Competitiveness Yearbook (2003)* (Lausanne, Switzerland: International Institute for Management Development, 2003).

[6] Wilbur Chung, Will Mitchell, and Bernard Yeung, "Foreign Direct Investment and Host Country Productivity: The American Automotive Components Industry in the 1980s," *Journal of International Business Studies*, 2003, Vol 34, Issue 2, pp. 199–218.

[7] For more on the history of international trade in Asia, see the sources for this discussion. Stuart-Fox, Martin, "A Short History of China and Southeast Asia: Tribute, Trade and Influence" (Australia: Allen & Unwin, 2003); Jones, Geoffrey, "The Evolution of International Business: An Introduction" (New York: Routledge, 1996); Wild, Oliver, "The Silk Road", 1992 (*http://ess1.ps.uci.edu/~oliver/silk.html#1*), 26 March 2003; C. M. Turnbull, *A History of Singapore, 1819-1988*, 2nd Ed (Singapore: Oxford University Press, 1989).

[8] Absolute advantage and comparative advantage are discussed much more extensively, with excellent examples and exposition, in most of the international trade and international economics textbooks.

[9] We could also consider other theories such as new trade theory as developed by economists such as W. J. Ethier, E. Helpman, and Paul Krugman. New trade theory is particularly important because it explains why we observe substantial amounts of intra-industry trade, especially between developed countries. According to new trade theory, countries trade goods because consumers like variety and trade is better than autarky when considering the trade-off between gains from economies of scale and rising transportation costs, that both accompany international trade. Issues such as these are covered in good detail in such texts as E. Leamer, editor, *International Economics*, Worth series in Outstanding Contributions, (Worth Publishers, 2001); J. Markusen, J. Melvin, W, Kaempfer and K Makus, *International Trade: Theory and Evidence* (McGraw Hill, 1995); E. Helpman and P. Krugman, *Market Structure and Foreign Trade* (Harvester Press, 1985); Gene M. Grossman and Elhanan Helpman, *Interest Groups and Trade Policy* (Princeton University Press, 2002); Paul R. Krugman, *Rethinking International Trade* (MIT Press, 1990).

[10] Raymond Vernon, "International Investment and International Trade in the Product Cycle," *Quarterly Journal of Economics*, May 1966, pp. 190–207.

[11] Michael E. Porter, *The Competitive Advantage of Nations* (New York: The Free Press, 1990).

[12] Alan M. Rugman, "Diamond in the Rough," *Business Quarterly*, Winter 1991, Vol. 55, No. 5, pp. 61–64.

3 THE CULTURAL ENVIRONMENT

Culture is a perplexing notion. We can each identify with the idea that specific groups of people, be it a nation or a group of people within a nation, share certain commonalities that provide attachment to a society, but it is not so easy to identify what are the commonalities. The definition of culture itself is a difficult one to pin down. Numerous definitions exist.[1] In one definition, culture is described as the learned beliefs, values and standards that are common to members of a group and help align interactions in the day-to-day life of group members.

In this definition, culture represents an adhesive force in a society that binds its people together at several points, whether it be by a commonality in beliefs, norms or values. Just as it can serve as a binding force, culture can also be a divisive force that separates people that come from culturally different groups. This latter concern is at the forefront of concerns for managers operating in global environments.

Managers in a multinational company must learn how to deal effectively with cultural differences. Understanding differences in culture across a company's host country markets helps managers in a company to develop successful marketing strategies for their company's products, it helps managers devise human resource management strategies that are consonant with the beliefs and practices of host country employees, and it helps align a company's strategy and organization with the external environment.

Levels of Culture

Our definition and description of culture has referred to a group of people, although some reference has been made to a national culture. It is important to use the word group to avoid the idea that culture is synonymous with a system of beliefs, values and norms at the level of a national culture. It is true that there is a concept such as national culture, but national culture is just one type of culture. We can also have a business culture, an organizational culture and an occupational culture.

Culture extends from a number of areas of influence in our lives. It comes from our interactions with different groups of individuals, and from our association with different institutions. These institutions include places of worship, schools, family, political systems, legal systems and economic systems. These work to shape the culture of a group of people. When considered together, these elements are the major shapers of national culture. But these elements also work in part to shape business, organizational and occupational cultures.

Although one can consider each level of culture as being important, the one most prominently featured for practitioners of international management is national culture. This prominence most likely extends from the high visibility of a national culture, particularly when juxtaposed against other national cultures. Given its prominence, it is important to try to understand what defines national culture, and differences across national cultures, and how we can contend with these differences.

National Culture

Researchers from a variety of disciplines, such as cultural anthropology, have tried to identify what defines national culture. In the international management field, several typologies of national culture have made their way into the lexicon of managers. One typology makes a simple, but powerful, distinction between high-context and low-context cultures. Another popular cultural framework is the Hofstede model of national culture. Other well-known cultural models and frameworks also exist. These include the 7d culture model created by Fons Trompenaars and the Kluckhohn and Strodtbeck model.

When looking at the descriptions of these models which are discussed below, it is important to consider the similarities in these models, as well as what are the implications of the descriptions of culture in these models for the practice of international management. One point of analysis is to look for similarities in terms of how individual cultures are defined across the models. Alternatively, we can look for similarities in the dimensions of the models used to define the values in a culture. As an example, several of the models have a dimension that refers to whether an individual or a group value orientation tends to be prevalent in a culture.

Hall's High- and Low-Context Cultural Model

Hall's cultural model differentiates between high- and low-context cultures.[2] In a high-context culture, the context is important for understanding the meaning of what an individual says. An understanding of a culture and its implicit cues to meaning in a conversation are key to fully understanding what somebody is saying. In a low-context culture, meaning is less reliant on the context, and it is more explicit in words. What the speaker says is more or less what the speaker means. Put another way, in a low-context culture unsaid words have little meaning. In a high-context culture, what is not said can carry substantial meaning, and perhaps more meaning than what is said.

Perhaps the foremost value of the high- and low-context culture model has been to aid business people from low-context countries such as the United States or the United Kingdom to understand communication in high-context cultures. The context cultural model was written by a US-based researcher, and published in journals and books in the United States. Interestingly, the model differentiates well between the prototypical US and European low-context business culture and many national cultures in Asia. German, Swiss, Scandinavian, US and British are each low-context cultures. Meanwhile, Vietnamese, Japanese, Korean and Chinese are each high-context cultures. Italian, Greek, Spanish and Arab societies fall somewhere between high- and low-context cultures.

The result is that the context approach to culture differentiates between cultures located in different parts of the world. Countries in the East – Japan, South Korea, Viet Nam and China – fall into the classic stereotype of the inscrutable, while Western cultures are typified as brazen and strident. The polarity between these stereotypes obscures vital differences between countries at the poles. In some respects, Vietnamese and Korean culture might be as much at odds with one another as Swiss and Korean culture are in the context model. This discrimination is lost by a focus on a solitary dimension of communicative exchange norms.

When we extend a cultural analysis framework beyond a single dimension it becomes more sensitive to subtler cultural differences, such as what might exist between geographically proximate nations. Along these lines, Hall's high- and low-context theory becomes more powerful as a tool for making fine-grained distinctions across cultures when we consider two other dimensions alongside the high- and low-context culture distinction. These two dimensions add considerations of a culture's view on space (proxemics) and time.

Proxemics refers to the way in which individuals in a culture use and perceive space. Cultures vary in their value of individual body space. A culture can have typical bodily distances that are close or far, given a situation of intimate personal-casual, social-consultive or public interaction. Cultures set different distinctive norms, and individuals from different cultures have different expectations for closeness in speaking and business situations. Standing too close or too far away in a given situation can lead to a cultural misunderstanding, in a feeling of apprehension akin to cultural shock.

The time value of Hall's model relates to idea of whether an individual in a culture tends to be in a monochronic time frame or a polychromic time frame. An individual in a monochronic time views time as critical, linear, tangible, and divisible. In monochronic time, events are scheduled sequentially. This schedule takes precedence over interpersonal relationships. Polychronic time involves the simultaneous scheduling of many events, where plans can change often and easily, and there is a high level of involvement in interpersonal relationships.

When we consider the space and time values along with the context dimension it becomes easier to distinguish cultures between nations in a region. If we compare Italy and Germany along these dimensions of time, context and space, we can readily see they are not alike as Italy is more high context, more polychronic and more proxemic than Germany.

In a cross-cultural situation it is important to try to understand and work with these distinctions. The challenge to any cultural frameworks model is whether it is able to aid an individual in making such a distinction. This challenge is magnified by the idea that a model of culture developed by a researcher based in one culture is also likely to have its greatest utility to people who are from a similar culture. Meanwhile, the model might not differentiate well in comparisons of cultures that are based outside the cultural context in which the researcher has been immersed. We will discuss this point more after we review several other cultural models.

Trompenaars' 7d Cultural Dimensions

Trompenaars developed the 7d cultural dimensions model based on traditional anthropological approaches to culture.[3] It contains elements similar to the Hofstede model, but not identical to Hofstede. The seven dimensions are articulated as polarities in values within a dimension. The dimensions can be grouped into three categories: relationships with people, perspectives on time and relationship with the environment, as given in Table 3-1.

Five dimensions fall into the relationships with people category. The universalism versus particularism dimension refers to whether individuals treat one another based on a set of rules or

Table 3-1:   **Trompenaars' 7d Cultural Dimensions**

Cultural Dimension	Definition	Sample issue
Relationships with people		
Universalism versus particularism	Social versus personal obligations	Are rules or relationships more important?
Collectivism versus individualism	Group versus personal goals	Do we act mostly as individuals or groups?
Neutral versus emotional relationships	Showing emotion in a business relationship	Can we express our emotions, or must we be restrained?
Specific versus diffuse relationships	Degree of involvement in personal relationships between superiors and subordinates	To what extent are we involved with the lives of other people?
Achievement versus ascription	The basis for determining status	Is status achieved through accomplishments or through situation in life (gender, age, social class)?
Perspective on time		
Sequential versus synchronic	Attitude towards time	Are tasks done in sequence or are several tasks done at the same time?
Relationship with environment		
Inner-directed versus outer-directed	Control over destiny	Do we control the environment, or does it control us?

Sources: Fons Trompenaars and Charles Hampden-Turner, *Riding the Waves of Culture: Understanding Cultural Diversity in Global Business* (New York: McGraw-Hill, 1998).

principles that provide guides to relationships, or by a judgment about what is right in a particular situation. The individualism versus collectivism dimension describes the extent to which a person is defined by their group memberships with family, school, work and other organizations. The neutral versus emotional dimension addresses the appropriateness of expressing emotions in daily interactions and when undertaking tasks. The specific versus diffuse dimension identifies how involved work is in a person's daily life, with a specific oriented culture having business separated from the rest of an individual's life. The achievement versus ascription describes the attainment of status in a society, with an ascription oriented culture leaning towards status by an individual's characteristics, instead of achievements.

The one dimension in the time category is sequential versus synchronic. This dimension expresses the importance of the time horizon, and whether the future, present or past receive prominence and are bounded.

The seventh dimension, inner-directed versus outer-directed, falls into the relationship with environment category. This dimension deals with the essential belief by individuals in a culture about whether they are dominated by nature, or they dominate nature. This belief identifies how people interact with the natural environment.

Kluckhohn and Strodtbeck's Value Orientations Framework

The Kluckhohn and Strodtbeck model identifies six orientations that define the attitudes of people in a culture to different parts of their lives and the world.[4] Interestingly, this model was not developed with managers nor an application to management in mind. Nevertheless, as given in Table 3-2, we can draw implications for the practice of management across cultures from the six value orientations.

These six orientations include items reflecting a culture's orientation towards the nature of people, the relationship to nature, the relationship to others, the modality of human activity, the temporal focus on human activity and the conception of space. For each of these orientations there are three prototypes of attitudes. Within an orientation, these prototypes of attitudes sometimes reflect a variance along a spectrum of attitudes, such as the endpoints of good and evil, and the mid-point of mixed for the nature of people orientation. Other attitudes of an orientation represent three distinct categories as in the doing, being and containing attitudes for the modality of human activity orientation.

As with the Trompenaars' framework, one of the consequences of this model for international managers is that it can point to important differences in basic attitudes across cultures. A firm in a culture that has an individualist attitude for its relationship to others orientation would likely have to adapt its internal organization practices if it sets up a factory or an office in a culture that has a collateral (collectivist) attitude. The firm's practices might have to change from a system of motivation and compensation based on individual merit towards one focused on the performance of groups.

Table 3-2:   **Kluckhohn and Strodtbeck's Value Orientations**

Orientation	Range of Attitudes	Implications for Managers
Nature of people	Good	Theory Y orientation, participation encouraged, direct communication valued, trusting and optimistic
	Evil	Pessimistic, Theory X orientation, secretive, suspicious of peers and subordinates
	Mixed	Use of intermediaries and consultants, a discrepancy between optimistic attitudes and behaviours
Relationship to nature	Dominant	Imposing one's will on the natural environment and the business environment
	Harmony	Coexistence, search for common ground, respect for diversity
	Subjugation	Fatalistic, ready acceptance of external control, aversion to independent planning
Relationship to others	Lineal (hierarchical)	Respect for authority and seniority, tall organizations, communication on a hierarchical basis
	Collateral (collectivist)	Relationships within the group influence attitudes towards work, superiors and other groups
	Individualist	People perceive themselves as individuals rather than as members of groups, competition encouraged
Modality of human activity	Doing	Performance valued, practical orientation, work central to an individual's life
	Being	Status derived from birth, age, sex and family connections more than achievement
	Containing	Focus on self-control, striving for balance between feeling and doing, self-inquiring
Temporal focus of human activity	Future	Future planning prioritized, past less important, concept of change valued
	Present	Immediate realities prioritized and used as basis of planning, long-term plans liable to modification
	Past	Past used as the model, respect for precedence, respect paid to aged
Conception of space	Private	Respect for personal ownership, what is private is valued, social distance
	Public	Suspicion of activities conducted in secret, public meetings valued
	Mixed	Private and public activities distinguished.

Sources: Adapted from Richard Mead, *International Management* (Oxford, U.K.: Blackwell, 1998), pp. 26–27.

Hofstede's Cultural Values Model

The Hofstede cultural values model has enjoyed great popularity since Hofstede's work was published in the 1980s. The Hofstede model defines national culture using five dimensions of cultural values. These five dimensions are typically labeled:

1. Power Distance – how a culture deals with inequality between superiors and subordinates
2. Uncertainty Avoidance – the level of tolerance for ambiguity
3. Individualism/Collectivism – the relationship between the individual and group
4. Masculinity – the cultural expectations for men and women
5. Confucianism (Long-Term Orientation) – a culture's perspective on time.

These value dimensions share overlaps with those values elucidated in the Trompenaars and Kluckhohn and Strodtbeck frameworks. Dimensions such as long-term orientation, power distance and individualism/collectivism have direct analogs in the other two frameworks.

Although the frameworks are similar along these value dimensions, the Hofstede framework is the most frequently referenced framework when describing cross-cultural issues, as they relate to the practice of international business. This popularity likely extends from the methodology of Hofstede's research, which attached a numerical score by nation for each value dimension. This scoring permits a relative ranking of a culture along a particular dimension to be made on a nation-by-nation basis.

If we refer to the scores in Table 3-3, we can use these scores to identify the ranking of a culture on the basis of one dimension or another. Among countries in the Asia-Pacific region, Japan scores the highest on the masculinity dimension, with the Philippines the next closest country, but still with a ranking considerably lower than Japan's. South Korea scores quite low on this dimension, which might be surprising given that South Korea and Japan are geographically proximate countries, with a shared history over centuries.

Using the values in Table 3-3, we can make similar comparisons for the other cultural dimensions. In the individualism category, there is not as substantial a differentiation across societies in Asia, as with the power distance dimension. These comparisons can yield some insight on a country-by-country, dimension-by-dimension basis, but the number of potential comparisons, with 40 countries and five dimensions, is too large to be of practical value.

Fortunately, the numerical scores facilitate another means of comparing cultures. We can compute a cultural distance that allows us to evaluate on an overall basis, how proximate one national culture is to another.[5] The cultural distance measure can be readily calculated using the scores found in Table 3.3. Typically, the Confucianism (Long-Term Orientation) dimension is not included in a calculation of cultural distance because this measure was added to the four core dimensions after the publication of Hofstede's original work in 1980. Further to this, the number of scores for countries on the Confucianism dimension is fewer than those for the other dimensions.

Table 3-3:   **Hofstede's Cultural Value Scores**

Country/ Region	Power Distance	Masculinity	Uncertainty Tolerance	Individualism	Confucianism
Argentina	49	56	86	46	—
Australia	36	61	51	90	31
Austria	11	79	70	55	—
Belgium	65	54	94	75	—
Brazil	69	49	76	38	65
Canada	39	52	48	80	23
Chile	63	28	86	23	—
Colombia	67	64	80	13	—
Costa Rica	35	21	86	15	—
Denmark	18	16	23	74	—
Ecuador	78	63	67	8	—
Finland	33	26	59	63	—
France	68	43	86	71	—
Germany	35	66	65	67	31
Great Britain	35	66	35	89	25
Greece	60	57	112	35	—
Guatemala	95	37	102	6	—
Hong Kong	68	57	29	25	96
Indonesia	78	46	48	14	—
India	77	56	40	48	61
Iran	58	43	59	41	—
Ireland	28	68	35	70	—
Israel	13	47	81	54	—
Italy	50	70	75	76	—
Jamaica	45	68	13	39	—
Japan	54	95	92	46	80
Korea (South)	60	39	85	18	75
Malaysia	104	50	36	26	—
Mexico	81	69	82	30	—
Netherlands	38	14	53	80	44
Norway	31	8	50	69	—
New Zealand	22	58	49	79	30
Pakistan	55	50	70	14	0
Panama	95	44	86	11	—
Peru	64	42	87	16	—

Table 3-3: **continued**

Country/ Region	Power Distance	Masculinity	Uncertainty Tolerance	Individualism	Confucianism
Philippines	94	64	44	32	19
Portugal	63	31	104	27	—
South Africa	49	63	49	65	—
Salvador	66	40	94	19	—
Singapore	74	48	8	20	48
Spain	57	42	86	51	—
Sweden	31	5	29	71	33
Switzerland	34	70	58	68	—
Taiwan	58	45	69	17	87
Thailand	64	34	64	20	56
Turkey	66	45	85	37	—
Uruguay	61	38	100	36	—
United States	40	62	46	91	29
Venezuela	81	73	76	12	—
Yugoslavia	76	21	88	27	—
East Africa	64	41	52	27	25
West Africa	77	46	54	20	16
Arab Countries	80	53	68	38	—
Mean	56.83	48.74	65.47	43.06	43.7
Standard Deviation	22	18	24	25	26
Variance	476	336	593	646	689

Sources: Geert Hofstede, *Culture's Consequences: International Differences in Work-related Values* (Beverly Hills, CA: Sage Publications, 1980); Geerte Hofstede and Michael Bond, "The Confucius Connection: From Cultural Roots to Economic Growth," *Organizational Dynamics*, 1988, Vol.16, issue 4, pp. 5–21.

The formula for calculating cultural distance is:

$$\text{Cultural Distance} = \Sigma\{(I_{ij} - I_{iu})^2 / V_i\} / 4$$

where I_{ij} equals index for cultural dimension i in country j
I_{iu} equals index for cultural dimension i in country u
V_i is the variance in the index for cultural dimension i

Using this formula, it becomes a fairly straightforward exercise to compare one country to another for the cultural distance scores. Table 3-4 shows countries ranked by cultural distance from the Netherlands, which is the home country for Hofstede. The countries that are the

Table 3-4:   Cultural Distance of Listed Countries from the Netherlands

Country	Rank	Cultural Distance	Country	Rank	Cultural Distance
Norway	1	0.11	Italy	21	2.27
Finland	2	0.24	Turkey	22	2.27
Sweden	3	0.36	Chile	23	2.29
Denmark	4	0.66	Brazil	24	2.30
Canada	5	0.91	India	25	2.54
New Zealand	6	1.38	Taiwan	26	2.55
Iran	7	1.40	Yugoslavia	27	2.59
Australia	8	1.42	Portugal	28	2.82
United States	9	1.51	Pakistan	29	2.86
Spain	10	1.52	Peru	30	3.05
France	11	1.59	Hong Kong	31	3.18
South Africa	12	1.67	Austria	32	3.47
Israel	13	1.68	Greece	33	3.78
Germany	14	1.83	Singapore	34	3.85
Great Britain	15	1.87	Colombia	35	4.20
Switzerland	16	2.04	Mexico	36	4.41
Ireland	17	2.07	Philippines	37	4.48
Argentina	18	2.11	Japan	38	5.38
Thailand	19	2.17	Venezuela	39	5.41
Belgium	20	2.20			

culturally closest to the Netherlands, using Hofstede's cultural distance scores, include the Nordic countries of Norway, Finland, Sweden and Denmark. This ordering generally matches intuition about which countries are the most culturally similar to the Netherlands. It is the same for the countries most distant from the Netherlands. These countries are located outside of Europe and are in the continents of South America and Asia. In order, the five most culturally distant countries from the Netherlands are Colombia, Mexico, the Philippines, Japan and Venezuela.

If we move to the case of Japan, the cultural distance rankings become a bit less clear. It is less clear in the sense that the countries culturally proximate and culturally distant from Japan do not in general match expectations. Typically, one would think that Asian countries, such as Taiwan and Singapore, might be the countries that are the culturally closest to Japan. However, this is not the case.

As shown in Table 3-5, the countries closest to Japan by the cultural distance measure are Italy, Argentina, Mexico, Greece and Colombia. Meanwhile, Taiwan and Singapore are respectively the 17th and 35th closest countries to Japan, in the ranking by cultural distance. This ranking

Table 3-5:   Cultural Distance of Listed Countries from Japan

Country	Rank	Cultural Distance	Country	Rank	Cultural Distance
Italy	1	0.89	India	21	2.46
Argentina	2	0.98	Ireland	22	2.52
Mexico	3	1.02	United States	23	2.53
Greece	4	1.15	Israel	24	2.57
Colombia	5	1.20	Canada	25	2.60
Germany	6	1.24	Philippines	26	2.68
Venezuela	7	1.33	New Zealand	27	2.73
Switzerland	8	1.34	Portugal	28	2.82
Belgium	9	1.46	Great Britain	29	2.90
Austria	10	1.56	Hong Kong	30	2.92
Brazil	11	1.60	Thailand	31	3.00
South Africa	12	1.60	Chile	32	3.08
Turkey	13	1.71	Finland	33	3.84
Spain	14	1.79	Yugoslavia	34	3.88
Pakistan	15	1.89	Singapore	35	4.96
France	16	2.08	Netherlands	36	5.38
Taiwan	17	2.14	Norway	37	6.04
Iran	18	2.18	Denmark	38	7.09
Peru	19	2.19	Sweden	39	7.37
Australia	20	2.43			

means Taiwan is at the mid-point in cultural distance from Japan and Singapore is among the most culturally distant countries from Japan.

Using the same methodology, we could compute cultural distance scores for any country-by-country comparison. Some scores would match expectations, but others such as when Japan or Singapore are the base, would not match expectations. This failure to match expectations in many cross-country comparisons of cultural distance means that the cultural distance measure may lack face validity.

Face validity refers to whether the tendencies in a measure concurs with our intuition and expectations. The cultural distance measure would have face validity if we found that the ranking of cultural distances between countries matches our expectations, or is at least close to what we expect.

In some cultural distance comparisons, such as for the Netherlands, the results match our expectations. In others, such as for the case of Japan, it does not. This lack of face validity for the cultural distance measure, particularly when it is taken out of the European setting, suggests that there might be an unintended bias in the research that developed the cultural values in the Hofstede cultural values framework. This unintended bias can emerge when an individual's own cultural background places an influence on how that person collects and interprets information. As it is based in the background of a person, this type of bias is almost inescapable.

It is possible for this bias to exist in any cultural values framework. Consequently, it is important to consider how that might influence our own interpretations of the cultural environment for international management decisions. The cultural frameworks we have reviewed, provide some insight into cross-national differences, and how to interpret these cross-national differences. We also have to be aware that such frameworks might mask important intra-regional cross-national differences, that would not be masked if the framework was developed by a researcher resident in the region in which the cultural comparisons were being made. In this sense, the frameworks might provide a better means of distinguishing across broad geographical regions of the world, than within countries in a region. This idea has lead to the creation of another categorization of cultures, called cultural blocks.

Cultural Blocks

We can think of cultural variation as occurring at three levels: within-country cultural variation, within-cultural block cultural variation and across cultural block cultural variation. Cultural blocks (or country clusters) emerged from the idea that the cultural variation between specific countries in a region is much less than the cultural variation between countries in different regions in the world.

Cultural blocks are by definition categories of countries that look similar on several cultural dimensions.[6] These dimensions include the importance of work goals, managerial and organizational variables, work roles and interpersonal satisfaction, and job fulfillment and satisfaction. As we have discussed above, many researchers have studied culture and compiled lists of cultural dimensions as well as scores on these. By looking at commonalties across these lists, we can categorize countries into cultural blocks (see Figure 3-1).

One of the principal utilities of cultural blocks is that it breaks down the world into more easily digestible pieces, than lists of countries ranked by a particular cultural value. Rather than trying to understand the wide range in cultural scores and values given across the countries listed in Table 3-3, a manager can look to the cultural blocks in Figure 3-1 as a way of defining the world into readily aggregated collections of culturally similar and dissimilar countries.

This aggregation of cultures can help pinpoint where uncertainty in the national environment might arise from the cultural environment, and what might be cultural dimension that creates the uncertainty. In this way, cultural analysis can help with decisions about international business decisions such as which country to enter, and how to enter it, or how to design a human resource management system.[7]

Figure 3-1: **Cultural Blocks**

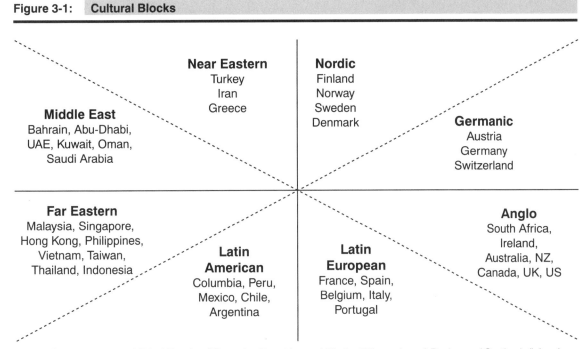

Source: Simcha Ronen and Oded Shenkar, "Clustering Countries on Attitudinal Dimensions: A Review and Synthesis," *Academy of Management Review*, 1985, Vol. 10, No. 3, pp. 435–454.

Culture and Management

The first part of this chapter makes it clear that culture varies across countries, along several important dimensions. This fact in itself is not surprising, but the forms of cultural variation across nations are not always immediately obvious. Effective international management in the cross-cultural domain begins with the development of an understanding of basic cultural differences. As that understanding develops, a manager can create strategies, structures and organizational systems that are consistent with the cultural values and beliefs in a region, such as how Nintendo has been doing in selling its game products (Box 3-1).

Trying to develop an understanding of culture in one country, let alone many countries, or even worldwide, is a daunting task. A memorization of the different cross-cultural values listed in Tables 3-1, 3-2 and 3-3 could be a first step in that direction, but it is a step that still leaves a manager far from the goal of an in-depth cross-cultural understanding.

One way to move closer to the goal is to understand differences in countries in terms of the determinants or reflections of national culture. Aspects of a society, such as its education systems, its languages, its religious beliefs, its family structures and its legal, economic and political systems, are knotted together to form national culture. Cultural norms, beliefs and values shared by members of a nation extend from these aspects of the society. As such, one point of departure for

Box 3-1   Nintendo in China

The Japanese video-games console maker Nintendo (*www.nintendo.com*) has developed a strategy to address the entrenched culture of software piracy in China.

The Chinese marketplace has posed problems for video-game console markers such as Nintendo, Sony and Microsoft, who are concerned with the protection of intellectual property rights. Nintendo estimates that it lost approximately US$650 million in sales as a result of software piracy in 2002. 'China remains the world's principal site for manufacturing pirated cartridge-based video games,' said Jodi Daugherty, director, anti-piracy, Nintendo of America.

When it chose to enter the Chinese marketplace, Nintendo designed its console system, released in late 2003, exclusively to address the piracy issue. Each console, named iQue Player, was equipped with a 64-megabyte flash memory card that was able to hold one game and would only work with one specific console. Customers could not purchase additional game cards. To purchase a new game, customers must download the new games at a designated retailer. When downloading a new game, the old game would be erased from the card, and replaced by the new game. The flash card records which games have been purchased, so that the consumer could download them again for free, at a later date.

Nintendo has also requested that the Chinese government pursue criminal prosecutions and impose sanctions against proven counterfeiters. In 2002, Nintendo confiscated nearly one million pirated products and video game components in China from 135 retail and manufacturing facilities, including pirated pieces of Nintendo's Game Boy Advance packaging, manufacturing components and counterfeit versions of its games, including Pokemon Ruby and Pokemon Sapphire.

To further harden its stance against the pirating of its games, Nintendo has undertaken legal action against individuals and firms pirating video games. In June 2003, Nintendo won a significant anti-piracy judgment when the High Court of Hong Kong ruled against Lik Sang International Limited (*www.lik-sang.com*), a global distributor of game copying devices.

By understanding and acknowledging the piracy issues in China, and in adjusting its entry strategy, Nintendo may be able to successfully enter a marketplace where the culture of video game piracy has become entrenched.

Sources:

"Nintendo Seeks Trade Sanctions to Combat Piracy, Designates China as Most Prominent Offender," *China Business News*, 18 February 2003.

"China – Nintendo to Launch iQue Video Games Console", *Asia Africa Intelligence Wire*, 25 September 2003.

"Nintendo to Launch New Game Console in China", *China Business News*, 25 September 2003.

"Hong Kong High Court Rules in Favor of Nintendo," *Business Wire*, 19 June 2003, p. 5163.

developing an awareness of a nation's culture, or national cultural differences, is to learn about a nation's religions, its languages, and its education systems.

Religion

Religion influences the development of culture in a region, and the practice of international business. Religious beliefs can have an impact on a society's attitudes towards individual entrepreneurship, to the types of lending practices used to finance businesses, to days of the week on which business can be conducted, and so forth.

Religion varies across world regions, but it also provides common ground to the nations of the world. Religions such as Buddhism, Christianity, Hinduism and Islam have large followings distributed worldwide (see Table 3-6). These religions can be found with a high concentration in any one particular country, or a country can have an eclectic mix of religions distributed amongst its people. India, for example, has a large majority of its population following Hinduism. Yet, a significant number of people in India follow Islam and Christianity. The strength of the numbers in these three religions, let alone others such as Sikhism or Jainism, reflect the need for international managers in a firm operating in India to consider the multi-faceted set of values and beliefs that stem from adherence to these religions.

In the Philippines, Christianity and Islam both thrive. There is somewhat of a geographical divide between the two, with Christianity being followed more strongly in the north and Islam more strongly in the south. The southern islands in the Philippines, where Islam tends to dominate

Table 3-6: Religions of the World

Religion	Number of followers (in millions)	Sample of countries and regions where religion is practiced
Atheist	850	Czech Republic, Slovakia
Buddhism	360	Bhutan, Brunei, Cambodia, Japan, Korea, Laos, Macau SAR, Malaysia, Mongolia, Myanmar, Sri Lanka, Thailand
Chinese Folk	225	China, Hong Kong SAR, Macau, Singapore, Taiwan
Christianity	2,000	Argentina, Australia, Austria, Belgium, Benin, Bolivia, Brazil, Canada, Chile, Costa Rica, Denmark, Dominican Republic, Fiji, Finland, France, Germany, Ghana, Greece, Hungary, Iceland, Indonesia, Ireland, Italy, Jamaica, South Korea, Mexico, Netherlands, New Zealand, Philippines, Spain, Ukraine, UK, US, Uruguay
Hinduism	900	Bangladesh, Bhutan, Fiji, Guyana, India, Mauritius, Nepal, Sri Lanka, Suriname, Trinidad and Tobago, Zambia
Indigenous	150	Angola, Benin, Botswana, Burkina Faso, Burundi, Cameroon, Central African Republic, Côte d'Ivoire, Ghana, Nigeria, Sierra Leone, Sudan, Swaziland, Togo
Judaism	14	Israel
Muslim (Islam)	1,300	Afghanistan, Albania, Algeria, Egypt, Ethiopia, Guyana, India, Indonesia, Iran, Iraq, Jordan, Kenya, Kuwait, Kyrgyzstan, Morocco, Nigeria, Oman, Pakistan, Saudi Arabia, Tajikistan, Tanzania, Togo, Turkey, Turkmenistan, Uganda, United Arab Emirates, Uzbekistan, Western Sahara, Yemen
Others	174	

Source: Adherents.com (*www.adherents.com*), 30 March 2003 and *The CIA World Book* 2002.
Note: Sikhism, Spiritism, Baha'i, Jainism, Shinto, Cao Dai, Tenrikyo, Neo-Paganism, Unitarian-Universalism, Rastafarianism, Scientology, Zoroastrianism and numerous other religions are included in the others category.

are close to Indonesia, which is also a country in which there are large numbers of Muslim adherents.

On one hand, national borders can instill a solidarity in culture, where different religions exist in a nation. On the other hand, the boundaries of cultural values can begin to blur across borders, especially where there is an absence of a clear distinction between the sets of religious beliefs in one country and those in another. The multi-faceted nature of religious beliefs within and across countries reinforces this idea.

Language

The richness of languages around the world is well-documented (see Table 3-7). The on-going increase in language commonalities across nations and the disappearance of a large number of languages is another trend that has continued and intensified over the past few decades.

Table 3-7:   Languages of the World

Language	First and Second Language Speakers (millions)	First Language Speakers (millions)	Countries and regions in which the language is commonly used
Mandarin	1,052	874	China, Indonesia, Malaysia, Singapore, Taiwan,
Hindi	487	366	India, Nepal, South Africa, Uganda
Spanish	417	358	Andorra, Argentina, Belize, Bolivia, Chile, Colombia, Costa Rica, Cuba, Dominican Republic, Ecuador, El Salvador, Guatemala, Honduras, Mexico, Nicaragua, Panama, Paraguay, Peru, Puerto Rico, Uruguay, United States, Venezuela
English	508	341	American Samoa, Antigua and Barbuda, Australia, Bahamas, Barbados, Belize, Bermuda, Botswana, Virgin Islands, Brunei, Cameroon, Canada, Cayman Islands, Cook Islands, Dominica, Eritrea, Ethiopia, Falkland Islands, Fiji, Gambia, Ghana, Gibraltar, Grenada, Guam, Guyana, India, Ireland, Israel, Jamaica, Kenya, Kiribati, Lesotho, Liberia, Malawi, Malta, Mauritius, Micronesia, Montserrat, Namibia, Nauru, New Zealand, Nigeria, Norfolk Island, Northern Mariana Islands, Pakistan, Palau, Papua New Guinea, Philippines, Pitcairn, Puerto Rico, Rwanda, Seychelles, Sierra Leone, Singapore, Solomon Islands, Somalia, South Africa, Sri Lanka, Swaziland, Tanzania, Tonga, Trinidad and Tobago, Uganda, United Kingdom, United States, Vanuatu, Zambia, Zimbabwe
Bengali	211	207	Bangladesh, India, Nepal

Table 3-7: continued

Language	First and Second Language Speakers (millions)	First Language Speakers (millions)	Countries and regions in which the language is commonly used
Arabic	200	175	Algeria, Bahrain, Chad, Comoros Islands, Djibouti, Egypt, Eritrea, Ethiopia, Iraq, Israel, Jordan, Kuwait, Lebanon, Libya, Mauritania, Morocco, Oman, Palestinian West Bank and Gaza, Qatar, Saudi Arabia, Somalia, Sudan, Syria, Tunisia, Turkey, United Arab Emirates, Western Sahara, Yemen
Portuguese	191	176	Angola, Brazil, Cape Verde Islands, France, Guinea-Bissau, Mozambique, São Tomé e Principe
Russian	277	167	Azerbaijan, Belarus, Bulgaria, Czech Republic, Estonia, Georgia, Israel, Kazakhstan, Kyrgyzstan, Latvia, Lithuania, Moldova, Russia, Tajikistan, Turkmenistan, Ukraine, US, Uzbekistan
Japanese	126	125	Japan
German	128	100	Austria, Belgium, Bolivia, Czech Republic, Denmark, Germany, Hungary, Italy, Kazakhstan, Liechtenstein, Luxembourg, Paraguay, Poland, Romania, Switzerland
French	128	77	Algeria, Andorra, Belgium, Benin, Burkina Faso, Burundi, Cameroon, Canada, Central African Republic, Chad, Comoros Islands, Congo, Côte d'Ivoire, Democratic Republic of Congo, Djibouti, France, Gabon, Guadeloupe, Guinea, Haiti, Italy, Lebanon, Luxembourg, Madagascar, Mali, Martinique, Monaco, New Caledonia, Niger, Reunion, Rwanda, Senegal, Seychelles, Switzerland, Togo, UK, Vanuatu
Cantonese	—	71	China, Malaysia, Singapore, Viet Nam

Source: Ethnologue: Languages of the World (*www.ethnologue.com*), 30 March 2003. Information on Arabic from 1999.
Note: The list of countries by language includes countries with up-to-date language information that have at least 50,000 people, 10 per cent of the population speaking the respective languages or the language is a national/official one.

The roots of language commonality are sunk in colonial ambitions. English, French, Spanish, Portuguese and Dutch became widely used in areas of North and South America, Asia and Africa and the Indian sub-continent during the 16th to 20th centuries. Mandarin became widely-used across China during the 20th century. Russian became a common language across the former republics of the Soviet Union during much of the 20th century.

The growth of these languages across regions of the world followed the colonization and political unification of different world regions. More recently, in the latter part of the 20th century, and on into the 21st, the integration of national economies has fostered the growth of English, Spanish and German, for example, as common languages in which to conduct business.

One of the results of these trends has been the growth of the numbers of speakers of several languages, whether a speaker uses a language as their first language or their second language. If we consider just the 12 languages in Table 3-7, we find that nearly two-thirds of people in the world speak one of these twelve languages as a first or second language. If we rely just on the first language criterion, half the world's population had one of these twelve languages as a first language.

Although those numbers are impressive, it still leaves a considerable portion of the world's population, two to three billion people, who speak another language predominantly. A key consideration for international managers is how to cope with this language variance.

The case of Japanese multinational firms is a case in point. Just one million people outside of Japan, South Korea and Taiwan, speak Japanese as a second language. Second language penetration of English, German, French or Mandarin within Japan still lags the efforts to promote language growth in Japan. Even by the year 2003, Japan was essentially a monolingual society, in which its populace spoke a language (Japanese) that was not shared widely across the world.

This homogeneity and isolation in language creates a unique set of challenges for Japanese multinational firms. For recruitment of staff and managers in a country such as Thailand, should Japanese firms impose a Japanese language criterion because that is the home country language? If so, the number of potential recruits will be quite low. An alternative is to use a language such as English, which is more widely spoken among graduates of Thai universities than Japanese, but that would entail providing similar efforts at training Japanese expatriates in English. Either way, the costs of recruiting and training are going to be substantial. Further, this scenario does not even consider the case of how to develop local marketing efforts in a local language.

This latter consideration, the language used to target a group of consumers in a host country, requires serious deliberation, when the society is multilingual. In polyglot societies such as Singapore and Malaysia, where it is not unusual for an individual to be fluent in Malay and English, and Mandarin along with perhaps other Chinese dialects, the selection of a language for communication with consumers has implications for which segment of the society the business reaches, as well as the visceral nature of the communication. Communication in Malay will carry a much different meaning than a literal translation of the same communication in Mandarin or English.

Even with the emergence of common languages among business people, a nation's mother languages are still an important means of communicating with a firm's buyers, suppliers and employees within a nation. Language also carries elements of a region's culture. How ideas are expressed, whether a particular idea or thought are expressed in words, how one refers to family members, teachers, colleagues, superiors and subordinates in a culture, are all captured in the language native to a region.

A more complete understanding of a nation's culture accompanies fluency in a nation's language, or its languages. Fluency permits an international manager to better understand a local culture, through a personal, instead of interpreted, experience of what is happening. Fluency permits direct communication with local employees, and it permits an international manager to move more easily in a society outside a work setting. Fluency coupled with a knowledge of norms and values in a society also reduces the chances of making critical mistakes in advertisements, brand names and communication.

Many such language blunders are infamous.[8] Even with the growing ubiquity of English in Asia, books and business magazines devote space to exposing odd and unusual uses of the English language. International managers whose native language is English are just as likely, or perhaps even more likely, to make similar blunders in verbal or written communications in languages such as Japanese, Vietnamese, Thai, Malay or Mandarin.

Education Systems

A nation's education system provides an individual with a form of acculturation that takes place over almost two decades. Just from the duration of education, it can be a strong force on the development of an individual's values, norms and beliefs. Numerous aspects of an education system can vary. Education systems can vary in the subject matter. Many schools in Europe focus on the teaching of one or more second languages. This focus promotes multilingualism in Europe, and leads to bilingual and trilingual capabilities in many of Europe's citizens.

In Australia, the response to the growing export wine market, has led to the creation of new educational avenues to promote the development of knowledge in this industry. The newly opened Australian College of Wine (*www.nmit.vic.edu.au/acw/*) provides diplomas, certificates and traineeships for those interested in pursuing a career in winemaking. The Wine MBA (*www.winemba.com*) covers major management topics applied to vine and wine business. Further, there are diploma and masters courses available in wine technology and marketing at Monash University (*www.buseco.monash.edu.au/units/Wine*). In this way, Australia's education system is shaped partly by its core industries, and the resultant developments in its education system help to develop values, norms and beliefs in Australia's citizens.

Aside from variance in subject matter, education systems can vary in their pedagogy. Is the typical form of instruction teacher-centred or student-centred? Is the typical form of instruction lecture and rote learning, or project-based learning? The type of instruction can be reflected in how comfortable and capable an individual in a nation is with a particular task environment. A rote-learning, teacher-centred system might be conducive to learning to work in highly structured environments (see Box 3-2).

Education systems can vary in the standards of relationships between students and between students and teachers. In some education systems, relationships can be formalized, with a strict hierarchy. The *senpai-kohai* distinction in Japanese schools and sports clubs, in which senior students (*senpai*) mentor junior students (*kohai*), is one example of this. Formal, hierarchical relationships in education can reflect cultures with a high power distance. A person educated in such a system might be the most comfortable in a work environment in which the hierarchy among superiors and subordinates is well-defined.

Box 3-2 The Thai Education System

The Thai government realized that it had to reform its largely rote-learning approach to education in order to remain competitive in the global marketplace. A government study in 1999 identified that the skills gap between Thailand and other ASEAN nations was a nationwide problem and a key issue that could negatively affect future development in Thailand.

The former education system did not encourage the creation of a pool of skilled workers. In 2000, Nattuwat Thiewthanom, an engineering graduate of Chulalongkorn University found it difficult to make use of his expertise, as Thailand was an assembler not a manufacturer. A typical Thai business enterprise did not house its own technology skills, let alone high-tech skills. Nitin Afzulpurkar, who is in charge of high-tech training programmes at the Asian Institute of Technology in Bangkok, supports this view, finding that designs, components and processes were usually developed abroad and then imported into Thailand. As a result, the lack of high-tech skills was impeding educated workers, like Thiewthanom, from successfully leveraging their education.

The system's impact was felt in the automotive sector. As the automotive sector continued to develop and expand and Thailand became an automotive manufacturing hub, it became apparent that the country lacked the human resource skills necessary to support this growth. To compete successfully, the auto industry had to source its talent from foreign countries, import auto parts from abroad, or invest in educating its employees. For example, from January 1998 to December 2000, GM had provided an average of about 120 hours of training for each member of its 700 to 800 strong Thai workforce.

The Thailand Ministry of Education (*www.moe.go.th/English/*) has been working to reform the system. However, the changes have been taking time to implement. The new education system was becoming more student-centred. The National Education Commission created 100 new educational zones around Thailand to ensure it would be better equipped to solve students' education problems. Education has become free for the first twelve years, and the Ministry was working on ways to promote life-long education. The Thai government hopes that these reforms will provide for greater opportunities for Thais and ensure that the country remains competitive into the twenty-first century.

Sources:

"Business Training: Skill Deficit; Thailand's Poorly Trained Workforce Costs the Country Business," *AsiaWeek*, 1 December 2000, Vol. 26, No. 47, *http://www.asiaweek.com/asiaweek/magazine/2000/1201/biz.training.html*, 26 December 2003. *http://www.moe.go.th/weberd/ministry__of_education.htm*, 26 May 2003

As with language and religion, knowledge of the education system, can provide these kinds of base insights into a culture. It can help with a design of the strategy, structure and systems implemented by a foreign firm when entering a country. It can help with the adjustment procedure an international manager must make when taking an expatriate assignment. Finally, it can help with the relationships international managers must establish with local employees, customers and other constituents of the firm in the local market.

Developing Cross-Cultural Knowledge

Even though it is difficult to precisely identify how and why national culture varies across the nations of the world, it is still a fairly easy task compared to learning how to deal with this variance. Numerous descriptions, such as that covered in the preceding sections of this chapter, outline basic national cultural differences, or differences along specific elements of a nation's culture. A person anticipating an international management career can read and learn about these cross-cultural characteristics, but this is just part of the training required.

To prepare managers for work in cross-cultural assignments, and to prepare managers to be able to develop effective strategies that account for cross-national variation in the cultural environment, companies frequently institute training programmes.

Training programmes usually begin with a language component, particularly in a national situation in which facility in a second or third language is not common. Training programmes will also devote some attention to developing cultural sensitivity. What are the typical mistakes one makes in common situations of interpersonal exchanges? As an example, should one bow, shake hands or wave when being introduced to someone new? The Executive Planet website (*http://www.executiveplanet.com/index2.jsp*) is one example of the kind of information available to guide one's conduct in various national environments.

Training programmes can involve indirect exposure to a nation's culture through the viewing of films, media reports, television shows or by reading books, magazines and newspapers published in a nation. Training can include a simulation component, in which situations such as a business negotiation are practiced with representatives from the local country.

These training activities range from the non-interactive to the interactive (see Figure 3-2). The idea in sequencing these activities in these ways is to provide increasing levels of exposure to a nation's culture. The intensity of exposure increases with each step, but the foundation is strengthened with each step. Clearly, this sequence of activities can be very time consuming. This reinforces the idea that culture is a tremendously amorphous notion that cannot be deduced but must be learned inductively.

Ultimately, the best way to develop cross-cultural knowledge is to experience a culture, or cultures, first-hand. Models of internationalization reflect this need to learn about culture in a gradual and sequential manner.[9] Unfortunately, this might mean that in an expatriate assignment, the expatriate is in a learn-as-you-go situation. The development of cultural knowledge occurs hand-in-hand with the performance of the expatriate's job.

Experiential learning about culture emphasizes the idea that travel and direct experience in other countries is a valuable means of preparing for a career in international management.[10] Business schools emphasize exchange programmes for this reason. Exchange programmes provide exposure to other cultures in a low-risk setting and the educational system of another country. Aside from exchange programmes, experience in other cultures can be achieved through one's own travels. Homestays and other forms of international travel that lead to integration in a local community provide a deep exposure to a nation's culture, and make for excellent opportunities to develop cross-cultural knowledge.

Figure 3-2: **Cross-Cultural Training Methods**

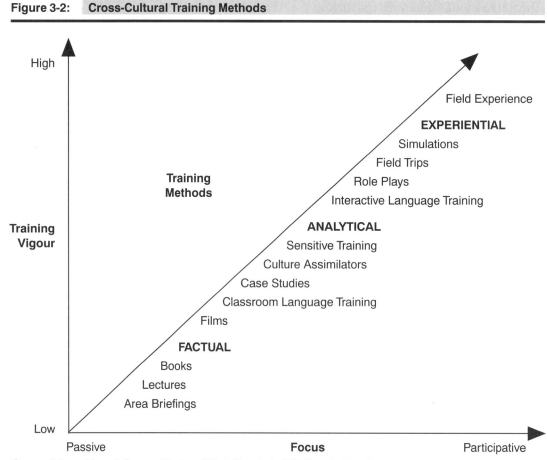

Source: Adapted from J. Stewart Black and Mark Mendenhall, "A Practical but Theory-Based Framework for Selecting Cross-Cultural Training Methods," in Mark Mendenhall and Gary Oddou, eds, *International Human Resource Management* (Boston: PWS-Kent, 1991), p. 188.

Local Managers

The difficulty and time consuming nature of learning about a culture necessarily means that any one manager would face a staggeringly daunting task to become conversant in several cultures of the world. Nevertheless, an international manager can become comfortable and effective in managing in more than one national culture. A few uniquely talented individuals might even develop a facility to operate equally well in several national cultures.

The challenges to managing diversity in the cultural environment are created in part by the difficulties in learning about new cultures. These challenges are only magnified as a firm increases the geographic scope of its operations. As a firm grows internationally, it will encounter an increasing variety of national cultures in its operating environments. In a firm with a wide spread across world regions, managers indigenous to the home country of the firm are less likely to be able to operate effectively in each of the firm's host country markets.

One option to deal with this challenge of managing cultural diversity is to undertake a series of training programmes, such as those detailed in the preceding section of this chapter. Another option is to focus recruitment activities on individuals from the local host country market. These recruitment activities can have the goal of developing a cadre of local managers who can one day move up into the upper echelons of a multinational firm's management hierarchy. The idea behind this form of recruitment strategy is that it is easier to train someone in the skills of a particular management job, and in the organizational culture, then it is to train someone to understand a new national culture.

Although this idea might seem obvious, multinational firms have been slow to offer real opportunities for advancement to host country nationals. This process has changed somewhat in recent years. Even Japanese firms, which had a reputation of having a rice paper ceiling that limited the upward advancement of non-Japanese employees, have shown a decrease in their reliance on the appointment of expatriates to manage foreign operations.[11] This decrease in the use of expatriates is a natural consequence of supply and demand. The demand for expatriates increased tremendously during Japanese firm's rapid international expansion in the late 1980s and early 1990s. The supply did not increase commensurately, leading to a shortfall in qualified expatriate managers. Local managers compensated for this shortfall.

The crux of this example is that a Japanese firm's impetus to the use of local managers has been more reactive than proactive. Yet, companies can be proactive in the recruitment, selection and training of local managers. As we discuss in Chapter 12, doing so, however, can entail a significant shift in the organizational mindset to one that embraces the contributions of host country managers.

Summary

Culture is one dimension of national institutional environments. As with each dimension of a national institutional environment, cultural variation heightens the level of uncertainty in decisions made by an international manager. It creates uncertainty because a national culture new to a firm encompasses new sets of beliefs, values and norms that can alter the keys to success in a firm's operations.

To minimize this uncertainty, and maximize the effectiveness of decisions, and the host country success of a firm's operations, it is necessary to develop skills in managers to run a firm's operations in its host countries. These skills can come from the development of cross-cultural knowledge in expatriate managers, or the development of host country nationals to work as managers in the firm.

The former training task is a daunting one. It begins with a recognition of how cultures vary across the world. Gradually, the training process moves to one of higher engagement with the local culture. It concludes with direct experience in the host country's culture, as one lives in a country, to build-up a visceral understanding of its culture.

As these skills are developed in a firm's management, important decisions about how to manage a firm's operations in the country can be made. These decisions encompass broad strategic issues such as the degree to which products and organizational systems are tailored to the local environment, as well as more specific decisions such as the entry mode used to establish operations in a host country. A successful firm in these decisions is one that has planned and taken the steps to proactively manage the cultural dimension in the international environment.

Notes

[1] Alfred Kroeber and Clyde Kluckhohn, *Culture: A Critical Review of Concepts and Definitions* (New York: Random House, 1995).

[2] Edward T. Hall, *Beyond Culture* (Garden City, New York: Anchor Press, 1976).

[3] Fons Trompenaars, *Riding the Waves of Culture* (Chicago: Irwin, 1993).

[4] Florence R. Kluckhohn and Frederick L. Strodtbeck, *Variations in Value Orientations* (Westport, CT: Greenwood, 1961).

[5] Kogut Bruce and Harbir Singh, "The Effect of National Culture on the Choice of Entry Mode," *Journal of International Business Studies*, 1988, Vol. 19, No. 3, pp. 411–432.

[6] Simcha Ronen and Oded Shenkar, "Clustering Countries on Attitudinal Dimensions: A Review and Synthesis," *Academy of Management Review*, 1985, Vol. 10, No. 3, pp. 435–454.

[7] Harry G. Barkema, John H. J. Bell, and Johannes M. Pennings, "Foreign Entry, Cultural Barriers and Learning," *Strategic Management Journal*, 1996, Vol. 17, No. 2, pp. 151–166.

[8] David A. Ricks, *Big Business Blunders* (Homewood, Illinois: Irwin, 1983).

[9] Jan Johanson and Jan-Erik Vahlne, "The Internationalisation Process of the Firm – A Model of Knowledge Development and Increasing Market Commitments," *Journal of International Business Studies*, 1977, Vol. 8, No. 1, pp. 23–32; Reijo Luostarinen, *Foreign Operations,* (Helsinki, Finland: Helsingin Kauppakorkeakoulun Kuvalaitos, 1970); Harry G. Barkema, John H. J. Bell, and Johannes M. Pennings, "Foreign Entry, Cultural Barriers and Learning," *Strategic Management Journal*, 1996, Vol. 17, No. 2, pp. 151–166.

[10] Paul W. Beamish, Alan J. Morrison, Philip M. Rosenzweig, and Andrew C. Inkpen, *International Management: Text and Cases*, 4th Ed (Irwin-McGraw-Hill, 2000), pp. 392–398.

[11] Paul W. Beamish and Andrew C. Inkpen, "Japanese Firms and the Decline of the Japanese Expatriate," *Journal of World Business*, 1998, Vol. 33, No. 1, pp. 35–50.

4 THE POLITICAL ENVIRONMENT

The word politics can almost never fail to inspire debate. Politics is a sensitive issue with many individuals. The political environment is an equally sensitive issue to a company. Just like the cultural environment, the political environment can vary considerably across nations. This variance creates uncertainty when a firm is entering a new host country market, and when it is operating in a host country.

To maximize the chances of making a successful and profitable entry in a foreign country, a firm's managers must be able to both measure and manage the political environment.[1] The political environment can inject uncertainty into a firm's operations.[2] To identify the extent of uncertainty, a firm's managers can turn to subjective measures of the political environment which are typically called political risk measures, or to objective measures of the political environment which we will call political hazards. Both of these types of measures help a manager assess the level of uncertainty in a political environment, which consequently helps with the management of this uncertainty.

Uncertainty from the political environment can impede a manager's ability to design structures, systems and strategies for its foreign subsidiaries.[3] Regardless of whether a firm and a host country government interact in a one-time or an on-going basis, the political environment is of foremost concern to a firm's management because a host country's political system is in the background of every business transaction.[4] The political environment contributes to the certainty of the business environment. It contributes to the costs of doing business in a country. It influences the types of skills and capabilities that managers in a firm must develop to be effective in operations in a host country.

Typically, international managers regard the political environment as a source of added costs, as an impediment to business operations and as a source of risk. The political environment introduces these elements through the possibility of a government's intervention in the activities of a multinational firm. Intervention can take various forms. A government can impose limitations on foreign ownership in subsidiaries. It can institute requirements for local content and export levels. At the extreme, it can expropriate a portion of the returns of a multinational firm's operations, or it can expropriate ownership of the foreign subsidiary.[5]

One of the principal difficulties in managing these forms of government intervention stems from a common perception of the political environment. More often than not, international managers perceive the political environment to be exogenous. Managers view it as being outside the realm of managerial influence and action, and therefore it cannot be managed.

Yet, this perception is not necessarily accurate. Like other facets of the environment, international managers can both measure and manage the political environment. This management does not only mean coping with the stresses placed on a firm's operations by the political environment. It also means developing the capabilities to make management of the political environment a source of competitive advantage in a multinational firm.

Hence, when thinking about the political environment, it is more than just a case that politics matters. A fundamental part of international business is that it involves business transactions that take place across nations. As such, national political environments and variation therein are of prime concern to multinational managers. The ability to measure and manage these differences can be a source of advantage for a firm.

Measures of Policy Uncertainty

The political process, from how laws and policies are made, to how individuals reach positions of power in a political system, clearly varies across countries. The structure of political systems and political institutions likewise vary across countries. Each of these sources of variance can create uncertainty in a firm. A new political system can be a point of uncertainty, just based on the unfamiliarity a firm's managers have with that particular system.

Another type of uncertainty engendered by a nation's political system, comes not from its novelty to a firm's management team, but from the fluctuations in policies and regulations – taxes, import and export quotas, employment conditions, input and output constraints, local content requirements – that govern a firm's business transactions in a host country. This form of uncertainty, which we can call policy uncertainty, is rooted in the nature of a nation's political system and in the structure of its political institutions. Policy uncertainty, sometimes thought of as political risk, is at the heart of the management challenge in the political environment.

Managers in a multinational company need to be concerned with, and are often frustrated by, unwanted and unforecasted changes in their operations that are a consequence of government intervention. Government intervention occurs when policy makers intervene in the operations of a foreign subsidiary by making or changing laws about the degree of foreign ownership and control, by regulating financial flows, by instituting local content requirements, by setting taxes and tariffs and by a host of other policy instruments. Policy makers are charged with the task of making and altering rules and laws, which can change the basic conditions under which a firm's subsidiaries operate and perform.

When a company enters a country, it has knowledge about the current state of a country's rules, regulations and laws regarding its operations in the country. Managers can devise a set of operations, and make forecasts about returns based upon the existing set of conditions in the host country. These conditions can change. It is important for the managers in a multinational company to be cognizant of the possibility of such change, and to devise strategies for dealing with, and perhaps influencing the possibility and direction of, change.

The starting point for managing this change is the measurement of the political environment. In the next two sections, we concentrate on identifying two specific types of measures of the political environment. The first, political risk, is a subjective rating of the political environment. A political risk measure can help assess where and when a firm might encounter difficulties in managing the political environment, but it is subject to biases in the individuals who provide the perceptual assessments of political risk and it might not reflect the micro-nature of political opportunities and risk.

The second measure, political hazards, is an objective measure that examines the threat that politics or political players will have a negative impact on a firm's asset values, costs or revenues.[6] Political hazards can provide a good first order, or overall objective view, of the political environment, but it does not identify the specific political institutions that are most relevant to a particular multinational firm.

Political Risk

The importance of the policy environment is marked by the attention given to measurements of political risk. The chance of a government taking action in way that is detrimental to the economic or operational viability of a subsidiary operation can be thought of as political risk. Political risk is often associated with the idea of unwanted and potentially drastic changes, culminating in perhaps the complete expropriation of a subsidiary's operations.[7]

Several well-known agencies produce political risk rankings. The Economist Intelligence Unit, Euromoney, the European Management Foundation, the World Bank[8] and IMD each produce measures of political risk. The scores are available by nation and are compiled on annual, semi-annual, and even monthly bases.

These political risk indices are generally compiled through a survey of international executives. The sum of the perceptions of the international executives becomes the political risk score for a country. This method has the advantage of having people intimately involved with a country producing assessments of the political risk levels of that country, or other nearby countries.

The result of these assessment methods is an ordinal ranking of the political risk levels of different countries. Using these political risk scores, we can rank countries into the most risky and least risky. Further, we even have a score that we can use to distinguish just how risky one country is to another.

Table 4-1 provides a sample of political risk scores as compiled from Euromoney's September 1992 and 2003 rankings. These scores range from zero to 20 in 1992, with 20 being a situation of least political risk and zero being a situation in which political risk is at its maximum. In 2003,

Table 4-1: Political Risk Scores by Country/Region

Country/Region	Political Risk 1992	Political Risk 2003	Country/Region	Political Risk 1992	Political Risk 2003
Afghanistan	1.3	2.71	China	13.3	16.84
Albania	2.1	6.08	Colombia	11.5	11.86
Algeria	5.8	11.58	Congo	4.5	5.31
Angola	5.9	4.98	Costa Rica	10.2	14.79
Antigua & Barbuda	—	10.68	Côte d'Ivoire	6.2	3.34
Argentina	10.6	3.26	Croatia	4.4	13.94
Armenia	3.1	6.54	Cuba	4.5	1.89
Australia	18.4	23.88	Cyprus	12.7	18.40
Austria	19	23.96	Czech Republic	10.5	18.37
Azerbaijan	2.8	9.31	Dem. Rep. of the Congo	—	2.60
Bahamas	13.7	18.15	Denmark	18.5	24.62
Bahrain	14.1	15.94	Djibouti	6.1	5.72
Bangladesh	5.3	9.12	Dominica	—	9.09
Barbados	12.8	19.09	Dominican Republic	—	9.12
Belarus	6.9	5.72	Ecuador	7.6	7.64
Belgium	17.9	23.08	Egypt	9.5	11.34
Belize	8.5	8.11	El Salvador	4.8	11.53
Benin	3.2	6.41	Equatorial Guinea	—	7.78
Bermuda	—	20.65	Eritrea	—	3.40
Bhutan	7.8	10.79	Estonia	8.9	17.91
Bolivia	7.8	7.34	Ethiopia	1.9	5.01
Bosnia-Herzegovina	1.7	6.82	Fiji	11.9	10.19
Botswana	9.9	17.33	Finland	17.6	24.59
Brazil	7.8	11.69	France	19.2	23.85
Brunei	17.7	17.72	Gabon	8.2	7.06
Bulgaria	5.7	12.10	Georgia	4.7	3.37
Burkina Faso	—	6.46	Germany	19.7	23.88
Burundi	4.8	3.67	Ghana	8.7	7.97
Cambodia	1.3	7.80	Greece	12.8	19.85
Cameroon	7	6.46	Grenada	8.8	12.57
Canada	18.6	24.64	Guatemala	6.1	10.30
Cape Verde	7.9	6.00	Guinea	5.1	4.30
Central African Republic	4.2	2.90	Guinea-Bissau	2.9	6.02
Chad	2.9	4.65	Guyana	—	8.90
Chile	14.3	19.17	Haiti	3.7	3.72

Table 4-1: **continued**

Country/Region	Political Risk		Country/Region	Political Risk	
	1992	2003		1992	2003
Honduras	—	8.60	Malta	14.7	19.66
Hong Kong	16.2	19.17	Marshall Islands	—	8.52
Hungary	11.5	18.04	Mauritania	2.6	5.31
Iceland	15.9	21.14	Mauritius	10.5	14.29
India	6.4	14.73	Mexico	13.7	16.87
Indonesia	12.6	8.98	Micronesia (Fed. States)	—	10.79
Iran	10.3	11.06	Moldova	2.6	5.12
Iraq	1.7	0.74	Mongolia	4.8	9.42
Ireland	16.4	23.60	Morocco	10.4	13.94
Israel	11.5	17.03	Mozambique	1.9	6.22
Italy	15.9	21.88	Myanmar	2.9	4.79
Jamaica	8	10.95	Namibia	8.9	9.61
Japan	20	22.26	Nepal	6.7	9.99
Jordan	7	11.64	Netherlands	19.8	24.51
Kazakhstan	6.7	10.87	New Caledonia	—	13.53
Kenya	7	8.05	New Zealand	17.3	22.67
Korea North	3.2	0.00	Nicaragua	—	4.93
Korea South	16.6	18.18	Niger	3.8	5.37
Kuwait	13	17.74	Nigeria	6.6	6.57
Kyrgyz Republic	5.7	6.00	Norway	18.5	24.51
Laos	—	7.97	Oman	14.4	16.51
Latvia	7.8	16.54	Pakistan	8.2	10.27
Lebanon	4.2	7.69	Panama	7.6	12.16
Lesotho	8.6	7.37	Papua New Guinea	8.2	8.79
Liberia	—	0.74	Paraguay	8.8	5.48
Libya	8.8	11.28	Peru	2.7	11.23
Lithuania	8.5	16.29	Philippines	8	13.36
Luxembourg	19.6	24.76	Poland	8.6	17.00
Macau	—	17.36	Portugal	15.9	21.58
Macedonia (FYR)	—	5.72	Qatar	14.6	17.17
Madagascar	4.8	5.39	Romania	7.2	11.88
Malawi	—	4.96	Russia	6.8	11.77
Malaysia	15.3	17.25	Rwanda	—	2.49
Maldives	—	12.16	Samoa	—	13.06
Mali	—	6.22	São Tomé e Principe	5.3	3.61

Table 4-1: **continued**

Country/Region	Political Risk		Country/Region	Political Risk	
	1992	2003		1992	2003
Saudi Arabia	16.1	14.92	Thailand	13.6	16.57
Senegal	7	8.43	The Gambia	7.4	7.34
Seychelles	9.3	9.34	Togo	—	5.31
Sierra Leone	—	2.57	Tonga	—	12.16
Singapore	18	23.47	Trinidad & Tobago	10.1	15.83
Slovak Republic	7.4	15.72	Tunisia	10.4	14.81
Slovenia	7.9	19.82	Turkey	11.8	10.90
Solomon Islands	—	9.42	Turkmenistan	6.2	6.16
Somalia	0	1.86	Uganda	4.2	7.34
South Africa	11.9	16.07	Ukraine	8.7	8.05
Spain	17.1	22.65	United Arab Emirates	14.9	18.98
Sri Lanka	7.4	12.27	United Kingdom	19.5	25.00
St Lucia	—	13.80	United States	19.6	24.95
St Vincent & the Grenadines	9.7	14.35	Uruguay	10	6.71
Sudan	0.3	3.92	Uzbekistan	5.7	5.83
Suriname	—	6.68	Vanuatu	7	10.10
Swaziland	—	6.96	Venezuela	10.2	6.60
Sweden	18.8	24.34	Vietnam	5.5	11.86
Switzerland	20	24.97	Yemen	—	6.96
Syria	8.5	8.16	Yugoslavia (Fed. Republic)	1.5	4.74
Taiwan	17.3	20.43	Zambia	4.8	4.52
Tajikistan	4.7	5.15	Zimbabwe	7.3	1.64
Tanzania	4.5	7.64			

Sources: Euromoney, "Nowhere to Lend to," *Euromoney*, September 1992, pp. 65–71; Euromoney, "Country Risk," *Euromoney*, September 2003, pp. 287–292.

the range was 0 to 25, with 25 being a situation of least political risk. Over time, from 1992 to 2003, the coverage of countries in the Euromoney political risk scores has become greater.

Perhaps not surprisingly to some, countries such as Afghanistan, Burundi, Rwanda, Tajikistan and North Korea show up as among the most politically risky. Meanwhile, Norway, Switzerland, the United Kingdom and the United States are among the countries with the lowest levels of political risk.

Interestingly, the People's Republic of China shows up as country with moderate and declining levels of political risk. In 1992, China's political risk score was above the mid-point on the scale at 13.3. By 2003, this political risk ranking had improved somewhat to 16.84. Singapore is a country in Asia that has shown a consistently low level of political risk in both 1992 and 2003. Taiwan, Japan, South Korea, Hong Kong, the Philippines, India, Australia and New Zealand each had some consistent or improving political risk scores, marking a general trend to less political risk in economies in Asia Pacific.

This general trend is not an all inclusive one. Indonesia had its score drop from a moderate level to a high level of political risk. In Pakistan and Malaysia, political risk levels remained essentially unchanged.

An interesting question to ask at this point is why have we observed these trends in political risk levels from 1992 to 2003. If there have been changes in political risk levels, have there been accompanying fundamental changes in the structure of the political institutions of these countries? Have the leaders of these countries changed attitudes towards domestic and foreign business activities? Have the policies with respect to foreign involvement in the local economy changed over time? Or is it just a matter of a more optimistic or pessimistic projection by international managers for a particular national environment?

One answer to this basic question rests in the last question. Political risk rankings are perceptual. A perceptual index means that the index tends to be heavily influenced by past events in the making of forecasts of future events. As a consequence, political risk indices such as Euromoney's, ranked countries in Asia in 1997, just before the onset of the Asian Financial Crisis, quite low on political risk dimensions. The International Country Risk Guide placed Malaysia, Indonesia, Thailand and South Korea in its least risk category in the mid-1990s. Yet, events in countries such as Malaysia, Indonesia and Thailand in the post-1997 period revealed the underlying latent political risk in these countries, that was eventually picked up by these risk indicators. Malaysia, as an example of the emergence of political risk, suspended the tradability of its currency forcing a dramatic change on the operations of foreign businesses in Malaysia.

An alternative to a perceptual measure of political risk would be a measure that permits one to forecast the likelihood of change from policy makers, independently of the immediate past actions of policy makers. Such a measure needs to consider the features of a political system that permit or facilitate policy change under the basic but important idea that policy outcomes are a function of policy structure.

Political Hazards[9]

Political hazards is another measure of the political environment, particularly the uncertainty in the policy environment. Unlike the perceptual measures of political risk, political hazards is an objective measure.

The measure of political hazards is built on the idea that policy makers design, implement and change a country's policies. Policy makers take these actions following the rules of the political system. In some situations, a political system can make it difficult for an individual policy maker to act with a considerable degree of discretion in implementing new policy. In other political systems, an individual policy maker can have considerable discretion in designing and implementing new policy.

The degree of discretion that an individual policy maker possesses is therefore dependent on the structure of a political system. Based on the degree of discretion permitted to individual actors, we can define a political system as being one that imposes or does not impose constraints on its political actors. A system that constrains political actors can limit the individual discretion of any one political actor. A system that does not constrain political actors offers a substantial amount of latitude to an individual political actor.

Restraint of individual discretion implies that more actors must be brought together to make a decision. As more actors are brought into a decision to create and implement new policy, it becomes more difficult to make new policy. As anyone has experienced, the greater the number of people in a group, the more difficult it is to reach a consensus. It can be particularly problematic to reach a consensus if the basic preferences of all the people in a group differ. This notion of group consensus is the core of the idea of why it becomes less easy to implement new policy when individual discretion is restrained.

In this sense, a system that has strong political constraints on its actors is one in which it is difficult to change policy. One with weak political constraints on its actors is one in which it is easy to change policy. The difference in the ease in which new policy is implemented stems from the idea that as individual discretionary behaviour is restrained, more actors must come into agreement to make new policy.

We can think of a political environment that has strong constraints as one with a *status quo* bias in policy making. This *status quo* bias means that policies are unlikely to change, which also implies that the policy environment will be stable. Policies are likely to remain the same, or only change slowly and in predictable ways, in a system with good constraints on its political actors. The converse of this is the idea that a system that lacks political constraints is one in which policies can change rapidly and unpredictably. Such a situation can be thought of one that has political hazards.

Diagnosing Political Hazards

When the political system in a country constrains the freedom with which individual political actors can make or change policy, there is less uncertainty in a nation's policies, and less political risk. Where there are fewer constraints, there is more uncertainty and political hazards are high. This point is easily understood, but the question remains – 'How can one diagnose the level of political hazards in a country?".

One method of diagnosis is to look at the past and extrapolate to the future. The past can be a good indicator of the future, although it is not perfect as other political risk measures have shown. The past is an imperfect predictor of the future because political actors and political systems can change.

Another method of diagnosis is to look at the structure of the policy making apparatus in a country. The policy making apparatus defines the steps that must be taken to create and implement new policy.

There are, therefore, two dimensions to look at when diagnosing the level of political constraints and political hazards. The first dimension is the preference of the political actors in the system. If the actors tend to have similar preferences, such as might be the case when the actors at each level are from the same political party, then it becomes easier to create new policy. The second dimension is the number of political and judiciary levels that have an influence in the policy making process. The fewer the number of levels, the easier it is to create new policy.

We can think of a policy making structure as first consisting of an executive, or the political actor who makes a new policy a reality. In a system with no constraints on its political actors, the executive does not have any other political actors that can veto or delay the implementation of new policy. Such a system might be thought of as a dictatorship.

Aside from the executive, we can think of another set of political actors at the national level as being the legislature. There can be one or two branches of the legislature in a policy making system. The legislature can be thought of as an upper and lower house of elected representatives in a parliamentary system, for example.

We can look for the existence of a legislature, but we also must be concerned with the degree of power a legislature has. In some cases, the legislature might just act as a rubber stamp for the implementation of new policy designed by the executive. In another case, the legislature might have some power but it is still effectively outweighed by the executive. In a third case, the legislature might have the same effective power as the executive and operates autonomously to veto or accept new legislation tabled by the executive. There can be one or two levels of the legislature. A key point is to identify if a legislature has a real role in policy making as identified by its independence from the executive.

After the legislature, there can be independent judiciary and sub-national entities, that can also influence the design and implementation of new policy. As with the legislature, the judiciary and a sub-national entity need to be independent of the executive in order to act effectively as a constraint in the policy making apparatus of a country.

When we compare these two dimensions, the structure of the policy making apparatus tends to be more stable over time than the preferences of the actors within each level of the policy making apparatus. Preferences of actors can change whenever there is an election, or anytime there is an appointment of a new actor. The result is that political hazards can show considerable variance over time. However, the largest variance comes with real changes in the policy making structure.

Some perspective on this process of change can be gained by examining the long-term time trends of policy making structures. From 1960 to 1998, the amount of policy uncertainty was reduced substantially in a number of countries in their process of democratization. Large decreases could be found in countries undergoing democratic transitions in Latin America, Asia and Eastern Europe.

For instance, since the first democratic election was held in 1992 in post-Soviet Mongolia, each successive government has pledged to transform the country's political and social structures, and ensure that economic reform is one of its declared priority areas. One Western diplomat in Mongolia stated that, 'No former Soviet state has come so far, and no former communist country in Asia has shown as much commitment to reform as Mongolia.'[10]

The Mongolian government (*www.pmis.gov.mn/indexeng.php*) is focusing on continued macroeconomic stability and structural reforms to maintain political and economic stability, and attract foreign aid and foreign direct investment. Since the fall of the Soviet Union, the Mongolian government has worked to reduce perceived threats of violence or kidnapping, while minimizing red tape and official discrimination against foreigners and foreign firms.

'We have a genuine open market,' says Mr. S. Otgonbat, the Vice Chairman of the five year old Foreign Investment and Foreign Trade Agency (*www.investmongolia.com/index.htm*). 'Prices are no longer fixed; they are free.'[11] The World Bank identified Mongolia as one of the most open economies in Central Asia (*www.worldbank.org.mn*). As a result of its political stability, foreign investors are funding restaurant, travel, textile, and mining companies in Mongolia, and the United States continues to donate large sums of foreign aid.

Meanwhile, countries such as Burundi, Chile (under Pinochet), Guyana, Jamaica (1985–1989), Lebanon, Nigeria, Panama, the Philippines (under Marcos), Sierra Leone, Sri Lanka, Somalia and Uruguay experienced decreases in effective political constraints, leading to increased levels of uncertainty in the policy environment for international managers.

The variance in the amount of political uncertainty by time and by country is shown in Table 4-2. Political uncertainty is marked by the political hazards measure. The political hazards measure can take a value between zero and one. A score of zero indicates minimal political hazards, as the policy makers in the country are highly constrained. A political hazards score of one is the maximum, indicating a highly uncertain policy environment, in which the policy makers are not constrained.

Two immediate and obvious differences emerge when comparing political hazards to Euromoney's political risk scores. These differences are found in the political risk and political hazards scores for China and Singapore. China is at the highest end of political hazards, as is Singapore. Yet, for political risk China is moderate and improving, while Singapore has consistently had low political risk. Why would there be this difference?

One reason rests in perceptions. Singapore has long held a positive stance towards foreign investment. It has created an investor friendly environment. After decades of isolationist economic policies, China has likewise followed a pro-foreign investment policy in the last 20 years. Although these positive stances to foreign investment, coupled with stability in the actors that inhabit the policy making structures, may seem to mark political stability, they do not equate to a lack of political risk.

Table 4-2: Political Hazard Scores by Country/Region

Country/Region	Political Hazards 1992	Political Hazards 2001	Country/Region	Political Hazards 1992	Political Hazards 2001
Afghanistan	1.00	1.00	China	1.00	1.00
Albania	—	0.64	Colombia	0.55	0.64
Algeria	1.00	0.58	Comoros	1.00	1.00
Andorra	—	0.59	Congo, Kinshasa	1.00	1.00
Angola	0.63	1.00	Congo, Brazzaville	0.69	1.00
Antigua	0.86	0.65	Costa Rica	0.63	0.59
Argentina	0.47	0.59	Ivory Coast	1.00	0.58
Armenia	0.49	1.00	Croatia	0.58	0.74
Australia	0.49	0.49	Cuba	1.00	1.00
Austria	0.57	0.45	Cyprus	0.82	0.51
Azerbaijan	1.00	1.00	Czechoslovakia	0.49	0.57
Bahamas	0.67	0.83	Denmark	0.48	0.47
Bahrain	1.00	1.00	Djibouti	1.00	0.81
Bangladesh	0.56	0.61	Dominican Rep	0.53	0.63
Barbados	0.68	0.91	Dominica	0.57	0.59
Belarus	1.00	0.80	Ecuador	0.91	0.45
Belgium	0.29	0.28	Egypt	1.00	1.00
Belize	0.66	0.87	El Salvador	0.55	0.81
Benin	0.93	0.90	Equatorial Guinea	1.00	1.00
Bhutan	1.00	1.00	Eritrea	—	1.00
Bolivia	0.41	0.39	Estonia	—	0.45
Bosnia-Herzegovina	—	0.93	Ethiopia	1.00	1.00
Botswana	0.89	0.82	Fiji	0.51	0.54
Brazil	0.89	0.86	Finland	0.46	0.46
Brunei	1.00	1.00	France	0.45	0.56
Bulgaria	0.61	0.60	Gabon	1.00	1.00
Burkina Faso	0.63	0.89	Gambia	0.84	1.00
Burundi	1.00	1.00	Georgia	—	0.67
Cape Verde	0.72	0.71	Germany	0.58	0.56
Cambodia	1.00	1.00	Ghana	1.00	0.69
Cameroon	1.00	1.00	Greece	0.62	0.63
Canada	0.55	0.54	Grenada	0.60	—
Cen. African Rep.	1.00	0.49	Guatemala	0.76	0.61
Chad	1.00	1.00	Guinea	1.00	1.00
Chile	0.60	0.35	Guinea-Bissau	1.00	1.00

Table 4-2:   continued

Country/Region	Political Hazards		Country/Region	Political Hazards	
	1992	2001		1992	2001
Guyana	0.76	—	Malaysia	0.70	0.46
Haiti	1.00	0.85	Maldives	1.00	1.00
Honduras	0.66	0.70	Mali	1.00	0.84
Hong Kong	1.00	—	Malta	0.66	0.66
Hungary	0.51	0.53	Marshall Islands	1.00	1.00
Iceland	0.50	0.53	Mauritania	1.00	1.00
India	0.41	0.59	Mauritius	0.59	0.84
Indonesia	1.00	0.50	Mexico	0.72	0.61
Iran	1.00	0.65	Micronesia (Fed.)	—	—
Iraq	1.00	1.00	Moldova	1.00	0.51
Ireland	0.56	0.55	Monaco	1.00	1.00
Israel	0.48	0.40	Mongolia	0.80	0.93
Italy	0.45	0.43	Morocco	0.86	0.92
Jamaica	0.65	0.80	Mozambique	1.00	0.67
Japan	0.46	0.42	Myanmar (Burma)	1.00	1.00
Jordan	1.00	1.00	Namibia	0.60	0.73
Kazakhstan	1.00	1.00	Nauru	1.00	1.00
Kenya	1.00	0.54	Nepal	0.60	0.61
Kiribati	—	0.55	Netherlands	0.40	0.60
Korea, North	1.00	1.00	New Zealand	0.75	0.52
Korea, South	0.52	0.76	Nicaragua	0.65	0.58
Kuwait	1.00	1.00	Niger	1.00	1.00
Kyrgyzstan	1.00	1.00	Nigeria	1.00	0.61
Laos	1.00	1.00	Norway	0.49	0.48
Latvia	1.00	0.45	Oman	1.00	1.00
Lebanon	0.88	—	Pakistan	0.54	1.00
Lesotho	1.00	1.00	Palau	—	1.00
Liberia	1.00	1.00	Panama	1.00	0.50
Libya	1.00	1.00	Papua New Guinea	0.43	0.46
Liechtstein	0.65	0.61	Paraguay	0.67	0.62
Lithuania	0.68	0.49	Peru	0.54	0.50
Luxembourg	0.48	0.47	Philippines	0.83	0.46
Macedonia	0.51	0.50	Poland	0.88	0.73
Madagascar	—	0.47	Portugal	0.63	0.57
Malawi	1.00	0.58	Qatar	1.00	1.00

Table 4-2: continued

Country/Region	Political Hazards		Country/Region	Political Hazards	
	1992	2001		1992	2001
Romania	0.70	0.41	Syria	1.00	1.00
Russia	1.00	0.88	Taiwan	0.78	0.68
Rwanda	1.00	1.00	Tajikistan	1.00	1.00
St Lucia	0.65	0.92	Tanzania	1.00	0.89
Samoa	—	0.57	Thailand	1.00	0.49
San Marino	0.54	0.51	Togo	1.00	1.00
São Tomé e Principe	0.66	0.61	Tonga	—	0.52
Saudi Arabia	1.00	1.00	Trinidad	0.53	0.53
Senegal	1.00	0.44	Tunisia	1.00	0.78
Seychelles	1.00	1.00	Turkey	0.55	0.47
Sierra Leone	1.00	1.00	Turkmenistan	1.00	1.00
Singapore	0.94	0.97	United Arab Emirates	1.00	1.00
Slovakia	—	0.48	Uganda	1.00	0.67
Slovenia	0.60	0.46	United Kingdom	0.64	0.65
South Africa	0.73	0.54	Ukraine	1.00	0.40
Solomon Islands	0.53	0.66	Uruguay	0.44	0.45
Somalia	1.00	1.00	United States	0.59	0.60
Spain	0.49	0.49	Uzbekistan	1.00	1.00
Sri Lanka	0.60	0.59	Vanuatu	0.51	0.83
St Kitt/Nev	0.55	0.68	Venezuela	0.53	1.00
St Vincent Islands	1.00	0.64	Vietnam	1.00	1.00
Sudan	1.00	1.00	Western Samoa	0.66	—
Suriname	0.73	0.90	Yemen	1.00	1.00
Swaziland	1.00	1.00	Yugoslavia	1.00	0.75
Sweden	0.49	0.49	Zambia	0.81	0.81
Switzerland	0.83	0.84	Zimbabwe	0.97	0.66

Source: Witold J. Henisz, POLCON Database (*http://www-management.wharton.upenn.edu/henisz/*), 2 April 2003.

The reason for this is the lack of constraints on actors in the policy making structures of China and Singapore. China, for example, did not possess an effective legislative in the 1990s. The executive in China could implement new policy with relative ease. Singapore did possess an effective legislative along with an effective judiciary, but the preferences of the actors were aligned.

The result is that new policy can be enacted fairly quickly. This new policy can be a substantial detriment to the operations and profitability of a firm's foreign subsidiaries. One example of the risks and uncertainty imposed by political hazards comes from a Hong Kong investor's experience in the construction and operation of tollroads. A tollroad is an infrastructure investment that requires a long time horizon to recoup the heavy upfront investment. Investments with long time horizons are the ones most sensitive to policy uncertainty, since policy long run stability allows for real returns to match projected returns.

The Cangtong Highway Co. of Hong Kong invested in the construction of Mafeng Highway in Handan city, Line 307 in Shijiazhuang city and National Road 205 in Cangzhou. Through the local joint venture used to construct the tollroads, the company invested more than 80 million yuan, or about USD10 million in the tollroad's construction. The contract with the Hebei provincial government entitled Cangtong Highway to collect tolls at the site for 20 years.

After two years of operations, disputes began to emerge between the Hong Kong developer of the tollroad and government officials. The dispute concluded with the provincial government in Hebei closing down the tollgates. The Hong Kong operator was notified of this decision by telephone. At the same time as the notification, the provincial government was dismantling the tollgates. When the Hong Kong investors sought recourse through explanation of the government's actions, they received no response from the provincial government in Hebei. The dispute has now reached Beijing, where Cangtong Highway is claiming the Hebei provincial government misled them to secure foreign investment in highway construction.[12]

This example is typical of the uncertainty that emerges when policy makers are unconstrained. The case is a bit severe in the sense that the changes in the rules to the operations of the tollroad ended any revenue streams the Hong Kong investor was receiving from the operation of the tollroad. Other changes in investment conditions, such as increases in tax rates, the imposition of duties, the introduction of new property taxes and the like, can similarly expropriate returns from a foreign investor's host country operations, although not at the cost of the closure of those operations. For these reasons, and countless other stories like the experience of the Hong Kong tollroad operator in Hebei, political uncertainty should be at the forefront of any foreign investment or trade decision.

The starting point, as always, for bringing a dimension of the institutional environment forward, is to develop an elementary cognizance of the variance in a dimension across countries and over time. We have already discussed the high and unwavering levels of political hazards in China and Singapore. Likewise, Indonesia shows high hazards. However, it has shown a general trend to decline in the 1990s. Malaysia is a similar case of declining political hazards, with an exception of a late 1990s rise. Bangladesh and India show more stability over the 1990s, with moderate levels of hazards, that fluctuate based upon the preferences of the actors in power. Pakistan has shown a substantial increase in political hazards since 1992, reflecting the emerging dominance of the military in the policy making structure in the late 1990s and early 2000s. Myanmar, Cambodia and Vietnam each score high and unwavering values on political hazards.

Many of these values in political hazards match intuition and expectations. Indeed, despite some of the variance between political hazards and traditionally used political risk measures, there is a reasonably strong correlation between these different measures over time.

Yet, if an international manager is concerned, as one should be, with the quality of political institutions in a host country, a measure of the constraints placed on the actors in a political system offers a relatively objective assessment of the policy environment. In this sense, political hazards has an advantage over perceptual measures that are based in experience, especially when there is rapid political change.

Perceptual measures will always lag change, because the change must be experienced for it to show up in an individual's perception. Meanwhile, an objective measure based in the structures of a policy making system that facilitate or impede change, can provide a reasonable forecast about the likelihood that future government policy will maintain the *status quo*. We can take the political transitions in Peru, the Philippines, South Africa and South Korea as examples. Political hazards changed in the year in which there was a transition in the policy making structure, but perceptual measures, such as that from the International Country Risk Guide, took up to five years to change, if any change was marked at all.

Other Dimensions of the Political Environment

Political risk and political hazards are two measures that identify the level of uncertainty in a policy environment. These measures provide a general but, nevertheless, important guide to how the policy environment can potentially influence a firm's operations. Other features of the political environment can and should also be considered when formulating and implementing international strategy. These other features have a stronger relationship to specific aspects of a firm's operations, than do political risk and political hazards.

These features can be considered as elements that influence the costs of doing business in particular ways. Costs can increase because information is difficult or easy to come by – this relates to the transparency of the business environment and the political system. Costs can increase when a nation has a system of informal payments to government officials to facilitate the processing of business transactions. Costs can increase, or returns can decrease, when the intellectual property protection regime in a country is weak. Costs can increase where legal systems do not promote strong adherence to a nation's set of laws.

Transparency

A commonly cited non-tariff barrier to trade is the lack of transparency in a country's rules and regulations. To be able to establish trading relations with a firm in another country, a manager must be able to identify what are the import and export regulations, and how one handles customs, transportation and goods storage in the host country. Transparency relates to the availability and clarity of such information from government sources. Where there is a lack of transparency about governmental regulations, a decision is likely to be impeded. Incorrect filing of applications, the failure to solicit or gain approval to conduct a particular business activity, extensive search to identify the relevant rules and regulations, time spent identifying officials and communicating with those officials about relevant government regulations, are all areas that may not only increase the time it takes to make a transaction, but also increase the costs associated with that transaction.

Not only can a lack of transparency increase costs and time associated with a transaction, it can also derail a firm from making inroads into a particular market. Where there is a lack of transparency, information about how to access a particular market, such as procurement procedures for government contracts, becomes a valuable and strategic resource. Typically, a host country firm would possess this resource, while a foreign competitor would be at a severe disadvantage in trying to secure this resource. Transparency, or a lack thereof, acts as a significant barrier to the competitiveness of foreign firms in a local market.

Aside from being transparent, a country can be perceived to be difficult to penetrate by a foreign firm because of the proliferation of business practices that favour local firms to foreign firms (see Table 4-3).

The United States, France, the United Kingdom and Japan score highly on this particular dimension. The high score for Japan is a reflection of the frequent accusation that domestic Japanese firms are unreceptive to foreign firms, preferring to remain in their traditional trading networks. The lack of a fair trade environment, in the sense that social connections rather than

Table 4-3: **Non-Bribery, Unfair Trade Practices in Business and Trade (2002)**

Country	Percentage	Country	Percentage
United States	58%	Switzerland	4%
France	26%	Malaysia	3%
United Kingdom	19%	Canada	3%
Japan	18%	Netherlands	3%
China	16%	Singapore	1%
Russia	13%	Belgium	1%
Germany	11%	Australia	1%
Spain	9%	Austria	1%
Italy	5%	Hong Kong	1%
Taiwan	5%	Sweden	<1%
South Korea	4%	Respondent's Country of Residence	12%

Total Sample: 567

Source: Transparency International Bribe Payers Index 2002 (*www.transparency.org*), 3 April 2003.
Note: The score reflects the percentage of responses where a country was featured among the three countries cited as principally associated with other unfair practices.

an economic rationale dictate a firm's preference in a transaction, can impede the penetration of foreign firms into a local market. Unlike the economic giants that head the list of the prevalence of perceived unfair trade practices, small open trading economies such as Canada, Australia, Singapore and Hong Kong are infrequently cited as having unfair trade practices.

Intellectual Property Protection

Another salient characteristic of national institutional environments is the level of intellectual property rights protection. Effective intellectual property rights protection provides the owner of a resource with the discretion to use the resource in the manners seen fit by the owner. Property rights protection ensures that the owner is able to secure returns from the uses to which the resource is put.

Effective intellectual property rights protection is important to an economy because it fosters investment in research and development and the creation of unique brands, and other forms of intellectual property that could otherwise easily be appropriated (see Box 4-1).

An international manager needs to scan potential sites for trade and investment in order to identify the security of the intellectual property rights regime. If the full value of a resource is not able to be secured by its owner when making an investment, such as in the case where the value of patents and trademarks cannot be fully achieved, the incentives to apply these resources via fixed investments is reduced.[13] Aside from reducing levels of foreign investment, a country with weak intellectual property rights is less likely to be a site for high value-added activities such as technology development or basic research.

Intellectual property rights regimes vary widely across Asia. Some countries, such as Singapore, have enacted stringent measures to cultivate the respect of intellectual property rights. Meanwhile, the lack of intellectual property rights protection is well-documented in several other countries in Asia.

News reports place software piracy in China at upwards of 90 per cent of all software used in China. Prior to crackdowns in Hong Kong in the late 1990s, the Mong Kok area was well known for small stores with large stocks of pirated compact discs of software and DVD movies. In Bangkok, shopping centers populated by small businesses selling pirated software, pirated movies and pirated music proliferate.

The risk does not stop at the consumer level. In an institutional environment in which the protection of property rights is lower, the cost of forming a joint venture is greater because of the increased risk of unwanted appropriation of a firm's unique resources. In host countries in which intellectual property rights protection is weak, the strategy for foreign subsidiaries moves towards the explicit protection of key resources by securing high ownership levels in joint ventures, or the choice of a greenfield, wholly-owned entry, over a joint venture. This incentive to avoid entry, or avoid partnering if entering, is strongest for those firms that possess valuable forms of intellectual property such as patents, trademarks and brands.[14]

Box 4-1   The Indian Pharmaceutical Industry

Historically, India's pharmaceutical industry has been characterized by heavy protectionist policies and weak drug patent laws. This has allowed Indian firms to make high-quality, low-costs copies of the latest drug innovations for the domestic marketplace. These laws will be changing as of January 2005, when India will have to implement the product patent regime in accordance with its obligations to the Trade Regulated Intellectual Property Rights (TRIPS). TRIPS is an attempt by the World Trade Organization to narrow the gaps in the way these intellectual property rights are protected around the world, and to bring them under common international rules (*http://www.wto.org/english/tratop_e/trips_e/trips_e.htm*). Once India's patent laws comply, the country will be allowed to manufacture and export generic versions of specific vital drugs.

The exploitation of India's patent laws has been extensive. As the soon-to-be-reformed laws do not allow chemical and pharmaceutical compounds to be patented, Indian firms are able to manufacture cheap copies of patented, brand-name drugs and sell them at deeply discounted prices on the domestic market. The government undertook this strategy to encourage the development of Indian drug companies and assist them in competing in the domestic market. In addition to the lenient patent laws, the National Pharmaceutical Pricing Authority (*http://nppaindia.nic.in/index1.html*), a governmental regulatory body, was established in 1995 to enforce the prices and availability of medicines. As a result of the government policies, a number of Indian pharmaceutical companies have become internationally successful, including Ranbaxy (*www.ranbaxy.com*) and Dr Reddy's (*www.drreddys.com*), both of which sell generic versions of off-patent drugs abroad.

The government's protectionist measures and poor intellectual property rights ensured that multinational companies did limited business in India. The latter deterred multinationals from undertaking research projects to develop drugs specifically geared to the Indian marketplace. Further, the marketplace itself, largely rural and poor, was undesirable as customers chose cheaper, domestic products rather than being enticed by the quality and brand image offered by multinational companies. Supply-chain inefficiencies and need for a large sales force to influence both Indian pharmacists and doctors are two additional factors that limited market involvement.

The beginning of the 21st century showed that the pharmaceutical industry in India is thriving and growing. The industry has grown at a compounded annual growth rate (CAGR) of 10 per cent over the last five years to USD6.3 billion (USD1 = RM3.80) in 2002. The strengthening of product patent regime in 2005 is set to change the Indian pharmaceutical marketplace. The new regime will benefit the India market in a number of ways. It will allow Indian companies to compete in the global marketplace as innovators and respecters of intellectual property, challenging patents that have not yet expired and directly selling their cheaper versions of generic brands abroad. Further, the reforms will better support research and development services, establish a more competitive domestic market, and provide an opportunity for Indian companies to offer contract research services and other IT-led development services. This has lead analysts to expect the market to increase to approximately USD25 billion by 2010, driven by global and Indian industry trends.

Sources:
http://www.wto.org/english/thewto_e/whatis_e/tif_e/agrm7_e.htm
The America's Intelligence Wire, 13 September 2003.
"India Offers ASEAN Huge Opportunities," *Business Times*, 12 September 2003, p. 4.

For businesses in Asia, a lack of knowledge of the importance of intellectual property can deter internationalization efforts. According to Pham Dinh Chuong, head of the Vietnamese Industrial Property Department under the Ministry of Science, Technology and Environment (*www.vista.gov.vn*), 'Not many enterprises [in Vietnam] understand the need to register their trademarks abroad.' He believes that this 'is the reason why they have trouble entering the world market.'[15]

A case in point is the family-owned company Ngoc Linh. This company is synonymous with famous Vietnamese rice pancakes. When the owners of Ngoc Linh decided to enter the Japanese marketplace they learned that their trademark brand had already been registered by a Japanese business whose associates had visited the Vietnamese factory, videotaped, and subsequently, duplicated the Ngoc Linh process and name. As Ngoc Linh was a widely recognized name by its patrons and the market alike, the family-owners of Ngoc Linh believed the name was theirs by default. Consequently, they had not registered the company's name. Another example of a similar failure to take steps to protect a firm's intellectual property is the Vietnamese national tobacco company Vinataba (*http://www.vinataba.com.vn/*). Vinataba saw its trademark usurped in Cambodia and 11 other countries by PT Putra Staba Industri from Indonesia.

The future of intellectual property rights protection in Asia depends as much on the actions of individual companies as it does on the development of local economies. In Viet Nam, the government has invested USD49 million to assist large companies to build their trademarks globally. The deputy chairman Vu Tien Loc of the Vietnamese Chamber of Commerce and Industry (VCCI) (*www.vcci.com.vn*) believes that supporting local brands are important because trademarks are not only connected to a company in terms of being important property of a firm, but trademarks also represent a nation's possessions and pride.

As local economies advance, and local firms move into higher value added activities and begin to produce valuable intellectual property of their own, domestic pressure to strengthen intellectual property rights will intensify. Until then, in the short term at least, the gains and losses from weak intellectual property rights are asymmetric, foreign firms lose out on returns, but domestic firms and local consumers gain.

Law and Order

A country's set of laws provide the grounding for the rules that govern transactions and other business activities. The legal system includes the set of laws and the institutions that are in place to monitor and enforce a nation's rules and regulations. The soundness of law and civil order within a country hence extends from the strength of political institutions.

Where there is a strong court system, where laws and their enforcement are consistent with a nation's citizens' expectations and are perceived to be fair, there will be a greater willingness among citizens to accept and behave in accordance with laws. This acceptance extends to the role that institutions have to play in making laws, implementing enforcement and adjudicating disputes.

If a country does not have a convention of sound law and order and good political institutions to enforce laws, a foreign investor can be at substantial risk in the event of a dispute. A weak law and order system can favour incumbents that have a high degree of familiarity with the system. A weak law and order tradition in a country means that a foreign firm is unlikely to be able to settle disputes satisfactorily through the legal system. Greater costs could be incurred than would be the case in a strong law and order system. As dispute resolution costs escalate, a firm remains exposed to illegal actions to prosecute claims or resolve disputes. In this way, a foreign firm's bargaining power is weaker when a host country's legal system is weaker.

Management of the Political Environment

Accurate measurement is a first step in contending with cross-national differences in various dimensions of the political environment. Post-identification, the second step is effective management of the political environment. Effective management can help forestall loses that come from corruption, lack of transparency, and judicial or political unpredictability. Managing policy uncertainty can buffer a firm from adverse changes in policy and, perhaps, even secure favourable changes in policy. The latter point suggests that the effective management of the political environment can be a source of advantage for a firm. Effective management is facilitated by understanding a firm's bargaining position with the host country government.

Bargaining Power

The various features of national political environments impose risks, uncertainty and potentially new sets of costs on a firm. At times, the risks, uncertainty and costs apply equally to domestic and foreign firms. At other times, direct discriminatory action can be taken by a host country government against a foreign firm. Although discriminatory action connotes a negative outcome for a firm, this is not always the case. Discrimination can be positive, if it emerges in the form of a favourable set of policies to encourage trade and investment by a foreign firm.

Discrimination is not necessarily exogenous to a firm. A multinational firm can have an influence on the conditions under which it makes an investment.[16] This influence is exerted in a process of bargaining with a host country government. When a multinational firm's bargaining power is high, the conditions of investment can be particularly favourable. Bargaining power refers to the relative distribution of power between a multinational firm and host country constituents, such as a host country government, in setting the terms of a multinational firm's operations in a host country.

In general, a multinational firm's bargaining power is greatest before an entry is made into a host country. Prior to entry, a host country government is still uncertain about receiving the flows of capital, assets, technology and management skills that can accompany a foreign entry. To the extent that the entry is desired by a host country government, managers in a multinational firm are in a position to establish favourable terms of investment. The tax concessions and fiscal incentives offered to automobile manufacturers to establish an assembly plant in a region is an example of the positive sets of incentives that can emerge when a firm is in a strong bargaining power position.

An automotive firm can encounter these positive incentives if considering investment in India or Thailand. To attract auto manufacturers to India, the Indian national government is encouraging the development of a globally competitive automobile industry. This encouragement takes the form of the introduction of an import tariff policy that will facilitate the development of manufacturing capabilities, ensure a balanced transition to open trade, promote increased competition in the market and enlarge purchase options for the Indian customer. The changes in regulations and policies have led to a 65.3 per cent increase in India's automobile exports in 2002–2003 as 'Made-in-India' vehicles continued to attract overseas buyers.[17]

Similarly, the Thai government has implemented policies to encourage competitiveness in its automobile marketplace. Policy makers shifted the focus of regulations from protection of domestic producers to liberalization. Policy makers reformed tax and regulatory policy to increase imports and pressure local assemblers to improve quality and efficiency. In 2003, domestic production in the automotive industry was approaching record highs, with domestic sales of at least 500,000 vehicles and export sales of 200,000.[18]

After a foreign entry has been made, particularly if it is in the form of a subsidiary, a multinational firm's bargaining power can begin to decline. A multinational firm is now faced with a new dynamic in the policy environment in which the terms of investment can be altered by the host country government, in an obsolescing bargaining scenario. The potential loss to a firm from a change in the policy environment can be particularly high if, prior to entry, a multinational firm's bargaining generated uniquely favourable conditions for investment.

As a consequence, a multinational firm needs to lobby or exert other influence strategies to guard against the overturning, alteration or reinterpretation of policy commitments made prior to entry, or even to secure their improvement over time. Thus, when considering the bargaining position of a firm, a before and after perspective needs to be taken. What are the sources of a firm's bargaining power prior to entry? What are the sources of bargaining power post-entry? If the latter is particularly weak, then a multinational firm risks diminishing levels of returns from its subsidiaries' operations.

A central element of the political strategy a firm adopts when entering a host country is how to minimize its post-entry reductions in bargaining power. A host country's relative bargaining power tends to increase the longer a subsidiary is in a host country. However, if a multinational company undertakes steps to maintain a wedge by which it can off-set the general increase in the bargaining power of the host country government, then it has the potential to minimize interventions in its operations. We discuss such strategies in the next section.

Managing Political Risk

A host country government possesses a legal monopoly on coercion. It is present in the background of every economic transaction. As such, it poses a threat to the revenue stream of all private firms. As we have discussed, this threat can take the form of regulatory or tax policy shifts or outright expropriation of private sector assets. Each of these forms of government intervention hold the potential to reduce the profitability of a firm.

Both domestic and multinational firms are exposed to risks stemming from intervention. Multinational firms face heightened exposure because of two main factors.

First, compared to domestic competition in a host country, a multinational firm has inferior knowledge of domestic factor markets. As a consequence of this inferior knowledge, and its superior knowledge of foreign factor markets, a multinational firm tends to use a lower percentage of domestic content in its operations than its host country competitors. With a lower percentage of domestically sourced inputs, the political costs, in the form of higher unemployment, lower tax revenue, lower political contributions or lower votes, to a host country government of intervention are lower than if it intervened in the operations of a host country firm.

Second, subsidiaries of multinational firms are relatively disadvantaged in their ability to adapt in a manner that reduces the costs of a given expropriation. As with information disparity about local factor markets, multinational firms are at an information disadvantage in the disposal of assets compared to host country competitors. If a host country government intervenes in a manner that makes continued operations undesirable, a multinational firm faces a higher opportunity cost than a host country competitor in transforming its assets to their next best use.

As an additional complication, foreign subsidiaries which are tightly integrated with a multinational firm need to seek permission from headquarters to make adaptive moves to proposed or actual intervention. The higher cost in adapting provides a government with additional leverage when contemplating an intervention that can discriminate negatively against the subsidiaries of multinational firms. In the long term, repeated interventions can reduce foreign investment, leading to a downward spiral in foreign sources of revenue, products and technical and managerial knowledge. Even so, politicians do not always have long time horizons, perhaps, due to a coming election or the need to appeal to support groups such as the military or other powerful political classes. As such, the short term benefits of intervention are likely to take precedence in the minds of policy makers, thus increasing the likelihood of such intervention occurring to the detriment of a multinational firm.

In sum, the heightened exposure to intervention for a multinational firm stems from two points of comparison with local firms. A multinational firm has a knowledge disadvantage compared to local firms. A multinational firm is less local than a domestic competitor. The successful management of intervention and political risks hinges on the reduction of knowledge disparities, and the development of a host country presence that hinges on being more local and less foreign.

Local Partner Joint Ventures

One strategy for alleviating knowledge disparities and for becoming more local in operations is to form a local partner joint venture.[19] By adding a host country partner as a legitimate equity partner in a foreign subsidiary, a multinational firm can partially alleviate both its knowledge disparity and organizational rigidity. A local partner increases the share of local content in a subsidiary's operations, which in turn shifts the political decision calculus of a government away from intervention. It does this by increasing the political costs of any interventionist act by a host country government.

In a joint venture, equity ownership tends to be positively related to a partner's involvement. With some equity ownership by a host country partner, comes involvement and a degree of control over day-to-day operations. The more a local partner is involved, the greater the potential for knowledge transfer about the host country environment. This information flow provides an important safeguard against government intervention by reducing the costs of asset disposal in the event of an intervention that harms the profitability of a subsidiary.

Type of Investment

A multinational firm can have a variety of motivations for investing in a particular host country market. Two of the most common motivations are entry to produce a particular product in a host country and entry to sell a particular product in a host country. In many instances, a multinational firm will eventually end up doing both of these activities in a host country. When considering the choice to enter first to sell a product or manufacture a product, an international manager involved with this decision needs to consider the political reaction and the possibility for intervention.

An export entry, or an export entry supported by the establishment of a local distribution facility, can have little appeal to a host country government. Although consumers can benefit from the wider choice and lower costs that accompany new foreign competition in a market, concentrated producer interests may be harmed by the increase in competition. The welfare of the economy as a whole might not be increased by an exporting or a distribution entry. There is unlikely to be substantive gains in employment. There are no hard currency or tax revenue gains that can cushion the negative impact of harm to domestic constituents in the manufacturing sector. In fact, there can be net outflows of currency in the form of profit repatriation and a net loss of jobs in the domestic economy. Individually, or together, these two outcomes can create substantial economic costs to a host country government. With these economic costs, comes a lower political and economic cost to intervention, and a greater likelihood of a policy change that expropriates some of the revenues of the foreign entrant.

A manufacturing entry brings a different set of costs and benefits. If a multinational firm makes an entry by building a manufacturing facility that exclusively sells its output abroad, it provides net economic benefits in the short term. The benefits can include net inflows of foreign currency and stimulation of demand in local supply markets through intra-industry and inter-industry linkages in supply and output markets. The discipline imposed on local firms by a foreign entrant, and the potential for knowledge transfer to domestic manufacturing firms, can stimulate the efficiency of domestic firms' production, and lead to improvements in international competitiveness.

The choice to establish a manufacturing plant or a distribution facility has substantively different repercussions for the perception of a foreign entry by local government interests. A distribution entry is more likely than a manufacturing entry to engender a negative response and some form of negative intervention, such as a restriction on profit repatriation, foreign exchange quotas for capital and other inputs, increased corporate tax rates and stricter local wage and employment laws that degrades firm performance. Of course, a manufacturing entry is still exposed to the risk of intervention but there are other steps a multinational firm can take to minimize the risks of intervention.

Post-Entry Strategy[20]

The post-entry stage of the foreign entry process is the point at which a multinational firm's bargaining power can be at its lowest. It will continue to decline the longer a multinational firm remains in a host country, provided the foreign entrant does not change the types of operations it has in a host country. The longer it maintains a similar profile of value chain activities, products and technologies, the greater chance it has of competitive obsolescence. When foreign or domestic competitors produce products in similar ways as a multinational's subsidiary, it is no longer a unique competitor. The erosion of a firm's uniqueness is its competitive obsolescence.

In addition to the direct economic consequences of obsolescence, comes a potential political cost. A multinational firm's bargaining power is ground down as its operational advantages fall. The chance of an intervention increases correspondingly, and the political and economic costs of an intervention to a host country government decrease.

To avoid this situation, a multinational firm needs to take steps to upgrade its bargaining power. It does this by moving and adjusting activities and management to maintain a competitive gap with local firms, and preserve its uniqueness. The critical points in this strategy are to monitor the competitive and political environment to know when an upgrade is necessary, and to successfully implement whatever upgrade is required.

As we will discuss in more detail in Chapters 6 and 10, this perspective on a multinational firm's entry involves an evolutionary component. A foreign entry is not a static entity. If it is static, it risks obsolescence on a number of fronts. To avoid becoming a relic on the political front, management needs to look at the technology a subsidiary employs. When competitors begin to catch up on technology, new technology can be introduced or the activities in the subsidiary can be expanded vertically. Backwards vertical integration can raise the sophistication of the activities conducted in the subsidiary, as it moves from basic product assembly, to component parts manufacture, and eventually to research and development. Each of these steps, while posing management challenges for staffing, inputs sourcing and so forth, can increase a multinational firm's bargaining power.

Forward vertical integration, for example, in the direction of adding management staff for the development of marketing campaigns can produce the same result. Along a similar vein, new products can be introduced to maintain differentiation against the product offerings of local competitors. As with the backwards vertical integration strategy, the introduction of new products can test management's ability to identify new distribution channels and communicate with a new set of consumers. Nevertheless, if this test is passed, the multinational firm can stay one step ahead of competitors and avoid an obsolescing bargaining scenario.

Political Management Capabilities

We began this chapter with the point that the political environment can be managed. This statement necessarily implies that international managers can develop political management capabilities. The development of such capabilities does not occur by chance, although the capabilities can be developed by opportunity. Further, the development of such capabilities is likely to be of greater advantage to a firm than sourcing political expertise through the home country government, international or domestic industry associations, consultants or lawyers because the political knowledge in a firm can be tied to its other areas of expertise.

The opportunity to sharpen political management capabilities is created by participation in areas with differing political environments. Operating in high and low political hazard countries and in countries with good and poor intellectual property protection provides important experience that can foster the growth of knowledge about, and skills to deal with, these dimensions of the political environment.

The knowledge and skill development process can be managed. Management involves sequencing the expansion of a firm to expose it in a sequential fashion to progressively more thorny political environments. It involves understanding the structure of political institutions to identify points of decision power, leverage and influence. It involves understanding the role and influence of local lobbying.

Participation in a host country economy provides these opportunities because it creates interactions with local consumers, businesses, politicians and other government officials. For example, when a multinational firm is trying to establish a manufacturing plant, its managers bargain with governments over the terms of entry such as land prices, tax rates and concessions, and local employment regulations. This process establishes relationships with local government officials, by which a firm's managers can gain knowledge about the local policy making apparatus.

Being on-the-ground ties a firm's expatriate and local managers to the local business and political community. These ties emerge as a firm builds exchange relationships with customers, suppliers and competitors. Exchange relationships provide a conduit for learning about local political conditions. Where this information is managed strategically, it can lead to improvements in a multinational firm's capabilities to understand, react to and, ultimately, influence the policy environment.

Summary

The nature of a political strategy depends much on the nature of the political environment. Clearly, political uncertainty, as measured by political risk and political hazards, transparency, and other aspects of the political environment vary across nations. In nations in which the political environment is strong, there can be less of a need to invoke specific strategies against intervention. The reason for this is that the chance of an intervention, in the form of a change in policy that expropriates revenues from a foreign entrant, is greater where there are fewer constraints on actors in a political system.

In this way, the starting point for an international manager is measurement, that is the accurate identification of differences in the political environment across nations, as well as the reasons why there are these differences. To identify reasons for variance in political environments, it can be useful to look to objective dimensions, such as the structure of a country's political institutions. The resultant strategy of a multinational firm will then be dependent on the nature and strength of the political institutions in a nation.

One particularly useful measure for identifying uncertainty in the policy environment is political hazards. As a first order assessment of a country's political environment, a manager can look at whether a nation has strong or weak constraints on its political actors. Even in a nation with strong constraints on its political actors, it still behooves the managers in a multinational firm to consider the policy environment. In cases where there are strong constraints, the political strategy will involve an understanding of the policy making process, including the importance and use of influence groups to help anticipate and shape policy outcomes.

In a nation with weak constraints on its political actors, the importance of understanding the policy environment is even greater. Where political institutions are weak, there is a greater likelihood that political actors will use discretionary policy instruments in a way that can harm the profitability of a foreign entry.

Even when strong constraints might be absent, a multinational firm has a variety of strategic options. It can avoid entry if policy uncertainty is sufficiently high. However, avoiding investment can mean foregoing otherwise attractive trade and investment opportunities. Instead of taking this reactive step to the policy environment, it can be treated proactively as a part of the firm's environment that can be managed. Once this viewpoint is taken, visible dimensions of a firm's international strategy can be altered.

A firm can use a joint venture for entry. It can alter the structure of its investment sequence to minimize the economic costs and maximize the benefits of its entry to a host country government. It can introduce new products and new technology to its subsidiary operations to maintain differentiation against local competitors and avoid competitive obsolescence. It can focus on politically-oriented staffing and knowledge development to better understand the policy environment in a country. In this way, a firm's managers will be better able to anticipate, mitigate and influence a nation's political process as it relates to the multinational firm's activities in a host country.

Notes

[1] Witold J. Henisz, "The Institutional Environment for Economic Growth," *Economics and Politics*, 2000, Vol. 12, pp. 1–31; Witold J. Henisz, "The Institutional Environment for Multinational Investment," *Journal of Law, Economics and Organization*, 2000, Vol. 16, pp. 334–364.

[2] Andrew Delios and Witold J. Henisz, "Political Hazards, Experience and Sequential Entry Strategies: The International Expansion of Japanese Firms, 1980-1998," *Strategic Management Journal*, 2003, Vol. 24, No. 11, pp. 1153–1164; Andrew Delios and Witold J. Henisz, "Political Hazards and the Sequence of Entry by Japanese Firms, 1980-1998," *Journal of International Business Studies*, 2003, Vol. 34, No. 3, pp. 227–241.

[3] Andrew Delios and Witold J. Henisz, "Japanese Firms' Investment Strategies in Emerging Economies," *Academy of Management Journal*, 2000, Vol. 43, pp. 305–323.

[4] S. Kobrin, J. Basek, S. Blank, and J. La Palombara J., "The Assessment and Evaluation of Noneconomic Environments by American Firms," *Journal of International Business Studies,* 1980, Vol. 11, pp. 32–47.

[5] Paul W. Beamish, Alan J. Morrison, Philip M. Rosenzweig, and Andrew C. Inkpen, *International Management: Text and Cases*, 4th Ed. (Irwin-McGraw-Hill, 2000), Chapter 12, pp. 196–213.

[6] Wilkin, Sam, "Why Political Risk is Important to You," *World Trade*, 2000, pp. 40–44.

[7] D. Bradley, "Managing against Expropriation," *Harvard Business Review*, July-August 1977, pp. 75–83; F.N. Burton and H. Inoue, "A Country Risk Appraisal Model of Foreign Asset Expropriation in Developing Countries," *Applied Economics*, 1987, Vol. 19, pp. 1009–1048.

[8] See the website *http://paradocs.pols.columbia.edu:8080/datavine/MainFrameSet.jsp* for an example of several measures of the political environment.

[9] For more on political hazards and its relationship to international business issues please see the following readings. Witold J. Henisz, "The Institutional Environment for Economic Growth," *Economics and Politics*, 2000, Vol. 12, pp. 1–31; Witold J. Henisz and Andrew Delios, "Uncertainty, Imitation, and Plant Location: Japanese Multinational Corporations, 1990-1996," *Administrative Science Quarterly*, 2001, Vol. 46, pp. 443–475; Witold J. Henisz and Bennet Zelner, "The Institutional Environment for Telecommunications Investment," *Journal of Economics and Management Strategy*, 2001, Vol. 10, pp. 123–147; Witold J. Henisz and Oliver E. Williamson, "Comparative Economic Organization – Within and Between Countries," *Business and Politics*, 1999, Vol. 1, pp. 261–277.

[10] Ron Gluckman, "A Post-Soviet Surprise," *Newsweek International*, 15 September 2003, p. 34.

[11] *Ibid.*

[12] "Hong Kong Investors Face Losses as Tollgates are Closed in Hebei," ChinaOnline LLC, 13 June 2001.

[13] David J. Teece, "Profiting from Technological Innovation," *Research Policy*, 1986, Vol. 15, pp. 285–305.

[14] Andrew Delios and Paul W. Beamish, "Ownership Strategy of Japanese Firms: Transactional, Institutional and Experience Influences," *Strategic Management Journal*, 1999, Vol. 20, No. 10, pp. 915–933; Andrew Delios and Paul W. Beamish, "Japanese Ownership Strategies for Subsidiaries in Asia," *Global Focus*, 2001, Vol. 13, No. 2, pp. 173–185.

[15] "Trade: Vietnam Jolted by Pancake Trademark Furor," *Interpress Service*, 8 April 2003.

[16] Witold J. Henisz and Bennet A. Zelner, "Legitimacy, Interest Group Pressures and Change in Emergent Institutions: The Case of Foreign Investors and Host Country Governments," *Academy of Management Review* (Forthcoming, 2004).

[17] "India: Automobile Exports up 65 Percent in 2002-03," *Asia Africa Intelligence Wire*, 6 May 2003.

[18] "Thailand's Automobile Production to Hit Unprecedented High, Xinhua," *The America's Intelligence Wire*, 21 April 2003.

[19] The topic of joint ventures is discussed in detail in Chapter 7.

[20] See Thomas A. Poynter, *Multinational Enterprises and Government Intervention* (New York: St. Martin's Press, 1985), for a more detailed discussion.

SECTION II

Managing International Growth

5 ENTRY MODE CHOICE

A firm becomes a multinational firm by making a foreign direct investment. A foreign direct investment, however, is not a firm's only means of international activity. Indeed, there are a considerable number of modes of international involvement. The choice of the mode of international involvement, sometimes called the entry mode or mode of entry, is an important and challenging one. Each entry mode comes with its own set of advantages and disadvantages that can differ in the firm making the foreign entry. The balance of advantages and disadvantages can also vary, within a firm, over time.

The optimal mode for a firm is highly contextual. It depends on several features of a firm as well as its position along its internationalization path. The entry mode choice is one that needs to be evaluated when an international entry is being considered and re-evaluated after an international entry has been made. To make this choice effectively, a manager must compare the set of advantages and disadvantages attributable to each mode, as well as the context that can alter the weighting of the advantages and disadvantages.

Aside from the international mode decision, there are three other important decisions to be made when entering international markets. One of these is the timing of entry, i.e. when should a firm enter a particular country and when and how fast should it go about its internationalization process. The second is the country choice, i.e. which countries, or regions within a country, should a firm enter when going international. The third is the product choice, i.e. what product or products should be moved into international markets, and what productive activities such as marketing, distribution or manufacturing, should accompany a product's move into international markets. We discuss these choices in detail in the next chapter. In this chapter, we concentrate on the entry mode choice.

The entry mode choice is an important one as it can influence the performance of a subsidiary. At times, wholly-owned subsidiaries have better performance than joint ventures or acquisitions.[1] At other times, joint ventures might perform better than an acquisition or a wholly-owned entry.[2] The performance of a particular mode is often times contingent on the context for the entry mode decision.[3]

The conclusion about the performance of a particular mode can depend on how performance is defined. There are multiple ways to define performance. Performance can be the financial profitability of a foreign entry. It can be the survival of that entry. It can be the success of technology transfer in an entry, or it can be any, or more, of the samples of types of performance listed in Table 5-1.

These multiple measures of performance complicate management's evaluation of the success of a subsidiary. This complication can be particularly profound in the case of strategic alliances, as discussed in Chapter 7. A further complication is the relationship an entry choice has to a firm's overall corporate performance. The entry mode choice does not only influence the success of the entry itself, it also influences the profitability and competitiveness of the corporate parent. As an example, exporting and foreign direct investment can become more profitable or less profitable at the corporate level for a multinational firm depending on prevailing exchange rates.[4]

Internationalization and Entry Modes

A firm can enter international markets for many reasons. Although the reasons might vary, one common outcome to most successful internationalization strategies is growth. A firm generally becomes larger as it internationalizes. Sales will increase as the firm moves into new foreign

Table 5-1:   **Performance Measures for Foreign Entries**

Performance Measure	Definition
Financial Indicators	Profitability of foreign entry, its ability to meet its cost objectives, or its receipt of royalty payments.
Technology Transfer	Technology successfully transferred to a foreign firm, or by a foreign firm to a local firm.
Parental Control	The foreign firm has retained strategic and operational control of an entry in the way it envisioned.
Survival	The entry continues to operate. It is not sold or liquidated.
Failure	The entry does not operate any longer.
Duration	The length of time an entry continues to operate. Generally, the greater the duration, the better the performance.
Instability	Unforeseen and unplanned changes to the structure or strategy of an entry are marks of a lack of success. No change equates to success.
Multiple/Composite Measures	Any combination of the above, or other performance measures.
Perceptions of Success	Managers in the entry perceive it to be doing well. This perception could be developed based on the above performance measures or others.

Source: Adapted from Paul W. Beamish and Andrew Delios, "Improving Joint Venture Performance through Congruent Measures of Success," in Paul Beamish and J. Peter Killing, editors, *Cooperative Strategies: European Perspectives* (San Francisco: New Lexington Press, 1997).

markets, and its employment and assets will increase accordingly as productive capacity needs to be enlarged to cope with growing sales.

Growth will occur in other areas of the firm. There can be growth in the range of product lines in a firm, as it produces more products for more markets. There can be growth in the underlying skills and capabilities in the employees in a firm. New skills and capabilities can be acquired through foreign market participation.

A firm's managers and employees can be exposed to new technologies and new methods of management as it competes in new product and geographic markets inhabited by new sets of competitors, buyers and suppliers. A firm is exposed to new national institutional environments. This exposure brings about a fundamental imperative – the managers in a firm need to acquire knowledge and learn how to operate a firm successfully in these new environments, otherwise the entry does not stand much chance of succeeding in the long term.

As a firm expands into international markets, its strategy and structure will become more complex. Management will face more difficult questions about the best way to structure the firm so as to maintain its core advantages, and reap the potential benefits of multinationality. Corporate and business strategy will have to assimilate environmental and competitive conditions from multiple, heterogeneous markets. Management skills and capabilities will have to grow accordingly to deal successfully with these new tests of the efficacy of a firm's strategy.

Internationalization is essentially growth in each of these aspects. As it involves growth, a fundamental question is how to structure and stage a firm's internationalization process such that it can capture benefits from internationalization while minimizing costs attributed to growing pains.

A critical part of internationalization, and the balancing of costs and benefits emerges in a firm's entry mode strategy. A firm's management must make a choice about the entry mode when entering a foreign market. One question to answer in entry mode strategy is: Will a foreign market entry be made by an equity or a non-equity mode of investment? (Table 5-2) If the mode is non-equity, is the entry to be made by exporting, licensing, franchising, or another non-equity mode? If the mode is equity, is the entry to be made by acquisition, joint venture or a wholly-owned subsidiary?

Entry Mode Decision

The entry mode decision starts with a comparison of equity and non-equity modes. Equity modes involve ownership of assets in the host country that is entered. Examples of equity modes of entry include joint venture, acquisition and greenfield wholly-owned subsidiaries. A non-equity entry mode means there is no ownership of assets in the host country that is entered. Licensing, franchising and exporting are typical forms of non-equity entry modes.

From the equity and non-equity categorization, we can move to a comparison of entry modes types in each category. As with the basic distinction between equity and non-equity modes, a key defining feature within each category is the degree of ownership and control a firm has

Table 5-2:   **Equity and Non-Equity Entry Modes**

Mode	Definition	Length of agreement	Typical Compensation Method
Equity			
Wholly-owned greenfield subsidiary	Establishment of a new subsidiary operation by one firm.	Unlimited	Profits
Acquisition	Purchase of an existing domestic firm.	Unlimited	Profits
Joint Venture	Establishment of a new subsidiary operation by two or more firms.	Unlimited	Fractions of shares/dividends
Foreign minority holding	Purchase of a minority equity stake in an existing domestic firm.	Unlimited	Fractions of shares/dividends
Fade-out agreement	Purchase of an equity stake, but agree to sell at a future date.	Limited	Fractions of shares/dividends
Non-Equity			
Exporting	Sale of a firm's products in foreign markets.	Unlimited	Profits
Licensing	Contractual agreement for a foreign firm to use a firm's technology or other assets.	Limited by contract	Royalty as percent of sales
Franchising	Contractual agreement to use a firm's trademarks and assets and its brands	Limited by contract	Royalty as percent of sales
Management contract	Supply of managers and technical staff to a foreign company.	Limited	Lump sum Royalty
Technical training	Provision of training to a foreign company using a particular technology.	Limited	Lump sum
Turnkey venture	Build an operational plant, then turn it over to another company.	Limited	Lump sum
Contractual joint venture	Contractual agreement for two or more firms to cooperate in an activity (*e.g.*, joint research).	Limited	Change in costs/revenues
International subcontracting	Engage local and foreign firms in a project outside of a firm's domestic markets.	Limited	Markups
Buyer-supplier coalition	Engage in an agreement with buyers or suppliers for the purpose of foreign market participation.	Limited by contract	Markups Change in costs/revenues

Sources: Adapted from Peter J. Buckley and Mark Casson, *The Economic Theory of the Multinational Enterprise* (New York: St. Martin Press, 1985); Farok Contractor and Peter Lorange, *Cooperative Strategies in International Business* (Lexington, MA: D. C. Heath, 1988); Paul W. Beamish, Allen J. Morrison, Philip M. Rosenzweig, and Andrew C. Inkpen, *International Management: Text and Cases*, 4th Ed. (Boston: McGraw-Hill, 2000).

with each entry mode. Entry modes involve varying levels of costs and benefits (see Figure 5-1), and resource commitments and risk (see Figure 5-2). Non-equity entry modes such as exporting and licensing have the lowest costs in terms of financial and managerial investment required.

Figure 5-1:   **Costs and Benefits and Entry Mode**

Entry Mode Trade-offs (4 = Highest, 1 = Lowest)				
	Exporting	Licensing	Joint Venture	Wholly-Owned
Costs				
1 Financial Investment Required	1	2	3	4
2 Managerial Investment Required	1	2	3	4
3 Constraints on Operating Flexibility	4	3	2	1
Benefits				
1 Total Payment Received	1	2	3	4
2 Stability of Payment	4	3	2	1
3 Contribution of New Knowledge	1	2	3	4
4 Contribution to Company Reputation	1	2	3	4

Source: Adapted from Paul W. Beamish, *Sterling Marking Products Inc., Teaching Note* (Ivey Publishing: University of Western Ontario, London, Canada, 8-89-G005), Exhibit 1, p. 54.

Figure 5-2:   **Ownership, Resource Commitment and Entry Mode**

Getting a Product into International Markets				
	Exporting	Licensing	Joint Venture	Wholly-Owned
Financial				
Capital Requirement	Low	Zero	Med	High
Profit Potential to Investor	Med	Low	Med	High
Financial Risk	Low	Low	Med	High
Managerial				
Management Requirement	Low	Low	Med	High
Operational Decisiveness	Med	High	Low	High
Speed of Market Entry	Low	High	High	Med
Technological				
Access to Customer Feedback	Low	Low	Med	High
Technological Risk	Med	High	Med	Low
Other				
Ability to Cope with High Tariffs	Low	High	High	High
Ability to Exploit High Economies of Scale	High	Low	Med	Med

Source: Adapted from Paul W. Beamish, *Sterling Marking Products Inc., Teaching Note* (Ivey Publishing: University of Western Ontario, London, Canada, 8-89-G005), Exhibit 2, p. 55.

As equity modes, joint ventures and wholly-owned subsidiaries entail a heavier financial and a greater managerial investment, which can be costly to a firm in the event of failure. Japan-based MOS Foods Services attempted expansion into America by entering the Hawaiian fast-food market first in the late 1980s. However, high rents, inventory problems and inconsistent food taste cut short expansion goals. As of 2003, only one MOS Burger remained open in Hawaii, serving mainly Japanese tourists on vacation.

Heavier investment is accompanied by a greater return in terms of payments received for a market entry. Equity modes also create substantial opportunities for learning about a market, thereby contributing new knowledge to a firm, and, in some cases, adding positively to the reputation of a firm, as in the case of Café de Coral.

Hong Kong-based Café de Coral Holdings (*www.cafedecoral.com*), the world's largest Chinese fast-food company, entered into a joint venture with New Asia Group (*www.newasia.sh.cn*), in March 2003, by purchasing 50 per cent of Shanghai New Asia Snack Co. (SNAS).[5] SNAS is the largest operator of Chinese fast-food restaurants in Shanghai, with 90 outlets under the brand name "New Asia Dabao," and USD24 million in revenues in 2001.

In the early 1990s, Café de Coral failed in its attempt to enter the mainland Chinese marketplace. With China's entry into the World Trade Organization (WTO), analysts expected the fast-food industry to develop like the US, where one-third of fast-food market is Chinese. Café de Coral wants to be prepared to capitalize on the opportunity. 'This is a good way to educate themselves about the market,' says Sun Hung Kai analyst Carrie Chan in Hong Kong.[6] The purchase also allows Café de Coral to acquire the skills of the local managers and use SNAS as a local launching pad to expand nationally, and finish what CEO Michael Chan had identified as the final pieces in a global jigsaw puzzle. SNAS also benefits from the deal. 'The move indicates our commitment to go more international,' said Kang Ming, board secretary of SNAS's parent-company, New Asia Group, and 'seek quicker expansion through certain business reform.'

Even though an equity mode can have these benefits, it is accompanied by heavy costs such as greater financial requirements than a non-equity entry mode. For a capital constrained firm, licensing can be an attractive form of entry because it does not require much, if any, financial commitment. The profit potential of licensing follows accordingly, being the lowest and most stable among the four entry modes in Figure 5-2.

The general pattern of low resource commitment accompanying low return on financial and other dimensions continues through the areas of comparison in Figure 5-2. Managerial resource requirements are limited for non-equity entry modes, but there is little gain from the market entry in terms of learning about local consumers through customer feedback. A low management commitment means a firm is less involved in a market than it would be where there is a high managerial commitment. Lower involvement comes with fewer opportunities for acquiring new knowledge related to a firm's penetration of its new markets.

These features of the various entry modes, as laid out in Figures 5-1 and 5-2, identify the core trade-offs encountered when deciding between one mode and the other. These trade-offs provide an initial guide to identifying whether to use one mode or another. Yet, other factors related to each of the major modes of investment can be prominent influences on the entry mode decision.

Exporting

Exporting is the entry mode most frequently used by a firm making its first foray into an international market. It is a low risk and low commitment entry mode that offers the potential for enhancing a firm's sales by expanding its market reach. From the initial beginnings in foreign markets using an export strategy, exports can become a major part of a firm's business, and a chief contributor to a firm's bottom line. As with any business function, as export operations become a larger part of a firm's business, the successful management of export operations becomes more important.

In the initial phases of international expansion, exports are often treated opportunistically, as an add-on, but not as a crucial component of existing markets. Continued expansion into international markets reinforces the need to begin to approach export markets at a strategic level.

A strategy for managing exports begins with being proactive in the search for market opportunities. Rather than waiting for unsolicited export contracts to roll in, a firm's management can begin to uncover market opportunities through a process of market segmentation. The material in Chapter 2 provides information on several of the key variables that help differentiate world markets. Table 6-2 provides a number of links to websites with specific information on a country-by-country basis for international trade opportunities. These, and similar sources at the level of a firm's products, can be used to understand which markets might be good destinations for a firm's products.

After identifying a market for export entry, consideration needs to be given to the strategy that will be used for penetrating that market. How will a firm's product offerings be tailored to the local market? Will there be any tailoring at all, or will a one-size-fits-all strategy be invoked? What pricing strategy will be adopted? Distribution channels are an equally central element of the strategy. Distribution begins with the type of export contract that is secured (see Table 5-3). Exports can be left at the gate of a factory, as in an ex-Factory Gate contract, or delivered to final consumers directly. Alternatively, exported goods can be shipped to some destinations between the above two.

To facilitate distribution, a firm's management can consider using an export agent, an import agent, a broker or a wholesaler in the host country. There is no clear guide as to which distribution route is the best, however, the further along the distribution channel a firm progresses, the more control it maintains over the process and the integrity of its product offerings. Further to this, if the goal of senior management in exporting is to make a successful long-term penetration of a market, the best chances for doing this can be raised by being close to the market. An export strategy that brings a firm's management and employees into contact with distributors or

Table 5-3:   Exporting Terminology

Phrase	Abbreviation	Meaning
ex-Factory Gate	—	Goods are placed in vehicle at the factory's gate.
Free Alongside Ship	F.A.S.	Goods are unloaded from a vehicle on wharf at the port of origin for a shipment.
Free on-Board	F.O.B.	Goods are loaded on a vessel at the port of origin.
Cost, Insurance and Freight	C.I.F.	Goods are loaded on a vessel, but left on the vessel when it arrives at the port of destination. Insurance is provided by the supplier of the goods.
Market Price	—	Price of goods as found in the final consumer markets for a good.

consumers in a host country maximizes opportunities for acquiring local market knowledge that can boost a firm's competitiveness.

Ultimately, exporting might yield to another mode of international involvement, such as an equity investment. The shift from trade to investment can be a natural consequence of a firm's evolution in international markets. This evolution does not mean that exporting eventually becomes a redundant or outdated part of a firm's international strategy, instead it means that the advantages of exporting need to be compared directly to equity modes of entry, or other non-equity modes of entry, such as licensing and franchising.

Licensing and Franchising

More so than even exporting, licensing and franchising can have a low level of commitment and resources in international expansion. Licensing and franchising operate on the principle that a firm is selling a transferable part of its resources to another firm for application in a geographically competitively separate market. In international business, this new market typically means a foreign country or a set of foreign countries.

The term 'licensing' tends to apply to situations in which a firm is transferring some of its technology to another firm through a contractual agreement. The agreement can stipulate a one-time payment for the use of a technology, or a set of royalty payments depending on the sales or profitability of activities associated with the application of a firm's technology. Indeed, the form of payment is one of the crucial areas for negotiation in a license agreement.

The term 'franchising' tends to apply in situations in which a firm is transferring its brand name or a trademark to facilitate another firm or individual to establish a service activity. Franchising is often found in the hotel, restaurant and tourism industries. As with licensing, franchising can be both a domestic and international form of expansion. A franchising contract can stipulate the terms of payment, the types of services that are provided by the franchisor to the franchisee, and the responsibilities of the franchisee. As a brand name is often a component of a franchise contract, the franchisor requires provisions in the contract that protect the brand name from erosion through neglect or misuse by a franchisee. Misuse of the brand name can not only hurt the offending franchisee's operations, but it can have widespread implications for the whole firm.

As with exporting, licensing and franchising can be a means to enter a foreign market with little risk and little resource commitment. It can also provide a means by which to penetrate a large number of foreign markets. By alleviating the capital constraints on expansion, franchising enables a firm to grow as quickly as it can secure franchisees and internally manage the new franchise establishment process, such as that done by Singapore's BreadTalk (see Box 5-1).

As a low commitment mode of market entry, franchising and licensing do not consume many resources of a firm. This reduces the risk in one way, but risks can arise in other areas. By using licensing, a firm risks the chance of creating a competitor by selling its technology to another firm. Although the licensing agreement might stipulate a specific geographic area to the market application of products developed by the licensee using the licensor's technology, minor modifications to that technology sufficient to justify a new patent, can bypass the terms of the contractual agreement. Care also needs to be taken when establishing a licensing or franchising agreement, that the licensor or franchisor is not frozen out of a market by the terms of the agreement. This suggests that licensing and franchising might not be a good option for a market that holds considerable opportunity for higher commitment modes of entry, such as an equity entry mode. Even in small markets, the terms of the licensing or franchising agreement should allow for the contingency of entry by exporting or direct investment, given that the economic appeal for a firm to launch an equity entry mode might increase as its internationalization process matures.

Equity Modes of Entry

We consider the case of equity modes jointly because there are several direct trade-offs made between one equity mode and another. One of the most important trade-offs in the equity entry mode case that is not present to a substantial degree in non-equity entry modes is the opportunity to deploy and access assets and resources in a host country. This specific point is at the crux of the decision of which equity mode – whether it is joint venture, acquisition or greenfield wholly-owned subsidiary – to use when entering a foreign market.

Aside from the vantage point of resources, several other influences can emerge in the choice of equity entry mode. Table 5-4 lists Japanese equity entry modes (with the exclusion of a category called plant expansion) by 131 economies in the world. The numbers in Table 5-4 are the cumulative totals for Japanese FDI into the respective economy by the year 2001. Overall, Table 5-4 lists 27,779 FDI (equity mode) entries, with 51 per cent in the wholly-owned subsidiary category, 45 per cent in the joint venture category and four per cent in the acquisition category.

Two notable aspects of the overall trends in entry mode use are the relative absence of acquisition entries and the comparative high presence of joint venture entries. Unlike counterparts

Box 5-1   The Franchising of BreadTalk

Singaporean-based BreadTalk uses franchising as part of its international growth strategy. BreadTalk is a boutique bakery that specializes in making a constantly changing variety of breads and confectionaries in an efficient and clean environment. Over 150 recipes have been created by BreadTalk, and new breads are constantly being introduced. After opening its first store in July 2000, BreadTalk had opened 22 stores in Singapore by April 2003. It plans to continue expanding through franchises, joint ventures and wholly-owned subsidiaries.

In the few years since BreadTalk opened its doors, it has become a household name in Singapore. The company focuses on three branding concepts: creativity, passion, and transparency. These commitments emerge from all facets of its business. From the open concept store interior, to the bread itself, which through both name and variety, show the passion and creativity from whence it was created. George Quek, managing founder and creator, stated that: 'Our bread has a life, a personality of its own. We are always looking for innovative changes, for breakthroughs. Nowadays, people like creativity... so we have a very strong six-member international research and development team that continues to develop new products.' BreadTalk's ability to successfully create its brand won it the Singaporean Promising Brand Award for 2002.

According to Frankie Quek, General Manager of BreadTalk, the company has been approached by countless investors. The company receives email every day from all parts of the world – US, Canada, UK, Europe, Australia, New Zealand, South Africa, Bangladesh, Nepal. From Indonesia alone, the company received more than 500 inquiries. BreadTalk has developed its franchising growth plan seriously. In April 2003, when the company opened its first franchised store in Jakarta, Indonesia, it selected the franchisee with careful consideration. In addition to stringent qualification criteria, the franchisee possesses a strong network of contacts and sound financial standing.

To ensure that its growth plans through franchising are successful, BreadTalk has created a specific franchise division which follows a proven methodology. As such, the division is directly responsible for supervising, monitoring and operating the company's franchises. Each franchise must abide by the company's core branding concepts. To ensure similarity, the franchise team will provide advice on the retail outlet, from interior design plans to the materials used, to ensure the franchisee maintains the unique BreadTalk brand. This team also provides administrative and logistical support, to preserve product distinction.

In addition to retail growth in Singapore and overseas through franchising, BreadTalk opened its first overseas, wholly-owned subsidiary in Shanghai in July 2003. The company is also undertaking a diversification strategy, by entering into a joint venture to open Taiwanese-originated 'Din Tai Fung' restaurants in Singapore. Din Tai Fung, specializing in dumplings, noodles and chicken soup, had restaurants located in Taiwan, China, Japan and the United States in 2003.

Sources:

Joyce Teo, "BreadTalk Spreads Its Wings: Fancy bread man George Quek ventures overseas and into new businesses," *The Edge Singapore*, 2 June 2003, *http://www.singaporeabroad.org.sg/*, accessed on 26 December 2003.

www.iesingapore.com/iejournal/oct2002/iej_22.jsp+Breadtalk+indonesia&hl=en&ie=UTF-8, Foreign investors hungry for a slice of BreadTalk.

"Singapore's BreadTalk Group Sets up Unit in Shanghai," *AsiaPulse News*, 30 July, 2003.

from the United States, the United Kingdom and Germany, where the percentage of entries made by acquisition can reach as high as 50 per cent, Japanese firms tend to eschew FDI entry by acquisition.[7] Instead, Japanese firms place a high reliance on joint venture entry modes.

Table 5-4:   Japanese Equity Entry Modes by Economy (2001)

Nation	Wholly-owned subsidiary	Joint venture	Acquisition	Total number of FDIs
Algeria	1	1	0	2
Argentina	33	20	1	54
Australia	468	255	40	763
Austria	53	17	9	79
Bahamas	25	8	1	34
Bahrain	12	6	0	18
Bangladesh	5	6	0	11
Barbados	1	1	1	3
Belgium	159	54	14	227
Bermuda	36	18	0	54
Bolivia	2	4	0	6
Brazil	263	216	18	497
Brunei	4	10	0	14
Bulgaria	3	2	0	5
Burkina Faso	0	1	0	1
Cambodia	0	2	0	2
Cameroon	6	0	0	6
Canada	315	141	29	485
Cayman Islands	74	10	1	85
Chile	43	29	0	72
China	735	2,409	17	3,161
Colombia	10	16	1	27
Congo	0	2	0	2
Costa Rica	7	6	1	14
Croatia	2	1	0	3
Cyprus	0	1	0	1
Czech	29	15	0	44
Denmark	28	8	5	41
Dominican Republic	2	1	0	3
Dutch Antilles	17	3	0	20
Ecuador	7	9	0	16
Egypt	3	9	0	12
El Salvador	2	7	0	9
Estonia	0	2	0	2
Ethiopia	1	2	0	3
Fiji	2	2	0	4

Table 5-4:   continued

Nation	Wholly-owned subsidiary	Joint venture	Acquisition	Total number of FDIs
Finland	16	10	3	29
France	349	145	61	555
Germany	668	210	54	932
Ghana	0	2	0	2
Greece	7	7	0	14
Guam	48	26	3	77
Guatemala	4	11	0	15
Guyana	0	1	0	1
Honduras	2	2	0	4
Hong Kong	1,056	594	42	1,692
Hungary	34	29	5	68
India	30	161	0	191
Indonesia	156	709	6	871
Iran	12	13	0	25
Ireland	48	16	5	69
Israel	5	7	1	13
Italy	157	84	22	263
Ivory Coast	1	1	0	2
Jamaica	1	1	0	2
Jordan	0	2	0	2
Kazakhstan	0	3	0	3
Kenya	1	2	0	3
Korea	170	524	6	700
Kuwait	0	5	0	5
Laos	0	4	0	4
Lebanon	2	1	0	3
Liberia	150	33	1	184
Luxembourg	53	8	2	63
Macao	2	5	0	7
Madagascar	0	1	0	1
Malaysia	392	728	10	1,130
Maldives	1	0	0	1
Malta	0	1	0	1
Mariana Islands	2	1	0	3
Mauritius	4	0	0	4
Mexico	165	95	2	262

Table 5-4: continued

Nation	Wholly-owned subsidiary	Joint venture	Acquisition	Total number of FDIs
Mongolia	1	3	1	5
Morocco	0	4	0	4
Myanmar	10	14	0	24
Nepal	1	2	0	3
Netherlands	481	103	47	631
New Zealand	62	53	13	128
Niger	0	1	0	1
Nigeria	6	30	0	36
Norway	21	12	3	36
Oman	0	2	0	2
Pakistan	1	30	1	32
Palau Islands	0	5	1	6
Panama	216	55	2	273
Papua New Guinea	7	2	2	11
Paraguay	0	2	0	2
Peru	16	14	0	30
Philippines	168	360	3	531
Poland	33	19	4	56
Portugal	17	29	0	46
Puerto Rico	16	4	0	20
Qatar	0	3	0	3
Romania	6	6	0	12
Russia	20	57	0	77
Saipan Island	10	21	1	32
Samoa	2	3	1	6
Saudi Arabia	0	40	1	41
Senegal	0	1	0	1
Singapore	1,001	524	27	1,552
Slovak	8	2	0	10
Slovenia	2	2	0	4
Solomon Islands	0	3	2	5
South Africa	15	18	1	34
Spain	124	70	19	213
Sri Lanka	8	25	2	35
Suriname	0	2	0	2
Swaziland	1	1	0	2

Table 5-4: continued

Nation	Wholly-owned subsidiary	Joint venture	Acquisition	Total number of FDIs
Sweden	53	25	6	84
Switzerland	92	41	8	141
Taiwan	438	772	11	1,221
Tanzania	1	6	0	7
Thailand	243	1,364	8	1,615
Tonga	0	1	0	1
Trinidad & Tobago	2	3	0	5
Tunisia	2	2	0	4
Turkey	11	26	0	37
UAE	17	13	1	31
Uganda	0	1	0	1
Ukraine	4	2	0	6
United Kingdom	972	324	107	1,403
Uruguay	1	0	0	1
USA	3,978	1,566	496	6,040
Uzbekistan	0	1	0	1
Vanuatu	3	3	1	7
Venezuela	19	21	1	41
Vietnam	45	158	2	205
Virgin Islands	15	16	2	33
Zaire	0	3	0	3
Zambia	1	3	0	4
Zimbabwe	0	1	0	1
Total	**14,034**	**12,610**	**1,135**	**27,779**

Source: Toyo Keizai, *Japanese Overseas Investment.* (Toyo Keizai: Tokyo, Japan, various editions).

This reliance on joint ventures is not the same everywhere in the world. The proportions of entry modes by economy and world regions are skewed. In North America, for example, entries by wholly-owned subsidiary appear to dominate. Sixty per cent of the FDI entries into Canada were made by wholly-owned subsidiary, a percentage just less than the 66 per cent recorded for the United States. Countries in Europe, such as Belgium, Luxembourg and Germany had even higher proportions of entries fall into the wholly-owned subsidiary category.

If we jump from the west coast of North America across the Pacific Ocean, we land in an area where there is a much higher proportion of joint venture use. In two of the largest recipients of Japanese FDI in Asia, China and Thailand, the percentage of entries made by joint venture exceeded 75 per cent. Among its 32 FDIs, Pakistan had 30, or 94 per cent, in the joint venture category. South Korea, the Philippines, Malaysia, Taiwan and Indonesia each had 60 per cent or more of Japanese entries made as joint ventures. Meanwhile, Australia, New Zealand, Hong Kong and Singapore had distributions in entry modes that resembled those in North America and Europe.

These cross-country trends in entry mode usage emerge for a number of reasons. First, managers in a firm might have little choice in the use of a joint venture. The host country government can stipulate a number of restrictions on foreign ownership. Thailand, China and Pakistan each had fairly stringent foreign ownership regulations in the 1990s, leading to high percentages of entries by joint venture.[8]

Second, the national institutional environment might not be conducive to a wholly-owned entry. Weaknesses in the policy environment might lead a firm to seek a local partner to reduce the chances of unfavourable policy change, much of which has been discussed in Chapter 4. This motivation must be balanced against other dimensions of the national institutional environment, such as intellectual property protection. Where intellectual property protection is weak, there can be a substantial risk in entering via a joint venture because the joint venture partner faces few consequences of appropriating the propriety knowledge of the other joint venture partner.

Third, countries might be sites for different kinds of FDI. Hong Kong and Singapore, for example, tend to be the sites for regional headquarters for manufacturing operations, or a site for foreign branches of banks for corporate banking activities, or headquarters for a firm's trading and distribution activities. These entries involve smaller levels of capital investment than a manufacturing subsidiary, although not necessarily inconsequential levels of investment, and a high need for control. When we evaluate these needs against the entry mode trade-offs listed in Figures 5-1 and 5-2, we can see that a wholly-owned entry tends to be the one with the best match.

Moving to the acquisition column, we find that in Asia, acquisitions occur rarely at best. The typical range among major Japanese FDI recipient countries in Asia, such as the Philippines, Viet Nam, India, Thailand, China, South Korea, Taiwan and Malaysia is zero to one per cent. Even in Hong Kong and Singapore, the percentage does not climb over two. In North America and Europe, the percentage of entries by acquisition still remains low, but can be as much as five to ten times as great as the numbers in Asia.

Setting aside the low propensity of Japanese investors to use acquisitions, we can still see a wide variance by region. Why might this be the case? The answer rests in a couple of areas. First, the number of desirable targets might be fewer in one area versus another. Many of Asia's economies have just emerged onto the world scene. Japanese firms might enjoy a substantial competitive advantage over most, but definitely not all, firms in Asia. Consequently, few firms in Asia emerge as desirable targets.

Second, even if a firm is a desirable target, how can another firm acquire it? If it is a private firm, the owner of the local company must agree to sell it to the prospective purchaser. If it is a public firm, the acquirer can purchase enough shares to take control of the company. This latter process assumes that equity markets are mature, function well, and have good information, which might not always be the case. It also assumes that ownership is dispersed. In Asia's public companies, concentrated ownership, with one individual owning the majority of a firm's shares, is more the rule than the exception. Meanwhile, in North America, shares are less concentrated in the hands of one individual. As a consequence, acquisitions can be difficult to implement in Asia.

Resources and Equity Entry Mode Choice

The selection of equity entry mode is clearly one influenced by a number of factors. These factors can emerge from a firm's external environment, much as discussed in the preceding section, or the factors can emerge from a firm's internal environment. One of the internal factors with the foremost influence is that related to the resources required to mount an entry.

When a firm is moving into international markets, it generally must cross a divide that separates its existing areas of business and new areas of business. The new area can be a new type of productive process, it can be a new geographic market, or it can be a new product. This newness implies that the managers in a firm might have to revise existing activities to accommodate the areas into which a firm is expanding, which might also necessitate the addition of new assets of resources to a firm.

If new resources are required to support a firm's expansion, managers must deal with the matter of how to acquire those new resources. The resources could be acquired by internal development or they could be sourced from another firm. If the internal development option is selected, then an entry made by wholly-owned subsidiary is a feasible means of entering a market. If the 'source from another firm' option is selected, then a joint venture or acquisition becomes the preferred route of entry into a market.

With this in mind, the driving consideration between an independent entry by wholly-owned subsidiary or shared entry by joint venture or acquisition, is whether a firm's managers perceive the resource hurdle to successful entry as one that can be independently cleared.

The height of the resource hurdle, and the corresponding ease of clearing it, depends on the characteristics of the resources that need to be added. In some cases, needed resources can be readily developed or acquired in a market-based exchange. When a firm makes a foreign entry to undertake manufacturing, it faces a need to build a manufacturing facility, which is a new resource in the host country. In most cases, this need can be readily matched by the application of capital to purchase needed inputs and by the use of existing knowledge about the construction of a manufacturing facility to create this resource.

In other instances, the required resource is not so easily built by a firm independently. Consider the case of a foreign entry made by a retailer. In this type of entry, one of the keys to successful entry is to tailor offerings to local consumer demands. A foreign entrant with little experience in a host country market could face a substantial barrier to learning about local consumer tastes. For this reason, an entry made by joint venture or acquisition could help overcome the resource deficiency faced by a foreign firm when trying to compete in a retail environment. Several companies have used this strategy, with Harvey Norman of Australia and Dairy Farm Group of Hong Kong being recent examples (see Box 5-2).

Continuing with the retail entry example, we can also consider the resource of location. For retailers, such as Carrefour, Mitsukoshi, Sogo and Daimaru, the location of a store is a key success factor. Entering a mature retail environment, such as that faced by a foreign entrant when entering Shanghai, Singapore or Hong Kong, can be extremely difficult, especially in locating prime retail space in the main, densely-packed shopping areas such as Nanjing Road,

Box 5-2   Growth of Dairy Farm International

First incorporated in 1889 by a Scottish surgeon and five Hong Kong businessmen, Dairy Farm International Group is now a leading Asian operator of supermarkets, hypermarkets, health and beauty, convenience and furniture stores. (*www.dairyfarmgroup.com*) The group's banners include Cold Storage, 7-Eleven and Guardian. Dairy Farm credits its success to its strong corporate focus: high quality, low cost retailing; multiple formats, shared services; long-term shareholder value creation; and an Asia focus.

Dairy Farm's growth strategy consists of market entry through joint ventures, acquisitions and strategic alliances. For example, in 1980, Dairy Farm became the first company to enter into a joint venture with the Chinese Government in order to operate a flight kitchen at Beijing International Airport. In 1999, the Group acquired a 228-outlet 7-Eleven convenience store chain in Hong Kong. More recently, a joint venture company was formed in 2000 between Dairy Farm and India-based Spencer and Company to operate Cash & Carry stores in India. In 2002, Dairy Farm commenced operations in South Korea through a 50/50 joint venture with CJ Corporation of South Korea, to operate health and beauty stores.

Although the company is geographically committed to only one continent, Asia, Dairy Farm acknowledges that each country is different and unique. This nation-by-nation uniqueness makes it a priority of Dairy Farm to tailor its retail operations to the local marketplace. For instance, Dairy Farm owns Giant Hypermarket, an ethnically-focused hypermarket located in Singapore and Malaysia. In both countries Giant provides customers with good value and large selection, but the stores cater specifically to the individual needs of the different ethnic groups in their respective countries. Giant's hypermarkets are designed to ensure strong local appeal and to be a one-stop shopping destination for the average local family, whether the family is Singaporean or Malaysian. In keeping with its growth strategy, Dairy Farm purchased 34 Tops supermarkets in Malaysia in May 2003, and converted them into Giant and Cold Storage banners. To gain and internalize the knowledge of the staff, Dairy Farm retained the current store operation staff from the Tops supermarkets as Giant and Cold Storage staff once the stores were converted.

Source:
http://www.dairyfarmgroup.com/dfarm_graphic/corporate/press/p030502.pdf.

Orchard Road or Causeway Bay. An acquisition of a competitor with retail space, or a joint venture with an owner of property in these prime areas, can provide this important resource.

Although resource shortfalls will be encountered in an entry, it does not always behoove a firm's managers to try to replace the missing resources. In some instances, the missing resource might not be crucial to a firm's competitive success. However, when it is, a strategy to replace that missing resource should be in place.

For the entry mode part of that strategy, we can think of the following heuristic for helping to guide the choice between entry by acquisition, joint venture or wholly-owned subsidiary. First, when contemplating an international expansion, identify a firm's key success factors in the home country. Second, ask the question of whether the resources required for those key success factors can be transferred to, or replicated in, the foreign market. Third, if yes, then a wholly-owned subsidiary entry can be made. Fourth, if no, then management needs to consider using a joint venture entry or an acquisition entry to bridge the divide between the sources of a firm's competitiveness in its home country and that in its host countries. As for the choice between acquisition and joint venture, there are a number of additional considerations that will be discussed in Chapter 7.

Notes

[1] C. Patrick Woodcock, Paul W. Beamish, and Shige Makino, "Ownership-based Entry Mode Strategies and International Performance," *Journal of International Business Studies*, 1994, Vol. 25, No. 2, pp. 253–273.

[2] Andrew Delios and Paul W. Beamish, "Joint Venture Performance Revisited: Japanese Foreign Subsidiaries Worldwide," *Management International Review*, 2004, Vol. 44, No. 1, pp. 47–58; Andrew Delios and Paul W. Beamish, "Ownership Strategy of Japanese Firms: Transactional, Institutional and Experience Influences," *Strategic Management Journal*, 1999, Vol. 20, No. 10, pp. 915–933.

[3] James Myles Shaver, *The Influence of Intangible Assets, Spillovers and Competition on Foreign Direct Investment Survival and Entry Time* (Unpublished PhD Dissertation, Ann Arbor, MI: The University of Michigan, 1994); Jaideep Anand and Andrew Delios, "Location Specificity and the Transfer of Downstream Assets to Foreign Subsidiaries," *Journal of International Business Studies*, 1997, Vol. 28, No. 3, pp. 579–604.

[4] Jane Lu and Paul W. Beamish, "Internationalization and Performance of SMEs," *Strategic Management Journal,* June–July 2001, Vol. 22, pp. 565–586.

[5] Press Release, *Café de Coral Holdings, http://202.66.146.82/listco/hk/cafedecoral/press/p030304.pdf*, 25 November 2003.

[6] Neil Weinberg, Kerry A. Dolan, and Justin Doebele, "Another Look," *Forbes Global*, 14 April 2003, Vol. 6, No. 8, p. 6.

[7] Jaideep Anand and Andrew Delios, "Absolute and Relative Resources as Determinants of International Acquisitions," *Strategic Management Journal*, 2002, Vol. 23, No. 2, pp. 119–134.

[8] Shige Makino and Paul Beamish, "Local Ownership Restrictions, Entry Mode Choice, and FDI Performance: Japanese Overseas Subsidiaries in Asia," *Asia Pacific Journal of Management,* Special Issue on "Government-Business Relations in Asia," 1998, Vol. 15, No. 2, pp. 119–136.

6 INTERNATIONAL EXPANSION

When a firm is undergoing international expansion, its managers must make decisions about the entry mode, entry timing, the geographic market for entry and the product market for entry (see Figure 6-1). As we will discuss in this chapter, each of these decisions has its own set of drivers. It is important to understand these drivers, to understand the advantages and trade-offs

Figure 6-1:   Key Internationalization Decisions

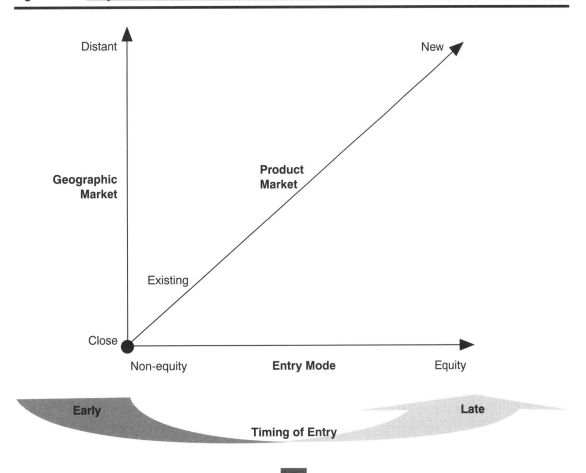

of entering a market early or late, of using one entry mode or another, of moving into a market that has a similar or a dissimilar national institutional environment, or of entering a product market in which a firm has strong or weak competitive advantages.

The four decisions outlined in Figure 6-1 – entry mode, timing of entry, geographic market of entry and product market of entry – are the pillars on which a firm's success in its internationalization process are founded. As we will review in the sections that follow, there are several key ways in which we can conceptualize these decisions to maximize the chances of success in any internationalization decision. At the most basic level, it is useful to think of these decisions along the parameters outlined in Figure 6-1.

As we discussed in Chapter 5, entry modes can range from non-equity to equity entry, with a number of types of equity modes within each category. Entry timing in a market can be early or late. The timing of a firm's entry into a market can be compared to that of a firm's competitors. Entry into a particular host country can also be identified as early or late, depending on its temporal sequencing in a firm's internationalization process. The geographic market for entry, the host country and the region within the host country selected for entry, can be distant or close to a firm's other home and host country markets. Distance can be defined at a number of levels, starting from geographic distance and ending in institutional distance. Finally, the products a firm introduces into its markets can be existing or new products.

Timing of Entry Decision

The timing of entry decision is one that has risen to more prominence in recent years. Part of the reason for this has been the opening of the Chinese market and the rush by foreign firms to enter China. The opportunity to capture a first mover advantage was a major driver of the rush to be among the first foreign firms to enter the Chinese market.

Timing of entry is most often a relative decision. It involves a comparison of when one firm enters a market versus when other firms enter a market. Rivalry between firms, social pressures to conform to the actions of other firms and the need to avoid being among the only firms that did not enter a market, drive firms to move in tandem into markets.

The tendency to move together is a characteristic common to much of foreign investment. In the 1950s and 1960s, US firms moved abroad together. One firm followed another because the managers in the following firms believed the home competitive position would be weakened if they did not imitate the international expansion moves of competitors. This co-dependence emerged from the oligopolistic structure of the industries in which many of these US firms competed.

Japanese firms have had the same behaviour in foreign entry. Japanese firms that competed in the tire industry for example had a great tendency to mimic the timing of the strategic moves of competitors. Japanese firms in other industries had similar behaviour.

In 1962, when Japanese firms began to take up foreign investment positions across the world, Nissan established its first automotive manufacturing plant in Thailand. Two months after Nissan's plant opened, Toyota's manufacturing subsidiary in Thailand began operations. Two years later, in October 1964, Mitsubishi established its own manufacturing facility and Honda set up a sales subsidiary. Another three years later, Honda likewise constructed a manufacturing plant in Thailand. Meanwhile, across the Pacific, the same Japanese firms were developing operations in Canada. In 1964, Toyota established its first sales subsidiary in Canada. Not one year later, this was followed by Nissan's entry. Mazda's came in 1968 and Honda's in 1969. Further, in the mid-1980s, this round of distribution subsidiary formation was followed by another series of grouped entries, this time for the manufacture of automobiles.

The prevalence of bunching in foreign entry raises questions about why it occurs. Are there advantages that come from being the first to enter a market? The answer to this is 'Yes', there can be a first mover advantage. Marketers have long been concerned with the question of whether there is any advantage to being the first to enter a market. The idea of a first mover advantage, or an advantage to early entry, can also apply to a foreign entrant. Several advantages can come from being an early entrant into a foreign geographic market (see Table 6-1). Even so, the case of foreign entry is not exactly like that for a new product entry. There are several notable differences that have implications for whether a firm should be among the first to try to penetrate a product area in a host country market.

Foreign entrants do not always enter a market unoccupied by other firms. A foreign firm might be the first among other foreign firms to enter a market, but that market might already be served by other domestic firms. When a foreign firm enters a market, it is not always for the purpose of selling a product in the country. Foreign subsidiaries can be established for market seeking, resource seeking, efficiency seeking and strategic asset seeking motivations.[1] Particularly, in the case of foreign investments motivated by resource seeking, efficiency seeking and strategic

Table 6-1:   **First Mover Advantages**

Advantage	Source
Cost	First mover can achieve larger sales outputs than late entrants, leading to economies of scale, experience curve gains, and advantages in marketing.
Technological	Establishment of industry standards by being among the first to enter a market.
Behavioural	Consumers establish a firm set of preferences with the early firms to enter a particular consumer market. These preferences translate into stronger loyalty than that enjoyed by late entrants, as switching costs can be high, and consumption experience can lead to consistency in purchasing habits.
Pre-emptive	Pre-emption of distribution channels, customers and suppliers can provide a firm with lowered costs and unique access to important buyer or supplier segments.

Source: Yigang Pan, Shaomin Li, and David Tse, "The Impact of Order and Mode of Market Entry on Profitability and Market Share," *Journal of International Business Studies,* 1999, Vol. 30, No. 1, pp. 81–104.

asset seeking goals, certain first mover advantages, such as pre-emption in supply side markets for labour and other local assets or favourable procurement arrangements, can be gained by early entry to a market. When a subsidiary is established in a foreign market under a motivation other than market seeking, certain first mover or early entrant advantages, such as the advantage of pre-emption, might be less prominent.

A foreign firm does not enter a market like a new firm, or one moving into a new product market. A foreign firm has a set of skills and capabilities that provide it with advantages in competition. In some cases, these advantages, such as a proprietary technology, a patent, a trademark or a brand, can be transferable to the host country market. This means that a foreign entrant does not necessarily have to build a complete set of new capabilities on foreign entry.

The timing of entry decision is thus more than just the choice to enter a foreign market as soon as possible. Some firms will gain more than others from early entry. Other firms face less of an imperative to enter early. The differences in motivations and rewards to early entry emerge by evaluating the reason for foreign entry, the intensity of existing competition from domestic and foreign firms, and the types of skills and capabilities a firm already possesses.

Gains can be had from being an early mover. There are first mover advantages. However, the pursuit of first mover advantages at all costs needs to be balanced against the potential to encounter first mover disadvantages. The first firms to enter a market do so under conditions of high uncertainty and less information as compared to late entrants. Uncertainty about a market can encumber decision making, leading to a less successful entry. For the timing of entry decision, managers should consider carefully whether the market can yield first mover advantages, whether resources required in an entry will be depleted if other firms enter the market first, and whether existing skills and capabilities can be transferred to the host country to provide a firm with competitive advantages. By examining these issues, and balancing the potential gains from early entry against the information deficiency and uncertainty costs that accompany early entry, an international manager can be better prepared to determine when, and if, a company should be a pioneer in entering a foreign market.

Geographic Market Decision

The geographic market decision is an important one in many respects. The choice of geographic location for an entry has an influence on the types of buyers and suppliers that a firm will be connected to in its entry. It has an influence on the costs of factors of production like raw material, skilled and unskilled labour, management, land, transportation, electricity and the like.[2] A firm's location also influences its access to knowledge and technology spillovers from other firms, educational and research organizations in a region.[3]

For example, if a company was in the fashion industry, it may want to open a national office in Hong Kong where garment manufacturers place a strong emphasis on original design. If a company specializes in biotechnology research, it could consider opening an office in Singapore, where the government is providing economic incentives with the objective of making the country a world-class hub for biomedical science activities. Likewise, if a company is focused on ceramic manufacturing, it could consider entry into Sri Lanka.

The geographic market decision attaches a firm to locational advantages and disadvantages. The locational advantages are bound to a region because the advantage is non-mobile. Natural resources such as oil, coal, iron ore and the like are clearly attached to a particular region. In the 1950s and 1960s, and even earlier, many foreign direct investments had the goal of accessing the right to mine raw materials, or harvest forests, where it was difficult to purchase these materials on open markets.

The people who work in skilled, unskilled and managerial positions in a firm can be immobile. The labour cost motive is one of the dominating incentives to foreign investment. Multinational firms moved a substantial portion of productive activities to Asia and Latin America in the 1980s and 1990s to access low cost sources of labour. Labour can become more mobile when trading agreements are put in place. Recall that in a common market or in an economic union, people from different nations can move freely across member states.

Somewhat surprisingly, knowledge can be location-bound. To access pockets of knowledge about productive activities, or about consumers, a firm needs to have an operation and its people in the region in which a type of knowledge is regarded as strong. Locating in a knowledge hotbed provides a firm's employees with direct access to employees in other firms, and university and government researchers and scientists. As we discuss in Chapter 11, the motivation to access knowledge drove large numbers of firms based in Taiwan, Singapore, Japan and now China, to enter the United States. This same motivation can drive firms to invest in other nations of the world, provided it is a leader in an industry.

Take the example of the Sri Lankan ceramics industry (*www.ceramics.lk*). Sri Lanka has a well-established, competitive ceramics industry that produces high quality tableware, porcelain, brick and tile. Historians estimate that ceramics production first began in Sri Lanka between 500–250BC.[4] The industry's strengths include knowledge by way of a highly trained workforce, excellent management at the factory level, and confidentiality of design integrity. The industry also boasts relatively low labour costs and an abundant supply of raw material.

Locating in a particular region can be motivated by access to location-bound knowledge and resources, it can also be done to access the consumer segment. Consumers can be location-bound in the sense that a firm might not be able to access a country's consumers unless it manufactures products in a consumer's home country. Governments can create this incentive through tariff and non-tariff barriers to entry. A firm can create advantages for itself by operating in a country. Foreign operations can enable a firm's managers to better understand local consumers than in the case where it exports or licenses its products for sale in a foreign market.

Access to markets for the production and sale of a firm's products are the major benefits that can accompany a foreign entry. A firm's management needs to evaluate both of these national and sub-national dimensions when considering making a foreign entry.

A complete evaluation of a market also requires a review of its comparative weaknesses as well as its strengths. Returning to the Sri Lankan example, further investigation reveals constraints, or weaknesses, that may be significant for an entrant. For example, there is little brand and quality recognition for Sri Lankan ceramics and, it appears, no movement to alter the current situation. Existing companies, such as Fernwood Porcelain (*www.fernwoodporcelain.com*), Dankotuwa (*www.dankotuwa.com*), Lanka Tile (*www.lankatile.com*) and Lanka Wall (*www.lankawall.com*) are highly proficient manufactures with little or no understanding of the end-user. For instance, Dankotuwa exports its products globally, producing tableware for Ralph Lauren (*www.rlhome.polo.com*) and Dansk (*www.dansk.com*). However, it does not design or manufacture tableware under its own name or brand. Other constraints emerge in the manufacturing process. The quality of raw materials have been inconsistent, energy prices have been high and the existing companies have not been prepared to adopt and use advanced technology.

National Analysis

A nation by nation analysis for investment opportunities involves deliberation of many of the items we outlined in Chapters 2, 3 and 4. A foreign investor needs to think about the economic environment of a country, the cultural environment and the political environment. This analysis should be made on an absolute level, i.e. is this a good country in which to make a foreign entry now? Similarly, on a comparative level – Is this the best country in which to make this particular entry at this time?

The economic, cultural and political analyses should be directed towards both the present situation and the future situation. The assessments can be made at a general level, but also with specific concern toward the type of entry being made. General information about the national institutional environment of a country can be obtained by a potential investor fairly easily. In addition to printed material available through embassies, trade offices and representative offices of national governments, many countries maintain information on websites devoted to the dissemination of basic information about the attractiveness of the country for foreign entry (see Table 6-2). This information can be quite extensive and detailed. Further, the information offered by an investment promotion agency tends to be standardized, meaning that cross-country comparisons can be made fairly easily.

In analyzing the cross-national investment environment with respect to the type of entry, it is important to consider trends in the product environment. If the entry is for automotive parts, information on the automotive assemblers and competing automotive parts suppliers and their patterns of foreign entry is required. Which countries have seen the strongest growth in automotive trade and investment in the past few years? Are there any changes in regional trading agreements that might create opportunities or threats in automotive trade and investment? What is a country's set of advantages for the production of automotives and automotive parts?

Table 6-2: **Web-based Investment Information**

Country/ Region	Website URL	Sample of information available on website
Afghanistan	N/A	N/A
Australia	www.investaustralia.gov.au	A B C F G H
Bangladesh	www.boibd.org	A C D E F G H
Brunei	www.industry.gov.bn	C F G H
Burma	www.myanmar.com/gov/trade/inv.htm	A C D E F G
Cambodia	www.cambodiainvestment.gov.kh	C D F H
China	www.chinafdi.gov.cn	A C D E F G H
East Timor	N/A	N/A
Hong Kong	www.investhk.gov.hk	A B C D E F G H
India	iic.nic.in	A B C D E
Indonesia	www.bkpm.go.id	A B C D E G H
Japan	www.investment-japan.net	A B C D F
Korea, North	crm.kotra.or.kr/main/info/nk/eng/main.php3	C D E F G
Korea, South	www.kisc.org	A B C D E F G H
Laos	www.laoembassy.com/news/index.htm	A C D G
Malaysia	www.mida.gov.my	A B C D E F G H
Mongolia	www.investmongolia.com	A C D E F G H
New Zealand	www.investnewzealand.govt.nz	A B C F G H
Nepal	www.catmando.com/gov/industry/fipd/fipd.htm	A C D E F G
Pakistan	www.pakboi.gov.pk	A B C D E F G H
Papua New Guinea	www.ipa.gov.pg	A C D E F
Philippines	www.boi.gov.ph	A B C D E F G H
Singapore	www.sedb.com.sg	A B C D E F G H
Sri Lanka	www.boisrilanka.org	A C D E F G H
Thailand	www.boi.go.th	A B C D E G H
Vietnam	www.invest.mpi.gov.vn	A C D E F G H

Legend

A	Statistics		E	Incentives / Support Policies
B	Official Publications		F	Industry News / Profiles
C	Business Environment		G	Investment Options / Project Database
D	Investment Legislations		H	Investment Services

Notes:

1. The information one can find on these websites is standardized in terms of structure and content. The main differences across websites are in the levels of detail, user-friendliness, methodology, terminology, language options, and website design.

2. The North Korean website is provided by a South Korean investment promotion agency.

This last question hinges in part on the competitive environment made by the foreign entry patterns of other firms in the automotive industry, as well as the state of domestic competitors. A country's attractiveness as a site for investment is not only defined by costs of inputs, and the economic, political and cultural environments. It is defined by the competitive environment. As laid out in Chapter 2, in our discussion of national competitiveness, certain countries are better sites for the production of a particular product than others.

One of the reasons for this is that the existing competitors, suppliers and buyers in a region create opportunities for spillovers of knowledge and technology.[5] Although this can be an opportunity, it can also be a risk. Spillovers come from somewhere, and that place is another firm. A concentration of firms in an area can lead to the erosion of a firm's competitive position.[6] If a leading foreign firm invests in an area already densely occupied by domestic and foreign competitors, it risks leakage of its competitive advantages to other firms. Furthermore, the risk is that costs might rise as many firms begin to compete for the same kinds of inputs such as skilled labour and management, or other raw materials. This concern about concentration is heightened when considering the question of where to locate within a particular country.

Sub-National Analysis

One important consideration for the geographic market decision is the country choice. Another important consideration is the choice of location within a country. In some cases, such as with entry into Singapore, the within-country, or sub-national location choice, is not complicated because the country is small. When investing in Singapore, the foreign investor might consider a location close to Changi Airport as of primary importance, or the investor might choose the other end of the country, and move 35 km west, to co-locate with other factories in the Jurong area.

In other cases, particularly when the country is large and diverse, the within-country location choice can be just as complicated as the across-country location choice. Taking entry into India and China as examples, a foreign investor is confronted with regions within these countries that vary tremendously in levels of economic development, language, culture and politics. In some ways, this variance might be as great as the difference between member states in the European Union.

As always, at the forefront of making a good sub-national choice is cognizance of how regions vary. In large countries, understanding regional variance can be vital to the success of an international expansion strategy. Such variance is well in evidence in the strength of various industries in India by region. The city of Ludhiana in northern India accounts for 95 per cent of the country's woollen knitwear, 85 per cent of the India's sewing machines and 60 per cent of the nation's bicycle and bicycle parts,[7] while Bangalore in the south is known as India's Silicon Valley.

Table 6-3 provides an example of the variance in the provinces and major municipalities in China, but it is just a part of the story of identifying sub-national differences in China. It only

Table 6-3: GDP, Population, Trade and FDI by Region in China (2001)

Province/ Municipality	Population (Million)	GDP (USD million)	GDP per capita (USD)	Inward FDI (USD million)	Exports (USD million)	Imports (USD million)
Anhui	59.00	39,736	673	337	2,282	1,338
Beijing	13.57	34,368	2,533	1,768	11,787	39,754
Chongqing	30.51	21,132	693	256	1,103	731
Fujian	34.10	51,373	1,507	3,918	13,926	8,704
Gansu	25.12	12,953	516	74	476	303
Guangdong	85.23	128,596	1,509	11,932	95,426	81,069
Guangxi	43.85	26,947	614	384	1,235	562
Guizhou	35.25	13,103	372	28	422	225
Hainan	7.56	6,594	872	467	798	949
Hebei	66.68	67,364	1,010	670	3,956	1,782
Heilongjiang	36.24	43,007	1,187	341	1,612	1,772
Henan	91.24	68,117	747	457	1,705	1,077
Hubei	59.51	56,308	946	1,189	1,797	1,780
Hunan	63.27	48,104	760	810	1,753	1,005
Inner Mongolia	23.32	18,669	800	107	627	1,408
Jiangsu	73.04	114,878	1,573	6,915	28,874	22,477
Jiangxi	40.40	26,276	650	396	1,039	492
Jilin	26.80	24,547	916	338	1,462	1,745
Liaoning	41.82	60,786	1,453	2,516	11,008	8,799
Ningxia	5.49	3,604	657	17	352	181
Qinghai	4.82	3,635	754	36	149	56
Shaanxi	35.37	22,274	630	352	1,108	954
Shandong	89.97	113,989	1,267	3,521	18,121	10,833
Shanghai	16.41	59,793	3,644	4,292	27,624	33,269
Shanxi	32.47	21,497	662	234	1,468	473
Sichuan	82.35	53,403	649	582	1,583	1,516
Tianjin	9.85	22,223	2,256	2,133	9,492	8,680
Tibet	2.62	1,675	640	..	82	11
Xinjiang	18.46	17,941	972	20	668	1,103
Yunnan	42.36	25,057	592	65	1,244	745
Zhejiang	45.93	81,499	1,774	2,212	22,976	9,822

Sources: National Bureau of Statistics, *China Statistical Yearbook 2002* (State Statistical Bureau of the People's Republic of China, various editions).

identifies economic, trade and investment differences across the 31 provinces and municipalities listed in Table 6-3 and not differences in culture, language, social customs and customary business practices.

As we have discussed in Chapter 2, there are numerous other dimensions we could consider. In the case of China, one of these dimensions is politics and political autonomy. China has a strong central government. Since the late 1970s, national government officials have been providing sub-national regions in China with increasing levels of autonomy. This freedom permits each province or municipality to design individualized incentive packages to attract foreign investors to China. This autonomy has emerged in a considerable variety of regional incentive packages for foreign investors.

Sub-National Incentives to Foreign Investment

Regional incentive packages are commonly used to attract foreign investment in all countries of the world. The packages can include tax breaks for foreign investors, reductions in tariffs for imported raw materials and equipment, subsidies for the construction of manufacturing plants and other forms of fiscal incentives. The incentive packages have had varying degrees of success, with perhaps one of the best examples of the success of an incentive package occurring in China in the 1980s and 1990s.

China followed a policy of economic self-reliance between 1949 and 1976. The institution of the Act of Joint Venture Enterprises in 1979 formally re-opened China's doors to FDI. The Act mandated that foreign firms take a minimum equity share of 25 per cent in foreign invested enterprises. The Act stipulated that foreign investment should be limited to four Special Economic Zones (SEZs): Shantou, Shenzhen Xiamen and Zhuhai (see Table 6-4). Hainan became the fifth SEZ in 1988.

The Act of Joint Venture Enterprises helped the resumption of FDI in China. In SEZs, foreign investors had tax holidays for the first two years of profitable operations. The third to fifth years faced taxes at 50 per cent of normal rates. Lowered duties applied to the import of equipment and the export of products, while the paperwork was reduced for imports and exports. Although there was considerable uncertainty in China in the 1980s, foreign investment did begin to flow in, marking some success to these SEZs (see Figure 6-2).

The initial success of the SEZs in attracting FDI inflows into China led to the creation of several other types of special policy zones for FDI. The first of these were the Opening Coastal Cities (OCCs), established in 1984. The OCCs had an advantage over the SEZs. Many of the OCCs had a higher level of economic and infrastructure development than did the SEZs in the 1980s. Foreign investors in OCCs could receive tax concessions similar to, but of a lesser magnitude, than those in SEZs. Foreign invested enterprises in SEZs faced a 24 to 30 per cent tax rate on profits, while those in SEZs enjoyed rates as low as 15 per cent.

The OCCs and SEZs can be found along the Eastern seaboard of China. This meant that

Table 6-4: **Opening Coastal Cities and Special Economic Zones in China**

Type of Economic Promotion	City	Province
Special Economic Zone	Shenzhen	Guangdong
	Zhuhai	Guangdong
	Shantou	Guangdong
	Xiamen	Fujian
	Hainan	Hainan
Opening Coastal City	Dalian	Liaoning
	Qinhuangdao	Hebei
	Tianjin	Tianjin
	Yantai	Shandong
	Qingdao	Shandong
	Lianyungang	Jiangsu
	Nantong	Jiangsu
	Shanghai	Shanghai
	Ningbo	Zhejiang
	Wenzhou	Zhejiang
	Fuzhou	Fujian
	Guangzhou	Guangdong
	Zhanjiang	Guangdong
	Beihai	Guangxi

Source: Changhui Zhou, Andrew Delios, and Jing Yu Yang, "Locational Determinants of Japanese Foreign Direct Investment in China," *Asia Pacific Journal of Management,* 2002, Vol. 19, No. 1, pp. 63–86.

the East coast region of China was receiving more investment than the other areas of China. In the early 1990s, the Chinese government attempted to rectify this situation by creating new and high-technology industrial zones (NTZs). Fifty-two newly-established regions had this designation by 1992.[8]

Another type of zone, created after the OCCs, is the Economic and Technology Development Zones (ETDZs). ETDZs are distributed widely across China, in many different cities. Only small areas within a city have this designation. A foreign investor must set up a plant in the designated area to be subject to its benefits. The benefits are oriented towards fiscal rewards for the development of productive capabilities and technology research. Infrastructure, telecommunications and energy improvements accompany the fiscal incentives.

A fifth type of zone, called Free Trade Zones (FTZs) or Tax Protection Zones, tried to foster international commerce. In an FTZ, a foreign investor faced reduced import quotas, reduced import duties and a tax structure that favoured the development of local and foreign businesses.

Figure 6-2: **Worldwide FDI Inflows into China (1979-2002)**

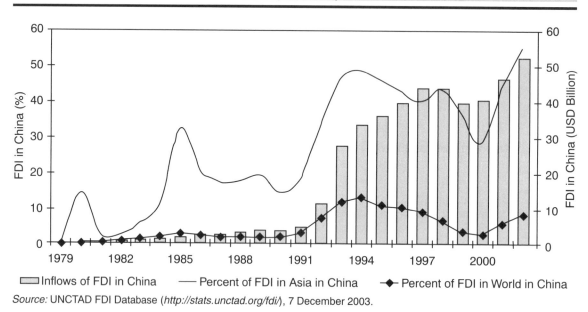

Inflows of FDI in China — Percent of FDI in Asia in China — Percent of FDI in World in China

Source: UNCTAD FDI Database (*http://stats.unctad.org/fdi/*), 7 December 2003.

These different policy areas contributed importantly to China's economic growth and integration in the world economy. Most foreign investment has flowed into areas that have one of these five policy designations. The creation of the newest zones, ETDZs, FTZs and NTZs, has drawn some of the FDI away from the OCCs and SEZs. The result has been a less skewed distribution of FDI in China, in which areas other than the Eastern Coastal cities are popular FDI sites.

Specialized economic zones do not only exist in China. Indeed, Vietnam and Malaysia, just to name two countries, have established similar zones. The Vietnamese government set up several industrial zones to stimulate foreign investment, and economic activity. These zones have been successful in doing so.[9]

In Vietnam, the Southern Economic Zone, spanning Ho Chi Minh City and the provinces of Dong Nai, Binh Duong, Ba Ria - Vung Tau, generates nearly 50 per cent of Vietnam's revenue. Ho Chi Minh City itself has built 13 specialized economic zones. In 2002, these zones attracted 227 new foreign-invested projects with a total prescribed capital of USD506 million. The provincial authorities in Binh Duong and Dong Nai offered specialized incentives that encouraged rapid growth in export-oriented production of goods such as footwear, garments, electronics, and processed food and beverages. Indeed, the growth of Binh Duong as a recipient of FDI has been one of the more prominent success stories in the first few years of the 21st century.

The coastal province of Ba Ria - Vung Tau focused on stimulating inward FDI by building infrastructure, including a steel plant, plastics and chemicals plant, and a power plant. In 2003, the more than 1,000 foreign investment projects in Vietnam were worth over USD10 billion, and provided jobs for 320,000 people.

As shown in Table 6-5, the majority of Japanese and overall investment in Vietnam has been directed to provinces that have an industrial zone. We can also observe that areas with high GDP, or high per capita GDP tend to be the major recipients of FDI in Vietnam. Even though Ho Chi Minh and Hanoi have been the major recipients of FDI, other areas such as Binh Duong have successfully implemented policies to stimulate inflows of FDI.[10]

A critical policy has been the creation of industrial zones, with dedicated land area for the foundation of foreign-owned manufacturing plants and offices. Even so, not all investment made in these provinces is in an industrial zone. In Ho Chi Minh, just three per cent of Japanese FDIs were in an industrial zone, but in other areas the percentage climbed as high as 60 per cent. The challenge for the Vietnamese government is to create a more even distribution of FDI across Vietnam's 61 provinces.

In the late 1990s and early 2000s, the Malaysian government extended considerable efforts to develop two special zones, Putrajaya and Cyberjaya, to create a suitable climate for domestic and foreign investment in the multimedia development industry. The Malaysian government funded the establishment of new infrastructure – new roads, buildings and telecommunications. It passed specialized laws and policies to attract foreign investment. It created fiscal incentives such as a five-year exemption from income tax, duty free importation of multimedia equipment and R&D grants for small- and medium-sized enterprises. It added a number of other FDI stimuli such as non-financial incentives, including no restrictions on foreign ownership and improved protection for intellectual property rights. Although these initiatives have had a measure of success, with Putrajaya and Cyberjaya attracting several world renowned multimedia development companies, the Multimedia Super Corridor in Malaysia faces stiff competition from other government sponsored incentive areas such as Hong Kong's Cyberport and the Singapore One project.

Whether in Malaysia, Vietnam, China or elsewhere in Asia these specialized policy areas add a layer of factors that need to be considered when evaluating geographic sites for entry. This added layer reinforces the notion that the sub-national locational choice is as important as the national location choice. It also suggests that a different set of factors often needs to come under the purview of a foreign investor for an effective location decision to be made.

Product Market Decision

The product market decision is a question of business diversification. For a single-business firm, there is no question about which product to move into which international market. For a multi-business firm, the product market decision is not a simple one. Should a firm make a full-scale jump into an international market with most of its products? Should it move products into a

Table 6-5: FDI, GDP and Population in Vietnam (2001)

Province	Number of all foreign subsidiaries	Number of Japanese subsidiaries	Province has an industrial zone(s)?	Population (million)	GDP (USD millions)	GDP per capita
Ho Chi Minh (City)	839	65	Yes	5.29	5,439.2	1,029.1
Binh Duong	365	5	Yes	0.77	447.0	580.6
Ha Noi	342	38	Yes	2.73	2,090.6	764.7
Dong Nai	273	18	Yes	2.04	670.4	328.8
Hai Phong	86	13	Yes	1.72	729.7	425.5
Ba Ria -Vung Tau	58	4	Yes	0.84	1,602.9	1,903.7
Lam Dong	41	2	No	1.08	250.0	230.5
Da Nang	35	1	No	0.73	369.7	507.3
Khanh Hoa	29	1	No	1.06	0.4	0.4
Ha Tay	26	2	No	2.41	—	—
Vinh Phuc	22	4	Yes	1.12	275.9	246.3
Hai Duong	20	2	No	1.69	430.3	255.3
Binh Thuan	15	1	No	1.06	139.1	131.4
Quang Nam	12	1	No	1.39	—	—
Thai Nguyen	11	1	No	1.08	184.7	171.0
Nghe An	8	1	No	2.90	441.7	152.3
Thanh Hoa	8	1	No	3.61	682.2	188.8
Hung Yen	7	0	No	1.10	285.6	259.6
Ha Tinh	6	1	No	1.27	172.1	135.4
Phu Tho	6	1	Yes	1.29	276.0	214.4
Bac Ninh	5	1	No	0.96	181.9	189.4
Binh Dinh	5	1	No	1.51	310.9	206.5
An Giang	4	1	No	2.11	627.6	297.7
Binh Phuoc	4	0	Yes	0.72	91.7	128.1
Bac Giang	3	1	No	1.52	250.9	165.1
Bac Lieu	3	1	No	0.75	176.9	263.3
Ca Mau	2	0	No	1.16	—	—
Song Be	1	1	No	—	—	—

Sources: Toyo Keizai, *Japanese Overseas Investment*, (Toyo Keizai: Tokyo, Japan, various editions). *http://www.mpi.gov.vn/ website_oda/English/Doitac/Province.asp*, 5 December 2003.
Note: Not all the provinces in Viet Nam are shown in Table 6-5.

market incrementally? The discussion at the outset of this chapter makes it clear that the latter choice is generally the most preferred route.

When internationalizing, product lines tend to be added sequentially. Eventually, a firm will reach a point where most of its existing product lines are active in a host country. Does this mean the process ends at this point? Generally, it will not. Being active in international markets creates new opportunities for a firm in the types of activities it can undertake and the products it can manufacture.

Take the case of Honda as one example of this process. Honda Motor Company (*www.hondacorporate.com*) first began as a small motorcycle manufacture, with a focus on small motors, fuel-efficiency and low-emission technology. By 2003, Honda was a globally recognized business that sold nearly 11 million products worldwide, including automobiles, motorcycles and power products.

As a global company with 100 factories in 33 countries, Honda was able to design and manufacture products for specific markets, such as the North American automobile marketplace. In this market, the company wanted to design a vehicle targeted to young, male, generation-Yers. This vehicle should coexist with its other product offerings and be faithful to Honda's brand.

To accomplish this, the development team gathered direct information on the target market's lifestyle; they visited fraternity houses and hung out with surfers and mountain bikers. When developing the final product, they blended Honda's strengths, small engines with their creativity, as sparked by their information gathered on the target market's lifestyle. The final product, the Honda Element, was a fun, functional and versatile automobile, which was also 'quite a good little vehicle' according to Car and Driver magazine.[11]

New opportunities for a firm can also arise from the differentiated nature of competition and consumer preferences in a firm's international markets. To satisfy such divergent sources of consumer demand in a host country market, a firm might have to develop new product lines.

Haier Group, discussed in detail in Chapter 1, has specific products, and corresponding websites, in each of its international markets. Haier America (*www.haieramerica.com*) has introduced Ribbit TV, a frog-shaped television, with parental controls, to provide educational television for children. It has also created the BrewMaster, a draft-beer dispenser aimed at the American marketplace where more than half the market prefers draft beer to bottled or canned beer.

Haier Europe (*www.haiereurope.com*) manufactures 'Extreme Line,' appliances, which are designed especially to cater to European tastes where aesthetic and design properties are as essential selling points as Haier's quality and brand name. Haier also provides targeted websites and products for its Middle Eastern market, (*www.haiermideast.com*), Chinese market (*www.haier.com*) and Spanish market (*www.haierspain.com*).

The development of new product lines can be supported by the competitive environment in a host country. Suppliers, buyers and competitors provide the opportunity for positive spillovers that can aid new product development. To be able to stay in touch with the American market, Haier America spent USD15 million on its US Headquarters with a purchase of the landmark Haier Building in New York City (*www.haieramerica.com/about_haier_building.php*). This central location, which houses the corporate offices and research and development labs of Haier America, also has a public restaurant and showroom. The restaurant and showroom provide an opportunity for Haier to acquire significant consumer information and feedback from its American consumers. As illustrated by the case of Haier, international expansion can start with a product exploitation imperative, but its endpoint can be new product development.

To reach this endpoint, foreign markets must be viewed by a firm's management as more than sites for production or sites for sales. Foreign markets can become part of the planning for all of a firm's productive activities. Manufacturing, marketing and distribution, research and development, product design, resource procurement, business planning, and strategy formulation and implementation are all functions that can yield advantages to a firm if carried out in international markets, at an appropriate time in a firm's international expansion. To achieve these advantages requires a mindset that international markets are more than a source for product and capability exploitation. Once this mindset is reached, managers must wrestle with coordination issues underlying the geographic dispersion of a firm's productive activities. We discuss this issue in depth in Chapters 10 and 11. Before that, we return to the matter of product expansion in international expansion in the context of the stages model.

The Stages Model

A stages model of international expansion places an emphasis on the sequence of activities by which a firm internationalizes. This sequence of activities can include the markets a firm's managers choose to enter, as well as the modes by which these markets are entered. The optimal markets and modes of international expansion depend on the stage of expansion, because the types of skills and capabilities found in a firm vary by the stage (see Figure 6-3).

At the earliest stage of international expansion, managers in a firm typically lack in-depth knowledge about international markets. This lack of knowledge creates uncertainty and makes effective decision making more difficult. One way to minimize the risk in an international expansion is to minimize the amount of new information with which a firm's managers must contend. This can be achieved by avoiding entering markets that are dissimilar along too many dimensions. Bringing an existing product into a new geographic market, or a new product into an existing geographic market, is a much less daunting challenge than bringing a new product into a new geographic market. It is not surprising that the dominant motive in internationalization is to bring existing products into new geographic markets.

Figure 6-3:   Stages in Entry Types in the Internationalization Process

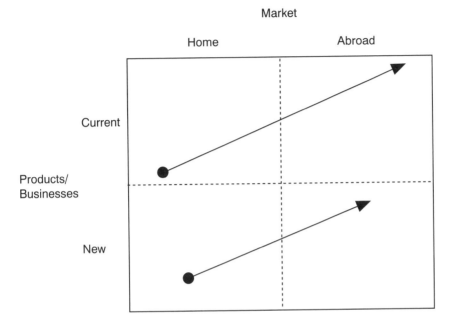

Motivation for International Investment

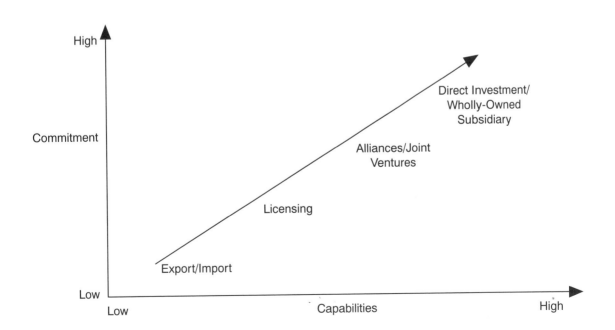

Steps in International Investment

Another way to minimize the risks that come with decision making under uncertainty is to minimize the commitment made to a foreign market. The lower the commitment, the lower the risk of failure in the event a poor decision is made.

Although risk is reduced by making a low commitment entry, the entry still provides a firm's managers with an opportunity to learn about conditions in foreign markets, and develop better sets of skills to compete successfully in foreign markets. Newly-developed skills and knowledge can aid a firm's subsequent entries, which can also be made by a higher commitment entry. A higher commitment entry provides even more opportunities for knowledge and capability development. In this sense, the virtuous cycle is repeated.

As indicated in Figure 6-3, entry modes come with different requirements for commitments of resources such as management time, human resources and capital. At the low end of the commitment continuum is an exporting or trading entry. This form of entry typically requires a firm to engage in a contract with a local distributor for the sale of a firm's products in the host country. By selling products in a host country, the managers in a firm should become more familiar with local consumers and local market conditions. This familiarity should promote the development of skills and capabilities to brand and market products to local consumers.

An exporting entry can provide this benefit, while minimizing the costs in the event of product failure. If a firm's products do not sell well as an export, perhaps because it is not suited to consumers in the foreign market, the loss is restricted to any costs associated with the export contract. Contrast that to the case in which an entry is made by forming a joint venture plant for the purpose of manufacture and sale of a product. There, if the product fails, the plant might have to be sold to the joint venture partner or to a third party, or the assets of the plant are liquidated. In each case, the foreign entrant risks losing a substantial amount of the investment made to establish the joint venture plant.

For these reasons, it can be beneficial to enter a country in a series of stages. Costs are minimized in a staged sequence of entry. The commitment made at each stage of entry is commensurate with the capabilities of the managers in a firm. At no point is the commitment greater than the capabilities required to operate in a host country, which is the situation in which there is the greatest risk for a foreign entering firm.

Aside from the concern about the type of entry used to move into a country, there is the concern about which countries are entered first. Each host country market represents a potential opportunity to a firm. Each host country market also represents a challenge to a firm. Not all the challenges are equal. Some host country markets will be easier to enter than others because the degree of uncertainty a firm's managers have about the institutional environment in the host country are less. This could be because the institutional distance or the difference in the culture, politics, language and economic systems between the foreign country and a firm's home country are less.[12]

For a newly-internationalizing firm, foreign expansion will be less of a trial if the expansion is made into familiar markets. A firm from Singapore should face less of a challenge by expanding into Malaysia first, rather then entering South Korea. A firm from Hong Kong could face a much easier route to foreign expansion by entering Guangdong province in China, rather than entering India. The general idea of using geographic proximity as a guide to expansion is a good one, but not all geographically proximate countries are the ones with the least amount of uncertainty to enter. As we have discussed in the preceding chapters, uncertainty stems from a number of dimensions of national institutional environments. These dimensions make certain countries more attractive and less attractive depending on a firm's stage of internationalization.

The next concern for an internationalizing firm is that of the product choice. The general idea is that the more products a firm can move into international markets, the greater its opportunities to boost revenues, and improve the bottom line. With that general goal in mind, the question is 'Which products should be moved into which markets when?'

For movement of products into foreign markets the essential concept remains the same. Consideration must be given to the risk and knowledge demands associated with the introduction of a particular product. The risk and knowledge demands are related to the competitive advantages a firm has in a particular product line. Those products in which a firm has its strongest advantages should lead the internationalization charge.

A strong advantage provides a competitive buffer against the disadvantages that accompany a foreign firm in its competition with domestic counterparts (see Figure 6-4). A strong advantage can buy time for the managers in a firm to develop the knowledge, skills and capabilities necessary to reduce competitive disadvantages in specific areas against local competitors. As these competitive disadvantages are reduced, other products can then be introduced into the host country, with less risk of failure than if these products had been introduced during the earliest stages of a firm's international expansion.

Figure 6-4:   Product Diversification in International Markets

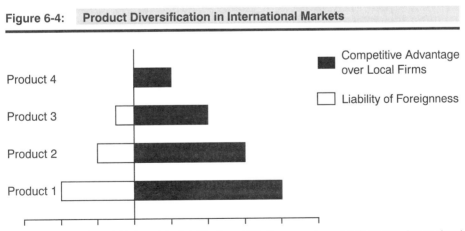

Source: Adapted from P.W. Beamish, A.J. Morrison, P.M. Rosenzweig, and A.C. Inkpen, *International Management: Text and Cases*, 4th Ed. (Boston: Irwin McGraw-Hill, 2002), Exhibit 10-1, pp. 171.

This process of entry into international markets can be thought of as line of business diversification, or product diversification. It begins with a firm's strongest product lines, that provide a significant competitive advantage over local firms. As time in a country helps reduce a firm's liability of foreignness, because of organizational learning and capability development, other lines of business can be introduced into a country. The process begins to reach a conclusion as product lines with little or no advantage are introduced into a country.

Business diversification in international markets happens through a process of growth, development of new capabilities, evaluation of opportunities and re-evaluation of opportunities. Monitoring and re-evaluation are important steps because a firm begins to evolve as it participates in international markets. Each time it enters a market successfully, new skills and resources can be added to a firm. It might develop a strong local brand, it can develop a good reputation with local firms and employees and it can better understand the operating environment, as time spent in the country progresses.

The evolution culminates in a multinational firm that has successfully moved most of its product lines into its international markets. Some of the products will be ones in which advantages can be exploited. Other product lines will be ones in which a firm is weak, but has the opportunity to develop better strengths through participation in a local market. This process has an element of the relocation of high value-added activities such as research and development and business planning and strategy to international markets, in a shift of important business functions to foreign subsidiaries. We cover how subsidiaries capture high value-added functions in Chapter 11.

Summary

An effective internationalization strategy involves the joint consideration of four key decisions: timing of entry, entry mode, geographic market of entry and product market of entry.

We introduced each of these four decisions in turn, and then considered these decisions jointly in the context of a stages model of international expansion. This joint consideration of the four decisions is the most important consideration for each of the individual decisions. Put another way, these decisions should not be evaluated in isolation from one another, as well as in isolation from a firm's other international expansion decisions.

The reason for this is that the sequencing of these four elements of a firm's international expansion provides a manager with control over the kinds and heights of barriers that will have to be crossed in firm's internationalization process. International expansion involves opportunities for extending a firm's strength into new markets, and chances to develop new competitive advantages. By thinking of these key internationalization decisions jointly, both market expansion and market development opportunities can be exploited as a firm moves through its internationalization process.

Notes

[1] This point is discussed in more detail in Chapter 8.

[2] John H. Dunning, *Multinational Enterprises and the Global Economy* (Addison-Wesley Publishing Company: Don Mills, Ontario, 1993).

[3] Wilbur Chung and Arturs Kalnins, "Agglomeration Effects and Performance: A Test of the Texas Lodging Industry," *Strategic Management Journal*, 2001, Vol. 22, No. 10, pp. 969–988; J. Myles Shaver and Frederick Flyer, "Agglomeration Economics, Firm Heterogeneity, and Foreign Direct Investment in the United States," *Strategic Management Journal*, 2000, Vol. 21, No. 12, pp. 1175–1193.

[4] *http://www.ceramics.lk*, 19 November 2003.

[5] Keith Head, J. Ries and Deborah Swenson, "Agglomeration Benefits and Location Choice: Evidence from Japanese Manufacturing Investment in the United States," *Journal of International Economics*, 1995, Vol. 38, pp. 223–247.

[6] J. Myles Shaver and Frederick Flyer, "Agglomeration Economics, Firm Heterogeneity, and Foreign Direct Investment in the United States," *Strategic Management Journal*, 2000, Vol. 21, No. 12, pp. 1175–1193; Wilbur Chung and Arturs Kalnins, "Agglomeration Effects and Performance: A Test of the Texas Lodging Industry," *Strategic Management Journal,* 2001, Vol. 22, No. 10, pp. 969–988.

[7] *https://www.unido.org/doc/4308*, 10 November , 2003.

[8] Changhui Zhou, Andrew Delios, and Jing Yu Yang, "Locational Determinants of Japanese Foreign Direct Investment in China," *Asia Pacific Journal of Management*, 2002, Vol. 19, No. 1, pp. 63–86.

[9] "Vietnam's Southern Economic Zone Fuels GDP Growth," *AsiaPulse News*, 15 January 2003, p. 136.

[10] Klaus E. Meyer and Vo Hung Nguyen. *Foreign Investors' Entry Strategies and Sub-National Institutions in Emerging Markets* (Mimeo: Copenhagen Business School, November 2003).

[11] *http://www.caranddriver.com/article.asp?section_id=19&article_id=2482*, November 2002.

[12] Dean Xu and Oded Shenkar, "Institutional Distance and the Multinational Enterprise," *Academy of Management Journal*, 2002, Vol. 27, No. 4, pp. 608–619.

7 STRATEGIC ALLIANCES AND JOINT VENTURES

A strategic alliance is a collaborative activity carried out by two or more firms, in which all firms involved in the alliance contribute inputs to the alliance. The firms have determined a set of goals for the strategic alliance which might include the technologies to be developed or markets to be entered. The firms, sometimes called strategic alliance partners or just partners, will typically have a defined duration for the strategic alliance.

Strategic alliances can take many forms (see Figure 7-1). A joint venture is at the end point on the cooperative continuum of alliances. Joint ventures have moved from the periphery of corporate activities to become an increasingly important component of a firm's international strategy. At the other end of the continuum, we have cooperation agreements. Licensing, franchising and R&D consortia, each represent a form of an interfirm strategic alliance.

R&D alliances in particular have been becoming increasingly popular as the pace of technological development has quickened. Figure 7-2 depicts the typical structure of an R&D alliance. In an R&D alliance, two firms jointly organize specific R&D activities. Specific aspects of a firm's technology and personnel are brought together to form the alliance. The alliance, if jointly organized and funded, will have its interim and final results shared between its alliance partners. The shared results from the pre-competitive joint development of R&D can be used to pursue independent and separate competitive activities, outside the domain of the alliance. As an R&D alliance might not have a specific product-market goal, the scope of the cooperation should be determined at the design stage. The design of a non-equity R&D alliance does not lead to the creation of a new organizational entity, unlike in the case of an equity alliance, such as a joint venture.

A joint venture is an equity alliance. A joint venture involves the creation of a separate organization in which each firm has an equity investment. A firm's equity investment should be substantial enough to confer some degree of control in, and commitment to, the joint venture. The lower bound to the amount of equity can be as little as five percent but, typically, at least 10 to 20 per cent is the minimum necessary to enable the firm to have some say in the operations of a joint venture.

Figure 7-1: **Range of Strategic Alliances**

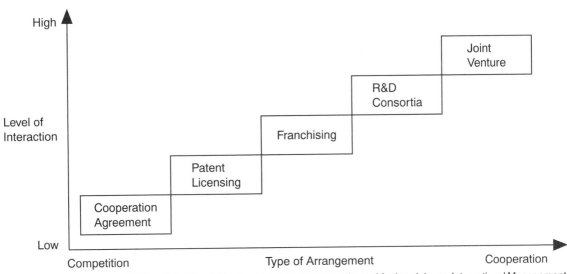

Source: Adapted from Paul. W. Beamish, Allen J. Morrison, Philip M. Rosenzweig, and Andrew Inkpen, *International Management: Text and Cases*, 4th Ed. (Boston: McGraw-Hill, 2002), Exhibit 7-1, p. 114.

Figure 7-2: **Joint R&D Non-Equity Alliance**

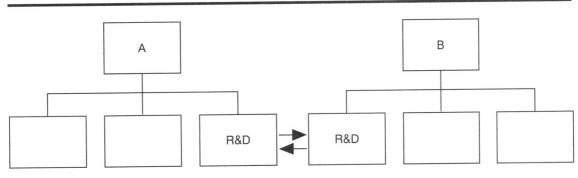

    – A and B jointly organize and fund the programme
    – A and B share results of collaborative R&D, but compete separately

Source: Adapted from Paul W. Beamish, J. Peter Killing, Donald J. Lecraw, and Allen J. Morrison, *International Management: Text and Cases*, 2nd Ed. (Burr Ridge, IL: Irwin), Figure 7-3, p. 121.

Figure 7-3 provides an example of an equity alliance; i.e. a joint venture. This example is a typical international joint venture, in which a foreign partner has technology but lacks market knowledge. Meanwhile, a local partner has market knowledge but lacks technology. Together, the two firms form a new company, the joint venture, which merges the market knowledge and technological knowledge of the two partners. Each partner shares a management role in the joint venture, although the extent to which each partner contributes to, and has control in, the joint

Figure 7-3:   **Joint Venture – An Equity Alliance**

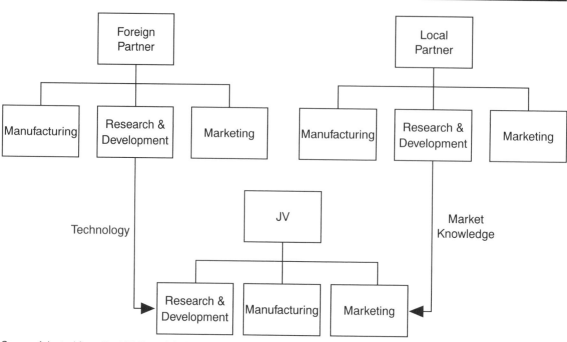

Source: Adapted from Paul W. Beamish, J. Peter Killing, Donald J. Lecraw, and Allen J. Morrison, *International Management: Text and Cases*, 2nd Ed. (Burr Ridge, IL: Irwin), Figure 7-5, p. 125.

venture is a matter for negotiation between the partners. The performance of the joint venture rests on the ability of the partners to satisfactorily decide on the design of the joint venture, as we discuss later in this chapter.

As part of the structural decision, joint ventures can take many forms. There can be two parties in a joint venture, in which both are from the same country or from different countries. Where the partners are from different countries, the strategic alliance is called an international joint venture. There can also be more than two equity partners in a joint venture or a strategic alliance. These multi-party strategic alliances can be common in such sectors as the construction industry where consortia are often formed to undertake large construction projects. Multi-party joint ventures are less common, but still do occur.

A basic distinction to make in international joint ventures comes from the division of equity ownership among the parties. There are three possible situations in a two partner international strategic alliance. To describe these, we can take the case of an international joint venture formed by a foreign firm and a local firm.

In one situation, a co-owned joint venture, both the foreign firm and the local firm hold an equal equity share (50 per cent each). In the second case, a foreign majority-owned joint venture, the foreign partner holds a greater equity share than the local partner. In the third case, the local partner holds a greater equity share than the foreign partner. This type of joint venture is a local majority-owned joint venture, or a minority joint venture, if we take the foreign partner's perspective.

The Growth of Strategic Alliances

Strategic alliances have been growing in popularity since the onset of the 1980s. It is difficult, if not impossible, to find a multinational firm that does not have some form of strategic alliance or joint venture in its operations.

The original perception that forestalled the use of strategic alliances was that they were difficult to manage. Managers were also reluctant to collaborate with competitors in case it potentially strengthens a competing firm. These two beliefs have not changed much. Alliances continue to be a difficult to manage entry mode, and there is a risk of disseminating knowledge to partner firms in an alliance. There has, however, been a growing realization that alliances can succeed if managed well. Good management can also limit the risk of unwanted knowledge dissemination to partner firms. If thought of in this way, it is not that strategic alliances are a sub-optimal entry mode – instead, the set of managerial challenges that come with a strategic alliance are different from those of other entry modes.

As international managers have become more familiar with the challenges of managing alliances, and as the environmental imperatives to strategic alliance formation have increased in force, the use of strategic alliances has increased. Even in the 1980s, the incidence of alliance use grew rapidly. Comparing the first half of the 1980s to the second half of the 1980s, alliances in the automotive industry increased by three times and in the biotechnology industry they doubled.[1] The growing incidence of strategic alliance is common across all Triad regions. Firms from Europe, the United States and Japan each formed larger number of strategic alliances as the 1980s and 1990s progressed.

This growth in strategic alliances came at a time when international trade and investment were increasing. Part of the growth of the incidence of strategic alliances came with this growth in international business activities. The demands of moving businesses into new geographic markets frequently necessitates the use of a strategic alliance, hence strategic alliance usage grows with international activities.

The trend to increased strategic alliance use includes growth in the annual numbers of joint ventures. Again, this growth is partly related to growth in foreign direct investment. Through the 1980s and 1990s, firms continued to use the international joint venture for 30 to 45 per cent of all foreign direct investments. Firms from the United States are at the bottom of that range, while Japanese firms are at the top. In Europe and the US, foreign entrants had a low rate of joint venture usage.

Meanwhile, joint ventures tend to be used more frequently in Asia, where countries such as Thailand and China had ownership or other regulations that dictated local ownership in most foreign entries. For example, the Chinese government retains a 20 titles a year quota on foreign-made film productions,[2] but films co-produced with Chinese companies are exempt from the limit. This encourages foreign companies producing films in China to enter into joint ventures with local production houses.

The growth in the incidence of strategic alliances reinforces the importance of this entry mode for firms competing in international markets. The prevalence of alliances underscores the need to develop capabilities to effectively manage strategic alliances and to make an alliance entry a successful one. To help understand the most important management issues in a strategic alliance, we identify reasons why firms engage in strategic alliances and joint ventures.

Motivations to Form Strategic Alliances

Managers form strategic alliances and joint ventures to combine the resources of two or more firms. The basic motivation of one firm to solicit another to form an alliance is a resource short-fall for a particular activity. The resource short-fall can come about because a firm is entering a new geographic market, because it is entering a new product market or because it is trying to become more competitive in its existing geographic and product markets. In each scenario, the strategic expansion might move the firm into an area in which it is resource deficient. In moving into a new geographic market, knowledge of the host country might be lacking. In moving into a new product market, technological resources for the production of the new product, or brand-related resources, might be lacking. In either case, a firm does not have a full-set of resources to pursue its strategic initiative.

A resource short-fall can be alleviated in one of four ways. A firm could undertake a process of internal development. It could acquire another firm that has the particular resource it requires. It could try to purchase the resource in an open market. It could engage in a strategic alliance.

The question as to why a strategic alliance should be formed then comes down to why a strategic alliance is used to mitigate a resource short-fall, instead of one of the other three options.

For internal development, there is the issue of time and the likelihood of success. If a firm requires a brand to enter a particular consumer segment, such as chocolate confectionaries or soft drinks, it can take considerable time and effort to develop such a brand. Even if a firm has the money and the luxury of time to take efforts to develop the resource, there is still no guarantee of success. The uncertainty of success, and speed of resource acquisition, can be increased by the pursuit of one of the other three options.

The next option is the purchase of a resource in an open market. At times this form of transaction is the easiest one to undertake. If a firm requires a particular piece of property or physical equipment to establish a manufacturing plant, these resources can easily be acquired through a market-based exchange. Well-established markets exist for the exchange of these kinds of resources, and price and quality are equally easy for the buyer and seller to discern.

In some cases, buyers and sellers can have asymmetric information about the worth of a resource. Such a case might occur for a new technology. The developer and seller of a technology will have a better idea of its worth than the buyer. In this case, there are considerable risks in the exchange because of asymmetric information. A market-based transaction is less likely to be satisfactory to both the buyer and the seller. Where the resource being sought by a firm is transacted infrequently, where it is difficult to define and where asymmetric information exists, purchase in a market becomes more difficult.

Where purchase in an open market is difficult, a firm could undertake an acquisition of another firm to acquire a needed resource. This option is used frequently. Up to 50 per cent of the foreign entries made into the US by firms from the United Kingdom, and 40 per cent of German firms' entries, have been by acquisition.[3] The frequency of entry by acquisition into countries in Asia has been much less. Acquisitions can be an effective form of entry, and a means to acquire a required resource, where there is an effective market for corporate control. If the stock market provides the means for a firm's shares to be traded in a fair manner, in which buyers have good information about a target firm, then the market could function well. Where the market does not function well, it is less common to see acquisitions.

Aside from the functioning of equity markets, a potential acquirer needs to consider what else comes with an acquired firm, aside from the required resource. The larger and more diversified a target firm, the less suitable it is as a target. The attractiveness of the acquisition option can be decreased by the difficulty of integrating a target firm's resources with a firm's own resources, particularly if key managers and employees leave the target firm after its acquisition.

As the acquisition, resource purchase and resource development options each have their own formidable sets of challenges, the strategic alliance option can at times be the best one. A strategic alliance can provide a well-defined means to acquire a needed resource. For Ranbaxy, the resources it required for its internationalization were a global reputation and a local presence (see Box 7-1).

One requirement for a strategic alliance to be implemented, that is generally not a requirement in the other three options, is that another firm has to be interested in forming an alliance as well. Generally, that other firm's interest in an alliance stems from its own need to acquire a resource.

Complementary Resource Needs

A strategic alliance generally occurs when two or more firms require a resource to undertake a particular business activity. Based on resource needs and the business activities that are pursued, we can find a great range in the types of strategic alliances. Figure 7-4 shows a number of these types for international joint ventures, using the traditional form of an international joint venture, which is one formed by a local partner and a foreign partner. We can divide traditional international joint ventures by the type of resources contributed by each partner. Two basic types of joint ventures emerged, which can be distinguished by the types of resource combinations that take place in the joint venture. One is a scale joint venture, the other is a link joint venture.

Box 7-1   Ranbaxy's Alliances

To carry out its internationalization strategy, Ranbaxy Laboratories (*www.ranbaxy.com*), India's largest pharmaceutical company, participated in alliances, joint ventures and other forms of collaborations with various drug companies worldwide. The strategy has proven effective. In 2003, Ranbaxy sold it products in over 70 countries, it had a ground presence in 25 countries, and manufacturing operations in seven countries.

Ranbaxy's first joint venture was with local producers in Nigeria in 1977. This venture led to the establishment of Ranbaxy Nigeria Ltd, the third largest branded generic pharmaceutical company in Nigeria in 2002. Since 1977, Ranbaxy has continued to expand its global presence through joint ventures and subsidiaries in China, Malaysia, Thailand, Brazil, India, South Africa, Egypt, Ireland, UK, Netherlands, Germany and the US. In the US, Ranbaxy had a now dissolved joint venture with US-based Eli Lilly (*www.lilly.com*). It had a joint venture with Schein Pharmaceutical, the US-based generic arm of Bayer, Germany (*www.schien-rx.com*), and one with South Africa-based Adcock Ingram (*www.adcock.com.za*). In addition to joint ventures, Ranbaxy participates in other forms of alliances such as strategic partnerships and it undertakes acquisitions to implement strategic plans.

Ranbaxy's focus on forming global alliances stemmed from its strategic choice to become an international company operating in key markets worldwide which in turn create a platform for future expansion. According to CEO and Managing Director, Davinder Brar, 'The inexorable force of our internationalisation strategy ensures presence in a portfolio of markets and helps us gain proximity to people who make us what we are – our customers.' The company's strategy has paid off. By 2002, Ranbaxy was one of the world's top 10 generic drug manufacturers, and in the mid-60s of the top 100 global pharmaceutical companies.

Sources:
http://www.ranbaxy.com/pressrelease_det.asp?sno=65, 16 November 2003.
http://www.ranbaxy.com/history60-80.htm, 16 November 2003.
http://www.ranbaxy.com/nigeria.htm, 16 November 2003.
Ranbaxy, *Annual Report 2002*, 7 May 2003.
Financial Times, 23 September 2002, p. 5.

Scale Joint Ventures

A scale joint venture is one in which the two partners contribute a similar resource. These resources can be technology, distribution or raw materials, as identified in the table. The purpose of such a joint venture is to achieve advantages through an increase in size, such as the competitive gains that can come from economies of scale. The motivation to form a scale joint venture to achieve economies of scale is pronounced when small firms must match the scale advantages of large firms.

Although US-based Delta Airlines and Korean Air are large airlines, their size is small compared to industry giants such as United Airlines and Cathy Pacific. To be able to compete more successfully against giant airlines and their alliances, Delta Airlines and Korean Air formed a scale alliance in which they codeshare their flight operations and have coordinated sales and

Figure 7-4:   Types of International Joint Ventures

Local Partner's Resources	Foreign Partner's Resources				
	Marketing skills	Technology	Distribution	Nationality	Raw materials/ other inputs
Country knowledge	*Link:* Market entry	*Link:* Market entry	*Link:* Market entry		
Technology		*Scale:* Technology			
Distribution	*Link:* Market entry	*Link:* Market entry	*Scale:* Distribution		
Nationality	*Link:* Nationality-based	*Link:* Nationality-based	*Link:* Nationality-based		
Raw materials/ other inputs	*Link:* Downstream vertical	*Link:* Downstream vertical	*Link:* Downstream vertical		*Scale:* Raw materials

Source: Adapted from Jean-François Hennart, "A Transaction Cost Theory of Equity Joint Ventures," *Strategic Management Journal,* 1988, Vol. 9, Figure 3, pp. 483–497.

marketing approaches. These combinations of the companies' resources help to improve quality and services, effectiveness and competitiveness.

Another purpose to scale is to achieve greater market power and lower cost through the joint sourcing of common sets of inputs. These inputs can include manufactured products such as small motors to run electrical appliances, or raw materials used in the manufacture of component parts. Where inputs become common to more than one firm through a scale joint venture, partner firms must make adjustments to accommodate a source of common inputs (see Box 7-2). Product designs and assembly processes might have to be altered, and the partners will have to agree upon a transfer pricing scheme for the common inputs.

Firms can combine common technology resources for a technology scale joint venture. The combination of technology resources, whether in a joint venture or a strategic alliance, can reduce costs and time in research and development initiatives. Although such R&D scale alliances have a considerable upside for developing a firm's technological base, managers involved in the alliance will have to think about issues of patent rights, licensing fees and other issues involved with the distribution of the returns from products of the joint research.

Box 7-2   Tsingtao's Joint Venture with Anheuser-Busch

China is the second-largest beer market in the world, surpassed only by the United States. With the opening of the market in the mid-1990s, Chinese and international breweries began to compete head-to-head to grab a share of the growing beer market. Historically, with the poor infrastructure that made large distribution networks intractable to manage, the Chinese market place for beer became fragmented with over 500 breweries developing to meet demand. Chinese-based Tsingtao (*www.tsingtaobeer.com*) has emerged as the market leader, as it held 11 per cent of the market in 2003. To help with the expansion of its distribution network and capture urban markets, Tsingtao acquired 45 local Chinese breweries in 2001.

Tsingtao's ambitions extend beyond the local Chinese market. It aims to be one of the top 10 global brewers. The brand strategy of Tsingtao is to develop the international and high-profile market in China with Tsingtao beer and to develop local popular consumption markets with the acquired local brands. As of 2003, Tsingtao was the number one selling Chinese beer in the United States. Its exports to 40 countries accounted for more than 80 per cent of China's beer exports.

In October 2002, to help achieve its international expansion goals and increase its exports, Tsingtao entered into a joint venture with American-based Anheuser-Busch, the number one brewer in the United States (*www.anheuser-busch.com*). Aside from a foothold in the American market, the venture provided Tsingtao with otherwise prohibitively costly acquisition of technical and financial resources. These resources strengthened Tsingtao's position in China by making it a leader in change and growth in the domestic Chinese beer industry. The joint venture gave Anheuser-Busch a greater role in a critical international market, namely China. Other foreign brewers' past attempts at entry into the Chinese market were problematic. For example, Denmark's Carlsberg (*www.carlsberg.com*) and Australia's Foster's (*www.fostersbeer.com*) initial attempts to enter China were unsuccessful as they lacked brand recognition and Chinese consumers deemed their beer to be too expensive.

Sources:

"Tsingtao's Long March: China Beer Battle," *Fortune International*, 27 May 2002, Vol. 145, No. 11, p. 25.

"Made in China: With a Hand from A-B, Tsingtao Pulls Ahead of the Pack in China," *Beverage World*, 15 December, 2002, Vol. 121, No. 12, p. 16.

http://www.tsingtaobeer.com, 14 November 2003.

"Scoring 100: Bud Light Helps A-B Barrel Past Volumetric Century Mark," *Beverage World*, 15 April 2003, Vol. 122, No. 4, pp. 29–31.

Link Joint Ventures

A link joint venture is one in which the two partners contribute different resources. These resources can be capital, technology, country knowledge, market knowledge, distribution, nationality and raw material or other forms of inputs.

Many traditional international joint ventures have a marketing skills, or a technology resource contribution from the foreign partner, and a country knowledge, distribution or nationality resource contribution from the local partner. These forms of international joint ventures can be thought of as market entry joint ventures, some of which are nationality-based.

A market entry joint venture combines a proprietary advantage of a foreign firm with a host market-related resource of a local firm. The foreign firm, particularly when making a first or early entry into a host country, can lack resources idiosyncratic to the local market. Such resources might include human resource management skills applicable to local employees, government contacts for negotiations about property, equipment, tax rates and other conditions related to entry, as illustrated in the Sinopec and PCCW joint venture.

In early 2002, China Petroleum and Chemical Corporation (Sinopec) (*www.sinopec.com.cn*), an integrated energy and chemical company, and Hong Kong-based Pacific Century CyberWorks Limited (PCCW) (*www.pccw.com*), a communications company, formed Petro-CyberWorks Information Technology Company Limited (PCITC) (*www.pcitc.com*). PCITC is an information technology joint venture focused on providing IT services in China.

PCITC leverages Sinopec's and PCCW's competitive advantages and resources such as IT services and market positioning, to provide benefits to both parents through the operation of this joint venture. The joint venture strengthens PCCW's presence in China's IT and telecommunications market by expanding its market reach by positioning it to serve large and small companies doing business with, and within, China. For Sinopec, the joint venture promotes the quality of its existing information systems and infrastructure and, according to Sinopec's Chairman Li Yizhong, it helps the corporation move towards its goal of digitalization of the petrochemical industry.[4]

The local resource can be a tangible asset such as a distribution system. Many markets, such as India, China and Vietnam have large rural populations distributed across an almost uncountable number of small towns and villages. A foreign firm would face a tremendously daunting task in building a distribution system to bring its products to local consumers. A joint venture with a local firm that possesses such a distribution system is one way to enter the market without having to take the time and resources to build a local distribution system.

The local resource can be something as simple as nationality. As mentioned earlier, governments can mandate a certain percentage of local ownership in any foreign-owned subsidiary.[5] In such a situation, a local firm or individual can be brought into a foreign entry as a partner solely for the purpose of satisfying the local ownership criterion. The local partner is often times a silent partner, providing a local presence in exchange for equity in the joint venture, but not participating in the day-to-day operations or strategic planning in the joint venture.

Another type of joint venture links the marketing, technological or distribution skills of a foreign firm and the raw material or other input resources of a local firm. A typical example is a joint venture mining operation. A local firm can possess local mineral rights to a deposit of iron ore, coal, oil or natural gas. Local laws could dictate that mineral deposits and mining rights cannot be owned by a foreign firm. In such cases, the only way for a foreign firm to gain secure access to local raw material supplies is to form a joint venture with a local partner. This type of joint venture is a variant on the nationality-based link joint venture. The motivation for formation is partially dependent on the nationality of a local partner that provides access to resources. However, in a link downstream vertical joint venture, a local partner might provide assistance in raw material extraction.

Within each type of joint venture, there are unique potential sources of conflict. Raw material markets can be volatile, with large fluctuations in markets prices. The price paid by the foreign firm for the joint venture's production can be a potential source of conflict between joint venture partners, if a system for pricing is not in place. Sales to third parties, such as a competitor of the foreign firm, is another point in the joint venture agreement that would have to be worked out before a link joint venture is formed.

Traditional International Joint Ventures

Are two-party joint ventures formed between a local and a foreign partner the only type of international joint venture? The answer is an unequivocal 'No'. Although the local-foreign partner joint venture is the archetype of an international joint venture, other types do exist.

Within the traditional joint venture category, as discussed at the outset of this chapter, we can define three types of joint ventures based upon equity ownership. Taking the perspective of the foreign partner, these three types are a minority joint venture, a co-owned joint venture and a majority joint venture. The basic distinction across these joint ventures is determined by the equity ownership of the partners. We could make a more fine-grained distinction and break the minority and majority categories into high majority and low minority categories. This distinction is based on identifying how strongly equity ownership is skewed in favour of the local partner or the foreign partner (see Table 7-1).

The five types of traditional joint ventures listed in Table 7-1 vary in their performance and in the partner's levels of control and commitment to the joint venture. In the high majority and low minority categories, the control of one partner is at its highest while the control and commitment of the other partner is at its lowest. Technically, high majority and low minority types are still joint ventures, but these are essentially pseudo-alliances.[6] One partner runs the joint venture, which minimizes control problems. Meanwhile, the other partner's equity stake and its share of the return from the joint venture are too low to motivate it to make a real

Table 7-1:   **Equity Ownership in Traditional International Joint Ventures**

Type of Traditional IJV	Foreign partner control	Local partner commitment	Financial performance	Survival
Low minority (5–20% foreign ownership)	Lowest	Highest	Lowest	Lowest
Moderate minority (21–49% foreign ownership)	Low	High	Moderate	Lowest
Co-owned (50% foreign ownership)	Moderate	Moderate	Highest	Moderate
Moderate majority (51–79% foreign ownership)	High	Low	Moderate	Moderate
High majority (80–95% foreign ownership)	Highest	Lowest	Lowest	Highest

Source: Andrew Delios and Paul W. Beamish, "Joint Venture Performance Revisited: Japanese Foreign Subsidiaries Worldwide," *Management International Review,* 2004, Vol. 1, pp. 78–92.

commitment to the joint venture. A low minority partner is unlikely to be involved in any substantive fashion in the joint venture, and unlikely to make a significant resource contribution. The consequence is that the financial performance of these types of joint ventures are the lowest among all types. A low minority joint venture also stands a substantial chance of being divested by the foreign partner.

The moderate majority, moderate minority and co-owned types are more like a true alliance. Ownership and control in the joint venture is divided equitably among the partners, leading to a good commitment and strong inputs to the operations of the joint venture. A consequence of this is that financial performance is higher than in the low minority and high majority categories. Survival rates are lowest in the moderate majority category as a foreign partner is unlikely to divest a high performing alliance, in which it has equity control.

Beyond Traditional International Joint Ventures

Another way to distinguish among types of joint ventures is to look at the nationality of the partners as well as their organizational affiliations.[7] Partners in a joint venture can be a local partner from the host country of the joint venture, a partner from the home country, or a partner from other foreign countries. A joint venture with one local partner and one foreign partner is a traditional international joint venture.

If there is no local partner in the joint venture, there are two possible combinations. One is that the partners in the joint venture are from the same country. Another is that the partners are from two different countries, and the joint venture is set up in a third country. We can call this type of joint venture, a tri-national joint venture. An example of a tri-national joint venture is the one being planned between Munich-based Wacker-Chemie (*www.wacker.com*) and US-based Dow Corning (*www.dowcorning.com*). In September 2003, these companies announced their intent to form a joint venture in Asia to manufacture silicone intermediates and fumed silica.[8] The companies expect that the joint venture will bring cost and quality advantages, benefit local customers and help to further develop local markets and communities.

Even with benefits such as the above tri-national joint ventures tend to have low performance compared to other forms of joint ventures (see Table 7-2). It is wrong to conclude, however, that all tri-national joint ventures will be unsuccessful ones. The venture between Wacker and Dow is still in the planning stages, and its success is yet to be seen; but the joint venture between US-based Dana Corporation (*www.dana.com*) and Daewoo-FSO Motor (*www.daewoo.com.pl/fso*), part of Daewoo Group Korea (*www.daewoo.com*) is an example of a successful tri-national joint venture. Dana Corporation designs, engineers, and manufactures components and systems for automotive manufactures. In 1998, the company entered a joint venture with Daewoo-FSO Motors to set up an automotive parts factory producing axles and driver shafts in Warsaw, Poland. While Daewoo-FSO, had entered 19 other joint ventures in this capacity, this was its first non-Korean joint venture.[9]

Table 7-2: **Japanese Joint Venture Ownership Structure and Performance**

International Joint Venture Type	Partner Nationality	Organizational Affiliation	Financial Performance	Survival
Traditional IJV	One local, one foreign	Different	High	Moderate
Trinational IJV	Both foreign, two different nationalities	Different	Low	Low
Cross-national JV	Both foreign, same nationality	Different	Moderate	High
Intrafirm JV	Both foreign, same nationality	Same	Moderate	High

Source: Shige Makino and Paul W. Beamish, "Performance and Survival of Joint Ventures with Non-conventional Ownership Structures," *Journal of International Business Studies*, 1988, Vol. 29, No. 4, p. 811.

The joint venture, named Spicer Axle ZPZP, provided Dana with a strategic foothold into the Eastern European market. Daewoo-FSO Motors gained a quality auto parts maker to supply its growing automotive manufacturing division. Under the terms of the joint venture agreement, Daewoo controlled 51 per cent of the USD40 million venture, with Dana gaining management control after five years.[10] In 2003, Spicer Axle ZPZP was a part of Dana's Spicer Driveshaft Group (*www.spicerdriveshaft.com*), the world's largest independent driveshaft supplier, and wholly owned by Dana Corporation.

If the partners are from the same country but the joint venture is set up in another country, we can call the joint venture a cross-national joint venture or an intrafirm joint venture. A cross-national joint venture is one in which joint venture partners are from the same country but do not share an organizational affiliation. An intrafirm joint venture is one in which the partners have the same nationality, but share an organizational affiliation. As an example, partners that are part of the same horizontal keiretsu, the same chaebol, or the same family-owned business group share an organizational affiliation.[11]

Clearly, joint ventures and strategic alliances take numerous and diverse forms. The diversity extends from the multiple motivations for alliance formation. Each type of joint venture comes with its own set of management challenges. The first challenge, as set out in our discussion of the internationalization process, is to understand when to use a strategic alliance versus other options for entry. Once this choice has been made, the task confronting managers is to design the strategic alliance, select a partner and manage it once it is up and running.

Design of Strategic Alliances

The design of a strategic alliance starts with the selection of the type of strategic alliance that will be used in entry. A comparison against the pros and cons of other entry modes, and other strategic alliances should help guide this choice. If entering by a joint venture, decisions will have to be made about the division of equity ownership. This decision cannot be made independent of the other parties involved in the joint venture, but parameters about minimum levels of acceptable ownership can be determined prior to negotiations about the joint venture. Another aspect of the basic structure of the joint venture concerns the nationalities and identities of the partners.

Moving beyond these basic issues brings the design task to specific operational and detailed structural parameters for the strategic alliance, or joint venture. The partners in a joint venture must identify how strategic and day-to-day decisions will be made. Will the joint venture's general manager (GM) have complete autonomy? At what point does the joint venture's GM have to turn to the joint venture's board of directors to implement a decision? What will be the composition of the board of directors? Will membership in the board be divided on the basis of equity ownership? If so, what happens in the case of a co-owned joint venture? If the two partners cannot agree on a particular decision, how will the impasse be resolved?

These questions are just a few of the issues that need to be discussed prior to the formation of a strategic alliance (see Table 7-3).[12] Among these, control issues need careful thought. Managers involved in the design of a strategic alliance must consider issues of strategic control and day-to-day operational control. If it is a joint venture, the most important decisions about control are

Table 7-3: Key Questions for the Design of a Strategic Alliance

Question	Question applies to all strategic alliances or only joint ventures
What products will be produced?	All forms of strategic alliances
Where is it to be located?	All forms of strategic alliances
Which country's set of laws govern the alliance's operations?	All forms of strategic alliances
What are the responsibilities of each partner?	All forms of strategic alliances
What are the contributions of each partner?	All forms of strategic alliances
How will the royalties or profits be divided?	All forms of strategic alliances
How will the alliance be controlled?	All forms of strategic alliances
What are the markets for the alliance's products?	All forms of strategic alliances
Is there a termination agreement? How will it be written?	All forms of strategic alliances
How will the partners resolve deadlocks in decisions?	All forms of strategic alliances
Have the partners' performance objectives been discussed?	All forms of strategic alliances
Who owns any new products, new technology, patents or processes developed in the alliance?	All forms of strategic alliances
What is the name of the joint venture?	Only joint ventures
What are the equity contributions of each partner?	Only joint ventures
What is the composition of the joint venture's board of directors?	Only joint ventures
Which partner supplies the joint venture's general manager?	Only joint ventures

Source: Adapted from John B. Cullen, *Multinational Management: A Strategic Approach*, 2nd Ed. (Cincinnati, Ohio: South-Western Thomson Learning, 2002), Exhibit 8.6, p. 313.

folded into choices about levels of equity ownership, the composition of the board of directors, the organizational affiliation of the joint venture's general manager, including the top management team.

To form the top management team in a joint venture, the instinctive inclination is to seek a composition that represents the interests of all alliance partners. A team with representatives from each partner can accomplish this objective as it provides the skills and perspectives from each partner, which were part of the logic for alliance formation. A mix of viewpoints and skills can provide healthy discussion and conflict, but it must be balanced against creating a large divide in the alliance's management team. This divide widens when there are compositional gaps, or systematic and consistent differences in the ages, genders, ethnic backgrounds, attitudes and skills of the managers brought together from the alliance partners.

For example, there would be a wide gap if all the managers from one alliance partner were below the age of 35, had a university education and valued collective work, while the members from the other alliance partner were each over the age of 35, did not attend university and valued individual work. The common divisions on these dimensions, accentuates the existing organizational divide, making it more difficult for these managers to work together effectively, with a minimal amount of conflict, and with accepted areas of control.[13]

Control over day-to-day functions comes from the top management team and from the lower-level managers in a strategic alliance. Control among functions can be divided among the managers from each partner firm, or it can be split according to the strengths of each partner. If the alliance is a traditional international joint venture, the foreign partner could retain control over manufacturing processes and management of the manufacturing plant, while the local partner could control the distribution and sale of the joint venture's products. In a scale alliance, in which partners contribute similar resources, the division of operational control is a more thorny matter. Both partners might not be willing to yield control to the other in an area in which a partner has expertise.

Control, the composition of alliance management teams and the degree of autonomy for the alliance are but a few of the issues that can influence an alliance's performance. Alliance partners can be of different size,[14] the partners can have different degrees of bargaining power,[15] the partners might or might not trust one another,[16] or the partners can have different levels of experience and expertise in operating alliances.[17] Each of these features can contribute positively or negatively to the satisfaction a partner has with the performance of an alliance. Partner satisfaction is an important dimension to consider, because the goals of each alliance partner for the alliance frequently do not align well.

Goal Alignment

The resolution to many of the potential problems that can be encountered in the design of a strategic alliance, including the division of control, can rest in a clear understanding of the goals of each partner in the alliance. If the goals of the partners are understood and aligned, the alliance can be designed in such a way as to meet those goals. If the goals of each partner are not understood, then the alliance might be destined to fail, because the partners will be pulling the alliance in different directions.

A task for partners in a joint venture during its formative stages is to define what constitutes the objectives of the joint venture and what performance measures will be used to examine the extent to which those objectives have been met. DHL and Cathay Pacific's joint venture in Hong Kong illustrates this point. In October 2002, DHL (*www.dhl.com*), the international air express carrier, and Cathay Pacific (*www.cathaypacific.com*), a Hong Kong-based airline, formed a joint venture to open and operate an express cargo terminal out of Hong Kong's international airport. Both companies entered the joint venture with the objective of making Hong Kong an aviation hub for both passenger services and express logistics. The joint venture also permitted the companies to pursue their individual objectives. For Cathay Pacific, it supported its objective of helping the economy and increasing jobs. For DHL, it supported its objective of strengthening its services and become more competitive in Hong Kong.

It is important for managers from the partners and the top management team from the joint venture to establish and agree upon the strategic objectives of the joint venture, *e.g.* its product-markets and its performance objectives. Several questions concerning a joint venture's objectives should be addressed. How will its financial performance be measured? What should be the rate of penetration into export and domestic markets? What is an acceptable rate of technology assimilation by the joint ventures? These questions are representative of the kind of objectives about which some form of agreement must be reached to establish congruity in purpose and to increase the likelihood of overall satisfaction with the joint venture's performance.[18] These issues were at the forefront of KFC's joint venture entry into China.

KFC in China[19]

In December 1986, KFC entered a joint venture agreement with two partners based in China. KFC had a 60 per cent equity position, the Tourist Bureau had a 27 per cent interest, and Beijing Animal Production had a 13 per cent stake. The JV was soon implemented, and by early 1988 the Beijing store had become the highest volume KFC store in the world. Although the first store was successful in terms of sales volume, several problems emerged when additional restaurants were to be opened in China.

In 1988, the Bank of China assumed a 25 per cent equity stake in the joint venture and KFC's interest became 51 per cent. New stores were soon opened in the Beijing area in April and December of 1988. As the joint venture expanded, it became apparent the objectives of the partners diverged (see Figure 7-5).

KFC regarded a rapid expansion into the whole of China as a measure of successful entry, whereas the rest of the partners considered the Beijing area as the limit of its geographic scope.

Figure 7-5:   Goal Alignment in KFC's Joint Venture in China

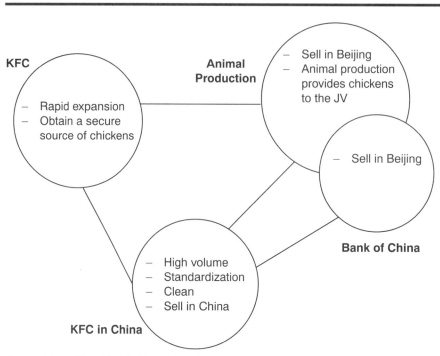

Source: Adapted from Paul W. Beamish and Andrew Delios, "Improving Joint Venture Performance through Congruent Measures of Success," in Paul. W. Beamish and J. Peter. Killing, eds, *Cooperative Strategies: European Perspectives* (San Francisco: The New Lexington Press, 1997).

Other goals likewise varied. The Animal Production partner wanted to use KFC as an outlet for its chicken, and be its sole supplier. If the Animal Production unit was producing at capacity in supplying the joint venture's restaurants in Beijing, it was satisfied with the scale of the joint venture's operations. KFC placed considerable emphasis on quality, service and cleanliness in its restaurants, but other partners were not as interested.

Several aspects of the joint venture's performance became issues as it expanded. Intracompany sales, hard and soft currency measures of financial performance, and the geographic scope of the joint venture were key items around which disagreement among the partners was centred. Dissatisfaction with the joint venture increased. Eventually, KFC founded a new joint venture with a different partner to pursue opportunities in China outside of Beijing.

Choice of Partner

Divergences in interests in strategic alliance partners can be resolved by discussing partner objectives during negotiations. Other issues related to the fit between the partners in a strategic alliance can likewise be determined prior to a strategic alliance beginning operations. Selecting a suitable partner is an important pre-emptive measure to controlling problems in a strategic alliance.

One dimension to examine when looking at partner suitability is the fit between the partners. Recall that the logic for a strategic alliance extends from a mutual need to obtain resources. Without this complementary resource need, the logic and prospects for the strategic alliance are weak from the outset. A potential alliance partner could have the resources required by the other partner, but it is not easy to accurately evaluate a partner's contributions prior to joint venture formation. Beginning with a non-equity alliance, or a small, short-term collaboration, is a low risk means of identifying the resources a partner has before committing to a larger scale alliance.

Once a potential partner has been identified in terms of the match between required resources and its resource attributes, the potential partner can be evaluated on a number of other dimensions. For a potential partner to become a valuable partner in the alliance, it must be committed to the alliance. If the management in the partner is not committed, the expected resource flows will not materialize.

Commitment means that the partner is willing to put forth the resources and make the efforts necessary to fulfill its obligations to the strategic alliance, and improve the chances for its success. Commitment can come about when a partner perceives its inputs to the strategic alliance to be matched by its share of the outputs, such as financial returns. If each partner's rewards are fairly matched to their contributions, commitment can be maintained from both partners. If one partner is marginalized, the commitment from that partner can easily decline.

A difficulty in the management of an alliance is gauging the commitment and contributions from a partner on an on-going basis. An alliance contract will define the roles of each partner, but these roles can change over time, as the alliance develops. High costs to monitoring, and the potential for change in an alliance, speak to the need to be flexible in the management of an alliance, while having trust in a partner.

Trust and commitment need to be built in an alliance, as part of the process of alliance management (see Table 7-4). It is a process that begins in the development stage of an alliance, but it is one that continues through the on-going management of a strategic alliance.

Trust is important in an alliance because of the difficulty of completely defining the roles and contingencies that might be encountered during the life of an alliance relationship. A contract can guide some of what should be undertaken in an alliance by the alliance partners, but it is impossible to specify all possible future scenarios. The managers in an alliance might have to make a decision in an area that has not been specified in the contract. The decision will be implemented with greater ease where the partners trust one another, and do not have to resort to a detailed by-the-book approval procedure.

Trust does not happen automatically. It needs to be cultivated in the partners over time. It can happen in a process of discovery. By identifying as clearly as possible the motivations and objectives of a partner in joining an alliance, fears about a partner's wish to acquire a particular capability or market from the other partner can be allayed. As described in Box 7-3, NCsoft (*www.ncsoft.net*) and Gamania (*www.gamania.com*) were well aware of the need for trust in a business relationship.

Table 7-4: **Key Factors to Building Trust and Commitment in an Alliance**

Factor	Reason
Partner Selection	Alliance partners must believe they can trust each other and that each is committed to the venture.
Identify your own and your partner's strategic goals	Identification of goals is an important step in the establishment of trust.
Seek win-win situations	A balance of commitment and rewards helps sustain commitment from both alliance partners.
Go slowly	Trust and commitment build in cycles over time.
Invest in cross-cultural training	Cross-cultural training minimizes the possibility for conflict and misunderstandings.
Invest in direct communication	Dealing with a partner face-to-face helps overcome potential cultural and organizational differences.
Identity the right level of trust and commitment	Trust and commitment levels must not be so high as to make a firm vulnerable to its partner, but must be high enough to permit the expected benefits to be gained in the alliance.

Source: John B. Cullen, *Multinational Management: A Strategic Approach*, 2nd Ed. (Cincinnati, Ohio: South-Western Thomson Learning, 2002), pp. 321–322.

Box 7-3   NCsoft and Gamania

NCsoft of South Korea was one of the world's largest developer and publisher of online computer games. Its most successful game, Lineage, holds a 42 percent market share for online games. NCsoft and Gamania have been developing a business relationship since June 2000, when NCsoft began to work with Taiwan-based Gamania's game distribution services. Gamania provides complementary services to NCsoft, such as marketing, management and distribution in Taiwan for NCsoft's top-selling game, Lineage. As of 2003, Lineage was Taiwan's leading online game with approximately 180,000 concurrent users.

The relationship between the two businesses continued to develop after their initial collaboration in Taiwan. In September 2003, the companies announced the establishment of a USD4 million joint venture called NC Taiwan (*www.nctaiwan.com*) to distribute and market the online game Lineage II, a much anticipated sequel to Lineage. Trust is a key motivation behind NCsoft's choice of Gamania as a partner for this joint venture. Tack Jin Kim, the CEO of NCsoft, identified that the cooperative ties built between Gamania and NCsoft have helped to prove that Gamania's marketing and service capabilities were the best in Taiwan. A longer term cooperation is a consequence of the mutual trust built in the initial business relationship and, hence, the formation of the joint venture. Lineage II will be among the first titles that NCsoft will provide for NC Taiwan, which will in turn use Gamania's resources to market, distribute, and provide user services in Taiwan, where the popularity of online games is second only to Korea. Figure 7-6 represents the structure of this joint venture.

As discussed earlier in this chapter, the motivations to form a strategic alliance require that both parties have an interest in the alliance. It is no different for the evolving relationship between NCsoft and Gamania. Both companies have been focused on global expansion and the alliance helps them to achieve their goal. Taiwan is the largest market for online games after Korea, and the NC Taiwan joint venture has been a milestone in NCsoft's globalization efforts to develop a worldwide network. For Gamania, the joint venture supports its strategic expansion plan to become the driving force behind videogaming in Asia. The partnership with NCsoft provided Gamania with a foothold into the Korean market and it allowed it to bring Taiwan's online game market to the world.

Trust, resource sharing, expansion of market power and aligned goals are all factors in the developing relationship between NCsoft and Gamania. NC Taiwan is another step towards solidifying a long-term business alliance that helps both companies' achieve their strategic goals.

Sources:
http://www.ncsoft.net, 15 November 2003.
"NCsoft to Establish Joint Venture in Taiwan; Deal Solidifies an Already Strong Relationship between Korea's NCsoft and Taiwan's Gamania," *Business Wire*, 26 August 2003, p. 5767.
"NCsoft Sets up Taiwan Deal," *Austin Business Journal*, 26 August 2003.
http://austin.bizjournals.com/austin/stories/2003/08/25/daily12.html, 15 November 2003.
http://www.gamespot.com/pc/rpg/lineage2thechaoticchronicle/news_6074106.html, 17 November 2003.
http://service.gamania.com/introduction/english/philosophy.html, 17 November 2003.
http://ir.gamania.com/english/IRNews.asp?NewsType=0&ID=20, 18 November 2003.
"How Korea Came To Have 67% Broadband Use," *The Online Reporter*, 21 October 2002.

Figure 7-6:   The NC Taiwan Joint Venture

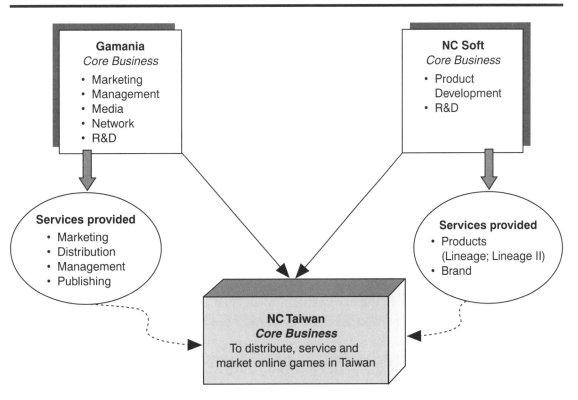

Management of Strategic Alliances

A strategic alliance needs to be managed as an on-going entity. It is not enough to devote senior management time to the alliance at its formative stages. An alliance needs continual monitoring and attention, to establish and maintain a good relationship between the partners involved in the alliance, and between each partner and the alliance itself.

Once an alliance is formed, there might be the temptation to not devote key resources to it. This temptation should be avoided. Capable individuals need to be sent to work in the alliance in order to maximize its chances for success. If the alliance is treated as a peripheral part of a multinational firm's network, it will perform accordingly.

As part of the on-going management of an alliance, its performance and the rationale behind its existence need to be examined at regular intervals. As markets and the needs of the partners change, the ways in which the performance of the alliance is interpreted by each partner can begin to diverge. With changing needs of a partner, it might employ a new set of objectives to evaluate the performance of an alliance. Changing needs can come about when the external environment experiences a change or a shock.

Following the onset of the Asian Financial Crisis in 1997, the survival of a substantial number of Japanese joint ventures in Thailand was placed in jeopardy because of the illiquidity of local Thai partners. The Thai partners reacted to this by relaxing their objectives for equity ownership in the joint ventures, permitting the Japanese partners to increase their equity stake in return for needed cash infusions into the joint ventures. The flexibility of each partner to alteration in a basic design element of a joint venture, the division of equity ownership between partners, made possible the continued operation of these joint ventures.[20]

Flexibility can be an essential element in alliance management. It is aided by allowing managers in the alliance a degree of strategic freedom in its operations. The partners in the alliance determine, during the negotiation stage, the freedom alliance managers should have for selecting markets, developing technologies, sourcing inputs and so forth. Alliance managers can be in the best position to make the most effective decisions about strategic issues such as these. It is a matter of identifying and providing an appropriate measure of freedom to an alliance's management to make these decisions.

Learning in Alliances

With freedom and flexibility in the management of an alliance, comes the risk that one partner can gain more than another partner, or that one partner can become a marginal contributor to the alliance. This risk relates to the biggest concern that most managers have when contemplating an alliance. This risk is one of the loss of a key resource to another firm, which would make that firm a stronger competitor.

This apprehension is captured by the idea that alliances can be learning races.[21] Two firms come together to form an alliance to satisfy mutual resource needs. Bringing together resources in an alliance creates a window by which one firm can view the key resources of another firm. This window can be used to acquire the resource of the other partner, for example, to learn a particular technological capability, or to develop knowledge about a certain manufacturing technique. Risks can be asymmetric, *e.g.* one firm's key resources and capabilities might be more exposed than another firm's, leading the more exposed firm to be the eventual loser in an alliance.

When partners regard an alliance to be a learning race, the chances of alliance failure are accordingly greater. Not only will this perception lower commitment and trust to the alliance, it will destabilize the alliance as its strategic logic is eroded by the flow of knowledge from the alliance to each partner. If the partners do not enter an alliance with an explicit objective to acquire the other partner's knowledge and capabilities, then the alliance can be more stable in the long term.

Figure 7-7 illustrates a key distinction in alliance management, which is that between resource access and resource acquisition.[22] If both partners provide an alliance with access to its key resources, and if both are committed to its use in the alliance, then the alliance has a fair chance of succeeding.

If the motive in an alliance becomes one of resource acquisition, the partner whose resource is acquired has decreased bargaining power in the alliance. This partner will eventually become a marginal participant in the alliance, with the likely outcome being the termination of the alliance.

Figure 7-7:   Resource Access and Acquisition and Alliance Instability

		Local Partner's Approach to Foreign Partner's Resources	
		Access	**Acquisition**
Foreign Partner's Approach to Local Partner's Resources	**Access**	The alliance tends to be very stable and cooperative	The alliance is potentially unstable
	Acquisition	The alliance is potentially unstable	The alliance is very unstable. It is a competitive alliance, in which partners are engaged in a race to learn

Source: Andrew Inkpen and Paul W. Beamish, "Knowledge, Bargaining Power, and the Instability of International Joint Ventures," *Academy of Management Review,* 1997, Vol. 22, No. 1, pp. 177–203.

This scenario is most often typified in the case of joint venture formation by developed firms in developing countries. These entries tend to be market access joint ventures in which a foreign firm would like to secure access to the local market knowledge of a local firm. As the market access joint venture operates, the foreign firm tends to acquire knowledge of the local market. In several years, the foreign firm can acquire enough knowledge about the local market to make a local partner redundant.[23] This knowledge acquisition, intended or not, destabilizes the joint venture, as it reduces the cogency of the strategic logic for the joint venture to exist.

Summary

Strategic alliances are an inescapable part of international business in the 21st century. Strategic alliances have been utilized by firms for decades, but with continued rapid growth in international markets, and a more rapid evolution in product markets, managers increasingly view alliances as integral to a firm's success.

As with any other aspect of a firm's operations, success comes with good management. The barriers to successful management of an alliance are substantial, but certainly not insurmountable. The growth in strategic alliance use since the 1980s speaks to the idea that managers are becoming increasingly comfortable with implementing and managing strategic alliances.

A part of the reality of strategic alliances is that however successfully managed, a strategic alliance will eventually be terminated. If the alliance is a joint venture, it might be taken over by one of the partners, it might be sold to a third party, or it might be liquidated. Whichever route is chosen, the endpoint is the same. Termination should not necessarily be viewed as a failure in alliance management unless its termination is much sooner than anticipated.

For some firms, the expected lifespan of an alliance can have a long horizon. Examples of joint ventures with a lifespan of more than 20 years is not unprecedented. The Toppan-Moore and Fuji-Xerox joint ventures, each of which lasted for more than a decade, are but two well-known examples.

The longevity of these alliances was aided in no small part by the development of strategic alliance management capabilities in the partner firms. Alliance management capabilities can be a resource of strategic value to a firm.[24] The development of alliance management capabilities, and a judicious use of alliances, should be regarded as crucial parts of a firm's internationalization strategy.

Notes

[1] Paul W. Beamish and Andrew Delios, "Incidence and Propensity of Alliance Formation by US, European and Japanese MNEs," in Paul. W. Beamish and J. Peter. Killing, eds, *Cooperative Strategies: Asian Perspectives* (San Francisco: The New Lexington Press, 1997).

[2] "Chasing the Tiger: Two Years after the Success of 'Crouching Tiger, Hidden Dragon,' the Hong Kong Film Industry Has yet to Follow through on Its Potential for Global Expansion," *Hollywood Reporter*, 21 May 2002, Vol. 373, No. 28, pp. 22–23.

[3] Jaideep Anand and Bruce Kogut, "Technological Capabilities of Companies, Firm Rivalry and Foreign Direct Investment," *Journal of International Business Studies*, 1997, Vol. 28, pp. 445–465.

[4] *http://www.pccw.com/NASApp/cs/*, 20 November 2003.

[5] Shige Makino and Paul Beamish, "Local Ownership Restrictions, Entry Mode Choice, and FDI Performance: Japanese Overseas Subsidiaries in Asia," *Asia Pacific Journal of Management,* Special Issue on "Government-Business Relations in Asia," 1998, Vol. 15, No. 2, pp. 119–136.

[6] Paul. W. Beamish, Allen J. Morrison, Philip M. Rosenzweig, and Andrew Inkpen, *International Management: Text and Cases*, 4th Ed. (Boston: McGraw-Hill, 2002), Chapter 7.

[7] Shige Makino and Paul W. Beamish, "Performance and Survival of Joint Ventures with Non-conventional Ownership Structures," *Journal of International Business Studies,* 1998, Vol. 29, No. 4, pp. 797–818; Shige Makino, *Joint Venture Ownership Structure and Performance: Japanese Joint Ventures in Asia* (Unpublished PhD dissertation. London, ON: The University of Western Ontario, 1995).

[8] *Adhesives & Sealants Industry*, September 2003, Vol. 10, No. 7, p. 16.

[9] Dana, "Daewoo Sign Joint Venture Agreement to Produce Rear Axles and Driveshafts in Poland," *PR Newswire*, 18 September 1998, p. 5429.

[10] "Daewoo to Set up Auto Parts Factory in Poland" *http://ssdc.ucsd.edu/news/korea/h98/korea.19981002.html*, 16 November 2003.

[11] For more detailed discussion on these forms of business groups, please see Chapter 9.

[12] Jean-Louis Schaan, "How to Control a Joint Venture even as a Minority Partner," *Journal of General Management*, 1988, Vol. 14, No. 1, pp. 4–16.

[13] Donald C. Hambrick, Jiatao Li, Katherine Xin, and Anne S. Tsui, "Compositional Gaps and Downward Spirals in International Joint Venture Management Groups," *Strategic Management Journal*, 2001, Vol. 22, pp. 1033–1053.

[14] Seung Ho Park and G. R. Ungson, "The Effect of National Culture, Organizational Complementarity, and Economic Motivation on Joint Venture Dissolution," *Academy of Management Journal*, 1997, Vol. 40, pp. 279–307.

[15] Aimin Yan and Barbara Gray, "Bargaining Power, Management Control, and Performance in United States-China Joint Ventures: A Comparative Case Study," *Academy of Management Journal,* 1994, Vol. 35, No. 5, pp. 1478–1517.

[16] J. P. Walsh, E. P. Wang, and Katherine Xin, "Same Bed, Different Dreams: Working Relationships in Sino-American Joint Ventures," *Journal of World Business*, 1999, Vol. 34, pp. 69–93.

[17] Andrew Delios and Paul W. Beamish, "Survival and Profitability: The Roles of Experience and Intangible Assets in Foreign Subsidiary Performance," *Academy of Management Journal*, 2001, Vol. 44, No. 5, pp. 1028–1038; Harry G. Barkema, John H. J. Bell, and Johannes M. Pennings, "Foreign Entry, Cultural Barriers and Learning," *Strategic Management Journal*, 1996, Vol. 17, No. 2, pp. 151–166.

[18] Paul W. Beamish and Andrew Delios, "Improving Joint Venture Performance through Congruent Measures of Success," in Paul. W. Beamish and J. Peter. Killing, eds, *Cooperative Strategies: European Perspectives* (San Francisco: The New Lexington Press, 1997).

[19] Description of the KFC JV is based upon the Richard Ivey School of Business case *Kentucky Fried Chicken in China (C),* case number 8-92-G001, and the accompanying teaching note.

[20] Andrew Delios and Timothy D. Keeley, "Japanese Foreign Direct Investment in Thailand: An Empirical and Qualitative Post-crisis Analysis," *Journal of International Business and Economy*, 2000, Vol. 1, No. 1, pp. 91–118.

[21] Gary Hamel, "Competition for Competence and Inter-partner Learning within International Strategic Alliances," *Strategic Management Journal*, 1991, Vol. 12, Special Issue, pp. 83–104.

[22] Andrew Inkpen and Paul W. Beamish, "Knowledge, Bargaining Power, and the Instability of International Joint Ventures," *Academy of Management Review*, 1997, Vol. 22, No. 1, pp. 177–203.

[23] Shige Makino and Andrew Delios, "Local Knowledge Transfer and Performance: Implications for Alliance Formation in Asia," *Journal of International Business Studies*, 1996, Vol. 27, No. 5, pp. 905–928.

[24] Harry G. Barkema, Oded Shenkar, Freek Vermeulen, and John H. J. Bell, "Working Abroad, Working with Others: How Firms Learn to Operate International Joint Ventures," *Academy of Management Journal*, 1997, Vol. 40, pp. 426–442.

8 MULTINATIONAL ENTERPRISE

Over the last few decades, multinational enterprises, or multinational firms, have increased both in number and size. This growth in multinational firms has been a major development that has contributed to rapid increases in the globalization of many national economies. The growth of multinational enterprises has been along two dimensions: growth in the size of existing multinational firms and growth in the absolute number of multinational firms. For the latter, the number of multinational firms from any one country has increased, as has the number of countries with a large number of multinational firms. Put another way, more and more multinational firms are coming from more and more countries worldwide.

The foreign subsidiary and parent multinational firm relationship, as captured in a multinational enterprise, is just one way to organize business activities. In this chapter, we outlined several rationales for why we have seen this form of business organization emerge. For an international manager operating in Asia, it is not only important to understand the competitive foundations of multinational firms, but it is also important to know which are the most prominent among these in the various countries in Asia.

Multinational Firms

In the popular and academic press, we frequently see references made to multinational firms, multinational corporations (MNCs), multinational enterprises (MNEs), multinational conglomerates, transnational corporations and the like. Are these the same types of companies? Do these names mean that these companies are different?

The answer to both of these questions is 'Yes'. These names all refer to companies that have an international scope of operations. To encompass all of these, we usually refer to a multinational enterprise, a multinational corporation, or a multinational firm. A multinational enterprise is a company that has productive operations in at least two countries in the world. Productive operations can mean manufacturing, sales, distribution, mining, agriculture, services or any other type of value-added activity that takes place using assets and a facility, usually called a foreign subsidiary, owned in whole or in part by the company.

This definition means that a company with a manufacturing facility in Taiwan and a distribution outlet in Hong Kong is a multinational firm, provided it has an ownership stake in both the manufacturing facility and distribution outlet. A company with a mining operation in Brazil and an iron ore processing plant in Argentina is considered to be a multinational firm. A company that extracts oil in Azerbaijan, and then refines that oil in Russia is a multinational firm.

A complementary way to look at whether a company is a multinational firm is to identify if it has made a foreign direct investment (FDI). A company must make a foreign direct investment for it to be a multinational firm. A foreign direct investment is the purchase of foreign assets for the purpose of controlling the use of those assets. National regulations usually stipulate that a foreign investing firm must own at least five to 20 per cent of the voting stock of a local company before the foreign investing firm can be considered as making a foreign direct investment. An investment in a subsidiary in an amount that does not confer some degree of control is not considered to be a foreign direct investment, instead it is a foreign portfolio investment. A foreign portfolio investment provides rights to the returns earned from a subsidiary's operations, but without the right of control over what a subsidiary does to earn its returns.

Why Do We Have Multinational Firms?

A company becomes a multinational firm when it makes a foreign direct investment. That is clear. Why, however, would managers in a firm want to establish operations in a foreign country? Having operations in a foreign country means that the managers and employees have to learn how to operate in a country with a different culture, in which the language is probably different. Legal and political systems, as well as the company's buyers and suppliers are also different. All of these differences represent a cost to a company. They represent a monetary cost as well as a competitive cost, in which a foreign company is at a competitive disadvantage to a local company in dealing with a host country's cultural, political, social, legal and competitive environments.

How does a company overcome this disadvantage to not only compete on an even footing with local companies but, in many cases, to be a superior competitor? The answer relates to advantages. Quite simply, to become a multinational firm, a company must have some unique advantage, called an ownership advantage, that provides it with a competitive edge in competition in a foreign market. This advantage can offset a company's disadvantage of being foreign, and provide it with a leg-up on domestic and foreign competitors.

One such ownership advantage is the technological advantage possessed by large pharmaceutical firms. Large pharmaceutical companies have begun to proliferate in world markets. These companies produce various prescription medications, called ethical pharmaceuticals. The companies have a limited time during which they have a proprietary right to monopolize production of a particular pharmaceutical product. This right is protected by a patent. A patent embodies the extensive research and development activities that a pharmaceutical company undertook to develop its unique drugs. This research and development and the resultant patent is an ownership advantage that can be used to support a pharmaceutical company's international expansion.

Another example of an ownership advantage is the brand name advantage possessed by the Walt Disney company. The Walt Disney brand is recognized in many countries around the world. The brand advantage comes from the worldwide distribution of Walt Disney's movies. This creates a brand recognition that can be used to support the sale of Walt Disney's other products such as its toys, stuffed animals, books and theme parks.

This ownership advantage, sometimes called a proprietary asset advantage, or a unique resource advantage, is the starting point for theories of multinational enterprise.

Theories of Multinational Enterprise

Theories of multinational enterprise began to multiply in the 1960s, and have continued to evolve to the present day.[1] The Product Cycle theory of Raymond Vernon (see Chapter 2) explained both trade and foreign direct investment. Other scholars began to address the existence of multinational enterprises from the perspective that a multinational enterprise emerged where there were market imperfections. The multinational structure exploited a market imperfection to achieve a more competitive set of operations than a company that did not.

The principal antecedent to current economic thinking on the existence of multinational firms rests in the market imperfections paradigm. Imperfect markets for competition lead to the development of oligopolistic and monopolistic competitive structures. A multinational firm can exploit market imperfections to develop more market power – a greater size and a reduction in the number of competitors in an industry – and grow into international markets. This perspective on multinational enterprise sees international expansion as an extended attempt to exploit a powerful competitive position brought on by size and concentrated market power.[2]

Internalization theorists extended this approach to consider the case of how imperfections in markets for cross-border business transactions can lead to the rise of multinational enterprise.[3] The internalization theory area is a tremendously rich one, and is a viewpoint that has spawned an impressive amount of inquiry into multinational enterprises.[4]

According to internalization theorists, a firm moves into international markets when the markets for the exchange of its proprietary assets and resources are imperfect. Market imperfections can arise because of information asymmetries, poor definitions of the assets to be exchanged and the intangible nature of the assets to be exchanged.

In summary, assets and markets have features that increase the costs and risks of using a market-based interface for the exchange of assets. As these costs and risks increase, it becomes more feasible to use an internalized exchange, *i.e.* the application of a firm's assets in a new market by the expansion of an organization into that market.

In this way, the rise of a multinational firm is a direct response to try to economize on the costs imposed on a firm by transactional market imperfections, for the exchange of intermediate products. A firm conducts international operations because there are advantages to the internalization of cross-border applications of its assets used in the production of intermediate inputs.

The OLI Framework

Notwithstanding the value of internalization theory, we now turn to what is sometimes called the OLI framework, or the eclectic paradigm.[5] The OLI framework helps to explain the extent and pattern of the foreign-owned production of multinational enterprises, by identifying the determinants of foreign production.

The eclectic paradigm draws on both micro- and macro-economic explanations of the existence and activities of multinational enterprises to create a comprehensive, economics-based theory of the activities of a multinational firm. The paradigm is a framework that can be used to explain the nature of foreign-owned productive activities of the MNE and identify determinants of foreign activities. By examining three discrete decisions that must be made in a foreign direct investment, the framework of the paradigm facilitates explanations of three specific questions: (1) why a multinational firm engages in cross border activities, (2) where those activities are located and (3) how those activities are structured.

Foundations

The eclectic paradigm is a melding of macro-economic theories of firm behaviour and micro-economic theories of firm behaviour. It begins with the macro-economic idea that where there is unequal location-bound resource distribution across nations, geographically scattered firms do not have equal access to spatially dispersed resources. In this scenario, there is the potential for efficiency-based productive gains from international trade.

Macro-economic theories of international trade concern variables at a country level. Micro-economic theories, conversely, are concerned with firm level variables. Micro-economic theories on the existence and growth of firms expand the scope of the eclectic paradigm's explanation of international activity and behaviour. In the eclectic paradigm, the market versus hierarchical transaction efficiency trade-off is the essential element in the reasoning behind how firms choose to operate. Managers in firms avoid market exchange when the costs of using a market-mediated transaction become high. The size and scope of a firm's operations are dependent on the cost savings of internal transactions versus market transactions. Inefficiencies in markets, which we can call transactional market failures, lead to the establishment of organizations that circumvent the costs of using the market.

Market failure explanations at the micro-level and macro-level provide a strong but incomplete argument for the existence and activities of multinational firms. It is not enough to have a rationale to economize on costs, a firm must also possess advantages relative to its competitors in an industry. It must have the ownership advantage that we discussed earlier.

Taken together, these three streams of economic thought form the theoretical foundation of the eclectic paradigm. The reason for the combination of these three theories in the eclectic paradigm rests in their complementarities and individual insufficiencies as explanations of foreign production. The principal deficiency of each theory, as an explanation of the existence and growth of multinational enterprises, is in their simplifying assumptions. Trade theory assumes all firms are equal in their capabilities and non-location bound endowments of resources. Micro-economic theories of the firm explain away industry-level and country-level variables. Industrial organization theory does not explicitly provide an explanation for the existence of efficiency-based, production-side competitive advantages. By combining these three theoretical perspectives, the eclectic paradigm removes the assumptions that limits the explanatory power of each, and combines them into a framework of three advantages of considerable explanatory power.

The Three Advantages (OLI Determinants)

Ownership Advantage (O)

An ownership advantage is an advantage specific to a firm, that provides it with the competitive edge required to undertake and sustain foreign direct investment activity. Originally, in the OLI framework, the ownership advantage was presented conceptually as a broad categorization of ownership related strategic factors. Recently, the ownership advantage has been split into two categories: intangible asset advantages and advantages of common governance. Intangible asset advantages are such things as the organization of work, non-codifiable knowledge, marketing and finance know-how and product innovations. Advantages of common governance arise from the organization of ownership advantages with complementary assets. For example, branch plants may enjoy lower costs of operation than solitary operations, as they can benefit from economies of scale and scope found in joint production, access to lower cost inputs, and access to resources at the marginal costs of the firm. Multinationality is a sub-classification of intangible asset advantages. The ability to learn about societal and cultural differences, opportunities for arbitrage, global sourcing and strategic factors are some of the potential benefits attributable to multinational operations. The ownership advantage, in considering firm and industry level factors, answers the 'what' question of economic activity, *i.e.* which firms will be active in foreign markets.

Locational Advantage (L)

Locational advantage is fundamental to trade theory.[6] International trade theory forms the underpinnings of the eclectic paradigm's explanation of locational advantage – the 'where' of economic activity. A locational advantage is an advantage that is specific to a geographical region, typically a country. Location specific advantages may be natural or created endowments of resources and include such things as: economic systems of governments, factor prices and endowments of labour and raw materials, and investment incentives. These advantages may favor the home country of a multinational firm or its host country.

Internalization Advantage (I)

The assumption of market imperfections and market failure is the basis for the internalization advantage. Where markets fail, it is more advantageous for a firm to internalize a transaction than it is to conduct the same transaction at arm's length in a market. By internalizing a transaction, firms can protect against market failure or exploit a failure in markets. An internal transaction reduces the costs of search, reduces buyer uncertainty, protects the quality of intermediate products and can result in the avoidance of government intervention – all forms of protection against market failure.

An example of internalization as protection against market failure is an aluminum producer that vertically integrates backwards to ensure a supply of bauxite and reduce input price uncertainty. Alternatively, a producer that internalizes an intermediate product market to create a more efficient transactional structure does so to gain from market failure. Internal transactions enable managers to control supplies, control the condition of sales of inputs, and control markets. The internalization advantage explains the 'how' of economic activity. Will a market be served by exporting or licensing, by a joint venture, or by a wholly-owned subsidiary?

Conditions for Foreign Activity

Building from the OLI set of advantages, we can outline four conditions that must be present for a firm to engage in international activities.

1. O advantages: The comparison point for O advantages is with other firms in the host country or home country of the prospective multinational firm.
2. Given (1), I advantages: Will a firm use markets, hierarchies or something in between to exploit its O advantage in international markets?
3. Given (1) and (2), L advantages: Will the uneven distribution of resources across nations confer advantages to a firm if it invests in another market?
4. Given (1), (2) and (3), that is, the presence of the OLI advantages: Is foreign production consistent with long-term management strategy?

The greater the strength of the advantages underlying each OLI determinant, the more likely a firm is to exploit these advantages by expansion into international markets. O advantages are a necessary condition for foreign operations. I advantages and L advantages influence the entry mode and location of foreign production. The fourth condition relates to the motivations for international activity, which we discuss below.

Motivations for Foreign Activity

A firm can invest abroad for a number of reasons. The most common reasons to invest abroad are to find a new market for products or to access resources in a host country that can lead to lower cost production. These two depictions of the motivations of multinational enterprise lead to the frequent characterization of multinational firms as exploiters of low-cost labour, or aggressive capitalists seeking to capture markets from local firms.

These motivations do undoubtedly exist, but they are a subset of what drives managers to make FDIs. The full range of the reasons to undertake FDI can be captured in four types of FDI: (1) market seeking FDI; (2) resource seeking FDI; (3) strategic asset seeking FDI; and (4) efficiency seeking FDI (see Table 8-1).

1. *Market seeking*: A company undertakes an FDI to capture new buyers for its products. Market seeking FDI is a form of international expansion that exploits a unique advantage a firm possesses in its home market that is transferable to a foreign market. FDI represents a means to extend the reach of a firm's unique advantages to capture new markets.

Table 8-1: Motivations for Foreign Direct Investment

Type of FDI	Strategic motivation of FDI	Examples of industries that favour the type of FDI
Market Seeking	• To protect existing markets. • To counter the moves of competitors. • To pre-empt or preclude existing and potential competitors from gaining a market.	• Computers, pharmaceuticals, motor vehicles, tobacco. • Airline services, fast-food services.
Resource Seeking	• To gain privileged access to resources. • To pre-empt resource access from competitors and thereby gain a new source of ownership advantages.	• Oil, copper, bauxite, bananas, forest products, hotels. • Export-processing, labour intensive industries.
Efficiency Seeking	• To enhance a regional product rationalization strategy. • To gain advantages in a process and production specialization strategy.	• Motor vehicles, electrical appliances, business services, R&D. • Consumer electronics, textiles, clothing.
Strategic Asset Seeking	• To strengthen global innovation capabilities. • To gain new product lines or markets. • To strengthen product competitiveness.	• Industries with a high ratio of fixed to overhead costs. • Industries in which there are substantial economies of scale and scope.

Source: Adapted from John H. Dunning, *Multinational Enterprises and the Global Economy* (New York: Addison-Wesley, 1993), Table 4.2, pp. 82–83.

2. *Resource seeking*: National markets differ in resource endowments. To capture those differences and improve the efficiency of production, a firm might undertake FDI. In this form of FDI a company establishes a subsidiary to capture a location-bound resource such as a raw material input, a mineral resource, or skilled and unskilled labour. Generally, this resource has a price or quality superior to what exists in a firm's other markets.

3. *Efficiency seeking*: This form of FDI relates mostly to the productive aspects of a firm's operations. FDI can take place to move a section of a firm's value chain into a country in which that value chain activity will have its greatest efficiency. Dynamism in technological and regulatory environments creates a series of new opportunities to move productive assets around countries in response to the efficiency seeking motive for foreign FDI.

4. *Strategic asset seeking*: FDI can incorporate a build component, in which foreign investment is meant to strengthen a firm's existing advantages. A firm can invest abroad via a joint venture or an acquisition to capture unique assets such as a distribution network, a technology, a brand or a unique location, that is possessed by a local firm. By capturing this strategic asset, a multinational firm should be able to strengthen its own existing ownership advantages. We discuss more on this particular motivation, in the next section of this chapter.

Developing Country Multinational Enterprises

Many of the ideas about multinational companies came from the analysis of the foreign activities of companies based in the United States. The time of the analysis was the 1950s, when companies from the US began to establish foreign operations in Canada and Europe, primarily, and also in other countries of the world. Later, also in the 1950s and on into the 1960s, firms from the United Kingdom, Western and Northern European countries and Canada, also began to move abroad in greater numbers.

As the foreign presence of companies from the United States and these other countries began to grow, academics, business people and public policy makers alike wanted to know why such companies could succeed when operating abroad. As we have discussed, the answer pointed to a strong ownership advantage, such as the technological lead that most American companies possessed over their foreign counterparts in the 1950s and 1960s.

As we entered the 1990s, and then the 2000s, a new set of companies began to enter international markets. These companies were coming from places like Taiwan, Singapore and Hong Kong, for example. These companies did not have the kind of technological advantage that US companies did in the 1950s. In fact, many of these companies had ownership disadvantages relative to companies in the countries that they were entering. Accordingly, a new question has emerged which is, 'How have companies without traditional ownership advantages taken part successfully in international activities?' This question becomes more profound when we consider the case that these investment flows increasingly have been from a developing country base to a developed host country.

This direction of flows is somewhat unique in the history of foreign direct investment (see Figure 8-1). The most typical case of FDI flows has been from one developed country to another (line 1 in Figure 8-1).

Next, developed country multinational enterprises began to explore opportunities in developing countries via FDI (line 2). In the 1970s and 1980s, a new phenomenon began to emerge, namely the case of developing countries outward FDI, which was also directed towards other developing countries as host sites (line 3). Most recently, in the 1990s and 2000s, we have seen the completion of this pattern, with developing country firms starting to invest in force in developed countries (line 4).

Although there is no strict reason why developing country multinational firms ought not to invest in developed countries, there is the question about whether these developing country multinational enterprises have an advantage that can provide an edge over leading firms in developed countries. At this point, it is important to bear in mind the first condition of the OLI paradigm: a firm must possess an ownership advantage for it to invest abroad. The developing country to develop country flow of FDI raises the question of whether this is always the case. That is, can a firm without an ownership advantage undertake foreign investment?

Figure 8-1:   Historical Patterns in Flows of Foreign Direct Investment

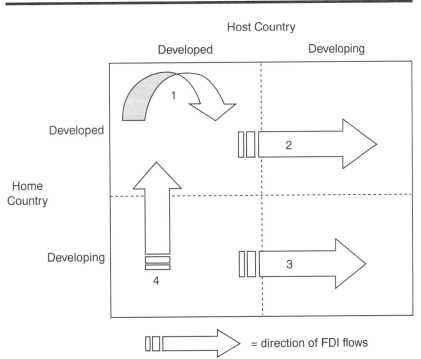

The answer to this question is 'Yes'. But this answer just raises the next question, which is 'How can a firm without an ownership advantage succeed in its foreign direct investments?'.

The answer to the second question rests in the motivation for an investment. The eclectic paradigm was formulated under the idea that a firm would go abroad with an asset exploiting motivation, *i.e.* to exploit its ownership advantage in international markets. The flip side of the asset exploiting argument is that a firm can go abroad under an asset seeking motivation. In this motivation, a foreign direct investment becomes a tool for improving the overall competitiveness of a multinational firm. A subsidiary established under an asset seeking motivation might be at a competitive disadvantage to host country firms, but this is just the condition that leads to an asset seeking investment. By establishing a subsidiary in a host country in which a firm is at a disadvantage, it creates new opportunities for knowledge and capability development that can mitigate this disadvantage.[7]

Firms in Indonesia in the late 1980s and early 1990s invested abroad under such a motive. Indonesian firms with advantages rooted in low-cost manufacturing and proprietary access to raw materials tended to first move abroad by exporting. Initial incursions by Indonesian firms into host countries by exports were then followed by foreign direct investments. The motive for these FDIs was to access management, technology and marketing expertise in the high income countries that were the host sites for the FDI. Although at a disadvantage in the FDI, capital earned from domestic operations supported by low-cost labour and raw material advantages, provided the buffer that enabled these Indonesian firms to support asset seeking FDI activities.[8]

Firms in Taiwan have also exhibited an asset seeking motivation to investments. Among the more than 100 FDIs made by Taiwanese firms in the electronics industry in the early 1990s, about half went to developed countries and half to developing countries. When the motivation for an FDI was asset seeking, the location for the investment tended to be in developed countries. When the motivation for FDI by a Taiwanese firm was asset exploiting, the location for investment tended to be in developing countries.[9] This pattern hearkens back to Figure 6-1, where the optimality of any one decision parameter for an FDI relates to the conditions underlying the other decision parameters.

The emergence of asset seeking and asset exploitation behaviours by firms from developing and newly industrializing countries also foreshadows developments among large multinationals that we will discuss in the next two chapters. More and more, an individual subsidiary is being looked at as a contributor to the competitiveness of the multinational firm as a whole, not just as a multinational firm's agent for the efficient exploitation of ownership advantages. With that changing role, comes new motivations for foreign direct investment and new assessments for the success of an FDI. Profitability or a lower cost structure are not the only relevant outcomes. Activities that can sharpen the overall competitiveness of a multinational firm can be just as valued.

Summary

This chapter identifies the main characteristics of multinational firms. A good understanding of why multinational firms exist and the common characteristics of multinational firms can aid the development of an internationalization strategy. It can also enable a better competitive response to the challenges of multinational firms, whether competing against these firms on their home soil or in foreign markets.

The strategies of a multinational firm can be thought of as existing at two levels – the strategy for a multinational firm as a whole, and the strategy for a multinational firm's individual subsidiaries. A successful development of these strategies hinges on the competitive advantages of a multinational firm, whether that advantage stems from its proprietary resources, its multinational system, or its knowledge of international markets. A strategy should also take into account the advantages of each individual location of a subsidiary operation. Locational advantages can benefit an individual subsidiary in local competition, or the whole multinational network in global competition.

The strategy of competing against a multinational firm can be thought of as engagement with a multinational firm in the domestic front, or the battle may be waged more widely across multiple fronts in international markets. A small domestic firm is likely to be more concerned with the first, while the second tends to characterize competition between multinational firms. In either case, knowledge of the advantages, weaknesses and strategies of competitors will certainly aid competition. An understanding of the impetuses and advantages to multinationality provides the groundwork for developing this knowledge.

Notes

[1] We can find many new ideas in theories of multinational enterprise in work such as Mauro F. Guillén and Sandra L. Suárez, "The Institutional Environment of Multinational Activity," in S. Ghoshal and E. Westney, eds., *Organization Theory and the Multinational Corporation*, 2nd Ed. (New York: St. Martin's Press, 2001); William N. Cooke, "The Influence of Industrial Relations Factors on U.S. Foreign Direct Investment Abroad," *Industrial & Labor Relations Review*, 1997, Vol. 51, No. 1, pp. 3–17; Mauro F. Guillén, "Organized Labor's Images of Multinational Enterprise: Ideologies of Foreign Investment in Argentina, South Korea, and Spain," *Industrial & Labor Relations Review*, April 2000, Vol. 53, No. 3, pp. 419–442; J. Delacroix, "The European Subsidiaries of American Multinationals: An Exercise in Ecological Analysis," in Sumantra Ghoshal and D. Eleanor Westney, eds., *Organization Theory and the Multinational Corporation* (New York: St. Martin's Press, 1993), pp. 105–135; Yves L. Doz and C. K. Prahalad, "Managing DMNCs: A Search for a New Paradigm," in Sumantra Goshal and E. Eleanor Westney, eds., *Organization Theory and the Multinational Corporation* (New York: St. Martin's Press, 1993); Yves L. Doz and C.K. Prahalad, *The Multinational Mission: Balancing Local Demands and Global Vision* (New York: The Free Press, 1987); Mauro F. Guillén, "Structural Inertia, Imitation, and Foreign Expansion: South Korean Firms and Business Groups in China, 1987–1995," *Academy of Management Journal*, June 2001, Vol. 45, No. 3, pp. 509–526; Xavier Martin, Anand Swaminathan, and Will Mitchell, "Organizational Evolution in the Interorganizational Environment: Incentives and Constraints on International Expansion Strategy," *Administrative Science Quarterly*, 1998, Vol. 43, No. 3, pp. 566–601; John

M. Stopford and Louis T. Wells, Jr, *Managing the Multinational Enterprise: Organization of the Firm and Ownership of the Subsidiaries* (New York: Basic Books, Inc, 1972); D. Eleanor Westney, "Institutionalization Theory and the Multinational Corporation," in Sumantra Ghoshal and D. Eleanor Westney, eds., *Organization Theory and the Multinational Corporation* (New York: St. Martin's Press, 1993), pp. 53–76.

[2] Charles P. Kindleberger, *American Business Abroad: Six Lectures on Direct Investment* (New York and London: Yale University Press, 1969); Stephen H. Hymer, *International Operations of National Firms – A Study of Direct Foreign Investment* (Cambridge, MA: M.I.T. Press, 1976).

[3] Alan M. Rugman, *International Diversification and the Multinational Enterprise* (Lexington, MA: Heath Books, 1979); Alan M. Rugman, *New Theories of the Multinational Enterprise* (New York: St. Martin's Press, 1982); Peter, J. Buckley and Mark C. Casson, *The Future of Multinational Enterprise* (Basingstoke and London: MacMillan, 1976); Jean-François and Hennart, *A Theory of Multinational Enterprise* (Ann Arbor: The University of Michigan Press, 1982).

[4] Richard E. Caves, *Multinational Enterprise and Economic Analysis,* 2nd Ed. (Cambridge, MA: Cambridge University Press, 1996).

[5] Statements on the eclectic paradigm can be found in a number of publications of John H. Dunning. See, John H. Dunning, "Explaining Changing Patterns of International Production: In Defence of the Eclectic Theory," *Oxford Bulletin of Economics and Statistics*, 1977, Vol. 41, No. 4, pp. 269–295; John H. Dunning, "Toward an Eclectic Theory of International Production: Some Empirical Tests," *Journal of International Business Studies*, 1980, Vol. 11, No. 1, pp. 9–31; John H. Dunning, "The Eclectic Paradigm of International Production: A Restatement and Some Possible Extensions," *The Journal of International Business Studies*, Spring 1988, Vol. 19, pp. 1–31; John H. Dunning, *Explaining International Production* (London: Unwin Hyman, 1988); John H. Dunning, "The Theory of International Production," *International Trade*, edited by Khosrow Fatemi (New York: Taylor and Francis Inc, 1989); John H. Dunning, *Multinational Enterprises and the Global Economy* (Addison-Wesley Publishing Company: Don Mills, Ontario, 1993).

[6] See Chapter 2 for more on trade theory.

[7] Shige Makino, Chung-Ming Lau, and Rhy-Song Yeh, "Asset-exploitation Versus Asset-seeking: Implications for Location Choice of Foreign Direct Investment from Newly Industrialized Economies," *Journal of International Business Studies*, 2002, Vol. 33, No. 3, pp. 403–421.

[8] Don Lecraw, "Outward Investment by Indonesian Firms: Motivation and Effects," *Journal of International Business Studies*, 1993, Vol. 24, No. 3, pp. 589–600.

[9] Shige Makino, Chung-Ming Lau, and Rhy-Song Yeh, "Asset-exploitation versus Asset-seeking: Implications for Location Choice of Foreign Direct Investment from Newly Industrialized Economies," *Journal of International Business Studies,* 2002, Vol. 33, No. 3, pp. 403–421.

9 BUSINESS GROUPS

The foreign subsidiary and parent multinational firm relationship, as captured in a multinational enterprise, is just one way to organize business activities. The discussion in Chapter 8 outlined rationales for why we have seen this form of business organization emerge. As we move into international markets, we can encounter diverse forms of business organization, other than the multinational enterprise. One important form of business organization in many countries in Asia, and elsewhere in the world, is a business group.

A business group is a collection of companies affiliated by ownership, shared goals, cross-shareholdings, diversification and commonalities in organizational culture. The companies in a business group are diversified across a number of industries. Individual companies can be large in their own right, as can be a business group in the aggregate.

Business groups are common in many parts of the world. Business groups in South Korea are called chaebol, those in Japan are called horizontal keiretsu or kigyou shudan, some of the largest of which are descendents of the pre-World War II groups called zaibatsu. Business groups in Taiwan can be considered to be family-centered collections of common business activities. Setting Korean chaebol and Japanese keiretsu at the two ends of the centralization continuum, the management system of Taiwan's business groups can be located in the middle (see Box 9-1).[1] Business groups in Latin America are called Grupo Economicos, or grupos. Those in India go by the name of family-owned trading houses.

Not all large companies in Asia are business groups. The Hongs, or the large diversified companies that dominate many sectors of Hong Kong's economy, are not business groups. The Hongs have their roots in the trading companies created in Hong Kong in the 1800s. Swire Pacific (*www.swirepacific.com*), Jardine Matheson Ltd. (*www.jardine.com*), Hutchison Whampoa Ltd. (*www.hutchison-whampoa.com*), New World Development (*www.nwd.com.hk*) and CITIC Pacific Ltd. (*www.citicpacific.com*) were among the largest, most well-known and most internationalized of Hong Kong's large diversified Hongs. These companies operated in a number of diverse sectors, typically having operations in property, construction, manufacturing and services such as banking and retailing.

Box 9-1   A Taiwanese Business Group: The Formosa Plastics Group

Established over 40 years ago, the Formosa Plastics Group (*www.fpg.com.tw*) in Taiwan is made up of over 20 domestic companies, including Formosa Plastics Corporation (*www.fpc.com.tw*), Formosa Chemicals & Fibre Corporation (*www.fpcc.com.tw*) and Formosa Petrochemical Corporation. The Group also holds numerous overseas investments, and positions in large educational and medical organizations. Table 9-1 identifies the companies in these various areas of business.

The rapid growth of the Formosa Plastics Group began in the late 1950s. At this time, management in Formosa Plastics, the Group's earliest venture, found that sales of its key product, polyvinyl chloride (PVC), were stagnating. To overcome this problem, the company set up activities in a secondary market by forming Nan Ya Plastics Corporation (*www.npc.com.tw*). Nan Ya purchased the PVC resins made by Formosa Plastics, and used these resins to manufacture products such as PVC pipes, PVC film and plastic leathers. With the success of Nan Ya, Formosa Plastics next established the New Eastern Corporation as a tertiary production site. New Eastern Corp. manufactured final stage goods which included luggage, handbags, shoes and raincoats, with secondary materials purchased from Nan Ya. (see Figure 9-1).

With its success in the plastics industry, Formosa Plastics expanded into textiles in 1965, and later, into the electronics and information industries. In the 2000s, the Formosa Plastics Group continued to expand. In 2003, it was engaged in a wide range of businesses including oil refining, petrochemicals, plastic raw materials and the secondary processing of plastics, fibres and textiles, electronic materials, machinery, and transportation.

The organization of the Formosa Plastics Group is characterized by its emphasis on both upstream and downstream vertical integration, commodities, and efficient production. The founder and Chairman, YC Wang, is known for his close involvement in all the related businesses. Wang puts in 100-hour work weeks, and expects his executives to put in 70 hours and his production workers to put in 48 hours. Although the Group's key businesses, Formosa Plastics, Nan Ya Plastics and Formosa Chemicals and Fiber, are not affiliated, they are recognized as part of a system of vertical integration. The Wang family owns at least 20 per cent of each affiliate company's stock, and each of the companies holds a one per cent to four per cent stake in the other two. This status and affiliation has given the Formosa group strong economies of scale and consolidated its influence in the petrochemical industry in Taiwan.

Sources:
http://www.fpg.com.tw/html/eng/his.htm, 12 November 2003.
Gale Data Base, Business and Company Resource Centre – Historical Backgrounder.
Andrew Tanze, "Y.C. Wang Gets up very Early in the Morning," *Forbes*, 15 July 1985, Vol. 136, pp. 88–93.

The Hongs are not business groups because the diverse businesses of a Hong are folded into one legal entity that is listed on the Hang Seng exchange in Hong Kong, or on other exchanges. Subsidiary operations in a Hong can be legal entities, but the ownership and control structure is distinct, unlike in a business group where control and coordination among members in different sectors of the economy can come without high ownership.

In this sense, business groups are a fascinating form of industrial organization – control can be high, but ownership positions are often low. Within a business group, the company affiliation mechanisms and structure straddle both a market and an organizational, or hierarchical, means of coordinating activities. A business group is not just one big company, nor is it a large number

Table 9-1: **The Formosa Plastics Group**[1]

Domestic Companies	Overseas Companies	Educational and Medical Companies
Formosa Plastics Corp.	Formosa Plastics Marin Corp.	Chang Gung Memorial Hospital
Nan Ya Plastics Corp.	Formosa Plastics Corp., U.S.A.	Chang Gung University
Formosa Chemical & Fiber Copr.	Nan Ya Plastics Corp., U.S.A.	Chang Gung Institute of Nursing
Formosa Petrochemical Corp.	Nan Ya Plastics Corp., America	Ming Chi Institute of Technology
Formosa Heavy Industries Corp.	Inteplast Group, Ltd—INTEPLAST	
Formosa Komatsu Silicon Corp.	P.T. Indonesia Nan Ya Indah Plastics Corp.	
Formosa Teletek Corp.	J-M Manufacturing Co., Inc	
Formosa Plasma Display Corp.		
Hwa Ya Power Corp.		
Formosa Asahi Spandex Co., Ltd.		
Formosa Daikin Advanced Chemicals Co., Ltd.		
Yung Chia Chemical Industries Corp.		
MIZ Port Management Corp.		
PFG Fiber Glass Corp.		
Nan Ya Technology Corp.		
Nan Ya Printed Circuit Board Corp.		
Weng Fun Industrial Co.		
Tah Shi Spinning Corp.		
Formosa Taffeta Corp.		
Formosa Transport Corp.		
Formosa Plastics Maritime Corp.		
Chang Gung Biotechnology Corp.		
Formosa Technology Corp.		

Source: Adapted from *http://www.fpg.com.tw/html/eng/org.htm*, 10 November, 2003.

of companies acting together under coordinated market incentives. The organization of the companies in a business group falls somewhere in between these two.

The mechanisms for coordination in business groups bring to light the idea of networks. A business group is a very tangible form of business network. The mechanisms that align activities in business groups typify those that exist in less overt networks. Cross-shareholdings, personnel exchanges, cross-appointments of staff, regular scheduled meetings between senior executives in group-affiliated companies, and in some cases hierarchical relationship structures, each act as a network mechanism. The resultant network acts to facilitate control and develop knowledge conduits. Control is exerted over the scope of activities and strategy invoked by a group-affiliated

Figure 9-1:   The Vertical Structure of the Formosa Plastics Group

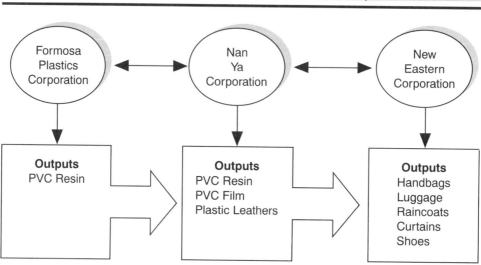

Source: Adapted from *http://www.fpg.com.tw/html/eng/org.htm*, 10 November 2003.

company. The conduit is one that permits knowledge and information to flow from one group-affiliated company to another, to perhaps enhance the overall competitiveness of each.

These latter two points are related to the three main questions we need to explore to understand how business groups influence the competitive landscape in Asia. These questions are:

1. What are business groups, and what are their main characteristics?
2. What is the rationale for the business group form of organization?
3. What are the strategic outcomes of business groups?

Business Groups – Characteristics

We have already defined a business group as a collection of companies that have legal independence, but are connected in other ways. These alternative connections include at least one, but not necessarily all, of the following: family ties, historical ties, cross-ownership, intra-group financing by a core bank, personnel exchanges and reciprocal trading agreements.

Business groups are common in many countries of the world, not just in Asia. Within Asia, business groups can be found in countries such as the Philippines, India, Indonesia, Malaysia, Japan and South Korea, to name a few. A few of the prominent business groups in these countries are outlined in Table 9-2, with profiles on business groups from several of these countries provided in the following sections.

Table 9-2:   Business Groups in Asia

Country	Type of Business Group	Examples of Companies	Website
India	Family-owned	Tata Group of Companies	www.tata.com
		Aditya Birla Group	www.adityabirla.com
		Reliance Industries Ltd.	www.ril.com
Indonesia	Business Groups	Berdikari Group	www.berdikari-pp.com
		PT. Indofood Sukses Makmur	www.indofood.co.id
		Bimantara Group	www.bimantara.co.id
		Lippo Group	www.lippo.co.id
		PT. Astra International TBK.	www.astra.co.id
		PT. Holdiko Perkasa	www.holdiko.com
Japan	Horizontal keiretsu	The Mitsubishi Companies	www.mitsubishi.com
		Sumitomo Group	www.sumitomo.gr.jp
		Mitsui & Co. Ltd	www.mitsui.co.jp
	Vertical keiretsu	Sony Corporation	www.sony.net
		Hitachi Ltd.	www.hitachi.com
		Kobe Steel, Ltd.	www.kobelco.co.jp
		Toshiba Corporation	www.toshiba.co.jp
		Fujitsu Ltd.	www.fujitsu.com
Malaysia	Business Groups	Renong Bhd	www.renong.com.my
		Multi-Purpose Holdings Bhd	www.mphb.com.my
		Pantai Holdings	www.pantai.com.my
		The Lion Group	www.lion.com.my
		Hong Leong Group Malaysia	www.hongleong.com
Philippines	Family Business Groups	Ayala Corporation	www.ayala-group.com
		JG Summit Holdings	www.jgsummit.com.ph
		SM Group of Companies	www.smprime.com.ph
		Benpres Holdings	www.benpres-holding.com
		Andres Soriano Corp.	
South Korea	Chaebol	Hyundai Corp.	www.hyundaicorp.com
		Samsung Corp.	www.samsungcorp.com
		LG Group	www.lg.co.kr
		Daewoo International Corp.	www.daewoo.com
Thailand	Family-owned	Siam Cement Group	www.siamcement.com
		Boon Rawd Trading Co, Ltd.	www.boonrawd.co.th
		Thonburi Automotive Group.	www.thonburi.com

Horizontal Keiretsu

Horizontal keiretsu (keiretsu) emerged from the pre-World War II family-controlled groups called zaibatsu. The zaibatsu had to change their structure after the 1947 institution of Japan's anti-monopoly law made holding companies illegal. The keiretsu emerged after the disbanding of the zaibatsu, where instead of a central company at the centre of a group, there were typically two or three companies: a major bank, a trading company and a major manufacturing company.

A keiretsu intercorporate alliance is defined formally as 'institutionalized relationships among firms based on localized networks of dense transactions, a stable framework for exchange, and patterns of periodic collective action'.[2] The number of firms formally involved in a keiretsu is often large with extensions across most sectors in the economy (see Table 9-3 and Figure 9-2).

Table 9-3: **Size of Japanese Horizontal Keiretsu (1996)**

Group	Number of Companies	Sales (Yen billion)	Number of employees
Mitsubishi	187	40,582	397,000
Sumitomo	173	41,846	425,000
Fuyo	154	34,519	363,000
Mitsui	154	29,864	187,000
DKB	135	44,012	385,000
Sanwa	124	33,062	256,000
Tokai	42	10,530	59,000
IBJ	31	3,018	52,000

Source: Dodwell Marketing Consultants, *Industrial groupings in Japan: The anatomy of the keiretsu,* 12th Ed. (Minato-ku, Tokyo, Japan: The Consultants, 1996-1997).

Figure 9-2: **The Mitsubishi Inner Group of Companies**

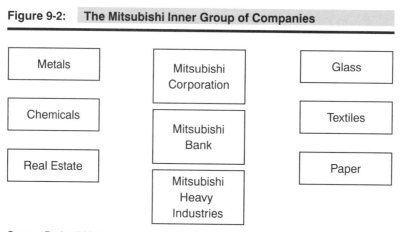

Source: Dodwell Marketing Consultants, *Industrial groupings in Japan: The anatomy of the keiretsu,* 12th Ed. (Minato-ku, Tokyo, Japan: The Consultants, 1996-1997).

The linking mechanisms in a keiretsu achieve integration across group members. Firms in a keiretsu are formally linked together by formal mechanisms, and informally by a patterned series of relationships developed over a long period of time. The formal mechanisms include:

- Cross shareholdings of stock
- Exchanges of personnel across member firms
- Formation of a president's club to hold regular meetings
- Joint investment in new or existing firms by member firms
- Bank financing to member firms by the keiretsu bank
- Trading transactions between member firms, sometimes transacted by the keiretsu's trading company.

The level of integration in a keiretsu achieved by these mechanisms is not as strict an institutional arrangement as can be found in a large, multinational firm. Rather, the functional integration in a keiretsu more closely approximates a market, with competition found within the keiretsu for the supply and purchase of intermediate products. The coordination of these functions is achieved via the intermediary functions performed by the trading company, and market opportunities arise for keiretsu member firms from the vertical or horizontal alignment of activities. For example, in large foreign investments, such as those in primary or extractive industries, the opportunities for profiting from the venture extend beyond the extractive activity. The firm involved in the actual extractive activity may not directly profit from the venture itself, but opportunities for profit for other keiretsu members are generated by new demands for plants and equipment, and technical and marketing assistance. Opportunities to capitalize on spillovers such as these arise from the linkages in the keiretsu and provide members with gains otherwise unattainable without group membership.

The keiretsu structure can offer member firms a number of advantages in their foreign activities. For small-sized and medium-sized manufacturing firms, keiretsu affiliation provides a member firm with the operational benefits of vertical integration: a steady and secure source of input supply, priced lower because of the large-scale of production of the supplier, and economies of scale in the distribution of output. A foreign subsidiary also has access to technological developments generated by keiretsu firms in Japan, and access to credit on favourable terms from other member companies involved in finance.

Because of these benefits, similar patterns are observed in international activities as in domestic activities. For example, trading company and steel manufacturers relationships are of the same order of importance in domestic and international transactions. Overseas business relationships follow established patterns of domestic relationships, with the nature of these relationships based on reciprocal trading. More than three-quarters of Japanese transplant automobile assembly plants and suppliers in the United States determined the location of their operations based upon the need to maintain close relationships, and to be situated in close proximity to a major Japanese customer. Other considerations, such as low labour costs, tax rates or subsidies had lesser influence on the choice of location.[3]

The keiretsu structure is a notable feature of Japanese business activity even in international markets. The inter-corporate alliances found in a keiretsu have been adapted to the varied conditions found in different host country markets, and there is no apparent decline in the use of these structures. While external pressures endure to change the keiretsu aspect of Japanese business, little evidence exists to indicate that change is happening either on domestic or international fronts. Hence, keiretsu remain a persistent aspect of Japanese business organization.

Anatomy of Chaebol

Chaebol share characteristics with Japanese horizontal keiretsu just as chaebol share characteristics with business groups in general. Chaebol are large business groups situated in South Korea. Chaebol are family-owned and family-managed. Examples of Chaebol include Samsung (*www.samsung.com*), Hyundai (*www.hyundai.com*), Lucky-Goldstar (LG) (*www.lg.co.kr*) and Daewoo (*www.daewoo.com*). These four chaebol are among the most recognized because they collectively accounted for about 60 per cent of all exports from South Korea and about a third of all South Korean companies' revenues. Chaebol in South Korea, however, are not limited to these four. In the 1990s, there were more than 50 chaebol in South Korea, with the top 30 accounting for at least 50 per cent of Korea's GDP.

As with other business groups, chaebol coordinate a series of activities of member companies using a number of mechanisms. In chaebol, these mechanisms include cross-shareholding among members, business interdependence among members, shared brands, and think tanks or corporate research groups, that contribute to the development of each member firm's businesses. For example, the Samsung Group of companies (*www.samsung.com*), including, among other companies, Samsung Electro-Mechanics (*www.sem.samsung.com*), Samsung Corning (*www.samsungcorning.com*), and Samsung Networks (*www.samsungnetworks.com*) all share the same corporate identity and logo in order to strengthen competitiveness.[4] These mechanisms also provide group members with flexibility in moving and exchanging capital, technology and personnel among member companies, which also work as a means to tighten the linkages across companies.

Chaebol share another characteristic with business groups. Member companies constitute a wide degree of horizontal diversification. In the case of chaebol, growth into new business areas has often been funded by issuing debt. A consequence of this is that after the onset of the Asian financial crisis a number of chaebol faced critical financial constraints. The size and financial difficulties faced by chaebol led many to associate their poor performance with the subsequent poor performance of the South Korean economy: 'After football, kicking the chaebol has become the favorite sport of South Koreans, who blame the conglomerates for dragging the country to the brink of default.'[5]

The Korean government stepped in at this point to arrange for a reduction in product line offerings by several chaebol. As examples, Samsung took over Daewoo's electronics business in exchange for Samsung's automobiles business. LG handed over its semi-conductor activities to Hyundai.

The Asian financial crisis in 1997 led to a considerable number of reforms in the chaebol structure. Some of the reforms were aimed at increasing the accountability of the owners of the chaebol to shareholders. The complicated series of cross-shareholdings in a chaebol has provided the family at the centre of a chaebol with a degree of control over member chaebol companies that apparently exceeds the level of investment in each. With seemingly small equity holdings, control remains concentrated on a few individuals' hands.

Government reforms have addressed this issue by requiring all listed companies to appoint external directors and to establish auditing committees. These structures provide an outside presence on the board of directors and other monitors of a firm's functions. The Korean government has also encouraged chaebol to sell shares to foreign investors, under the idea that foreign investors are more activist and more likely to raise voices about the accountability of owner-managers to minority shareholders.

A consequence of government and chaebol initiated reforms can be found by looking at the LG group (see Table 9-4). The LG group began as a chemicals company in 1947. It made one of its first business diversifications when it went into the electronics business in 1958. The 1960s and 1970s was a fast growth period in which LG undertook substantial diversification. In 1995, LG gained its current moniker opting for the short form of its original name, Lucky-Goldstar.

Table 9-4:   Organization of LG Group (2000)

Business Area	Businesses
Chemicals & Energy	LG Chemical Investment Ltd, LG Chem Ltd, LG Household & Health Care Ltd, LG Petrochemical Co., Ltd, LG Siltron Inc., LG MMA Corp, LG Down Polycarbonate Ltd, LG-Caltex Oil Corp., LG-Caltex Gas Co., Ltd, KukDong City Gas Co., Ltd, LG Energy Co., Ltd, LG Power Co., Ltd, Seorabul City Gas Co., Ltd, Haeyang City Gas Co., Ltd
Electronics and Telecommunications	LG Electronics Inc., LG N-Sys Inc., LG Philips LCD Co. Ltd, LGIBM PC Ltd, LG Innotek Co., Ltd, LG Micron Ltd, LG TeleCom Ltd, DACOM Corp., Dacom IN Corp., Dacom System Technologies, Dacom Multimedia Internet Inc., DACOM Crossing Corp., Korea Internet Data Center Inc., Customer Interaction Center Korea, Inc., SIMMANI Inc., LG CNS Co., Ltd, LG Industrial Systems Co., Ltd, LG Cable Ltd, LG-Nikko Copper Inc.
Finance	LG Investment & Securities Co., Ltd, LG Investment Trust Management Co., Ltd, LG Futures Co., Ltd, LG Card Co., Ltd, Bumin Savings & Finance Corp.
Services	LG International Corp., LG Engineering & Construction Corp., Han Moo Development Co., Ltd, LG Mart Co., Ltd, LG Department Store Co. Ltd, LG Home Shopping Inc., LG Ad Inc., LG Sports Ltd, LG Economic Research Institute, LG Academy

By the year 2000, LG was a USD81 billion company. It had more than 50 affiliated subsidiaries, 300 offices and 150,000 employees. It had made substantial inroads into international markets in its four core business areas: chemicals and energy, electronics and telecommunications, finance and services.

In the early 2000s, LG was yet undergoing restructuring by moving to a holding company structure which would fold its chemicals, electronics, telecommunications and services business under the umbrella of one holding company, as this form of company becomes recognized under Korean law. The objective of this process is to provide a separation of strategic and operating decisions, and provide a separation of ownership and control. Corporate governance issues should become more transparent, which would benefit minority shareholders as they could obtain better information about each constituent company's performance. Whether this restructuring process will continue through the remainder of the decade depends in part on how well the restructured chaebol companies perform.

Rationale For Business Groups

Business groups are a common form of organization, that much is clear. A more difficult issue is captured by the question: 'Will business groups continue to proliferate as globalization and the pace of technological innovation continue at rapid rates?' Part of the answer to this question rests in the rationale for why business groups exist.

The rationale for business groups' existence rests in comparisons of performance of business-group affiliated firms. In general, research on the comparative performance of companies has found that group-affiliated companies have better performance than non-group-affiliated companies, in countries such as India. In Japan, group-affiliated companies have a better performance than non-group companies along dimensions such as the reduction in risk, or the variability in performance in companies across a number of years. In South Korea, group-affiliated companies tend to have superior innovation performance.

India's Business Groups and Firm Performance

What could account for the fact that India's business-group affiliated firms tend to perform better than non-group-affiliated firms? To answer this question, we need to consider the environmental context of business groups in developing economies such as India.

As with any analysis of the environmental context, we need to look at the state of the national institutional environment. Recall that a national institutional environment defines the conditions under which business transactions occur. Dimensions of the national institutional environment can exhibit strengths that facilitate the efficiency and effectiveness of business transactions. Dimensions can exhibit weaknesses that impede business transactions.[6]

Where dimensions of the national institutional environment such as capital markets, labour markets, product markets and regulatory frameworks are weak, we have a situation in which firms in the nation must incur additional costs and risks and bear inefficiencies in transactions (see Table 9-5). Weaknesses in the institutional environment can strike all firms equally, unless the strategy of a firm can cushion it from the negative performance effects of weak institutions. One such strategy is to replace national institutions that are weak with an internally-developed function. For a small firm, the replacement costs can easily exceed the costs imposed by inefficiencies that accompany the weak institution. Even for a large firm, the costs of a grin-and-bear-it strategy are likely to be considerably lower than an institutional replacement strategy.

Unlike a single company, a business group, which is a collection of a considerable number of large and small firms, can have the size to justify an internal replacement for an institutional weakness. For example, in India several business groups own their own power supply companies to ensure that business is not hampered by power failures. Recently, these businesses have been given the freedom to sell excess power in the open market.[7]

For example, if labour market institutions are weak, a business group can establish labour markets for the exchange and development of human resources. Where movement across companies in an open market is impeded by restrictive labour laws, poor flows of information, or mistrust about qualifications and educational attainments, a business group structure can make for an efficient internal market. With a substantial number of companies in a business group, there are a corresponding number of opportunities for personnel to move to be at the best position for their qualifications.

Table 9-5:   **Institutional Strengths by Country**

Institutional Feature	United States	Japan	India
Market for Finance	Equity-focused Disclosure rules Active market for corporate control	Bank-focused Interlocking Investments	Illiquid equity markets Weak monitoring by bureaucrats
Market for Labour	Many business schools Consulting firms Certifications	Few business schools In-house training	Few business schools Little in-house training
Market for Products	Enforced liability laws Activist consumers Efficient information dissemination	Enforced liability laws Few activist consumers Efficient information dissemination	Limited enforcement of liability laws No activist consumers Little information dissemination
Government Regulation	Low regulation Low corruption	Moderate regulation Low corruption	High regulation High corruption

Source: Adapted from Tarun Khanna and Krishna Palepu, "Is Group Affiliation Profitable in Emerging Markets? An Analysis of Diversified Indian Business Groups," *Journal of Finance*, 2000, Vol. 55, No. 2, pp. 867–892.

Further, a training school, such as a management development programme, can be established by the business group to improve the skills of managers in group-affiliated companies. These training schools and services can be very specialized within the group. In the Indian business group, Tata, the air-conditioning and refrigeration group, Voltas Ltd ACnR (*www.voltasacnr.com*), of Voltas Ltd. (*www.voltas.com*), both enterprises associated with the Tata Group (*www.tata.com*), provides heating, ventilation and air-conditioning training to existing and new Voltas engineers.[8]

A business group can take similar initiatives to replace other forms of market inefficiencies or institutional voids in areas in which there is an institutional weakness. Internal markets can replace external markets for intermediate goods or raw materials. Internal capital markets can replace external capital markets, when the market for capital is plagued by a poor flow of information or poor corporate accountability. Weaknesses in capital markets can prevent entrepreneurial initiatives from receiving needed funding, thus strangling growth and new opportunities. If a business group has an internal market for capital, it can bypass the constrictions on capital flows, and internally fund entrepreneurial initiatives with good growth potential. A case in point is Mitsubishi Corporation (*www.mitsubishicorp.com*). Mitsubishi Corp. owns MIC Capital (*www.miccapital.com*), a financial services company that makes private equity investments in the Americas to generate financial returns and strategic benefits for its parent company.[9]

The internalization of each of these markets provides an opportunity for a business group to bypass market inefficiencies. The cost of bypassing market inefficiencies is not zero, and it is not inconsequential. The relevant point is not the absolute cost of market replacement but the relative cost. If internal costs are less than market costs, then the institution can be internalized.

Interestingly, this perspective on the performance of business groups has parallels with our discussion of the rationale for the multinational firm. A multinational firm emerges as a consequence of its ability to bypass costs for the trans-border, market-based exchange of its proprietary resources, by internalizing the market via an FDI. A business group can do the same for market inefficiencies that emerge as a result of institutional weaknesses. The result of replacing a market transaction with an international transaction is the same in both case: a firm in countries such as India and South Korea[10] can gain an advantage from reducing the costs of these transactions.

Keiretsu and Firm Performance

Next we can move to the cases of Japanese companies. In the case of Japanese companies, the performance benefit of business group affiliation comes from a moderation of fluctuations in performance. Performance moderation means that a firm is less likely to record a year or years of exceptional profit or a year/years of exceptional losses. This moderation in profits comes from the ability of group-affiliated companies to extend financial assistance. This ability is a consequence of the cross-shareholdings and the common central sources of financing that come with being a part of a horizontal keiretsu.[11]

Figure 9-3 displays the profit moderation effect graphically. This figure shows the performance of independent firms in Japan, and group-affiliated firms (members of horizontal keiretsu) in Japan. The lines depicting the performance for each show how performance in one year is related to performance in the next year. In Figure 9-3, the two years of performance comparison are 2002 and 2003.[12]

As can be seen in the figure, the plot for independent firms has a steeper slope than that for group-affiliated firms. This steeper slope indicates that if an independent firm had high (low) profitability in 2002, it was likely to have high (low) profitability in 2003. Meanwhile, for a group-affiliated firm high (low) profitability in 2002, was less strongly correlated with high (low) profitability in 2003. The reason for this weaker correlation is that a group-affiliated firm has a variety of means of transferring unusual profits (losses), outside of the firm, to other member firms. Hence, unusual profits of a member firm will be spread around group members, or losses will be jointly borne by group members.

This moderation in accounting profitability means that Japanese firms that are part of horizontal keiretsu are less profitable than unaffiliated firms but can recover more quickly from periods of poor financial performance. This moderation comes from a group objective to make resource allocations according to need, and the long-term collective performance of the keiretsu in aggregate. To implement this, profits move from strong member firms to weak member firms, reducing the risk associated with the reporting of any one year's performance numbers, while facilitating the reporting of year-on-year improvements in sales.

Figure 9-3: **Group Affiliation and Profit Moderation**

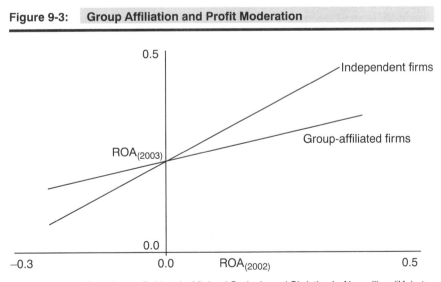

Source: Adapted from James R. Lincoln, Michael Gerlach, and Christina L. Ahmadjian, "Keiretsu Networks and Corporate Performance in Japan," *American Sociological Review*, 1996, Vol. 61, No. 1, pp. 67–95.

These performance benefits do not emerge through a series of haphazard, sporadic interventions by the group on a member firm. Instead, keiretsu tend to operate as a network organization, in which collective action can be observed at the level of financial performance. This collective rationality anticipates the goals of multinational networks, as outlined in the concluding parts of Chapter 10. Individual companies in a keiretsu network have some freedom to chart their own direction. However, the charting is done in the context of movements of the fleet of companies in the keiretsu network. Individual company action is thus taken with explicit recognition on the implications of an action on the keiretsu as a whole.

Although the ability to spread profits and losses among all member firms can provide a group with advantages, it also creates risks to these firms and to the shareholders of these firms. One such risk is that member firms are insulated from market conditions, and that profits earned by one member, will be used to sustain growth into unprofitable and non-sustainable businesses of other member firms. This problem plagued many of the chaebol through the mid-1990s. Their high debt levels, and poor levels of profitability in many member firms, placed these business groups in dire financial conditions at the onset of the Asian Financial Crisis in 1997. The result for many of these chaebol was extensive corporate restructuring to make decision-making more transparent, and accountable to shareholders, with profitability, not growth as one of the overarching goals of the business group (Box 9-2).

Chaebol and Firm Performance

Chaebol, along with independent South Korean firms, did experience considerable financial challenges in the latter half of the 1990s. Even though financial performance was poor, a different form of performance benefit emerged for group-affiliated companies. This performance benefit was the superior innovation performance of chaebol members.[13]

Innovation performance is particularly important to firms in Asia in competing in the 21st century. As Asian economies continue to progress up the ranks of country wealth by aggregate and per capita GDP numbers, the focus of these economies moves increasingly to an innovation stage. Given this environmental transition, companies in Asia will need to innovate in ways that provide advantages, as marked by patenting activity. As we can see in Table 9-6, Korean chaebol have been instrumental in developing South Korea's domestic strengths in innovation, unlike in other Asian countries where small and medium-sized firms, such as in Taiwan, or large multinational firms, as in Singapore, dominate patenting activity.

Why do we see these patterns in innovation performance? The answer rests in two strategic consequences of business group affiliation. A business group can stimulate innovation in the same way in can augment the performance of its member firms – it can replace institutional infrastructures necessary for innovation that are otherwise absent from a national institutional environment. A business group can constrain innovation, however, by creating a barrier to the

Box 9-2   Restructuring in Chaebol

In 1997, a survey by the Central Bank of Korea found that 21 of the 39 largest chaebol were refocusing investment on their core businesses, and 23 were reducing operating expenses. Samsung was one of the first companies that began to implement restructuring initiatives, such as slashing salaries and eliminating guaranteed pay raises, to cut costs. At the time, Mika Sarkkinen, spokesman for the Samsung Group stated 'We are getting ready for the worst. We are taking some pretty active measurements to increase our competitiveness.'

In addition to financial restructuring, investors in the late 1990s were calling for the chaebols to establish a stronger performance ethic. Some believed that strong family ties led the chaebol to overrule sound management judgment in order to follow family tradition. The chaebol began to respond to these external pressures. In 1998, the government and some of the larger chaebols agreed to restructuring plans aimed at improving transparency. This included the publishing of better accounts, appointing outside directors, making chairmen legally accountable, and listening to the concerns of minority shareholders.

Implementation of these plans, however, was slow. It was not until 2000, that LG Group announced the reorganization of its two holding companies into a single holding company to improve transparency. Kang Yu-sig, Chief Restructuring Officer stated that with the changes the 'stakes of LG's top shareholders, including group chairman Koo Bon-moo, will be limited to the holding company, while all holding-company affiliates will be independently run by board members and professional managers to increase managerial transparency.'

Around the same period, Hyundai announced plans to concentrate on its core business by cutting its number of companies to 28, from a high of 63 in 1997, and focusing on as few as five businesses. The focus on restructuring and transparency has continued into 2003. South Korea's new president, Roh Moo-hyun, was elected in part because his promise to reform the chaebol. The indictment of ten senior executives from the SK Group (*www.sk.com*) in early 2003 for inflating profits by 1.5 million won (USD1.2 billion) indicates that pressures to reform have been continuing as we approach the mid-2000s.

Sources:

Michael Zielenziger, "Samsung Group Tightens Its Belt," *Knight Ridder/Tribune News Service*, 28 November 1997.

Yuji Akaba, Florian Budde, and Jungkiu Choi, "Restructuring South Korea's Chaebol," *The McKinsey Quarterly*, Autumn 1998, No. 4, p. 68.

"The Chaebol Spurn Change," *The Economist (US)*, 22 July 2000, Vol. 356, No. 8180, p. 59.

"As Chaebol are Pressured to Reform, Many Consider Forming Holding Companies," *Korea Herald*, 6 July 2000.

"The Chaebol Spurn Change," *The Economist (US)*, 22 July 2000, Vol. 356, No. 8180, p. 59.

"Chaebol Trouble; Business in South Korea," *The Economist (US)*, 15 March 2003, Vol. 366, No. 8315, p. 78.

entry of small, entrepreneurial firms, and thereby inhibit the introduction of new ideas and skills into an economy.[14]

Innovation is a complex topic. There is no handbook that describes how a firm can innovate successfully. Nevertheless, we do generally know that for a firm to innovate it requires access to adequate financing, talented and skilled employees and technology. As with any input, a firm can gain access to financing, employees or technology through a market interface. It can transact with another party to purchase technology, hire employees, or secure capital. But, as we also know, markets seldom work perfectly, and in many cases imperfections in markets make the cost of transactions high.

Table 9-6:   Domestic Patenting Activity by Investor Type

Economy	Period	Multinational Firms	Business Group Firms	Private Individuals	Other Domestic Firms
Taiwan	1970–79	2.9%	0.0%	87.7%	9.4%
	1990–99	1.9%	3.5%	59.0%	35.6%
South Korea	1970–79	14.7%	2.9%	69.1%	13.2%
	1990–99	0.8%	80.7%	6.8%	11.7%
India	1970–79	54.5%	0.6%	24.7%	20.1%
	1990–99	29.6%	11.1%	18.3%	41.9%
Hong Kong	1970–79	26.1%	—	45.5%	28.4%
	1990–99	16.6%	—	30.7%	52.7%
Singapore	1970–79	50.0%	—	43.3%	6.7%
	1990–99	45.7%	—	9.6%	44.7%
China	1970–79	14.5%	—	76.8%	8.7%
	1990–99	17.2%	—	40.1%	42.7%

Source: See Ishtiaq P. Mahmood and Jasjit Singh, "Technological Dynamism in Asia," *Research Policy*, Vol. 32, Iss. 6, pp. 1031–1050.

If markets are sufficiently bad, then a firm will face considerable difficulty in securing access to the capital, people and knowledge it requires to pursue innovation. In such a setting, a business group can exploit its internal sources of financing to fund innovation attempts, its size to develop internal training programmes, and its reputation to secure access to technology. Each of these steps can help a business group amass resources necessary for innovation that are otherwise too costly for an individual firm to acquire when institutions are weak. The consequence of this is that innovation performance can be higher for business group affiliated firms, than for non-affiliated firms. These advantages for business groups are most pronounced when the group is large in a particular sector of the economy, and can bear the costs of replacing the absent institutions that support market-based exchanges.

Strategic Outcomes of Business Groups

The main strategic outcome for a business group affiliated firm is its heightened performance based on advantages gained from the internalization of activities that are costly to undertake in the market. This efficiency gain, however, is not the only advantage that comes from business group affiliation.

Internationalization and Member Advantages

The affiliation itself can provide an advantage to a firm. This advantage can emerge in terms of the profit subsidiary effect we discussed for Japanese firms. It can emerge in terms of a secure and stable source of inputs or outputs for member firms. In an international business setting, it can emerge as a unique motivation for the internationalization of group-affiliated firms, that would otherwise be at a disadvantage when competing in a foreign market.

Recall that a firm usually requires an ownership advantage to undertake a foreign direct investment. Not all firms, however, possess the brand, reputation, technology or knowledge advantages that can support internationalization. In many instances, the lack of an ownership advantage can forestall a firm's internationalization. In the case of group affiliated firms, however, this traditional form of ownership advantages can be absent, even among internationalizing firms.

The reason for this is that the group affiliation provides the advantage. When leading group-affiliated firms go abroad, weaker member firms can follow to replicate domestic relationships in international markets. As an example, if Toyota establishes an automotive assembly plant in North America, other members of Toyota's vertical keiretsu can also set up a subsidiary in North America. The motivation for these supplier firms to follow Toyota is to continue the domestic supply relationship in this new market. In this way, production networks in Japan's vertical keiretsu have been replicated in North America by Japanese firms. These same supplier networks, as founded on vertical keiretsu networks, have also been replicated in Asia.

Horizontal keiretsu firms use a similar strategy. When the large general trading companies such as Sumitomo Corp. (*www.sumitomocorp.co.jp*) and Mitsubishi Corp. (*www.mitsubishi.com*) go overseas, these companies often set up joint ventures with other companies from the same horizontal keiretsu. Mitsui & Co. (*www.mitsui.co.jp*) is involved in almost 100 subsidiaries in China. Many of these investments are in the textile industry and involve joint ownership with Toray Industries (*www.toray.co.jp*), a member of the Mitsui keiretsu and a manufacturer of synthetic fibres. In one more complicated example, Mitsui & Co., Toray Industries and Mitsui Toatsu Chemicals Inc. (*www.mitsui-chem.co.jp*) each have a 17 per cent share subsidiary in Shanghai, China called Shanghai Mitsui Plastics Compounds Ltd.

An important result of these chains of investments is that Japanese firms have become an important part of the competitive landscape in many Asian companies. If a foreign-investing firm fails to consider the state of Japanese competitors when entering markets in Thailand, Singapore or Malaysia, for example, the entry is more likely not to be successful. The chaebol from South Korea are also posed to become significant competitors in countries such as China, as Taiwanese firms have already become in China, and are becoming in other Asian countries such as Viet Nam.

Domestic Market Competition and Member Advantages

Aside from international competition, there is also the issue of competing against business group affiliated firms in their home markets. There are a number of challenges to this form of competition, many of which are also typified by competing against large, dominant firms in their home markets.

One of the more pronounced competitive advantages of a business group in its home market is its ability to erect barriers to entry for foreign firms to enter the market. This barrier to entry comes from the vertical nature of relationships in many business groups.

Vertical relationships are those found between buyer and supplier firms in an industry. In a business group, manufacturing firms are often linked to consumers by group-affiliated firms that act as wholesalers, distributors and retailers. The wholesalers, distributors and retailers in this vertical chain can, and often do, provide preferred access to the distribution channel to member firms from the same group. At the same time, the firms involved in the distribution chain can discriminate against other firms, such as foreign entrants, and thereby introduce a formidable barrier to entry.

These vertical relationships have created a real barrier to entry for foreign firms contemplating competition in Japan. As an example of the types of barriers that a firm can face, take the case of the electronics industry in Japan. Hitachi is one of the dominant firms in the electronics industry in Japan. Hitachi has a number of firms involved in its sales distribution network in Japan (Figure 9-4).

Figure 9-4:   Hitachi's Sales-Distribution Keiretsu

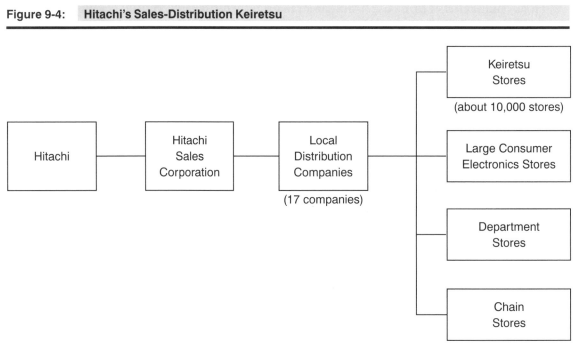

Source: Adapted from Shige Makino, *A note on the Japanese Keiretsu*, Case No. 9A92G008, Ivey Management Services, Richard Ivey School of Business, University of Western Ontario.

The vertical chain of relationships in Hitachi's sales keiretsu is not unique to Hitachi. Other electronics companies, such as Matsushita Electric Ind, have a similar system of sales and distribution relationships. Companies outside of the electronics and manufacturing sectors likewise have a similar arrangement. One such company is Kirin Breweries.

There are several types of companies in the Kirin keiretsu: beverage producers, food producers, service sector firms, agribusiness companies and restaurants, among others (Figure 9-5). The vertical linkages between these companies can impede foreign entry attempts. The result is that foreign entrants in the beverage sector often seek partnerships with Kirin. When Seagrams entered Japan, it engaged in a joint venture with Kirin. Beer producers Anheuser Busch and Heineken N.V. likewise used a joint venture with Kirin for entry, respectively forming the Budweiser Japan and the Heineken Japan joint ventures.

Although the distribution keiretsu have been a dominant part of business in Japan for decades, their prominence has been declining in recent years. Retail stores affiliated with keiretsu tend to charge high prices, which has opened the door to competition from discount retailers. New competition has reduced sales in keiretsu stores, which are also hampered by a higher cost structure. Keiretsu stores tend to stock shelves based on the availability of products from the manufacturer, not based on sales demand. As a consequence, inventory carrying costs are high, and product development efforts by the manufacturer are hampered. Even so, the barriers erected by these sales distribution networks are still a substantial barrier to competition by foreign entrants.

Figure 9-5:   The Kirin Brewery Group (1996)

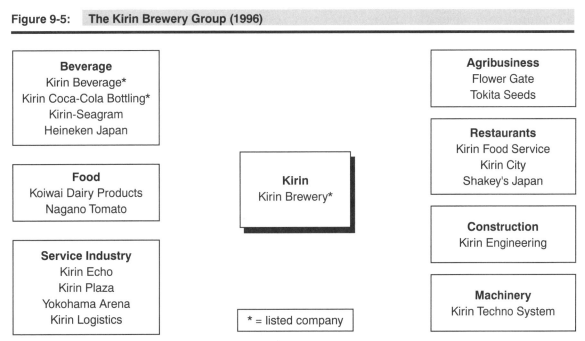

Source: Dodwell Marketing Consultants, *Industrial groupings in Japan: The anatomy of the keiretsu,* 12th Ed. (Minato-ku, Tokyo, Japan: The Consultants, 1996-1997).

Summary

This chapter identifies the characteristics of multinational firms and business groups. A joint understanding of why multinational firms exist and why business groups exist, combined with knowledge about the common characteristics of multinational firms and business groups, can aid the development of an internationalization strategy. It can also enable a better competitive response to the challenges of multinational firms, and business groups, whether competing against these firms on their home soil or in foreign markets.

The strategies of a multinational firm can be thought of as existing at two levels – the strategy for a multinational firm as a whole, and the strategy for a multinational firm's individual subsidiaries. A successful development of these strategies hinges on the competitive advantages of a multinational firm, whether that advantage stems from its proprietary resources, its multinational system, or its knowledge of international markets. A strategy should also take into account the advantages of each individual location of a subsidiary operation. Locational advantages can benefit an individual subsidiary in local competition, or the whole multinational network in global competition.

The strategy of competing against a multinational firm can be thought of as engagement with a multinational firm in the domestic front, or the battle may be waged more widely across multiple fronts in international markets. A small domestic firm is likely to be more concerned with the first, while the second tends to characterize competition between multinational firms. In either case, knowledge of the advantages, weaknesses and strategies of competitors will certainly aid competition. An understanding of the impetuses and advantages to multinationality provides the groundwork for developing this knowledge.

Along a similar vein, the strategic implication of business groups needs to be considered on both home and international fronts. The size and industrial scope of business groups means that their affiliated firms enjoy substantial competitive advantages from potentially low cost financing, barriers to entry, preferred networks of suppliers and buyers and good reputation effects. The result of these advantages is that business group affiliated firms tend to be superior competitors compared to independent domestic counter-parts. A challenge to business groups is not only to contend with foreign competition but to see if the advantages of business group affiliation can be extended to overseas markets.

Japanese firms are leading the way in this regard, with the formation of the same industrial networks from Japan in foreign countries. South Korean and Taiwanese business groups are engaging in similar strategies, particularly in their foreign investments in Asia. Competitors in the region must be aware of and able to respond to the competitive challenges posed by the international operations of internationalized business group firms.

At this point, it bears reiteration that the formulation and implementation of an effective international strategy begins with a good understanding of the context. In this case, the contexts are a multinational enterprise and business groups: types of organizations that take unique forms in different parts of the world, but are prominent in world markets.

Notes

[1] Chi-Nien Chung and Ishtiaq P. Mahmood, *Chandler Revisited: Interface between Strategy and Structure during Institutional Transition*, Korea University, September 2003.

[2] Michael L. Gerlach, *Alliance capitalism: The social organization of Japanese business* (Berkeley, CA: University of California Press, 1992), p. 3. See also Michael L. Gerlach, "Business Alliances and the Strategy of the Japanese Firm," *California Management Review*, 1987, Vol. 30, No. 1, pp. 126–142.

[3] Richard Florida and Martin Kenney, "Transplanted Organizations: The Transfer of Japanese Industrial Organization to the U.S.," *American Sociological Review*, 1991, Vol. 56, No. 3, pp. 381–398.

[4] *http://www.samsung.com/AboutSAMSUNG/CompanyProfile/CorporateIdentity/index.htm*, 14 November 2003.

[5] "The Chaebol in Denial," *The Economist (US)*, 24 January 1998, Vol. 346, No. 8052, p. 66.

[6] For more on this particular area of business group performance, please see the following articles: Tarun Khanna and Krishna Palepu, "Why Focused Strategies May be Wrong for Emerging Markets," *Harvard Business Review*, 1997, Vol. 75, No. 4, pp. 41–51; Tarun Khanna and Krishna Palepu, "Is Group Affiliation Profitable in Emerging Markets? An Analysis of Diversified Indian Business Groups," *Journal of Finance*, 2000, Vol. 55, No. 2, pp. 867–892; Tarun Khanna and Krishna Palepu, "The Future of Business Groups in Emerging Markets: Long-run Evidence from Chile," *Academy of Management Journal*, 2000, Vol. 43, No. 3, pp. 268–285.

[7] Adapted from presentation given by Christian Luetkehaus, Managing Director, Portelet, 2 October 2003.

[8] *http://www.voltasacnr.com/training.htm*, 18 November 2003.

[9] *http://www.miccapital.com*, 17 November 2003.

[10] Sea Jin Chang and Jaebum Hong, "Economic Performance of Group-Affiliated Companies in Korea: Intragroup Resource Sharing and Internal Business Transactions," *Academy of Management Journal*, Vol. 43, Iss. 3, pp. 429–448.

[11] For more on keiretsu and performance see James R. Lincoln, Michael Gerlach, and Christina L. Ahmadjian, "Keiretsu Networks and Corporate Performance in Japan," *American Sociological Review*, 1996, vol. 61, no. 1, pp. 67–95.

[12] For more on keiretsu and performance see James R. Lincoln, Michael Gerlach, and Christina L. Ahmadjian, "Keiretsu Networks and Corporate Performance in Japan," *American Sociological Review*, 1996, Vol. 61, No. 1, pp. 67–95.

[13] See Ishtiaq P. Mahmood and Jasjit Singh, "Technological Dynamism in Asia," *Research Policy*, Vol. 32, Iss. 6, pp. 1031–1050.

[14] Ishtiaq P. Mahmood and Will Mitchell, "Two Faces: Effects of Business Groups on Innovation in Emerging Economies," *Mimeo*, 2003. (NUS Business School, Singapore).

SECTION III

Multinational Management

10 MANAGING A MULTINATIONAL ENTERPRISE

The management of a multinational enterprise is a challenging task at any stage of its internationalization process. At the early stages, many of the challenges extend from coping with what can be rapid growth into new and diverse markets. At later stages, many of the challenges come from organizing diverse sets of activities across a large number of markets.

The growth of a multinational firm is stimulated by a number of pressures for globalization. Advances in telecommunications and transportation technology, declining barriers to trade between national markets, the internationalization of markets for capital and consumer goods, and the emergence of competitors from all parts of the globe, each push a firm to greater depths in international markets.

Throughout its 90 year history, Hong Kong-based Li & Fung (*www.lifung.com*) has adapted its business to globalization pressures, such as these. Li & Fung began as a small trading company in 1909, when it exported products such as porcelain and silk to China. The dynamic environment that emerged in the aftermath of World War II brought changes to the company. Hong Kong's population began to swell with refugees and immigrants from China, and the Hong Kong economy began to develop as a light manufacturing base, that exported labour-intensive consumer products to developed country markets. In response, Li & Fung expanded the range of products they exported to include garments, toys, electronics and plastic flowers.

The opening up of China in 1979 and the rapid industrialization of developing Asian markets in the 1980s and 1990s brought new globalization pressures. Li & Fung was able to adapt to these pressures by moving manufacturing to China where labour was inexpensive, and it developed access to a wide choice of suppliers from other developing Asian markets. In an effort to serve its customers better, Li & Fung restructured to focus on two core businesses: export trading and retail operations, and strategically grew these business through acquisitions. The dynamic environment since the turn of the twentieth century stimulated these changes in strategy and structure that has transformed Li & Fung into a multinational trading company.

With a movement into international markets, such as what Li & Fung has undertaken, comes competitive gains from a wider geographic scope of operations. These gains frequently stem from the integration of activities across a firm's markets. To achieve these gains from multinationality, there is a concurrent need to structure the activities in an organization to match its global strategy. A coordinated structure of activities comes at a cost. Integration implies the coordination and homogenization of activities. Economies of scale and scope, for example, are more difficult to achieve if product lines are diverse. With greater integration comes less of a focus on individual national markets. Subsidiaries operate under a cost imperative in a coordinated global strategy, losing the autonomy of a profit-centred orientation in an internationalizing firm. Management practices become less individualized to demands of individual markets, as recruitment, training and promotion practices become standardized.

An alternative to experiencing this cost in a multinational firm comes if activities are not coordinated and homogenized. Diversity across markets could be embraced in a strategy that remains sensitive to differences across national markets. This strategy places an emphasis on national markets. Subsidiaries operate under a high degree of autonomy. Senior management in national markets can design and implement strategy. Managers in a subsidiary can have a national focus, with the objective being to recruit locally and retain local management in the subsidiary for the long term. In essence, a subsidiary in a multinational firm that places an emphasis on the local environment, operates as an independent entity, but with ultimate reporting responsibilities to its parent multinational.

The costs and benefits of integration and responsiveness in a multinational firm's operations are an inescapable dilemma in the management of a multinational firm. Certain pressures push a firm towards higher levels of multinationality, in which dispersed activities are integrated. Yet, other pressures direct a firm towards a set of activities that are responsive to local market conditions. Managers in a multinational firm are confronted with the task of determining how integrated or how responsive a firm should be in its international operations.

Depending on how the managers in a firm judge the trade-offs between integration and responsiveness, and how they balance and merge the two, various archetypes of a multinational firm can emerge. Two polar organizations on these dimensions are the multi-local and the global organization.[1]

The Organization of Activities

Multi-local and global are just two of the organizational forms that are possible in a multinational firm. The range of organizational forms mirrors that in an entirely domestic organization, but with a greater degree of complexity.

Managers in all firms are faced with the question of how to organize the activities in a firm. Three basic levels of organization are functional, product and geographic. These levels of organization reflect the primary choices for a firm's growth – vertical expansion, geographic expansion and product expansion.

In a single product, and single geographic market firm, organization tends to fall along functional lines, once a firm is large enough to have collections of employees specializing in different functions. A functionally organized firm has units devoted to research and development, logistics, marketing, finance, accounting and so forth. A functional structure provides gains in competitiveness by coordinating employee activities in specialized tasks that can improve the efficiency of performance within each task.

A functional structure is, however, notorious for creating walls that bring communication between functional areas to a standstill. There is a trade-off in a functional structure between the efficiency and coordination of tasks. A similar set of trade-offs exist if management implements a geographic organizational structure or a product organizational structure.

Growth of a single product market, single geographic market firm into new geographic markets brings an increasing need to organize activities along geographic lines. Growth into new product markets brings a similar need to organize activities along product lines. In either case, a firm can gain from a coordinated set of specialized activities to pursue the production of a particular product or to pursue a particular geographic market. These gains relate to advantages in competition that come from a greater efficiency in production, or a greater responsiveness to market needs. The trade-offs between these two types of advantages meet on the drawing board for the formulation of a multinational firm's strategy and structure.

Multi-Local Organization

As the name suggests, a multi-local organization places an emphasis on being responsive to conditions in local markets. In pursuing a multi-local strategy, a firm tends to develop products in its home market, and then sells these products in its host country markets. The product can be adapted by an overseas subsidiary to suit the needs of the local market. As such, product manufacture is done by an overseas subsidiary for its national market, such as the case for Sony VAIO's US-based operations.

Located in California, the marketing team of Sony America's Video Audio Integrated Operations (VAIO) division (*www.sony.com* and *www.vaio.net*) studied the newest technology and techno-toys coming out of Japan. The team determined which innovations could be translated to the US market. For some products, no adaptation was necessary and they could be marketed as is. For others, small or large changes needed to be made so that they met the needs and tastes of the local market. Some products were ultimately too different to suit the US market.

According to Mark Hanson, Vice President and General Manager of VAIO, the environment is a key determinate as to whether or not a product will suit the local market. 'A typical house in Japan is 1,000 to 1,100 square feet,' Hanson says. 'They just can't have as much stuff! The stuff they do have, they want to be unique, whereas in the United States, we want to have one of everything.'[2] Products adapted by VAIO's California team include Sony VAIO series notebooks and PCs.

In order to successfully adapt products to local markets, a subsidiary often requires the same manufacturing technology as the parent, as it must be able to manufacture an adapted product for local sale. A subsidiary should at least have marketing and distribution facilities, to enable sales in the local market.

In a pure multi-local organization, each subsidiary can be thought of as a miniature replica of the parent. Each subsidiary performs almost all the same functions of the parent, but perhaps at a smaller scale, particularly if the local market is smaller than the parent multinational's home country market.

To pursue a multi-local strategy, a multinational firm would be organized along country lines (see Figure 10-1). In this organizational structure, countries or world regions become the individual divisions in a firm. This organizational design provides the maximum amount of flexibility to implement country-focused strategies.

Flexibility comes from the individual autonomy senior management has to coordinate the functions to meet a local customer's needs with a particular product. The miniature replicas of the parent organization in each geographic unit enable decisions to be made quickly and effectively when focused on satisfying local market demands. For product development issues within a particular function, such as research and development, there is a loss of efficiency and scale, because this function is not coordinated and integrated on a worldwide basis. A multi-local organization structure tends to be most appropriate when competition is localized and the need for product specialization by region is high.

In considering a multi-local organization design, the geographic region requires as much thought as the product drivers that propel a firm to implement this particular strategy. Take the case of Singapore-based Popular Holdings (*www.popular.com.sg*) as an example. Singapore-based Popular Holdings (Popular) was a regional integrated internet media company that focused on the Asia-Pacific region. Popular had a network of franchise outlets spanning Singapore, Malaysia, Hong Kong and Taiwan and it also operated publishing activities through its subsidiaries.

Geography was a key consideration when Popular expanded its e-learning services division in East Asia. Popular was attracted to the East Asian market because 'Asian parents place great emphasis on their children's academic success, and consider the ages of 3-12 as pivotal years.'[3]

Figure 10-1:   Multi-Local Organization Structure

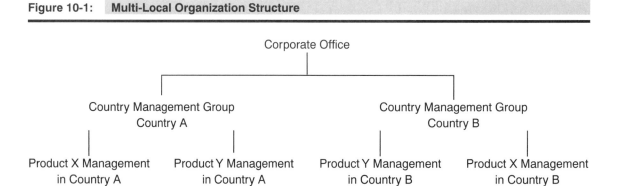

The company chose the East Asian marketplace to leverage the popularity of its e-learning services in the region, particularly China.[4] Popular expanded its e-learning capabilities through strategic partnerships with companies that provided e-learning services, including software companies and kindergartens, aiming to be the "edu-channel of choice for e-learning companies".[5] The company identifies this initiative as leveraging and complementing its established infrastructure.

In thinking about the geography of this decision, the appropriate level of aggregation merits consideration. At one extreme, the world can be treated as one geographic market necessitating just one geographic unit. At this extreme, we have the imperative to form a global organization structure. At the other extreme, each country, or even regions within countries, need to be treated as individual markets. For Popular Holdings, the East Asian market, including China, Hong Kong and Taiwan, was considered to be its aggregate market for e-learning services. To help support this initiative, Popular opened marketing offices in Beijing and Taipei. These offices focused on promoting its regional e-learning services.

As demonstrated by Popular's decision to focus on the East Asian market, the reality of a geographic focus most frequently falls somewhere between the two extremes of global and national markets. A global market is too broad a level of aggregation, while treating each national market as an individual one is too fine a level of aggregation. Identifying the appropriate level of aggregation is an imposing task, and one fundamental to the successful implementation of a global strategy. Two points to evaluate in determining an appropriate number of geographic divisions are the size of a market and its level of homogeneity with other markets (see Figure 10-2).

Where a market is sufficiently large, it can merit consideration as a separate division in a multi-local organization structure. If it is not large, the costs of adding an extra division will exceed any potential benefits from being able to tailor products and strategies to a particular market. If a market is too small to merit consideration as an autonomous division in a multi-local organization structure, then it would need to be folded into another regional unit in the multinational firm.

The determination about which countries can be folded into regional units comes from an assessment of the level of heterogeneity of geographic markets. Managers can assess heterogeneity along a number of dimensions of national institutional environments. Are the markets

Figure 10-2:   Pressures to Create Geographic Divisions

		Size of Regional Market	
		Small	**Large**
Similarity of region to other geographic regions	**Homogeneous**	Low	Moderate
	Heterogeneous	Moderate	High

geographically proximate to one another? Are there similarities in culture, politics, levels of economic development? The more the answers to questions like these point to similarity across markets, the greater the strength of the argument to fold these markets together into one geographic division.

Even if a market is large, and it shares substantial similarities with other markets, the markets can be treated as one geographic unit. This prescription becomes a bit more intricate when we have the case of a small market that is unique in many respects. Its uniqueness creates a rationale to form a separate regional market, yet its size suggests there is little potential payoff, even in the case of a successful entry, given the costs of creating a separate division for this market. In such a scenario, entry could be delayed until the market increases in size, or other similar markets emerge.

Global Organization

A global organization places an emphasis on achieving gains that come from the integration of a multinational firm's activities. In pursuing a global strategy, products can be developed in many parts of the world, and then sold in each of a firm's host country markets. Products tend to be standardized, as managers search for efficiencies and advantages that come from large-scale coordinated production. As such, product manufacture occurs in the location that has the highest economic rationale, be it a low-cost or high technology site for manufacturing.

A foreign subsidiary has the functions that support the production and sale of a product on a worldwide basis. A product can be manufactured in a country, then exported to other countries, but not sold in the country in which it was manufactured. This division of activities typified much of the production in the footwear, apparel and toys industries in the early 2000s. Multinational firms in these sectors established manufacturing and assembly plants.

In a global organization, each subsidiary can be thought of as performing a specific task, for the goal of improving the overall competitiveness of the parent organization. The functions performed in an individual subsidiary can be quite diverse, with no explicit need for any overlap or duplication in functions across geographical regions, unless some regional specialization is required.

An example of this is LG (*www.lg.co.kr*), Korea's second largest business group. The Group comprises 49 affiliates and over 300 subsidiaries. It coordinates its business into four fields: Chemicals & Energy (*www.lgchem.com*), Electronics & Telecommunications (*www.lge.com*), Finance (*www.iflgkorea.com*), and Services (*www.lgicorp.com*). Each field and its related companies share the LG brand and business philosophy, with the goal of being among the top companies in their respective industries (see Figure 10-3).

To pursue a global strategy, a multinational firm should be organized along product lines. In this organizational structure, businesses or product groups become the individual divisions. This organizational design provides the maximum amount of integration to implement global strategies

Figure 10-3:   **LG's Businesses and its Organization**

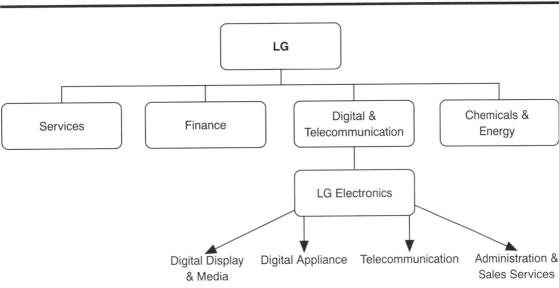

Source: Adapted from *www.lge.com*, 3 December 2003.

for a firm's products. It is worth looking more closely at one of LG Group's sectors, for instance LG Electronics & Telecommunications, to gather a better understanding of how a multinational firm can choose to organize its business lines.

LG Electronics, with 73 subsidiaries worldwide in 2003, was a global player in the electronics and telecommunications sector.[6] The corporation separated itself into three main companies: Digital Appliances, Digital Displays and Media, and Telecommunications Equipment and Handsets (see Figure 10-4). Each company globally manages their own particular R&D and product development. For example, Digital Display and Media, which focuses on multimedia-related products, display products and core components, has R&D offices throughout North America, Europe and Asia. Administrative and sales services are external to the companies, reducing overlap and duplication and allowing for integration of the necessary downstream functions.

Integration comes from the autonomy a product division has for producing and selling its products around the world. The global structure is an effective way to centralize the functional structures for each product division. Subsidiaries implement the global strategies within a product division, by performing the specific activities dictated by management in the headquarters for the product division.

In LG, just as each field works to enhance the status of LG Group, each company within a field works to enhance its respective profitability. For LG Electronics, each company strives to meet the overall top priority of raising shareholder value. This goal is to be reached by increasing brand power, developing products to meet customer's needs and expanding sales overseas. Each company under the LG Electronics umbrella conducts business with these objectives in mind.

Figure 10-4:   Organization of LG Electronics

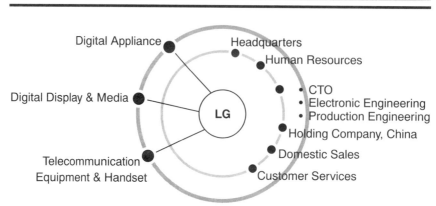

Source: Adapted from *www.lge.com*, 3 December 2003.

Within a broad set of objectives such as these, individual subsidiaries can perform specialized functions, with concern for local markets secondary to concerns about the efficiency and competitiveness of the multinational firm as a whole. The multinational firm gains efficiency and scale through integration, but losses responsiveness to local demands. A global organization structure tends to be most appropriate when competition is globalized and the need for global integration in activities is high.

In a global organization design (see Figure 10-5), products need to be aggregated in product lines, or lines of business. As a guide to this decision, managers need to consider how similar different product lines are in the various business functions. As the basis for competition in a global structure is one of efficiencies that come from integration, the greater the scope of efficiencies that can be gained through the combination of functions in different product lines, the greater the competitiveness of a firm.

The automotive industry provides an example of this principle. The search for new sources of productive efficiency has driven many of the trends in the automotive industry. In the 2000s, worldwide overcapacity and price competition characterized the competitive environment. As a

Figure 10-5:   Global Organization Structure

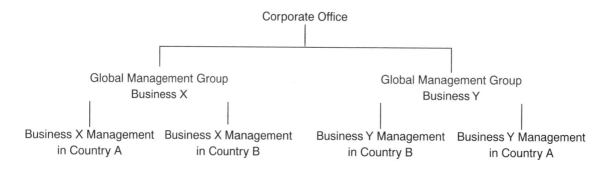

consequence, two common trends in the automotive industry were growth by merger and acquisition, and the increasing homogenization of product lines.

Both of these trends had the goal of lowering costs through the efficient manufacture and assembly of automobiles. Growth by acquisition and merger leads to increases in the size of a firm, both in terms of the number of geographic markets in which it participated and the type of automobiles an automotive manufacturer produced. The merger between Chrysler and Daimler typified this strategy as it brought together two companies from the two sides of the Atlantic. The result was a firm with substantial activities in both North America and Europe, as well as other regions of the world, with a broad product line.

The increase in geographic coverage brought about by the merger of Chrysler and Daimler creates opportunities for economies of scale in production, reductions in the costs of sourced inputs through greater purchasing power, and greater volumes of purchased components. Economies of scope could be achieved by the introduction of more automotive makes and models in existing distribution channels. Automotive development costs could be shared across a broader base by using a common platform across more makes and models of vehicles.

These cost and efficiency-related objectives provided a substantial rationale and motivation for undertaking the merger between Chrysler and Daimler. In combining product lines into divisional lines of business, a similar set of objectives can drive the decision. Are there economies of scope to be gained in centralizing the functions for various products? What commonalities are there in the productive activities for each product? As the answers to these questions point to the potential for combining functions, or spreading costs across a similar input, the arguments to combine the products under one business division in a global organization become more persuasive.

Selecting an Organizational Structure

The distinctions between a multi-local and a global organization strategy and structure are quite clear. A multi-local structure is oriented to local markets to make the maximum of gains from being responsive to local conditions. A global structure is oriented to global markets to make the maximum of gains from being globally integrated.

Selecting between the two structures becomes a matter of deciding which sets of gains is greater, and which set of costs is lower. The gains and costs are the ones that come with an integrated organizational structure, or a responsive organizational structure.

To identify gains and costs in selecting one or the other, managerial attention should be directed at the products of the firm. The pressures for global integration and local responsiveness emerge from the nature of competition in an industry, and developments in markets worldwide. Trends across the globe affect competition in most product sectors, but trends in an industry are specific to a product sector. Where we see pressures that point to the universalization of consumer demands, the emergence of global competitors, the intensification of research and development, the shortening of the product cycle and so forth, we have specific forces driving an industry to become more globalized.

In a single product, multinational firm, it is a comparatively easy task to identify an appropriate organizational structure. The pressures to globalize, and the concomitant gains and costs from integration can be compared to the rationale, gains and costs from local responsiveness. Management can conduct this assessment for a single product line of a firm.

As shown in Figure 10-6, products can be categorized along two dimensions: pressures for global integration and pressures for global responsiveness. When a product is high on the global integration dimension and low on the local responsiveness dimension, it is a clear candidate for a global strategy and organization approach. Meanwhile, a product that is low on the global integration dimension, but high on the local responsiveness dimension is a good candidate for a multi-local strategy and organization.

The products placed in Figure 10-6 afford several examples. Agricultural products such as wheat, rice and so forth can gain from a worldwide distribution network, with sourcing and selling strategies set to move according to fluctuations in demand and supply across world regions. Although different varieties of rice, for example, might be more commonly consumed in one region of the world versus another, the pressure for local responsiveness in the product characteristics of rice is low.

Another product in the food sector offers an example of one that would gain from a multi-local strategy. Consumer tastes for confectionaries such as candy and chocolate tend to be highly

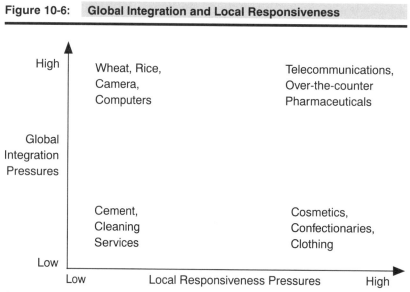

Figure 10-6:   Global Integration and Local Responsiveness

Source: Adapted from Christopher A. Bartlett and Sumantra Ghoshal, *Managing Across Borders – The Transnational Solution* (Cambridge, MA: Harvard Business School Press, 1989).

localized. Pricing, packaging and product design must be local for a confectionary to have a good chance of success. Although economies of scale in purchasing could be gained if manufacturing and procurement activities were centralized, other sources of scale economies in areas such as manufacturing are limited because of the customization that must occur for each market. As a consequence, confectionaries tend to favour a multi-local organization and strategy.

Another example of a product type that favours a multi-local organization and strategy is the ethnic cosmetics and toiletries category. The tastes of many consumers in Asia have moved toward an emphasis on skincare.[7] Among Asian women, there is a strong emphasis in cosmetics on skin-whitening products. As a result, cosmetics manufacturers are adapting their products to tap into the demand for skin-whiteners by adding whitening agents to many of their products. Japanese cosmetics manufacturer, Kose (*www.kose.com.jp*), has developed *White-Science*, a product line designed to whiten the skin.[8] Other cosmetic companies that have adapted their skin care products include: L'Oreal with *White Perfect* with Melano-Block, and Nivea with *White* and Neutrogena with *Fine Fairness*.

Figure 10-6 provides examples of products in which there is no clear choice between a multi-local and global organization and strategy. Over-the-counter pharmaceuticals can have gains from standardization worldwide, to support research and development efforts. Illnesses and diseases can vary in their rate of incidence worldwide, but causes remain common, and this supports integration in product development efforts. At the same time, advertising remains an important component of sales. Consumers have substantial differences in tastes for particular kinds of over-the-counter pharmaceuticals. Purchasing power differs across countries as well, leading to distinctive types of packaging and product sizes across world regions. For over-the-counter pharmaceuticals, both the pressures for global integration and local responsiveness are high.

Even though some products might not offer a clear alternative for the organization of a single product, multinational firm, it is still a comparatively easy task to select between one structure or another. It is easy when the comparison point is a multi-product, multinational firm. It is exceptionally easy, when the comparison point is a multi-product, multinational firm that has product lines that could gain from a multi-local approach, and product lines that could gain from a global approach.

In such a case, there is no clear answer about how to structure the operations of the firm. A multi-local strategy and structure will augment the competitiveness of one or more product lines, but hamper the competitiveness of others. A global strategy would provide the same set of mixed results. This mixture of product lines creates a Catch-22 situation for the managers in a firm. No matter which structure and strategy is implemented, there will be losses in the firm. There is no decision that creates a winning scenario for all product lines.

Faced with such a situation, once a choice is made, it has substantial implications for the future strategy of a multinational firm. By deciding on a multi-local or global strategy and structure, the managers in a firm are explicitly identifying one set of product lines as being more important to the firm than another. The set is the one that matches the strategy. If a global strategy and organization is the endpoint of the decision, products that would be strongest in a multi-local firm become less central to the firm's future success. Ultimately, these product lines might be destined to be divested.

Divestment of existing product lines that do not suit the newly implemented global or multi-local product structure, and investment in new product lines that do, can reshape the firm to have a greater consistency in product lines, geographic scope, and organizational strategy and structure.

This divestment strategy is often implemented hand-in-hand with expansion elsewhere in the world, as given in the experiences of Dairy Farm. To its strategic goal of focusing on the Asian marketplace, Dairy Farm International divested the grocery store chains of Woolworth's in New Zealand and Franklins' in Australia in early 2000. To further pursue this Asian-focus goal, Dairy Farm purchased the 'Shop and Save' supermarkets in Singapore in November 2003. These divestments and acquisitions have, according to Ronald J. Floto, Group Chief Executive of Dairy Farm, allowed the company 'to develop the largest retail group in Singapore'[9] while re-focusing its operations to Southeast and East Asia.

This type of restructuring is a part of a multinational firm's growth in international markets. It involves substantial shifts in many of a firm's core products and activities. It has implications for the success of particular product areas in a firm, and ramifications for the tasks, responsibilities and careers of a firm's employees. Accordingly, organizational resistance to change in the strategy and structure of a multinational firm can be substantial. Implementation can have its own series of trials and tribulations.

Implementing Structural Change

A large or small change in the structure of organization is likely to face some opposition. Any change will be accompanied by gains and losses among units, divisions and individuals in a firm. In a large change, from a multi-local to a global structure, or from a global to a multi-local structure, product and country managers will either gain a greater amount of power, or lose some power in the organization. Responsibilities, reporting practices, accountability, autonomy and flexibility will be transformed, as part of the metamorphosis in the organizational structure of a multinational firm.

Anticipating and planning for this resistance is central to the success of the implementation of a new or varied organizational structure. As a starting point, when planning for organizational change, senior managers can look at distinct groups of managers and employees that will gain or lose in the change. When the shift is large, such as from a multi-local to a global strategy, the winners and losers will be obvious. Country managers stand to lose power and autonomy as their decision become subordinate to product managers. Product managers will lay down product strategy, with country managers providing input into the ways the product could be managed in their own locale. The opposite shift, from a global to a multi-local strategy, would necessarily entail an opposite swing in the power and responsibilities of country and product managers.

Recognizing the loci of gains and losses among managers is important because the changes to the organization can yield results only if individual employees reorganize their activities in a way consistent with the diagrammed structure. Drawing a new organizational chart and defining new reporting relationships does not automatically assure that meaningful change will occur. Management and staff need to reorient attitudes and habits to be consistent with the new structure. The more effectively senior management can obtain buy-in from other management and staff, the more quick can be the institution of the new organizational structure.

Control Systems

As part of a revised organizational structure, managers should consider what control systems need to be altered or put in place. Control systems facilitate the coordination of activities in a firm. Control systems help to make sure that managers act in ways consistent with the overall goals of a firm.

Control becomes an increasingly important issue the more diverse a firm. Product, functional and geographic diversity each increase the chance that an individual division, subsidiary or group of managers will act in a way inconsistent with the overall objectives of a firm.

Changing the organizational structure creates an explicit need to revisit its control systems. The organizational structure itself is a part of the control system. It defines at the broadest level the types and nature of interactions that should occur between divisions, subsidiaries and headquarters. The remaining mechanisms in a control system provide a set of incentives and mechanisms to help align the decisions of management with the overall strategy of the multinational firm.

Managers can exercise and enforce control through a variety of mechanisms. Control can be formal or informal. Formal control includes the sets of rules and procedures that define a job or an employee's responsibilities. Formal control mechanisms define reporting requirements and identify performance objectives. Formal controls provide a rigid and well-defined collection of mechanisms by which to coordinate activities.

Informal controls include communication between staff, and cultural mechanisms. Person-to-person communication provides a means for a manager to assess how a staff members tasks, or a subsidiary's performance, aligns with the expectations of the firm. Corporate and national culture likewise can help define the parameters of activities and performance. The acculturation of employees into a firm defines expectations and inculcates organizational goals. National culture can imbue an individual with a sense of responsibility to specific individuals, whether the individual is a colleague, a superior or a subordinate. National and corporate culture can lead to the creation of shared values that minimize deviations from organizational goals.

The issue of control systems is more complicated and involved than this presentation. The point with discussing control systems at this juncture is to emphasize the need to consider the mix of mechanisms that will be used to motivate and reward management and staff to work in the ways envisioned in the organizational strategy, and as outlined in an organization's structure. This need is particularly profound in a multinational corporation that is undergoing change in its strategy and structure.

Multinational Strategy and Structure

A firm's strategy and structure evolve as it moves into international markets. This evolution is marked by several organization milestones. As a firm expands into international markets, it grows new organizational appendages to facilitate this expansion.

One of the first appendages to develop is an exporting arm. As exports become a more and more important component of a company's sales, it is not uncommon to see a department arise to deal with a firm's international customers. Reporting practices in a firm can be modified to identify domestic and international (export) sales. The export department's performance is reflected in export sales. A primary objective with pursuing export markets is to increase firm sales. Year-on-year increases in export sales are a sign of meeting this objective.

The formation of an export department indicates the seriousness with which a firm approaches its international markets. Too frequently, during the early stages of international expansion, managers view international markets as a windfall and not a key part of a firm's strategy. With this perspective in place, the dominant attitude to international markets is one of opportunism. When an opportunity for a sale in international markets arises, it is taken, regardless of its match with the strategic objectives of the organization. Matching this is a failure to approach international markets in a systematic and strategic fashion, which in turn, makes for a large divide between the potential and actual sales and returns from international markets.

With the formation of an export department, a firm's managers provide a strong sign of their interest in approaching international markets strategically. Managers in the export department concentrate on securing sales in international markets. Sales growth comes from developing an understanding of consumer tastes, and acceptable levels of pricing and distribution channels in international markets. If the managers in an export department are successful in their tasks, international sales will become an increasingly large component of a firm's overall sales, and an increased intensity of international market participation could well follow.

Eventually, an export department can be overwhelmed by the task of managing international sales, and international production. Its increasing responsibilities can lead to the formation of an international division. An international division will manage exporting activities as well as international sourcing and productive operations. Initially, a single international division organizes a firm's trading and investment activities in all regions of the world.

An international division can be an effective means of organization when there is still an international-domestic dichotomy in the perceptions of senior management. Its effectiveness can be hindered by growth in international markets that leads to more products being introduced into international markets and a greater scope of geographic coverage. This growth can be particularly problematic for a firm when it occurs within a mindset of domestic versus international markets where domestic markets are perceived to be of the greatest strategic importance to a firm.

These attitudes towards domestic and international markets are not just restricted to small, internationalizing firms. Even the largest firms in the world can harbour this kind of attitude despite decades of exposure to international markets and global competitors. General Motors' senior management acknowledged that it took until 2003 for senior executives to begin to consider international markets as being as important to strategy formulation as the domestic market. This epiphany was brought about by the opening and growth of the automobile market in China, which had the potential to rival the US market in the coming decades. In this sense, the cause of strategy reformulation in General Motors in 2003 is a consequence of relentless pressures to globalize.

Strategy Choice in International Markets

Strategic choices in international markets often emerge from dynamic environmental conditions that create competing tensions within a firm. As we have already discussed, these tensions are global integration pressures and local responsiveness pressures. The pressures vary by industry, resulting in unique competitive approaches to global markets that depend on the product profile in a firm.

Figure 10-7 shows four prime examples of strategic choices in international markets. Three of these should already be recognizable. International, global and multi-domestic strategies bear a strong resemblance to our earlier reviews of an international division, global organization and multi-local organization. The new form of strategy listed in Figure 10-7 is a transnational strategy.

Each of these strategy types emerges as a more or less favourable option for a firm depending on the types of pressures encountered in a firm. Where pressures for global integration and local responsiveness are low, an international strategy is preferred. An international strategy emerges more from a firm's search for new opportunities, than from an external environmental imperative for international market participation. A global strategy is favoured in a situation in which global integration pressures are high, but local responsiveness pressures are low. A multi-domestic strategy is the best option when local responsiveness pressures are high and global integration pressures are low. Finally, we have a transnational strategy which satisfies the strategic demands placed on a firm competing in areas in which global integration and local responsiveness pressures are both high.

Figure 10-7:   **Strategy Choice**

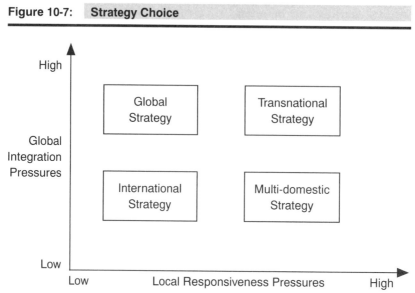

Source: Adapted from Sumantra Ghoshal and Nitin Nohria, "Horses for Courses: Organizational Forms for Multinational Corporations," *Sloan Management Review*, Winter 1993, pp. 27–31.

International Strategy

An international strategy emerges in a firm as it begins to expand into international markets in a serious and coordinated manner. International strategy is facilitated by the formation of an international division. An international division has some autonomy to approach international markets in terms of the planning and administration of international activities. The international structure makes this autonomy distinctive by forming a unique division to deal with a firm's international market activities (see Figure 10-8).

International market activities represent extensions of domestic market activities. International markets are a place for the exploitation of whatever products and advantages are developed in a firm's domestic market activities. MOS Food Services Inc. (MOS Burger) is a multinational company with an international strategy (see Box 10-1).

Even though the international structure provides some autonomy to an international division, as the solid-line arrows indicate, its activities are coordinated by the corporate office in the home country of the firm, which in Figure 10-8 is Hong Kong. The corporate office provides formal planning for subsidiary operations in places such as Singapore, the USA, China, Japan, India and Germany, through an international divisional office. In this way, the corporate office retains control over foreign operations. Specific decisions and responsibilities can fall under the purview of the international division or its subsidiaries, but these decisions are still made in a situation in which each subsidiary's operations are linked to the rest of the firm through the international divisional office and the corporate office.

Figure 10-8: **International Multinational Firm**

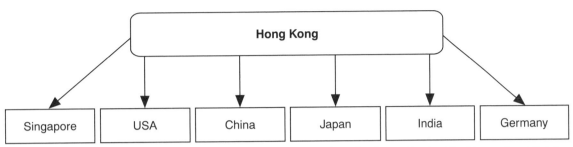

Source: Adapted from Christopher A. Barlett and Sumantra Ghoshal, *Managing Across Borders-The Transnational Solution* (Boston: Harvard Business School Press, 1989).

Box 10-1   MOS Burger's International Strategy

The Japanese fast-food hamburger company, MOS Burger (*www.mos.co.jp*), focuses its international efforts on exploiting the products and activities that have contributed to it's success in its home market.

MOS Food Services is the second largest fast-food restaurant in Japan with over 1,500 stores in Japan, and outlets in Taiwan, Singapore and Hawaii. MOS is an acronym for Mountain, Ocean and Sun, which refers to MOS Foods founder Satoshi Sakurada's personal philosophy of clean living. His philosophy extends to the MOS brand, which is known for emphasizing taste, food safety and health, over low prices.

In its domestic market of Japan, MOS Burger has followed a tradition of introducing new products and activities in its restaurants. This included the introduction of a more expensive burger that had 1.8 times as much meat as its predecessors, was made from a better cut, and took 10 minutes to make. MOS introduced wireless internet access in many of its outlets, and a new tea store concept called Mother Leaf. In its international markets of Taiwan, Singapore and Hawaii, MOS Burger has followed a strategy of simply extending its successful domestic activities into these international markets. It delivers its basic format of fast food that tastes good and is safe, reliable and healthy.

This strategy has proven to be successful. In Taiwan, where market shares of major fast-food restaurants have been declining in recent years, only MOS Burger has not shown declining shares. This stability extends from the preferences of its customers, 70 per cent of whom are female. MOS's customer segment tends to be health conscious and is consequently drawn to the restaurant's low-fat and low-calorie meals as served-up in a homey atmosphere. In response to its success, MOS Burger announced in August 2003 that it would increase the number of its stores in Taiwan from 51 to 66 by the end of 2003.

In Hawaii, MOS Burger serves Asian-style food and burgers, capitalizing on the number of Japanese tourists who visit the island each year and are familiar with the menu. For MOS Burger in Hawaii, the outlet was company-owned to ensure quality control.

Sources:

"Looking for a Competitive Edge in a Deflationary Environment," *Asahi Shimbun/Asahi Evening News*, 14 February 2002.

Jessie Ho, "McDonald's Turns to Love in a Bid to Revive Business," *Taipei Times*, 24 September 2003, p. 10.

Annabel Lue, "MOS Burger Beefing Up Presence in Local Markets," *Taipei Times*, 12 August 2003, p. 10.

Jacob Kamhis, "Three Hawaii Burger King Sites Will Get New Menus MOS Burger, L&L Drive-Inn Negotiating for Oahu Eateries," *Pacific Business News*, 22 June 1998.

"The Big MOS Attack," *Hawaii Business*, March 1990, Vol. 35, No. 9, pp. 79–81.

This form of strategy and structure can be appropriate to coordinate dispersed forays into international markets. As international market activity grows, the limitations to the pursuit of market opportunities that accompany direct control by the corporate office can become burdensome. A shift in orientation, to a multi-domestic strategy can provide the flexibility required to deal with localized competitive threats and opportunities.

Multi-domestic Strategy

In the pursuit of a multi-domestic strategy, a considerable number of activities retain commonalities between domestic and international markets (see Figure 10-9). No longer, however, is there a strict international-domestic market dichotomy in a firm. There is still a differentiation between the two, but that differentiation is broken down further as the firm's strategic approach to each host country market becomes somewhat unique in its own right. International markets, however, remain a place for the exploitation of whatever products and advantages are developed in a firm's domestic market activities.

A multi-domestic strategy is a viable option when the limited flexibility afforded by an international strategy constrains a firm in its internationalization. The development of a multi-domestic strategy is facilitated by a shift to a multi-domestic organizational structure. The multi-domestic structure affords a firm's subsidiaries with the autonomy to be responsive to demands in local markets. It provides this autonomy through the decentralization of operations, decisions and responsibilities. This autonomy is marked by the dashed-lines in Figure 10-9, which indicate that subsidiaries still maintain their primary connection to the multinational firm through the head office in Hong Kong, but Hong Kong does not provide explicit control over a subsidiary's activities. This form of decentralization means that local subsidiaries pickup the decisions and responsibilities to implement strategies in a firm's host country markets.

The multi-domestic structure provides autonomy to subsidiary operations in each host country, but subsidiary managers still bear a responsibility to report to the corporate office.

Figure 10-9:   Multi-domestic Multinational Firm

Source: Adapted from Christopher A. Barlett and Sumantra Ghoshal, *Managing Across Borders-The Transnational Solution:* (Boston: Harvard Business School Press, 1989).

Reflecting the growing autonomy of the subsidiaries, corporate controls can shift from detailed formal reporting requirements, to an informal set of controls. Simple financial controls in the form of sales growth targets, profitability objectives or cost objectives can be the limit of formal controls. In this regard, a firm's foreign subsidiaries operate like independent businesses that contribute to the bottom-line profitability of a firm, but are not integrated in their operations.

A multi-domestic strategy enables a rapid penetration of multiple markets, while coordination costs are minimized. Provided a firm's core advantages are great enough to sustain competitiveness in each market, this structure can be maintained. As global competitors emerge, or as domestic competitors strengthen, the multi-domestic structure might not be sufficient to maintain a firm's competitive advantages. New sources of advantage might have to be sought, such as those that come with an integrated set of global operations. To the extent that there are pressures for global integration, this competitive imperative becomes more acute.

Global Strategy

A global strategy befits a firm faced with a situation in which pressures for global integration in operations are substantive. A global structure helps with the implementation of a global strategy as it provides strong links between the corporate office and geographically scattered subsidiary operations. As an example of this global implementation, McDonald's (*www.mcdonalds.com*) undertook its very first global marketing campaign in September 2003. The new 'I'm lovin' it!' campaign is a unified brand theme line used in over 100 countries in which McDonald's has restaurants. The company has called this campaign a 'new era of marketing in McDonald's' as it believes the campaign is 'not only an advertising line but an expression of a new attitude at McDonald's.'[10]

The success of global strategy, such as the one new branding strategy being implemented by McDonald's, hinges on the ability of a firm's managers to centralize key assets, responsibilities and decisions in the corporate office. Centralization means that the corporate office acts as the hub for the coordination of activities carried out in different regions of the world.

In a global strategy, subsidiaries lose autonomy (see Figure 10-10). There is even less differentiation between international markets and domestic markets in a firm's operations than in the case of a multi-domestic strategy. The key distinction is in the locus for the organization of activities, which tends to remain in the home country. Other activities are moved to the place in which the economic or competitive rationale is strongest. Hence, subsidiaries have less autonomy as compared to those in a multi-domestic structure. The dashed borders around the subsidiaries in Figure 10-10 symbolize the idea that each subsidiary is a functional component in the multinational firm, and might not have a full range of functional activities to operate independently.

Tight control, as marked by the solid-lines in Figure 10-10 that connect Hong Kong to each subsidiary, over the operations means that manufacturing, distribution, research and development

Figure 10-10:   Global Multinational Firm

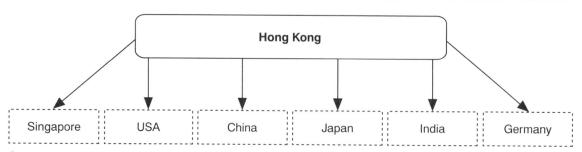

Source: Adapted from Christopher A. Barlett and Sumantra Ghoshal, *Managing Across Borders – The Transnational Solution* (Boston: Harvard Business School Press, 1989).

and marketing activities can still be coordinated even if geographically separated. International operations provide the inputs and serve as the markets for a firm's output, with the corporate office serving as the nexus that matches the flows of productive inputs and a firm's products.

A global strategy enables substantial gains to be made in competitiveness through the pursuit of economies of scale and scope, low-cost production strategies, and a widening of consumer markets. A firm's core advantages can be augmented from optimizing production to improve competitiveness, although tight centralized control can limit local responsiveness. Central control not only limits possibilities for being more reactive to local consumer needs, it can also limit opportunities for developing new areas of competitive advantage in a firm. A structure that permits a firm to be both locally responsiveness and global integrated overcomes this limitation of a global strategy.

Transnational Strategy

A transnational strategy addresses localization and integration pressures. A transnational structure is necessary for the implementation of a transnational strategy as it provides the autonomy and linkages to be both local and global. In a transnational strategy, subsidiaries can act independently, yet still have connections to the corporate office, as well as other dispersed subsidiaries. The closest analogy to a transnational structure is a matrix organization. Although similar these are not the same, as a transnational organization most closely resembles a networked organization. Assets, responsibilities and decisions are distributed across the subsidiaries in a transnational organization.

In a transnational strategy, subsidiaries regain the autonomy lost in the shift to a global strategy, but with no substantial loss in the strength of linkages to the rest of the firm (see Figure 10-11). International and domestic market activities enjoy little real distinction in a transnational organization. The corporate office becomes less of a defining aspect of the centrality of the organization, instead nodes emerge to coordinate dispersed pieces of information, knowledge

Figure 10-11:   Transnational Multinational Firm

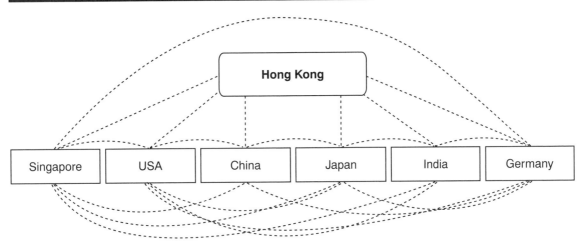

Source: Adapted from Christopher A. Barlett and Sumantra Ghoshal, *Managing Across Borders – The Transnational Solution* (Boston: Harvard Business School Press, 1989).

and activities in the firm. In this sense, as shown in Figure 10-11, the Hong Kong corporate office does not necessarily have the size to dominate the subsidiaries activities. The corporate office and subsidiaries are more equal. Lines of communication exist between each subsidiary, but importantly, these lines are not means of explicit control, as in the case of a global or international structure and strategy.

A transnational organization is characterized by substantial flows of people, information, products, components and technologies through nodes to subsidiaries. Flows of individuals between subsidiaries enlarge intra-firm communication networks that assist with the coordination of activities and the future flows of tangible and intangible items.

The basic structural unit in a transnational organization is the subsidiary. Subsidiary operations are autonomous, but maintain a logic for existence based upon providing an advantage to the whole of the transnational organization. The provision of an advantage can come from the specialization of operations, in the form of the production of a particular product, the development of a unique expertise in a functional area such as marketing or basic research, or by being able to tap into key resources that are specific to a world region.

With specialization, each subsidiary can be incomplete to compete alone in a market. It requires inputs from other subsidiaries. Substantial interdependencies across subsidiaries means that there is a complex process of coordination and cooperation in a transnational firm. Decisions are shared throughout the network, but decisions must be aligned.

A transnational strategy carries the best of all worlds. Integration, responsiveness, communication and specialization are its cornerstones, with the subsidiary as its foundation. Just as an internationalizing firm's foreign market competitiveness rests on the advantages a firm has in its home market, a transnational firm's competitiveness is rooted in the strengths and capabilities of its subsidiaries. The complexity of the organizational design of a transnational firm draws attention to the necessity of establishing good communication and coordination for it to succeed. Subsidiaries with strong, unique capabilities are equally crucial to the success of a transnational firm. This is the topic for the next chapter.

Summary

International managers are faced with a constant imperative to optimize the organization of the international activities of a multinational firm. The intensity of this imperative varies with the extent of globalization pressures encountered by a firm. One thing is constant – globalization pressures continue to increase over time, with greater numbers of industries moving to regional and global-based competition. As industries evolve into a greater degree of global activity, managers in firms will have to respond. In some cases, the response will involve a complete overhaul of a firm's organizational structure. In other cases, it will be a fine-tuning of a strategy and structure.

In responding to external pressures and modifying the organizational structure, it is critical to maintain an alignment between the international strategy and organizational structure. If the strategy of a firm is oriented towards coordinated product development efforts on a worldwide basis, but it has a structure that fosters subsidiary autonomy and flexibility, then a lack of integration of dispersed subsidiary operations can become a problem. Changes in strategy, need to be accompanied by commensurate changes in organizational structure. By moving strategy and structure together with environmental transformations, managers in a firm have a good chance of maintaining alignment across these three important elements.

If current trends in national environments continue towards a greater globalization of markets and a continued decline in government regulated barriers to competition, firms will face even greater imperatives to move towards a global strategy and organizational structure. This does not mean that all firms will end up structured as global organizations. Most will end up with a hybrid solution among the organizational structures described in this chapter. Even though a hybrid structure can be more difficult to manage than an unadulterated structure, it has a greater chance of meeting the multiple strategic needs of a multi-product, multinational firm.

Notes

[1] The material in this chapter is drawn from a variety of sources. For more details on the various topics that comprise this chapter, please see any one or all of the following. Christopher A. Barlett and Sumantra Ghoshal, "Tap Your Subsidiaries for Global Reach," *Harvard Business Review*, November–December 1996; Christopher A. Barlett and Sumantra Ghoshal, "Organizing for Worldwide Effectiveness: The Transnational Solution," *California Management Review*, Fall 1988; Christopher A. Barlett and Sumantra Ghoshal, *Managing Across Borders – The Transnational Solution* (Boston: Harvard Business School Press, 1989); William G. Engelhoff, "Strategy and Structure in Multinational Corporations: A Revision of the Stopford and Wells Model," *Strategic Management Journal*, January–February 1988; Gunnar Hedlund, "The Hypermodern MNC-A Heterarchy?," *Human Resource*

Management, Spring 1986, Vol. 25, No. 1; Allen J. Morrison, David Ricks, and Kendall Roth, "Globalization Versus Regionalisation: Which Way for the Multinational?," *Organizational Dynamics*, Winter 1991; C. K. Prahalad and Yves Doz, *The Multinational Mission: Balancing Local Demands and Global Vision* (New York: The Free Press, 1987).

[2] Douglas McGray, "Translating Sony into English," *Fast Company*, January 2003, p. 38.

[3] POPULAR's Strategic Vision for 2002 & Beyond – Press Release, 24 January 2002.

[4] POPULAR's Strategic Vision for 2002 & Beyond – Press Release, 24 January 2002.

[5] *Investor Report by Popular Holdings*, *http://202.66.146.82/listco/sg/popular/interim/2003/pre.pdf*, 31 October, 2002.

[6] *http://www.lge.com*, 19 November 2003.

[7] *Marketing*, Singapore's Marketing Advertising Public Relations and Media Bible, November 2003, p. 35.

[8] *http://www.kose.co.jp/office/pdf/annual/2000/annual_03.pdf*, 14 November 2003.

[9] "Dairy Farm Acquires Shop and Save Supermarkets in Singapore," *Company Press Release*, 14 November 2003.

[10] McDonald's 'I'm Lovin' It' New Brand Theme Exudes a New Attitude!," *News Release*, 12 September 2003.

11 MANAGING A FOREIGN SUBSIDIARY

The management of a foreign subsidiary is a vital part of a multinational firm's operations. As a multinational firm's international operations grow in extent and intensity, subsidiaries can assume increasingly important roles and responsibilities within the multinational. Managers in a firm's foreign subsidiary implement the corporate and business level strategies of a multinational firm. In some cases, senior management in a firm's foreign subsidiaries can have substantial input into the formulation of a multinational firm's strategies.

In this sense, a firm's foreign subsidiaries reflect its strategies. The distribution of subsidiaries across regions of the world define the geographic scope of a multinational firm's strategy. The functions undertaken in a firm's subsidiaries – research and development, manufacturing, assembly, distribution, marketing – define the product scope and functional orientation of a multinational firm's strategy.

Subsidiaries can also vary in entry mode, size and performance. These parameters identify entry strategies that have been used in different parts of the world at different times in a multinational firm's internationalization. The size and performance of a firm's subsidiaries indicate the importance and success of a multinational firm's operations across the world regions in which it is active.

When we splice together these pieces of information derived from the subsidiaries of a multinational firm, we have a picture of its strategies and operations. Yet, this is just a surface view of the strategy invoked by a multinational firm in its subsidiaries. It is a static picture that shows us the where, what and how of a multinational firm's approaches to its strategy in international markets. As a static picture, the dynamic component is missing. This dynamic component is the evolution of a subsidiary's role in a multinational firm over time.

Historically, there have been two routes to a subsidiary's evolution. The first route is one led by the headquarters of a multinational firm. This route is one in which a subsidiary receives its schedule and scope of activities as an assignment from headquarters. The second route is one led by a subsidiary itself. In this route, managers in a foreign subsidiary take responsibility for leading the development of the subsidiary, through their own initiative and lobbying efforts in the multinational firm.

These two routes to a subsidiary's development both fall under the broad topic of subsidiary management. A central concern in subsidiary management is how a subsidiary's role in a multinational firm evolves over time. To understand the evolution of a subsidiary's role, we need to be aware of the environment in which a subsidiary operates, both in terms of its external environment and its internal organizational environment. With respect to the internal organization environment, it is useful to take a perspective on a multinational firm that encompasses all of a firm's subsidiaries, not just one subsidiary and the headquarters unit.

In adopting this perspective, we need to define what is a subsidiary. In some cases, a subsidiary can take a very technical definition, in which it is defined as a distinct organizational unit owned at least 51 per cent by the parent multinational firm. For our purposes, we can adopt a broader definition of a subsidiary. Essentially, a subsidiary can be thought of as a value-adding unit of a multinational firm, that is situated in a foreign country.[1]

A value-adding unit means that a subsidiary performs an activity, or activities, that augment the value of the products and services produced by the multinational firm. A subsidiary does not have to manufacture or assemble products to be a value-added entity. It can be a sale office, it can be a trading office, or it can be a financing office. The key consideration is that the subsidiary performs a function that benefits a multinational firm's competitiveness.

A subsidiary can fulfill this role in a multinational firm either by conducting a single activity, such as manufacturing, or a full range of value-added activities – research and product design, input sourcing, manufacturing, distribution and marketing. A subsidiary can be one separate factory, or it can comprise a number of distinct physical entities in a host country, such as a factory, a sales office and a distribution warehouse. A subsidiary can be formed by a joint venture, by an acquisition or by constructing a wholly-owned new unit in a host country. In essence, our definition of a subsidiary considers a subsidiary to be an entity owned in full or in part by a multinational firm. This entity carries out an activity or a set of operations in a host country, and these activities add value to the multinational firm at various points in the firm's value-chain.

Subsidiary Mandates and Development

As we defined above, a subsidiary performs value-added activities for a multinational firm. Simply put, the types of activities a subsidiary performs can be called its role in the multinational firm, or more formally, we can call a subsidiary's set of activities its mandate or charter.[2] The businesses in which a subsidiary operates, and its responsibilities in the multinational firm, can also be thought of as its charter. Charters can be accorded to internal and external units. The production of a product can be outsourced, in an external grant of a charter, or it can be assigned to a subsidiary in a multinational, as an internal grant. Essentially a subsidiary's charter captures the products it produces, the technology it houses, the markets it serves and the functional areas included in its operations.

A subsidiary's role, or its mandate or charter, can and does change over time. It changes over time because the international business environment is a dynamic one. The competitive challenges to a multinational firm are in flux. A multinational firm itself is in constant development as it seeks new product and new geographic market opportunities. A subsidiary evolves in response to environmental dynamism.

This evolution can lead to a declining importance of a subsidiary in a multinational firm, and perhaps its eventual closure, or it can lead to an augmentation of the role of a subsidiary. For example, the Australian (Mitsubishi Motors Australia, Ltd.) and Thai (MMC Sittipol Co. Ltd.), subsidiaries of the Japanese car maker Mitsubishi adapted their strategies and their mandates in response to changing business environments in their host countries (see Box 11-1).

Box 11-1   Mitsubishi Motors in Australia and Thailand

Mitsubishi Motors (*www.mitsubishi-motors.com*) is a Japanese company that dates back to the 1870s. It specializes in the manufacture of passenger vehicles, which are sold in more than 170 countries worldwide. The company has many subsidiaries located globally, including subsidiaries that are situated in Australia and Thailand. Mitsubishi's foreign subsidiaries have had to be dynamic, adjusting their mandates in response to changing economic environment in their host country markets.

In the 1980s, the removal of Australia's protectionist policies and the subsequent liberalization of the Australian automotive market, increased domestic competition and improved the quality of locally built vehicles. These changes to the business environment encouraged Australian vehicle manufacturers to expand production. Mitsubishi Motors Australia's (*www.mitsubishi-motors.com.au*) response was to focus production on a medium-sized car that was popular domestically, but could still be exported. This focus allowed the company to achieve the necessary production volumes to be an efficient producer and remain a player in the Australian market. Mitsubishi Motors Australia's response to the economic changes of the 1980s has contributed to it becoming one of Australia's largest exporters by 2003.

Mitsubishi's Thai subsidiary, MMC Sittipol Co. Ltd. (*http://www.mitsubishi-motors.co.th*), had to quickly respond to a changing business environment when the Asian Financial Crisis hit in 1997. High demand for pick-up trucks in South East Asia in the early 1990s led the subsidiary to focus on the pick-up truck market. It built two plants, one for domestic production and one for export production. When the market crashed in the throes of the Asian Financial Crisis, MMC Sittipol quickly closed the plant that manufactured domestic models, and focused solely on export models. MMC Sittipol's export business has since prospered. By 2003, the company was exporting pick-up trucks to 139 countries worldwide and it was Thailand's biggest automobile exporter.

Sources:

Takahiro Fujimoto and Shinya Orihashi, *The Strategic Effects of Firm Sizes and Dynamic Capabilities on Overseas Operations*, University of Tokyo, January 2002.

http://www.mitsubishi-motors.com.au/, 19 November 2003.

http://www.mitsubishi-motors.co.th, 19 November 2003.

A key point in this example of Mitsubishi Motor's subsidiaries is that both had changes in their mandates emerge from changes in the external operating environment. In the Australian case, liberalization in product markets led to the Australian subsidiary to expand the geographic market of its sales, as its domestic market operations became more competitive. In the Thai case, the Thai subsidiary expanded the product portion of its mandate to capture rapidly emerging opportunities in the pick-up truck market.

In this sense, the external environment is an important influence on a subsidiary's development, and the type of role it assumes in a multinational firm. A subsidiary's role in a multinational firm emerges in part from the constraints and opportunities it faces in its markets in its host country. Its role also emerges from the assignments it receives from the head office or regional office of the multinational firm, and it emerges from the initiatives and opportunities pursued by a subsidiary's own management. These latter issues – the assignment of roles to a subsidiary by its parent, and the entrepreneurial pursuit of roles by a subsidiary's management – are two of the more critical in subsidiary management and subsidiary strategy.

A Multinational Firm's Network of Subsidiaries

When looking at subsidiary strategy from the perspective of the multinational firm, it is essential to consider how a subsidiary receives its roles by assignment from the parent firm. We can illustrate the roles a subsidiary receives by resorting to various typologies of the activities pursued by a subsidiary. When doing so, it is important to keep in mind that an individual subsidiary is in reality part of a network of subsidiaries in a multinational firm. This network of subsidiaries works together to complete all the activities of the multinational firm. Hence, what one subsidiary does often bears a relationship to the activities conducted by the other subsidiaries in the multinational firm.

As part of a multinational firm's network of subsidiary operations, a subsidiary can enjoy different degrees of integration with a multinational firm's operations. Integration and localization of activities can take place along a number of dimensions of a firm's operations including:

1. where inputs are sourced (locally or from the multinational firm)
2. whether purchases are made individually or together with other subsidiaries
3. the degree of local content in locally sourced inputs
4. the amount (percentage) of production that is exported
5. the extent of alignment of a subsidiary's manufacturing activities with those of other subsidiaries in the multinational firm
6. the level of local, versus global, research and development
7. the extent of product adaptations for the local market
8. the extent to which marketing programmes are tailored to the host country market

To consider the general idea of how a multinational firm decides on the extent of integration for these various facets of its activities, let's take the case of the degree of integration that accompanies a multinational firm's globalization, as an example.[3]

If a multinational firm's subsidiary operations enjoy greater levels of integration as it globalizes, this can have several important repercussions for a subsidiary's operations. As integration tightens, the strategic independence of a foreign subsidiary is lessened. Its amount of local autonomy in its operations can become less, especially if its operations become less general in scope. As the scope of its operations lessen, it can move, for example, from having in-house R&D for the development of its own technology, to the use of technology imported from the multinational.

Although it might suffer these losses in autonomy, there are clear gains from greater integration into the network of a multinational firm's subsidiaries. The loss of strategic independence can be accompanied by a growing influence on the overall strategic direction of the multinational. As a consequence, the geographic scope of a subsidiary's operations can change from one focused on the local market, to a regional or global one. If the scope of a subsidiary's product activities are contracted, it can develop depth in a particular area. It can become specialized in the manufacture of a particular product, or it can develop strengths in a defined area of the value chain. If it is strong in the downstream end of operations, it can focus on this particular area of operations, while still having access to the multinational firm's in-house R&D.

This sequence of changes that accompanies the increasing integration of subsidiaries in a globalizing multinational network is what has traditionally been regarded as a standard development path for a foreign subsidiary. In the initial stages of a multinational firm's expansion, a subsidiary has a generalist role, with a substantial degree of autonomy. As a multinational firm continues its expansion, the role of a subsidiary can become more circumscribed, as its level of autonomy is reduced and it adopts more of a specialized function.

This process is especially likely to occur for subsidiaries that were established by an acquisition entry or, as a case of an external environmental influence, in an economic environment that is becoming increasingly liberalized. An acquired firm can have a full range of independent operations at the time of its acquisition. Once acquired, the target can face a reduction of the scope of its operations, as products or functions redundant to those in the multinational network are shut down. Further, its autonomy is likely to be reduced as its operations are integrated with the parent multinational.

For the case of the external environmental influence, barriers to trade can lead a multinational firm to adopt a miniature replica strategy. In this strategy, a foreign subsidiary replicates most of the functions and products of the multinational, but in another country. Tariff and non-tariff barriers to trade make a host country an unattractive place to which to export. A foreign subsidiary operation becomes the most economical way to serve that host country market. As economies liberalize, and barriers to trade drop, this motivation to form a foreign subsidiary decreases. The rationale for having a full function, full product subsidiary is no longer as strong. A potential consequence is that the subsidiary will be closed, or that the scope of its operations will be reduced. We will discuss more of these types of assigned subsidiary development. Before doing so, we will develop a more concrete notion of the general types of roles a subsidiary can pursue in being part of a multinational firm's network of operations.

A Transactional Network of Subsidiaries

A network is a commonly used phrase to describe a series of interactions among many different individuals or entities. We think of networks in a variety of ways: we have a network of friend, a network of business contacts, even a family can be thought of as a network of relatives. In an organizational context, a network can be considered to be those business entities with which a firm enjoys a relationship. The relationships can be transactional where one firm buys a product and the other sells a product; it can be informational where the two firms exchange information about consumers, suppliers or governments; or it can be organizational where two or more business units are part of the same corporate entity. This latter type of network is the one we most frequently associate with a network of multinational firms.

Figure 11-1 shows this type of intra-organizational network. We can see that in a multinational firm the focal subsidiary has a variety of relationships with other subsidiaries in the multinational firm. The connections defined by these relationships comprise its intra-organizational network. The focal subsidiary also has connections with businesses that are outside the multinational firm. These connections with outside firms form the subsidiaries' inter-organizational network. Although both networks have important implications for the strategy and performance of the

Figure 11-1:   Internal and External Networks for a Subsidiary

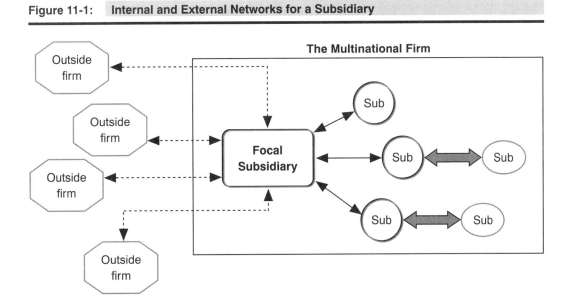

focal subsidiary in Figure 11-1, the network with the most profound implications for the role a subsidiary pursues in a multinational firm is its intra-organizational network.

In an intra-organizational network, there is a need for mechanisms to control and coordinate the activities carried out by the individual components in the network, namely a firm's subsidiaries. In a market, the coordinating mechanism is frequently the price and conditions that underlie a transaction between two firms. In an intra-organizational network, the coordinating mechanism is often a bit more complicated.

A traditional, and still often utilized means of coordination in a multinational network, is centralized parental control. Parental control, sometimes called corporate control, means that the headquarters of a multinational firm identifies the activities each subsidiary undertakes. In a corporate control system, subsidiaries are assigned roles. The parent then monitors and controls a subsidiary, often using different mechanisms for monitoring and control depending on the type of role a subsidiary is assigned.

In a multinational network coordinated by centralized corporate control, subsidiary strategy emerges as a consequence of activities and assignments of the corporate parent. In a sense, the corporate control of headquarters over a multinational firm can be thought of as a way to regulate the transactions, that is the exchanges, between a firm's subsidiaries. Inter-subsidiary transactions can occur along three dimensions: capital (monetary) flows, product flows and knowledge flows. A multinational firm is then a network of capital, product and knowledge flows and transactions, in which subsidiaries in the network are located in different countries worldwide.

Depending on the role assigned by headquarters to a subsidiary, each subsidiary in this network can vary in the magnitude of transactions it undertakes in the multinational firm, and the direction of the transactions. The magnitude of transactions refers to the quantity and importance of the inter-subsidiary transactions for capital, products and knowledge. The directionality of transactions refers to whether the flow is from the multinational firm to the subsidiary or from the subsidiary to the rest of the multinational firm.

The design of a multinational firm, and its subsidiaries' strategies, must take into account the idea that it needs to coordinate, and sometimes regulate, both the direction and magnitude of capital, product and knowledge flows. Across these three types of flows and transactions, knowledge has begun to emerge with an increased prominence.

The first typology of subsidiaries that we discuss in this chapter, emerges from a consideration of how knowledge flows between and across subsidiaries in a multinational flow.[4] Depending on the directions of flows of knowledge in a multinational firm, we can identify a subsidiary as having one of four potential roles to play in a multinational firm's knowledge transactions: (1) a local innovator; (2) a global innovator; (3) an implementer; (4) an integrated player (see Figure 11-2).

Figure 11-2: **Knowledge Flows and Subsidiary Types in a Multinational Firm**

Magnitudes of knowledge flows:
Subsidiary to the Multinational Firm

	Low	High
High	Global Innovator	Integrated Player
Low	Local Innovator	Implementer

Magnitudes of knowledge flows:
Multinational Firm to the Subsidiary

Source: Adapted from Anil K. Gupta and Vijay Govindarajan. "Knowledge Flows and the Structure of Control Within Multinational Corporations," *Academy of Management Review*, Vol. 16, Iss. 4, Figure 1, p. 774.

Local innovator

A local innovator has low levels of knowledge flows from it to the multinational firm and from the multinational firm to it. A local innovator has complete responsibility for its own knowledge creation. It operates independently and autonomously, and is typically found in a firm that has implemented a multi-domestic strategy.

Global innovator

A global innovator has high levels of knowledge flows from it to the multinational firm, but low levels of knowledge flows from the multinational firm to it. This type of subsidiary is the source of much of the knowledge of a multinational firm. Historically, these subsidiaries were located in the home country of a multinational firm, but in more recent years, subsidiaries of this sort have been emerging in host countries, when a firm adopts a transnational strategy.

Implementer

An implementer has low levels of knowledge flows from it to the multinational firm, but high levels of knowledge flows from the multinational firm to it. An implementer does not rely heavily on its own knowledge generation, instead it relies on knowledge inflows from the rest of the multinational firm. This type of subsidiary was found in the early development of a multinational firm, in ones that implemented an international or multi-domestic strategy.

Integrated player

A local innovator has high levels of knowledge flows from it to the multinational firm and from the multinational firm to it. An integrated player is similar to a global innovator. It is different from a global innovator as it is reliant on knowledge flows from the rest of a multinational firm, for its own development. It is typically found in a multinational firm that has implemented a global strategy.

The typology illustrated by Figure 11-2 shows the differences a multinational firm's subsidiaries can have in just one general aspect of its network relationships. A subsidiary can utilize or develop the knowledge that flows through a multinational firm's network of subsidiaries. Aside from the notion that knowledge can be generated at multiple points in a multinational firm, Figure 11-2 is important because it raises our awareness of the differences in the strategic contexts of subsidiaries in multinational firms. This strategic context must be at the forefront of considerations when deciding on roles for subsidiaries and when planning the mix of formal and informal corporate controls for a subsidiary and its management.

A Role Assignment For Subsidiaries

Aside from the idea of the types of transactions a subsidiary undertakes, we can also consider the broad role it has in a multinational firm's network of subsidiaries. Each subsidiary in a network can have specific functions to fulfill. These functions might or might not have overlap with those functions of other subsidiaries in the multinational firm's network. As with transactional typology shown in Figure 11-2, we can illustrate the various functions, or activities, a subsidiary can be assigned by using a series of figures that break down a subsidiary's activities into product scope, market scope and value-added scope.

We can define product scope as the flexibility and independence a subsidiary has to make improvements and extensions in its existing product mandate, as well as introduce new products. Market scope refers to the number and extent of geographic markets a subsidiary can serve. Value-added scope is the types of functional activities – research and development, manufacturing, new product development, marketing – that a subsidiary is charged to undertake.[5]

As we have discussed, part of the influence on the product, market and value-added scope of a subsidiary's operations comes from its external environment. Environmental forces might dictate a global approach, or these forces might favour a local approach. Another feature influencing the extent of the a subsidiary's product, market and value-added scopes is its assignment from headquarters. A subsidiary's parent might provide it with a mandate to pursue the multinational firm's full range of product lines, but with only a manufacturing value-added scope that applies to a specific country market.

Figures 11-3 and 11-4 illustrate the types of subsidiaries associated with different product, market and value-added scopes. In these figures, we can see different types of subsidiary roles emerge with different configurations of product, market and value-added scopes. A strategic

Figure 11-3:   Product and Market Scope in a Subsidiary of a Multinational Firm

Market (Geographic) Scope

	Narrow	**Wide**
Wide	Product Specialist	Strategic Independent
Narrow	Miniature Replica: Adopter	Miniature Replica: Innovator

Product Scope

Source: Adapted from Roderick E. White and Thomas A. Poynter, "Strategies for Foreign-owned Subsidiaries in Canada," *Business Quarterly*, 1984, Vol. 48, No. 4, Exhibit 1, p. 60.

Figure 11-4:   Value-Added and Market Scope in a Subsidiary of a Multinational Firm

Market (Geographic) Scope

	Narrow	**Wide**
Wide	Specialist Manufacturer	Strategic Independent
Narrow	Marketing Satellite	Miniature Replica

Value-Added Scope

Source: Adapted from Roderick E. White and Thomas A. Poynter, "Strategies for Foreign-owned Subsidiaries in Canada," *Business Quarterly*, 1984, Vol. 48, No. 4, Exhibit 1, p. 60.

independent subsidiary is one charged with a wide scope along all dimensions. This type of subsidiary is permitted to explore global market opportunities independently. It can pursue new product development initiatives, and it can tailor a product to a local market, or it can produce a common product for global consumption.

A specialist manufacturer and a product specialist both share the characteristic of selling to a wide geographic market, but with the product specialist focusing on a specific product, such as a component part. A specialist manufacturer undertakes a narrow range of functional activities, such as manufacturing with no research and development.

A marketing satellite also has a narrow range of functional activities, but these functions are also constrained to a specific geographic market. A marketing satellite is typified by a sales subsidiary that push a firm's products in local markets. A marketing satellite can be an importing company, or it can be a complex marketing entity that distributes products, designs marketing programmes, and provides after-sales service in a specific geographic market.

A miniature replica has a specific role to serve a local market. It does so generally by replicating a multinational firms full range of functional activities, as it has a wide value-added scope. It can produce a full range of products or a narrow range of products. It can have the freedom to introduce new products, in which case it is considered to be an innovator, or it can be constrained in its introduction of new products, in which case it is an adopter.

These various subsidiary types help identify the types of roles to which a subsidiary can be assigned by a multinational firm. When making the assignment of subsidiary strategy to a subsidiary, it is not as simple a task as defining the role on paper and then issuing this strategy directive to a subsidiary's management. Implementation of subsidiary strategy requires consideration of the control and coordination mechanisms that will be instituted to support the strategy and to meet the administrative challenges associated with the strategy. This administrative challenge returns us to the issue how headquarters must plan the mix of formal and informal corporate controls for a subsidiary and its management.

Formal and Informal Control Mechanisms

We have been working with the idea that a subsidiary's role is assigned to the corporate parent. This assignment extends from the perceptions the corporate parent has with respect to the capabilities of the subsidiary as well as the influence of the external environment, such as the strategic importance of the local market.[6] After making this assignment, the corporate parent should monitor and control the subsidiary.

There are a variety of mechanisms available to a multinational firm to facilitate the coordination of the activities carried out with its network of subsidiaries. These control mechanisms can be divided into two categories: (1) structural and formal mechanisms, and (2) informal and subtle mechanisms.[7]

Structural and formal controls include several specific mechanisms. One of these is departmentalization, or the formal structure of the organization. An organizational chart, such as illustrated in Chapter 10, is an example of departmentalization. Centralization, formalization and standardization of decisions, policies, jobs and other rules in an organization is another formal means of coordination. Planning, such as that encompassed in budgeting and goal setting activities is another mechanism. Finally, the corporate parent can rely on output control as found in the provision of formal reports and data from the subsidiary to the corporate parent.

Informal controls are more subtle. Personnel placements and relationships can provide information and knowledge to facilitate control and coordination. Informal communication through business trips, meetings, conferences and the like can also help with control and coordination. Likewise, an organizational culture can be a powerful force for aligning activities, goals and behaviours in managers dispersed across a firm's network of subsidiaries.

Over time in multinational firms, there has been a shift from a concentration on structural and formal control mechanisms to informal and subtle controls. This shift is a consequence of the controls that are most effective given the type of multinational strategy being invoked, and the type of roles being assigned to a firm's subsidiaries (see Figure 11-5). In a highly centralized organization, such as in a firm that has implemented an international strategy, structural and formal control mechanisms are effective, given the objective and clear definition of the roles of a subsidiary. In a multinational firm that has a transnational strategy, it is difficult to demarcate lines of communication and responsibility. If activities among autonomous subsidiaries, with wide product, market and value-added scopes are to be coordinated, then a firm needs to rely on informal and subtle control mechanisms. Similarly, knowledge creation and flows among subsidiaries can be stimulated by informal control mechanisms, and by having subsidiary input into decision-making that can culminate in a subsidiary influencing the role it takes in a multinational firm.

Figure 11-5: **Coordination Mechanisms in Multinational Firms**

Multinational Strategy	Subsidiary Roles	Coordination Mechanisms
International	Marketing Satellite Local Innovator	*Formal Mechanisms* International division Centralized decision-making Financial performance control Intensive use of expatriates
Multidomestic	Miniature Replica Implementer	*Formal Mechanisms* Personal reporting Financial performance control Strong use of expatriates
Global	Product/Manufacturing Specialist Global Innovator	*Formal Mechanisms* Worldwide product/geographic division Centralized decision-making Formal policies and rules Standard planning and production systems
Transnational	Strategic Independent Integrated Player	*Formal Mechanisms* Global matrix Centralized decisions, but have subsidiary input Complex output control *Informal Mechanisms* Temporary teams, tasks forces, committees Informal managerial communication channels Strong organizational culture in shared values

Source: Adapted Jon I. Martinez and J. Carlos Jarillo, "The Evolution of Research on Coordination Mechanisms in Multinational Corporations," *Journal of International Business Studies*, 1989, Vol. 20, No. 3, Table 4b, p. 506.

Subsidiary Choice

We have looked at subsidiary strategy from the perspective of the headquarters unit of a multinational firm. We can also consider subsidiary strategy from a subsidiary perspective in which the managers in a subsidiary exhibit choices about the roles and strategies pursued by a subsidiary. A crucial concept in a subsidiary choice perspective on subsidiary strategy is subsidiary development.

The concept of subsidiary development, or subsidiary evolution, comes from an extension of the perception about the roles a subsidiary has in a multinational firm. This changing perception of a subsidiary's role, which accompanies growth in a multinational firm, leads to new issues for management in a multinational firm.

During the early stages of growth in a multinational firm, when key functions are still largely centralized in a firm's headquarters, the foremost management issue is the dyadic relationship between a subsidiary and its headquarters. The relationship is well-defined, with the subsidiary controlled by headquarters.

As a multinational firm matures, the nature of the management challenge shifts from relationship to role management. The multinational firm becomes more differentiated in its functions, in a shift towards a network form. Subsidiary roles begin to become more distinctive, and the management task is one of contending and leveraging this diversity in a way that benefits individual subsidiaries and the firm as a whole.

Continued maturation in a multinational firm, brings with it increased opportunities for subsidiaries to begin to chart the direction of their own development. A subsidiary's role can and will change over time. Rather than this role development being a result of forces outside a subsidiary – such as changing goals of the parent multinational and changing environmental conditions – subsidiary managers can assume the challenge to steer the subsidiary to new destinations in the multinational network.

That said, the course that managers need to steer, even when adopting a self-directed subsidiary strategy, is often dictated by currents in the external environment. A powerful current in the late 20th and early 21st centuries has been the devolution of technological leadership from a few areas in North America and Europe to many more sites in the world. This current has guided multinational firms to a new technological imperative, in which a firm relies less on its home site as the source of its competitiveness, and more on its host country sites.

The Technological Imperative

Technology has had a central role in explanations about the behaviour of multinational firms. Technology provided early multinational firms with the advantage required to succeed in overseas markets. Central to a technological advantage is research and development.

Initial thinking on the process of research and development was that it had to be centralized to be effective. When centralized, there was a greater opportunity for making the groundbreaking innovations that could be translated into a competitive advantage spread throughout the multinational firm. Localized research and development activities did have a role in a multinational firm, but that role was primarily limited to be in the domain of local product and process adaptations.

The premises of this perspective on research and development were twofold. First, centralization provided the coordination necessary to have success in innovation activities. Second, the home site of the multinational firm was the best site at which to conduct these activities because it was the leading area for the technology of a firm. This second premise was particularly strong for the case of US, European, and later, Japanese multinational firms.

The second premise began to weaken with rapid technological developments in specific areas of the world. A growing number of countries have developed advanced capabilities in technology. This has been accompanied by a growing specialization of capabilities across countries over time. As a consequence, the home site of a multinational firm was not necessarily the best site for its technological activities. New hotbeds of technology – whether for the development of pharmaceutical products, electronic products, semi-conductor chips, small motors, automobiles and so forth – began to emerge around the world.

With the weakening of the second premise came a challenge to the first premise. How can research and development activities be centralized in the home country, if the home country is not the source of leading edge technological developments in a particular field? One response to this question is to shift all research and development activities to a new location, perhaps outside the home country. Doing so, assumes that technology will be leading edge for all a firm's products in that new site. This assumption is not always correct.

In this way, we land at the solution of distributing research and development activities to the location that provides the best opportunities for being at the leading edge of a technology or product development. TDK Corporation is an example of a company that has strategically situated research and development subsidiaries in a variety of locations to leverage geographical advantages. Established in Japan, TDK (*www.tdk.co.jp*) is a manufacturer of recording media, electronic materials and components. The company had R&D facilities in Japan, and through its TTDC-Japan subsidiary and TDK Electronics Ireland it had R&D facilities in Europe. In January 2001, TDK developed R&D facilities in the United States with the establishment of its subsidiary, TDK R&D Corp.

TDK created a worldwide network of R&D facilities so that it would be able to 'determine and react to market and technology trends within their respective local markets and engage in more effective technology and product development.'[8] Looking specifically at the US market, TDK Corp. had a number of R&D facilities to leverage geographic advantages and areas of expertise.

For example, in mid-2000, TDK acquired Headway Technologies of California, a manufacturer of recording heads for hard drives (*www.hdwy.com*). The ownership of Headway

Technologies not only provided TDK with a research and manufacturing base in the US, but this was a company that was already located close to the R&D facilities of many other leading US hard drive makers. To further develop its R&D capabilities in the US, TDK established the wholly-owned subsidiary, TDK R&D Corp., This subsidiary helped TDK strengthen its basic technology and market products specifically designed for the US market.

Decentralized research and development, such as that undertaken by TDK, can increase the richness of a firm's knowledge base. But decentralization will provide little benefit without some coordination or research and development activities. Surprisingly, the answer to coordination rests in autonomy, but in the direction of increased, not decreased, autonomy of subsidiaries engaged in research and development. The increase in autonomy comes at the level of the activities pursued to fulfill the core goal of developing new products and processes through research and development activities. Autonomy does not, however, mean complete independence or isolation from the rest of the multinational firm. Instead, a system of coordinative mechanisms need to be developed that allow managers in subsidiaries in other areas of the multinational firm to be cognizant of developments in subsidiaries engaged in basic research and development, and likewise for the other direction.

As necessarily complicated as this series of relationships and processes seem, few firms have been able to successfully decentralize their research and development in this way. One organization that is an exception to this is the Finnish firm, Nokia, a worldwide leader in mobile communications.

Nokia was founded as a wood pulp mill in 1865. In the intervening 140 years, Nokia has developed into a global mobile communications firm that in 2003, sold five phones every second.[9] The company held a 35 per cent share of the global mobile phone market, greater than the share of its nearest three rivals combined.[10]

In the spring of 2002, the Nokia Mobile Phones (NMP) business unit altered its organizational structure to ensure the continuation of its innovative and creative business culture. This restructuring involved the creation of nine small autonomous business units backed by cost-effective central services. Each unit tapped into Nokia's central research lab for basic technology and product design, with end products being handed over to a shared operations-and-logistics group. Autonomy in these business units is preserved by making each unit a profit-and-loss centre with the capacity to create its own business model, conduct its own advanced R&D and marketing, and draft its own product road maps.[11]

'By allowing teams the space they need to dig deeper into their area of interest, we've enabled them to create a big business and do it fast,' says Matti Alahubta, president of NMP. 'Big companies lose sensitivity. People need to feel that they can make a difference. And they need to have the power to make their ideas happen. We've created a small-company soul inside a big-company body.'[12] Nokia, like TDK, ensures it is exposed to the best opportunities by distributing its R&D sites in a variety of locations worldwide, usually adjacent to leading universities and relevant industry clusters.

As a subsidiary competes in its own geographic and product market, it is exposed to the market forces that are an important contributor to the success of innovation efforts. Nokia believes that continuous product development should also be emphasized. Alahubta makes the point that, 'It's a combination of putting people in the right environment to generate ideas and giving them the power to make those ideas happen.'[13] New product developments can happen in dispersed subsidiaries. The advantages of multinationality can be further leveraged if other subsidiaries in the multinational network have the opportunity to capture and internalize these new products and processes.

Technology and the Multinational Firm

In following this perspective on recent developments in technology in a firm, management becomes involved in making attempts to selectively tap into dispersed pockets of knowledge via foreign direct investments. Dispersed subsidiaries are then linked together in the multinational network. Not all connections across subsidiaries will be the same, making for idiosyncratic patterns in network connections, and a corresponding uniqueness in the knowledge and information to which a subsidiary is exposed. Unique sources of knowledge should contribute to the development of specialized capabilities and specialized contributions to the competitiveness of a multinational firm.

Unique sources of knowledge can come from within and from outside a firm. Innovation involves combining knowledge from a variety of places, that are situated within and outside a firm. Multiple connections to sources of information and pressures for advancement of a firm's technological capabilities, can push the innovation process forward. There is no recipe to guarantee the success of innovation efforts, but establishing multiple connections within the organization, and outside of it to other firms, universities and government research institutes, buyers and suppliers, can improve the chances of success.

If we turn to the experience of foreign investors in the United States, we can begin to see that such efforts to build connections do yield rewards in the form of enhanced technological competence, and the development of new capabilities and advantages.

Firms from outside the United States have viewed the United States as a vibrant source of technological knowledge. A considerable number of foreign direct investments have been made in the United States with the goal of tapping into local hotbeds of technological knowledge, to improve the technological capabilities of the multinational firm, and foster new innovations. For example, the India technology firm, Infosys (*www.infosys.com*), set up global development centres in US and other countries, in order to expand the capabilities of their 'global delivery model to leverage talent and infrastructure in different parts of the world.'[14]

New technological innovations are generally marked by a patent. A patent is accorded to an inventor, when the invention, or innovation, is substantially new. A tremendous number of new patents can be granted in a country in a given year. In the 1980 to 1990 period in the United

States, more than 16,000 patents were granted to subsidiaries of foreign companies based in the United States.[15] These patents related directly to research and development activities done by these foreign subsidiaries of non-US companies.

About 30 per cent of these patents came from former US firms that were acquired by a non-US firm, in an acquisition foreign direct investment. This observation reinforces the idea that acquisitions can be a way for a multinational firm to increase its technological competences.

The other 70 per cent of the patents came from wholly-owned subsidiaries of non-US companies. These foreign subsidiaries were able to tap into local networks of knowledge. Both TDK Corporation, discussed earlier in this chapter, and Haier America, established wholly-owned subsidiaries in the United States to garner a full understanding of, and develop products for, the US market. Having a subsidiary in the United States permitted a foreign firm to embed itself in the local context. The local context provided a new source of knowledge to a subsidiary, and to the multinational firm, which when linked to other sources of knowledge as resident in the multinational network, created opportunities for innovation.

Back to Subsidiary Evolution[16]

We can think of subsidiary evolution as the accumulation and development of resources and capabilities in a subsidiary over time, as it moves into a changed role, or charter, in a multinational firm. Managers in a subsidiary can compete for charters, and thereby change the responsibilities of a subsidiary and alter its development path. A subsidiary manager's ability to compete for a charter is dependent on how attractive the subsidiary appears to be to managers in the multinational firm. A convincing case for charter change, or new charter acquisition, can be built when a subsidiary has strong capabilities. If managers in a subsidiary permit its capabilities to atrophy, or to show no improvement, then the subsidiary risks being left behind as the multinational itself evolves.

The process of subsidiary evolution and charter change and extension is not solely related to the maintenance and enhancement of a subsidiary's capabilities. Other factors come into play. Some of these are outside the discretion of management. The location of a subsidiary dictates in no uncertain terms its attractiveness as a house for a particular technological initiative. If a subsidiary is not located in a technological hotbed, it is not likely to accommodate the research and development processes associated with a technology initiative.

The organizational context is important as well. This discussion is premised on the idea that that there is latitude for managers in a subsidiary to act. This means the organizational context must be one in which there is decentralization of management tasks and decision making, that there is a global perspective adopted by management, and that there is a competitive internal resource allocation process. Where these are missing, it can be a foregone conclusion that subsidiary initiatives to secure new charters will fail. If senior management has a strong home country bias, it can stop any host country subsidiary initiatives cold. If there is no competitive resource allocation process, there is no competition to win in the first place.

Given that the host country and organizational context are conducive to subsidiary initiatives, what can subsidiary managers do to enhance the chances of securing new charters, that enable a subsidiary to climb the evolutionary ladder? Three managerial actions are particularly important: build a track record of subsidiary success, build the credibility of subsidiary management, and cultivate an entrepreneurial orientation in a subsidiary's management and employees.

1. *Track record of subsidiary success:* A good track record of success in a subsidiary makes it much easier for decision makers in the multinational firm to award the subsidiary favourably in an investment decision. Past success builds a strong justification, for permitting a subsidiary to undertake new and expanded initiatives, that enhance its charter.

2. *Credibility of subsidiary management:* Managers in a multinational firm cannot be sure of the success of a new initiative in a subsidiary, regardless of the assurances and the strength of proposal put forward by a subsidiary's managers. Where a subsidiary's management is more credible in the eyes of managers in the parent multinational, a proposal is likely to be more compelling. Credibility comes from a variety of sources, but an important one in the context of a distributed multinational network is the informal ties between decision makers in the multinational firm and subsidiary management. Where informal ties are strong, and the subsidiary managers are well-known, their personal credibility will be higher. Combining high personal credibility with a strong proposal helps build a better case for charter change.

3. *Entrepreneurial orientation:* Employees with an entrepreneurial orientation are on a constant lookout for new opportunities. Entrepreneurship in the context of a multinational firm refers to a watch for ways in which a subsidiary can capture new chances to add value to the multinational firm's operations. Without an entrepreneurial orientation, a status quo bias can begin to permeate subsidiary management. This status quo bias can be detrimental in an organizational context characterized by decentralization and internal competition, as it can lead the subsidiary to charter losses, because of its neglect to pursue opportunities.

Accepting that these three subsidiary factors are in place, success in pursuing charters will not come automatically. The capabilities in the subsidiary need to be commensurate with the type of opportunity offered by the multinational firm, in whatever investment decision is being contemplated. It is clear, however, that separation from the process of charter enhancement can reduce chances for capabilities to be upgraded, which will ultimately contribute to the lessening of a subsidiary's role and responsibilities in a multinational firm.

This is just one possible destination for a subsidiary. It can become a negligible part of a multinational's firms operations through neglect, and ultimately it can lose its charter. An alternative route is one of continual charter and capability improvement that takes a subsidiary to a position of considerable value in a multinational firm. This latter destination, which can be considered an extension of a world product charter, can be achieved when a subsidiary becomes a centre of excellence in a multinational firm.

Centres of Excellence[17]

A desirable endpoint for a subsidiary seeking an improved value-added, high responsibility mandate in a multinational firm is to become a centre of excellence. Aside from being a centre of excellence, a subsidiary can end up as a central point for other activities in a multinational firm. It can be a dormant centre, an administrative centre, a global headquarters, or a strategic centre of excellence.[18]

A dormant centre is one that has little influence on the overall operations of a multinational firm, perhaps because the capabilities housed in the subsidiary do not hold value for the rest of the multinational firm. A dormant centre has a limited scope in its operations and a low domain of influence. A dormant centre tends to be one that implements directives from headquarters and follows local market opportunities. It is possible that a dormant centre can have unique capabilities that would be useful to the organization as a whole, but those capabilities are not picked up by the multinational firm.

When capabilities do exist and are picked up by the multinational firm, then a subsidiary has a chance to move into a more central role in the multinational network. One of those roles is an administrative centre. An administrative centre has a wide scope of responsibilities. Management in an administrative centre influence a broad range of activities in the part of the multinational network over which the administrative centre has control and responsibilities.

Although an administrative centre has a central role in coordinating functions across many other subsidiaries, it still has some responsibility to the central administrative functions of the multinational firm. In the early stages of a firm's internationalization, the central functions of administration generally fall into the domain of the global headquarters. Global headquarters are common to highly centralized companies. The global headquarters maintains tight control over a large number of functions of individual subsidiaries. As part of decentralization in a multinational network, the importance of a global headquarters is usually slated to decline.

As operations and responsibilities become more dispersed in a multinational network, there is greater opportunity for individual subsidiaries to assume more prominent roles in a multinational firm. When a subsidiary develops a particular capability, that is valued throughout the organization, it can become a centre of excellence. A centre of excellence has two unique defining characteristics. First, it is a subsidiary, or group of subsidiaries in one host country, that has a set of capabilities that are recognized by senior management as being an important source of value creation in a multinational firm. Second, the capabilities in the subsidiary should be leveraged throughout the entire organization to strengthen its competitiveness. Hence, it is not enough that a centre of excellence is at the leading edge in a particular area of a multinational firm's activities, it must augment the competitiveness of the multinational firm as a whole.

As an example of a centre of excellence, we can turn to Hewlett Packard's operations in Singapore. The Singaporean unit has been charged with the task to move low value-added manufacturing activities outside of Singapore to areas in Southeast Asia and China where a lower cost structure can be achieved. This task could be a prelude to the end of Hewlett Packard's manufacturing activities in Singapore. Instead, the Singaporean subsidiary has successfully gained a worldwide mandate to improve on existing technology to make and market Hewlett Packard's handheld information products such as calculators, palm tops and mobile printers.[19]

As we have discussed in Chapter 8 and earlier in this chapter, the traditional source of the leading capabilities in a multinational firm has been the headquarters of its operations in its home country. A secondary source of leading edge capabilities could be other organizational units, but also those stationed in the home country. Increasingly, however, high value-added activities have been moved outside the home country. Eventually, business units in host countries undertaking high value-added activities can become the source of a firm's advantage in a particular area. When this happens, and the business unit improves the overall competitiveness of a multinational firm, then we have a centre of excellence. What naturally follows is the question of how a multinational firm can create, or how a subsidiary can evolve into, a centre of excellence.

Development of Centres of Excellence

The first step to understanding the development process of centres of excellence crosses the dimensions that are characteristic to all centres of excellence. Four dimensions are common to all centres of excellence: a physical presence; a superior set of capabilities; explicit recognition; and derivation of value for the organization as a whole.

1. *Physical Presence:* a centre of excellence is based in one unit in an organization. This unit can be an individual subsidiary, or it can be a group of subsidiaries.

2. *Superior Set of Capabilities:* The capabilities in a centre of excellence must be at the leading edge of competence for a multinational firm. The capabilities do not need to be unique; that is, several different units can each have leading edge capabilities, but the capabilities do need to be at the forefront of what is available in a firm. The capabilities can be in areas such as technology and marketing to create patents and brands, that can be applied to one or more product lines.

3. *Explicit Recognition:* A multinational firm must proclaim that a particular organizational unit is a centre of excellence, for it to be one. Explicit recognition is important as it facilitates the achievement of the fourth dimension.

4. *Derivation of Value:* A multinational firm must derive value from the leading edge capabilities of a particular organizational unit for it to be considered a centre of excellence. Value can be derived by distributing technology developed in a centre of excellence throughout the whole organization, or by flows of intangible assets such as knowledge to the rest of the organization.

With these dimensions in mind, we can take the next step down the road to understanding the development of centres of excellence. In considering the forces behind the development of a centre of excellence, it is useful to revisit a couple of the key defining aspects of multinational enterprise. Recall that in Chapter 8, we discussed the ideas of locational and ownership advantage. A locational advantage is an advantage that is specific to a geographic region, that can be captured in whole or in part by a multinational firm's foreign direct investment in that particular geographic region. An ownership advantage is an advantage specific to a firm that provides a firm with the competitive edge required to undertake and sustain foreign direct investment activity.

We can combine the ideas of locational and ownership advantage to envision the case of a firm undertaking a foreign investment with a particular set of capabilities, which then might become augmented because of specific features of the location in which it has invested. Put another way, the site of a firm's foreign direct investments can have the building blocks that can be used to heighten or extend a firm's competitive advantages. In this way, both locational factors and international organizational factors need to be in place for a subsidiary, or organizational unit, to develop into a centre of excellence.

Locational Factors

The idea of location contributing to the development of a firm's competitive advantages is not new to theories of international business. The archetype of a multinational firm is one that has a unique advantage developed in the home country context. Presumably, conditions in the home country contributed to the development of a firm's advantage.

In the same way, the host country context holds the potential to influence the evolution of a firm's existing advantages. As described in Chapter 2, the sets of factors that contribute to national competitive advantage – demanding customers, availability of specific factors of production, related and supporting industries, firm strategy, structure and rivalry – can likewise create the competitive conditions in a host country to promote the growth of competitive advantages in new ways for a firm.

It almost goes without saying, but just being in a country that has good competitive conditions for a particular industry does not automatically lead a firm to develop strong capabilities in that industry. Organizational factors, in the form of subsidiary management processes, and incumbent capabilities and advantages, work jointly with locational factors to lead a subsidiary to evolve into a centre of excellence.

Organizational Factors

The internal organization helps create and mold the competitive conditions necessary for the intensification of a firm's unique capabilities advantages. It can create supportive conditions when the organizational structure and systems are oriented towards an internal competition for business, or towards creating linkages between dispersed subunits to coordinate activities. The network that surfaces as a consequence of structures and systems that increase the density of inter-unit transactions, creates opportunities for knowledge exchange and new capability development.

The flows of intangible knowledge and resources across units within a firm can propagate capability development provided other resources are available. These resources are not necessarily the intangible elements in an organization, but rather the tangible resources, *i.e.* capital and human resources, that can permit a subsidiary or an organizational unit to engage in the transformational activities that build new knowledge and capabilities. If the multinational firm, or its network of subsidiaries, provide both tangible and intangible resources, the likelihood of capability development will be greater. A subsidiary will not develop without some organizational investment.

With the resources in place, and the competitive pressures providing explicit motivation, management in a subsidiary next requires the autonomy to pursue the development initiatives that will lead to capability advancement. In a situation in which the managers in a subsidiary have some control over the day-to-day operations, but not the broader strategic direction of the subsidiary, the likelihood is low that it can pursue activities that will enhance its capabilities. With strategic autonomy comes an implicit endorsement to hunt down new sources of value creation for a subsidiary's operations.

With both organizational and locational features in place, managers in a subsidiary and the multinational firm have an opportunity to turn host country operations into sites that can augment the overall competitiveness of the firm. The importance of this process is an off-shoot of continued globalization in which home country, or localized sources of advantage, have become a less fundamental part of a firm's success. Increasingly, a multinational firm's competitive success is premised on identifying and creating multiple national houses of capabilities, that are applied throughout the multinational firm.

Summary

Our discussion of the management issues in international business in Chapters 10 and 11 has come almost full circle. It has moved from the management of a home country's initial ventures into international markets, to the centralized management of a dispersed set of subsidiary organizations, to the management of individual subsidiary functions that contribute back to the competitiveness of the multinational firm.

These shifts in the focus of a manager's attention are a consequence of the evolution of a multinational firm, as inscribed by its internationalization process. The evolution leads to a point where individual subsidiaries achieve heightened importance in a multinational firm, and managers in individual subsidiaries can take steps to expand the roles and responsibilities of a subsidiary in its multinational firm.

To be successful in the pursuit of a new and expanded charters, subsidiary managers need to be aware of the organizational context. Understanding the key success factors of the multinational and the goals of key decision makers in the multinational, provide a good starting point for anticipating and reacting to opportunities to gain new charters. Once an opportunity is recognized, a proposal needs to be developed. The chances of the proposal being met favourably will be greater where subsidiary managers understand the organizational context underlying the decision making process.

The proposal needs to build on the advantages and existing competencies of the subsidiary. Does the local infrastructure or local market provide any advantage relative to competitors both inside and outside the firm? Are the current competencies of the subsidiary suited to the pursuit of this particular charter? Are the competencies in the subsidiary equal to or better than those in other subsidiaries in the multinational firm? Does the proposal have a sound economic basis?

As we have discussed, building a good proposal is just part of the process. There will be internal competition. If a subsidiary's management has maintained personal connections with key decision markers in the multinational firm, if the subsidiary is not an organizational stranger, if it has a good reputation and track record, then a sound proposal for an investment decision is more likely to be accepted. Throughout this process, a subsidiary can build its competencies, and improve or expand its charter to capture new technological initiatives, new product lines or new geographic markets.

As multinational firm's internationalization process matures, its success is increasingly predicated on the strengths of its subsidiary operations in host countries, and less on strengths drawn from its home markets. Subsidiary development, charter expansion, and the growth and extension of subsidiary capabilities, hence become fundamental to the continued expansion and performance of a multinational firm.

Notes

[1] Julian M. Birkinshaw and Neil Hood, "Multinational Subsidiary Evolution: Capability and Charter Change in Foreign-owned Subsidiary Companies," *The Academy of Management Review*, 1998, Vol. 23, No. 4, pp. 773–795.

[2] Julian M. Birkinshaw and Neil Hood, "Multinational Subsidiary Evolution: Capability and Charter Change in Foreign-owned Subsidiary Companies," *The Academy of Management Review*, 1998, Vol. 23, No. 4, pp. 773–795.

[3] J. Carlos Jarillo and Jon I. Martinez, "Different Roles for Subsidiaries: The Case of Multinational Corporations in Spain," *Strategic Management Journal*, 1990, Vol. 11, No. 1, pp. 501–512, provide a detailed illustration of the types of processes described in the paragraphs that follow.

[4] Anil K. Gupta and Vijay Govindarajan, "Knowledge Flows and the Structure of Control Within Multinational Corporations," *Academy of Management Review*, Vol. 16, Iss. 4, pp. 768–792.

[5] Roderick E. White and Thomas Poynter, "Strategies for Foreign-Owned Subsidiaries in Canada," *Business Quarterly*, 1984, Vol. 49, No. 2, pp. 59–69.

[6] Christopher A. Barlett and Sumantra Ghoshal, "Tap Your Subsidiaries for Global Reach," *Harvard Business Review*, November-December 1996.

[7] For more on control and coordination mechanisms see Jon I. Martinez and J. Carlos Jarillo, "The Evolution of Research on Coordination Mechanisms in Multinational Corporations," *Journal of International Business Studies*, 1989, Vol. 20, No. 3, pp. 489–514.

[8] *http://www.tdk.co.jp/teaah01/aah05100.htm*, 25 November 2003.

[9] Ian Wylie, "Calling for a Renewable Future: How Nokia Has Tackled the Ultimate Creative Act: Building Innovation into the Company's Culture," *Fast Company*, May 2003, pp. 46–47. (Next: Smart Company).

[10] "Worldwide Mobile Phone Shipments Up 21.2% in Third Quarter Year-over-Year, According to IDC," *PR Newswire*, 5 November 2003.

[11] Ian Wylie, "Calling for a Renewable Future: How Nokia Has Tackled the Ultimate Creative Act: Building Innovation into the Company's Culture," *Fast Company*, May 2003, pp. 46–47. (Next: Smart Company).

[12] Ian Wylie, "Calling for a Renewable Future: How Nokia Has Tackled the Ultimate Creative Act: Building Innovation into the Company's Culture," *Fast Company*, May 2003, pp. 46–47. (Next: Smart Company).

[13] Ian Wylie, "Calling for a Renewable Future: How Nokia Has Tackled the Ultimate Creative Act: Building Innovation into the Company's Culture," *Fast Company*, May 2003, pp. 46–47. (Next: Smart Company).

[14] *http://www.infosys.com/infrastructure/global.asp*, 23 November 2003.

[15] Tony Frost, "The Geographic Sources of Foreign Subsidiaries' Innovations," *Strategic Management Journal*, 2002, Vol. 22, No. 2, pp. 101–123.

[16] For more on subsidiary evolution see Julian M. Birkinshaw and Neil Hood, "Multinational Subsidiary Evolution: Capability and Charter Change in Foreign-owned Subsidiary Companies," *The Academy of Management Review*, 1998, Vol. 23, No. 4, pp. 773–795 and the collected chapters in Julian M. Birkinshaw and Neil Hood (editors), *Multinational Corporate Evolution and Subsidiary Development* (New York: St. Martin's Press, Inc., 1998); Julian M. Birkinshaw, *Entrepreneurship in the Global Firm* (London: Sage Publications, 2000); Julian M. Birkinshaw, *Entrepreneurship in Multinational Corporations: The Initiative Process in Canadian Subsidiaries* (Western Business School: London, Ontario, Canada, Unpublished Doctoral Dissertation, 1995); Julian Birkinshaw and Neil Hood, "An Empirical Study of Development Processes in Foreign Owned Subsidiaries in Canada and Scotland," *Management International Review*, 1997, Vol. 37, No. 4, pp. 339–364; Julian M. Birkinshaw, Neil Hood, and S. Jonsson, "Building Firm Specific Advantage in MNCs: The Role of Subsidiary Initiative," *Strategic Management Journal*, 1998, Vol. 19, No. 3, pp. 221–242; Gunnar Hedlund, "The Role of Foreign Subsidiaries in Strategic Decision Making in Swedish Multinational Corporations," *Strategic Management Journal*, 1980, Vol. 1, pp. 23–36; J. C. Jarillo and J. Martinez, "Different Roles for Subsidiaries: The Case of Multinational Corporations," *Strategic Management Journal*, 1990, Vol. 11, pp. 501–512; Thomas Malnight, "The Transition from Decentralized to Network-based MNC Structures: An Evolutionary Perspective," *Journal of International Business Studies*, 1996, Vol. 27, No. 1, pp. 43–66; James Taggart, "Autonomy and Procedural Justice: A Framework for Evaluating Subsidiary Strategy," *Journal of International Business Studies*, 1997, Vol. 28, No. 1, pp. 51–77; Rod E. White and Thomas A. Poynter, "Strategies for Foreign-owned

Subsidiaries in Canada," *Business Quarterly*, 1984, Vol. 48, No. 4, pp. 59–69; Thomas A. Poynter and Alan M. Rugman, "World Product Mandates: How Will Multinationals Respond?," *Business Quarterly*, Autumn 1982, pp. 54–61.

[17] For more on the centre of excellence concept, see Tony Frost, Julian Birkinshaw, and Scott Ensign, "Centers of Excellence in Multinational Corporations," *Strategic Management Journal*, 2002, Vol. 23, pp. 997–1018.

[18] Bernard Surlemont, "A Typology of Centers Within Multinational Corporations," in Julian M. Birkinshaw and Neil Hood (editors), *Multinational Corporate Evolution and Subsidiary Development* (New York: St. Martin's Press, Inc., 1998), pp. 162–188.

[19] D. Leonard Barton, *Wellsprings of Knowledge* (Harvard Business School Press: Boston, MA, 1995). As reported in Tony Frost, Julian Birkinshaw, and Scott Ensign, "Centers of Excellence in Multinational Corporations," *Strategic Management Journal*, 2002, Vol. 23, pp. 997–1018.

chapter 12 MULTINATIONAL MANAGER

International human resource management (IHRM) is a key function in a multinational firm. HRM concerns how a firm organizes its activities to use the people in the organization most effectively. HRM in multinational firms is becoming an increasingly taxing task as more and more individuals in the multinational firm work outside of their home country. International placements of staff complicate the HRM functions as functions such as recruitment, selection and training become tough to harmonize across the countries in which a firm operates.

Essentially, international HRM involves many of the same functions – recruitment, selection, training, performance appraisal and compensation – as human resource management in domestic corporations. When thinking of HRM in a multinational firm, one of the principal challenges in designing an international HRM system is identifying the extent to which policies and practices can be harmonized throughout the corporation, and the extent to which they must be individualized by host country. To some extent, globalization and international organizations are creating pressures in the international environment for the convergence of standards of labour employment practices worldwide. Even so, there is still considerable pressure to allow practices to diverge by nation.

What is International Human Resource Management?

International HRM is an important function within a firm as it helps to develop the people that staff key management, technical and operational positions in a multinational firm (see Table 12-1). An international HRM system in a firm must have systems to identify candidates to staff key positions. It must incorporate systems to develop these candidates so that they have the skills to fulfill the mandates of their organizational position. It must have a system to adequately compensate people working in their home country, or in a foreign country. When a manager takes the second of these positions; that is, a person from one country who is working abroad in another country, that individual is referred to as an expatriate manager.

A challenge that has emerged with respect to the development of these systems for the management of the HRM function internationally is that nations have different standards for the various functions in a firm's HRM systems:[1] recruitment; selection; training; performance

Table 12-1:	Key Functions in an International HRM System
Function	**Description**
Recruitment	A company must have a system to identify and attract the most qualified individuals to work in specific positions.
Selection	A company must have a system to choose individuals to work in specific positions.
Training	A company must have processes by which it can provide individuals with the knowledge, skills and abilities they require to be able to succeed in their position in the company.
Performance Appraisal	A company must have processes by which it can identify and evaluate how well individuals perform in their job functions.
Compensation	A company must have a means to compensate individuals for the work they do in the company. Compensation can include a monetary component as in a salary, as well as a non-monetary component as in child care benefits.

Source: Adapted from John Cullen, *Multinational Management: A Strategic Approach*, 2nd Ed., 2001 (South-Western: Mason, Ohio), p. 428.

appraisal and compensation. These different standards can be reflected in local employees' expectations for the job conditions under which they might work, and in the adaptations a firm must make in compensation and performance appraisal, for example, when assigning a manager to an international position.

The different standards emerge in perceptions of equity and fairness in a multinational firm as its HRM systems will inevitably involve a comparison with other organizations in the host country, and with other organization sub-units within the organization. These two points of comparison magnify the importance of striving to balance demands for localization and standardization in a firm's HRM systems.

National HRM Systems

In the first part of this book, we discussed the various dimensions of national environments that inject sources of variance in a multinational firm's operations. These same dimensions influence national HRM systems. In general, standards for business practices in a nation are rooted in national institutional features.

At times a nation's institutions can produce obvious and easily recognizable influences on HRM practices. For example, the laws of a country might prohibit certain forms of union organization, or a country's labour laws in a country might mandate specific levels of employee compensation. Many nations have minimum wage laws that explicitly identify the minimum compensation for an employee. Employment equity laws is another area that varies by nation. If employment equity laws are absent, a manager might use different procedures for recruitment and selection, than for the case in which a firm is operating in a nation with employment equity laws.

At times a nation's institutions can produce less obvious and less easily recognizable influences on HRM practices. For example, a nation's culture might place a high premium on work rather than leisure. Such an influence could appear in a higher reliability and responsibility in employees, than in a setting where this attribute is less prominent. Returning to the elements of national cultures we discussed in Chapter 3, where a culture is particularistic, managers might select employees based on personal qualities, such as a family affiliation. Meanwhile in a universalistic culture, employee selection is likely to be based on specific criteria such as an applicant's education and prior experience.

These differences in national HRM systems often have important implications for a multinational firm. Frequently, a lack of familiarity with national HRM systems and practices, can place a multinational firm at a disadvantage. A further complication is that existing corporate standards might be at odds with typical practices in a host country. As a consequence, a multinational firm does not only face a knowledge disadvantage for developing its local HRM systems, it faces the challenge of adapting existing corporate practices to what is required in the local environment.

This scenario returns us to the basic dilemma in multinational management – go local or global. The pressure on a multinational firm is often to go local with its HRM practices, but its resources and knowledge, and its existing corporate standards, lead to the idea that global strategy for managing HRM functional might be the best strategy. There is no clear answer, whether global or local, but there are considerations that should be made when managing the global and local aspects of an international HRM system.

Managing the International HRM Function

The management of the international HRM function in a multinational firm is not an easy task. A manager charged with such a task must meet both local and corporate standards for recruitment, selection, training, performance appraisal and compensation.

The first step in meeting local and corporate standards is to understand what those standards are. As an employee in the multinational firm, an international HRM manager should be fully cognizant of corporate standards. The task then becomes one of developing a deep cognizance of national standards.

The discussion earlier in this chapter suggests that some of the variance in national HRM systems, are rooted in dimensions of national environments. Aside from appreciating the role of national institutional environments to understand a nation's HRM system, it is also useful to look at how these differences are manifest in common HRM practices across nations.

A list of common HRM practices on a country-by-country basis would be a dauntingly long one. Minimum wage rates, wage rates by position or job, recruitment procedures, performance appraisals, training procedures and responsibilities, often have little resemblance from one nation to the next. This lack of commonality emphasizes the importance of being local in approach and developing localization in management.

Although nations can have substantial variance in HRM standards, there are features of the globalizing economy that create a current trend towards greater uniformity across nations in standards for HRM practices. Multinational firms help to drive this trend as they bring corporate standards for HRM policies and procedures to a number host countries. International organizations that seek to establish common standards in work practices across nations also help to drive this trend.

International Labour Organization

One of the organizations helping to drive convergence in national HRM systems is the International Labour Organization, known more commonly by its acronym, ILO (*www.ilo.org*). The ILO was established in 1919 to aid calls for social reform in international labor practices. It was founded on the idea that reform had to take place at an international level. Since its inception, the ILO has worked within an international institutional framework to improve working conditions worldwide.

The ILO has four principal strategic objectives:

1. To promote and realize standards, fundamental principles and rights at work
2. To create greater opportunities for women and men to secure decent employment
3. To enhance the coverage and effectiveness of social protection for all
4. To strengthen tripartism and social dialogue.

Consistent with these objectives, the ILO has instituted a number of key conventions (Table 12-2) aimed at specific problem areas in employment practices worldwide.

One of the implications of a multinational firm's HRM system of the activities of international bodies such as the ILO is that it limits opportunities to arbitrage national differences in HRM standards. As standards converge, albeit at a slow pace, multinational firms face fewer advantages from moving labour practices to the nations that have the most favourable national standards. Instead a multinational firm's advantages in HRM practices, will come from the effective management of the resources in the firm itself, such as its expatriate managers.

Managing Expatriates

Expatriate managers are an important component of a firm's international operations. The task of being an expatriate manager is a demanding position in a multinational firm. A multinational firm cannot compete successfully without skillful and well-trained expatriate managers. At the same time, the training, preparation and placement costs of expatriate managers can be an expensive and resource-consuming endeavour for multinational firms.

In thinking about the expatriate issue, there are several key issues that must be broached. One issue involves the type of approach a multinational firm can use to staff its foreign subsidiaries.

Table 12-2:   **Key ILO Conventions**

Convention Number	Convention	Description
29	Forced Labour Convention	Requires suppression of forced or compulsory labour with the exception of military service, convict labour and labour in the times of emergencies
87	Freedom of Association and Protection Right to World	All workers have the right to form and join organizations of their own choosing. Guarantees the free functioning of such organizations without interference from public authorities.
98	Right to Organize and Collective Bargaining	Protects against anti-union discrimination, protects workers' and employers' organizations against interference, allows for collective bargaining
100	Equal Remuneration	Equal pay and benefits for men and women for work of equal value
111	Discrimination	National policies should eliminate discrimination in recruitment, selection and training on the basis of race, colour, gender, religion, national or social origins, and promote equality of opportunity and treatment.
138	Minimum Age	Stipulates minimum age for admission to employment should not be less than the age for compulsory schooling. Has the goals of eliminating child labour.
182	Worst Forms of Child Labour	Calls for the elimination of the worst forms of child labour.

Source: http://www.ilo.org, 15 June 2003.

Will a multinational firm's management adopt an ethnocentric approach, a polycentric approach and a geocentric approach?

A second issue involves consideration of the trade-offs involves in employing an expatriate employees versus host country or third country nationals in the multinational firm. These trade-offs relate to matters of cost, skills and ease of recruitment, selection and training.

A third issue relates to the types of policies that are used to manage a firm's expatriate employees, when expatriate employees are used. A multinational firm should have policies in place to minimize the use and cost of expatriate managers, yet, when expatriate employees are used, these same policies need to optimize the performance of expatriates by focusing on easing an expatriate's adjustment to a foreign assignment.

Approaches to Staffing Policy

Several decades ago, back in the 1960s and 1970s, multinational firms had a very clear guideline to their international staffing policies. With few exceptions, the guideline was to use expatriate managers in all key overseas positions. Multinational firms made the explicit choice to absorb the high cost of using expatriates, to have an expatriate manager placed in every important position in an overseas subsidiary.

In the last years of the 20th century and on into the 21st century, such a policy has become less prevalent. Multinational firms across all regions of the world increasingly turned to local managers in place of expatriates to manage overseas operations. An AT Kearney study in 1999 in China determined that the desired ratio is two or more locals to every expatriate manager. [2]

The trend from expatriate to local management represented a change in mindset in multinational firms from an ethnocentric orientation to a geocentric orientation.[3] In essence, we can distill a multinational firm's staffing policies in its foreign subsidiaries to one of three types: an ethnocentric approach, a polycentric approach and a geocentric approach. Table 12-3 illustrates key features of each approach.

Table 12-3:   Approaches to Staffing in a Multinational Firm

Staffing Philosophy	Management Staffing	Strategic Orientation	Pros	Cons
Ethnocentric	Use expatriates in key positions throughout the multinational firm	International	• Facilitates coordination of activities across subsidiaries and the transfer of core skills across subsidiaries • Maintains uniform corporate culture and practices	• low diversity in opinion • common sets of skills • creates potential for perceptions of inequity and resentment by host country managers • high attrition rate of host country managers because of few opportunities for advancement
Polycentric	Use host country managers in key positions in host country subsidiaries	Multidomestic	• high levels of diversity, opinions and skills in management staff • avoid high costs of using expatriates	• coordination lower, and subsidiaries can be isolated from multinational firm's headquarters • potential for dilution of corporate culture
Geocentric	Best person for key positions, independent of person's nationality and independent of geographic location	Global and Transnational	• makes best use of a firm's human resources • strengthens management issue • strengthens retention through creation of internal opportunities for advancement	• expensive • complicated compensation systems • can achieve some uniformity but still must be responsive to local differences in employment laws

Source: Adapted from Charles W. L. Hill, *Global Business Today*, 2nd Ed. (New York: McGraw Hill, 2001), Table 14.1, p. 462.

By comparing the columns 'Staffing Philosophy' and 'Strategic Orientation' we can see that ethnocentric, polycentric and geocentric orientations match-up with the international, multidomestic and global/transnational strategies and structures we identified in Chapter 10. As such, a shift from an ethnocentric staffing philosophy to a polycentric staffing philosophy, usually accompanies a change from an international to a multidomestic strategy. A key point in implementing a multidomestic strategy involves the change in reliance on expatriate managers to manage foreign subsidiaries to local managers.

A shift to a geocentric staffing philosophy is one that accompanies a transition to a global or transnational strategy. If a transnatoing strategy is to be implemented in its purest form, then there should be no set preference for the nationality of a subsidiary's management given the location of a subsidiary. Instead, managers should be assigned to the position for which they are best suited, with job qualifications, not nationality, being the principal selection criterion.

Most organizations are involved, or have been involved, in a shift from an ethnocentric, to a polycentric and finally to a geocentric approach to staffing. This shift has important implications for the type of policies and practices instituted by a multinational firm, as shown in Table 12-4.

Multinational firms from various nations in the world are at different stages in terms of this shift, but even traditionally ethnocentric firms, such as those from Japan, are beginning to adopt polycentric and geocentric staffing philosophies, and, as a consequence, rely less on expatriate managers.

Expatriates in Japanese Multinational Firms

Japanese firms have been characterized as being among the most ethnocentric of multinational firms. This ethnocentrism has lead to the perception that that Japanese firms have a rice-paper ceiling policy.[4] A rice-paper ceiling is analogous to the glass-ceiling that was thought to be common in many corporations in the US in the 1980s.

A glass-ceiling is a metaphor used to describe an invisible barrier to upward advancement for female employees in US corporations. The rice-paper ceiling is a barrier to the upwards advancement of non-Japanese managers in Japanese corporations. A rice-paper ceiling has been thought to be a common characteristic of Japanese multinational firm, but recent studies point to an increase in the use of local management staff in place of expatriate managers in Japanese multinational firms.[5]

Just as in multinational firms from other countries, those from Japan use expatriates to help meet several corporate objectives. Expatriate managers play an important role in representing and implementing the corporate objectives of an MNE. Expatriates help align the operations of a subsidiary with that of the parent firm. Expatriates also help in a variety of other ways. An expatriate assignment helps facilitate the transfer of technology skills a subsidiary.

Take the example of Pro-Tec Coating Co., a joint venture between United States Steel Corp. (*www.usx.com*) and Kobe Steel Ltd. (*www.kobelco.co.jp*). This joint venture relocated managers

Table 12-4:   International HRM Practices by Staffing Philosophy

International HRM practice	International HRM staffing philosophy		
	Ethnocentric	**Polycentric**	**Geocentric**
Recruitment	Give priority to home country managers over host country managers.	Give priority to homes country managers at top positions. Host country managers staff middle management and technical positions.	No nationality pre-requisite for recruitment.
Selection	Select a home country manager based on the manager's qualifications for position and performance record.	Select manager based on technical, experience and other objective qualifications.	Assign most qualified, as defined by experience, skills and prior training and performance, to position.
Training	Concentrate on job training, provide limited emphasis for cultural training.	Emphasis is on job training. For home country managers, provide limited training in language and culture of host country.	Provide extensive training in language and culture in which a manager works. Training continuous throughout duration of assignment.
Performance evaluation	Use a home country standard for all positions independent of location, in the multinational firm.	Use a home country standard, with consideration given to standards in the world region in which a subsidiary operates.	Use global standards for subsidiary and individual performance.
Compensation	Increase compensation for expatriates, relative to same position in the home market.	Home country managers receive higher compensation than host country managers, as host country managers paid at rates consistent with those in the host country.	Compensation packages standardized on a global basis, across the multinational firm. Can make cost of living adjustments based on the nation in which a manager is situated.

Sources: Adapted from Nancy Adler and Fariborz Ghadar, "International Strategy from the Perspective of People and Culture: The North American Context," *Research in Global Business Management*, 1990, Vol. 1, pp. 179–205; D. A. Heenan and H. V. Perlmutter, *Multinational Organization Development* (MA: Addison Wessley, 1979); John Cullen, *Multinational Management: A Strategic Approach,* 2nd Ed. (South-Western: Mason, Ohio, 2001).

and engineers from Himeji, Japan to Ohio, USA to transfer their technological knowledge and skill from Kobe Steel to the joint venture. The companies also relocated sales and purchasing personal so that Japanese-speaking customers and suppliers could speak to each other in their mother tongue.[6] These expatriate assignments were used to put promising managers in a challenging position, and to provide managers with valuable developmental experience, both in functional areas and in international markets.[7]

These reasons are but a few of why expatriate managers have been so commonly used in

Japanese multinational firms, as well as those from other nations. Even so, there has been a chance in Japanese staffing philosophy, towards a polycentric approach. These changes have been occurring for a number of reasons.

The first reason is a simple matter of supply and demand. Japan's FDI has grown extensively since the mid-1980s. This growth has placed a considerable demand for qualified expatriate managers, but Japan's population growth, and the growth of its management pool has not kept pace. The result is that the growth in demand for expatriate managers has outstripped the growth in supply.

The second reason is that local managers can bring valuable sets of complementary skills to a subsidiary. Expatriate managers facilitate the transfer of core organizational management and technical skills. Local managers bring a unique knowledge of the host market context that can aid with local product development efforts, and strategic planning for the local market. Provided a foreign subsidiary can integrate local management staff effectively into its senior management teams, it can realize these benefits of employing local managers.

The integration of local management staff into an overseas Japanese firm can be challenging. According to Rochelle Kopp, president and founder of Japan Intercultural Consulting (JIC), the biggest challenge is communication. 'For Japanese, the hardest thing is learning how to be specific and forthcoming. They hear one thing and understand ten. There's lots of nonverbal communication.' To prevent problems in communication, Kopp believes that Japanese expatriates working overseas, especially in North America, have to be more explicit and explain themselves more fully when participating in intercultural situations.[8]

The second reason relates to a revenue-enhancement effect. The third reason relates to a cost reduction effect. Expatriates are expensive to employ. Local managers, even if paid at a level equitable with other management staff, are a lower cost option than expatriates, as their compensation packages do not have to include the perks that accompany an expatriate assignment. We discuss this point in more details later in this chapter.

The fourth reason relates less to these revenue and supply related issues and more to the organizational culture in Japanese firms. Companies in Japan are developing a broader acceptance of foreign participation at senior management levels. New opportunities for advancement are reflected in growing participation by local managers. Even with growing participation by local managers, the number of Japanese nationals employed as expatriate managers is still a sizeable number.

Expatriate managers form a large contingent of personnel in Japanese foreign subsidiaries. There is a large contingent as Japan is one of the world's largest foreign investing nations. In 2003, Japanese firms had placed more than 19,000 foreign subsidiaries in more than 130 countries worldwide.

These 19,000 foreign subsidiaries employed approximately 4,000,000 people in 2001. Among these 4,000,000 employees, more than 60,000 were Japanese expatriates. Hence, 1.5 per cent of all employees in Japanese foreign subsidiaries were a Japanese national.

The worldwide average of 1.5 per cent was not common to all Japanese foreign subsidiaries in all nations (see Table 12-5). Expatriate employment exhibited a considerable range. Among major recipients of Japanese foreign investment, the high in expatriate employment (in percentage terms) was Singapore, with 4.8 per cent expatriate employment. The low was 0.9 per cent, for Japanese subsidiaries in the Philippines.

One reason for the cross-country variance in the intensity of use of expatriates is in the types of functions that expatriates perform. As we discussed above, expatriates can perform a control function, to help to ensure that a subsidiary's activities are aligned with those in the multinational firm. Expatriate employees can help to transfer organizational knowledge from the parent corporation to a subsidiary, and from a subsidiary to the parent corporation.

In countries such as the US, both the control and knowledge transfer function are important to a subsidiary's success. Meanwhile, in countries such as China, Malaysia and the Philippines, the knowledge transfer role, at least on a long-term basis, is often less important than the control role.

In the short term, the knowledge transfer role can be very important. When a subsidiary is formed, it is not unusual to see a Japanese multinational firm initially devote a large number of expatriates to the foreign subsidiary, to help ensure it operates as the parent expects it should. This high deployment of expatriates is followed by a lower deployment, as expatriate managers shift from a knowledge management function to a control and monitoring function.

When Yamaha wanted to increase its participation in India in the early 1990s, in response to liberalization initiatives, it went from being an arms length technology provider, to its Indian partner, Escorts Ltd., to a joint venture partner. One of the goals of establishing this joint venture was to bring the manufacturing standards for Yamaha motorcycle production in India up to those in Japan. To accomplish this objective, Yamaha took an active approach to the development of the joint venture manufacturing plant. Yamaha used expatriate managers extensively during

Table 12-5:   **Employment in Japanese Foreign Subsidiaries**

Country	Number of Employees	Number of Expatriates	Percent of employees that are expatriates
Singapore	91,000	4,412	4.8%
United Kingdom	93,000	3,421	3.7%
United States	733,000	18,000	2.5%
Thailand	397,000	5,416	1.4%
Malaysia	261,000	2,930	1.1%
China	675,000	6,775	1.0%
Philippines	169,000	1,520	0.9%

Source: "Japanese Overseas Investments," various editions. (Toyo Keizai Inc.: Tokyo, Japan)

the start-up phase. To train local staff in Yamaha's production techniques, Yamaha sent teams of ten managers to the Indian joint venture. By using these teams of expatriates, Yamaha could transfer and establish its cellular production system, as well as other practices such as just-in-time inventory and production management.[9]

This case of Yamaha in India is not an isolated one. Multinational firms frequently use expatriates to bring a firm's key knowledge and skills to a newly-founded subsidiary. When doing so however, management needs to consider other elements in the trade-off to use expatriate managers in place of local or third-country staff. Sometimes, as in the case of the transfer of knowledge during the start-up phase of a plant, the benefits of using expatriate managers is quite clear. In other cases, it is not as clear.

Expatriate and Local Management

A firm can use expatriate, host country or third country nationals to staff its foreign subsidiaries and positions in its regional and head offices. As we have discussed, expatriates are commonly used in foreign subsidiaries, particularly during the start-up phase of a subsidiary's operations. Expatriates can be used in a foreign subsidiary because they provide a unique skill or have special knowledge that is useful for the functioning of the subsidiary.

When home country personnel and host country personnel have similar skill and knowledge sets, the choice is less clear about which to use. If a firm has an ethnocentric staffing policy, expatriate managers will tend to be preferred over host country nationals. Yet such a policy can impose a significant cost burden on a firm. Cost is a major driver of management localization, or the use of increasing numbers of host country nationals in management positions in a firm's foreign subsidiary. An international relocation can cost two and three times more than an employee's annual salary.[10] Aside from cost considerations, host country nationals can aid the localization of a subsidiary's operations in terms of the subsidiary utilizing local suppliers, and developing locally relevant products. The understanding a local manager has of a host country's cultural, legal and political environments permits a greater level of adaptation to local conditions to be made, provided local managers have the responsibility and authority to make decisions related to the localization of a subsidiary's operations.

Even though local managers and expatriate managers have complementary sets of skills and knowledge to bring to a subsidiary, in some cases a third country national (someone from neither the home or host country) will be used in senior management positions. A third country national can replace a host country national, where the supply of qualified host country nationals is constrained, and the third country national is a less expensive option than an expatriate from the home country. A third country national is likely to be found in a subsidiary in a multinational with a geocentric staffing approach. This approach assigns the most-qualified candidate to a position in an organization, irrespective of that individual's nationality.

Cost of Employing Expatriates

There are numerous implications of employing expatriate, host-country nationals or third country nationals in management positions in a subsidiary. Often, the issue of who to employ can be driven down to the single issue of cost. Indeed, one of the principal challenges to utilizing expatriates successfully in an organization is managing the cost of an expatriate assignment.

An expatriate assignment can represent a tremendous cost to a firm. In 2002, the total remuneration for an expatriate in mainland China was close to US$1million.[11] For BP America Inc. (*www.bp.com*) in 2001, the total cost of using an expatriate manager approached three times the expatriates actual salary.[12] The cost is often of such a magnitude, that it can reduce any benefits that can come from placing a subsidiary in a foreign country. To realize the expected gains from foreign direct investment, the costs of employing expatriates must be minimized.

There are two basic ways in which a firm's overall costs of expatriate assignments can be managed in a multinational firm. First, as we discussed earlier, the number of expatriates can be optimized by focusing on the use of local managers. If a firm's staffing philosophies are not ethnocentric, then local managers can occupy important managerial positions in a subsidiary when qualified to do so.

Second, the cost associated with an individual expatriate assignment need to be minimized. Unfortunately, the costs associated with an expatriate assignment are usually more difficult to reduce than the number of expatriates used. Expatriates require a large compensation package. This large magnitude is created by several unique components of expatriate compensation. An expatriate's compensation packages should provide an expatriate with a standard of living equal to what an expatriate had in the home country, prior to being assigned to an overseas subsidiary. In the Asia-Pacific this can be significant as the area possesses twenty of the world's most expensive cities, with Tokyo being the world's most expensive city in 2003.[13] The compensation package frequently includes a premium to counterbalance the non-monetary costs borne by an expatriate when taking an overseas assignment.

In practice, an expatriate's compensation package involves five components. Each component must be managed to control the costs associated with each expatriate's assignment.

1. *Base Salary*: The base salary tends to be the same for an expatriate, as for a similar position in the home country.
2. *Expatriate Assignment Premium*: The premium is the extra pay an expatriate receives to compensate for the non-monetary costs associated with working overseas.
3. *Allowances*: A number of items are included in this component: a hardship allowance to compensate for living in difficult environments; a housing allowance to compensate for inequities in housing prices between the host and home country; an education allowance to compensate for providing equal education opportunities to an expatriate's children; and a cost-of-living allowance.
4. *Taxation*: If an expatriate has to pay income taxes in both the home and host countries,

then a taxation benefit can be provided to offset the costs to an expatriate of paying incomes taxes in two countries.

5. *Benefits*: If an expatriate must pay for services such as health care in the host country, than a heath care benefit can be provided.

These features of an expatriate managers compensation package complicate the design of an appropriate package. Parent company and host country legal and financial practices influence the magnitudes of these various components. Even with these complications, the driving idea behind the design of an expatriate's compensation should be to maintain a standard of living equivalent to what an expatriate had at home, with consideration for whatever extra compensation is necessary, given that an expatriate will be working in a foreign country.[14]

Ultimately, the compensation system for an expatriate has to be designed with the aim that it should help to attract, reward and retain valuable employees. An expatriate compensation system has implications for the retention of expatriate staff. Along a similar vein, the compensation package used for attracting, rewarding and retaining local employees should be designed accordingly. The design of local and expatriate compensation packages need to give consideration to each other, in the interests of maintaining perceptions of equity in foreign subsidiaries. The local manager package in particular has to give consideration to the competitiveness of the local environment for managers.

In China, where FDI routinely exceeded USD40 billion annually in the 1990s, demand for qualified local managers has grown considerably. As a consequence, salary increases for local managers have been substantial on an annual basis. Pay increases for local managers puts the same stresses on the profitability of a local operation in China, as does the high compensation required for expatriates. Yet, if a foreign subsidiary in China wanted to retain its local managers it had to increase compensation levels for local managers using a mix of salary increases and increased benefits, such as housing.[15]

In many cases, this process of providing adequate housing and other benefits has been aided by initiatives undertaken in the host country itself. Firms in countries that see substantial amounts of FDI and foreign trade have responded to the needs created by the compensation packages designed for expatriates. The arrival of large numbers of expatriates to Shanghai, China, has lead to the development of accommodation at international standards, new educational facilities and the creation of leisure activities and services aimed at expatriates. Hampton Woods, a new housing development in the Songjiang district of Shanghai has Western-style villas built around a large lake with a restaurant, gym, pool, concierge and free shuttle buses to international schools.[16]

China's entry into the World Trade Organization in 2001 has had a large impact on the demand for foreign talent in China. A 2002 study by Hewitt Associates (*www.hewittasia.com*), a global outsourcing firm, found that China was not considered as much of a "hardship posting" as it was in prior years. Rather, expatriates see a posting in China as a good career move and an important asset for their resumes.[17]

Expatriate Training

Given the various challenges and costs associated with management it is incumbent on a firm's management to maximize the chances of success of expatriate managers. To be able to increase success chances, a firm must have effective recruitment and selection procedures in place. It must also prepare its managers for living overseas, and returning from an assignment overseas.

The training challenge for expatriate managers is critical because expatriate failure rates tend to be higher than failure rates for other types of managerial assignments.[18] Up to 20 per cent of expatriates return back to the home country earlier than expected, which is one mark of failure.[19] Further, not all expatriates are as effective in their jobs as expected, which is another mark of failure.

The reasons for expatriate failure are numerous. Expatriates can fail in their assignments because:[20]

- The expatriate cannot adjust to the challenges of living in a foreign country.
- A family member, such as the expatriate's spouse, cannot adjust to the challenges of living in a foreign country.
- The expatriate can have trouble coping with the expanded set of responsibilities that comes with an overseas assignment.
- The expatriate can have a lack of technical competence for the overseas assignment.

An important measure to take to try to avoid these sources of expatriate failure is selection. Firms with overseas operations need to develop procedures for identifying good candidates for overseas assignments, and for training and preparing potential candidates for the rigors of an expatriate assignment. Considerable effort has been devoted to identifying the characteristics of individuals that tend to be associated with success in an overseas assignment (Table 12-6).

Table 12-6: Characteristics of Successful Expatriates

Characteristic	Description
Self-orientation	The greater the levels of an expatriate's self-confidence, self-esteem and sense of well-being, the greater the chances of success in a foreign assignment.
Relational abilities	The stronger an expatriate's relational skills, the greater their capacity to relate to individuals in the host country, and to adapt to relationships established with host country nationals.
Perceptual abilities	The greater the empathy of an expatriate, the better the understanding of host country nationals, and the greater the fairness in evaluating and working with host country nationals.
International motivation	The greater the commitment of an expatriate to a firm's internationalization initiatives, the greater the willingness to persevere through the exigencies of an overseas assignment.
Language and culture	Good language and cultural adaptation skills contribute to the success an expatriate has in working with local employees and adapting to the local culture.

Sources: Mark Mendenhall and Gary Oddou, "The Dimensions of Expatriate Acculturation: A Review," *Academy of Management Review*, 1985, Vol. 10, pp. 39–47; J. Stewart Black and Hal B. Gregersen, "The Right Way to Manage Expats," *Harvard Business Review*, 1999, Vol. 77, No. 2, pp. 52–61.

As part of the procedure for selecting and training expatriates, a series of tests can be used to identify which candidates have the personality characteristics associated with success in overseas assignments. Once a candidate has been selected appropriate training should be provided.

As the list of reasons for failure in an expatriate assignment suggest, training for an overseas assignment needs to cover issues such as the expatriates *and* the expatriate's family's adjustment to living in the new culture. The training should also prepare the expatriate for any new dimensions of the job that are likely to be encountered when on assignment.

As successful expatriate assignment is critical to a multinational firm's success, considerable effort has been devoted by corporations to developing programmes for successful expatriate placement. Many of these programmes are based on the results of research into the personal and organizational determinants of an expatriate's success in an overseas assignment.[21]

Areas of training in a multinational firm's programme for expatriate managers include language training, cross-cultural training and training for repatriation. The first of these is a fairly straightforward, even if a time-consuming form of training. Cross-cultural training and as with preparation for repatriation is a more complex task. One of the more critical areas for cross-cultural training is the preparation of an employee for culture shock.

Culture Shock

Culture shock is a state of disorientation or discomfort that comes with encountering new social conventions and new rules that disrupt the normal behaviour patterns of an individual in an unfamiliar culture.[22] Culture shock creates a disruption in a person's behaviour and routines, as the cues and norms that are used to guide a person's actions in their daily lives are set in a context of new cultural expectations and cues.[23]

Culture shock can have a variety of deleterious effects. A person suffering from culture shock can be simply irritable at work or at home, or the person can develop feelings of panic in hostility. Culture shock is manifest in the workplace as lower performance than expected, as the expatriate manager suffering from culture shock feels stress, is unable to work effectively, and has poor relations with local and expatriate staff.

Business misunderstandings are not necessarily a result of a conscious feeling of cultural superiority by an expatriate suffering from culture shock. Often a relocated employee might try to scrupulously observe surface differences such as etiquette, but fail to comprehend why another person's way of doing things is so foreign.[24] Learning to understand such differences is part of the adjustment process. The stages of adjustment to a culture, and the appearance of culture shock, occur in fairly regular patterns. The four typical stages are: the honeymoon period; culture shock; adjustment; and mastery.[25]

1. *Honeymoon period*: This stage lasts for up to three months. It is the period during which an expatriate is new to a host country, is excited about the host country, and has positive feelings and expectations about living and working in the host country.

2. *Culture shock*: This stage is the crisis period of adjustment to the host country in which negative feelings, irritability and stress are at their greatest. If an expatriate does move past this stage, then the overseas assignment is likely to end in failure.

3. *Adjustment*: This stage is the one in which an expatriate undertakes their recovery from the crisis of the culture shock stage. Gradually, the expatriate learns to cope with the host country culture, and begins to accept and adapt to the patterns of behaviour and daily life in the host country.

4. *Mastery*: This stage is the most advanced one. Once this stage is reached an expatriate is essentially literate in the host country culture and able to function in the host country as well, or almost as well, as the expatriate can function in their home culture.

Culture shock can be addressed by cross-cultural training programmes. The number and diversity of cross-cultural training programmes are too numerous to identify, but the main intent of these programmes is similar. These programmes are designed to ease the process of cross-cultural adjustment, and minimize the duration and severity of the culture shock, or crisis stage.[26] Most programs involve learning about a culture through the accumulation of facts about the host country, attribution training to identify explanations for behaviour, experiential exercises to simulate living and working in the host country and cultural awareness training to better appreciate the culture and patterns of behaviour in a host country.

Repatriation

Repatriation is the return of an expatriate manager to their home country. Even though repatriated employees bring an expanded set of skills to parent company, repatriated employees tend to have higher turnover rates then other employees. This high turnover extends from a lack of familiarity with the existing home operations, and a lack of appreciation in the multinational firm for the unique perspective and skills a repatriated employee can bring to the organization.[27]

Given the potential for turnover, and the unsuccessful readjustment of a repatriated employee to the parent company, a firm's HRM system should have processes in place to facilitate the repatriation of expatriates. Although repatriation programmes can be expensive, the potential cost of not successfully reintegrating returning expatriates can be almost as great as an unsuccessful international assignment. Repatriated employees possess valuable skills and experiences that can aid a multinational firms operations. The repatriated employee can be a window on the host country in which they served as an expatriate manager.

The types of programmes used for repatriation can be as diverse as those used for cross-cultural adjustment, but the number of companies with a repatriation programme is less than that with cross-cultural adjustment programmes.[28] Even so, a programme that focuses on developing ties with home country staff, links returning expatriates to one another, provides a forum for the distilling of an expatriates overseas experiences and develops realistic expectations in the expatriate about the nature of their job on return to the parent company, can aid with the repatriation process.

Summary

International human resource management is a key function in a firm's international expansion. Although many functional areas in a corporation, such as finance, accounting and marketing, are not the same when conducted on domestic and international bases, the human resource function is one that becomes particularly complicated when internationalized. These complications extend from the direct association a firm's HRM systems have with the national institutional environment in its host countries, as well as the very real difficulties individuals face when operating in a culture other than their home culture.

National differences in HRM standards and practices can be quite pronounced. These differences lead to the questions of whether and how a firm should adapt its existing HRM systems to local standards. There is no apparent answer to the question whether to globalize or localize. However, there is a need to consider the trade-offs in either approach. One factor promoting the globalize approach is cross-national convergence in the standards for human resource management practices worldwide. Even with this convergence, practices often times still remain distinct across nations creating the need to mobilize both expatriate and local employees as senior management in a firm's foreign subsidiaries.

A firm's staffing policies are a consequence of external forces driving convergence and divergence in HRM practices, and internal philosophies with respect to the staffing policy that is used. The ethnocentric staffing policies that dominated in the past have given way to polycentric and geocentric approaches to staffing. With this change in staffing philosophy has come a greater opportunity for managers who are not from the home country of a multinational firm.

Even with an increase in local managers, expatriate managers remain a key component of any firm's international operations. The challenges of successfully managing the HRM activities for an expatriate are profound. Recruitment, selection and training are complicated by the multiple needs and demands of an expatriate. The monetary and non-monetary costs encountered in an expatriate assignment add a layer of complications to the determination of an expatriate's compensation. Performance evaluations need to be made on several fronts including how well an expatriate performs with the technical aspects of the position, as well as how well an expatriate adapts to the host country culture.

The cross-cultural adaptation process, and the related issue of culture shock, is one that has scuppered many expatriate assignments. The demands of coping with a host country culture, while performing the functions of the job, and while ensuring that the expatriates spouse and family adjust to a host culture are considerable. But it is also these forms of challenges that make an expatriate assignment an exciting and enriching educational experience for an individual committed to an organization's international expansion.

Notes

[1] John Cullen, "Multinational Management: A Strategic Approach," 2nd Ed. (South-Western: Mason, Ohio, 2001).

[2] "New Forms of Corporate Mobility: Will the Long-term Expatriate Become a Figure of the Past?," *China Staff*, November 2002, Vol. 9, No. 1, pp. 1–5.

[3] Howard V. Perlmutter, "The Tortuous Evolution of the Multinational Corporation," *Columbia Journal of World Business*, 1969, pp. 9–18.

[4] Rochelle Kopp, *The Rice-paper Ceiling: Breaking through Japanese Corporate Culture* (Berkley, California: Stone Bridge Press, 1994).

[5] Paul W. Beamish and Andrew Inkpen, "Japanese Firms and the Decline of the Japanese Expatriate," *Journal of World Business*, 1998, Vol. 33, No. 1, pp. 35–50.

[6] "Language an Issue for Japanese Workers at Steel, Auto Firms in Ohio," *Knight Ridder/Tribune Business News*, 2 November, 2003.

[7] Peterson, R.B., Sargent, J., Napier, N.K., and Shim, W.S., "Corporate Expatriate HRM Policies, Internationalization, and Performance in the World's Largest MNCs," *Management International Review*, 1996, Vol. 36, pp. 215–230.

[8] "American Lifts Corporate Culture's Lid," *Asahi Shimbun/Asahi Evening News*, 30 March 2002.

[9] Jaideep Anand and Andrew Delios, "Competing Globally: How Japanese MNCs Have Matched Goals and Strategies in India and China," *Journal of World Business*, 1996, Vol. 31, No. 3, pp. 50–62.

[10] "Cutting the Cost of Relocation," *Personnel Today*, 18 November 2003, p. 18.

[11] "Mainland Proves Too Tough for Some Overseas Firms," *Asia Africa Intelligence Wire*, 16 September, 2002.

[12] Frank Hayes and Peggy Creveling, "Tighter Times to Slow the Flow of Americans Working Overseas," *Crain's Cleveland Business*, 2 April 2001, Vol. 22, No. 14, p. 28.

[13] "Seoul`s Cost of Living Ranks Eighth Globally," *Asia Africa Intelligence Wire*, 17 June 2003.

[14] C. Reynolds, "Compensation of Overseas Personnel," in J. Famularo, *Handbook of Human Resource Administration,* 2nd Ed. (New York: McGraw-Hill, 1989).

[15] Ingmar Bjorkman and Yuan Lu, "The Management of Human Resources in Chinese-Western Joint Ventures," *Journal of World Business*, Fall 1999, Vol. 34, No. 3, p. 306.

[16] "Expatriate Families Seek Homes away from Home," *Asia Africa Intelligence Wire*, 26 March 2003.

[17] *http://www.hewittasia.com/hewitt/ap/resource/articleindex/articles/article_05_15_03.htm*, 20 November 2003.

[18] J.S. Black, M. Mendenhall, and G. Oddou, "Towards a Comprehensive Model of International Adjustment," *Academy of Management Review*, 1991, Vol. 16, pp. 291–317.

[19] Rosalie L. Tung, "Selection and Training Procedures of U.S., European and Japanese Multinationals," *California Management Review*, 1982, Vol. 25, pp. 57–71.

[20] Rosalie L. Tung, "Selection and Training Procedures of U.S., European and Japanese Multinationals," *California Management Review*, 1982, Vol. 25, pp. 57–71.

[21] Oddou, Gary R., "Managing Your Expatriates: What Successful Firms Do," *Human Resource Planning*, 1991, Vol. 14, No. 4, pp. 301–308; Black, J. Stewart and Hal B. Gregersen, "The Right Way to Manage Expats," *Harvard Business Review*, 1999, Vol. 77, No. 2, pp. 52–61.

[22] Adrian Furnham and Stephen Bochner, *Culture Shock: Psychological Reactions to Unfamiliar Environments* (New York: Routledge, 1989).

[23] J. Stewart Black, Hal B. Gregersen, and Mark E. Mendenhall, *Global Assignments: Successfully Expatriating and Repatriating International Managers* (San Francisco: Jossey-Bass Publishers, 1992).

[24] "You Talkin' to Me," *Asia Africa Intelligence Wire*, 9 April 2003.

[25] K. Oberg, *Culture Shock,* Report No. A-329 (Indianapolis: Bobbs-Merrill Series in the Social Sciences, 1954).

[26] P. C. Early, "Intercultural Training for Managers: A Comparison of Documentary and Interpersonal Methods," *Academy of Management Journal,* 1987, Vol. 30, No. 4, pp. 685–698; J. Kline Harrison, "Developing Successful Expatriate Managers: A Framework for the Structural Design and Strategic Alignment of Cross-cultural Training Programs," *Human Resource Planning,* 1994, Vol. 17, No. 3, pp. 17–35.

[27] J. S. Black and Mark Mendenhall, *Global Assignments: Successfully Expatriating and Repatriating International Managers* (San Francisco, CA: Jossey-Bass, 1992).

[28] Michael Harvey, "Repatriation of Corporate Executives: An Empirical Study," *Journal of International Business Studies,* 1989, Vol. 20, No. 1, pp. 131–144.

chapter
13 ETHICAL AND SOCIAL RESPONSIBILITY IN MULTINATIONAL MANAGEMENT

Managers in a company are responsible to its shareholders and its other stakeholders. Typically, shareholders, who tend to have profit-related goals, are the stakeholder group to whom managers often feel the greatest responsibility. Yet, a firm has a variety of other stakeholders – its employees, its customers, the people in the communities in which a firm is situated, to name a few – to whom it also has responsibilities.

The decisions a firm's managers make will have an impact on each of these groups of stakeholders. In many cases, a firm's decisions have an influence beyond the immediate corporation itself. A decision by an electronics company to close a VCR assembly plant in Singapore, and to setup a new one in Zhejiang province in China, affects the members of the community in both Singapore and Zhejiang. This decision might be taken in response to better economic opportunities presented by shifting assembly operations to Zhejiang. The decision in this sense should be regarded as a positive one by the firm's shareholders, but it might not be regarded as a positive one by other stakeholder groups such as the firm's Singapore employees and suppliers.

When a firm operates in international markets issues of social responsibility and ethics become much more complex. This complexity extends from the multiplication in a firm's stakeholders that comes with international operations. It also extends from the potential for multiple ethical standards and common business practices that can be encountered across regions of the world.

Social Responsibility

A basic question to be evaluated when considering issues of responsibility and ethics is what are the responsibilities of the managers in a firm? Do managers just have a responsibility to pursue profits, or is there a broader mandate of responsibilities?

Increasingly, the common perspective is that managers have a responsibility beyond the pursuit of profits, or other activities that satisfy the objectives of shareholders. The issue of social responsibility concerns management's duties to a firm's various stakeholders. Pursuing activities commensurate with the goals of all stakeholders means that a firm engages in a number of activities, including creating sound and safe work conditions even where local laws do not require such, sponsoring local athletes or scholars, adopting sound environmental practices, providing free services, and so forth.

Benpres Holdings Corp. (*www.benpres-holdings.com*), a holding company for the Lopez Group of Companies, tries to appeal to a broad base of stakeholders in its activities. Benpres Holdings is a provider of public services and one of the largest family business groups in the Philippines. As far back as the 1950s, Eugenio Lopez Sr., the CEO of Benpres Holdings at the time, was known for his social activism. When speaking to the business community in 1958 he said:

> 'We sincerely believe that a greater proportion of the earnings accrued from business should be returned to the people whether this be in the form of foundations, grants, scholarships, hospitals or any other form of social welfare benefits. We consider this a sound policy and a good investment which, in the long run will pay off because it will mean more business and goodwill for the company and would minimize, if not prevent, the social unrest and disorder which are prevalent nowadays.'[1]

Under the direction of the Lopez family, with Oscar M. Lopez at the helm of the corporation in 2003, the corporation continued with this social activist approach to establish a number of foundations. These include the Eugenio Lopez Foundation, the ABS-CBN Foundation, the First Philippine Conservation, and the SKY Foundation. The Group continues to publicly emphasize the important role that corporations play in society. Oscar Lopez, speaking at the Asian Forum on Corporation Social Responsibility in September 2003 stated that 'CSR [corporate social responsibility] must be part of the overall corporate strategy backed up by resources and management expertise, and not just an afterthought, a "feeling good" statement, or merely a supplemental undertaking'.[2]

As part of its corporate strategy, there is a long list of activities, including those that fall into the realm of corporate social responsibility, that a corporation could undertake. This list could be condensed if we consider these as types of activities that a business pursues as part of fulfilling its mandates to its stakeholders. We can categorize all activities into four types of responsibilities.[3]

1. *Economic Responsibilities*: This responsibility is most often at the forefront of a firm. A business firm is an economic unit that makes products society desires, and should do so in a profitable manner.

2. *Legal Responsibilities*: This responsibility concerns the rules and regulations to which a firm must conform as it operates. A firm's pursuit of profits must be done within the framework of a nation's or society's legal requirements. Part of the challenge in international business comes with the differing legal responsibilities that accompany activities in various world regions.

3. *Ethical Responsibilities*: This responsibility concerns the standards of behaviour, and norms of conduct, to which a business is expected to conform, but are not embodied in laws or regulations. Ethical responsibilities are not always well-defined but society generally expects that businesses should satisfy ethical responsibilities, even when not defined by laws.

4. *Discretionary Responsibilities*: This responsibility concerns those activities for which there is no clear message from the societal or legal framework about whether a firm should pursue it. Fulfilling this responsibility is largely an issue of choice for a firm, in terms of deciding where to devote its philanthropic and other voluntary activities that meet a firm's social responsibility mandate.

The largest grey area in the above four categories falls in the third type – ethical responsibilities. A firm's economic and legal responsibilities are often well-defined. A firm's discretionary responsibilities are ones that a firm might do, but they are not activities that a firm should do. The challenges for a firm to meet its ethical responsibilities are multiple, as only complicated by participating in international markets. Consequently, we focus the discussion in the remainder of this chapter on the issues of ethics.

Ethical Responsibility

Ethical responsibility is an issue that has gained heightened importance as firms globalize, and experience the debacles that befall the corporate world in Asia and the US in the 1997–2003 period. Indeed, ethics is at the root of a society's and an individual's understanding about the norms and standard in social interactions, social responsibilities and business practices.

The emergence of several high profile cases of corporate irresponsibility in the form of wealth shifts from one stakeholder group to another, and management irresponsibility in failing to protect the interests of all shareholders, are but two typical examples of ways in which managers failed to meet expectations about ethical responsibility. The price for failing to maintain responsible behaviour towards stakeholder such as shareholder can carry penalties. In October 2003, Korea's Fair Trade Commission fined six chaebol for making illegal transactions to support failing parts of their business.[4] Cases such as these form a strong impetus to make managers more sensitive and responsive to calls for increased ethical responsibility.

These calls emerge from a variety of interested parties, or stakeholders, in these firms. National governments, multi-lateral governmental and regulatory bodies, special interest groups and non-governmental organizations collectively represent the stakeholders of a multinational firm, as they have interests in the organizational practices of a multinational firm.

Stakeholders and Ethics

An analysis of ethical responsibility clearly involves a consideration of how one's actions can affect others. In the setting of an organization, a decision by a manager will influence a number of other people, who have some association with the organization. Typically the people most interested in, and most affected by, the decisions of a firm's management are a firm's stakeholders.

A firm's shareholders is the group most commonly identified as being a firm's stakeholders. This association leads to the idea that organizational profitability should be the main organizational objective, because it is the shareholders' dominant interest. Yet, an organization often needs to satisfy the interests of stakeholders other than shareholders. Management pursues profits as a consequence of the shareholder's interests. Similarly, management can pursue other goals, such as organizational continuity and growth, to meet the interests of other stakeholders such as its employees.

The difficulty of meeting the multiple interests of stakeholders is magnified when a firm grows into the international environment. This magnification comes from the increasing diversity of stakeholders. Management in a multinational firm needs to consider its stakeholders in the home country, those in its host country and those in society in general (Table 13-1).[5]

Table 13-1 illustrates many of the potential stakeholders in an organization. These stakeholders can have different goals and different perspectives on what is the ethical responsibilities of a firm's management (Table 13-2). In many instances, it can be difficult to act in such a way that

Table 13-1: Stakeholders in a Multinational Corporation

Location	Stakeholders
Home Country	Owners
	Customers
	Employees
	Suppliers
	Distributors
	Community
	Government
Host Country	Employees
	Consumers
	Strategic allies
	Distributors
	Community
	Government
Society	Global environment
	Resources
	Living standards

Source: Adapted from Helen Deresky, *International Management: Managing Across Borders and Cultures,* 4th Ed. (Upper Saddle River, New Jersey: Prentice Hall, 2003), Exhibit 2-2, p. 39.

Table 13-2:   Ethical Scenarios and Stakeholder Conflicts

Ethical Scenario	Stakeholder 1	Stakeholder 2	Ethical Dilemma
Scenario 1 This multinational firm operates in the pharmaceutical industry. It has developed a unique drug that can be used to treat HIV infections before the infection progresses to become acquired immunodeficiency syndrome (AIDS). Substantial time and development costs went into the discovery of this drug. Clinical trials have been completed, and the drug has been launched successfully. The substantial development costs need to be recouped by the price charged for this patent-protected drug.	*Shareholders* Would like to receive a good return on money invested in the pharmaceutical company, hence the objective is to see the drug priced high enough to recoup development costs, plus provide a return.	*Host country community* In many countries of the world, people do not have the financial resources to be able to pay enough for a new drug to even cover its development costs.	What should be the price adopted by the multinational firm for the drug?
Scenario 2 This multinational firm has placed two large manufacturing subsidiaries in a country in which it was offered a tax break on its operations for its first five years. Now that the five year period has expired, the multinational firm is considering adjusting its transfer pricing policy to show low profits in the these two large manufacturing subsidiaries and thereby avoid paying the high tax that will accompany any profits it shows in the host country.	*Employees* Would prefer to continue to work for the multinational firm in the host country, and not see it relocate if it deems its cost structure to be too high.	*Host country community* Would like the multinational firm to pay its fair share of tax to reflect its social responsibilities to the countries in which it operates.	What should be the transfer pricing policy of the multinational firm?
Scenario 3 This multinational firm has been producing a low priced automobile that minimizes on its costs by using light-weight body parts that are structurally sound. These body parts do not, however, provide much cushion in the event of a collision between the automobile and another object. If stronger parts are used, the price of the car will rise substantially.	*Customers* Would like an affordable car, and can make the trade-off between safety features and costs in the purchase decision.	*Society in general* Would like products to be safe as many of the costs of accidents are borne by society.	Should a multinational firm delete safety features to make a product more affordable for people in a low income nation?

Table 13-2:   continued

Ethical Scenario	Stakeholder 1	Stakeholder 2	Ethical Dilemma
Scenario 4	*Customers*	*Shareholders*	
This multinational firm competes in the electronics industry. It has attempted to design easy-to-use interfaces for its television, VCR, DVD and other electronics products, but the operation of sophisticated functions in these products requires reference to the product manual. Like its competitors in Thailand, for example, the existing product manual is not available in Thai. A similar situation, no product manual available in a local language, exists for sales in many other countries.	Would like to have product information available in a local language.	Would like the firm to maximize profitability, by avoiding the addition of costs where the competitive situation does not require such.	Should a multinational firm assume the cost of translating all of its product information into other languages?

Source: Adapted from John B. Cullen, *Multinational Management: A Strategic Approach*, 2nd Ed. (Mason, Ohio: South Western, 2003), Exhibit 4.1, p. 111.

all stakeholders regard management's decisions as ethically responsible behavior. Often difficult choices need to be made about the course of action that will be followed.

In such cases, managing ethical issues involves a broad understanding of ethical standards and business norms across a firm's national institutional environments. When there is a conflict in perspectives on ethical responsibility, consideration needs to be given to the balance between global and local in managing ethical considerations. To help achieve this balance, and to deal with these thorny decisions, explicit corporate policy grounded in a perspective on ethics can provide a good guide to a manager.

BHP Billiton's has adopted such an explicit corporate policy to guide its future growth with a zero harm aspiration. BHP Billiton (*www.bhpbilliton.com*) is an Australian-based, diversified resouces company with an international presence. Its focus on major commodities includes large positions in aluminum, copper and iron ore. Chris Pointin, the President of Stainless Steel Materials explains that 'Zero harm is good ethics, but zero harm is also good business. It means upfront thinking and planning and ensuring optimum development of an asset over its full life cycle. It also means helping people to do their jobs with lower risk, more forethought and less waste.'[6]

In line with the zero harm aspiration, BHP Billiton has composed a charter (see Figure 13-1), which outlines the company's purpose, and unifies the company's values and its success measures. This charter serves to guide managers and all employees in their actions. To ensure that employees support the Charter, BHP uses it in both the recruitment and selection of employees, and in the performance measurement process.

Figure 13-1:   BHP Billiton Charter[7]

Our purpose is to create value through the discovery, development and conversion of natural resources, and the provision of innovative customer and market-focused solutions.

To prosper and achieve real growth, we must:

- Actively manage and build our portfolio of high quality assets and services.
- Continue the drive towards a high performance organization in which every individual accepts responsibility and is rewarded for results.
- Earn the trust of employees, customers, suppliers, communities and shareholders by being forthright in our communications and consistently delivering on commitments.

We value:

- Safety and the Environment
- Integrity
- High Performance
- Win-Win Relationships
- The Courage to Lead Change
- Respect for Each Other

We are successful in creating value when:

- Our shareholders are realizing a superior return on their investment.
- Our customers and suppliers are benefiting from our business relationships.
- The communities in which we operate value our citizenship.
- Every employee starts each day with a sense of purpose and ends each day with a sense of accomplishment.

Ethics

A society's and individual's ethics help define acceptable and unacceptable practices, given the context of a certain business activity. Ethics concerns the moral duties and obligations that are beyond the economic and legal consequences of any decision. Ethics extend from individual, corporate and societal values. These values are rooted in the institutions that pervade a society and a firm – the societal culture, the organizational culture, the legal system and the religious authorities in a nation.

Ethics in this sense can vary depending on the nature of the institutions in a particular geographic context. Much of the challenge of dealing with ethical responsibility in international business, comes from the basic duality of global versus local that pervades many decisions in multinational management. In the case of ethical responsibility, this duality is the question of whether to adopt a localized approach to ethical responsibility, or to adopt global set of norms, as in the case of BHP Billiton.

There are numerous ways to approach this question of global or local. Even before attempting to address this question, a firm's management can identify whether it is worthwhile to place themselves in the situation of having to contend with this question. To do this a series of three simple questions can be explored, as part of the decision process to enter a country.

1. Are there differences in ethical standards in the country we are considering entering, versus the ethical standards in the countries in which we currently operate?

2. If there are different ethical standards, are we able to compete if we maintain standards of practice consistent with what we are currently doing; that is, we do not localize our standards of ethical responsibility?

3. If we are at a disadvantage by not localizing our standard of ethical responsibility, will there be organizational acceptance of adapting our standard to those commonly used in the nation?

Exploring these questions helps to identify the potential ethical ramifications of a market entry decision. More often than not, a firm's management will decide to enter a country, even if there are ethical differences. When this is the case, the managers who must operate in the newly-entered country are either on their own in dealing with the variances in ethical standards, or the multinational firm has procedures, policies and codes to help guide its managers handle conflicting ethical standards.

Clearly, a situation in which a company has developed procedures, policies and codes for managing ethical responsibility is one that places a manager in a situation with reduced ambiguity. The foundation for developing such a corporate code is the basic philosophical perspective a firm adopts for managing national differences in ethics, coupled with an organization's perspective on its stakeholders.

National Differences in Ethics

There are four main perspectives on the nature of differences in ethical standards across nations.[8] These perspectives tend to vary on their statements on the degree of differences across nations and individuals, and the way in which one views which ethical standard is the most applicable one.

1. *Individual Ethics*: This perspective places variance in ethics at the level of the individual. Each individual in a nation has their own ideas about what is ethical or not. Accordingly, individuals and firms operate to their own ethical standards, and there is little commonality in ethical standards across individuals or organizations in a nation.

2. *National relativism*: This perspective places the variance in ethics at the level of the nation. Although people in one nation have ethical standard's different from people in another nation, not one nation's standard is inherently superior to another. A manager operating with a national relativism perspective would suggest a localization approach

to corporate ethical standards, and advocate adapting practices to the norms in each nation in which a firm operates.

3. *Ethical imperialism*: This perspective sees the home nation's ethical standards as being superior to those in all other nations. If there is a difference in ethical standards, the ethical standard in the home nation should prevail and emerge as the standard adopted in each host country. A manager operating with an ethical imperialism perspective would suggest that the firm adopts global corporate ethical standards and practices.

4. *Universalism*: This perspective sees individuals as having fundamentally similar ethical standards. There might be variance in minor points of ethics, but basic and essential beliefs about what is ethical exist in all individuals, regardless of national origins. These common points of belief can be called hypernorms, or core human values.[9] A manager operating with a universalism perspective would suggest that the firm adopts global corporate ethical standards and practices.

These viewpoints provide some guidance as to how national differences in ethics can be approached. As suggested in the above definitions, the perspective distill down to the managerial implication of whether to use a global or a local approach to managing ethical responsibility in a multinational firm. The resolution to this management of ethics issue can emerge in an organization's corporate code of ethics.

Management of Ethical Issues

There is no easy or black-and-white solution to the management of ethical issues. Ethics almost by its very definition is an individual issue. That said, standards of ethical responsibility can be a part of broader setting, such as a particular society or nation. Standard of ethical responsibility in a group emerge as a collection of beliefs about what constitutes norms in business practices and the social environment. These standards are typically bounded at the national, or even perhaps, the sub-national level.

Increasingly, these bounds of ethical responsibility are becoming less opaque at the national level, and more consistent across nations. Initiatives advanced by multilateral and worldwide organizations, both at the governmental and non-governmental levels, facilitate this advance of standards of ethical responsibility from a national to a regional or even a global level.

Even with these multinational initiatives, managers can still be placed in a quandary when confronting standards of ethical responsibility across nations. In this context, an organization can provide good guidance to help contend with the sticky situations that ethical questions can create.

Corporate Codes of Conduct

One of the guiding principles for a company designing a corporate guide to dealing with multinational ethical issues is to differentiate between cross-national practices that are just different, from practices that are different *and* not ethically responsible. An individual with an ethical imperialism perspective might be tempted to equate difference with ethically irresponsible actions, but this might not always be the case. Often the interpretation of an event or action as being ethically responsible or not depends on the context of the event or action, the types of local traditions that accompany that event or action, and the types of core human values that might be involved in the event or action.[10]

Core human values refers to the idea that there are minimal ethical standards that apply to all organizations. A search for core human values leads to attempts to identify similar kinds of values across societies and religious systems, for example. Although difficult to identify such ideas as respect for an individual's rights, support for a community's institutions and the recognition and respect of each individual in an organization as a person, are potential starting points for elucidating core human values.

By establishing guidelines as to what a company identifies as core values, it can clearly identify practices that are consistent with those values, or those that violate those values. This identification immediately reduces ambiguity about issues, and consequently provides unmistakable guidance to decisions made in cross-national settings.

A company's code of conduct can encompass its management's perspective on what are its core values. Developing a written statement of a code of conduct is one step in this process of instilling those same values in the organization, but it is a step that might not advance the organization far enough. The management in the company must reinforce the materials in the code of conduct through actions that make the words in the document meaningful. For example, consumers and other stakeholders can have access to the code of conduct, and be given a means of communicating to the company when any violations of the code take place. Further, a company's management must be committed to uphold the code of conduct when violations of it are detected.

Codes of conduct are not just for firms in the manufacturing or finance industries. Australian-based Tabcorp Holdings Ltd. (*www.tabcorp.com*), a provider of gambling and entertainment facilities in Australia, has an extensive Responsible Gambling Code to ensure and promote responsible gambling initiatives. The Code is prominently displayed on Tabcorps' website. All employees of the company are expected to uphold the code. To ensure the latter and meet the Code's goals, Tabcorp provides thorough training toward reducing the incidences of problem gambling.[11] An abbreviated version of the Responsible Gambling Code can be found in Figure 13-2.

Although a set of core values can be identified and placed in a company's code of conduct, it is not enough to cover all situations. Not all actions can be simply identified as an ethically responsible one or not. Inevitably, there is a context-dependency to a decision. The contextual overlay of any decision means there can be an ethical grey area, in which it is not clear what should be done to be ethically responsible when faced with a particular decision.

The contextual interpretation of a situation can revolve around two points. First, 'Is there a cultural explanation for what appears to be a cross-national conflict in ethics?'. If a practice emerges from a strong cultural or religious belief, it is likely to be fairly entrenched in a society. In such a case, a respect for local traditions might have to guide a company's decision-making. Second, 'Is there a stage of development explanation for what appears to be a cross-national conflict in ethics?'.

To approach the second question, a manager can apply the test of whether a similar standard might apply if their home country was at a similar level of economic development. If the manager is from a high GDP country such as Singapore, the standard minimum age for an individual to enter the workforce might be 18 years old. In developing countries in Asia, it might be more common for someone to enter the workforce at the age of 14. Is it the case of a difference in standards of ethical responsibility that lead to this difference, or is it a consequence of the economic context. Given the same economic situation in Singapore, such as in the late 1960s, would individuals entered the workforce at a younger age than 18?

Figure 13-2:   TABCORP Holdings Limited Responsible Gambling Code[12]

---

1. Background

TABCORP has a strong commitment to responsible service of gambling in all areas of its business. It is essential both to corporate social responsibility, and the long-term sustainability of the industry.

2. Goals

The TABCORP Code promotes four goals:

- Fully informed customer choice
- Staff training and awareness of observable behaviours which may be associated with problem gambling, and procedures to assist customers who display these behaviours
- Monitoring and assessment aimed at continuous improvement
- Research and consultation

We commit to adherence to the Code and procedural guidelines on the responsible service and delivery of gambling including staff training, advertising and promotions, and monitoring the effectiveness of these initiatives.

3. Purpose

By adopting the TABCORP Responsible Gambling Code, the company will endeavour to:

- ensure all employees receive training in the responsible service of gambling at a level appropriate to their role in the service of products;
- make available to customers product information with the aim of customers being able to make an informed choice regarding their decision to participate in gambling products;
- provide a secure and attractive environment while highlighting for customers the risks and issues associated with problem gambling.

The anchoring point for this process of managing ethical issues is the development of a company's code of conduct. Once a code is in place, and it is being used proactively, it can provide a set of rules that help communicate to managers what they can and cannot do given a certain situation. This guidance to implementing ethically responsible behaviour in multinational firms has also been aided by the creation of codes of conduct by international bodies.

Multinational Codes of Conduct

A variety of international bodies have created guidelines on ethical responsibility for various facets of a multinational firm's operations. The United Nations has been proactive in this regard, as have other bodies, as listed in Table 13-3.[13]

These bodies establish guidelines, which can aid managerial decision making. These guidelines are seldom put into law, or a set of formal and enforceable rules and regulations. Consequently, managers in a multinational firm retain the option of following the principles created by these various bodies. Nevertheless, guidelines, such as the APEC Forum Business Code of Conduct,

Table 13-3:   International Codes of Conduct

International Body	Guideline or Code of Conduct	Website (if available)
The United Nations	Universal Declaration of Human Rights	www.un.org/Overview/rights.html
The United Nations	Code of Conduct on Transnational Corporations	N/A
The European Convention	The European Convention on Human Rights	www.hri.org/docs/ ECHR50.html#Convention
The International Chamber of Commerce	Guidelines for International Investment	N/A
The Organization for Economic Cooperation and Development	Guidelines for Multinational Corporations	www.oecd.org/dataoecd/56/36/1922428.pdf
Conference on Security and Co-operation in Europe	The Helsinki Final Act	www.osce.org/docs/english/1990-1999/ summits/helfa75e.htm
The International Labour Office	Tripartite Declaration of Principles Concerning Multinational Enterprises and Social Policy	www.ilo.org/public/english/standards/norm/ sources/mne.htm
The International Labour Organization (ILO)	International Labour Standards, such as The Fundamental ILO Conventions	http://www.ilo.org/public/english/standards/ norm/whatare/fundam/index.htm
The Asia Pacific Economic Cooperation	Business Code of Conduct	www.cauxroundtable.org/APECForum BusinessCodeofConduct.html

can help with the development of an organization's corporate code of ethics, and its management of ethical responsibilities.

APEC Forum Business Code of Conduct

The Asia Pacific Economic Cooperation (APEC) forum *Business Code of Conduct* originated in the discussion undertaken in the 1999 APEC CEO Summit in Auckland, New Zealand. The APEC *Business Code* draws from two principle sources: The Caux Round Table *Principles for Business* and the OECD *Guidelines for Corporate Governance*.

The purpose of the APEC *Business Code* is to create a model code that companies can use to develop, supplement or strengthen their own codes of conduct. The CEO of any enterprise that will use the APEC *Business Code* should become a signatory to the *Code*, as an expression of a formal agreement to uphold the moral and ethical obligations outlined in the code.

The standards outlined by the APEC *Business Code* help to encourage transparency and predictability in corporations. The APEC *Business Code* provides guidance to national governments in APEC nations to improve their own levels of transparency and predictability in public sector operations. By focusing on both the public and private sectors, the APEC *Business Code* will help to improve the match between public sector expectations and regulations and private sector business practices. The APEC *Business Code* attempts to develop these private and public sector standards through the statement of seven standard for corporate conduct. These standards are outlined in Table 13-4.

Current Issues in Ethics in International Business

International business is rife with ethical issues. As we have discussed, many of the challenges to a manager in international business come with the need to coordinate activities across various national environments. Different issues tend of be of greater prominence in one country versus another, because of these differences in national environments. Hence, what might not be an contentious issue for a firm in one part of the world, can become a contentious issue for a firm in another part of the world.

Some of the most prominent issues facing international managers at the onset of the 21st century were corruption, sweatshops, child labour, the environment and drug prices. There are issues other than these ones, but these tend to be among the most prominent. To illustrate these issues, we can consider the examples of intellectual property rights, corruption and sweatshops.

Corruption

A lack of transparency in a particular country is often manifested in corruption. Where there is a lack of transparency for the actions of government officials, there emerges an opportunity for government officials to misuse their vested powers. Corruption emerges when government officials

Table 13-4:   **Standards for Corporate Conduct**

Number	Standard for Corporate Conduct	Definition
1.	International and local communities	A company must recognize its responsibilities to its international and local communities, and to the individuals in the communities in which it operates
2.	Respect for laws	A company must respect and comply with international and local laws, while avoiding legal behaviour that might yet have undesirable consequences.
3.	Stakeholder responsibility	A company must recognize the rights of stakeholders and encourage cooperation between the company and its stakeholders to create wealth, jobs, and financially viable and sustainable business enterprises.
4.	Responsibility for the environment	A company must sustain and improve the natural environments in which it operates, while avoiding the waste and depletion of natural resources.
5.	Free and fair competition	A company must not undertake anti-competitive actions in the interests of promoting and sustaining free and fair competition.
6.	Company governance	A company should have a framework for its corporate governance that leads to the timely and forthright disclosure of all materials of the company relevant to its stakeholders.
7.	Illicit actions	A company must not conduct or excuse extortion, bribery, money laundering or other forms of corrupt financial or business practices.

Adapted from: www.cauxroundtable.org/APECForumBusinessCodeofConduct.html, 30 March 2003.

take advantage of the lack of transparency. Corruption is the abuse of a government office by a public official to gain private benefits. Bribe taking to seal a land purchase or to award a contract is an example of corruption. In most nations, corruption is illegal, and offenders can be punished under a country's laws. But a lack of transparency, and the failure to enforce laws, allows corruption to flourish in some settings.

It is important to understand corruption because it influences the norms and standards of business in a country. It influences the growth rates of a country. It skews competition in favour of those firms and individuals that are comfortable and capable in dealing with situations in which corrupt practices are common.

As corruption is a part of the business environment that independent bodies are trying to root out and expose, several agencies are devoted to identifying areas of the world in which corruption is common. These agencies, such as Transparency International (*www.transparency.org*), identify the wealth distorting and wealth destroying outcomes of corruption.

To help with the identification and tracking of corruption, Transparency International produces a measure called the Corruption Perceptions Index (CPI). CPI evaluates a country on a scale of one to ten. A score of ten indicates a country is not characterized by public sector corruption, while a score of one marks a country that is corrupt. The measure was compiled by Transparency International by drawing on numerous independent surveys of business people, academics and country analysts. The Corruptions Perceptions Index thus represents the degree to which corruption is perceived to exist among a nation's public officials and politicians (see Table 13-5).

Table 13-5:   Corruption Perceptions Index, 1995 and 2002

1988–92 Rank	2002 Rank	Country	1995 CPI	2002 CPI	1988–92 Rank	2002 Rank	Country	1995 CPI	2002 CPI
6	1	Finland	9.1	9.7	25	33	Hungary	4.1	4.9
6	2	Denmark	9.3	9.5	29	33	Malaysia	5.3	4.9
1	2	New Zealand	9.6	9.5	—	33	Trinidad & Tobago	—	4.9
—	4	Iceland	8.6	9.4	—	36	Belarus	—	4.8
2	5	Singapore	9.3	9.3	—	36	Lithuania	—	4.8
8	5	Sweden	8.9	9.3	20	36	South Africa	5.6	4.8
5	7	Canada	8.9	9.0	—	36	Tunisia	—	4.8
—	7	Luxembourg	6.9	9.0	—	40	Costa Rica	—	4.5
3	7	Netherlands	8.7	9.0	23	40	Jordan	—	4.5
10	10	United Kingdom	8.6	8.7	—	40	Mauritius	—	4.5
11	11	Australia	8.8	8.6	36	40	South Korea	4.3	4.5
9	12	Norway	8.6	8.5	31	44	Greece	4.0	4.2
4	12	Switzerland	8.8	8.5	35	45	Brazil	2.7	4.0
21	14	Hong Kong	7.1	8.2	—	45	Bulgaria	—	4.0
19	15	Austria	7.1	7.8	—	45	Jamaica	—	4.0
13	16	United States	7.8	7.7	—	45	Peru	—	4.0
23	17	Chile	7.9	7.5	27	45	Poland	—	4.0
12	18	Germany	8.1	7.3	—	50	Ghana	—	3.9
16	18	Israel	—	7.3	—	51	Croatia	—	3.8
17	20	Belgium	6.9	7.1	27	52	Czech Rep.	—	3.7
18	20	Japan	6.7	7.1	—	52	Latvia	—	3.7
30	20	Spain	4.4	7.1	—	52	Morocco	—	3.7
14	23	Ireland	8.6	6.9	—	52	Slovak Rep.	—	3.7
—	24	Botswana	—	6.4	—	52	Sri Lanka	—	3.7
15	25	France	7.0	6.3	42	57	Colombia	3.4	3.6
24	25	Portugal	5.6	6.3	44	57	Mexico	3.2	3.6
—	27	Slovenia	—	6.0	32	59	China	2.2	3.5
—	28	Namibia	—	5.7	—	59	Dominican Rep.	—	3.5
—	29	Estonia	—	5.6	—	59	Ethiopia	—	3.5
28	29	Taiwan	5.1	5.6	48	62	Egypt	—	3.4
33	31	Italy	3.0	5.2	—	62	El Salvador	—	3.4
—	32	Uruguay	—	5.1	47	64	Thailand	2.8	3.2

Table 13-5: **continued**

1988–92 Rank	2002 Rank	Country	1995 CPI	2002 CPI	1988–92 Rank	2002 Rank	Country	1995 CPI	2002 CPI
34	64	Turkey	4.1	3.2	43	81	Venezuela	2.7	2.5
—	66	Senegal	—	3.1	—	85	Georgia	—	2.4
—	67	Panama	—	3.0	—	85	Ukraine	—	2.4
—	68	Malawi	—	2.9	—	85	Vietnam	—	2.4
—	68	Uzbekistan	—	2.9	—	88	Kazakhstan	—	2.3
22	70	Argentina	5.2	2.8	50	89	Bolivia	—	2.2
—	71	Cote d'Ivoire	—	2.7	37	89	Cameroon	—	2.2
—	71	Honduras	—	2.7	38	89	Ecuador	—	2.2
41	71	India	2.8	2.7	—	89	Haiti	—	2.2
38	71	Russia	—	2.7	—	93	Moldova	—	2.1
—	71	Tanzania	—	2.7	38	93	Uganda	—	2.1
—	71	Zimbabwe	—	2.7	—	95	Azerbaijan	—	2.0
46	77	Pakistan	2.3	2.6	52	96	Indonesia	1.9	1.9
45	77	Philippines	2.8	2.6	49	96	Kenya	—	1.9
—	77	Romania	—	2.6	—	98	Angola	—	1.7
—	77	Zambia	—	2.6	—	98	Madagascar	—	1.7
—	81	Albania	—	2.5	—	98	Paraguay	—	1.7
—	81	Guatemala	—	2.5	51	101	Nigeria	—	1.6
—	81	Nicaragua	—	2.5	53	102	Bangladesh	—	1.2

Source: Transparency International CPI 2002 (*www.transparency.org*), 3 April 2003.

By this measure, countries such as Finland, Denmark, New Zealand, Iceland and Singapore emerge as essentially non-corrupt countries. These countries show a stability in CPI over time indicating that once a battle against corruption has been won, the business environment is likely to remain corruption-free.

In some countries in Asia, there has been a strong stand taken against corruption. Singapore is one of these, as are Australia and Hong Kong, which also score among the least corrupt countries in the world. Malaysia maintains modest levels of perceived corruption, as does Japan and Taiwan. Other countries in Asia have been less successful at containing corruption. China, Thailand, Pakistan, the Philippines and India each have below average CPI scores, placing these countries among the more corrupt ones in the world. Bangladesh, Viet Nam and Indonesia score low on the CPI indicating very high levels of corruption, which in Indonesia's case has not changed from 1995 to 2002.

Indeed, Indonesia has been called the most corrupt place in the world.[14] Despite the introduction of various measures by the government to eradicate the practices of corruption, collusion, and nepotism, they continue to exist. Indonesian President Megawati Soekarnoputri recently stated that 'Despite numerous legal efforts made against corruptors, [corruption, collusion, and nepotism] is still practiced collectively by those sitting in provincial legislative bodies.'[15] The government continues to try to eliminate corruption. Recently, in response to an International Monetary Fund reform programme and to bolster foreign investment and trade, the government recently announced reforms to increase transparency of the notoriously corrupt public service.[16]

The existence of, and potential for, corruption is a reality underlying any business transaction. The reality is a good deal stronger in some nations than in others, as shown in Table 13-5. If one compares the nations that score highly on corruption with the data on economic growth provided in Chapter 2, you would find that nations that score highly on corruption have low rates of economic growth and small economies. Corruption forestalls the pursuit of economic opportunities and it can impede the growth of a nation.

As can be seen in Table 13-5 Bangladesh, like Indonesia, is considered one of the most corrupt nations in Asia, and indeed in the world. The law enforcing agency has been one of the most corrupt sectors in Bangladesh, along with the local government, education and health sectors. Corruption at all these levels hurts the economy. An example of this cost to the economy is given in the following: 211 incidents of corruption resulted in a government loss of 115 billion taka (USD21 billion) during the first six months of 2000. A World Bank study on corruption suggested that Bangladesh could post two to three per cent more GDP growth, and double its per capita income, if the extent of corruption could be reduced.[17]

This corruption also affects foreign investors. As a result, it increases the risk of investing in the nation. A recent World Bank report, *Reforming Governance in Bangladesh*, stated that 'inefficiency and corruption of the public sector remains a huge drag on the economy and a major constraint to improving the welfare of ordinary citizens.'[18] Further, the weak rule of law and order is hampering investment. In September of 2003, it was reported that an extortionist in Bangladesh demanded one million taka (USD17,241), and threatened to kill an Indian national doing business in the country.[19] The Federation of Bangladesh Chamber of Commerce and Industry (FBCCI) (*http://www.fbcci.org/*) made the point that countrywide extortion, the abduction of businessmen, and other criminal activities have worried the business community.

A second comparison that could be made is that between corruption and the political risk and political hazard scores found in Chapter 4, in Tables 4-1 and 4-2. Perhaps not surprisingly, countries considered to be politically risky are also frequently perceived to have high levels of corruption. Political hazards, or the absence of political constraints, can also foster a corrupt environment. An environment absent of political constraints is one in which political actors have more freedom to act at their own discretion. Such freedom can readily spill-over to individual transactions, where a payment to an official might be required to complete a transaction.

Corruption emerges as a part of the business environment. In places such as Indonesia, India and Vietnam, where foreign trade and investment have grown rapidly in recent decades, corruption is a reality in the business environment facing an international manager. Even before entering a country in which corruption has been institutionalized, managers need to consider if they would like to compete in such an environment. Once the entry has been made, more difficult questions begin to be encountered such as how to deal with a situation involving interaction with a corrupt official.

Corruption can become part of the informal norms in a country. When a foreign firm is operating in a country characterized by corrupt practices, the expectation is that a business will follow these informal norms. In essence, corruption, in whatever form it emerges, is a part of the rules of the game. Unfortunately, the rules of the game as played in one area of the world, can often be punishable offences in other areas of the world. In this sense, there are no easy answers on how to deal with a situation of corruption. However, the easiest question to ask is whether to make an entry in a country in which corruption is likely to be encountered.

Sweatshops

Sweatshops, textile production and multinational firms became siblings in the world media in the 1990s. A sweatshop is a low wage factory, in which employees work long difficult hours in rudimentary conditions for low wages relative to those for similar work in developed countries.

Multinational firms were often vilified for being the creators and sustainers of sweatshops. In many cases, these accusations were accurate. Yet, managers in multinational firms would argue that they were only providing jobs with above average wages in a country that required the employment. Many of the issues of sweatshops come from a contrast between what is an acceptable ethical business practice in the host country, and what is one in the home country. As with the case of oil extraction in the Sudan, stakeholders can have different opinions on sweatshops. Labour and consumer advocacy groups often see these as unethical. Host country employees, and managers striving to keep costs as low as competitor's, see sweatshops as ethical. There is no clear answer, which is part of what kept the controversy strong, but there are initiatives such as the Worldwide Responsible Apparel Production (WRAP) Principles (see Box 13-1 and Table 13-6), being undertaken to reduce the severity and prevalence of sweatshops.

The WRAP principles established core standards for production facilities that participate in the Worldwide Responsible Apparel Production Certification Program. The objective of this programme is to independently monitor and certify companies that exhibit compliance with socially responsible global standards for manufacturing as embodied in the WRAP Principles. These principles also help to ensure that sewn products are produced under lawful, humane and ethical conditions. Notably, companies that voluntarily take part in this programme voluntarily agree that their production as well as that of their sub-contractor's complies with these standards.

International Labour Standards and Child Labour

An issue just as pernicious as sweatshops, yet one more viscerally discomforting, is that of child labour. Conventions outlined by the WRAP Principles as well as the International Labour

Box 13-1   Sweatshops in Asia

Stories of horrific conditions in sweatshops are widespread. The Trade Union Congress of the Philippines (*www.tucp.org.ph*) documents sweatshop conditions as a part of its project to assert workers rights in Philippine sweatshops. According to the Congress, sweatshop workers are often subject to anti-union practices, low wages, maternity, discrimination, and sexual harassment, forced overtime, unpaid or underpayment of overtime, and locked exits.

Consumers, retailers, governments, shareholders, and the media pressure companies to hold themselves accountable for the conditions of their manufacturing facilities in developing countries. Nike (*www.nike.com*), the sports and fitness company, had serious public relations difficulties when their labour practices were exposed to the public. In 1996, the CBS News programme, 48 Hours, reported that Nike workers in Vietnam earned an average wage of 20 cents per hour. Fifteen women workers were hit on the head by their supervisor, and 45 women were made to kneel on the ground for 25 minutes with their hands in the air.

Poor working conditions at a specific Nike manufacturing facility was further documented in an Ernst & Young Environmental and Labour Practice Audit of Tae Kwany Vina Industrial Co., Vietnam, on 13 January 1997. Nike had hired Ernst & Young to determine if its subcontractors' factory conditions were in line with the Nike Code of Conduct. Findings, leaked to the public, concluded that the facility had inadequate ventilation, poor water supply and chemical storage facilities; heat, noise and dust conditions that exceeded industry standards. Further, protective devices were minimal and not widely available.

In line with these allegations, anti-Nike activism began to grow. Students rallied and called to boycott Nike products. The negative publicity directly affected Nike's financials, with sales dropping 20 per cent in the last quarter of 1997. Activism against other American companies with manufacturing facilities in Asia also began to grow, with Wal-Mart and The Gap being two of the targets.

In response to these issues, stakeholders, including government, industry members and consumers, worked together to develop the Worldwide Responsible Apparel Production Principles (WRAP Principles) consisting of basic standards that address labour practices, factory conditions, and environmental and customs compliance (see Table 13-6) Participating organizations to the WRAP Principles include American Apparel & Footwear Association (USA), Cámara Sectorial Algodón-Fibras-Textiles-Confecciones De Colombia (Colombia), Cámara Nacional De La Industria Del Vestido (México), Confederation Of Garment Exporters Of The Philippines, Inc. (Philippines), Hong Kong Exporters' Association (Hong Kong) and Sri Lanka Apparel Exporters Association (Sri Lanka).

At the corporate level, numerous goods manufacturers including Levi Strauss and Co. (*www.levistrauss.com*) and Avon Company (*www.avon.com*) have adopted codes of conduct, standards or guidelines to ensure that their contractors and the public are aware of their labour practices.

Sources:

http://www.tucp.org.ph/projects/sweatshops/sweatshopscampaign/index3.htm, 15 November 2003.

Russell Mokhiber and Robert Weissman, "Beat the Devil: the 10 Worst Corporations of 1997," *Multinational Monitor*, December 1997, Vol. 18, pp. 9–18.

http://www.corpwatch.org/issues/PID.jsp?articleid=2488, 17 November 2003.

Debra Goldman, "That Can-do Spirit: It's about Time Nike Paid Less Attention to Itself in its Communications and Devoted More Time to its Restless Customers," *ADWEEK Eastern Edition*, 12 January 1998, Vol. 39, No. 2, p. 50.

http://www.wrapapparel.org/index.cfm?page=participating, 15 November 2003.

http://www.levistrauss.com/responsibility/conduct, 15 November 2003.

http://www.avoncompany.com/about/responsibility.

Table 13-6:   **WRAP Principles**

WRAP Principle	Description of Principle
Compliance with Laws and Workplace Regulations	Manufacturers will comply with laws and regulations in all locations where they conduct business.
Prohibition of Forced Labour	Manufacturers will not use involuntary or forced labour – indentured, bonded or otherwise.
Prohibition of Child Labour	Manufacturers will not hire any employee under the age of 14, or under the age interfering with compulsory schooling, or under the minimum age established by law, whichever is greater.
Prohibition of Harassment or Abuse	Manufacturers will provide a work environment free of harassment, abuse or corporal punishment in any form.
Compensation and Benefits	Manufacturers will pay at least the minimum total compensation required by local law, including all mandated wages, allowances and benefits.
Hours of Work	Manufacturers will comply with hours worked each day, and days worked each week. Manufacturers will provide at least one day off in every seven-day period, except as required to meet urgent business needs.
Prohibition of Discrimination	Manufacturers will employ, pay, promote, and terminate workers on the basis of their ability to do the job, rather than on the basis of personal characteristics or beliefs.
Health and Safety	Manufacturers will provide a safe and healthy work environment. Where residential housing is provided for workers, apparel manufacturers will provide safe and healthy housing.
Freedom of Association and Collective Bargaining	Manufacturers will recognize and respect the right of employees to exercise their lawful rights of free association and collective bargaining.
Environment	Manufacturers will comply with environmental rules, regulations and standards applicable to their operations, and will observe environmentally conscious practices in all locations where they operate.

Source: Adapted from *http://www.wrapapparel.org/index.cfm?page=principles*, 7 December 2003.

Organization both address the issue of minimum work ages. According to the International Labour Organization, weak economic growth, political unrest, HIV/AIDS, and even global information networks have helped to encourage the growth of child labour in certain parts of the world.

In 2000, the ILO estimated that 246 million children were engaged as child labour. The Asia-Pacific region has the largest number of child workers in the 5–14 age category at 127.3 million (Figure 13-3). Myanmar has one of the highest number of child soldiers in the world, with Sri Lanka and Cambodia also affected. Child labour for domestic and agricultural work is also prevalent in several countries in Asia. In Cambodia, children are exposed to hazardous materials and situations when working in salt production, on rubber plantations and in the fish/shrimping process. In the Philippines, children working in gold mines show respiratory illness and ear injuries almost four times higher than the national average.

Figure 13-3:   The Prevalence of Child Labour Worldwide

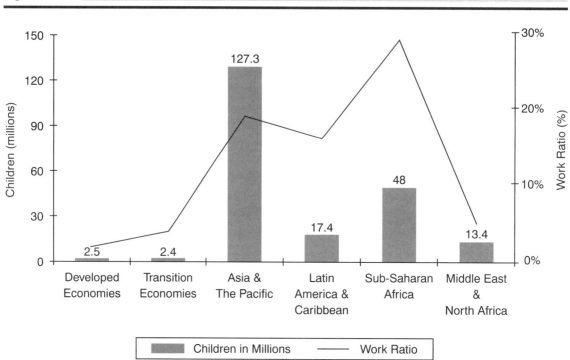

Source: Adapted from "IPEC Action Against Child Labour," 2002–2003, *Progress and Future Priorities*, October 2003, Geneva.

According to the ILO, and contrary to some viewpoints, child labour does not help to eliminate poverty, but rather, encourages its existence. As child labourers, children do not go to school and cannot acquire the skills or education they need to help the their own development or the development of their communities. The International Programme on the Elimination of Child Labour (IPEC) (*www.ilo.org/childlabour*), a body of the ILO, aims to progressively eliminate child labour worldwide through country-based programmes, awareness raising, and the implementation of ILO Child Labour Conventions. In Asia, IPEC is working to translate child labour issues into government policies, strategies, plans and budgets. By 2003, child labour issues had been more publicly addressed in Nepal, Cambodia, Philippines and Vietnam.[21]

Exportation of Hazard or Toxic By-Products

Another area in which multinational firms have been subject to criticism is in their treatment of the environment. Environmental responsibility concerns stakeholders directly related to a corporation – its customers, suppliers, shareholders and employees – but it also indirect stakeholders, namely society at large. As societal shareholders are limited in their direct influences on the activities of a corporation, social groups work through lobbying efforts, publicity and other forms of public awareness campaigns to avoid situation in which environmental damage can be substantial.

One example of concern in the area of environmental responsibility is the export of waste products from one nation of the world to another. An example of this practice can be found along what was pristine coastline in India. At Alang, India, a six mile stretch of oily and smoky beach has become a disposal site for the world's discarded ships.[22] More than 40,000 men work to dismantle these ships. These ships come from around the world. In fact, 90 percent of the next 700 ships slated for disposal worldwide will be dismantled on a beach somewhere in Pakistan, India or Bangladesh.[23] The exportation of ships, and other hazardous waste materials to countries in the Asia-Pacific and other developing nations has become a charged topic.

As with labour concerns, international bodies developed directives for the international disposal and movements of waste. One of these is the Basel Convention (*www.basel.int*), an international treaty to control inter-country movements of hazardous wastes and their disposal (Table 13-7).

Controversy developed after the 22 March 1989 adoption of the Basel Convention as some parties felt that the treaty allowed developed nations to more easily export their hazardous wastes to developing nations. A coalition of developing countries, and several countries from East and West Europe along with Greenpeace, passed an amendment to the Convention in 1994, known as the Basel Ban. The Basel Ban prohibited all forms of hazardous waste exports from OECD countries to non-OECD countries.[24] As of December 2003, the amendment has only been ratified by 32 parties, which leaves it short of the three-fourths of signatories it requires to be binding on its members.

Table 13-7:   **Elements of the 1989 Basel Convention**

Objectives	Measures
1. Reduce transboundary movements of hazardous wastes while minimizing their generation	A. Prohibited exports of hazardous wastes to Antarctica and countries that have banned such imports as national policy
2. Promote the disposal of such wastes as close as possible to their places of origin	B. Prohibited exports to nonparties unless they are subject to an agreement that is at least as stringent as the Basel Convention
3. Prohibit the shipment of hazardous wastes to countries lacking the legal, administrative, and technical capacity to manage them in an environmentally sound manner	C. Permitted transfers of hazardous wastes only with the prior notification and consent of a "competent authority" in the importing country
	D. Promoted the environmentally sound management of hazardous wastes.

Source: http://www.basel.int/, 9 December, 2003.

Pharmaceuticals

An area in which multinational firms have faced considerable challenges in operating at the consumer-level concerns the degree of localization adopted for the sale of pharmaceutical products in different countries worldwide. A rallying point for consumer and social activism with respect to the pricing and distribution policies for a multinational firm's patented pharmaceutical products has been those chemical compounds that can be used to treat AIDS/HIV cases.

On World AIDS Day (1 December 2003), the World Health Organization (WHO) announced an initiative called '3 by 5': the treatment of 3 million developing country HIV patients by 2005. A key to the successful implementation of the "3 by 5" initiative is the easily accessibility of a drug. The drug for treatment needs to both low priced and highly effective.

In August 2003, the World Trade Organization reached an agreement to remove the limit placed on the export of generic AIDS drugs. This agreement will help the WHO achieve '3 by 5' by allowing Indian pharmaceutical companies, who have patent protection, to make and export inexpensive drugs to patients in designated developing countries. The price of these drugs could be less than USD130/per year in developing countries.[25] Similar treatment in the United States is priced at approximately $15,000 per year.[26] The low cost of the drug will not only help spread treatments across more patients, it will encourage high-risk individuals to be tested and treated.

AIDS/HIV is not the only disease where cost-effective, defined as treatment costing less than USD1 per day, and efficient treatment is needed. The millions of individuals that contract Malaria, Leishmaniasis, Human African Trypanosomiasis, Tuberculosis, and Meningitis often cannot receive appropriate treatment due to high drug costs.

Summary

Issues of social responsibility and ethics are of considerable importance to a multinational firm. In today's business culture and environment, this statement is not very controversial. It is difficult, however, to identify how a firm's management can act in an ethical and socially responsible manner.

In terms of a firm's responsibilities, it is a fairly clear-cut exercise to identify the economic and legal responsibilities of a firm. Fulfilling a firm's economic responsibilities means pursuing activities that have a strong economic logic, that will improve the profitability of a firm. Fulfilling a firm's legal responsibilities means pursuing economic activities within the rules and regulations prescribed by a nation's legal framework. The principal complication with legal responsibility for a firm competing in international markets comes from the possibility of a conflict in laws across nations, or the possibility to arbitrage legal requirements across nations.

The issue of ethical responsibility is not as black-and-white as that of legal and economic responsibilities. A firm's ethical responsibility extends from the expectations that a society has about what a firm's managers should be doing. Unfortunately, there is no clear uniform statement about what is ethical, as ethics are intrinsically linked with morals, values and implicit expectations.

The challenges to a firm to meet its ethical responsibilities begin with trying to identify what is and is not ethical behaviour. In the international context, this challenge is extended to dealing with different ethical standards across nations. Part of how a firm deals with this challenge involves identifying what are national differences in ethics, and then determining what will be a firm's basic approach to dealing with this cross-country variance. As part of the identification process it is useful to consider the perspectives of a firm's various stakeholders.

Given that much of the challenge extends from the ambiguity in defining what is ethical behaviour, there have been attempts to codify a firm's ethical responsibility. This codification emerges in terms of a firm's code of conduct. Such a code of conduct can help managers in the field deal with ethical issues that fall into grey areas, for which there is no clear or easy answer. Similarly, standards for corporate conduct, either for corporations as a whole, or for individual corporate professions such as accounting or finance, have been emerging. The emergence of such standards also helps international managers avoid ethical quagmires.

The issue of ethics and social responsibility is not one that can be avoided. The consequences for a firm's reputation, as given in our examples of corruption, child labour, sweatshops, hazardous wastes and pharmaceuticals, can be severe for both a firm and its employees. Ultimately, the effective management of a firm's ethical and social responsibilities is an essential part of the successful management of a firm's international business activities.

Notes

[1] *http://www.benpres-holdings.com*, 8 December 2003.

[2] *Ibid.*

[3] Archie B. Carroll, "A Three Dimensional Conceptual Model of Corporate Performance," *Academy of Management Review*, October 1979, Vol. 4, No. 4, pp. 197–505.

[4] *http://news.bbc.co.uk/1/hi/business/3167302.stm*, 1 December 2003.

[5] Helen Deresky, *International Management: Managing Across Borders and Cultures,* 4th Ed. (Upper Saddle River, New Jersey: Prentice Hall, 2003).

[6] "BHP Billiton Ltd Stainless Steel Materials CSG Briefing Conference Call – Final," *Fair Disclosure Wire*, 25 September 2003.

[7] Adapted from *www.bhpbilliton.com/bb/aboutUs/charter.jsp*, 6 December 2003.

[8] Rajib N. Sayal, *International Management: A Strategic Perspective* (Upper Saddle River, New Jersey: Prentice Hall, 2001).

[9] T. Donaldson and T. Dunfee, "Ties that Bind: A Social Contracts Approach to Business Ethics," (Cambridge, MA: Harvard University Business School Press, 1999).

[10] T. Donaldson, "Values in Tension: Ethics away from Home," *Harvard Business Review*, September–October 1996, pp. 502-510.

[11] *http://www.tabcorp.com.au/responsible_gambling/Training.asp*, 8 December 2003.

[12] *http://www.tabcorp.com.au/responsible_gambling/Training.asp*, 8 December 2003.

[13] John B. Cullen, *Multinational Management: A Strategic Approach*, 2nd Ed. (Mason, Ohio: South Western, 2003).

[14] "A Matter of Law... (corruption of Indonesian legal system)," *The Economist (US)*, 8 July 2000, Vol. 356, No. 8178, p. 9.

[15] "Corruption Continues to Thrive in Indonesia, President Says," Ant – LKBN Antara (Indonesia), 1 August 2003.

[16] Shawn Donnan, "Indonesia Seeks to Build on Economic Gains as IMF Reform Programme Nears the End," *The Financial Times*, Asia-Pacific, 17 September 2003, p. 14.

[17] "Law Enforcers Top List of Corruption in Bangladesh: TIB," *Xinhua News Agency*, 26 September 2000.

[18] *http://www.worldbank.org/bd*, 28 November 2003.

[19] "Indian Business Man Extorted in Bangladesh," *Xinhua News Agency*, 10 September, 2003.

[20] *http://www.ilo.org*, 6 December, 2003.

[21] *http://www.ilo.org/childlabour*, 6 December 2003.

[22] William Langewiesche, "The Shipbreakers," *The Atlantic Monthly*, August 2000, Vol. 286, No. 2, p. 31.

[23] William Langewiesche, "The Shipbreakers," *The Atlantic Monthly*, August 2000, Vol. 286, No. 2, p. 31.

[24] *http://www.basel.int/pub/baselban.html*, 9 December 2003.

[25] "Bush AIDS Plan an Unfunded Mandate," *Africa News Service*, 2 December 2003.

[26] *Ibid.*

SECTION IV

Cases

BEIJING MIRROR CORPORATION

In January 1996, Mr. Ming Tian, Manager of the Strategic Management Department of Beijing Rearview Mirror HighTech Corporation (Beijing Mirror Corp.), was pondering a development strategy for the corporation. Beijing Mirror Corporation owned the patent for a newly invented type of rearview mirror. This mirror could effectively increase view width and eliminate the blind spot. Its invention and development had the potential to make a tremendous contribution to the transportation industry, by radically reducing traffic accidents. Small-scale production had already started and the goal of Beijing Mirror Corp. was a swift entry into domestic and international markets, as well as a high market share. However, at present it was nearly impossible for the Corporation to achieve its goal solely on its own. Many domestic and overseas companies had submitted offers concerning possible joint ventures or investments. These strategic decisions involved financial, marketing, R&D and production problems, and were now occupying Mr. Tian's thoughts.

Product Background

The importance of a rearview mirror to driving safety was well-known to every driver and members of the auto and transportation industries. Existing external rearview mirrors suffered universal defects such as narrow view width, a large blind spot and serious image distortion. The common remedies were to install more mirrors on both sides in different directions, or to glue a small convex mirror onto the original. The result was a broken image and difficulty for the driver in

Richard Ivey School of Business
The University of Western Ontario

determining the distance between the object and the vehicle. Furthermore, it was even harder for the driver to glance over two or more mirrors simultaneously. Consequently, traffic accidents could not be effectively avoided. According to some statistics, traffic accidents relating to rearview mirror defects amounted to some 30 per cent of the total traffic accidents in China and 20 per cent in the United States. Such problems were especially severe on expressways.

Mr. Zhang Lixin, an ordinary worker at Tsinghua University, found a solution by combining his personal experience with insight and research. The mirror was designed with different curvature radii both in vertical and horizontal sections. In other words, the reflective surface had a composite curved surface with smooth transition. Such rearview mirrors successfully solved the narrow view width and blind spot problems that were common to mirrors with a single-curved convex or a flat reflective surface. Moreover, because the mirror provided the driver with a satisfactory object image with little distortion, it was a further enhancement to driving safety. High product quality was guaranteed through the use of well-selected raw materials and imported manufacturing equipment. Formal tests by the Research Institute of Automobiles and Research Division of Optical Instruments, Tsinghua University, showed that this mirror thoroughly fulfilled drivers' requirements. This was followed by the praise of experts and drivers after installation and try-out.

Patent

The increased view-width and non-blind spot rearview mirror invented by Mr. Zhang Lixin was patented at the Chinese Patent Office. The patent would expire in ten years. To overcome its shortage of funds as well as its unfamiliarity with the foreign patent act and the patent application procedure, Beijing Mirror Corp. signed an agency agreement with the C&S Technology Company of the United States to apply for an overseas patent for the product. By January 1996, patents had been granted to Beijing Mirror in 19 different countries and regions. Mr. Zhang Lixin possessed 30 per cent of the total ownership of the patent held by Beijing Mirror Corp. S Department of Tsinghua University, and consequently, Tsinghua University owned the remaining 70 per cent. The patent value was assessed at 200 to 400 million RMB after technical appraisal of the mirror and a rough estimation of its market by domestic experts. (In January 1996, there were 8.31 RMB per US dollar.)

Beijing Mirror Corp.

In April 1990, the domestic patent was granted for the rearview mirror. Since then, Mr. Zhang Lixin had devoted his life to bringing his achievement into production. During the following years, he contacted numerous factories to seek a manufacturer. However, his approaches were turned down because of the risk and complications associated with the transition process, or because the company was unwilling to compensate Mr. Zhang Lixin for previous research. At a crucial juncture, Mr. Wang Yan, vice-dean of S Department, who had just returned from an overseas training course, suggested that his department cooperate with Mr. Zhang Lixin to support and finance the translation of the high-technology proposal into real products. Thus, the Beijing Mirror Corp. came into existence as a subsidiary of Tsinghua Enterprise Group.

However, difficulties and challenges continued. One year passed. Hundreds of thousands of RMB appeared to have achieved very little in controlling the distortion created during the production process of the mirror. Opposition to further investment was getting stronger. During this period, Mr. Wang Yan and Mr. Zhang Lixin sold off their personal properties to pursue their goal. S Department decided to make a final investment of 80,000 RMB. Not long afterwards, the first successful mirror was produced. Under the warrant of Tsinghua Enterprise Group, a further low-interest loan of 20 million RMB was obtained from Bank J, a state-owned commercial bank of China, which contributed a great deal toward enlarging the production scale of Beijing Mirror Corp. The current total book value of Beijing Mirror Corp.'s assets amounted to some 30 million RMB. Trial orders from various parts of the country were encouraging. Beijing Mirror Corp. had also acquired a certificate from the Beijing High and New Technological Industrial Development Zone. In addition, the Government provided favorable terms for hi-tech enterprises with respect to finance and taxation to accelerate the development of such an industry. All these conditions worked to Beijing Mirror Corp.'s advantage.

Industry And Market

Market Capacity

The annual production of vehicles in China was approximately 1.4 million. Auto production had been soaring recently, with an annual growth rate of 15 to 20 per cent. However, this rate was predicted to decline. The Chinese auto market now accommodated some 20 million vehicles. In both existing vehicles and in yearly production, roughly 50 per cent were large- or medium-sized; that is, the current number of large- and medium-sized vehicles in China was about 10 million, with an annual increase of 700,000. In the world auto market, the yearly production was 50°million or so. Its growth rate was more stable, but lower, than that of the domestic market. Moreover, the proportion of large- and medium-sized vehicles in the international market was far less than in that of the domestic market. The medium- and short-term target market of the Beijing rearview mirror was chiefly external use in large- and medium-sized vehicles because the blind spot problem was most serious in large- and medium-sized vehicles.

Market for Ordinary Rearview Mirrors

Ordinary rearview mirrors in the domestic market were divided into three categories: foreign-made; made by joint-venture; and domestic-made. Domestic-made rearview mirrors were usually priced around 50 RMB each, while foreign-made mirrors or those made by joint-ventures were priced from 150 RMB to 1200 RMB. Although entry into this industry did not require much input of capital and technology, it did demand an obvious technological or price advantage over existing products to earn a desirable market share, because it was a common practice for the mirror manufacturers to have long-term contracts with auto factories, or to conduct their sales through agents. The domestic price of the Beijing rearview mirror was around 250 RMB per piece. The tentative overseas price was $30 to $35 per piece. The final price would be determined according to the ordered quantity.

Technology Environment

Research to eliminate the blind spot of rearview mirrors was being conducted in various countries. There were three types of non-blind spot rearview mirrors. The first was the navigation security system, which provided a clear and stable rearview, while eliminating the blind spot, visual error, and time error. However, owing to the exorbitant cost, it could not be widely applied. The second type was the camera system, which required a lot of maintenance and lacked durability. The third involved a fibre optical system. It shared the same defects as the first type, with a unit price of $200. All these types of rearview mirrors necessitated modification of the auto design. Furthermore, if the mirror broke down, it could cause enormous risk to safe driving. The Beijing Mirror seemed to be quite the opposite. It had already passed numerous tests.

In preparing a development strategy for the company, Mr. Tian prepared the analysis which follows, including the calculations contained in the exhibits.

Beijing Mirror Corp.

Strengths:

1. The patent eased entry into the market to a large extent.
2. In the foreseeable future, no substitute or other competitive products were anticipated to match both the price and function of the patented product.
3. The quality and function of the product were guaranteed.
4. The Corporation enjoyed a monopoly on the manufacturing technology.
5. The patented product had been tested and certified by the China Motor Vehicle Safety Appraisal and Inspection Centre. A national standard requirement would be established based upon the patent. The Appraisal and Inspection Centre was going to be the sole domestic agent for the product.
6. Since it was a high technology enterprise, most favorable tax treatment had been granted to Beijing Mirror Corp. by the Government. Income tax was exempted in the initial three years and levied only on a reduced rate (50 per cent of the normal rate) for the following three years.

7. A loan with a favorable interest rate was available from Bank J, a state-owned commercial bank of China. The domestic interest rate had been as much as 20 per cent, while the rate required by Bank J from Beijing Mirror Corp. was only 12 per cent.

8. Research and development capability as well as high quality personnel were available with the support of Tsinghua University.

Weaknesses:

1. The bottleneck in the manufacturing process resulted in a high spoilage rate. This was a considerable obstacle for general efficiency and large-scale production.

2. The product could be easily imitated, and thus the technology could be stolen.

3. Since Beijing Mirror Corp. was a newly established company, the management still needed strengthening. The production and marketing capabilities also required improvement.

4. The degree to which the market would accept this new product remained unknown. Drivers were accustomed to the ordinary rearview mirror and were able to correctly judge the distorted image. Though no serious accidents happened during the try-out, drivers had to adjust to the undistorted image. This adjustment would certainly take time. During the probation period, more problems and accidents would emerge, possibly involving complex regulations and litigation. All this could block the successful entry of the Beijing rearview mirror into the market.

5. The rearview mirror was directly linked with safe driving, as well as life and property security. Consequently, stringent control over quality and function standards was imposed by all the involved countries. Although the Beijing rearview mirror had qualified under the national standard of China, it still could be incompatible with international standards and corresponding regulations. In such a case, Beijing Mirror Corp. would miss the optimal time to enter the world market unless it could promptly comply with foreign regulations and standards.

Marketing

The present Marketing Department of Beijing Mirror Corp. had only a few staff members, and had not conducted any vigorous marketing activity. Most of the orders that the company currently had were the result of articles in the press or of public interest aroused by domestic and overseas product exhibitions. Moreover, they were chiefly trial orders for small quantities. In addition to the contract with the C&S Technology Company of the United States, Beijing Mirror Corp. had signed a domestic-exclusive agency agreement with the Appraisal and Inspection Center of China. It was the American company's obligation to enlarge the overseas market and promote the sales of the product vigorously for Beijing Mirror Corp. Apart from these, Beijing Mirror

Corp. had no long-term contracts with any other enterprises. The overseas business had not yet started.

Finance

The Corporation had very high financial leverage. Production had not reached the optimum scale, with an annual output of only 100,000 pieces. Since the majority of costs were fixed, there was a net loss in the current year, resulting in a negative Owner's Equity. The total amount of the liabilities exceeded the total book value of the Corporation's assets. The Corporation's current ratio did not look good. Receivables tied up a great deal of funds. These were all common problems for domestic enterprises. Advances on sales constituted the greatest proportion of the Corporation's current liability; thus, the Corporation's liquidity could be better than the current ratio indicated.

Research and Development

Experts in various fields, such as optics, the chemical industry, electric-vacuum technology, the auto industry and thermal technology, etc., employed by Beijing Mirror Corp. had made a major theoretical breakthrough and were engaged in perfecting the manufacturing process. Small-scale production was now underway. The current problem was in the heat-forming process. Since the mirror had a composite curved surface, it was very difficult to heat it and cool it evenly; uneven heating or cooling resulted in distortion of the mirror. The spoilage rate of the entire manufacturing process was as high as 40 per cent. Consequently, production efficiency was relatively low, while the cost was fairly high. Research was being conducted by the Corporation to perfect the manufacturing technology and process, and the spoilage rate would ultimately be expected to decline. The Corporation was also considering the adaptation of the rearview mirror to small-sized vehicles, in order to form a complete product series.

Production

The existing production line of the Corporation was imported from Taiwan. Many of the most advanced technologies in the world had been applied to the manufacturing process. Furthermore, Tsinghua University could serve the Corporation with solid technology support. The Corporation also had adopted Computer Assisted Design. No matter what the vehicle model, once the required data (such as the size of the vehicle, the driver's position, and the position of the mirror) were input, a final optimized design of the mirror could be obtained immediately. The mould of the mirror was processed by the CIMS, one of the key experimental projects of the Government, which appeared to be highly efficient and precise.

Management

The Corporation currently had a small staff. It was in urgent need of supportive intermediate management. The Sales Department and Financial Department were especially weak, merely performing the most basic functions, and leaving unfulfilled their proper contribution to the Corporation's development. Some essential functions for manufacturing enterprises such as costing and cost control had not yet been set up in the Financial Department (not to mention the decision-assistance function such as financing the Corporation's development). These defects were mainly due to the short history of the Corporation. Before the business was operating normally, it could hardly be expected to attract high-quality management personnel.

Joint-Venture Proposal

The Beijing rearview mirror aroused a great deal of public interest after winning the Gold Prize in the National Patent Exhibition and through its presentation in the Selected Quality Exhibition held in Singapore in April 1995. Many trial orders followed. Several other companies submitted requests to be Beijing Mirror Corp.'s agent, or to cooperate with Beijing Mirror Corp. in developing the product. Among the joint-venture proposals, only two came to the negotiation stage.

1. Negotiation with the Domestic PAC Company

PAC Company accepted almost all the terms asked by Beijing Mirror Corp. in the negotiation. Under their proposal, a new firm (Firm X) would be established. The sole asset of the firm would be the ownership of the patent. The original stockholders of the Beijing Mirror Corp. would own 100 per cent of Firm X. The present Beijing Mirror Corp. (without the patent ownership) plus a 20 million RMB input from PAC Company would then become the joint-venture (PAC Company insisted on acquiring 30 per cent ownership of Beijing Mirror Corp.). The joint-venture would be the exclusive licensee of the rearview mirror. It would also be responsible for the production and sales of the mirror. Five per cent of the sales would be paid to the patent owner (Firm X) as the royalty. The negotiation did not refer to the influence that the 30 per cent stock ownership would exert upon the manufacturing and managing decisions. Since PAC Company did not demand the right to take part in the management, the original stockholders would still have control over Beijing Mirror Corp. However, the technology secret would be shared by both sides, although PAC Company's business scope had never been in the high technology area. Its entry was presumed to be motivated by a desire to increase its own profitability, and to find an appropriate investment opportunity for its huge cash surplus.

2. Negotiation with Cantise Co. of the United States

Cantise Co. Ltd. was an American company with branches in Canada, China and various other Asian countries. Mr. Huang Wei, the president of the company, was born in Mainland China and received his bachelor's degree there before he went to the United States. Cantise Co. Ltd. was founded immediately after he acquired his MBA degree in the United States. The negotiating delegation of Cantise Co. consisted of Chinese, with masters or higher degrees granted overseas before they entered Cantise Co. Cantise Co. did not reveal its overall business information to Beijing Mirror Corp., but the business performance report of the company's brochure showed that the company acted as the overseas agent for Chinese mainland enterprises or as the mainland agent for foreign companies. Cantise Co. could ease Beijing Mirror Corp.'s entry into the North American market, and help to establish a relationship with American manufacturers of vehicle components. Cantise Co. also promised that, once agreement was reached, it would arrange visits to the United States and Canada for the CEOs of Beijing Mirror Corp., and organize meetings for them with the American and Canadian manufacturers to discuss the production and selling of the rearview mirror in North America.

The proposal submitted by Cantise Co. was similar to that of the PAC Company. A new firm (Firm Y) would be planned. The sole asset of the new firm would be the ownership of the patent. The original stockholders of Beijing Mirror Corp. would own 100 per cent of Firm Y. The present Beijing Mirror Corp. (without the patent ownership) plus the 20 million RMB fund input from Cantise Co. would then become the joint-venture (Cantise Co. agreed to take no more than 30 per cent of the total ownership of the joint-venture). The joint-venture would have the exclusive licence of the rearview mirror, and could conduct its business worldwide. However, Cantise Co. would require a say in the management and decision-making of the new Beijing Mirror Corp. and access to the licence of the rearview mirror as well. It would not, however, engage in any domestic manufacturing or sales activities, but only carry out such activities overseas. When overseas sales of Cantise Co. reached two million pieces per year, the original stockholders of Beijing Mirror Corp. would get 10 per cent of the ownership of the Cantise Co.'s overseas division specializing in the rearview mirror business. As soon as the annual sales of Cantise Co.'s overseas business exceeded four million pieces, the original stockholders of Beijing Mirror Corp. could then increase their equity in that division to 20 per cent, which was the upper limit of its ownership of the division. Before the specified annual sales volume of four million pieces was reached, Beijing Mirror Corp. was authorized to sell the product directly overseas. As soon as Cantise's sales surpassed four million pieces overseas, Beijing Mirror Corp. would have to limit its sales within the country. No other business organization or individual would be granted the licence except Beijing Mirror Corp. and Cantise Co.

As mentioned above, capital and human resources were the two most crucial factors for Beijing Mirror Corp.'s successful entry into the world market. The reasons were as follows:

1. The existing rearview mirror market was served by all types of products with various functions. Therefore, interest in the new product had to be aroused by systematic advertising and sales promotion activities. Consequently, a huge amount of sales promotion expense was the first consideration for entry into the target market.

2. The current manufacturing capacity of the Corporation was still quite limited. More long-term assets would have to be purchased to increase the scale of production; this also created demand for more capital. However, the Corporation was currently experiencing a net loss. Although there might be greater cash inflows when sales increased, it was unrealistic to expect that advertising and expansion would be financed solely by operating cash inflow. The Corporation already had a high proportion of debts, which made further borrowing difficult.

3. The staff of the Corporation was still weak, especially in the Sales Department. It lacked the personnel not only for international marketing, but also for domestic sales promotion.

Therefore, one of the most practical approaches to encourage faster development of Beijing Mirror Corp. was to cooperate with other enterprises. The companies intending to cooperate with Beijing Mirror Corp. had long operating histories as well as considerable knowledge and experience in marketing and management. In addition, they were generally more familiar with the market, each having its own sales network. Cooperation with such companies would not only provide Beijing Mirror Corp. with adequate funds for development, but could also solve the problem of insufficient qualified personnel. However, to get such support, Beijing Mirror Corp. would have to give up part of the ownership, and possibly part of the management authority as well.

The Decisions

Beijing Mirror Corp. was aiming at a relatively high market share both in domestic and in overseas markets. To realize such a goal, the following issues were those Mr. Tian would have to consider in order to draft a strategy for the Corporation's development.

1. Whether Beijing Mirror Corp. should develop independently, or enter a joint venture with other companies?
    A joint venture would support Beijing Mirror Corp. with urgently needed funds and other kinds of resources, at the price of losing partial control over the corporation.

2. Whether Beijing Mirror Corp. should join with a domestic enterprise or with an overseas enterprise?
    Since Beijing Mirror Corp. had already been recognized as a high technology enterprise, most favorable tax treatment was granted by the Government. This eliminated one of the most important motivations for joint-venture with foreign companies, since no more favorable tax treatment could be obtained. However, there were other advantages

to joint venture, such as a smoother entry into the international market, the easier adoption of foreign advanced equipment, technology, and management as well as foreign capital and staff. The joint venture would also have to obey the laws and regulations of the two countries, and different countries had different taxation and regulatory policies toward the international remittance of royalties and profits. At the same time, problems such as accounting treatment and information disclosure might also exist. A joint venture with Cantise Co. would involve conflicts with the C&S contract as well, which might lead to arduous litigation. Nonetheless, Cantise Co. believed this was a minor problem.

Since Beijing Mirror Corp. was completely ignorant of the overseas market, it was difficult to find an appropriate way to assess whether the four per cent royalty and the 20 per cent upper limit of the division's equity were reasonable.

3. Which kind of pricing strategy should be adopted?

Cost was temporarily irrelevant in the pricing of the mirror, since there would be no competitors in the market in the near future. Therefore, a demand-oriented pricing method could be applied. The key here was to determine the sensitivity of demand to price, as well as the influence of price upon the goal of quick market entry.

4. What distribution pattern should be used?

Beijing Mirror Corp. had signed an exclusive agency agreement with the China Motor Vehicle Safety Appraisal and Inspection Centre. It would effectively prevent counterfeit and imitation, thus safeguarding the Corporation's reputation. However, the Corporation would be overly dependent on its sole agent, whose efforts to sell the consigned products would directly affect the Corporation's profit. To ensure consistent revenue, the Corporation would have to provide continuous incentives for the agent. Such incentives were usually not only costly but also highly risky. These concerns could be partially reduced by using a competitive distribution pattern, whether it involved an agency agreement or a goods delivery contract, long-term or short-term, with fixed price or floating price. This would increase both the distribution channels to the markets and the speed of market penetration. The new task of evaluating and controlling the performance of the numerous agents would then emerge.

5. Which promotion method should be applied?

Products like the rearview mirror were directly related to people's life and property security. Therefore, rigorous standards and regulatory controls concerning the quality and function were imposed by all governments. Although sales promotion through mass media might produce a wide coverage and a fast reaction, regulatory limits might restrict growth. If all required regulations were precisely followed, low efficiency might then result, and optimal timing might be missed.

These were the major aspects under consideration. Mr. Tian was well aware that he had to submit his proposals for Beijing Mirror Corp.'s development strategy as soon as possible. A detailed and well-documented explanation was also expected.

Exhibit 1   Organization Chart of Beijing Mirror Corp.

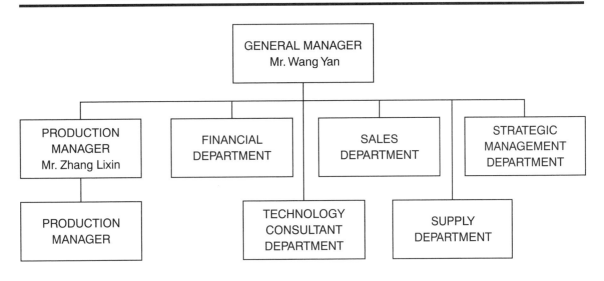

Exhibit 2   Balance Sheet Beijing Mirror Corp.

December 31, 1995 (10,000 RMB)

Current assets	
Cash	180
Accounts receivable	230
Inventory	328
Other receivables and prepaid items	42
Subtotal	780
Fixed assets	**2,400**
Less: depreciation	353
Net fixed assets	2,047
Other assets	20
Total assets	2,847
Current liabilities	
Bank loans	300
Sales advances	553
Other payables	17
Long-term Liabilities	**2,000**
Owner's equity	
Paid-in capital	400
Capital surplus	200
Retained earnings	(623)
Total of owner's equity	(23)
Total of liabilities and owner's equity	2,847

Exhibit 3   Partial Income Statement Beijing Mirror Corp.

for the year ended December 31, 1995
(10,000 RMB)

Sales revenue	2,500
Less: operating cost	2,883
Operating income	(383)
Less: Financial expense	240
Earnings before tax	(623)
Less: income tax	0
Net income	(623)

Exhibit 4   Fixed Assets of Beijing Mirror Corp.

	Cost (10,000 RMB)	Life Expectancy (year)	Production Capacity (10,000 Ps/year)	Depreciation Method
Imported manufacturing line	380	5	50	S/L
Complementary equipment	150	5	50	S/L
Multi-layer coating machine	400	5	50	S/L
Testing mchine	100	5	50	S/L
Interim-test machine	150	3		S/L
Moulding machine for mirror case	370	2.5 million pieces		Units of production
Moulding machine for mirror glass	150	2.5 million pieces		Units of production
Factory buildings	440	10	100	S/L
Office facilities	200	10	100	S/L
Set-up of factory building	60	5	100	S/L
Total	**2,400**			

Exhibit 5   Sales Forecast and Schedule of Long-Term Asset Investment and Depreciation (for 10 years)

Sales Forecast

The production volume of Beijing Mirror Corp. reached 100,000 pieces in 1995. The predicted volume for 1996 was 300,000 pieces. The target production volume for 1997 was around 700,000 units, roughly 50 per cent of the rearview mirror market for large and medium-sized vehicles. In 1998, with the further penetration of the domestic market, the Corporation would aim for the international market. A total production of 1.5 million was predicted with 1.2 million for the domestic market (80 per cent of the total market share) and 0.3 million for the overseas market. With the domestic market share secured, 1998 would be devoted to the campaign for the international market. The forecasted production volume was two million pieces, which would then remain constant afterwards. Therefore, the sales forecast within the valid period of patent was as follows:

Year	1995	1996	1997	1998	1999	2000	2001	2002	2003	2004
Production (10,000 Ps)	10	30	70	150	200	200	200	200	200	200

Schedule of Long-term Asset Investment and Depreciation (10,000 RMB)

Year	1994	1995	1996	1997	1998	1999	2000	2001	2002	2003	2004
Investment	2,400		1,030	2,250	1,030	1,610	520	1,550	1,610		
Depreciation		(353)	(394)	(684)	(1,082)	(1,392)	(1,392)	(1,392)	(1,392)	(1,392)	(1,392)
Net investment	2,400	(353)	636	1,566	(52)	218	(872)	158	(362)	(158)	(1,392)

Exhibit 6   Cost Behavior Analysis

1. **Variable Costs** (RMB/piece)

	Raw materials	74.3
	Package	12.0
	Instruction booklet	2.0
	Utilities	5.6
	Direct labor	4.0
	Depreciation of moulding machines	2.1
	Total	*100.0*

2. **Semi-variable Costs** (10,000 RMB)

Volume (10,000 pieces)	Below 50	50–100	100–150	150–200	200–250
Promotion expenditure	200	600	1,000	1,000	1,000
Depreciation of the manufacturing line and testing equipment	206	412	618	824	1,030
Maintenance expense	50	100	150	200	250
Fixed part of raw material	50	100	150	200	250
Depreciation of factory building and office facilities	76	76	152	152	228
Indirect labor and salary of non-manufacturing staff	110	110	220	220	330

3. **Fixed Costs**

Land rent:	400,000 RMB/year
Consultant fee:	1,000,000 RMB/year
R&D:	10,000,000 RMB/year (for the initial three years)
	5,000,000 RMB/year (for the following seven years)
Depreciation of interim-test equipment:	500,000 RMB/year (for the initial three years)

Exhibit 7   Pro-Forma Income Statement (10,000 RMB)

Ignore the influence of capital structure and assume the business to be entirely equity-financed.

Year	1995	1996E	1997E	1998E	1999E	2000E	2001E	2002E	2003E	2004E
Sales Revenue	2,500	7,500	17,500	37,500	50,000	50,000	50,000	50,000	50,000	50,000
Variable Cost	1,001	3,002	7,004	15,008	20,010	20,010	20,010	20,010	20,010	20,010
Contribution Margin	1,499	4,498	10,496	22,492	29,990	29,990	29,990	29,990	29,990	29,990
Fixed Cost	1,882	1,882	2,588	2,930	3,236	3,236	3,236	3,236	3,236	3,236
EBIT	(383)	2,616	7,908	19,562	26,754	26,754	26,754	26,754	26,754	26,754
Income Tax	0	0	0	0	4,013	4,013	4,013	8,829	8,829	8,829
Net Income	(383)	2,616	7,908	19,562	22,741	22,741	22,741	17,925	17,925	17,925

Exhibit 8   Forecasted Statement of Cashflow (10,000 RMB)

Year	1994	1995	1996E	1997E	1998E	1999E	2000E	2001E	2002E	2003E	2004E
Net income		(383)	2,616	7,908	19,562	22,741	22,741	22,741	17,925	17,925	17,925
Less: net investment of long-term asset	2,400	(353)	636	1,566	(52)	218	(872)	158	(362)	(158)	(1,392)
Less: working capital input (1)	500	1,000	2,000	4,000	2,500						
Residual value (2)											28,000
Net cashflow	(2,900)	(1,030)	(20)	2,342	17,114	22,523	23,613	22,583	17,707	17,767	47,317

(1) The turnovers of work-in-process, raw material inventory and accounts receivable were all assumed to be 12. Therefore, the net working capital need was 20 per cent of the marginal sales revenue.

(2) The validity of the patent would expire in 10 years. By then, the competition would be accelerated and Beijing Mirror Corp. would have to keep its market share by reducing the price. In that fully competitive market, no enterprise could earn more than the average profit, which was around 25 per cent with a unit price of 185 RMB or so. Also assume that the Beijing Mirror Corp. would maintain annual sales of two million pieces in 10 years. If the scale of production were kept constant, the annual depreciation would roughly equal the annual investment of long-term asset. Therefore, the net cashflow would approximately equal the net income, about 70 million RMB per year. Using a discount rate of 25 per cent, we get a residual value of 280 million RMB.

Exhibit 9   Valuation of the Patent

When estimating the cashflows, inflation factors were deliberately left out of the consideration of sales price and out-of-pocket expense. The replacement cost was also assumed constant when estimating the investment of a long-term asset. As a result, inflation should not be taken into account in determining the discount rate, where the intrinsic risk of the project ought to be the major concern. In the case of the rearview mirror, a discount rate of 20 to 30 per cent was used.

Discount rate	NPV (10,000 RMB)
20%	44,307
30%	25,190
50%	8,810
90%	107
100%	−659

IRR = 92 per cent

The patent was valued between 250 million and 440 million RMB.

Exhibit 10   Joint-Venture Scheme of Beijing Mirror Corp. with the Domestic Pac Co.

Original State:

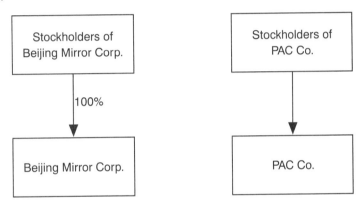

Joint-venture:

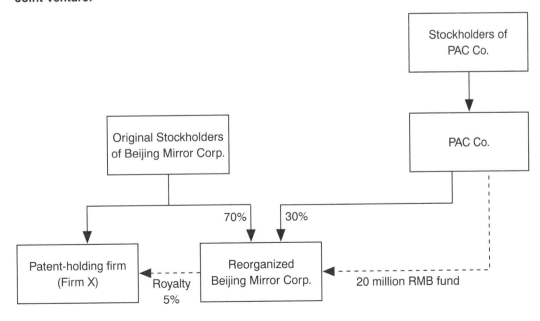

Exhibit 11   Joint Venture Scheme Of Beijing Mirror Corp. With Cantise Co.

Original State:

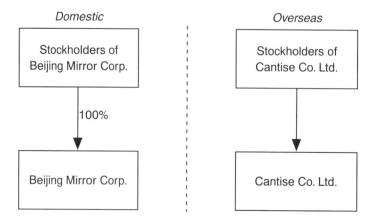

Joint-venture:

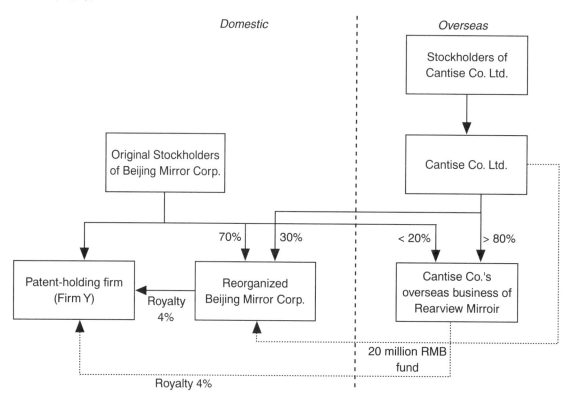

Exhibit 12   Value of Beijing Mirror Corp. after Joint Venture

Ignore the influence of capital structure and assume the business to be entirely equity-financed.

1. Joint venture with the domestic company

    (a) Value of the reorganized Beijing Mirror Corp.

    Assume the formal start of the joint venture was to be in 1997. Due to the 20 million fund input, the production volume and the market penetration pace of Beijing Mirror Corp. would be greatly increased. The predicted sales for 1997 were 1.5 million pieces. It could be further improved to two million in 1998. Since the domestic market was the target basis for Beijing Mirror Corp. only 30 to 35 per cent of the total sales would be made overseas. The domestic market could be considered well-captured with total annual sales of two million pieces. Therefore, sales of two million pieces could be assumed to remain afterwards.

    The pro-forma income statement is as follows: (10,000 RMB)

Year	1997E	1998E	1999E	2000E	2001E	2002E	2003E	2004E
Sales revenue	37,500	50,000	50,000	50,000	50,000	50,000	50,000	50,000
Variable cost	16,883	22,510	22,510	22,510	22,510	22,510	22,510	22,510
Contribution margin	20,617	27,490	27,490	27,490	27,490	27,490	27,490	27,490
Fixed cost	2,930	3,236	3,236	3,236	3,236	3,236	3,236	3,236
EBIT	17,687	24,254	24,254	24,254	24,254	24,254	24,254	24,254
Income tax	0	0	3,638	3,638	3,638	8,004	8,004	8,004
New income	17,687	24,254	20,616	20,616	20,616	16,250	16,250	16,250

Since the scale of production was relatively stable, the annual depreciation could be assumed to equal the annual investment in long-term assets. Similarly, the cashflow could be assumed to equal the net income. When the validity of the patent expires, the profitability of the business would decline. The residual value of the reorganized Beijing Mirror Corp. was the same as in Exhibit 8.

The forecasted statement of cashflow is as follows: (10,000 RMB)

Year	1997E	1998E	1999E	2000E	2001E	2002E	2003E	2004E
Residual value								28,000
Net cashflow	17,687	24,254	20,616	20,616	20,616	16,250	16,250	16,250

Discounting the cashflows at the beginning of 1996 with a rate of 30 per cent, we get: NPV = 484 million RMB.

    (b) Value of the patent-holding firm (the applicable tax rate is 33 per cent)

Year	1997E	1998E	1999E	2000E	2001E	2002E	2003E	2004E
Royalty	1,256	1,675	1,675	1,675	1,675	1,675	1,675	1,675

These cashflows were much safer than the operating cashflows of Beijing Mirror Corp. Therefore, a lower discount rate should be applied. Discounting them back to the beginning of 1996 with a rate of 20 per cent, we would get: NPV = 50.65 million RMB.

(c) Value held by original stockholders of Beijing Mirror Corp.

	Value (10,000 RMB)	Share held by original stockholders of Beijing Mirror Corp.	Value held by original stockholders of Beijing Mirror Corp. (10,000 RMB)
Reorganized Beijing Mirror Corp.	48,440	70%	33,908
Patent-holding firm	5,056	100%	5,056
Total			38,964

2. Joint venture with Cantise Co. Ltd.

(a) Value of reorganized Beijing Mirror Corp.

The value of the reorganized Beijing Mirror Corp. when forming a joint venture with Cantise Co. was the same as when forming a joint venture with the domestic company.

(b) Overseas business of Cantise Co.

Assume that Cantise Co. started its overseas business of rearview mirrors from 1998. Due to its powerful support of capital and technology, as well as its global distribution network, sales could grow rapidly to a volume of 4,000,000 pieces annually. Also assume that the manufacturing cost and sales price were the same for both the Cantise Co.'s overseas business and the reorganized Beijing Mirror Corp. The Pro-forma Income Statement would appear as follows: (10,000 RMB)

Sales revenue	100,000
Less: variable cost	44,020
fixed cost	7,000
Income before tax	48,980
Less: income tax (T = 30 per cent)	14,694
Net income	34,286

Since the scale of production was relatively stable, the annual depreciation could be assumed to equal the annual investment of long-term assets. Therefore, the net cashflow would equal the net income. Estimation of the residual value of the reorganized Beijing Mirror Corp. was also as before. The forecasted statement of cashflow is as follows: (10,000 RMB)

Year	1998E	1999E	2000E	2001E	2002E	2003E	2004E
Residual value							56,000
Net cashflow	34,286	34,286	34,286	34,286	34,286	34,286	34,286

Discounting the cashflows to the beginning of 1996 with a rate of 30 per cent, we get: NPV = 621.29 million RMB.

(c) Value of the patent-holding firm (The applicable tax rate is 33 per cent): (10,000°RMB)

Year	1997E	1998E	1999E	2000E	2001E	2002E	2003E	2004E
Royalty	1,005	1,340	4,020	4,020	4,020	4,020	4,020	4,020

These cashflows were much safer than the operating cashflows of Beijing Mirror Corp. Therefore, a lower discount rate could be applied. Discounting them back to the beginning of 1996 with a rate of 20 per cent, we get: NPV = 92.10 million RMB.

(d) Value held by original stockholders of Beijing Mirror Corp.

	Value (10,000 RMB)	Share held by original stockholders of Beijing Mirror Corp.	Value held by original stockholders of Beijing Mirror Corp. (10,000 RMB)
Reorganized Beijing Mirror Corp.	48,440	70%	33,908
Overseas business of Cantise Co.	62,129	20%	12,426
Patent-holding firm	9,210	100%	9,210
Total			55,544

Exhibit 13   Agency Agreement

In order to develop international business, the two parties, on the basis of equality and mutual benefit, came to a formal agreement as follows:

I.   Party A (Licensor): Beijing Mirror Corp.

Party B (General Agency): C & S Technology Corp.

Party A agrees to designate Party B as its exclusive general agent outside China for the increased view width and non-blind spot rearview mirror. Party B agrees to bear the expense of applying for the patent and to undertake to develop the market.

II. Rights and Obligations of the General Agent (Party B)

Based on the initial market analysis, Party B agrees to take the following responsibilities:

1.   Bearing the necessary disbursements when applying for the patent in relevant foreign countries.

2.   Vigorously advancing the overseas market, product promotion, after-sale service, information feedback, etc., in order to form a complete set of services.

3.   Keeping commercial secrets and promoting Party A's overseas interests.

4.   Enjoying the exclusive right of selling the above-mentioned product outside China.

5.   Operating independently and setting up its own distribution network.

III. Rights and Obligations of the Licensor (Party A)

Party A is willing to cooperate with Party B to develop the overseas market jointly and herein promises:

1.   To defend the overseas market developed by Party B and to hold Party B blameless.

2.   To maintain a regular goods supply of fair quality and adequate quantity.

3. To negotiate with Party B on a price suitable to the market.

4. To keep commercial secrets and to defend Party B's overseas interests.

5. To check and keep aware of Party's B's performance from time to time.

6. Without the approval of Party B, not to sell in any form, by any means, the above-mentioned product anywhere outside China.

IV. Patent

The patent belongs to the original inventor regardless of the country or region where an application is sought.

V. Commission

Party B requests 30 per cent of the sales price, with 15 per cent as the market development fee; 10 per cent for the coverage of expenses; and the rest, five per cent, as its own profit. The percentage shall be renegotiated if Party A is trapped in a net loss.

VI. Other Items

This agreement becomes effective as soon as it is signed by the two parties, with a validity of two years. When the validity expires, the agreement would automatically roll over with the agreement of the two sides. If the agreement is violated by either party, that party would be held responsible for any loss and damage.

This agreement is expressed both in Chinese and in English, with two copies for each party. However, only the Chinese version could be legally referred to, or be used for litigation purposes.

Party A:	*Party B:*
Beijing Mirror Corp.	C&S Technology Co., USA
Date: November 6, 1994	Date: November 6, 1994
Signature:	Signature:

INTERNATIONAL DECORATIVE GLASS

In June 1996, Delta, British Columbia, remained overcast and rainy. Frank Lattimer, vice-president operations of International Decorative Glass (IDG), mused that it really didn't matter, as there would be little time for golf this year. Rapidly increasing demand for decorative glass panels by steel door manufacturers in the United States, IDG's primary market, had its two production facilities in Delta and Shuenyi, China scrambling to keep up.

Lattimer had been asked to develop a recommendation for capacity expansion for consideration by the board of directors. The board had emphasized the need to move quickly as sales were increasing faster than IDG's ability to meet them. Although either existing plant could be expanded, IDG also had recently been approached about considering further off-shore sourcing in the rapidly developing country of Vietnam. Frank knew that any decision would have significant ramifications for the company's long-term positioning and ability to meet its ambitious goals for growth.

The Industry

Decorative glass panels typically are inserted into residential steel doors, and were increasingly being used by builders and home renovators to add architectural interest and a customized appearance to doorways (Exhibit 1). Growth in the industry was being fuelled by the general trend away from wooden exterior doors to steel doors. Forestry restrictions, lumber prices, energy efficiency and increasing criminal activity all contributed to the growing demand for retrofitting

Richard Ivey School of Business
The University of Western Ontario

Jim Barker prepared this case under the supervision of Professors Robert Klassen and Paul Beamish solely to provide material for class discussion. The authors do not intend to illustrate either effective or ineffective handling of a managerial situation. The authors may have disguised certain names and other identifying information to protect confidentiality. Ivey Management Services prohibits any form of reproduction, storage or transmittal without its written permission. This material is not covered under authorization from CanCopy or any reproduction rights organization.

Copyright © 1997, Ivey Management Services

wood doors with steel replacements, often with decorative glass panels. In addition, the lower price of steel doors relative to the traditional wood door, with wholesale prices starting as low as Cdn$300, further eroded market share in new home construction. Decorative glass was now being incorporated into 10 per cent of new home construction.

The total North American sales for decorative glass panels was conservatively estimated at $2 billion in 1995 (all figures are reported in Canadian dollars), and the market showed signs of continued strong growth. Industry experts predicted that annual sales could reach $4.5 billion in the United States alone, within five years. Canada's weighting of the North American market was disproportionately high, at 15 per cent, reflecting the somewhat earlier development of the market there for these panels. By 1996, panels were found in approximately 85 per cent of steel doors in Western Canadian homes.

Manufacturers in Canada tended to be more vertically integrated than their U.S. counterparts, with plants fabricating both the steel door and the decorative panel. Locally, British Columbia's supply capacity grew well past the sustainable growth rate during the late 1980s and early 1990s as new market entrants scrambled to ramp up production capability to capitalize on the residential construction boom. The result was steadily eroding margins, followed quickly by industry consolidation, with high cost producers closing or being absorbed by more competitive operations. In spite of these changes, Canadian industry continued to be characterized by oversupply, underutilized capacity and commodity pricing. Lattimer had recently completed a basic competitive assessment of several key Canadian competitors as part of IDG's business plan (Exhibit 2).

By contrast, U.S. manufacturers of decorative glass panels acted as original equipment manufacturers (OEMs) for large residential steel door fabricators and retail chains. The industry was quite fragmented, with the largest three producers in the United States each having less than six per cent of the total market. Unfortunately, information on these producers was limited (Exhibit 3). Manufacturers ship panels to predetermined central warehousing and assembly points where their panels are fitted into the steel doors and distributed by the door fabricators through their retail channels. In general, the U.S. marketplace demanded high quality, fast service and increasingly, low price.

At this time, the United States, unlike Canada, was rapidly growing and underserved. In addition, Canadian manufacturers generally were about three years ahead of their U.S. counterparts in product functionality and design and, thus, able to develop strategic partnerships with steel door manufacturers. An undervalued currency also provided Canadian suppliers, such as IDG, with an initial competitive advantage. Combined, these factors created a significant market opportunity for any Canadian supplier who could meet rigorous quality standards and maintain a high level of customer responsiveness to design customized panels.

Early attempts by Canadian firms to develop their export sales quickly revealed that a customer would pay only so much for quality, service and product differentiation, and price was becoming an increasingly important driver in the purchase decision. In response, manufacturers on both sides of the border began to source production of the glass panels at lower cost to facilities located abroad. Because labor represented a large portion of cost of goods sold, production was increasingly being moved to countries with low labor costs, such as Mexico, Thailand and China. At this time, only a few Canadian manufacturers had been able to address all of these challenges successfully.

Production of Decorative Glass Panels

The production process for decorative glass panels was quite standardized, with little variation among firms and plants. As might be expected with a product that until recently was considered a "craft," the process was very labor intensive, with the equivalent of up to two person-days required for each panel. Production equipment was generally quite flexible, and could be purchased from several suppliers.

Decorative glass panels consist of multiple glass panes of different sizes, colors and grades assembled between soldered brass rods to form a decorative picture. The production of the panels used a multistep process that cut and formed the glass and brass components, and assembled the parts into sealed decorative glass units that could withstand the harsh exposure needed for exterior doors.

The manufacturing process began with the cutting of raw glass sheets of various colors and finishes into pieces of the precise shape and size needed for the final design. Some of these pieces were then bevelled to give a more attractive final appearance. The specialized cutting and bevelling of the glass pieces were the most capital intensive steps in the production process.

In a separate area, brass rods were cut and shaped into segments that ultimately serve to hold and separate the glass pieces. The correct set of glass pieces and brass rods were grouped into panel-specific "kits." These kits were assembled and soldered into predetermined patterns that formed semifinished panels. Several cleaning and touch-up steps followed.

Next, clear solid glass panes were added to each side of the inlay, creating a "sandwich" that protected the more delicate decorative inlay. Swizzle, a sealant material, was added around the edge to insulate and protect the panel from water damage. The panel was then put through an automated sealing machine, washed and inserted into a frame. Finally, the finished panel was labelled and packaged for shipment. These operations typically were performed in small batches of panels.

The Company

Located near Vancouver, British Columbia, IDG was founded in 1984 by Michael Jeffrey, decorative glass designer and entrepreneur. Initially, the company started as an integrated manufacturer of steel doors and decorative glass panels, and IDG enjoyed modest prosperity through the 1980s as the housing market boomed in that province. During this period, numerous firms entered the market, hoping to share in the prosperity of the industry. As real estate development slowed and even stagnated in the early 1990s, and the competitive basis shifted to cost, Jeffrey realized that the company was losing money in their manufacturing of steel doors. He felt that IDG could significantly enhance profitability by concentrating exclusively on decorative glass panels.

Jeffrey also recognized the need for a senior operations and business development person to make the operations more competitive in that market. Lattimer was hired in 1991 with the mandate to grow the international market, to improve cost efficiency, to set up a fully integrated management information system, and to create a corporate structure and culture that would support continued expansion. To meet these objectives, contacts and sales were further developed with several U.S. steel door manufacturers, the largest being Midwest. Lattimer also gained concessions in wage rates and flexibility in staffing requirements during collective bargaining with the union. Finally, a management information system, including materials requirements planning (MRP), was installed and brought on line to improve access to timely information and to raise customer responsiveness.

Historically, IDG's sales had been driven by custom orders for the glass panels. However, with recent efforts to increase sales volume, an increasing number of higher volume orders were being pursued, although often at much lower margins. In spite of labor concessions, high wage rates and limited flexibility continued to make IDG's plant in Delta increasingly less cost competitive. To reduce production costs, Lattimer was forced to explore alternative, off-shore sources of production.

Century Glass

In January 1995, IDG began sourcing some of its high volume, low skill production through a strategic partnership with Century Glass, located in Shuenyi, approximately an hour's drive outside of Beijing, China. This manufacturing facility was developed solely to meet the production needs of IDG, although the actual plant was owned and operated by the father of a former employee, Jianwei (Jerry) Lo. Lo had returned to China to set up the joint venture with IDG.

When IDG first arrived, the Shuenyi facility was little more than a deserted warehouse, situated across the highway from the village of 2,000 people where Lo had been born. The Lo family was well respected in the area, even though they came from modest means relative to Canadian standards. There was no electricity, telephone or plumbing in the village, and fresh water was unavailable.

With minimal infrastructure in place, power requirements, communication and capital equipment challenges all needed to be addressed. Co-generation power supplies and inverters were supplied by IDG; satellite and cellular phones were used until Century received a land line (faxes were sent from Beijing in the interim). Basic production equipment needed to cut glass sheets and brass rods were sourced locally; however, one large panel sealing machine was imported from Korea. Practically everything else at the facility was built by the local workforce. Approximately one-third of the workers lived in four-person dormitory rooms located on the premises, and the production plant also included space for the workers to grow their own food in the courtyard.

Family ties of the Los facilitated the shipment of goods, as Chinese bureaucracy was legendary. Jerry's uncle was the police chief of the local district and, thus, extremely well connected politically; IDG benefited from the association. The movement of raw materials into China and finished goods out of China, via Tientsin to the Gulf of Chihli, was expedited through Jerry's uncle.

Because of differences in proximity to the market and cost structure, the Chinese production facility concentrated on producing high volume, low cost glass panels for IDG. These panels were then shipped in bulk to the Delta production facility for final processing, followed by packaging and shipment to U.S. or Canadian customers. The additional processing in Canada resulted in a change in product classification under the North American Free Trade Agreement (NAFTA), which allowed the finished product to be imported duty-free into the U.S. market. (By contrast, if complete, sealed panels were imported directly from China into the United States, a 60 per cent duty would apply.)

For some customers, the standardized panels produced at Shuenyi were modified and further assembled at Delta to form larger, more complex, customized panels. By necessity, these arrangements required a long lead time, currently 18 to 20 weeks (Exhibit 4), well above that of the Delta plant, where lead times averaged one month.

Initial start-up problems in 1995 centered on logistics and quality. Rather than allow IDG's reputation for excellent customer service to suffer by missing delivery dates, orders of panels were, at times, air freighted to Delta from China, at an extra cost of $250,000 in the first year. These problems were gradually overcome as typical production lead times were reduced to their current levels. Low yields and high waste/breakage also plagued the start-up. However, as the skill levels of the local workforce improved, yields increased dramatically. By mid-1996, finished panel yields consistently surpassed 99 per cent, although in-process breakage and other losses remained a problem.

Current Status

By June 1996, Century Glass produced 80 per cent of IDG's panels, representing 60 per cent of revenues. The remaining somewhat more specialized, lower volume panels were produced by 70 employees in the Delta plant. The Century plant was operating close to capacity, with approximately 100 employees producing 8,000 panels per month. Dorms were overcrowded and people were elbow-to-elbow in the manufacturing area.

The joint venture agreement specified that IDG purchase all materials, own all inventories, and specify all finished product standards. The production arrangement with Century stipulated a fixed charge per employee and a variable cost per finished panel. Specifically, IDG paid $140 per employee, per month. In addition, IDG also paid Century a product transfer price of $4 for each panel that met IDG's rigorous quality standards for finished panels. Employment levels could be varied as needed to match sales volumes. Employees worked seven, eight-hour days per week, every week. This was high by Chinese standards, where the five- or six-day work week was more common.

By comparison, in Canada, unionized employees received $9.75 per hour, per 40-hour work week. Combined, these differences in labor translated into a significant cost advantage for Shuenyi, without accounting for the operational advantages of increased labor flexibility. Relative product costs are illustrated in Exhibit 5.

Labor savings were offset to some degree by a higher working capital investment necessary to finance larger inventories and longer payment cycles. For example, inventory turnover at Century Glass was only two turns per year in 1995, whereas Delta averaged six. In addition, banks refused to finance or factor raw material and work-in-process (WIP) inventories located in, or in transit to or from, China as the risk of recouping funds in the case of insolvency was considered too high. This risk varied by country. Some developing countries, such as Mexico, were viewed as less risky, while others, such as India, offered government guarantees for export-oriented manufacturers.

The Lo family was anxious to keep 100 per cent of IDG's business at their facility. However, Lattimer was very concerned about having only a single supplier in China, where political risks were perceived to be significant for such a large portion of their production. For example, the repatriation of Hong Kong in 1997, adverse trade tensions and possible trade restrictions between China, the United States and Canada, all indicated that a move to establish another production source might have strategic and operational merits.

Financial Results

IDG's revenue growth had been impressive since 1990, increasing from $2.6 million to $5.4 million for fiscal 1995. Financial results for the last two years are summarized in Exhibits 6 and 7. Revenues were projected to reach $10.5 million this year, with 95 per cent of sales being made in the United States. As noted earlier, margins had eroded during the early 1990s as residential construction slowed, and competition increased. Sales levels had risen significantly in 1995 as new production capacity became available at Shuenyi. However, profitability fell as a result of poor initial yields and air freight shipment costs at this new plant. Looking forward, Lattimer expected margins to increase as productivity further improved in Shuenyi.

Both Jeffrey and Lattimer strongly felt that the market for strong growth by IDG was there. IDG had already been turning away business as they struggled to meet existing customer commitments from their two production facilities. Current plans called for revenue growth to $30 million by the year 2000. Critical to achieving these long-term results was an increase in production capacity to match the forecasted sales volumes.

This aggressive growth necessitated access to additional capital to finance investment in new capacity and additional working capital. In August 1995, IDG approached a venture capital firm, Working Opportunity Fund, for $2 million of equity financing. The structure of the investment was negotiated, due diligence conducted, and the deal finalized in November of that year. In addition, IDG paid down its line-of-credit from the bank by financing its inventory in China with a guarantee from Canada's Export Development Corporation. This effectively reduced IDG's investment in working capital and made the sourcing of manufacturing to Asian facilities increasingly attractive. Combined, these additional sources of capital enabled IDG to increase its operating flexibility, and further develop its presence in the U.S. market.

Capacity Expansion

Lattimer had narrowed the options for expansion of production to three alternatives. Expansion was possible at either existing plant. In addition, another strategic partnership could be developed in another low labor-cost country, similar to IDG's earlier decision to expand into China. After exploring options in other developing nations with low labor costs, Lattimer, in consultation with senior management, had narrowed the candidate list of countries to one: Vietnam. This country offered a critical advantage in Lattimer's mind over other developing nations: a potential local partner, Dan Kim. Kim's firm currently supplied raw glass to IDG, and Kim had approached Lattimer about establishing a manufacturing joint venture.

Expansion in Delta

At this time, company-wide capacity could be doubled by investing a relatively modest amount of capital, $30,000, in the Delta plant. Labor costs would rise based on existing wage levels. Given the close proximity of this plant to the U.S. market, the existing production planning system could be further leveraged and customer responsiveness further improved.

Expansion in Shuenyi

Because production at the Shuenyi plant was already very tight, any expansion would involve a significant increase of middle management and support staff, and an expanded production planning system, mirroring the earlier MRP investment made in Delta. Existing arrangements for labor would be maintained, where IDG would pay a flat monthly fee per person, plus a variable rate per panel.

Although some of the existing production equipment still had excess capacity, additional equipment would be needed. In total, an estimated capital investment of $30,000 would be needed in new cutting equipment to double company-wide capacity. Incremental manufacturing overhead costs would be approximately $150,000 per year. Direct labor costs would increase proportionately with production volumes. These costs did not include either a desperately needed new building or additional inventory carrying charges. Timing for ramp-up to this volume level would be approximately six to eight months.

The most significant concerns with expansion at Shuenyi were related to further dependence on a single supplier and issues related to political risks associated with production in China. Trade uncertainties between China and the United States also aggravated long-term planning efforts. Management was apprehensive that existing tensions could escalate over any, or all, of repatriation of Hong Kong in 1997, intellectual property rights (software piracy and patents), dissident protests, strained relations with Taiwan and a general trade imbalance.

Smaller manufacturers that supply the U.S. market, like IDG, inadvertently have been punished by short-term high tariffs, customs delays and other non-tariff barriers. Although quite unlikely now, the worst case scenario would be a ban on importation from China. Unfortunately, because of the general income levels in China and construction norms, there was little local market for IDG's products at this time, although it did look promising in the longer term.

Foreign Operations in Vietnam

Vietnam had only recently begun to exhibit the economic growth characteristic of other countries in Asia-Pacific. Like many developing countries, infrastructure at this time was terribly inadequate. Lattimer estimated that development was at least five years behind China, and conditions were even more challenging than those first faced by IDG when they established their joint venture in China.

In recent years, Vietnam had been plagued by internal political problems, and foreign investors were apprehensive to invest. This situation now was beginning to change, as the United States had moved to reestablish diplomatic relations with the Socialist Republic of Vietnam in 1995. In turn, this thawing of the political climate had encouraged foreign investment which had grown rapidly as a result. Vietnam also had a strategic location for re-export to other markets in Asia.

Although a Communist state, the central government had instituted the beginnings of "Doi Moi" or "open door" policy as early as 1986. The objectives of Doi Moi were to develop export-oriented production capabilities that create jobs and generate foreign currency, to develop import substitutes, to stimulate production using natural resources, to acquire foreign technology and to strengthen Vietnam's infrastructure. Incentives offered included: the option to establish wholly-owned foreign subsidiaries; favorable corporate income tax and tax holidays; waivers on import/export duties; and full repatriation of profits and capital.

With 75 million citizens and a labor force of 32 million, Vietnam had the second lowest wage rate in the Pacific Rim. Only about 11 per cent of the working population was employed in manufacturing, another 19 per cent in the service sector, and the remainder in agriculture. Inflation was high, at 14 per cent in 1995, partially because of the devaluation of the "new dong" as the government had allowed the currency to float in world markets for the first time. The primary industries of Vietnam included food processing, textiles, machinery, mining, cement, chemical fertilizers, tires, oil and glass. Vietnamese companies already supplied some of the standard glass and bevelled glass components used by IDG.

Generally, the labor force was energetic, disciplined and hard working, although unemployment remained high, at 20 per cent. English and French were widely spoken but literacy was relatively low, at 88 per cent. Unfortunately, basic human rights and freedoms had received little attention. There was widespread conflict between local and central governing bodies, extensive corruption and exhaustive bureaucracy at both levels.

Production of Decorative Glass Panels in Vietnam

The State Committee for Cooperation and Investment (SCCI) identified seven areas of the Vietnam economy where foreign investment would receive preferential tax treatment. Of particular relevance to IDG, labor-intensive manufacturing was one such area. The SCCI would assist the new venture in whatever way they could, typically through the development of contacts with customers and suppliers, as well as guiding the investor through the government bureaucracy that approved any business venture.

The Vietnamese government also had legislated five approaches for establishing a business venture in the country. Of the five, the international business community and the government widely favored the joint venture approach. Under this approach, a foreign firm such as IDG would sign a contract with one or more Vietnamese parties to create a new legal entity with limited liability. Foreign capital had to constitute at least 30 per cent of the new entity's total capital. A foreign investor could then leverage the local partner's contacts, knowledge of the local market, and access to land and resources.

The Vietnamese had a saying: "*Nhap gia tuy tuc,*" which means "When you come into a new country, you have to follow the culture." Clearly, identification of a strong local partner would be critical for meeting the cultural norms in Vietnam and ensuring the success of any investment by IDG; this had been a major obstacle for many other foreign firms.

Lattimer saw many parallels with the earlier joint venture into China. That investment had succeeded largely as a result of IDG's strategic partnership with Century Glass and the Lo family. IDG had been able to limit their investment risk to supplying capital equipment for the facility and inventories. By contrast, other decorative glass suppliers operating in China were paying higher costs, and making larger investments in plant and infrastructure. The partnership with Century also had provided IDG with additional political clout and allowed them to bypass much of the Chinese bureaucracy.

One obvious choice for a local partner was IDG's beveled glass supplier, managed by Dan Kim. Kim operated a glass plant in Da Nang, which was well under capacity, and had an oversupply of qualified labor. Kim had approached both IDG and government authorities and essentially paved the way for IDG to begin joint venture operations within a six- to 12-month time frame.

Labor and product transfer prices were likely to be significantly lower than either the Delta or Shuenyi plants, with these costs being approximately half those of Shuenyi. Additional overhead costs were estimated at $50,000 annually. Finally, a significant investment would be needed in new equipment to reach the same, company-wide production volume possible with the other options (Exhibit 8). Lattimer wondered whether he might be able to extract more favorable terms for any joint venture relationship, such as shifting responsibilities for financing inventories to Kim.

The Decision

As Lattimer was putting together his proposal for the board, he reflected on a conversation he had with Jerry Lo last month. Lo had indicated that Century would soon expect their piecework compensation to increase from $4 to $7 per finished panel. While seemingly a small fraction of total production costs, Lattimer worried that further requests for increases would follow unless other alternatives were developed. He also was only too aware that with up to $1 million invested in inventory at Century at any given time, IDG was in a very precarious position. Single sourcing had given Century a level of bargaining power that might limit IDG's future options and cost competitiveness.

Lo had become agitated as Lattimer described IDG's exploration of additional manufacture sourcing arrangements, but had to agree it made sense from IDG's perspective. Lattimer reassured Lo that IDG wanted to add capacity, not replace it. This discussion had reinforced the need to delicately handle IDG's existing relationships. Any recommendation for locating new production capacity would have to take into account the skilled Canadian workforce, Century Glass and the Lo family, and Dan Kim's offer for an expanded relationship in Vietnam.

Exhibit 1   Sample of decorative glass panel applications

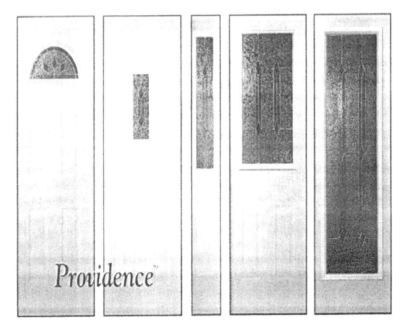

Exhibit 2   Summary of major canadian competitors

COMPANY	ACCENT	JCX GLASS	ROSEVIEW
Target Market	Small regional distributors.	Anyone who calls.	Small regional distributors.
Supply	Custom — None Volume — Langley, B.C. and Tacoma, WA	Custom — None Volume — New Westminster, B.C. Georgia Buy from China	Custom — None Volume — Surrey, B.C.
Positioning	Good Quality.	Copy designs of others.	Design Leader. Lower Quality.
Cost Base	- Two locations, 38,000 sq. ft. - Heavy overheads. - Non-union. - Small orders, but purchase materials in volume. Thus very high raw material & finished goods inventory. - Efficient production system.	- Two locations, 105,000 sq. ft. - Heavy overheads. - One year left on collective agreement. - Volume purchase. - Finished goods inventory of $3.2 million. - Efficient production system.	- One location, 38,000 sq. ft. - Heavy overheads. - Non-union. - High raw material costs. - Finished goods inventory of $1.6 million.
Sales (est. 1995)	$11 million Down, some of their lowest months.	$14 million Up 39 per cent.	$3 million Down.
Warranty	One year.	10 years.	One year.
CAD	Yes.	No.	No.
MRP	Some implementation.	Some implementation.	No.
Reputation/Customer Relations	Very good in Pacific Northwest with the "old boys" network.	Generally poor, can let the customer down.	Generally poor, always lets customer down
Management	Good, but have lost their spark and desire.	Aggressive, but weak in the middle management.	Generally weak.

Exhibit 3 **Summary of major U.S. competitors**

COMPANY	SPANNER DOOR	WESTERN DESIGN	BILLINGS	NEW ENGLAND GLASS
Target Market	National (U.S.)	National (U.S.)	National (U.S.)	Eastern (U.S.)
Positioning	Good quality. Simple, high volume panels.	Broad product line.	Broad product line; focus on high volume commodities, although some lower volume panels	Fast delivery, high quality.
Supply	Good operations in Mexico, with long-term commitment.	Plants in Mexico and Thailand.	No offshore production.	High cost producer. Focus on automation.
Est. 1995 Sales	$120 million	$85 million	$60 million	$25 million
Reputation/Customer Relations		Extensive distribution system.	Product line is narrower than IDG.	Strong, dependable supplier.
Management		Three top managers have left recently.		

Exhibit 4 Order cycle time for production at shuenyi plant

Raw materials ordered and received for shipment	2-4 weeks
Components in transit to China facility	5 weeks
Raw materials conversion to WIP and semi-finished goods	4 weeks
Sub-assemblies shipped to Canada	5 weeks
Final assembly completed at Delta, B.C. facility	2 weeks
Finished goods shipped to customer	1/2 week
Total Time	*18-20 weeks*

Exhibit 5 Typical production costs

Product	Production location	
	Shuenyi	*Delta*
#677, Oval-San Marino		
Materials	95.19	92.97
Labor	6.61	69.44
Freight	7.82	1.25
Total direct costs	*$109.62*	*$163.66*
#936, 22" x 36" panel		
Materials	44.27	44.27
Labor	3.18	40.27
Freight	7.08	1.25
Total direct costs	*$54.53*	*$85.79*
#445, 7-1/2" x 18-1/2" panel		
Materials	15.51	15.51
Labor	1.10	10.13
Freight	1.08	0.50
Total direct costs	*$17.69*	*$26.14*

Exhibit 6   **Income statement for international decorative glass as of September 30 (all figure reported as $000s)**

	1995	1994
Sales	$ 5,404	$ 3,634
Cost of Sales	4,365	2,610
Gross profit	1,039	1,024
Expenses		
administration and marketing	388	413
travel and promotion	97	44
rent and assessment	120	138
amortization of debt	48	55
bank charges and interest	141	48
interest on long-term debt	18	17
other expenses	182	258
subtotal	994	973
Income (loss) from operations	45	51
Other income	28	-
Income (loss) before taxes	73	51
Income taxes		
current	24	-
deferred	(6)	11
Net income (loss) for the year	$ 55	$ 40

Exhibit 7 **Balance sheet for international decorative glass as of September 30 (all figure reported as $000s)**

	1995	1994
Current		
cash	1	2
accounts receivable	1,513	474
income taxes recoverable	15	22
inventories	1,422	988
prepaid expenses	54	28
	3,005	1,514
Capital assets	233	296
	3,238	1,810
Current		
bank loans	1,435	593
accounts payable	886	482
income taxes payable	17	-
current portion of long-term debt	32	39
	2,370	1,114
Long-term debt	152	177
Deferred income taxes	13	20
Due to (from) affiliated company	522	372
	3,057	1,683
Share capital	0.1	0.1
Contributed surplus	45	45
Retained earnings	136	82
	$ 3,238	$ 1,810

Exhibit 8   Production equipment required for start-up in Vietnam as of September 30 (all figure reported as $000s)

Production equipment	Cost
Electrical back-up generator	$13
Air compressor	2
Glass equipment	
two-shape cutter (pneumatic, from Korea)	7
shape cutter (CNC, from Canada)	110
glass washer	60
Brass equipment	
roll-former	55
roll-forming dies	22
circle rollers (large and small)	5
saws (4)/blades/sharpeners	4
Bevelling equipment	
straight-line beveller	125
curved bevelling machines (12)	30
Miscellaneous equipment	
small forklift	7
pallet jack	2
computer, fax, etc.	3
hand tools, tables, etc.	5
Total capital equipment	*$449*

3

THE GLOBAL BRANDING OF STELLA ARTOIS

In April 2000, Paul Cooke, chief marketing officer of Interbrew, the world's fourth largest brewer, contemplated the further development of their premium product, Stella Artois, as the company's flagship brand in key markets around the world. Although the long-range plan for 2000-2002 had been approved, there still remained some important strategic issues to resolve.

A Brief History of Interbrew

Interbrew traced its origins back to 1366 to a brewery called Den Hoorn, located in Leuven, a town just outside of Brussels. In 1717, when it was purchased by its master brewer, Sebastiaan Artois, the brewery changed its name to Artois.

The firm's expansion began when Artois acquired a major interest in the Leffe Brewery in Belgium in 1954, the Dommelsch Brewery in the Netherlands in 1968, and the Brassiere du Nord in France in 1970. In 1987, when Artois and another Belgian brewery called Piedboeuf came together, the merged company was named Interbrew. The new company soon acquired other Belgian specialty beer brewers, building up the Interbrew brand portfolio with the purchase of the Hoegaarden brewery in 1989 and the Belle-Vue Brewery in 1990.

Interbrew then entered into a phase of rapid growth. The company acquired breweries in Hungary in 1991, in Croatia and Romania in 1994, and in three plants in Bulgaria in 1995. Again in 1995, Interbrew completed an unexpected major acquisition by purchasing Labatt, a large Canadian brewer also with international interests. Labatt had operations in the United States, for example, with the Latrobe brewery, home of the Rolling Rock brand. Labatt also held

Richard Ivey School of Business
The University of Western Ontario

Professors Paul W. Beamish and Anthony Goerzen prepared this case solely to provide material for class discussion. The authors do not intend to illustrate either effective or ineffective handling of a managerial situation. The authors may have disguised certain names and other identifying information to protect confidentiality. Ivey Management Services prohibits any form of reproduction, storage or transmittal without its written permission. This material is not covered under authorization from CanCopy or any reproduction rights organization.

Copyright © 2000, Ivey Management Services

a substantial minority stake in the second largest Mexican brewer, Femsa Cervesa, which produced Dos Equis, Sol, and Tecate brands. Following this major acquisition, Interbrew went on, in 1996, to buy a brewery in the Ukraine and engaged in a joint venture in the Dominican Republic. Subsequently, breweries were added in China in 1997, Montenegro and Russia in 1998, and another brewery in Bulgaria and one in Korea in 1999.

Thus, through acquisition expenditures of US$2.5 billion in the previous four years, Interbrew had transformed itself from a simple Belgian brewery into one of the largest beer companies in the world. By 1999, the company had become a brewer on a truly global scale that now derived more that 90 per cent of its volume from markets outside Belgium. It remained a privately held company, headquartered in Belgium, with subsidiaries and joint ventures in 23 countries across four continents.

The International Market for Beer

In the 1990s, the world beer market was growing at an annual rate of one to two per cent. In 1998, beer consumption reached a total of 1.3 billion hectolitres (hls). There were, however, great regional differences in both market size and growth rates. Most industry analysts split the world market for beer between growth and mature markets. The mature markets were generally considered to be North America, Western Europe and Australasia. The growth markets included Latin America, Asia, Central and Eastern Europe including Russia. Although some felt that Africa had considerable potential, despite its low per capita beer consumption, the continent was not considered a viable market by many brewers because of its political and economic instability (see Exhibit 1).

Mature Markets

The North American beer market was virtually stagnant, although annual beer consumption per person was already at a sizeable 83 litres per capita (lpc). The Western European market had also reached maturity with consumption of 79 lpc. Some analysts believed that this consumption level was under considerable pressure, forecasting a decline to near 75 lpc over the medium term. Australia and New Zealand were also considered mature markets, with consumption at 93 lpc and 84 lpc, respectively. In fact, volumes in both markets, New Zealand in particular, had declined through the 1990s following tight social policies on alcohol consumption and the emergence of a wine culture.

Growth Markets

Given that average consumption in Eastern Europe was only 29 lpc, the region appeared to offer great potential. This consumption figure, however, was heavily influenced by Russia's very low level, and the future for the large Russian market was unclear. Further, some markets, such as the

Czech Republic that consumed the most beer per person in the world at 163 lpc, appeared to have already reached maturity. Central and South America, on the other hand, were showing healthy growth and, with consumption at an average of 43 lpc, there was believed to be considerable upside. The most exciting growth rates, however, were in Asia. Despite the fact that the market in this region had grown by more than 30 per cent since 1995, consumption levels were still comparatively low. In China, the region's largest market, consumption was only 16 lpc and 20 to 25 lpc in Hong Kong and Taiwan. Although the 1997 Asian financial crisis did not immediately affect beer consumption (although company profits from the region were hit by currency translation), demand in some key markets, such as Indonesia, was reduced and in others growth slowed. The situation, however, was expected to improve upon economic recovery in the medium term.

Beer Industry Structure

The world beer industry was relatively fragmented with the top four players accounting for only 22 per cent of global volume — a relatively low figure as compared to 78 per cent in the soft drinks industry, 60 per cent in tobacco and 44 per cent in spirits. This suggested great opportunities for consolidation, a process that had already begun two decades prior. Many analysts, including those at Interbrew, expected that this process would probably accelerate in the future. The driver behind industry rationalization was the need to achieve economies of scale in production, advertising and distribution. It was widely recognized that the best profit margins were attained either by those with a commanding position in the market or those with a niche position. However, there were several factors that mitigated the trend towards rapid concentration of the brewing industry.

One factor that slowed the process of consolidation was that the ratio of fixed versus variable costs of beer production was relatively high. Essentially, this meant that there was a limited cost savings potential that could be achieved by bringing more operations under a common administration. Real cost savings could be generated by purchasing and then rationalizing operations through shifting production to more efficient (usually more modern) facilities. This approach, however, required large initial capital outlays. As a result, in some markets with "unstable" economies, it was desirable to spread out capital expenditures over a longer period of time to ensure appropriate profitability in the early stages. A second factor that may have had a dampening effect on the trend towards industry consolidation was that local tastes differed. In some cases, beer brands had hundreds of years of heritage behind them and had become such an integral part of everyday life that consumers were often fiercely loyal to their local brew. This appeared to be a fact in many markets around the world.

Interbrew's Global Position

Through Interbrew's acquisitions in the 1990s, the company had expanded rapidly. During this period, the company's total volumes had increased more than fourfold. These figures translated to total beer production of 57.5 million hls in 1998 (when including the volume of all affiliates), as compared to just 14.7 million hls in 1992. Volume growth had propelled the company into the number four position among the world's brewers.

Faced with a mature and dominant position in the declining Belgian domestic market, the company decided to focus on consolidating and developing key markets, namely Belgium, the Netherlands, France and North America, and expansion through acquisition in Central Europe, Asia and South America. Subsequently, Interbrew reduced its dependence on the Belgian market from 44 per cent in 1992 to less that 10 per cent by 1998 (total volumes including Mexico). Concurrently, a significant milestone for the company was achieved by 1999 when more than 50 per cent of its total volume was produced in growth markets (including Mexico). Interbrew had shifted its volume so that the Americas accounted for 61 per cent of its total volume, Europe added 35 per cent, and Asia Pacific the remaining four per cent.

Taken together, the top 10 markets for beer accounted for 86 per cent of Interbrew's total volume in 1998 (see Exhibit 2). The Mexican beer market alone accounted for 37 per cent of total volume in 1998. Canada, Belgium, the United States and the United Kingdom were the next most important markets. However, smaller, growing markets such as Hungary, Croatia, Bulgaria, and Romania had begun to increase in importance.

Adding to its existing breweries in Belgium, France and the Netherlands, Interbrew's expansion strategy in the 1990s had resulted in acquisitions in Bosnia-Herzegovina, Bulgaria, Canada, China, Croatia, Hungary, Korea, Montenegro, Romania, Russia, the Ukraine, the United States, in a joint venture in South Korea, and in minority equity positions in Mexico and Luxembourg. Through these breweries, in addition to those that were covered by licensing agreements in Australia, Italy, Sweden and the United Kingdom, Interbrew sold its beers in over 80 countries.

Interbrew's Corporate Structure

Following the acquisition of Labatt in 1995, Interbrew's corporate structure was divided into two geographic zones: the Americas and Europe/Asia/Africa. This structure was in place until September 1999 when Interbrew shifted to a fully integrated structure to consolidate its holdings in the face of industry globalization. Hugo Powell, formerly head of the Americas division, was appointed to the position of chief executive officer (CEO). The former head of the Europe/Africa/Asia division assumed the role of chief operating officer, but subsequently resigned and was not replaced, leaving Interbrew with a more conventional structure, with the five regional heads and the various corporate functional managers reporting directly to the CEO.

Recent Performance

1998 had been a good year for Interbrew in terms of volume in both mature and growth markets. Overall, sales volumes increased by 11.1 per cent as most of the company's international and local brands maintained or gained market share. In terms of the compounded annual growth rate, Interbrew outperformed all of its major competitors by a wide margin. While Interbrew's 1998 net sales were up 29 per cent, the best performing competitor achieved an increase of only 16 per cent. Of Interbrew's increased sales, 67 per cent was related to the new affiliates in China, Montenegro and Korea. The balance was the result of organic growth. Considerable volume increases were achieved also in Romania (72 per cent), Bulgaria (28 per cent), Croatia (13 per cent), and the United States (14 per cent). While volumes in Western Europe were flat, duty-free sales grew strongly. In the U.S. market, strong progress was made by Interbrew's Canadian and Mexican brands, and Latrobe's Rolling Rock was successfully relaunched. In Canada, performance was strong, fuelled by a two per cent increase in domestic consumption. Labatt's sales of Budweiser (produced under license from Anheuser Busch) also continued to grow rapidly.

Given that the premium and specialty beer markets were growing quickly, particularly those within the large, mature markets, Interbrew began to shift its product mix to take advantage of this trend and the superior margins it offered. A notable brand success was Stella Artois, for which total global sales volumes were up by 19.7 per cent. That growth came from sales generated by Whitbread in the United Kingdom, from exports, and from sales in Central Europe where Stella Artois volumes took off. The strong growth of Stella Artois was also notable in that it was sold in the premium lager segment. In Europe, Asia Pacific and Africa, Interbrew's premium and specialty beers, which generated a bigger margin, increased as a proportion of total sales from 31 per cent in 1997 to 33 per cent in 1998. This product mix shift was particularly important since intense competition in most markets inhibited real price increases.

Success was also achieved in the United States specialty beer segment where total volume had been growing at nine per cent annually in the 1990s. In 1998, Interbrew's share of this growing market segment had risen even faster as Labatt USA realized increased sales of 16 per cent. The other continuing development was the growth of the light beer segment, which had become over 40 per cent of the total sales. Sales of Labatt's Blue Light, for example, had increased and Labatt Blue had become the number three imported beer in the United States, with volumes up 18 per cent. Latrobe's Rolling Rock brand grew by four per cent, the first increase in four years. Interbrew's Mexican brands, Dos Equis, Tecate and Sol, were also up by 19 per cent.

Following solid volume growth in profitable market segments, good global results were realized in key financial areas. Net profit, having grown for each of the previous six consecutive years, was 7.7 billion Belgian francs (BEF) in 1998, up 43.7 per cent from the previous year. Operating profit also rose 7.9 per cent over 1997, from 14.3 to 15.4 BEF; in both the Europe/Asia/Africa region and the Americas, operating profit was up by 8.5 per cent and 4.9 per cent respectively. Further, Interbrew's EBIT margin was up 58.1 per cent as compared to the best performing competitor's figure of 17.0 per cent. However, having made several large investments in Korea and Russia, and exercising an option to increase its share of Femsa Cerveza in Mexico from 22 per cent to 30 per cent, Interbrew's debt-equity ratio increased from 1.04 to 1.35. As a result, interest payments rose accordingly.

Interbrew also enjoyed good results in volume sales in many of its markets in 1999. Although Canadian sales remained largely unchanged over 1998, Labatt USA experienced strong growth in 1999, with volumes up by 10 per cent. There was a positive evolution in Western European volumes as well, as overall sales were up by 6.5 per cent overall in Belgium, France and the Netherlands. Central European markets also grew with Hungary showing an increase of 9.6 per cent, Croatia up by 5.5 per cent, Romania by 18.9 per cent, Montenegro by 29 per cent, and Bulgaria with a rise of 3.6 per cent in terms of volume. Sales positions were also satisfactory in the Russian and Ukrainian markets. Further, while South Korean sales volume remained unchanged, volumes in China were 10 per cent higher, although this figure was still short of expectations.

Interbrew Corporate Strategy

The three facets of Interbrew's corporate strategy, i.e., brands, markets and operations, were considered the "sides of the Interbrew triangle." Each of these aspects of corporate strategy was considered to be equally important in order to achieve the fundamental objective of increasing shareholder value. With a corporate focus entirely on beer, the underlying objectives of the company were to consolidate its positions in mature markets and improve margins through higher volumes of premium and specialty brands. Further, the company's emphasis on growth was driven by the belief that beer industry rationalization still had some way to go and that the majority of the world's major markets would each end up with just two or three major players.

Operations Strategy

Cross fertilization of best practices between sites was a central component of Interbrew's operations strategy. In the company's two main markets, Belgium and Canada, each brewery monitored its performance on 10 different dimensions against its peers. As a result, the gap between the best and the worst of Interbrew's operations had narrowed decisively since 1995. Employees continuously put forward propositions to improve processes. The program had resulted in significantly lower production costs, suggesting to Interbrew management that most improvements had more to do with employee motivation than with pure technical performance. In addition, capacity utilization and strategic sourcing had been identified as two areas of major opportunity.

Capacity Utilization

Given that brewing was a capital-intensive business, capacity utilization had a major influence on profitability. Since declining consumption in mature markets had generated excess capacity, several of Interbrew's old breweries and processing facilities were scheduled to be shut down. In contrast, in several growth markets such as Romania, Bulgaria, Croatia and Montenegro, the opposite problem existed, so facilities in other locations were used more fully until local capacities were increased.

Strategic Sourcing

Interbrew had begun to rationalize its supply base as well. By selecting a smaller number of its best suppliers and working more closely with them, Interbrew believed that innovative changes resulted, saving both parties considerable sums every year. For most of the major commodities, the company had gone to single suppliers and was planning to extend this approach to all operations worldwide.

Market Strategy

The underlying objectives of Interbrew's market strategy were to increase volume and to lessen its dependence on Belgium and Canada, its two traditional markets. Interbrew dichotomized its market strategy into the mature and growth market segments, although investments were considered wherever opportunities to generate sustainable profits existed. One of the key elements of Interbrew's market strategy was to establish and manage strong market platforms. It was believed that a brand strength was directly related to a competitive and dedicated market platform (i.e., sales and distribution, wholesaler networks, etc.) to support the brand. Further, Interbrew allowed individual country teams to manage their own affairs and many felt that the speed of success in many markets was related to this decentralized approach.

Mature markets

Interbrew's goals in its mature markets were to continue to build market share and to improve margins through greater efficiencies in production, distribution and marketing. At the same time, the company intended to exploit the growing trend in these markets towards premium and specialty products of which Interbrew already possessed an unrivalled portfolio. The key markets in which this strategy was being actively pursued were the United States, Canada, the United Kingdom, France, the Netherlands and Belgium.

Growth Markets

Based on the belief that the world's beer markets would undergo further consolidation, Interbrew's market strategy was to build significant positions in markets that had long-term volume growth potential. This goal led to a clear focus on Central and Eastern Europe and Asia, South Korea and China in particular. In China, for example, Interbrew had just completed an acquisition of a second brewery in Nanjing. The Yali brand was thereby added to the corporate portfolio and, together with its Jingling brand, Interbrew became the market leader in Nanjing, a city of six million people.

In Korea, Interbrew entered into a 50:50 joint venture with the Doosan Chaebol to operate the Oriental Brewery, producing the OB Lager and Cafri pilsener brands. With this move, Interbrew took the number two position in the Korean beer market with a 36 per cent share and sales of 5.1 million hls. The venture with Doosan was followed in December 1999 by the purchase of the Jinro Coors brewery. This added 2.5 million hls and increased Interbrew's market share to 50 per cent of total Korean volume. Thus, the Interbrew portfolio in Korea consisted of two mainstream pilsener brands, OB Lager and Cass, the two local premium brands, Cafri and Red Rock, and Budweiser, an international premium brand.

In Russia, Interbrew expanded its presence by taking a majority stake in the Rosar Brewery in Omsk, adding the BAG Bier and Sibirskaya Korona brands. Rosar was the leading brewer in Siberia with a 25 per cent regional market share, and held the number four position in Russia. New initiatives were also undertaken in Central Europe with acquisitions of a brewery in Montenegro and the Pleven brewery in Bulgaria, as well as the introduction of Interbrew products into the Yugoslavian market. Finally, although Interbrew had just increased its already significant investment in Mexico's second largest brewer from 22 per cent to 30 per cent, Latin America remained a region of great interest.

Brand Strategy

A central piece of Interbrew's traditional brand strategy had been to add to its portfolio of brands through acquisition of existing brewers, principally in growth markets. Since its goal was to have the number one or two brand in every market segment in which it operated, Interbrew concentrated on purchasing and developing strong local brands. As it moved into new territories, the company's first priority was to upgrade product quality and to improve the positioning of the acquired local core lager brands. In mature markets, it drew on the strength of the established brands such as Jupiler, Belgium's leading lager brand, Labatt Blue, the famous Canadian brand, and Dommelsch, an important brand in the Netherlands. In growth markets, Interbrew supported brands like Borsodi Sor in Hungary, Kamenitza in Bulgaria, Ozujsko in Croatia, Bergenbier in Romania, Jingling in China, and OB Lager in Korea. In addition, new products were launched such as Taller, a premium brand in the Ukraine, and Boomerang, an alternative malt-based drink in Canada.

A second facet of the company's brand strategy was to identify certain brands, typically specialty products, and to develop them on a regional basis across a group of markets. At the forefront of this strategy were the Abbaye de Leffe and Hoegaarden brands and, to a lesser extent, Belle-Vue. In fact, both Hoegaarden and Leffe achieved a leading position as the number one white beer and abbey beer in France and Holland. The Loburg premium pilsener brand also strengthened its position when it was relaunched in France. Further, in Canada, Interbrew created a dedicated organization for specialty beers called the Oland Specialty Beer Company. In its first year of operation, the brands marketed by Oland increased its volumes by over 40 per cent. More specifically, sales of the Alexander Keith's brand doubled and the negative volume trend of the John Labatt Classic brand was reversed. The underlying message promoted by Oland was the richness, mystique and heritage of beer.

To support the regional growth of specialty beers, Interbrew established a new type of café. The Belgian Beer Café, owned and run by independent operators, created an authentic Belgian atmosphere where customers sampled Interbrew's Belgian specialty beers. By 1999, Belgian Beer Cafés were open in the many of Interbrew's key markets, including top selling outlets in New York, Auckland, Zagreb and Budapest, to name a few. The business concept was that these cafés were to serve as an ambassador of the Belgian beer culture in foreign countries. They were intended to serve as vehicles to showcase Interbrew's specialty brands, benefiting from the international appeal of European styles and fashions. Although these cafés represented strong marketing tools for brand positioning, the key factors that led to the success of this concept were tied very closely to the individual establishments and the personnel running them. The bar staff, for example, had to be trained to serve the beer in the right branded glass, at the right temperature, and with a nice foamy head. It was anticipated that the concept of the specialty café would be used to support the brand development efforts of Interbrew's Belgian beers in all of its important markets.

The third facet of Interbrew's brand strategy was to identify a key corporate brand and to develop it as a global product. While the market segment for a global brand was currently relatively small, with the bulk of the beer demand still in local brands, the demand for international brands was expected to grow, as many consumers became increasingly attracted to the sophistication of premium and super-premium beers.

The Evolution of Interbrew's Global Brand Strategy

Until 1997, Interbrew's brand development strategy for international markets was largely *laissez faire*. Brands were introduced to new markets through licensing, export and local production when opportunities were uncovered. Stella Artois, Interbrew's most broadly available and oldest brand, received an important new thrust when it was launched through local production in three of the company's subsidiaries in Central Europe in 1997. This approach was consistent with the company's overall goals of building a complete portfolio in high growth potential markets.

By 1998, however, the executive management committee perceived the need to identify a brand from its wide portfolio to systematically develop into the company's global brand. Although the market for global brands was still small, there were some growing successes (e.g., Heineken, Corona, Fosters and Budweiser) and Interbrew believed that there were several basic global trends that would improve the viability of this class of product over the next couple of decades. First, while many consumers were seeking more variety, others were seeking lower prices. It appeared that the number of affluent and poor consumer segments would increase at the expense of the middle income segments. The upshot of this socioeconomic trend was that eventually all markets would likely evolve in such a way that demand for both premium and economy-priced beers would increase, squeezing the mainstream beers in the middle. A second trend was the internationalization of the beer business. As consumers travelled around the world, consuming global media (e.g., CNN, Eurosport, MTV, international magazines, etc.), global media were expected to become more effective for building brands. A global strategy could, therefore, lead to synergies in global advertising and sponsoring. In addition, the needs of consumers in many markets were expected to converge. As a result of these various factors, Interbrew believed that there would be an increasing interest in authentic, international brands in a growing number of countries. Interbrew had a wide portfolio of national brands that it could set on the international stage. The two most obvious candidates were Labatt Blue and Stella Artois.

The Labatt range of brands included Labatt Blue, Labatt Blue Light and Labatt Ice. To date, however, the exposure of these brands outside of North America had been extremely limited and they were not yet budding global brands. Of the total Labatt Blue volume in 1998, 85 per cent was derived from the Canadian domestic and U.S. markets, with the balance sold in the United Kingdom. The Labatt brands had been introduced to both France and Belgium, and production had been licensed in Italy, but these volumes were minimal. The only real export growth market for Labatt Blue appeared to be the United States, where the brand's volume in 1998 was some 23 per cent higher than in 1995, behind only Corona and Heineken in the imported brand segment. The Labatt Ice brand was also sold in a limited number of markets and, after the appeal of this Labatt innovation had peaked, its total volume had declined by more than 25 per cent since 1996. Total Labatt Ice volume worldwide was just 450,000 hls in 1998, of which 43 per cent was sold in Canada, 33 per cent in the United States, and 21 per cent in the United Kingdom.

Stella Artois as Interbrew's International Flagship Brand

The other potential brand that Interbrew could develop on a global scale was Stella Artois, a brand that could trace its roots back to 1366. The modern version of Stella Artois was launched in 1920 as a Christmas beer and had become a strong market leader in its home market of Belgium through the 1970s. By the 1990s, however, Stella's market position began to suffer from an image as a somewhat old-fashioned beer, and the brand began to experience persistent volume decline. Problems in the domestic market, however, appeared to be shared by a number of other prominent international brands. In fact, seven of the top 10 international brands had experienced declining sales in their home markets between 1995 and 1999 (see Exhibit 3).

Stella Artois had achieved great success in the United Kingdom through its licensee, Whitbread, where Stella Artois became the leading premium lager beer. Indeed, the United Kingdom was the largest market for Stella Artois, accounting for 49 per cent of total brand volume in 1998. Stella Artois volume in the U.K. market reached 2.8 million hls in 1998, a 7.6 per cent share of the lager market, and came close to 3.5 million hls in 1999, a 25 per cent increase over the previous year. By this time, over 32,000 outlets sold Stella Artois on draught.

Apart from the United Kingdom, the key markets for Stella Artois were France and Belgium, which together accounted for a further 31 per cent of total brand volume (see Exhibit 4). With these three markets accounting for 81 per cent of total Stella Artois volume in 1999, few other areas represented a significant volume base (see Exhibit 5). Beyond the top three markets, the largest market for Stella Artois was Italy, where the brand was produced under license by Heineken. Stella Artois volume in Italy had, however, declined slightly to 166,000 hls in 1998. Licensing agreements were also in place in Sweden and Australia, but volume was small.

Stella Artois was also produced in Interbrew's own breweries in Hungary, Croatia and Romania, with very pleasing 1998 volumes of 84,000 hls, 120,000 hls, and 60,000 hls, respectively. After only three years, the market share of Stella Artois in Croatia, for example, had reached four per cent — a significant result, given that the brand was a premium-priced product. In all Central European markets, Stella Artois was priced at a premium; in Hungary, however, that premium was lower than in Croatia and Romania where, on an index comparing Stella's price to that of core lagers, the indices by country were 140, 260 and 175 respectively.

Promising first results were also attained in Australia and New Zealand. Particularly in New Zealand, through a "seeding" approach, Interbrew and their local partner, Lion Nathan, had realized great success in the Belgian Beer Café in Auckland where the brands were showcased. After only two years of support, Stella Artois volume was up to 20,000 hls, and growing at 70 per cent annually, out of a total premium segment of 400,000 hls. Interbrew's market development plan limited distribution to top outlets in key metropolitan centres and priced Stella Artois significantly above competitors (e.g., 10 per cent over Heineken and 20 per cent over Steinlager, the leading domestic premium lager brand).

The evolution of the brand looked very positive as world volumes for Stella Artois continued to grow. In fact, Stella Artois volume had increased from 3.4 million hls in 1992 to a total of 6.7 million hls in 1999, a rise of 97 per cent. Ironically, the only market where the brand continued its steady decline was in its home base of Belgium. Analysts suggested a variety of reasons to explain this anomaly, including inconsistent sales and marketing support, particularly as the organization began to favor the rising Jupiler brand.

Overall, given Interbrew's large number of local brands, especially those in Mexico with very high volumes, total Stella Artois volume accounted for only 10 per cent of total Interbrew volume in 1999 (14 per cent if Femsa volumes are excluded). Interbrew's strategy of nurturing a wide portfolio of strong brands was very different as compared to some of its major competitors. For example, Anheuser-Busch, the world's largest brewer, focused its international strategy almost exclusively on the development of the Budweiser brand. Similarly, Heineken sought to centre its international business on the Heineken brand and, to a lesser extent, on Amstel. While the strategies of Anheuser-Busch and Heineken focused primarily on one brand, there were also great differences in the way these two brands were being managed. For example, Budweiser, the world's largest brand by volume, had the overwhelming bulk of its volume in its home U.S. market (see Exhibit 6). Sales of the Heineken brand, on the other hand, were widely distributed across markets around the world (see Exhibit 7). In this sense, Heineken's strategy was much more comparable to that of Interbrew's plans for Stella Artois. Other brands that were directly comparable to Stella Artois, in terms of total volume and importance of the brand to the overall sales of the company, were Carlsberg and Foster's with annual sales volumes in 1998 of 9.4 million hls and 7.1 million hls, respectively. While Foster's was successful in many international markets, there was a heavy focus on sales in the United Kingdom and the United States (see Exhibit 8). Carlsberg sales volume profile was different in that sales were more widely distributed across international markets (see Exhibit 9).

Stella's Global Launch

In 1998, Interbrew's executive management committee settled on Stella Artois, positioned as the premium European lager, as the company's global flagship brand. In fact, the Interbrew management felt that stock analysts would be favorably disposed to Interbrew having an acknowledged global brand with the potential for a higher corporate valuation and price earnings (P/E) multiple.

As the global campaign got under way, it became clear that the organization needed time to adapt to centralized co-ordination and control of Stella Artois brand marketing. This was, perhaps, not unexpected given that Interbrew had until recently operated on a regional basis; the new centralized Stella brand management approach had been in place only since September 1998. In addition, there were often difficulties in convincing all parties to become part of a new global approach, particularly the international advertising campaign that was the backbone of the global plan for Stella Artois. Belgium, for example, continued with a specific local advertising program that positioned Stella as a mainstream lager in its home market, and in the United Kingdom, Whitbread maintained its "reassuringly expensive" advertising slogan that had already proved to be so successful. For other less-established markets, a global advertising framework was created that included a television concept and a series of print and outdoor executions. This base advertising plan was rolled out in 1999 in 15 markets, including the United States, Canada, Italy, Hungary, Croatia, Bulgaria, Romania, New Zealand and France (with a slightly changed format) after research suggested that the campaign had the ability to cross borders. The objective of this campaign was to position Stella Artois as a sophisticated European lager. It was intended that Stella Artois should be perceived as a beer with an important brewing tradition and heritage but, at the same time, also as a contemporary beer (see Exhibit 10).

In 1998, an accelerated plan was devised to introduce Stella Artois to two key markets within the United States, utilizing both local and corporate funding. The U.S. market was believed to be key for the future development of the brand since it was the most developed specialty market in the world (12 per cent specialty market share, growing 10 per cent plus annually through the 1990s), and because of the strong influence on international trends. Thus, Stella Artois was launched in New York City and Boston and was well received by the demanding U.S. consumer and pub owner. Within 1999, over 200 pubs in Manhattan and 80 bars in Boston had begun to sell Stella Artois on tap. To support the heightened efforts to establish Stella Artois in these competitive urban markets, Interbrew's corporate marketing department added several million dollars to Labatt USA's budget for Stella Artois in 2000, with commitments to continue this additional funding in subsequent years.

Current Thinking

Good progress had been made since 1998 when Stella Artois was established as Interbrew's global brand. However, management had revised its expectations for P/E leverage from having a global brand. The reality was that Interbrew would be rewarded only through cash benefits from operational leverage of a global brand. There would be no "free lunch" simply for being perceived as having a global brand. In addition, in an era of tight fiscal management, it was an ongoing challenge to maintain the funding levels required by the ambitious development plans for Stella Artois. As a result, in early 2000 the prevailing view at Interbrew began to shift, converging on a different long-range approach towards global branding. The emerging perspective emphasized a more balanced brand development program, focusing on the highest leverage opportunities.

The experience of other brewers that had established global brands offered an opportunity for Interbrew to learn from their successes and failures. Carlsberg and Heineken, for example, were two comparable global brands that were valued quite differently by the stock market. Both sold over 80 per cent of their total volumes outside their domestic market, and yet Heineken stock achieved a P/E ratio of 32.4 in 1999 versus Carlsberg's figure of only 17.1. According to industry analysts, the driving force behind this difference was that Heineken maintained a superior market distribution in terms of growth and margin (see Exhibit 11). The key lesson from examining these global brands appeared to be that great discipline must be applied to focus resources in the right places.

In line with this thinking, a long range marketing plan began to take shape that made use of a series of strategic filters to yield a focused set of attractive opportunities. The first filter that any potential market had to pass through was its long-term volume potential for Stella Artois. This volume had to trace back to a large and/or growing market, the current or potential sizeable premium lager segment (at least five per cent of the total market), and the possibility for Stella Artois to penetrate the top three brands. The second screen was the potential to achieve attractive margins after an initial starting period of approximately three years. The third filter was whether or not a committed local partner was available to provide the right quality of distribution and to co-invest in the brand. The final screen was the determination that success in the chosen focus markets should increase leverage in other local and regional markets. For example, the size and stature of Stella Artois in the United Kingdom was a significant factor in the easy sell-in of Stella Artois into New York in 1999.

Once filtered through these strategic market development screens, the global branding plans for Stella Artois began to take a different shape. Rather than focus on national markets, plans emerged with an emphasis on about 20 cities, some of which Interbrew was already present in (e.g., London, Brussels, New York, etc.). This approach suggested that the next moves should be in such potential markets as Moscow, Los Angeles and Hong Kong. Some existing cities would receive focused efforts only when distribution partner issues had been successfully resolved to solidify the bases for sustained long term growth. The major cities that fit these criteria provided the right concentration of affluent consumers, who would be attracted to Stella's positioning, thus providing scale for marketing and sales, investment leverage, as well as getting the attention and support of motivated wholesalers and initial retail customers. These venues would thereby become highly visible success stories that would be leveragable in the company's ongoing market development plans.

Thus, the evolving global branding development plan required careful planning on a city-by-city basis. Among the demands of this new approach were that marketing efforts and the funding to support them would have to be both centrally stewarded and locally tailored to reflect the unique local environments. A corporate marketing group was, therefore, established and was charged with the responsibility to identify top priority markets, develop core positioning and guidelines for local execution, assemble broadly based marketing programs (e.g., TV, print advertising, global sponsorships, beer.com content, etc.), and allocate resources to achieve the accelerated growth objectives in these targeted cities. To ensure an integrated development effort the company brought all pivotal resources together, under the leadership of a global brand development director. In addition to the brand management team, the group included regional sales managers who were responsible for licensed partner management, a customer services group, a Belgian beer café manager, and cruise business management group. Another significant challenge that faced the corporate marketing group was to ensure that all necessary groups were supportive of the new approach. This was a simpler undertaking among those business units that were wholly owned subsidiaries; it was a more delicate issue in the case of licensees and joint ventures. A key element of managing brands through a global organizational structure was that the head office team had to effectively build partnerships with local managers to ensure their commitment.

Fortunately, much of the initial effort to establish Stella Artois as a global brand had been done on a city-by-city basis and, as such, there was ample opportunity for Interbrew to learn from these experiences as the new global plan evolved. In the late 1990s, for example, Stella Artois was introduced to various Central European cities (e.g., Budapest, Zagreb, Bucharest and Sofia). In each of these cities, Interbrew's marketing efforts were launched when the targeted premium market was at an early stage of development. Further, distribution and promotion was strictly controlled (e.g., product quality, glassware, etc.) and the development initiatives were delivered in a concentrated manner (e.g., a media "blitz" in Budapest). In addition, results indicated that the presence of a Belgian Beer Café accelerated Interbrew's market development plans in these new areas. These early successes suggested that brand success could be derived from the careful and concentrated targeting of young adults living in urban centres, with subsequent pull from outlying areas following key city success.

The key lessons of these efforts in Central Europe proved to be very valuable in guiding the market development plan in New York City. In this key North American city, the rollout of Stella Artois was perceived by the analysts as "one of the most promising introductions in New York over the last 20 years" and had generated great wholesaler support and excitement. Among the tactics used to achieve this early success was selective distribution with targeted point of sale materials support. In addition, a selective media campaign was undertaken that included only prestigious outdoor advertising (e.g., a Times Square poster run through the Millennium celebrations). Similarly, the sponsoring strategy focused only on high-end celebrity events, Belgian food events, exclusive parties, fashion shows, etc. Finally, the price of Stella Artois was targeted at levels above Heineken, to reinforce its gold standard positioning. This concerted and consistent market push created an impact that resulted in the "easiest new brand sell" in years, according to wholesalers. The success of this launch also built brand and corporate credibility, paving the way to introductions in other U.S. cities as well as "opening the eyes" of other customers and distribution partners around the world.

To pursue this new global development plan over the next three years, a revised marketing budget was required. Given that the corporate marketing department was responsible for both the development of core programs as well as the selective support of local markets, the budget had to cover both of these key elements. To achieve these ends, total spending was expected to more than double over the next three years.

While great progress had been made on the global branding of Stella Artois, Cooke still ruminated on a variety of important interrelated issues. Among these issues was the situation of Stella Artois in Belgium — would it be possible to win in the "global game" without renewed growth in the home market? What specific aspirations should Interbrew set for Belgium over the next three years? Further, what expectations should Interbrew have of its global brand market development (e.g., volumes, profit levels, number of markets and cities, etc.)? How should global success be measured? With respect to Interbrew's promotional efforts, how likely would it be that a single global ad campaign could be successful for Stella Artois? Was there a particular sponsorship or promotion idea that could be singled out for global leverage? And what role should the Internet play in developing Stella Artois as a true global brand?

Exhibit 1   The World Beer Market in 1998

Region	% of Global Consumption	Growth Index ('98 vs 92)	Per Capita Consumption
Americas	35.1%	112.6	57
Europe	32.8%	97.7	54
Asia Pacific	27.2%	146.2	11
Africa	4.6%	107.7	8
Middle East/Central Asia	0.4%	116.0	2

Source: Canadean Ltd.

Exhibit 2   Interbrew's 1998 Share of the World's Top 10 Markets

Rank	Country	Volume (000 HL)	Market Share
1	USA	3,768	1.6%
2	China	526	0.3%
3	Germany	–	–
4	Brazil	–	–
5	Japan	–	–
6	UK	3,335	5.5%
7	Mexico	21,269	45.0%
8	Spain	–	–
9	South Africa	–	–
10	France	1,915	8.4%
Total		30,813	3.6%

Source: Canadean Ltd.

Exhibit 3   Domestic Sales HISTORY of Major International Brands (million hectolitre)

	1995	1996	1997	1998
Budweiser (incl. Bud Light until '98)	69.48	71.10	72.43	40.00
Bud Light	n/a	n/a	n/a	30.00
Heineken	3.87	3.78	3.85	3.78
Becks	1.68	1.71	1.72	1.78
Carlsberg	1.47	1.39	1.31	1.22
Stella Artois	1.08	1.00	0.96	0.92
Fosters	1.48	1.11	1.40	1.43
Kronenbourg	5.65	5.53	5.35	5.60
Amstel	2.30	2.23	2.21	2.18
Corona	12.89	14.09	14.80	15.18

Exhibit 4   1999 World Sales Profile OF STELLA ARTOIS

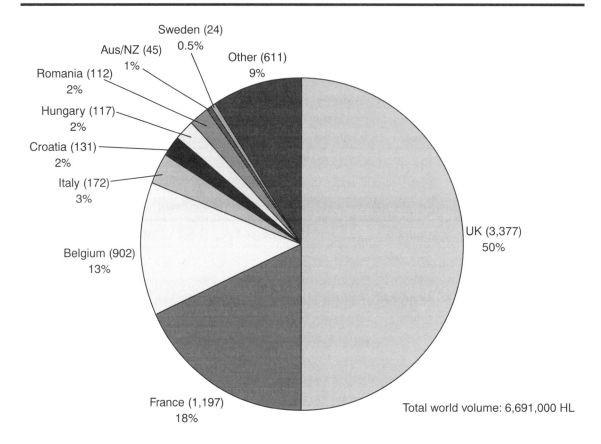

Sweden (24)
0.5%

Aus/NZ (45)
1%

Romania (112)
2%

Hungary (117)
2%

Croatia (131)
2%

Italy (172)
3%

Belgium (902)
13%

France (1,197)
18%

Other (611)
9%

UK (3,377)
50%

Total world volume: 6,691,000 HL

Exhibit 5   Stella Artois Sales Volume Summary (000 hectolitre)

	1997	1998	1999
Production:			
Belgium	965	921	902
France	1,028	1,110	1,074
Hungary	59	84	117
Croatia	54	120	133
Romania	17	60	112
Bulgaria	–	–	3
Bosnia-Herzegovina	–	–	2
Montenegro	–	–	0
Total Production	**2,123**	**2,295**	**2,343**
License Brewing:			
Italy	162	166	172
Australia	6	11	22
New Zealand	7	11	22
Sweden	29	27	24
Greece	7	7	10
UK	2,139	2,815	3,377
Total Licensed	**2,350**	**3,037**	**3,627**
Export:			
USA	–	·	7
Canada	–	–	5
Other Countries	92	49	202
Duty Free	245	389	507
Total Export	**337**	**438**	**721**
Overall Total	**4,810**	**5,770**	**6,691**

Exhibit 6   Top 10 Brewers by International Sales

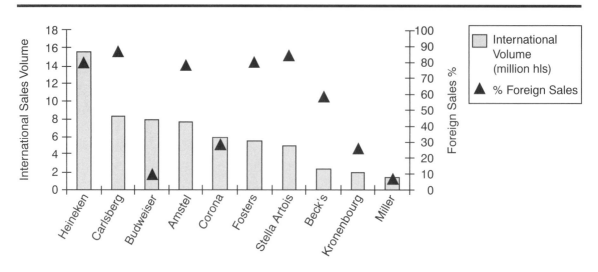

Exhibit 7   1998 Heineken World Sales Profile

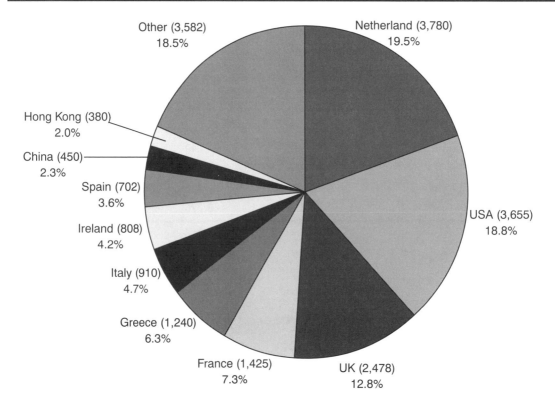

Exhibit 8   1998 Foster's World Sales Profile

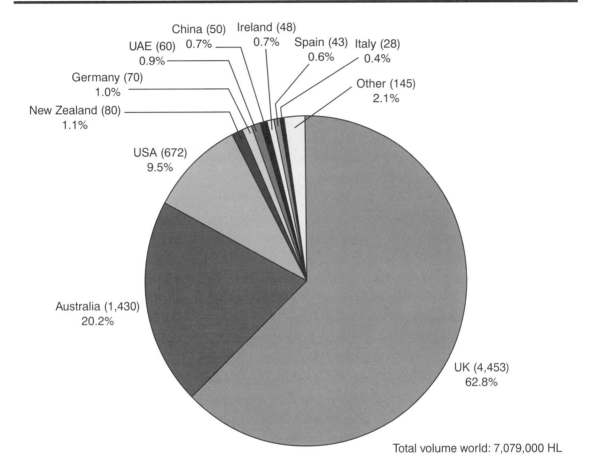

China (50)
0.7%

Ireland (48)
0.7%

Spain (43)
0.6%

Italy (28)
0.4%

UAE (60)
0.9%

Germany (70)
1.0%

New Zealand (80)
1.1%

Other (145)
2.1%

USA (672)
9.5%

Australia (1,430)
20.2%

UK (4,453)
62.8%

Total volume world: 7,079,000 HL

Exhibit 9   1998 Carlsberg World Sales Profile

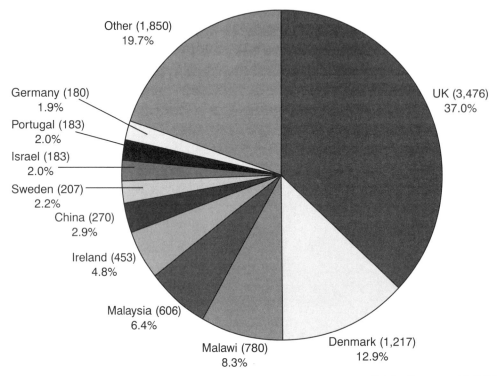

Other (1,850)
19.7%

Germany (180)
1.9%

Portugal (183)
2.0%

Israel (183)
2.0%

Sweden (207)
2.2%

China (270)
2.9%

Ireland (453)
4.8%

Malaysia (606)
6.4%

Malawi (780)
8.3%

Denmark (1,217)
12.9%

UK (3,476)
37.0%

Total volume world: 9,405,000 HL

Exhibit 10   Global Positioning Statement

Brand Positioning

To males, between 21 to 45 years of age, that are premium lager drinkers, Stella Artois is a European premium lager beer, differentially positioned towards the product.

Stella Artois offers a modern, sophisticated, yet accessible drinking experience with an emphasis on the very high quality of the beer supported by the noble tradition of European brewing.

The accent is on the emotional consequence of benefit: a positive feeling of self esteem and sophistication.

Character, Tone of Voice

Sophistication

Authenticity, tradition, yet touch of modernity

Timelessness

Premium quality

Special, yet accessible

Mysticism

European

Exhibit 11   A comparison of Carlsberg and Heineken

Profit Exposure by Market Type

		Low	High
Market Return	High	Carlsberg = 19% Heineken = 2%	Carlsberg = 22% Heineken = 46%
	Low	Carlsberg = 56% Heineken = 2%	Carlsberg = 3% Heineken = 50%

Market Growth

TECHNOPHAR IN VIETNAM

As Gary Dube, vice-president of Technophar Equipment & Service Ltd. (Technophar), a leading manufacturer of hard and soft gelatin capsule machines, proceeded to his meeting with Mark Habuda, vice-president of marketing, and Herman Victorov, president, he reviewed the history of their recent venture in Viet Nam. Negotiations had proceeded smoothly since the initial contact 18 months ago, and an agreement had been reached with the Vietnamese partner, Cuulong Pharmaceutical Import and Export Company (Cuulong). However, the initial deposit, due on December 15, 1994, had not arrived, and now, on January 15, 1995, concern about the Viet Nam contract had intensified. Dube wondered if Technophar should re-negotiate the contract, cancel the contract, or continue to wait patiently for a payment that might not ever arrive. In the back of his mind, Dube re-evaluated their approach to securing foreign contracts.

The Gelatin Capsule Industry

Hard gelatin capsules were invented in 1833 by the French pharmacist A. Mathes. Originally produced in a hand process by Parke Davis (Capsugel), they were first machine-processed by Eli-Lilly (Elanco) in the late 19th century. The first semi-automatic machine was developed in 1909 by Arthur Colton who continued to innovate and improve the capsule manufacture process through the first half of the 20th century. He introduced the first fully automatic machine in the 1930s and eventually sold his company and machine design patents to Snyder Co. of Detroit, Michigan. In 1963, Snyder Co. was purchased by Cherry-Burrell Corporation, the company from which Technophar was spun-off.

Technophar's position in the gelatin capsule industry was that of a supplier of machines and turn-key plants for the manufacture of hard and soft gelatin capsules (see Exhibit 1). Two other firms, one in Canada and the other in the United States, competed directly with Technophar. Technophar manufactured machines that were widely considered technologically superior in design and operating performance. In 1995 it was the industry leader with an 80 per cent share of the growing worldwide market for capsule machines. However, high price sensitivity among machine purchasers required Technophar to price their machines on par with competitors' machines.

Capsule machine manufacture and gelatin capsule production existed as niche businesses within the larger pharmaceutical industry. Large pharmaceutical firms, with the exception of Shinogi and Capsugel, were not involved in gelatin capsule production. Pharmaceutical firms were reluctant to integrate backwards for three reasons: (1) pharmaceutical firms preferred to concentrate on the production of fine chemicals used in pharmacological products, (2) a small capsule factory produced 1.5 billion capsules per year and most pharmaceutical firms filled fewer than a billion capsules annually, and (3) gelatin capsule production was a notoriously difficult and finicky process. Capsules were easier to buy than produce; as a result, the gelatin capsule industry was initially a duopoly.

In the early 1970s, the U.S. based R. P. Scherer Co. (Scherer) entered into capsule production, joining the first two producers of hard gelatin capsules: Capsugel and Elanco. By the 1990s, these three producers had secured an 80 to 85 per cent share of the worldwide gelatin capsule market and were protective of their processes and technology. Dube commented on the impression these capsule producers had created:

> For many years Capsugel and Elanco portrayed the technology of making capsules as an exclusive, painstaking craft which few people had the God-given ability to do well, and these few were employed by Capsugel and Elanco. Consequently these two companies put factories in a few key countries around the world, and really controlled the market until the early 1970s. Then R. P. Scherer came in and took a little bite out of it. Finally we started to sell the technology which opened up the industry.

Capsugel was the largest producer of hard capsules with 140 hard capsule machines located in eight countries around the world (see Exhibit 2). Shinogi, a Japanese pharmaceutical firm and previously Elanco's joint venture partner in Japan, purchased Elanco's capsule production business in the 1990s. Shinogi operated 80 hard capsule machines and had centralized capsule production to facilities in the United States, Spain and Japan. Scherer, the third largest producer of hard capsules with 40 machines in three different countries, was the dominant firm in the soft capsule market. Scherer had a 60 to 65 per cent world share in this rapidly growing segment of the capsule market.

The hard capsule factory location decision was driven mainly by transportation cost considerations. Gelatin capsules, a light, voluminous product consisting mostly of air, were expensive to transport because of their low value per unit volume. Accordingly, to minimize transportation costs, capsule factories had been located close to pharmaceutical firms' manufacturing facilities in Europe and North America. However, in recent years, pharmaceutical firms had been shifting production to developing countries to take advantage of lower labour costs and tax incentives, and to be closer to the source of fine chemicals used as filler in encapsulated products. Indonesia, Puerto Rico and China had emerged as popular host sites for manufacturing investments by pharmaceutical firms.

The relocation of pharmaceutical facilities created new opportunities for capsule producers. Capsule factories placed in developing countries had a transportation cost advantage in supplying these new pharmaceutical plants. Also, pharmaceutical firms from developing countries were entering the worldwide market for pharmacological products and, for similar reasons, these firms required nearby capsule factories.

Market Development

Capsule production technology became available to firms around the globe through Technophar's innovative efforts. Technophar simplified and standardized capsule production enabling the process to be transferred with relative ease. Dube stated, "We took the production process and broke it down so that you could teach it to a 10 year old." The company developed procedures and manuals to support its simplified process. These manuals detailed the intricacies of the production process and explained machine operations, maintenance and repair.

Technophar's innovations led to demand growth in less-developed regions of the world such as Eastern Europe, Africa, Latin America and regions of Asia. For example, prior to Technophar's technology transfer to China, the market for hard capsules had been small because capsules were expensive to produce. Capsules were produced in a labour-intensive, hand-dipping process which had a very low productivity. As automated capsule production technology became available to producers in China through Technophar's efforts, the market for hard capsules began to grow. Hard capsules produced with Technophar's technology became inexpensive to produce (US$3 per thousand) or purchase. As a result, developing countries could produce their own capsules which facilitated upstream entry into the pharmaceutical industry.

Company History

Herman Victorov, president and founder of Technophar, had been a plant engineer for Scherer. During his tenure there, he developed a process modification which nearly doubled the hourly yield of capsule production from 28,000 to 48,000. In 1983, a subsequent process improvement increased output another 4,000 capsules per hour. In 1984, he left Scherer and established Multi-Motion Engineering Inc. in Windsor, Ontario, which was purchased by Cherry Burrell in 1985.

Technophar, a spin-off of the Canadian division of Cherry Burrell, came into existence as a private company in 1988. Technophar was, in the words of Dube, "a company of machine builders led by Victorov's desire to be an engineer and machine designer." Technophar employed 50 people, many of them highly-skilled technicians who had worked with Victorov at Cherry Burrell's Canadian division.

Technophar, building on Victorov's experience in Bulgaria, Germany, China and Romania, quickly emerged as an international supplier of hard capsule machines. Sales, while initially slow at seven machines for the 1988-1990 period, increased dramatically in 1992 when eight machines were sold. This rapid growth rate continued, and 20 machines were sold in 1994. Revenues in 1994 were US$12 million and the company was moderately profitable.

Technophar's customers were primarily in developing countries. The company's management team, experienced in the pharmaceutical industry and in international markets, was well-suited to dealing with the uncertainty and risk in these emerging markets. Dube commented on the nature of Technophar's business:

> When you are doing business internationally, quite often you are dealing with countries that are relying on aid money and it tends to be a feast or famine business. Our employees were either working 60 hours a week building machines, or they were painting doorknobs.

Technophar was accustomed to a high variability in orders. When the order book was empty, management was more willing to accommodate riskier contracts. Four or five contracts represented the company's annual business and Dube was well aware of the cost of a lost contract.

> If you are planning on two or three projects and a major one crumples on you, it can be devastating to a small company like ours. With our uneven stream of revenues, we have to be a private company. We could not be a public company with quarterly reporting requirements.

Technophar manufactured hard capsule machines in its Oldcastle, Ontario location for distribution and re-assembly in a variety of countries around the world. New capsule machines were list priced for US$535,000 to US$635,000. The company designed and constructed a number of different models for different needs, though components were readily interchangeable between models. Hence, machines tailored to specific customer needs were essentially identical across customers. The Oldcastle facility could produce 20 capsule machines annually with a single shift.

Technophar's Activities

International Operations

Technophar participated in several international alliances. Most alliances were manufacturing joint ventures and three of these were located in Romania, Victorov's country of birth. In Bucharest, Technophar had established a model turn-key plant for prospective clients. While this plant vertically integrated the firm forward, it was not an entry into the hard capsule market. Technophar did not want to compete with its own customers in the hard capsule market. Output from this plant was used to demonstrate the quality of Technophar's machinery and hard capsule product. A second joint venture in Bucharest operated as an engineering and trading company. The third joint venture, located in Odorheiu, was a manufacturing facility which produced components used in the assembly of capsule machines.

To date, China was Technophar's largest purchaser of hard capsule machines and factories (see Exhibit 3). For that reason Technophar had devoted considerable resources to serving the Chinese market and was positioned to exploit the huge untapped potential (see Exhibit 4). Mark Habuda was stationed in Guangzhou, Guangdong and two joint ventures had been established: the one in Qingdao, Shandong assisted with Technophar's projects in China; the other located in Guangzhou, Guangdong was a complete manufacturing facility which employed both local personnel and Canadian technicians. It produced capsule machines and support equipment for turn-key plants in China.

Turn-Key Plants

Technophar's main business was turn-key projects in developing countries. The sale of a turn-key plant was a complicated and time-consuming process: contracts were often courted for several years. Once the contract had been negotiated, a 10 to 15 per cent deposit and a letter of credit for the balance was sent to Technophar. Because Technophar did not stock inventory, it would not begin capsule machine manufacture until these two items had been received. Technophar shipped the completed machines when it received the remaining portion of the contracted amount, less 10 per cent. When the turn-key plant had been certified as fully operational, it was turned over to the purchaser in exchange for the 10 per cent hold back amount.

The technology transfer consisted of four major components: preliminary building designs, the equipment necessary for the production of hard capsules, auxiliary equipment, and training in plant operations. Under the terms of the technology transfer agreement, the purchaser was responsible for the construction and cost of the Technophar-designed facility. Technophar used a standardized design which was adapted to local operating criteria. Once the facility had been constructed, a team of Technophar's technicians accompanied the machinery and equipment to the purchaser's facility.

The machines and auxiliary equipment were manufactured in one of Technophar's three manufacturing facilities. The auxiliary equipment included items such as dehumidifiers, air-conditioners and operational controls. Half of the turn-key contract's value was in this auxiliary equipment and the other half in the hard and soft capsule machines. The machines and auxiliary equipment, once manufactured and tested, were disassembled and shipped to the purchaser's facility, where they were re-assembled by the plant set-up team.

The plant set-up team comprised five technicians. The first technician, who arrived in the purchaser's country toward the end of facility construction, inspected the new building and supervised installation of the climate control equipment. The next crew was responsible for auxiliary equipment set-up and capsule machinery installation. The final crew made the plant operational and subjected the plant to a 72-hour test run, termed the production test protocol (PTP). If the plant operated well under the PTP, Technophar completed instruction about machine operations, formulations, and gelatin preparations. Technophar's contractual obligations ended when it formally turned the plant over to the purchaser.

Service Business

Throughout the facility construction process, Technophar's technicians had the opportunity to interact with people who would be operating the plant. They emphasized to the purchaser's staff the importance of following Technophar's well-documented operating procedures. Despite this stress on conformity with procedures, factories often "went to hell in a handbasket. After the keys had been handed over, the purchaser would take shortcuts and forget about the operating rules."

Although Technophar's guarantee did not cover operational difficulties arising from equipment misuse, company technicians were available to help repair machines. This form of after-sale service was offered for a fee, but purchasers seldom took advantage of it. Plants located in developing countries typically did not have discretionary funds for maintenance and repairs. Also, the efficiency imperative found in private companies was not present in many of these state-supported plants. Thus, machines capable of operating 24 hours per day and producing 65,000 capsules per hour, were operated for 13 or 14 hours each day, and when operated, the machines ran at 60 per cent efficiency.

Technophar was also engaged in the service, repair and upgrading of existing capsule machines, a number of which had been operating for many years. These machines were much slower and produced lower quality capsules than the newer machines. Technophar had refurbished a few machines, but managers were uncertain of the size of the existing market for machine upgrades.

Auxiliary Businesses

Technophar's expertise in machine manufacture and design facilitated the company's entry into other related businesses. The company had designed and manufactured various mechanical systems and machinery for firms in the metallurgical, chemical and automotive industries. A major food processing company in North America had purchased original machines and prototypes for use in packaging. Technophar was also engaged in the manufacture of machinery for the small but rapidly expanding soft capsule industry.

Markets

Hard Gelatin Capsule

Estimates of annual worldwide capsule consumption ranged between 100 billion and 200 billion capsules: North America, the largest market for capsules, consumed 50 billion to 55 billion; Western Europe, the second largest market, consumed 40 billion. The size of other large regional markets was uncertain. Technophar's management estimated worldwide market growth to be three to five per cent per annum (see Exhibit 5).

Gelatin Capsule Machine

Firms in developing countries and newly industrializing countries formed the large majority of Technophar's customers. One gelatin capsule plant was often sufficient to satisfy domestic demand in these countries and Technophar was continually challenged to find new market opportunities. However, Technophar lacked formal marketing procedures and did not employ a sales force or agents dedicated to seeking and developing opportunities.[1] Trade shows, in which Technophar could display its product and meet potential customers, were deemed of little value because the North American market for gelatin capsule machines was saturated.

Technophar relied on two processes for accessing opportunities. The first was internal: managers were experienced both internationally and in the pharmaceutical industry. Dube, Victorov and Habuda had, respectively, 30, 17 and 13 years of experience in this industry and direct experience in the countries of Asia, Latin America and Eastern Europe. Dube expanded on the importance of experience and industry contacts:

> Over a period of time we had learned who was buying capsules. When I worked at R.P. Scherer I knew who was buying capsules because we had agents in 13 or 14 countries. We also knew where our competitors had factories.

> In determining opportunities for Technophar, we used our industry experience and went either through the gelatin end or through the pharmaceutical industry. We asked ourselves, 'Is a pharmaceutical company interested in making capsules?' Or a group of people may leave these companies and become entrepreneurs. They would want to start a capsule-making business and would be natural customers for our product.

In determining opportunities, these managers operated a lot on "gut feel," and each brought a unique perspective to their joint evaluation of a country. Entering into their intuitive assessment were a number of factors, one of which was the type of capsule consumption. Capsules were used for some ethical pharmaceutical products (prescription drugs and over the counter drugs), and for health food products, a rapidly growing market segment in North America and Europe. Ethical pharmaceutical consumption was multiplying in developing countries, particularly with the increased emphasis on health care.

The managers also considered the location of existing hard capsule factories. The Middle East, for example, was a promising region because only one small company produced capsules there. Other factors included the type of government in a country, its emphasis on health care (and by association, hard capsule consumption), and the openness of the country to international trade.

The second process for finding markets was also informal. Technophar gathered market information through a network of non-company agents and contacts. For example, it had an arrangement with Marubeni, a large Japanese trading company with offices around the world, to use its agents for information about potential markets. Canadian embassies and consulates had also been helpful by providing leads and by disseminating Technophar's promotional literature within their regional spheres of responsibility. American embassies, host country nationals residing in Canada, and agents within China provided an informal source of information and often approached Technophar with unsolicited orders. An agent whose efforts resulted in an actual delivery received a commission of three to eight per cent of the value of the contract. Contract values for a four-machine turn-key plant averaged US$3 million to US$4 million.

Developing Opportunities

Technophar's unblemished reputation for honesty, integrity and reliability was instrumental in securing new contracts. The company had gone to considerable lengths in the past to protect its highly valued reputation. In 1992 for example, it had received a deposit of US$1.3 million from Saudi Arabia for a turn-key plant. Technophar had begun machine manufacture and had invested a considerable amount of time and money in bringing the deal to fruition. However, a change in priority in Saudi Arabia led to the cancellation of the contract. Technophar was under no obligation to return the deposit; nevertheless, to protect its reputation and to promote the likelihood of future business in the region, it refunded all but accrued out-of-pocket expenses. From the goodwill created by this gesture, Technophar had secured contracts with other countries in the Middle East (e.g., Jordan) and was presently speaking with representatives from the United Arab Emirates, Qatar and a new Saudi group about capsule machine sales.

Technophar continually cultivated new clients, as winning contracts often required an extended period of negotiations. It was not unusual for managers to spend US$10,000 on travel plus weeks of management time exploring an opportunity which might not ever result in a contract. Dube and Habuda, for example, travelled more than 140 days in 1994.

During the early stages of negotiation, Technophar assisted the purchaser with market and feasibility studies for the proposed plant. Technophar had a series of standard schedules for assessing manufacturing costs which were adaptable to factor conditions in the purchaser's country. Using these schedules, the purchaser plugged in the relevant figures to make projections of its production costs and profitability.

The Viet Nam Opportunity

Technophar received an unsolicited order for the Viet Nam contract. The deal had a *Viet Kieu* connection, as Mr. Ly Van Phi, the owner of an import-export business in Montreal, originally approached Technophar with officials of Cuulong about supplying hard-capsule-making equipment to Viet Nam.[2] The proposed project was valued at US$4 million and the agreement to provide the plant and equipment was signed on November 15, 1994, during Canadian Prime Minister Chretien's two-day visit to Viet Nam.

Though Technophar had been handed this opportunity, management had to evaluate the viability of the Viet Nam technology transfer as compared with other potential projects. The company, which normally had seven or eight projects in the process of negotiation, was also developing opportunities in Russia, France, Thailand, Malaysia, India, China and in three other countries of the former Soviet Union. An issue was: Why enter Viet Nam when other opportunities existed in China and South-East Asia? (see Exhibits 6 and 7).

Technophar had a number of reasons for entering Viet Nam. The central government's support was a major consideration because it was an active participant in larger projects. It supported this technology transfer because of its favourable balance of payments effects. Imports of gelatin capsules would be reduced, and exports would be upgraded in the forward integration of Viet Nam's pharmaceutical industry. Also, the government's position on health care implicitly supported the deal. A state-supported health industry was thought to lead to increased encapsulated drug consumption.

A second set of reasons for entering Viet Nam entailed a longer term perspective. Although Technophar did not perceive a market there for more than one or two capsule plants, opportunities existed for the company's related, but as yet undeveloped, businesses. Victorov, an entrepreneur and inventor, had a patent on a sugar extraction process which greatly increased the yield of sugar from sugar cane. Viet Nam had a sizable sugar cane industry but the country's poor infrastructure hampered processing. Victorov's process was uniquely suited to the country's needs as sugar processing units could be built individually and located close to the supply of sugar cane. A second opportunity existed in the development of processing machinery for the extraction of gelatin from pig skins, beef skins and cow bones, which were usually discarded by the Vietnamese. The introduction of this technology would enable Viet Nam's pharmaceutical industry to further integrate backwards. However, the two projects involved a much greater financial commitment and would not likely materialize in the next three to four years.

Offsetting these reasons for entering the Viet Nam market was Technophar's limited experience in this country. Previously, sales in developing markets had been to those countries in which managers had prior experience — Victorov in Romania and Bulgaria, and Habuda in China. Technophar's managers were inexperienced in Viet Nam and needed to know more about the basic characteristics of the country to which they were actually committed.

Viet Nam — Country Study[3]

Market Promise

Viet Nam was positioned in the heart of the dynamic countries of the Pacific Rim (see Exhibit 8). While slow to reach the economic growth levels of other countries in the region and saddled with a turbulent past, recent reforms had positioned Viet Nam to become the next tiger in the region (see Exhibit 7).

The package of economic renovations (*Doi Moi*) instituted in 1986 had been a turning point for the country's economy. Viet Nam had made significant progress in recent years moving away from the planned economic model toward a more effective, market-based economic system. Most prices were now fully decontrolled, and the Vietnamese currency had been devalued and floated at world market rates. In addition, the scope for private sector activity had been expanded, primarily through decollectivization of the agricultural sector and the introduction of laws giving legal recognition to private business.

Sectorally, economic growth was not evenly dispersed as industries in the economy were treated differently under the guidelines of *Doi Moi*. Land reforms had created more autonomy. Light industries, such as textiles and food manufacture, had been emphasized, as export promotion and diversification were seen to be key variables in Viet Nam's future economic success. In 1994, nearly three-quarters of export earnings were generated by only two commodities, rice and crude oil. Led by industry and construction, the economy did well in 1994 with GNP rising 4.8 per cent.

In response to *Doi Moi*, foreign direct investment (FDI) in Viet Nam had surged dramatically in recent years. From US$360 million in 1988, FDI approvals had grown ten-fold to US$4 billion in 1994. FDI was dominated by firms from Asian countries; European and North American firms had been slow to invest in the region (see Exhibit 9). Firms from the United States had not been permitted to invest in Viet Nam prior to February 3, 1994, though only hours after President Clinton announced the lifting of the U.S. embargo against Viet Nam, both PepsiCo and Coca-Cola made commitments to begin bottling and distributing in Viet Nam.

Foreign investors were attracted to Viet Nam for a number of reasons. Investors were permitted to have 100 per cent equity ownership in their ventures, unlike in some countries in the Asia Pacific region. Low corporate tax rates, tax holidays, potential waivers on import and export duties, and full profit repatriation were other government-centred investment incentives. Investors were also encouraged by market conditions. Wage rates were low, Viet Nam was considerably well-endowed with natural resources such as forests, marine life, minerals, crude oil and a workforce of 32 million people. Infrastructure was poor, which hampered economic development, but created considerable opportunity for companies in this sector.

Risks

Social

Other factors mitigated these attractions. Viet Nam was classified as a "least developed nation" by the United Nations. Malnutrition was high, double that in China, and diseases not prevalent in other countries in South-East Asia were found in Viet Nam. Infant mortality (45.5 deaths per 1,000 live births) was high and literacy rates (88 per cent) comparatively low. A significant proportion of children did not complete secondary (high school level) schooling. Improved living standards had been given priority, though little attention had been paid to human rights and basic freedoms. Viet Nam's natural resource advantages were suffering from environmental degradation. Deforestation, water pollution, overfishing and soil degradation were issues of concern.

Economic

While wealthy in natural resources and people, Viet Nam was still one of the poorest countries in the South-East Asia region. The industrial sector remained burdened by uncompetitive state-owned enterprises that the government was unwilling or unable to privatize. The economy was primarily agrarian, with 40 per cent of GDP accounted for by agricultural products, and 65 per cent of employment in agriculture. Eighty per cent of Viet Nam's 70 million people lived as peasant farmers without the income to spend on items other than necessities such as food and shelter.

Unemployment loomed as a serious problem. Roughly 25 per cent of the workforce was without work and population growth swelled the ranks of the unemployed yearly. The government ran a five per cent budget deficit in 1993, and imports at US$3.1 billion exceeded exports (US$2.6 billion). Moreover, the government would issue no information on foreign currency reserves. Doubts existed as to the ability of the central government to exhibit sound fiscal management, and inflation had reached 14.4 per cent by 1995.

Political

The political risk in Viet Nam was still considerable (see Exhibit 7). Viet Nam was a one party state in which political power came from the Communist party and its politburo. Although the Communist party enjoyed little support from the populace and was widely disliked in the south, there was no real challenge to the government's authority. However, as a vocal generation of Vietnamese emerged in the thrills and throes of economic freedom, the potential for conflict between political authoritarianism and growing market freedoms was increasing.

The central government, despite its free-market preaching, often participated overtly in markets by restricting competition and by acting as a partner in the majority of foreign ventures. Its market participation was not always valued because Vietnamese government officials had little experience in dealing with multinational agencies and corporations or in formulating and implementing projects. Also, Vietnamese security officials were suspicious of foreigners to the point of paranoia, which created apprehension in many foreign investors.

Conflict still remained between central and regional governments. Similar to the situation in China, economic power was fragmented and economic policies varied by province in their internal competition for foreign investment. Laws and regulations were interpreted differently in each region and, in cases, were disregarded. For example, officials in Ho Chi Minh City had developed their own income tax laws and had threatened to prevent foreigners from leaving the country until all personal taxes had been reconciled.

Corruption, bribery, copyright and patent infringement were not uncommon for want of effective legal enforcement. Institutions supporting free enterprise were absent. Without a legal framework, a viable banking system or private land ownership (all land was the property of the state), business in Viet Nam involved considerable risk. Thus, the raw potential and attractiveness of the country was countervailed by these social, economic and political risk factors. Consequently, only one-third of the US$12 billion in FDI committed to Viet Nam since 1988 had been implemented and US$1 billion of projects had been cancelled.

The Viet Nam Contract

Negotiations for the Viet Nam contract transpired smoothly and quickly. The initial discussions went well when Habuda visited the Vietnamese purchasers during one of his trips to China. He returned for a second set of meetings, during which he assisted with local market and feasibility studies. Cuulong completed these evaluations and recognized the large domestic market for pharmaceuticals as well as the export potential of hard capsules. After his transfer to China, Habuda visited Viet Nam for a third time and completed the technology transfer package. The final task was to get all of the political players in place, and the contract was signed when Prime Minister Chretien's Asian trade mission arrived in Viet Nam.

The deal, though quickly negotiated, had been dragging on for a number of months. Internal changes on the Vietnamese side had caused some delays and Technophar's costs had changed considerably since the contract had been negotiated. For example, stainless steel, a large component of the auxiliary equipment, had increased in price by 30 to 35 per cent in the last six months. Technophar's management recognized the difficulties faced by Cuulong because of the poor infrastructure in the country, but concern about the contract became acute when the December 15 deposit did not arrive.

Management at Technophar communicated weekly with Pharmexco, the official importer of the equipment, and Cuulong. In these communications, a great deal of uncertainty began to develop about the project and the partners. Technophar's managers, who were having difficulty sorting fact from fiction in their dealings with Pharmexco and Cuulong, had no way of judging the validity of the many reasons given for the delay. Much of what was said had to be taken on faith.

Despite the increased uncertainty, Technophar's managers were reluctant to cancel the contract outright. Doing so would tarnish the company's reputation, and the contract, even with the cost increases, was still profitable. However, with additional orders coming onto the books, Technophar could keep its plant producing for at least the next six months. Thus, Technophar could legally cut the order off and renegotiate at a later date.

A more fundamental issue was Technophar's presence in Viet Nam. Largely, the company's growth had been in developing countries in markets where the managers had previous experience. Otherwise, large sales had been to developed countries such as Germany and France. The few sales that had been to riskier, developing countries involved a smaller stake: one machine had been sold to each of Brazil, Columbia, Venezuela and Indonesia. The sale of a plant, complete with four machines and auxiliary equipment, to Viet Nam, one of the least developed countries, was a considerable departure from Technophar's established practices. Dube wondered whether Technophar should even be in Viet Nam.

Technophar's entry into Viet Nam had also been one of chance. How many of these opportunities were slipping through the cracks because Technophar was not systematically seeking out and evaluating potential markets? Was the same kind of innovation which allowed for simplification and systemization of capsule production required in their approach to international markets?

Exhibit 1   The Gelatin Capsule Industry

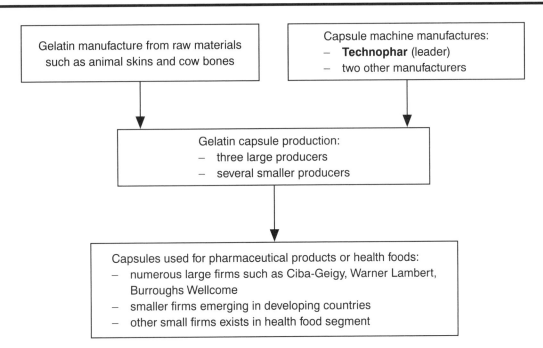

Exhibit 2   Location of Hard Capsule Factories and Machines (as of 1995)

Manufacturer	Country	No. of Machines
Capsugel	Belgium	
	Brazil	Total: 140 machines
	China	
	France	
	Japan	
	Mexico	
	Thailand	
	United States	
Shinogi	Japan	
	Spain	Total: 80 machines
	United States	
Scherer	Brazil	
	Canada	Total: 40 machines
	Germany	

Source: Company Records

Exhibit 3   Technophar's Worldwide Market (as of 1995)

Country	No. of Machines Sold
Brazil	1
Bulgaria	4
Canada	2
China	31
Colombia	1
France	5
Germany	4
Indonesia	1
Israel	2
Korea	1
Romania	4
Taiwan	3
United States	1
Venezuela	1

Source: Company Records

Exhibit 4   Market Penetration In China (No. of Machines as of 1995)

Province or Major Municipality	1994 est. Population (million)	1993 GDP (US$ billion)	Per Capita GDP (US$)	GDP Annual Growth Rate (%)	Known No. of Hard Capsule Machines*
Anhui	60	28	469	17	
Beijing	11	20	1,806	0	
Fujian	31	23	744	10	
Gansu	23	10	426	18	
Guangdong	71	91	1,277	21	7
Guangxi	44	19	434	21	
Guizhou	34	9	262	8	
Hebei	64	37	577	−1	
Heilongjiang	39	26	673	11	2
Henan	89	37	417	−2	4
Hubei	57	37	649	19	
Hunan	65	29	442	13	
Inner Mongolia	23	11	492	22	
Jiangsu	73	102	1,398	10	
Jiangxi	40	18	249	11	
Jilin	27	19	720	18	
Liaoning	43	54	1,251	16	
Ningxia	5	2	516	17	
Qinghai	5	2	443	33	
Shaanxi	35	15	442	11	
Shandong	89	76	853	1	12
Shanghai	14	52	3,683	21	2
Shanxi	30	15	506	2	
Sichuan	120	52	432	15	
Tianjin	9	18	1,962	0	
Tibet	2	1	182	0	
Xinjiang	16	11	692	29	
Yunnan	39	15	393	22	
Zhejiang	47	53	1,127	5	4
Total for China	**1,205**	**882**			**31**
Mean for China			743	11	

*Technophar machines only.

Sources: Department of Population Statistics, State Statistical Bureau, People's Republic of China, Beijing, July 1985, Table 34. World Bank Atlas 1995. Company records.

Exhibit 5   Worldwide Capsule Consumption (as of 1995)

Region	1995 est. Population (million)	Estimated GDP in each Region (US$ billion)	Average GDP per person (US$)	Capsule Consumption (Est.)
North America	300	7,350	24,500	55 billion
Western Europe	465	8,439	18,148	40 billion
Eastern Europe	447	1,879	4,203	not known
Asia/Pacific	3,294	6,670	2,025	not known
Latin America*	494	1,416	2,866	not known
Africa	683	463	678	not known
Middle East	212	1,007	4,750	not known
World	**5,895**	**27,224**	**4,618**	**100–200 billion**

*Includes the countries of South and Central America.
Note: The worldwide market for capsules was estimated by Dube to be growing at three per cent to five per cent per year.
Source: World Bank Atlas 1995. Company records.

Exhibit 6   Market Penetration in Asia (as of 1995)

Country	Hard Capsule Machine
Bangladesh	No
Burma	No
Cambodia	No
China	Yes
Hong Kong	No
India	Yes (old, inferior quality)
Indonesia	Yes
Japan	Yes
Laos	No
Malaysia	No
Nepal	No
North Korea	??
Pakistan	No ?
Philippines	No
Singapore	Yes
South Korea	Yes
Taiwan	No ?
Thailand	Yes
Viet Nam	Contracted

Source: Company Records

Exhibit 7   Characteristics of Countries in South East Asia and South Asia

	1994 GNP/ Capita (US $)	GNP: Growth Rate (%)	Inflation Rate, 1993 (%)	1993 Population (000)	Political Risk*	Life Expectancy (years)	Mftg. Wages (US$/hr.)
Viet Nam	170	4.8	5.2	73,103	C	67	0.24
China	743	6.5	18.0	1,164,908	D	69	0.37
Malaysia	3,160	5.7	3.6	19,032	B	71	1.90
Singapore	19,310	6.1	2.4	2,867	A	75	NA
Thailand	2,040	8.4	4.1	58,824	B	69	0.92
Indonesia	730	4.8	10.0	187,151	B	60	0.17
Philippines	830	1.6	7.6	65,775	C	65	0.67
Burma	950	5.0	30.0	44,277	NA	60	NA
Cambodia	600	7.5	60.0	10,265	NA	49	NA
Hong Kong	17,860	5.3	9.5	5,865	B	78	NA
India	290	3.0	8.0	900,543	D	61	NA

*A = Low; D = High

Sources: World Bank Atlas 1995. The Vietnam Business Journal, 1(3), 1993. Economist Intelligence Unit. Business Asia, January 16, 1995.

Exhibit 8   Map of Asia

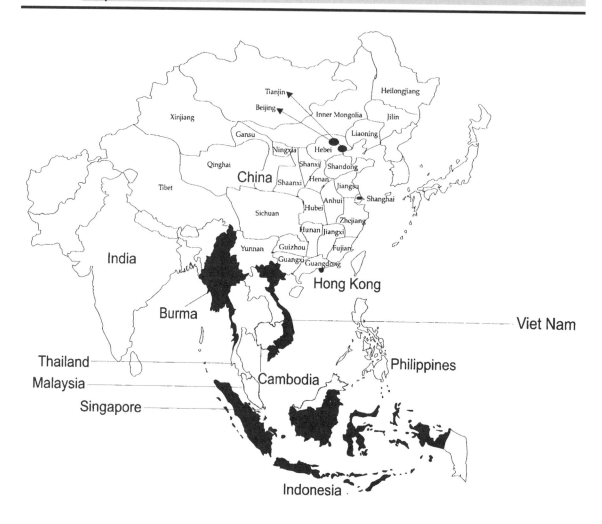

Exhibit 9   FDI in Viet Nam by Country (as of 1995)

	Country	No. of Projects	Total Capital Committed(US$ million)
1	Taiwan	179	1,964
2	Hong Kong	171	1,788
3	Singapore	76	1,070
4	South Korea	97	884
5	Japan	73	783
6	Australia	42	655
7	Malaysia	31	581
8	France	58	534
9	Switzerland	14	463
10	Britain	15	376
11	Netherlands	16	348
12	United States	28	270
13	Thailand	43	236
14	Indonesia	11	160
15	Russia	34	125
16	Ireland	13	81
17	Sweden	7	78
18	Canada	9	66
19	Philippines	12	58
20	Ukraine	6	45

Source: Vietnam Business Journal, III(1), 1995

Footnotes

[1] An agent would travel extensively, incurring expenses of US$400 per day, and would receive salary and benefits of approximately US$60,000 per year. A secretary for this agent could be employed at an annual cost of US$30,000. (Source: John W. Wright, "The American Almanac of Jobs and Salaries," 1995.)

[2] Viet Kieu refers to members of the 1975 exodus from Viet Nam to countries such as Canada, the United States and Australia after the collapse of South Viet Nam. The 180,000 Canadians of Vietnamese origin were, with their valuable ties and business connections, becoming increasingly important for doing business in Viet Nam. While it had been stated that Viet Kieu were welcome to assist in rebuilding Viet Nam, their exact status under Vietnamese law was still uncertain.

[3] Sources: Joseph P. Quinlan, "Vietnam: Business Opportunities and Risks," Pacific View Press: Berkeley, CA, 1995. The Economist Intelligence Unit reports.

TIME WARNER INC. AND THE ORC PARTNERS

In early July 1992, John Adamson, president of Optical Recording Corporation (ORC), sat depressed and second-guessed his company's decision to sue Time Warner Inc. for patent infringement. An in-house patent counsel from the U.S. Philips Corporation, whose parent firm developed and licensed the compact disc (CD) technology in partnership with Sony Corporation, had just finished his testimony in the Wilmington, Delaware, courtroom.

The Philips attorney had just advised the court that Philips International N.V. had indeed signed a license agreement with ORC but only to "get rid of ORC with a modest nuisance payment." He had gone on to say that in spite of their decision to accept a license from ORC, the Philips engineers and attorneys had never believed that the Russell patents owned by ORC were valid nor that any compact disc products infringed these patents. Adamson watched in shock as the Philips man made his way out of the courtroom.

Given that Time Warner had mounted a very credible defense and that ORC's entire licensing program might be at risk, Adamson needed to decide whether he should make a modest settlement with Time Warner, just to save the licensing program.

Background

Optical Recording Corporation (ORC) was incorporated in 1984 to exploit a technology invented by James T. Russell, an American inventor, then working in laboratories in Salt Lake City, Utah. Due to the desperate financial straits of SLC[1], his employer, Russell had made little progress in the previous two years and both he and SLC were anxious to secure a buyer for the technology.

Richard Ivey School of Business
The University of Western Ontario

Through Wayne White, a fellow MBA 1972 graduate from the University of Western Ontario, then working with Dominion Securities in Toronto, John Adamson was put in contact with Dr. R. Moses and Dr. A. Stein. These two Toronto businessmen had been working for close to a year to buy Russell's technology. By happenstance, Adamson had contacted White looking for business opportunities to start his next business, preferably in electronics or software, just days after Moses and Stein had advised White that they were going to throw in the towel on their Russell project. In spite of the considerable time that they had spent, it appeared unlikely that they would be successful in securing the necessary finances to proceed.

Adamson negotiated an option with these gentlemen to assume their "interests" in the Russell project, on the condition that he secure the necessary funding for a technology transfer by April 1, 1985, a propitious date as it would turn out. In return, Adamson agreed to reimburse their expenses to date and to give to each, a five per cent equity interest in the incorporation formed to exploit the Russell project in Toronto.

After completing a "due diligence" investigation of the Russell technology, with the assistance of Warner Sharkey, an alumnus and friend from the Royal Military College of Canada and a senior technology consultant, who operated from offices in New York and Toronto, Adamson began planning in earnest. He wanted to transfer the Russell technology to Toronto, where he expected a well qualified team of scientists and engineers could be assembled to pursue a cost-effective development of a pocket-portable digital storage device.

For the next nine excruciating months, he worked to find investors for an issue of special debentures from his Toronto start-up. These debentures also offered a very attractive cash-back feature under a research tax credit program of the Canadian government. Funding was secured and the technology transfer agreements were signed on March 28, 1985, only three days before the option agreement with Moses and Stein would have expired. Adamson had resisted the temptation to request an extension of time on his option agreement with Moses and Stein. He feared that, better informed, they might rekindle their interest in the Russell technology and work to obstruct what little chance he still had to find funding prior to the option expiry on the first of April.

With the debenture funding and the transfer agreements signed, the new Toronto company, soon to be called Optical Recording Corporation (ORC), was now ready to hire Russell and transfer SLC's technology to Toronto.

Jim Russell

By 1984, Jim Russell had worked for close to 20 years toward an improvement in recorded music beyond what was possible with the analog magnetic tape technology. This quest was motivated in part by his love of opera and a desire to listen to more accurate playbacks of recorded performances. When Adamson first visited Russell's lab in Salt Lake City, he was treated to the playback of a recording of Richard Wagner's "Ride of the Valkyries" (or "Die Walkure" in the original German). It was a most rousing introduction to a technology!

Russell had accomplished this playback by shining an argon ion laser beam onto a pre-recorded glass plate, the size of an index card. This was the latest of his laboratory prototypes designed to demonstrate his patented techniques. These techniques were claimed in his extensive portfolio of 26 U.S. patents with corresponding foreign issues in seven other countries.

In Russell's way of recording music, the acoustic signal of the music was first pre-processed into a single *digital* bit stream from a series of time-coincident frequency samples. A laser, an *optical* device, was then used as the energy source to mark the music, as digital bits, onto a glass plate in the recording step and then used to read the music, as digital bits, in the playback step. This technology was known as *digital optical* audio recording.

Adamson was not the first to visit Russell's lab, far from it. Over the course of the previous 10 years, both at SLC in Salt Lake City, and at Battelle Northwest Laboratories in Richland, Washington, electronics manufacturers around the world beat a path to Russell's laboratory door and at his invitation. SLC had been trying to sell technology licenses to the Russell technology but with virtually no success. Prominent among the visitors to SLC's labs were representatives from Philips International N.V., the multinational electric/electronics giant headquartered in Eindhoven, the Netherlands. They had made three separate visits over that 10-year period.

Prior to the commercial availability of the diode laser in the early 1980s, Russell's recording and playback devices were operated with the use of a gas ion laser and as such could be made no smaller than the dimensions of an office desk. Gas ion lasers were too bulky, complicated and expensive to be used in consumer products. This may explain SLC's lack of success in licensing and their resultant financial distress. With the advent of the diode laser, essentially a powerful light source on a silicon chip, a light, compact and economical consumer product such as the compact disc was possible. Although never well funded, SLC's money troubles really began in 1981, just as the mass commercialization of a digital optical audio recording device became feasible.

From Adamson's viewpoint, Russell's greatest achievement was not any one of his inventions, but his success in demonstrating the technical feasibility of recording a digital audio signal optically. Before Russell had successfully demonstrated this technical feat in 1975, no one else had even attempted it. By early 1984, however, the electronics trade papers were reporting that Sony and Philips were developing a so-called compact disc player. SLC and Russell must have felt that they were being left on the sidelines in Salt Lake City, a bitter fate for the inventor and his investors who had all contributed so much.

In bringing Russell and his technology to Toronto, Adamson had decided that there was little point in continuing audio research toward a digital optical tape recorder. The opportunity to develop a massive random access data storage device using credit card-sized media was seen a less ambitious technical challenge and possibly of greater commercial value than a music device like the CD. With the insight of Russell, Adamson envisioned books, medical records, equipment schematics, maintenance instructions and records on this type of device — and all pocket-portable.

In order to determine what protection the existing Russell patents would provide to the new research focus, Adamson employed the services of John Orange, a patent agent, then with the Toronto law firm of McCarthy & McCarthy. (Orange was recommended by Daniel Cooper, a corporate attorney with the same law firm, who earlier had prepared all of the financing and technology transfer agreements for ORC.)

After working with Russell for several months, Orange advised Adamson in early 1986 that the Russell patents may not provide much protection to the new company's research focus, as the most relevant patents appeared to be limited in their claims to audio applications. Adamson had already understood that it was the precise language of the claims within a patent that determined the patent's intellectual property rights.

Discovering a Treasure

In completing his study of ORC's patents with the assistance of Russell, Orange also concluded that the newly released compact disc players and discs might infringe one or more of the claims in the Russell patents. What a finding!

Russell had mentioned this possibility to Adamson during their first meeting in the Salt Lake City lab; however, Adamson had put little faith in Russell's remark at the time, as no consumer electronics firm had bothered to license the technology, in spite of SLC's efforts. Furthermore there were no CD products on the market then and its commercial success could not be anticipated.

Encouraged by the report from Orange and the early market success of the compact disc by the spring of 1986, Adamson retained the services of Adrian Horne, an established patent licensing professional of Dolby acoustic research fame. With Horne's assistance, ORC set out to advise every electronics firm likely to market a compact disc player anywhere in the world that "they may infringe the Russell patents" by doing so. Horne was most clear on the point that ORC must not appear to threaten legal action in their notice, as it may give grounds to the recipients to file a preemptive request for Declaratory Judgment and thereby force ORC into premature legal proceedings that ORC could ill afford.

In conjunction with the initial contact of alleged infringers, Adamson prepared cost estimates for the licensing effort and started to gain some early information on what it would cost to sue for patent infringement. He knew that once launched, any investment in the licensing program was certain to be incurred, whereas the return by way of royalty revenues would be anything but certain. He also made early estimates of the royalty potential for the licensing program, but these royalty estimates carried an enormous emotional impact.

Simple arithmetic established that if 100 million CD players were sold in ORC's patent-protected territories at an average manufacturer's selling price of US$100 and if ORC licensed their patent rights for this product at two per cent of revenues, ORC's projected royalties would total US$200 million. And this figure ignored the royalties to be earned on the manufacture and sale of the compact disc media itself! It was clear that a successful licensing program could be mounted given these simple estimates. Adamson chose not to dwell on these figures, however, as his typical reaction oscillated between a measured excitement and a raw fear of the business of licensing beyond what little he knew.

ORC's first meeting with a suspected infringer took place in the early summer of 1986 in Tarrytown, New York, in the offices of N.A. Philips Corporation. Legal representatives for both N.A. Philips and their Philips parent in Eindhoven, the Netherlands, and for the DuPont Corporation of Wilmington, Delaware, were in attendance. For ORC there were Cooper, Orange, and Adamson and a lawyer from Battelle Laboratories of Columbus, Ohio, Jim Russell's first employer, and the original owner and assignor of the Russell patents, first to SLC and then to ORC.

This first meeting with the Philips and DuPont people ended three and one-half hours later, after a full exchange of views and some acrimony, but no progress toward a licensing agreement. The attorneys representing both Philips and DuPont were of the view that no patents were infringed and further that there was some question about the validity of the Russell patents in the first place. There seemed little point in a further meeting and it seemed very likely that ORC might get no further without filing a patent infringement suit.

In August 1986, Adamson made a first trip to Tokyo on behalf of ORC, with Horne and Russell. A week-long series of company presentations had been arranged by Horne, with the assistance of Far East Associates, a technology licensing agency based in Tokyo, with whom Mr. Horne had collaborated in his Dolby days. Only one prominent manufacturer was invited to each meeting.

On Horne's advice, ORC had booked conference room space at the prestigious Okura Hotel, located directly across from the American Embassy in Minato-ku, a district of central Tokyo. Adamson choked on the daily expense of US$2,000 per day for a meeting room that comfortably held only six people. Horne, however, had stressed the importance of the location to ensure that the status-sensitive Japanese gained the best initial impression of ORC and its business offering.

The ORC team was overwhelmed by the turnout to their presentations. Each firm sent at least four executives and engineers; and in two instances, a group of over 10 people arrived, forcing the ORC team to scramble for a larger meeting room. Many guests recognized Horne from his previous Dolby research licensing days and more than a few appeared quite knowledgeable of Russell's research and patents. In fact, three firms clearly had comprehensive files on Russell's work and appeared very familiar with the technology.

The ORC presentations were made in English. Horne had advised that the executives in the international departments of all Japanese companies were invariably fluent in English. The younger members, however, tended to be more at ease in English, while some of the more experienced guests appeared to be there simply to witness the process and tone of the meeting and to gage the visitors as adversaries. Adamson concluded that some of the groups had arrived en masse, ready to take notes, in order to do a team translation, once they returned to their corporate offices. This would explain the large numbers of guests from some companies.

Nonetheless, this initial series of meetings convinced the ORC team that their patent infringement claims were being taken seriously by the Japanese firms. Apart from Philips, only the Japanese had announced CD player products by the fall of 1986.

During this initial trip by the ORC team to Tokyo, Yoshihide (Josh) Nakamura, then senior general manager, Intellectual Property, Sony Corporation invited the ORC team to Sony's headquarters for another meeting on their next visit to Japan.

Adamson returned to Tokyo with Orange and Horne in November 1986, for another series of presentations and meetings, but this time at each company's offices as prearranged again by Far East Associates. The most important of these meetings was with Sony Corporation, as the ORC team felt certain that Sony's decision on whether to license the Russell patents, would predetermine ORC's success with all other firms in Japan. (It was a Philips-Sony partnership that had launched the compact disc and taught an industry how to make them.)

On a schedule of two and even three meetings each day, including shuttles between companies located around Tokyo and Osaka, the ORC team made 12 more presentations. All discussions were held in English, again with only a perfunctory objection from the Japanese hosts. Everyone appreciated that the United States represented the largest domestic market for the compact disc industry and as Jim Russell had first filed his patents in the United States, it was also likely to be the site of ORC's most comprehensive patent protection.

In fact, ORC's patents were most comprehensive in the United States, Britain and Canada, but appeared to provide a weaker protection in Germany, France and the Netherlands. The prosecution of ORC's patents before the Japanese Patent Office had been stalled for many years, partly due to SLC's lack of funds. As such, while virtually all of the CD players were being manufactured in Japan, apart from those made by Philips, the greatest exposure of these Japanese manufacturers to ORC's claims of infringement lay in their export shipments to North America and Europe. Their shipments within Japan and to the rest of the world would only be exposed if ORC succeeded in getting the Japanese Patent Office to issue a key patent. (ORC never succeeded at having their Japanese patent issued.)

Some firms, including Sony, had gone to the expense of having an U.S. patent attorney present at all meetings with ORC, but Sony appeared the most ready to enter into substantive discussions. In this second round of discussions, Sony's team of six or seven engineers and executives presented ORC with a package of over 25 U.S. patents, all cited as Prior Art against the Russell patents.

Publishing the "Blue Book"

Adamson had been warned by both Horne and Orange to expect such a patent defense from Sony. He understood that if the techniques that Russell had claimed in his patents as inventions could be found in any reference that had been published or made public prior to the filing of his patents (i.e. Prior Art), Russell's patents would be found "invalid" and unenforceable. In spite of the warnings, Adamson was highly alarmed and wondered whether ORC was in for a challenge.

On returning to Toronto and on the suggestion of Orange, Adamson tasked him to collaborate with Russell in a review of documents that Sony had provided. Orange prepared a technical response for each reference and compiled these results in a bound booklet for distribution to each prospective licensee. Thus, the so-called "Blue Book" was born. It was thought that by making a general distribution of the "Blue Book," any duplication of effort from one set of technical discussions to another could be minimized, while hopefully speeding all talks toward the signing of licenses.

Adamson had no sense whether one or other of the Prior Art references might hold a "golden arrow" that would pierce the assumed validity for the Russell patents. He knew that a patent was generally assumed to be valid as issued, and therefore enforceable before the courts, but any unanswered Prior Art reference could quickly dispose of ORC's credibility and their licensing prospects.

Distractions Along the Way

Adamson had another more urgent reason to wish the licensing talks to progress quickly. As a research firm, ORC was funding its operations from its initial financing, gained through a tax credit program of the Canadian government. With an initial net investment of just Cdn$6.5 million and a monthly "burn-rate" approaching Cdn$250,000 for the research program, Adamson knew that ORC would likely run out of cash by the end of 1987, at the latest. (Luckily for ORC, the mid-1980s were a period of rampant inflation and ORC was earning 10 per cent, and 12 per cent per annum on its cash hoard.)

To add to the general instability of the situation, the Canadian government, SLC (the firm that had transferred the Russell technology to ORC) and the inventor himself, Russell, were now all objecting to the terms of the agreements that had brought the technology to Toronto. The Canadian government wished to rescind their tax credits and were demanding an immediate cash reimbursement while SLC and Jim Russell were both interpreting their respective agreements in their favor, to secure some respective right to ORC's potential licensing windfall from the compact disc industry.

Adamson remained of the view that all claimants were incorrect in their positions and vowed privately to resist their claims even into bankruptcy. Despite all of these distractions, he also knew that ORC had to maintain the appearance of complete stability, control and competence, in order to avoid "losing face" before their Japanese prospective licensees. Many hours of sleep were lost during this desperate period.

The Sony Protocol

By their second meeting with ORC, the Sony team were stating that they wished to deal directly with ORC and not through Far East Associates, as Sony reportedly had for their patent licence with the Dolby firm. They also indicated that if Sony agreed to a licence, they would want the right to act as ORC's exclusive agent to license all other manufacturers based in Japan, for their CD player production. As only Japanese manufacturers were then making CD players, apart from Philips in the Netherlands, this was difficult to agree to, given that ORC had resisted a similar proposal from Far East Associates.

Both the services of Horne and Far East Associates had been contracted on a fee-for-service basis, with ORC retaining all licensing rights to the Russell patents. Both could be terminated without cause in the normal course of business. As consultants, their services were required only as long as the client thought they were adding value. Far East Associates had indicated a desire to assume a full agency role on behalf of ORC with the full authority to license ORC's patents on behalf of ORC, but Adamson had resisted this overture, convinced that ORC would be better served by dealing with each manufacturer directly.

Now Sony was asking ORC to terminate Far East Associates and to make presentations directly to Japanese manufacturers, in anticipation of Sony agreeing to a patent licence. This licence, however, would only apply to CD players, with Sony assuming the role of exclusive agent, possibly for all of Asia. Adamson accepted this protocol with Sony, but he had to trust that Sony was in earnest in their desire to be the exclusive agent and not just leading ORC toward a dead end.

Further, as with Far East Associates, he had no idea how ORC was to monitor the work and licensing progress of an exclusive agent based in the Far East, directly licensing Asian manufacturers. How was one to know when a licence signed and royalties collected, if not by the exclusive agent? In any case, as co-licencer with Philips of the CD technology, Sony's support was clearly paramount to ORC.

So a pattern developed. Every four to eight weeks, Adamson and Orange traveled to Tokyo, Osaka and other cities in Japan to hold patent infringement and licensing discussions with the major Japanese consumer electronics firms such as Matsushita (Panasonic), Toshiba, Hitachi, Sanyo, Pioneer, Sharp and particularly Sony.

With each visit, new Prior Art references were put forward by one or other of the manufacturers, and ORC, in the person of Orange, would respond "on the fly" if an obvious separation from the art could be discerned. If not, ORC would fax a response to all participants upon returning to Toronto.

As the months passed, it was becoming increasingly clear to all that the Russell patents as presented by the ORC team, could withstand the invalidity challenges from the Prior Art. Equally important, the compact disc technical standard that ensured manufactured compatibility across all compliant CD products included techniques claimed in the Russell patents. To comply with this CD standard was to infringe the Russell patents! In short it appeared that the Russell patents were valid and infringed by all CD products!

To balance this rosy picture, however, it was equally clear that, month by month, ORC's cash was disappearing into its research program. The company had lost any of the financial strength with which to mount a credible court challenge against even one of the established manufacturers: Sony, Philips or any of the twenty other firms of similar bulk.

The End Game?

Finally in the fall of 1987, Adamson realized that neither Sony nor any other firm was likely to accept a license without more pressure being applied and more pressure than ORC could bring to the negotiating table. With nothing left to lose, Adamson flew to Tokyo in mid-January 1988, for a final meeting with Sony Corporation. No other firm was as advanced in discussions with ORC as Sony and Adamson reasoned that Sony had become fairly certain of the profit potential as ORC's master licensee for Japan. Sony would also have something to lose if the talks with ORC failed.

To add to this pressure, he could advise Sony that ORC was close to bankruptcy and, if ORC went into bankruptcy, the Russell patents would revert to their former owner, SLC, a firm that, in his direct experience, proved to be very litigious. The Sony team requested a lunch break.

Over lunch Josh Nakamura asked Adamson whether he would continue to be involved with the Russell patent licensing if ORC went bankrupt. Adamson replied that while his ownership of the patents would be lost, he could no doubt strike a deal with SLC such that the licensing program would not "skip a beat." However the program would then be well financed by a very litigious American backer and, under the circumstances, Adamson would have little interest in favoring Sony in any way. Given his rocky relations with SLC, Adamson painted a most optimistic view of his future.

Returning to the Sony offices after lunch, the Sony team requested a further break and Adamson and Cooper sat quietly for an hour and a half in the meeting room at the Sony corporate head offices in Kita-Shinagawa; Adamson pondering his fate.

ORC's First License

Back in the meeting, Nakamura advised that Sony would be ready to sign a license with ORC. The license, however, would only cover CD players, not compact disc media. Further, ORC had to significantly reduced their royalty demands, accept Sony as the exclusive agent with full authority to license all CD player manufacturers based in Asia and pay Sony an administrative fee for their exclusive agency representation out of the royalties to be received. The proposal also required that ORC transfer the right to sue Asian CD player manufacturers for patent infringement to Sony as their exclusive agent. Adamson felt he had no choice but to accept this proposal if he wished to maintain his control of the Russell patents.

It was then agreed that the outline of the license and agency agreements be developed that very afternoon with a final negotiation of royalty rates to occur by telephone in the following week. Cooper took on the task of drafting the required changes to ORC's standard patent license agreement. Negotiations were then completed by telephone the following week and the Sony CD player agreement was signed in early February 1988.

From this shaky last-minute effort, Adamson had managed to retain his full ownership of the Russell patents through ORC. By licensing Sony, ORC now had a royalty cash flow with which to maintain the research program underway in Toronto, as well as the resources to fend off the law suits from the Government of Canada and SLC. For the first time in its existence, ORC was cash flow positive and in that sense, time was now on ORC's side; however, when measured against industry norms, the license with Sony cost ORC plenty. Nakamura and the Sony team had done their job well.

Apart from Sony's hard bargain, they were always gracious but now as business partners, Nakamura and Sony's negotiating team seemed to relish this role even more.

Adamson came to look forward to an invitation to dine at one restaurant in particular. High above Akasaka in central Tokyo, directly overlooking the Diet, Japan's national parliament, there was a restaurant laid out in a series of private dining rooms, each in a unique Western décor of a particular color and at least one Monet or similar Old Master painting dominating the room. Their chefs were trained at the Paul Bocuse culinary school in France and the wine list read like a vintners' award booklet.

Adamson also came to realize that the superb ambiance and staff service of the Hotel Okura was very habit-forming and in spite of the expense, he opted to stay there whenever he was in Tokyo. Horne had been right. Being invited to lunch or dinner at the Hotel Okura, was also a great treat for ORC's licensing prospects and other business associates in Tokyo.

Onward

Among the more difficult challenges that ORC faced in mounting the licensing program was the determination of the size of the infringing production unit volumes and sales revenues. A prospective licensee is not about to divulge this data, as it would impair their negotiating position and possibly increase their chances of being sued before one of their competitors. Nevertheless in the case of CD media, it was pretty obvious that the five sisters of sound; Philips (Deutsche Grammophon), Sony (Columbia), Time-Warner (Warner), EMI (London and Angel) and

Bertelsmann (RCA) were the largest manufacturers of CD media. After Philips and Sony, Time-Warner was likely to be the largest compact disc maker in the United States.

Government agencies and industry trade associations publish trade statistics, but this data is usually on an industry-wide basis (not by company) and for broad product categories, not for individual products, such as a CD player. Beyond these sources, there are industry consultants of varying usefulness and reliability. Nevertheless the licenser must develop estimates of the production and sales volumes for the infringing product by manufacturer and for each year from the start of the infringement to the expiry of the patent or the end of the infringement, whichever comes first.

Without such numbers it is not possible to decide which companies are the more lucrative licensing prospects and more importantly whether a licensing program is even feasible. Without this data the licenser cannot know which infringer to sue or in which jurisdiction to bring the suit, to ensure the most favorable cost-benefit ratio for such an action.

In the ensuing 12 months, Sony sub-licensed over 50 per cent of the remaining Japanese production for CD players and ORC began to develop a substantial "war-chest." Still unresolved were ORC's equivalent infringement claims against the manufacturers of the discs, the compact disc media. Sony had refused to include this item in the initial license as they advised that they needed more time to study the matter. They also stated the view that the Russell patents were less likely to be infringed by the discs.

In the summer of 1988, however, ORC succeeded in licensing the Philips Corporation for both CD players and media and with this success, somewhat confirming Sony's earlier license commitment, Sony agreed to sign a license for CD media in November 1988. By the end of 1988, ORC had a cash position well in excess of US$10 million and the licensing program was on a roll.

The next largest manufacturer of CD media in the United States, by production volume, after American subsidiaries of Sony and Philips-Dupont, was known to be WEA Manufacturing, a subsidiary of Time Warner Inc. Commencing in 1987, Adamson held several discussions, by mail, telephone and face-to-face meetings, with Time Warner's in-house counsel. These discussions lead nowhere however as Time Warner's often-repeated view was the standard "non-infringement and invalid patents" position of an alleged infringer.

Enforcing ORC's Patent Rights

In early 1990, ORC had retained Davis Hoxie Faithfull & Hapgood, a patent law firm. just next door to Time Warner's corporate head office in the Rockefeller Centre in New York City. Charles Bradley, a senior patent litigating attorney with Davis Hoxie had been recommended to Adamson on a chance encounter, while in Tokyo, with an American attorney who had the misfortune of opposing Bradley in a previous patent case. Bradley and Lawrence Goodwin, his partner, were engaged to pursue ORC's interests with the respect to the alleged infringement by WEA

Manufacturing, a subsidiary of Time Warner Inc. Goodwin became the "lead" attorney on the ORC file with Bradley providing oversight, senior counsel and strategic advice to Goodwin.

On ORC's behalf, the Davis Hoxie firm filed a patent infringement complaint against WEA Manufacturing in the Federal District Court in Wilmington, Delaware, in June 1990. Like many other major American corporations, Time Warner and its subsidiary, WEA Manufacturing, were incorporated in the State of Delaware.

Not the least of Adamson's concerns in deciding to sue Time Warner in early 1991, was a looming patent expiry date in July 1992, for a U.S. patent, the key to ORC's infringement claims against CD media manufacturers.

The greatest threat that a patent-holder has against a recalcitrant infringer is a court injunction to stop the infringer's production lines. By 1991, this threat was all but lost to ORC as the July 1992 expiry date of ORC's key U.S. patent was likely to pass before any court could rule on the matter.

Without the threat of a court order to stop an infringing production, the patent-holder's leverage is reduced to the probability of a favorable court award being considerably more arduous for the infringer than the royalty payable if a license had been accepted. Even this leverage is diminished by the reality that, at any time prior to an appeal court ruling on a lower court award, the infringer is free to negotiate a settlement with the licenser, even well past a court decision which declares them to be infringing. The infringer can also hope that the patent-holder will capitulate before the end of a full trial, for lack of sufficient funds.

These considerations were very much on Adamson's mind in March 1992 as he drafted a letter (see Exhibit 1) to be sent directly to Time Warner's in-house counsel with a copy to Goodwin. Goodwin had advised against sending the letter, given that ORC had filed their patent infringement suit against Time Warner almost two years earlier, however, Adamson felt certain that Time Warner should be willing to settle for the modest sum of US$3 million, just to avoid the patent infringement trial now scheduled for June 1992, with all of its costs and disruption. Of no surprise to Goodwin, Time Warner politely declined ORC's settlement proposal, perhaps thinking that the letter was a clear indication that ORC was about to capitulate, if they had not already, with their modest US$3 million settlement offer.

Will They Like Us in Wilmington?

Now faced with the certainty of a trial in the United States, Adamson had to deal with a personal overriding concern. Could an American jury be prejudiced against a Canadian company such as ORC? Goodwin had told him not to worry about it, but Adamson was concerned that Goodwin simply did not know.

Too embarrassed to advise Goodwin of his continuing concern with a potential American prejudice toward a Canadian company, Adamson hired the New York office of Goldfarb Consultants, a Canadian market survey firm. Their assignment was to conduct an opinion survey on attitudes, toward Canadian companies, of people drawn from the "jury-pool" population around Wilmington, Delaware. The Goldfarb team suggested that they conduct this survey with focus group interviews based on a set of questions pre-cleared by ORC.

In April 1992, Adamson traveled to Wilmington to witness the interviews firsthand by watching the proceedings on a video monitor in an adjacent room. There were three sessions comprising a total of 35 participants, who gave up a part of their evening for the survey in return for dinner and a modest stipend.

The interviews were conducted in two parts. The first part was designed to solicit an unprompted reference to Canada, in its role as a trading partner of the United States. The second part was designed to solicit directly any opinions that they may hold toward Canadian companies and then specifically a Canadian company's right to protect their American rights by suing an American company in Delaware.

The survey was of great benefit to Adamson as it quickly became clear that he should not be concerned about an American prejudice toward Canadian companies. If a prejudice did exist, it could only be positive because the survey, in every focus group, turned into a love-fest for Canada and Canadians.

Each focus group became frustrated with the first part of the survey. In trying to find the trading partner that they might be concerned about, Canada was never mentioned, even in their desperate attempts to finally yell out the "correct answer." This desperation was then followed by groans when Canada was finally noted by the session moderator at the beginning of the second part of the survey. Very few of those surveyed knew that Canada was indeed the largest trading partner of the United States.

With Canada now on the table and not hiding as in a trick question, many positive views were openly expressed. In fact more than a few had vacationed in Canada, some had close Canadian relatives and one woman was so effusive as to simply say, "I love Canadians," quickly adding that she and her husband vacationed regularly in the Montreal area.

A little sheepishly, Adamson returned to Toronto and phoned Goodwin to advise him that "the ball was now in his court" and that ORC would see the Time Warner case through to appeal, if necessary. He did not mention the survey.

The Rubber Meets the Road

Lead by Goodwin, the Davis Hoxie team was comprised of one other full-time attorney, Robert Cote, and a support staff of three, all of whom stayed in Wilmington for the duration of the trial (with some weekends at home in New York). This Delaware team worked from the offices of a Wilmington law firm. This law firm in turn provided its own legal and support staff to ORC's team on an as-required basis. At Davis Hoxie in New York, at least one additional full-time attorney, Peter Bucci, and various other support staff were employed in research and document preparation for the duration of the trial. This entire trial effort was monitored and when appropriate, coached by Charles Bradley.

The trial began in the last days of May 1992, and it was to run for five and one-half weeks. Throughout the trial period, the Davis Hoxie team worked a daily double shift, one in courtroom and then a second in their law offices and hotel rooms, debriefing the day's events and preparing for the next day's court sessions. This preparation included a review of salient facts, prior affidavits, deposition testimony and then general court procedures with each individual witness, in preparation for the court appearance.

It also included a daily review of defendant witness testimony for discrepancies. The review of the court plan for the following day might include witness questioning, preparing motions that pulled together now-important facts and revising presentation materials imperiled by the day's events.

Adamson had decided to remain in Wilmington and attend every court session, given the importance of its outcome for ORC. Having watched the jury selection a few days before, he was highly stressed on the morning of the first day of the trial. He took some comfort in the size and evident competence of the Davis Hoxie team until the Time Warner team appeared.

Either by chance or design, 20 minutes prior to the official court start-time, opposing attorneys began to file into the courtroom. First they filled to overflowing the small defendant's bench in front of the commons rail, and then gradually they occupied the entire commons observer section on the defendant side of the courtroom, spacing themselves comfortably. Adamson sat as a lone observer for ORC directly behind the Davis Hoxie team of five on the plaintiff's side until three more groups of attorneys whom he had never met, filed in to sit behind him, also on the plaintiff's side.

Possibly the entire recording industry, including a few Japanese firms with still unlicensed CD plants in the United States, had sent attorneys, some 30 in all, to observe the start of the trial. The contrast between the sizes of the defendant and plaintiff legal teams was so evident that, prior to the jury entrance, lead counsel for Time Warner told the attorneys behind him to scatter into the plaintiff's observer benches.

Apparently unfazed by the obvious imbalance, a few minutes later, Goodwin stood up to address judge, jury and courtroom on behalf of ORC in a calm, humble but masterful tone. He was to continue as he had started through five and one-half weeks of trial, through surprise, setback, equipment failure, client panic and one or two staff confusions.

ORC's case was further strengthened by the skill of a superb expert witness, Leonard Laub. Laub was responsible for explaining ORC's highly technical infringement case, to a jury with no technical training except for one retired man with an engineering degree dating back to the 1930s. This was accomplished with Laub's testimony guided by questioning from Goodwin and with the use of circuit diagram blow-ups and point summaries on white three feet by five feet storyboards. Adamson was satisfied that if there were a chance that the jury could come to understand ORC's case, it would be solely through the ample teaching skills of Goodwin and Laub.

ORC asked the court and jury for an award in lieu of royalty of six cents per disc against Time Warner and their American subsidiaries and a tripling of that award in punitive damages for willful infringement. The decision to ask for six cents per disc was partly based on ORC's initial licensing request of three cents per disc. Legally, licensers are able to change their royalty demands at any point in a negotiation, before or after the filing of a suit, just as infringers are free to agree to previously unacceptable terms.

(In normal licensing practice, it is simply wise to give active infringers, some substantial incentive to sign a license prior to the filing of a suit. This is usually accomplished by increasing the royalty rate by some multiple of the original, say two, three, five or even 10 times. The practical upper limit of a royalty rate is, of course, at that point where the manufacturer can make little profit after paying the royalty, as it is unlikely that any judge or jury would endorse a more onerous royalty request.)

Hearing Goodwin make this request for six cents per disc in open court was a thrilling moment early in the trial. Weeks later the Time Warner attorney was obliged to produce for the court, the unit volumes of their subsidiary's infringing production of compact discs. Their infringement for the period covering the start of production in 1986 through July 1992, the month of the expiry of ORC's patent, totalled over 450 million discs and, at six cents per disc, represented a potential court award for ORC of over US$27 million. The addition of pre-judgment interest and a possible tripling of those damages were more than Adamson could fathom or entertain.

In spite of the good efforts of the Davis Hoxie team with Laub and several other strong witnesses, including Russell, the inventor, and the prospect of an enormous court award, all was not well. After the court appearance by the Philips attorney, Adamson believed that ORC's decision to sue Time Warner might have been taken too lightly.

Goodwin had warned that corporate litigation in the United States was a very expensive enterprise. It was also very demanding of management time, given the need to find, assemble and organize relevant business records, to educate the attorneys in the minutiae of events that usually had happened long ago and to attend court hearings as observers and witnesses. He had also noted that, in the normal course of a robust cross-examination, the combatants and their witnesses could expect personal insults and general verbal abuse. Adamson observed somewhat ruefully that Goodwin had been correct on all counts.

Preliminary motions, production and review of plaintiff and defendant business records and correspondence files, witness depositions, private investigators and trial preparations for the attorneys, company personnel and expert witnesses had already consumed close to US$750,000 of ORC's hard won royalties all before the actual trial had begun. Adamson had budgeted an additional US$1.5 million for fees and expenses to be incurred from the trial itself; however, after the first three weeks of the trial, Adamson saw no end in sight to the trial or its expense.

As was its right as the plaintiff, ORC had chosen to have its case against Time Warner heard before a jury. Even this decision seemed to backfire as it was clear that the jury was putting a good deal of attention and apparent credence into what the defendant's attorneys had to say. The Time Warner litigating team had mounted a very credible defense. They seemed to cloud the technical issues of patent validity and product infringement as these related to the Russell patent claims and the compact disc technology, so that even Adamson found himself confused with ORC's claims from time to time. He had little hope left that the jury would be able to sort through the haze.

With this technical complexity and possible jury confusion, Adamson worried that the direct and damning statements of the Philips attorney toward the Russell patents and ORC's infringement claims could be disastrous for ORC, as these arguments gave the jury, a reasonable and easy "out," from all the confusing technical jargon. Perhaps he was simply someone who knew better about these matters than they could ever hope to know.

Adamson also reflected on the fact that he had been forced to curtail the on-going licensing program for the other CD manufacturers. He had been concerned that some event within ORC's licensing program, such as an agreement with a royalty rate for CD discs below the six cents per disc demanded in the court case, might affect the outcome of the case; however this concern was made mute by the simple fact that the other CD manufacturers had displayed little interest in signing a license with ORC as long as a major record company such as Time Warner was challenging ORC's infringement claims in court.

Should the court case result in anything less than a complete endorsement of ORC's infringement claims, ORC's entire licensing program could collapse including the all important quarterly payments from Sony. The CD player license with Sony may have been a "done deal." As a matter of practicality, Adamson wondered whether ORC would be prudent to take Sony to court, should Sony simply stop paying royalties to ORC after a jury verdict had cleared Time Warner of ORC's patent infringement claims.

Over the course of the six years from 1986 to 1992, Adamson had been drawn away from ORC's research effort and future prospects and ever deeper into patent licensing and then this litigation struggle. As he had testified in the Time Warner trial, "there seems little point in investing in the creation and development of new intellectual property rights if major industrial firms are prepared to ignore and infringe existing patent rights that you already own." Playing somewhat to the jury, he knew that he had purposefully overstated his predicament but the basic truth of his simple observation resonated in the momentary silence of the court that day.

Adamson had made the very difficult decision early in 1991, to temporarily shelve ORC's research program and to reduce the Company's technology development team to a skeleton staff of five team leaders. This move had been made for reasons other than the need to focus the Company's resources on the Time Warner litigation. Nonetheless as he sat in that Delaware courtroom, watching the door close after the hasty exit of the Philips attorney, Adamson felt that he had bet ORC's entire future on the outcome of the court case against Time Warner.

Exhibit 1   draft letter to time warner's in-house counsel

CONFIRMATION ONLY!

FACSIMILE MESSAGE OF TWO PAGES TO: 1 (212) 522-1252

March 4, 1992

WITHOUT PREJUDICE

Dear

RE: ORC vs Time Warner Inc.

Over the past week, we have prepared estimates on the costs and probable outcome of this case. We share this information with you now, in the hope of developing a common understanding from which a mutually satisfactory settlement might result. Our New York counsel is aware of this communication but, the views expressed here may not necessarily coincide with theirs.

Assuming that your costs to date equal ours, Time Warner has spent US$1,000,000. in out-of-pocket expenses alone,. Assuming that we will each spend another US$1,000,000. to the end of trial and then another US$200,000. on an appeal, we will each have spent another US$1,200,000. for a total of US$2,200,000 on this case. Give or take a few $100,000., these costs have a 100% probability of being incurred, if we proceed.

As to the outcome, it is our view that ORC has a significantly stronger case, as Justice Farnan's recent rulings might suggest. Further, we have substantial confidence in our representation. Nevertheless, we accept that the trial process is highly unpredictable. Therefore, we would attach a conservative estimate of perhaps 50% to the probability of ORC winning at both, trial and appeal.

Our licensing program had been based on the royalty rate of US$0.015 per disk and against the estimated and actual production totals for WEA and Allied of 400 million disks, a royalty amount of US$6,000,000. can be estimated. The size of award by the court could vary up or down from this royalty estimate but, it is our view that US$6,000,000 is a good average to assume of all possible court awards. If we assume a 50% probability that ORC will win, then it follows that there is a 50% probability that Time Warner will be required to pay the average award of US$6,000,000.

.../...

OPTICAL RECORDING CORPORATION

141 JOHN STREET, TORONTO, CANADA M5V 2E4 · TELEPHONE (416) 596-6862 · FAX (416) 596-0452

OPTICAL RECORDING CORPORATION

- 2 -

To summarize, at this point in time, Time Warner has a 50% probability of paying out $6,000,000 in award and a 100% probability of paying $1,200,000 in continuing litigation costs, if we proceed.

We believe that a final attempt at settlement is in the interest of both companies at this time. Therefore, we now propose a patent license to Time Warner for their manufacture of Compact Disc in the United States, for $3,000,000.; that is, for 50% of the $6,000,000. which we contend that Time Warner has at least a 50% probability of incurring as a court award.

This offer will remain open until 5:00pm, Friday, March 6, 1992, after which, this and all previous offers will be withdrawn.

We would appreciate your comments on the logic presented here, particularly if you have a significantly divergent view on any point. Please feel free to call me directly if you wish to discuss any point in this letter.

Yours very truly,

G. John Adamson
President

GJA/gj
Source: Company files.

Footnotes

[1] Due to a series of commercial lawsuits lasting 10 years with Russell's former employer, the author prefers to omit any real name reference to this company that had been a party to the technology transfer agreements with ORC. It is referred to here as "SLC." In all other references herein to persons, places or businesses, the actual names are used.

SELKIRK GROUP IN ASIA

From their modern brick building in Victoria, Australia it seemed a long way from the economic crisis that had engulfed Asia in the past 18 months. At one side of the board table sat Bernie Segrave, the Managing Director of the Selkirk Group of Companies and the person who had taken direct charge of the group's export marketing strategy across Asia. On the other side, and with a view of the large brick chimney that announced Selkirk Brick's presence in the local community, sat Peter Blackburn, Export Manager and the person being groomed to progressively take over the exporting responsibilities. Both were looking at the export performance graphs of the group over the past five years as background preparation for their forthcoming trip.

Ahead of them (in late October 1998) was an overseas tour to meet their existing network of agents and potential customers in Singapore, Thailand, Hong Kong and Taiwan. Their largest market, Japan, was not included in this tour. The reasons for the tour were quite straightforward in Segrave's mind:

> We have made a strategic decision to continue developing and building relationships in Asia in these bad times. We went to Japan earlier this year. In this downturn, we are very lucky we have good agents in Japan. If Japan goes, we don't want to think about it — but I guess the rest of the world goes as well.

> Asia is very important in the long term because we continue to develop products of excellent technical quality which are appreciated by Asians. It's very important to us in terms of sales and output. Within five years we expect to have either a subsidiary or a selling arm in an Asian destination.

Richard Ivey School of Business
The University of Western Ontario

Lambros Karavis prepared this case under the supervision of Professor Paul Beamish solely to provide material for class discussion. The authors do not intend to illustrate either effective or ineffective handling of a managerial situation. The authors may have disguised certain names and other identifying information to protect confidentiality. Ivey Management Services prohibits any form of reproduction, storage or transmittal without its written permission. This material is not covered under authorization from CanCopy or any reproduction rights organization. *Copyright © 1999, Ivey Management Services*

At issue was how to continue developing their business in Asia. Both Segrave and Blackburn were wondering about the business opportunities they would uncover and whether it was time to review their export strategy and organisation for the region.

Selkirk Brick — A Family Business for over 100 Years

Selkirk Brick was established in 1883 when the gold rush in colonial Victoria brought together fortune seekers and entrepreneurs from across the world. Chinese, Scots, Irish and even Californians were among the immigrants who saw the opportunity to prosper in the colony. Among them was Robert Selkirk, a Scottish stonemason, who sought to capitalise on the building boom accompanying the wealth generated from gold and wool. He started making bricks using a local clay deposit in Allendale but moved to nearby Ballarat in 1900 where suitable clay deposits had been identified on ten hectares of land in Howitt Street, the present-day site of the works and head office.

Though clay bricks and pavers were often seen as a low-tech product, there was, in fact, considerable technical expertise required to produce a high quality product. Apart from selecting the right clays as the raw material for firing into bricks and pavers, a number of other factors needed to be managed carefully. The moisture content in the clay was critical to both moulding and firing outcomes achieved. Various oxides and other additives were used to achieve specific colors and finishes. Kiln temperature, length of time in the kiln and airflows also needed to be carefully controlled to achieve consistency in strength and color characteristics.

The high quality of Australian clay bricks and pavers has led to their extensive use as a building material for external cladding. Many houses had been traditionally built with double brick walls, particularly in the more temperate climate zones in Australia ranging from New South Wales, through Victoria, South Australia and Tasmania (refer to Exhibit 1 for geographic locations in Australia). In recent years, the use of brick had declined as brick veneer, steel frames, timber, concrete and even mud-brick homes gained popularity with the home buyer. Increasingly, clay bricks and pavers were being used as architectural features rather than simply as a construction material.

From a study of the company's history (see Appendix 1), Selkirk Brick could be characterised as a company which was managed in a financially conservative manner but which embraced (world-class at the time) technological innovation to maintain technical superiority and cost efficiency in the marketplace. It was a company which had resisted buyouts and generational fragmentation in the process.

The shareholders were well aware that by the time a family company reached the fifth generation, it was unlikely to accommodate the needs of all who might expect to work there. Robert Selkirk, who became Chairman in 1985 and was in charge of marketing, commented on the roles of the working shareholders:

It's something that you have to work at every day of your life. There are conflicts; we all see things differently. The challenge is to try to put personal and family disagreements to one side when in the office.

Jim Selkirk, Finance Director since 1986, suggested a few basic requirements for a family company: no gamblers, squanderers or alcoholics; no tendency to over-borrow or be over-acquisitive; be prepared to spend most of your time with the company; and no expensive or messy divorces.

Overall, the Selkirk family believed their success stemmed from a number of features: a mix of family and non-family directors, conservative finance, market leadership through technology, maintaining a good reputation in the market and a belief that nothing happens until you make a sale. They saw themselves as adaptable, able to make decisions quickly, having a close rapport with repeat customers, and constantly examining their strategies to produce long-term success.

The Selkirk Group — Diversification in the 1980s and 1990s

Between 1982 and 1992, the company made three major acquisitions, none of which were cheap but all of which were easily absorbed into the balance sheet:

- Phillips Bricks and Pottery Pty Ltd was acquired in 1982. This Bendigo-based company had a strong market-presence in north-western Victoria and was converted from the traditional extruded to the higher-priced pressed brick production in 1986. (Segrave became Managing Director of Phillips in 1983).
- In 1987, Selkirk purchased Hick Timbers in Altona (a suburb of Melbourne) in a move that took it outside bricks but still serving the needs of the building industry. Hick was a specialised supplier of structural timber importing softwoods from the USA, Canada, New Zealand and Finland and supplying engineered timber beams.
- Shepparton Bricks and Pavers, one of Victoria's largest concrete building and landscaping products manufacturers was acquired in 1992. While Selkirk had been supplying clay pavers since 1983, this acquisition took the company into the less expensive concrete paver business in a booming market for pavers.

At a time when Australian entrepreneurs like (the subsequently convicted) Alan Bond and (the fugitive) Christopher Skase had created conglomerates through leveraged acquisitions, Selkirk Brick had been tempted to the brink of over-expansion, according to Jim Selkirk, but was saved at the eleventh hour by a bidder with deeper pockets. To date, its diversification had been within the confines of its perceived area of expertise, the building industry. Each of the acquisitions was valuable for adding manufacturing capacity and for providing additional sales outlets. Each office and outlet sold the complete range of Selkirk products.

Hick Timbers was closed down in 1997 though the company name was retained. Margins in the timber business were falling for players and the company was being outmuscled in the marketplace by large integrated timber and hardware groups such as Bunnings (which had established a series of home/trade superstores across the Melbourne metropolitan area). The Board of Selkirk had taken a common-sense but courageous strategic decision to quit while they were ahead.

While diversifying through acquisition, Selkirk Brick also embarked on a three-stage, A$5 million program of modernisation between 1982 and 1986 which resulted in world-class product quality outcomes. This investment program involved modernising the processes for extrusion and material preparation in the first stage, improving the productivity and energy efficiency of the drying tunnel in the second stage, and replacing the 25-year-old tunnel kiln with an energy-efficient one in the final stage.

By 1988, pavers had come to represent 20 per cent of the company's production volume and Selkirk Brick was recognised as the only brick company supplying products compliant with Australian Products Standard AS1225. While most of the product sales were in Victoria, the sales region was progressively being extended into the South Australian and New South Wales marketplace where product quality and service were being used to overcome price and transport barriers to competition. Selkirk was reputed to have a 15 per cent share in the Victorian clay building products market and was the largest privately owned brick company in Australia.

Selkirk Brick survived the severe economic recession that hit Victoria in the early 1990s by halving production at one stage and closing one plant for ten months in 1991. By late 1993, utilisation had recovered to 75 per cent and by 1998 the plants were operating again at full capacity. Selkirk Brick acquired Stratblox, a manufacturer of quality concrete building products located in the Gippsland region of Victoria in 1998. This acquisition meant that Selkirk had geographically encircled the Melbourne metropolitan area through a series of country acquisitions and had established itself as the dominant player in rural Victoria.

The capacity of the Selkirk Group of Companies exceeded 70 million bricks and pavers prior to that acquisition. Production capacity at Bendigo was 10 million units (bricks and pavers) per annum while Shepparton capacity was 23,000 tonnes per annum. The Gippsland acquisition added 27,000 tonnes per annum of capacity. Total Victorian sales were in the range of A$25 million and A$30 million per annum (refer to Exhibit 2 for external estimates of group revenue). The company employed 170 people, 100 people at the Ballarat head-office and operations alone. With the acquisition of Stratblox, Selkirk Brick could no longer be seen as a specialist clay brick and paver company (refer to Appendix 2 for additional information on the Australian Brick and Paver Industry) but as a more broadly diversified company in the clay and concrete brick and paver business.

Company documents indicate that each of the acquisitions was a wholly owned subsidiary of Selkirk Brick Pty Ltd but they were managed autonomously, each with its own Board of Management and Board of Directors. In 1998, Robert Selkirk was Non-Executive Chairman of the Board, Bernie Segrave was the Managing Director, Jim Selkirk was the Finance Director, and

Iain Selkirk was the Works Director. In 1994, Jamie Selkirk (son of the Chairman) became the first of the fifth-generation to join the family company.

Asia — a Selkirk Success Story of the 1990s

The export trading activities of Selkirk Brick began in earnest in 1992 when Robert Selkirk attended a Global Business Opportunities Convention in Osaka, Japan. A Japanese company had been looking at securing a supply of sandstone from Australia and had seen Selkirk pavers extensively used at Bond University in Queensland. (A major Japanese construction and development company was a joint-venture partner in the university at the time). Selkirk pavers had been selected for their ability to withstand the high traffic and high humidity requirements of Australia's first private university in 1988. Following a visit of Japanese personnel to the plant in Ballarat, a trading alliance was formed and Selkirk began to export to Japan. As Robert Selkirk reminded people within the company, not everybody had approved of the move at the time:

> Six years ago, we wouldn't have believed where we are now. It was all done on an exploratory "try it and see" basis. We had (Prime Minister) Paul Keating telling us that Australian companies had to be in Asia. There was considerable criticism at the time on the expense and management attention being directed to the export efforts. We were advised that we had to be patient. Then we got the first order within twelve months and it was done on a handshake.

Total exports had grown strongly from the first export order to Japan of 49,000 paving units (approximately six containers) in 1992. Exports to all destinations increased by 735 per cent in 1993, followed by a 69 per cent increase in 1994 and a 150 per cent increase in 1995. Flat sales in 1996 and 1997 were followed by a massive increase in 1998 to approximately four million units. While initial sales were to Japan, by 1998 Selkirk Brick was exporting pavers and some bricks across Asia to countries such as Hong Kong ('94) and Taiwan ('96) as well as Singapore, Indonesia, New Zealand and Malaysia. Japan was the largest export destination but healthy sales were beginning to be experienced in Taiwan where product quality and service were considered to be key selling features.

By 1998, Asian exports had become a small but increasingly important part of Selkirk Brick's business. Exports accounted for just under 10 per cent of total sales volume (slightly higher in terms of sales value) in the 1997/98 financial year and that figure was expected to increase. Well over 25 per cent of paver manufacturing volume was now being exported. The clay paver market had been facing low growth and market share losses in the highly competitive Australian market to cheaper pavers made from concrete and other composite materials. Exports were an important sales outlet for the company.

Selkirk had a policy of appointing non-exclusive distributor agents in the marketplace and currently had 18 distributors across Asia: five in Japan, four in Hong Kong, three in Taiwan, two in Singapore, and one each in Malaysia, Indonesia, Thailand and New Zealand. Letters from overseas parties interested in purchasing directly and offering their local services were inevitably referred back to the nearest agent. Product was usually sold C.I.F. (Cost, Insurance and Freight to Destination Port). Prices ex-factory and loaded into containers were generally 70 per cent of the C.I.F. price. Anecdotal data suggested that a unit price of A$0.47 F.O.B. (Free on Board at Shipping Port) for shipped products could be sold for as high as A$2.00 per unit in Japan to end-users (refer to Exhibit 3 for Export Pricing Nomenclature and Value-Added). The use of agents did mean, however, that there was a lack of information on who was the ultimate user of products and what margins were being charged locally.

Information on the clay brick and paver market across Asia was otherwise limited and generally anecdotal in nature. Housing construction materials varied considerably across the region and clay bricks were not traditionally used. Local brick manufacturers in countries such as Malaysia ran "cottage-industry" facilities using kilns with inadequate temperature controls and with a poor understanding of quality control mechanisms. Brick walls were often rendered and thus considered a "filler" material which did not require high quality standards. Clay brick and pavers were being increasingly seen in large "upper middle class" housing estates across the region where developers were taking the lead in developing suburban housing and shopping communities.

Exports to the region came from a number of countries, with Canada, the United States, the United Kingdom, South Africa and Australia mentioned frequently. Export data often lumped clay bricks and pavers with other construction materials such as timber and composite materials. The Australian data on exports were derived from shipping data collected at ports of origin but some ports used different classification methods, making accurate information difficult to ascertain. Australian brick and paver products were reputed to have more durability, better water repelling capability and more vibrant color attributes than the cheaper product sourced from local or imported Asian producers.

Sales Distribution Agreement in Japan

Exports to Japan had grown steadily from 900,000 units in 1995/96 to 1.8 million units in 1996/97 and 3.5 million units in 1997/98. One reason for the growth was a five-year distribution agreement that had been signed in 1997 with a leading Japanese building products company and that agreement was expected to triple current export figures within two years. Segrave commented on his experiences in doing business with their Japanese agents:

> We find the Japanese are very tough negotiators — but also very fair. We are thrilled they fully appreciate the technical qualities of our products. So often here in Australia, aesthetic requirements dominate a specifier's consideration. Mind you, we have been developing a clay brick with smaller width dimensions and new colors to suit the Japanese market (in conjunction with the Stonehenge Group, a major builder in urban Victoria.) Our wide variety of pavers and special shapes also meets their needs.

> Understand that the Japanese do not tolerate mediocrity which means you must send your most senior people to negotiate with them. In 1992 we had employed a retired General Manager of a large

clay brick and paver company in Western Australia who had the requisite seniority, technical knowledge and excellent sales skills to become our first Export Manager.

One must also be courteous, pleasant and respectful with the Japanese and become practised in Nemawashi: the art of building relationships and personal trust over time. Our success can be measured by the fact that the 1997 distributor agreement had everybody from the Managing Director down to the most senior functional managers attending the Agreement Signing ceremony. What may look like a simple commercial arrangement to us was a symbol of strategic intent and business partnering in their eyes.

While exact details of the 1997 Sales License Agreement were confidential, certain aspects of the Agreement have been disclosed (refer to Appendix 3).

Selkirk retained the brand and trademark for its range of products in Japan, prohibited the transfer of distribution rights to other companies without its approval, had the ability to terminate the agreement with 90 days' notice and ensured any arbitration was done through "officially approved" channels. The term of the agreement was for five years and required 90 days' written notice on either side to terminate. Advertising and sales promotions in Japan were at the expense of the agent.

The Japanese agent had secured a number of conditions in the agreement as well. No new agents were to be appointed without their prior agreement. The primary language of the agreement was English but it was to be interpreted under Japanese commercial law. The bricks and pavers were to carry a Japanese logo and meet the requirements of the Japanese Industrial Standard but to be labelled as "Made in Australia". All products were to be inspected and certified by Selkirk Brick as meeting the product and shipping standards specified in the agreement, with the agent being able to reject shipments in Japan if these conditions were not met.

The Export Function in Selkirk Brick

The Group Managing Director, Bernie Segrave, was directly responsible for overseeing all export matters including communication with the main agents, creating new relationships across Asia and being one-half of the trade show that travelled to Asia every four to five months. He spent approximately 15 per cent of his time on export-related matters across a year but this time allocation varied between 100 per cent and zero per cent on a weekly basis. Having started in sales and marketing with Selkirk Brick in 1968, Segrave brought significant experience and credibility to the role. He reported directly to the Board of Directors (see Exhibit 4: Organisation Chart).

The Export Manager, Peter Blackburn, spent between five and 20 per cent of his time on export matters during the course of a week. He reported directly to the Group Managing Director on these export matters. The rest of the time, Blackburn was officially the Regional Sales Manager for Western Victoria. In addition to maintaining relationships with agents across Asia, Blackburn was involved in developing products for export markets and ensuring that products exported met the highest technical standards. One of his current projects was working with an Australian residential building group to develop smaller, thinner bricks for the Japanese market.

Blackburn had joined Selkirk Brick four years ago though he had extensive industry experience with NuBrik. He was in the process of gradually assuming responsibility for all export business matters and had accompanied Segrave on all the recent overseas export development tours. In his view, Selkirk had been successful in Asia because it spent time building relationships with its agents, delivered products required in the marketplace on the basis of technical excellence and service rather than price alone, was committed to helping agents secure orders and maintained face-to-face relationships in order to avoid "long-distance communications and language" barriers.

Assisting the senior export marketing duo was Clare McGuinness, Export and Agency Sales Coordinator, who spent some 80 per cent of her time specifically on export matters. Among her responsibilities were receiving export orders, arranging all aspects of an export order (stock, shipping, letters of credit and export documents) and preparing all correspondence for Segrave on export related matters. All product for export markets was palletised and containerised at the brick yard adjacent to the head office in Ballarat. Selecting the appropriate bricks and pavers to ensure that they met required quality and aesthetic standards was considered to be critical in meeting customer needs. The Yard Stock Controller, Steve Banks, played an important role in this.

Overseas trips to visit agents and develop new business opportunities were generally scheduled every four to five months with Segrave and Blackburn travelling together to visit two to three countries over a two- or three-week period. Accompanying them on these trips was a technical reference manual, "The Selkirk Technical Advantage", that contained over 400 pages of technical specifications, photos of significant building projects where Selkirk bricks and pavers had been used across Asia, and a whole range of information on Frequently Asked Questions. This manual was provided for the exclusive use of agents in each country as a selling tool but was not to be distributed further.

The cost of these overseas trips was substantial for a small family-owned company, each in the range of A$15,000 to $25,000 depending upon the countries visited and the length of the trip. Typically, these trips involved more than meeting with existing agents. They included talking to customers, meeting with architects and providing technical information on products and services offered. Often these visits coincided with local trade fairs and with Austrade government missions to specific countries. The company tried to see each overseas agent at least once per annum. Most of the agents had visited Selkirk Brick's operations at head-office at least once and some of the Japanese agents had visited three or four times each.

Looking to the Future of Asia

The future of the Australian export business to Asia was in some doubt in early October 1998. According to the internationally respected newsmagazine *Business Week*, Asia was experiencing a widespread social backlash to the collapsing economic situation and stringent conditions imposed by the IMF (International Monetary Fund). The headlines of one issue (August 17, 1998) were quite pointed:

- Joblessness is soaring in Japan.
- Bitterness is growing in Korea.
- Political opposition is rallying in Thailand.
- Will the repercussions of recession scuttle Asia's economic reforms?

The Asian crisis had, in fact, spread to create global financial risk from collapsing economies and the flight of capital needed to underpin economic growth. Malaysia had already imposed currency controls on the Ringgit and in China there was strong evidence that Beijing was resorting to import controls and other measures to keep the Asian crisis at bay. Indonesia was still an open currency economy (despite moves earlier that year to establish a Currency Board) but the value of the Rupiah (R12,000 to the US$1.00) meant that imports were effectively priced out of the market.

During the months of August and September, the Australian dollar had suffered a significant decline against the U.S. dollar, dropping to a low of US$0.56 per A$1.00 before recovering to US$0.63. In 1997 the Australian dollar had traded at US$0.73. Though not suffering as high a devaluation as the Thai Baht or the Indonesian Rupiah, the Australian dollar had devalued in line with the decline in the Japanese Yen and Korean Won against the U.S. dollar because Japan and South Korea were the major export market destinations for Australian products. The Australian balance-of-trade data suggested that a falling Australian dollar rate and an aggressive shift to European and North American markets had reduced the (potentially negative) impact of the Asian crisis on the Australian economy.

In this global economic context, the prospects for future export business were difficult to predict. Segrave was expecting a large export order from the Greater China triangle (China, Hong Kong and Taiwan) but the strength of home startups in the local building industry in Victoria meant that export orders would be competing with local orders in the short term. The forthcoming trip would be useful in providing first-hand evidence on the future prospects for their export business across Asia. This would be another factor to consider in developing a strategy and organisational structure for their Asian export business.

At this stage, Selkirk did not have any licensing agreements, joint-venture operations or subsidiaries overseas. Segrave thought it was an interesting question:

> These types of strategic alliances are all useful. In fact, we have a new product right now which we are considering licensing to Asian companies.

> We would consider a licensing agreement (for bricks and pavers) if someone wanted to do it on their own in Asia. We would joint-venture if that was more appropriate (and it was commercially viable). These both have great benefits as we don't really know much about the Asian marketplace. Establishing an Asian subsidiary would depend upon the state of our core business in Australia.

It also depends upon the state of Asia and the business opportunities that arise. We have thought of dedicating one plant here in Ballarat to meeting (the higher standard) needs of the Asian marketplace. This would allow us to ensure product quality and still take advantage of our unique clay deposits.

Thus far Selkirk Brick had concentrated on exporting product to Asia and using existing production capacity to meet market needs. The current strategy of appointing export agents made sense in that context.

Nevertheless, there was some concern that increasing exports to the region and a future recovery of the Asian marketplace would change the economics of competing locally as brick and paver utilisation increased. In that case, product and brand licensing would become attractive alternatives and technical support agreements would become viable. Segrave was also concerned that new technologies could make "mini-kilns" economically viable and change the economic attractiveness of local production. This would require a change not only in their international export strategy but also to their whole way of doing business in Asia.

Exhibit 1   Geographic Locations

Exhibit 2   Group Sales Estimates

Year	Sales Revenue ($A millions)
1987/88	$19.9
1988/89	$24.8
1989/90	$25.5
1990/91	$20.7
1991/92	$19.0
1992/93	$23.5
1993/94	$24.9
1994/95	$25.8
1995/96	$23.2
1996/97	$22.2
1997/98	$27.8

Note: Estimates derived from industry data

Exhibit 3   Export Pricing Nomenclature and Value-Added

ex-Factory Gate

Goods in vehicle at factory gate.   **A$3,500/container**

Free Alongside Ship (F.A.S.)

Goods unloaded off vehicle on wharf at port of origin.   **A$3,800/container**

Free on-Board (F.O.B.)

Goods loaded on vessel at port of origin.   **A$4,000/container**

Cost, Insurance and Freight (C.I.F.)

Goods on vessel at port of destination   **A$5,000/container**

with insurance premiums included.

Market Price

Price of goods at final consumer market.   **A$12,000 to $17,500/container**

Exhibit 4   Organisation Chart

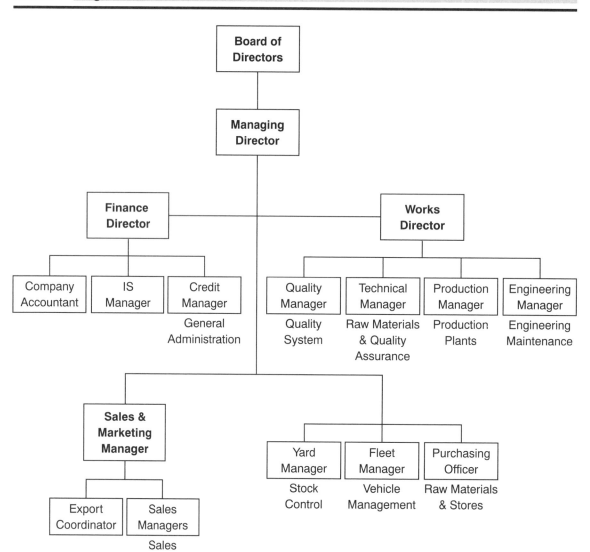

Appendix 1 Historical Highlights of Selkirk Brick

Extracted from a profile of Selkirk Brick, one of eight companies examined by Edna Carew and published in *Family Business: The Story of Successful Family Companies in Australia*.

- In 1883, Robert Selkirk began making bricks using a clay deposit in Allendale, Victoria. Bricks were hand-made using moulds. A brick press and engine purchased in 1892 signalled the beginning of mechanised production.
- In 1905, Selkirk was using coal-fired kilns to produce five brick types in batches. During that year, they began continuous firing of bricks on a three-shift, 24-hour, seven-day a week basis.
- In 1921, James Selkirk assumed control of Selkirk Brick (upon the death of his father) and was assisted by Bill Gillman, his brother-in-law, as company secretary.
- In 1935, James Selkirk suffered a heart attack and was ultimately succeeded by his two sons, Bill and Ron Selkirk. They managed the business until they enlisted and handed over control to Bill Gillman (Uncle Willy) during the war years.
- The post-WWII years saw Bill and Ron return to the family business, with Bill managing operations and staffing while Ron handled management and accounting.
- The late '40s and '50s were years of a great (re)building boom for Australia and Selkirk often needed to resort to a lottery to allocate bricks to customers. Innovation was central to its continued success; mechanised claypit in 1952, forklifts in 1953, its own transport company in 1954, "packaged" bricks in 1955 and the appointment of its first Sales Rep in 1959.
- By 1962, the brick works was completely redeveloped and a tunnel-kiln was built that allowed a clean-burning butane gas and an automated plant, both of which substantially enhanced the quality of bricks produced but also left the company with debt that stretched it financially for the next decade.
- During the '60s, the boom market evaporated and Selkirk Brick began to market its bricks across state boundaries into New South Wales and Canberra (the national capital). In 1969, Bill and Ron Selkirk became joint chairmen of the company.
- In 1974, production capacity was doubled to 50 million bricks a year with Plant No. 2 commissioned in Ballarat and in 1978 the fourth generation of Selkirks (Robert, Iain and Jim) was appointed to the Board.
- Bill and Ron Selkirk retired from day-to-day management in 1981; Ian McCoy (who had joined the company in 1951) became Chairman and several other long-term employees, who had joined the Board in 1969, were also promoted.

Appendix 2 The Australian Clay Brick Manufacturing Industry in 1998

The Australian clay brick industry was small, accounting for 0.09 per cent of GDP in 1997/98. Products included clay bricks and pavers used in new housing construction (70 per cent), housing renovations (15 per cent) and commercial construction (15 per cent). The state of New South Wales had the largest market share (36.3 per cent) followed by Queensland (18.9 per cent), Western Australia (17 per cent) and Victoria (16.9 per cent). Exports were low at 2.3 per cent of turnover in 1997/98 and imports were negligible.

Market Demand and Prices
Industry turnover reached $906 million in 1992/93 but then declined to $728 million in 1996/97 before climbing to $780 million in 1997/98. Clay brick production was estimated to be 1,532 million bricks in 1997/98. Approximately 87 per cent of housing was constructed using clay brick (typically as brick veneer, with the external walls using brick and interior walls using plaster or fibre board). Premium bricks (used in

exterior walls) cost approximately $500 per 1,000 bricks while seconds (used as fill-in) cost in the order of $300 per 1,000. Pavers represented 15 per cent of production but less than 10 per cent of sales revenue.

The outlook for 1998/99 was for a solid increase in sales to $880 million due to a strong residential housing construction demand fuelled by low mortgage interest rates, a strong domestic economy (despite the Asian crisis) and widespread concerns that the proposed 10 per cent value-added tax in July 2000 would increase housing costs. (Clay bricks and pavers were currently exempt from wholesale sales tax). The long-term market demand was expected to decline as new materials (concrete bricks, steel panels, and prestressed concrete) and new construction techniques (steel frames in particular) acted as substitutes. Steel-framed buildings using steel or corrugated iron cladding were reputed to cost about two-thirds the cost of brick-veneer.

Prices across markets were believed to be stable with competition based on product differentiation and distribution networks. High transportation costs and fear of price wars in a concentrated marketplace led to careful geographic competition. The industry cost structure had been estimated as follows:

- Material Purchases   9%
- Electricity and Fuel   12%
- Freight and Cartage   8%
- Repairs and Maintenance   7%
- Wages and Salaries   22%
- Other (Overheads/Profits)   42%

Industry Competition

Industry concentration was considered to be relatively high with the top five competitors accounting for 85 per cent of sales: the top four competitors also accounted for 35 of the 75 enterprise units in the Australian market.

Company	Market Share	Industry Revenue
Boral Limited	33%	$235 million
CSR Limited	21%	$150 million
Pioneer International	13%	$95 million
Futuris Limited	10%	$72 million
Brickworks Limited	8%	$56 million

The industry could be divided into three strategic groups:

- National Competitors Boral, Pioneer and CSR were competitors nationally with operations in a number of states. They were all diversified building products companies with manufacturing interests in related markets and with significant overseas manufacturing interests. Boral and CSR were each reported to have brick manufacturing capacity of 500 to 550 million bricks across Australia. Boral, Pioneer and CSR had recently been penalised by the Australian Consumer and Competition Commission for collusive pricing in the Queensland cement market.
- Regional Competitors Futuris (Western Australia), Brickworks (NSW/Queensland) and Selkirk (Victoria) were considered to be regional players. They were specialist clay brick and paver companies, with a number of plants and brands under their umbrella. Futuris had a manufacturing capacity of 200 million bricks.
- Local Competitors A number of small companies with local distribution and very small production capacities. Pioneer was the dominant player in Victoria with a 50 per cent market share followed by Boral with 25 per cent. Victoria's share of national production had fallen from 21 per cent in 1990/

91 to less than 17 per cent in 1993/94. Overcapacity was considered to be high. Production in 1997/98 had reached 2,177 million bricks.

International Business

Australian bricks were gaining export markets across Asia due to their natural colors and strength. Boral was successfully exporting through its Western Australian subsidiary, Midland Bricks. Exports had risen to $14.9 million in 1993/94 but had fallen subsequently to $14.0 million in 1994/95 and remained at that level in the two years that followed. The three largest companies all had overseas brick-making operations though the scale and importance of these varied considerably.

Appendix 3   Outline of Distributor Sales Agreement

1.1   Definitions
1.2   Appointment Period
1.3   Terms and Conditions of Sale
1.4   Trademarks
1.5   Advertising and Sales Promotions
1.6   Management Reports
1.7   Product Specifications
1.8   Acceptance Test and Inspections
1.9   Termination, Extensions and Revisions
1.10   Transfer of Rights
1.11   Business Secrecy
1.12   Force Majeure
1.13   Arbitration
1.14   Notice Addresses
1.15   Governing Laws

case

7

NORA-SAKARI: A PROPOSED JOINT VENTURE IN MALAYSIA

On the morning of Monday, July 13, 1992, Zainal Hashim, vice-chairman of Nora Holdings Sdn Bhd[1] (Nora), arrived at his office about an hour earlier than usual. As he looked out the window at the city spreading below, he thought about the Friday evening reception which he had hosted at his home in Kuala Lumpur (KL), Malaysia, for a team of negotiators from Sakari Oy[2] (Sakari) of Finland. Nora was a leading supplier of telecommunications (telecom) equipment in Malaysia while Sakari, a Finnish conglomerate, was a leader in the manufacture of cellular phone sets and switching systems. The seven-member team from Sakari was in KL to negotiate with Nora the formation of a joint-venture between the two telecom companies.

This was the final negotiation which would determine whether a joint-venture agreement would materialise. The negotiation had ended late Friday afternoon, having lasted for five consecutive days. The joint-venture company, if established, would be set up in Malaysia to manufacture and commission digital switching exchanges to meet the needs of the telecom industry in Malaysia and in neighbouring countries, particularly Indonesia and Thailand. While Nora would benefit from the joint-venture in terms of technology transfer, the venture would pave the way for Sakari to acquire knowledge and gain access to the markets of South-east Asia.

The Nora management was impressed by the Finnish capability in using high technology to enable Finland, a small country of only five million people, to have one of the fastest-growing economies in the world. Most successful Finnish companies were in the high-tech industries. For example, Kone was one of the world's three largest manufacturers of lifts, Vaisala was the world's major supplier of meteorological equipment, and Sakari was one of the leading telecom

Richard Ivey School of Business
The University of Western Ontario

R. Azimah Ainuddin prepared this case under the supervision of Professor Paul Beamish solely to provide material for class discussion. The authors do not intend to illustrate either effective or ineffective handling of a managerial situation. The authors may have disguised certain names and other identifying information to protect confidentiality. Ivey Management Services prohibits any form of reproduction, storage or transmittal without its written permission. This material is not covered under authorization from CanCopy or any reproduction rights organization.

Copyright © 1995, Ivey Management Services

companies in Europe. It would be an invaluable opportunity for Nora to learn from the Finnish experience and emulate their success for Malaysia.

The opportunity emerged when in February 1990, Peter Mattsson, president of Sakari's Asian regional office in Singapore, approached Zainal[3] to explore the possibility of forming a cooperative venture between Nora and Sakari. Mattsson said:

> While growth in the mobile telecommunications network is expected to be about 40 per cent a year in Asia between 1990 and 1994, growth in fixed networks would not be as fast, but the projects are much larger. A typical mobile network project amounts to a maximum of a few hundred million Finnish marks, but fixed network projects can be estimated in billions. In Malaysia and Thailand, billion-mark projects are currently approaching contract stage. Thus it is imperative that Sakari establish its presence in this region to capture a share in the fixed network market.

The large potential for telecom facilities was also evidenced in the low telephone penetration rates for most South-east Asian countries. For example, in 1990, telephone penetration rates (measured by the number of telephone lines per 100 people) for Indonesia, Thailand, Malaysia and the Philippines ranged from one to 11 lines per 100 people compared to the rates in developed countries such as Canada, Finland, Germany, United States and Sweden where the rates exceeded 50 telephone lines per 100 people.

The Telecom Industry in Malaysia

In November 1990, Syarikat Telekom Malaysia Sdn Bhd (STM), the government-owned telecom company, became a public-listed company, Telekom Malaysia Berhad (TMB). With a paid-up capital of RM2.4 billion,[4] TMB was given the authority by the Malaysian government to develop the country's telecom infrastructure. It was also given the mandate to provide telecom services that were on par with those available in developed countries.

In a corporate statement, TMB announced that it would be investing in the digitalization of its networks to pave the way for offering services based on the ISDN (integrated services digitalized network) standard, and investing in international fibre optic cable networks to meet the needs of increased telecom traffic between Malaysia and the rest of the world. TMB would also facilitate the installation of more cellular telephone networks in view of the increased demand for the use of mobile phones among the business community in KL and in major towns.

As the nation's largest telecom company, TMB's operations were regulated through a 20-year licence issued by the Ministry of Energy, Telecommunications and Posts. In line with the government's Vision 2020 program which targeted Malaysia to become a developed nation by the year 2020, there was a strong need for the upgrading of the telecom infrastructure in the rural areas. TMB estimated that it would spend more than RM6 billion between 1991 and 1995 on the installation of fixed networks, of which 25 per cent would be allocated for the expansion of rural telecom. The objective was to increase the level of telephone penetration rate to 25 per cent by the year 2000.

Although TMB had become a large national telecom company, it lacked the expertise and technology to undertake massive infrastructure projects. In most cases, the local telecom companies would be invited to submit their bids for a particular contract. It was also common for these local companies to form partnerships with large multinational corporations (MNCs), mainly for technological support. For example, Pernas-NEC, a joint-venture company between Pernas Holdings and NEC, was one of the companies that had been successful in securing large telecom contracts from the Malaysian authorities.

Nora's Search for a Joint-venture Partner

In mid 1991, TMB called for tenders to bid on a five-year project worth RM2 billion for installing digital switching exchanges in various parts of the country. The project also involved replacing analog circuit switches with digital switches. Digital switches enhanced transmission capabilities of telephone lines, increasing capacity to approximately two million bits per second compared to the 9,600 bits per second on analog circuits.

Nora was interested in securing a share of the RM2 billion forthcoming contract from TMB and more importantly, in acquiring the knowledge in switching technology from its partnership with a telecom MNC. During the initial stages, when Nora first began to consider potential partners in the bid for this contract, telecom MNCs such as Siemens, Alcatel, and Fujitsu seemed appropriate candidates. Nora had previously entered into a five-year technical assistance agreement with Siemens to manufacture telephone handsets.

Nora also had the experience of a long-term working relationship with Japanese partners which would prove valuable should a joint-venture be formed with Fujitsu. Alcatel was another potential partner, but the main concern at Nora was that the technical standards used in the French technology were not compatible with the British standards already adopted in Malaysia. NEC and Ericsson were not considered, as they were already involved with other local competitors and were the current suppliers of digital switching exchanges to TMB. Their five-year contracts were due to expire by the end of 1992.

Subsequent to Zainal's meeting with Mattsson, he decided to consider Sakari as a serious potential partner. He was briefed about Sakari's SK33, a digital switching system that was based on an open architecture, which enabled the use of standard components, standard software development tools, and standard software languages. Unlike the switching exchanges developed by NEC and Ericsson which required the purchase of components developed by the parent companies, the SK33 used components that were freely available in the open market. The system was also modular, and its software could be upgraded to provide new services and could interface easily with new equipment in the network. This was the most attractive feature of the SK33 as it would lead to the development of new switching systems.

Mattsson had also convinced Zainal and other Nora managers that although Sakari was a relatively small player in fixed networks, these networks were easily adaptable, and could cater to large exchanges in the urban areas as well as small ones for rural needs. Apparently Sakari's small size, compared to that of AT&T, Ericsson, and Siemens, was an added strength because Sakari was prepared to work out customized products according to Nora's needs. Large telecom companies such as AT&T, Ericsson and Siemens were alleged to be less willing to provide custom-made products. Instead, they tended to offer standard products that, in some aspects, were not consistent with the needs of the customer.

Prior to the July 1992 meeting, at least 20 meetings had been held either in KL or in Helsinki to establish relationships between the two companies. It was estimated that each side had invested not less than RM3 million in promoting the relationship. Mattsson and Ilkka Junttila, Sakari's representative in KL, were the key people in bringing the two companies together. (See Exhibits 1 and 2 for brief background information on Malaysia and Finland respectively.)

Nora Holdings Sdn Bhd

The Company

Nora was one of the leading companies in the telecom industry in Malaysia. It was established in 1975 with a paid-up capital of RM2 million. In 1991, the company's paid-up capital increased to RM16.5 million and recorded a turnover of RM320 million. Nora Holdings consisted of 30 subsidiaries, including two public-listed companies: Multiphone Bhd, and Nora Telecommunications Bhd. As at August 1991, Nora had 3,081 employees, of which 513 were categorized as managerial (including 244 engineers) and 2,568 as non-managerial (including 269 engineers and technicians).

The cable business

Since the inception of the company, Nora had secured two cable-laying projects, one in 1975 and the other in 1983. For the 1983 project worth RM500 million, Nora formed a joint-venture with two Japanese companies, Sumitomo Electric Industries Ltd (held 10 per cent equity share) and Marubeni Corporation (held five per cent equity share). Japanese partners were chosen in view of the availability of a financial package that came together with the technological assistance needed by Nora. Nora also acquired a 63 per cent stake in a local cable-laying company, Selangor Cables Sdn Bhd.

The telephone business

Nora had become a household name in Malaysia as a telephone manufacturer. It started in 1975 when the company obtained a contract to supply telephone sets to the Telecom authority, which would distribute the sets to telephone subscribers on a rental basis. The contract, estimated at RM130 million, lasted for 15 years. In 1980 Nora secured licenses from Siemens and Northern

Telecom to manufacture telephone handsets and had subsequently developed Nora's own telephone sets — the N300S (single line), N300M (micro-computer controlled), and N300V (hands-free, voice-activated) models.

Upon expiry of the 15-year contract as a supplier of telephone sets to the government-owned Telecom authority (STM) in 1989, Nora suffered a major setback when it lost a RM32 million contract to supply 600,000 N300S single line telephones. The contract was instead given to a Taiwanese manufacturer, Formula Electronics, which quoted a lower price of RM37 per handset compared to Nora's RM54. Subsequently, Nora was motivated to move towards the high end feature phone domestic market. The company sold about 3,000 sets of feature phones per month, capturing the segment of the Malaysian market that needed more sophisticated sets than the ones supplied by STM.

Nora had ventured into the export market with its feature phones, but industry observers predicted that Nora still had a long way to go as an exporter. The foreign markets were very competitive and many manufacturers already had well-established brands. In 1989, exports amounted to RM2 million and were expected to increase to RM5 million after orders were filled for its N300M and N300V models from Alcatel and Tokyo Telecommunications Network. Nora's N300V had been recently approved in Germany and a shipment of 2,000 sets would be distributed through its subsidiary, Nora GmbH, to test the German market.

The payphone business

Nora's start-up in the payphone business had turned out to be one of the company's most profitable lines of business. Other than the cable-laying contract secured in 1975, Nora had a 15-year contract to install, operate and maintain payphones in the cities and major towns in Malaysia. By 1992, Nora had started to manufacture card payphones under a license from GEC Plessey Telecommunications (GPT) of the United Kingdom. The agreement had also permitted Nora to sell the products to the neighbouring countries in South-east Asia as well as to eight other markets approved by GPT.

While the payphone revenues were estimated to be as high as RM60 million a year, a long-term and stable income stream for Nora, profit margins were only about 10 per cent because of the high investment and maintenance costs.

Other businesses

Nora was also the sole Malaysian distributor for Northern Telecom's private automatic branch exchange (PABX) and NEC's mobile telephone sets. The company had ventured into the paging market through a subsidiary, Unikom Sdn Bhd, and was capturing 50 per cent of the paging business in Malaysia. It was also an Apple computer distributor in Malaysia and Singapore. In addition, Nora was involved in: distributing radio-related equipment; supplying equipment to the broadcasting, meteorological, civil aviation, postal and power authorities; and manufacturing automotive parts (such as the suspension coil, springs, and piston) for the local automobile companies.

The Management

When Nora was established in 1975, Osman Jaafar, founder and chairman of Nora Holdings, managed the company with his wife, Nora Asyikin Yusof, and seven employees. Osman was known as a conservative businessman who did not like to dabble in acquisitions and mergers to make quick capital gains. He was formerly an electrical engineer who was trained in the United Kingdom and had held several senior positions at the national Telecom Department in Malaysia.

In 1980, Osman recruited Zainal Hashim to fill in the position of deputy managing director at Nora. Zainal held a master's degree in microwave communications from a British university and had several years of working experience as a production engineer at Pernas-NEC Sdn Bhd, a manufacturer of transmission equipment. In 1984, he was promoted to the position of managing director and in 1990, the vice-chairman.

Industry analysts observed that Nora's success was attributed to the complementary roles, trust, and mutual understanding between Osman and Zainal. While Osman "likes to fight for new business opportunities," Zainal preferred a low profile and concentrated on managing Nora's operations.

Industry observers also speculated that Osman, a former civil servant and an entrepreneur, was close to Malaysian politicians, notably the Prime Minister. Zainal, on the other hand, had been a close friend of the current Finance Minister since the days when they were both active in the Malaysian Muslim Youth Movement (a group that had developed a reputation for idealism, integrity and progressive interpretation of Islam). Zainal disagreed with allegations that Nora had succeeded due to its close relationships with Malaysian politicians and stressed that Nora's success was not due to its political skills. However, he acknowledged that such perceptions in the industry had been beneficial to the company.

Osman and Zainal had an obsession for high-tech and made the development of research and development (R&D) skills and resources a priority in the company. About one per cent of Nora's earnings was ploughed back into R&D activities. Although this amount was considered small by international standards, Nora planned to increase it gradually to five to six per cent over the next two to three years. Zainal said:

> We believe in making improvements in small steps, similar to the Japanese *kaizen* principle. Over time, each small improvement could lead to a major creation. To be able to make improvements, we must learn from others. Thus we would borrow a technology from others, but eventually, we must be able to develop our own to sustain our competitiveness in the industry. As a matter of fact, Sakari's SK33 system was developed based on a technology it obtained from Alcatel.

To further enhance R&D activities at Nora, Nora Research Sdn Bhd (NRSB), a wholly-owned subsidiary, was formed, and its R&D department was absorbed into this new company. NRSB operated as an independent research company undertaking R&D activities for Nora as well as private clients in related fields. The company facilitated R&D activities with other companies as well as government organizations, research institutions, and universities. NRSB, with its staff of 40 technicians/engineers, would charge a fixed fee for basic research and a royalty for its products sold by clients. Thus far, NRSB had developed Nora's Network Paging System, which was the system presently used by the company's paging subsidiary, Unikom Sdn Bhd.

Zainal was also active in instilling and promoting Islamic values among the Malay employees at Nora. He explained:

> Islam is a way of life and there is no such thing as Islamic management. The Islamic values, which must be reflected in the daily life of Muslims, would influence their behaviours as employers and employees. Our Malay managers, however, were often influenced by their western counterparts, who tend to stress knowledge and mental capability and often forget the effectiveness of the softer side of management which emphasizes relationships, sincerity and consistency. I believe that one must always be sincere to be able to develop good working relationships.

Sakari Oy

Sakari was established in 1865 as a pulp and paper mill located about 200 kilometres northwest of Helsinki, the capital city of Finland. In the 1960s, Sakari started to expand into the rubber and cable industries when it merged with the Finnish Rubber Works and Finnish Cable Works. In 1973 Sakari's performance was badly affected by the oil crisis, as its businesses were largely energy-intensive.

However, in 1975, the company recovered when Aatos Olkkola took over as Sakari's president. He led Sakari into competitive businesses such as computers, consumer electronics, and cellular phones via a series of acquisitions, mergers and alliances. Companies involved in the acquisitions included: the consumer electronics division of Standard Elektrik Lorenz AG; the data systems division of L.M. Ericsson; Vantala, a Finnish manufacturer of colour televisions; and Luxury, a Swedish state-owned electronics and computer concern.

In 1979, a joint-venture between Sakari and Vantala, Sakari-Vantala, was set up to develop and manufacture mobile telephones. Sakari-Vantala had captured about 14 per cent of the world's market share for mobile phones and held a 20 per cent market share in Europe for its mobile phone handsets. Outside Europe, a 50-50 joint-venture was formed with Tandy Corporation which, to date, had made significant sales in the United States, Malaysia and Thailand.

Sakari first edged into the telecom market by selling switching systems licensed from France's Alcatel and by developing the software and systems to suit the needs of small Finnish phone companies. Sakari had avoided head-on competition with Siemens and Ericsson by not trying to enter the market for large telephone networks. Instead, Sakari had concentrated on developing dedicated telecom networks for large private users such as utility and railway companies. In Finland, Sakari held 40 per cent of the market for digital exchanges. Other competitors included Ericsson (34 per cent), Siemens (25 per cent), and Alcatel (one per cent).

Sakari was also a niche player in the global switching market. Its SK33 switches had sold well in countries such as Sri Lanka, United Arab Emirates, China and the Soviet Union. A derivative of the SK33 main exchange switch called the SK33XT was subsequently developed to be used in base stations for cellular networks and personal paging systems.

Sakari attributed its emphasis on R&D as its key success factor in the telecom industry. Strong in-house R&D in core competence areas enabled the company to develop technology platforms such as its SK33 system that were reliable, flexible, widely compatible and economical. About 17 per cent of its annual sales revenue was invested into R&D and product development units in Finland, United Kingdom and France. Sakari's current strategy was to emphasize global operations in production and R&D. It planned to set up R&D centres in leading markets, including South-east Asia.

Sakari was still a small company by international standards (see Exhibit 3 for a list of the world's major telecom equipment suppliers). It lacked a strong marketing capability and had to rely on joint-ventures such as the one with Tandy Corporation to enter the world market, particularly the United States. In its efforts to develop market position quickly, Sakari had to accept lower margins for its products, and often the Sakari name was not revealed on the product. In recent years, Sakari decided to emerge from its hiding place as a manufacturer's manufacturer and began marketing under the Sakari name.

In 1988, Sakari's revenues increased but margins declined by 21 per cent when integration of the acquired companies took longer and cost more than expected. In 1989 Mikko Koskinen took over as president of Sakari when Olkkola died. Koskinen announced that telecommunications, computers, and consumer electronics would be maintained as Sakari's core business, and that he would continue Olkkola's efforts in expanding the company overseas. He believed that every European company needed global horizons to be able to meet global competition for future survival. To do so, he envisaged the setting up of alliances of varying duration, each designed for specific purposes. He said, "Sakari has become an interesting partner with which to cooperate on an equal footing in the areas of R&D, manufacturing and marketing."

In 1991, Sakari was Finland's largest publicly-traded industrial company and derived almost 80 per cent of its total sales from exports and overseas operations. However, export sales were confined to other Scandinavian countries, Western Europe and the former Soviet Union. Industry analysts observed that Finnish companies had a privileged relationship with the former Soviet Union, which was considered an easy market with minimal trading costs and high margins. As a result, until recently, these companies failed to invest in other parts of the world and were not making the most of their advantage in high-tech industries.

The recession in Finland which began in 1990 led Sakari's group sales to decline substantially from FIM22 billion[5] in 1990 to FIM15 billion in 1991. The losses were attributed to two main factors: weak demand for Sakari's consumer electronic products, and trade with the Soviet Union which had come to almost a complete standstill. Consequently Sakari began divesting its less profitable companies within the basic industries (metal, rubber, and paper), as well as leaving the troubled European computer market with the sale of its computer subsidiary, Sakari Macro. The company's new strategy was to focus on three main areas: telecom systems and mobile phones in a global framework, consumer electronic products in Europe, and deliveries of cables and related technology. The company's divestment strategy led to a reduction of Sakari's employees from about 41,000 in 1989 to 29,000 in 1991.

In June 1992, Koskinen retired as Sakari's President and was replaced by Visa Ketonen, formerly the President of Sakari Mobile Phones. Ketonen appointed Ossi Kuusisto as Sakari's vice-president.

The Nora-Sakari Negotiation

Since mid-May 1990, Nora and Sakari had discussed the potential of forming a joint-venture company in Malaysia. Nora engineers were sent to Helsinki to assess the SK33 technology in terms of its compatibility with the Malaysian requirements, while Sakari managers travelled to KL mainly to assess both Nora's capability in manufacturing switching exchanges and the feasibility of gaining access to the Malaysian market.

In November 1991, Nora submitted its bid for TMB's RM2 billion contract to supply digital switching exchanges supporting four million telephone lines. Assuming the Nora-Sakari joint-venture would materialise, Nora based its bid on supplying Sakari's digital switching technology. Nora competed with seven other companies short listed by TMB, all offering their partners' technology — Alcatel, AT&T, Fujitsu, Siemens, Ericsson, NEC, and Samsung. In early May 1992, TMB announced five successful companies in the bid. They were companies using technology from Alcatel, Fujitsu, Ericsson, NEC, and Sakari. Each company was awarded one-fifth share of the RM2 billion contract and would be responsible in delivering 800,000 telephone lines over a period of five years. Industry observers were critical of TMB's decision to select Sakari and Alcatel. Sakari was perceived to be the least capable in supplying the necessary lines to meet TMB's requirements, as it was alleged to be a small company with little international exposure. Alcatel was criticised for having the potential of supplying an obsolete technology.

The May 21 Meeting

Following the successful bid and ignoring the criticisms against Sakari, Nora and Sakari held a major meeting in Helsinki on May 21, 1992 to finalise the formation of the joint-venture. Zainal led Nora's five-member negotiation team which comprised Nora's general manager for corporate planning division, an accountant, two engineers, and Marina Mohamed, a lawyer. One of the engineers was Salleh Lindstrom who was of Swedish origin, a Muslim and had worked for Nora for almost 10 years.

Sakari's eight-member team was led by Kuusisto, Sakari's vice-president. His team comprised Junttila, Hussein Ghazi, Aziz Majid, three engineers, and Julia Ruola (a lawyer). Ghazi was Sakari's senior manager who was of Egyptian origin and also a Muslim who had worked for Sakari for more than 20 years while Aziz, a Malay, had been Sakari's manager for more than 12 years.

The meeting went on for several days. The main issue raised at the meeting was Nora's capability in penetrating the South-east Asian market. Other issues included Sakari's concerns over the efficiency of Malaysian workers in the joint-venture in manufacturing the product, maintaining product quality and ensuring prompt deliveries.

Commenting on the series of negotiations with Sakari, Zainal said that this was the most difficult negotiation he had ever experienced. Zainal was Nora's most experienced negotiator and had single-handedly represented Nora in several major negotiations for the past 10 years. In the negotiation with Sakari, Zainal admitted making the mistake of approaching the negotiation applying the approach he often used when negotiating with his counterparts from companies based in North America or the United Kingdom. He said:

> Negotiators from the United States tend to be very open and often state their positions early and definitively. They are highly verbal and usually prepare well-planned presentations. They also often engage in small talk and 'joke around' with us at the end of a negotiation. In contrast, the Sakari negotiators tend to be very serious, reserved and 'cold.' They are also relatively less verbal and do not convey much through their facial expressions. As a result, it was difficult for us to determine whether they are really interested in the deal or not.

Zainal said that the negotiation on May 21 turned out to be particularly difficult when Sakari became interested in bidding a recently-announced tender for a major telecom contract in the United Kingdom. Internal politics within Sakari led to the formation of two opposing "camps." One "camp" held a strong belief that there would be very high growth in the Asia-Pacific region and that the joint-venture company in Malaysia was seen as a hub to enter these markets. This group was represented mostly by Sakari's managers positioned in Asia and engineers who had made several trips to Malaysia, which usually included visits to Nora's facilities. They also had the support of Sakari's vice-president, Kuusisto, who was involved in most of the meetings with Nora, particularly when Zainal was present. Kuusisto had also made efforts to be present at meetings held in KL. This group also argued that Nora had already obtained the contract in Malaysia whereas the chance of getting the U.K. contract was quite low in view of the intense competition prevailing in that market.

The "camp" not in favour of the Nora-Sakari joint-venture believed that Sakari should focus its resources on entering the United Kingdom, which could be used as a hub to penetrate the

European Union (EU) market. There was also the belief that Europe was closer to home, making management easier, and that problems arising from cultural differences would be minimized. This group was also particularly concerned that Nora had the potential of copying Sakari's technology and eventually becoming a strong regional competitor. Also, because the U.K. market was relatively "open," Sakari could set up a wholly-owned subsidiary instead of a joint-venture company and consequently, avoid joint-venture-related problems such as joint control, joint profits, and leakage of technology.

Zainal felt that the lack of full support from Sakari's management led to a difficult negotiation when new misgivings arose concerning Nora's capability to deliver its part of the deal. It was apparent that the group in favour of the Nora-Sakari joint-venture was under pressure to further justify its proposal and provide counterarguments against the U.K. proposal. A Sakari manager explained, "We are tempted to pursue both proposals since each has its own strengths, but our current resources are very limited. Thus a choice has to made, and soon."

The July 6 Meeting

Another meeting to negotiate the joint-venture agreement was scheduled for July 6, 1992. Sakari's eight-member team arrived in KL on Sunday afternoon of July 5, and was met at the airport by the key Nora managers involved in the negotiation. Kuusisto did not accompany the Sakari team at this meeting.

The negotiation started early Monday morning at Nora's headquarters and continued for the next five days, with each day's meeting ending late in the evening. Members of the Nora team were the same members who had attended the May 21 meeting in Finland, except Zainal, who did not participate. The Sakari team was also represented by the same members in attendance at the previous meeting plus a new member, Solail Pekkarinen, Sakari's senior accountant. Unfortunately, on the third day of the negotiation, the Nora team requested that Sakari ask Pekkarinen to leave the negotiation. He was perceived as extremely arrogant and insensitive to the local culture, which tended to value modesty and diplomacy. Pekkarinen left for Helsinki the following morning.

Although Zainal had decided not to participate actively in the negotiations, he followed the process closely and was briefed by his negotiators regularly. Some of the issues which they complained were difficult to resolve had often led to heated arguments between the two negotiating teams. These included:

1. Equity Ownership

In previous meetings both companies agreed to form the joint-venture company with a paid-up capital of RM5 million. However, they disagreed on the equity share proposed by each side. Sakari proposed an equity split in the joint-venture company of 49 per cent for Sakari and 51 per cent for Nora. Nora, on the other hand, proposed a 30 per cent Sakari and 70 per cent Nora split. Nora's proposal was based on the foreign equity regulations set by the Malaysian government that allowed a maximum of 30 per cent foreign equity ownership unless the company would export a certain percentage of its products (see Exhibit 4 for these regulations). In addition, formal approval from the Malaysian authorities would have to be obtained to enable the foreign partner to hold an equity share of more than 30 per cent. Nora was concerned that this would further delay the formation of the joint-venture.

Equity ownership became a major issue as it was associated with control over the joint-venture company. Sakari was concerned about its ability to control the accessibility of its technology to Nora and about decisions concerning the activities of the joint-venture as a whole. The lack of control was perceived by Sakari as an obstacle to protecting its interests. Nora also had similar concerns about its ability to exert control over the joint-venture because it was intended as a key part of Nora's long-term strategy to develop its own digital switching exchanges and related high-tech products.

2. Technology Transfer

Sakari proposed to provide the joint-venture company with the basic structure of the digital switch. The joint-venture company would assemble the switching exchanges at the joint-venture plant and subsequently install the exchanges in designated locations identified by TMB. By offering Nora only the basic structure of the switch, the core of Sakari's switching technology would still be well-protected.

On the other hand, Nora proposed that the basic structure of the switch be developed at the joint-venture company in order to access the root of the switching technology. Based on Sakari's proposal, Nora felt that only the technical aspects in assembling and installing the exchanges would be obtained. This was perceived as another "screw-driver" form of technology transfer while the core of the technology associated with making the switches would still be unknown.

3. Royalty Payment

Closely related to the issue of technology transfer was the payment of a royalty for the technology used in building the switches. Sakari proposed a royalty payment of five per cent of the joint-venture gross sales while Nora proposed a payment of two per cent of net sales.

Nora considered the royalty rate of five per cent too high because it would affect Nora's financial situation as a whole. Financial simulations prepared by Nora's managers indicated that Nora's return on investment would be less than the desired 10 per cent if royalty rates exceeded three per cent of net sales. This was because Nora had already agreed to make large additional investments in support of the joint-venture. Nora would invest in a building which would be rented to the joint-venture company to accommodate an office and the switching plant. Nora would also invest in another plant which would supply the joint-venture with surface mounted devices (SMD), one of the major components needed to build the switching exchanges.

An added argument raised by the Nora negotiators in support of a two per cent royalty was that Sakari would receive side benefits from the joint venture's access to Japanese technology used in the manufacture of the SMD components. Apparently the Japanese technology was more advanced than Sakari's present technology.

4. Expatriates' Salaries and Perks

To allay Sakari's concerns over Nora's level of efficiency, Nora suggested that Sakari provide the necessary training for the joint-venture technical employees. Subsequently, Sakari had agreed to provide eight engineering experts for the joint-venture company on two types of contracts, short-term and long-term. Experts employed on a short-term basis would be paid a daily rate of US$700 plus travel/accommodation. The permanent experts would be paid a monthly salary ranging from US$12,000 to US$15,000. Three permanent experts would be attached to the joint-venture company once it was established and the number would gradually be reduced to only one, after two years. Five experts would be available on a short-term basis to provide specific training needs for durations of not more that three months each year.

The Nora negotiation team was appalled at the exorbitant amount proposed by the Sakari negotiators. They were surprised that the Sakari team had not surveyed the industry rates, as the Japanese and other western negotiators would normally have done. Apparently Sakari had not taken into consideration the relatively low cost of living in Malaysia compared to Finland. In 1991, the average monthly rent for a comfortable, unfurnished three-bedroom apartment was US$920 in Helsinki and only US$510 in Kuala Lumpur.[6]

In response to Sakari's proposal, Nora negotiators adopted an unusual "take-it or leave-it" stance. They deemed the following proposal reasonable in view of the comparisons made with other joint-ventures which Nora had entered into with other foreign parties:

Permanent experts' monthly salary ranges to be paid by the joint-venture company were as follows:

(1) Senior expert (seven to 10 years experience).......RM13,500–RM15,500
(2) Expert (four to six years experience)...............RM12,500–RM14,000
(3) Junior expert (two to three years experience)......RM11,500–RM13,000
(4) Any Malaysian income taxes payable would be added to the salaries.
(5) A car for personal use.
(6) Annual paid vacation of five weeks.
(7) Return flight tickets to home country once a year for the whole family of married persons and twice a year for singles according to Sakari's general scheme.
(8) Any expenses incurred during official travelling.

Temporary experts are persons invited by the joint-venture company for various technical assistance tasks and would not be granted residence status. They would be paid the following fees:

(1) Senior expert...RM750 per working day
(2) Expert...RM650 per working day
(3) The joint-venture company would not reimburse the following:

- Flight tickets between Finland (or any other country) and Malaysia.
- Hotel or any other form of accommodation.
- Local transportation.

In defense of their proposed rates, Sakari's negotiators argued that the rates presented by Nora were too low. Sakari suggested that Nora's negotiators take into consideration the fact that Sakari would have to subsidize the difference between the experts' present salaries and the amount paid by the joint-venture company. A large difference would require that large amounts of subsidy payments be made to the affected employees.

5. Arbitration

Another major issue discussed in the negotiation was related to arbitration. While both parties agreed to an arbitration process in the event of future disputes, they disagreed on the location for dispute resolution. Because Nora would be the majority stakeholder in the joint-venture company, Nora insisted that any arbitration should take place in KL. Sakari, however, insisted on Helsinki, following the norm commonly practised by the company.

At the end of the five-day negotiation, many issues could not be resolved. While Nora could agree on certain matters after consulting Zainal, the Sakari team, representing a large private company, had to refer contentious items to the company board before it could make any decision that went beyond the limits authorized by the board.

The Decision

Zainal sat down at his desk, read through the minutes of the negotiation thoroughly, and was disappointed that an agreement had not yet been reached. He was concerned about the commitment Nora had made to TMB when Nora was awarded the switching contract. Nora would be expected to fulfil the contract soon but had yet to find a partner to provide the switching technology. It was foreseeable that companies such as Siemens, Samsung and AT&T, which had failed in the bid, could still be potential partners. However, Zainal had also not rejected the possibility of a reconciliation with Sakari. He could start by contacting Kuusisto in Helsinki. But should he?

Exhibit 1   Malaysia: Background Information

Malaysia is centrally located in South-east Asia. It consists of Peninsular Malaysia, bordered by Thailand in the north and Singapore in the south, and the states of Sabah and Sarawak on the island of Borneo. Malaysia has a total land area of about 330,000 square kilometres, of which 80 per cent is covered with tropical rainforest. Malaysia has an equatorial climate with high humidity and high daily temperatures of about 26 degrees Celsius throughout the year.

In 1991 Malaysia's estimated population was 18 million, of which approximately seven million made up the country's labour force. The population is relatively young, with 40 per cent between the ages of 15 and 39 and only seven per cent above the age of 55. A Malaysian family has an average of four children and extended families are common. Kuala Lumpur, the capital city of Malaysia, has approximately 1.5 million inhabitants.

The population is multiracial; the largest ethnic group is the Bumiputeras (the Malays and other indigenous groups such as the Ibans in Sarawak and Kadazans in Sabah), followed by the Chinese and Indians. Bahasa Malaysia is the national language but English is widely used in the business circles. Other major languages spoken included various Chinese dialects and Tamil.

Islam is the official religion in Malaysia but other religions (mainly Christianity, Buddhism and Hinduism) are widely practised. Official holidays are allocated for the celebration of Eid, Christmas, Chinese New Year and Deepavali. All Malays are Muslims, followers of the Islamic faith.

During the period of British rule, secularism was introduced to the country, which led to the separation of the Islamic religion from daily life. In the late 1970s and 1980s, realizing the negative impact of secularism on the life of the Muslims, several groups of devout Muslims including the Malaysian Muslim Youth Movement (ABIM) undertook efforts to reverse the process, emphasizing a dynamic and progressive approach to Islam. As a result, changes were introduced to meet the daily needs of Muslims. Islamic banking and insurance facilities were introduced and prayer rooms were provided in government offices, private companies, factories, and even in shopping complexes.

Malaysia is a parliamentary democracy under a constitutional monarchy. The Yang DiPertuan Agung (the king) is the supreme head, and appoints the head of the ruling political party to be the prime minister. In 1992 the Barisan Nasional, a coalition of several political parties representing various ethnic groups, was the ruling political party in Malaysia. Its predominance had contributed to the political stability and economic progress of the country in the late 1980s and early 1990s.

The recession of 1985 through 1986 led to structural changes in the Malaysian economy which had been too dependent on primary commodities (rubber, tin, palm oil and timber) and had a very narrow export base. To reduce excessive dependence on primary commodities, the government directed resources to the manufacturing sector. To promote the establishment of export-oriented industries, generous incentives and relaxed foreign equity restrictions were introduced. A pragmatic approach toward foreign policy and heavy investments in modernizing the country's infrastructure (highways, air and seaports, telecommunications, industrial parks) led to rapid economic growth in 1988 through 1991 (Table 1). In 1991, the manufacturing sector became the leading contributor to the economy, accounting for about 28 per cent of gross national product (GNP). Malaysia's major trading partners are Singapore, United States, United Kingdom, Japan, Korea, Germany and Taiwan.

MALAYSIA: ECONOMIC PERFORMANCE
1988 to 1991

Economic Indicator	1988	1989	1990	1991
Per capita GNP (in RM)	5,065	5,507	6,206	6,817
Real economic growth rate	9.5%	9.3%	11.4%	9.1%
Consumer price index	2.5%	2.8%	3.1%	4.4%

Source: Ernst & Young International. 1993. "Doing Business in Malaysia."

Exhibit 2   Finland: Background Information

Finland is situated in the north-east of Europe, sharing borders with Sweden in the west, Norway in the north and the former Soviet Union in the east. About 65 per cent of its area of 338,000 square kilometres is covered with forest, about 15 per cent lakes and about 10 per cent arable land. Finland has a temperate climate with four distinct seasons. In Helsinki, the capital city of Finland, July is the warmest month with average mid-day temperature of 21 degrees Celsius and January is the coldest month with average mid-day temperature of –3 degrees Celsius.

Finland is one of the most sparsely populated countries in Europe. In 1991 Finland had a population of five million, 60 per cent of whom lived in the urban areas. Currently the city of Helsinki has a population of about 500,000. Finland has a well-educated work force of about 2.3 million. About half of the work force are engaged in providing services, 30 per cent in manufacturing and construction, and eight per cent in agricultural production. The small size of the population led to scarce and expensive labour. Thus Finland had to compete by exploiting its lead in high-tech industries.

Finland's official languages are Finnish and Swedish, although only six per cent of the population speaks Swedish. English is the most widely spoken foreign language. About 87 per cent of the Finns are Lutherans and about one per cent Finnish Orthodox.

Finland has been an independent republic since 1917, having previously been ruled by Sweden and Russia. A President is elected to a six-year term, and a 200-member, single-chamber parliament is elected every four years.

In the 1980s, Finland's economy was among the fastest growing economies in the world, with gross domestic product increasing at an average rate of over 10 per cent a year. Other than its forests, Finland has few natural resources. The country experienced a bad recession in 1991 leading to a drop in GDP (Table 2). Finland's economic structure is based on private ownership and free enterprise. However, the production of alcoholic beverages and spirits is retained as a government monopoly. Finland's major trading partners are Sweden, Germany, the former Soviet Union and United Kingdom.

Finland's standard of living is among the highest in the world. The Finns have small families with one or two children per family. They have comfortable homes in the cities and one in every three families has countryside cottages near a lake where they retreat on weekends. Taxes are high, the social security system is efficient and poverty is virtually non-existent.

Until recently, the stable trading relationship with the former Soviet Union and other Scandinavian countries led to few interactions between the Finns and people in other parts of the world. The Finns are described as rather reserved, obstinate, and serious people. A Finn commented, "We do not engage easily in small talk with strangers. Furthermore, we have a strong love for nature and we have the tendency to be silent as we observe our surroundings. Unfortunately, others tend to view such behaviour as cold and serious." Visitors to Finland are often impressed by the efficient public transport system, the clean and beautiful city of Helsinki with orderly road networks, scenic parks and lakefronts, museums, cathedrals, and churches.

FINLAND: ECONOMIC PERFORMANCE
1988 to 1991

Economic Indicator	1988	1989	1990	1991
Per capita GDP (in FIM)	88,308	99,387	104,991	102,083
Increase in GDP	12.8%	12.2%	6.0%	−2.8%
Inflation	5.1%	6.6%	6.1%	4.1%
Unemployment	n.a.	3.5%	3.4%	7.6%

Source: Ernst & Young International. 1993. "Doing Business in Finland."

Exhibit 3   Ten Major Telecommunication Equipment Vendors

Rank	Company	Country	1992 telecom equipment sales (US$ millions)
1	Alcatel	France/Netherlands	19,359
2	Siemens	Germany	11,877
3	AT&T	United States	10,809
4	Northern Telecom	Canada	8,029
5	Ericsson	Sweden	7,742
6	Motorola	United States	7,724
7	NEC	Japan	7,591
8	Bosch	Germany	5,221
9	Fujitsu	Japan	3,738
10	Philips	Netherlands	3,412

Source: International Telecommunication Union. 1994. "World Telecommunication Development Report 1994."

Exhibit 4   An Extract of the Malaysian Government's Policy on Foreign Investment

The level of equity participation for other export-oriented projects are as follows:

For projects exporting between 51 per cent to 79 per cent of their production, foreign equity ownership up to 51 per cent will be allowed; however, foreign equity ownership of up to 79 per cent may be allowed, depending on factors such as the level of technology, spin-off effects, size of the investment, location, value-added and the utilization of local raw materials and components.

For projects exporting 20 to 50 per cent of their production, foreign equity ownership of 30 to 51 per cent will be allowed, depending upon similar factors as mentioned above; however, for projects exporting less than 20 per cent of their production, foreign equity ownership is allowed up to a maximum of 30 per cent.

For projects producing products that are of high technology or are priority products for the domestic market, foreign equity ownership of up to 51 per cent will be allowed.

Source: Malaysian Industrial Development Authority (MIDA). 1991. "Malaysia: Your Profit Centre in Asia."

Footnotes

[1] Sdn Bhd is an abbreviation for Sendirian Berhad, which means private limited company in Malaysia.

[2] Oy is an abbreviation for Osakeyhtiot, which means private limited company in Finland.

[3] The first name is used because the Malay name does not carry a family name. The first and/or middle names belong to the individual and the last name is his/her father's name.

[4] RM is Ringgit Malaysia, the Malaysian currency. As at December 31, 1991, US$1 = RM2.73.

[5] FIM is Finnish Markka, the Finnish currency. As at December 31, 1991, US$1 = FIM4.14.

[6] IMD & World Economic Forum. 1992. The World Competitiveness Report.

8 STUDDS NOLAN JOINT VENTURE

In February 1995, Mr. Madhu Khurana, the managing director of Studds, Ltd. (Studds) of Faridabad, India, was considering breaking off Studds' joint venture agreement with Nolan of Italy. The Studds Nolan Joint Venture was Studds' first equity venture with a foreign partner and the preliminary negotiations for this venture had been completed six months earlier. However, as the two parties worked to finalize the joint venture agreement, they had reached an impasse. The current negotiations were marked by tension and distrust, and Mr. Khurana, while anxious to have a foreign partner for access to world markets, was concerned about several problems which had arisen since the joint venture was initiated. He had serious doubts about the long-term viability of the venture.

Company History

Gadgets India (Gadgets), the first company in the Studds group, was formed by two brothers, Ravi and Madhu Khurana, in 1969. Trained as engineers, the brothers first manufactured, in a house garage, injection and compressed molded engineering items on a custom basis for the automotive, textile, and white goods industries. In 1973, a motorcycle helmet manufacturing process was developed in-house and the first sale was in 1974. The motorcycle helmet line was marketed under the brand name 'Studds.'

Studds' development of indigenous technology contrasted with the way in which other companies grew in the regulated environment of India in the 1970s and 1980s. Most large

Andrew Delios prepared this case under the supervision of Professor Jaideep Anand solely to provide material for class discussion. The authors do not intend to illustrate either effective or ineffective handling of a managerial situation. The authors may have disguised certain names and other identifying information to protect confidentiality. Ivey Management Services prohibits any form of reproduction, storage or transmittal without its written permission. This material is not covered under authorization from CanCopy or any reproduction rights organization. *Copyright © 1996, Ivey Management Services*

Richard Ivey School of Business
The University of Western Ontario

Indian companies formed equity and non-equity alliances to access and acquire foreign technology. As the chairman of one of these conglomerates noted, most of these alliances were cultivated over a period of time and negotiations were often concluded by handshakes.

In the mid-1970s, motorcycle helmet usage was not popular in India. Consequently, early sales were low and only grew slowly. Two competitors existed in this embryonic market: Steelbird, who peddled high-priced helmets, and Concorde, a low-end manufacturer of cheap, industrial helmets. Studds competed in both ends, producing a premium helmet priced 10 per cent lower than Steelbird's, and lower quality helmets for more price-conscious consumers. Studds quickly secured a leading position in both the high and low end of the budding motorcycle helmet market. The 'Studds' brand became synonymous with helmets in India, and its market leadership was virtually uncontested through the remainder of the 1970s and into the first half of the 1980s.

Organizational Characteristics

In 1994, Studds consisted of Gadgets and Studds Accessories Pvt. Ltd. (Studds Accessories). Studds Accessories, formed in 1984, took over the marketing function for the Studds brand from Gadgets. Thus, Studds Accessories conducted all marketing activities, while Gadgets performed all manufacturing for Studds. By the 1990s, Studds Accessories had established a dealership network that penetrated all the nooks and crannies of the vast, dispersed Indian market; 800 chosen dealers provided Studds Accessories with the extensive network needed to reach into all of India.

These two companies were family-owned and controlled, with equity split equally between the families of the brothers, Ravi and Madhu Khurana. Gadgets remained a partnership, while Studds Accessories was a public limited company, wholly owned by the two Khurana families, friends and relatives.

Gadgets manufactured all products sold by Studds Accessories. As well, it had testing facilities for ensuring that products complied with the relevant country or regional standard. Gadgets employed 380 people of which 60 were supervisory staff, 145 were skilled labor and 175 were semi-skilled or unskilled labor. The main manufacturing facility was located in Faridabad, India and could produce 370,000 bi-wheeler helmets per year when operated at capacity. In 1994, 320,000 helmets were manufactured.

Gadgets was led by Ravi Khurana, the group chairman. A general manager reported to Ravi Khurana and the division of responsibility and control was along functional lines, with six managers reporting directly to the general manager. Studds Accessories was organized in a similar fashion. Madhu Khurana, the managing director, had a general manager and four functional managers reported to him. Twenty-five people were employed in Studds Accessories which had an advertising budget of Rs200,000 (in mid-1994, US$1 equaled Rs30.77).

Managers, responsible for a specific functional area, did not have much cross-communication. Where responsibilities overlapped and conflicts developed, resolution was sought through discussion with either Ravi or Madhu Khurana. Managers were reluctant to assume responsibility for decisions, and the general managers were reluctant to release such responsibility to the managers. Consequently, both Ravi and Madhu Khurana were intimately involved with the day-to-day operations of their companies.

Labor Relations

Employees of Studds were heavily unionized. Unions were active and vocal in India, and possessed considerable bargaining power because of the Indian government's 'no fire' policy. Under the terms of this policy, once an employee had been hired, the company was obligated to employ this individual for the lifetime of the company or employee. Dismissals were rare and were often accompanied by a considerable payout.

Other union activities sporadically disrupted activities inside and outside the Faridabad plant, and consumed upper management time. Studds helmets were distributed throughout India by trucking companies. Deliveries were subject to interruptions based on the relations of the trucker's union with the trucking companies. Also, a 1994 strike by dockworkers at the Bombay port delayed a recent shipment of Studds helmets to the North American market.

The strength of the union made changes in the manufacturing process difficult. In 1992, an injection molding machine was purchased. This machine was to be used for the manufacture of plastic, molded helmets for the lower-end segment of the market. Injection molding was a capital-intensive process, utilizing less labor than that used in the production of fiberglass helmets, a premium product. However, unions resisted the implementation of this process, and the injection molding machine remained idle, inhibiting expansion of Studds helmets in growing lower-end market segments.

Studds' Products

Approximately 70 per cent of the revenues for the Studds group came from motorcycle helmet sales. Studds marketed helmets in both the lower and premium segments of the market, though lower-end models were priced higher than inexpensive locally made brands. Studds produced both open-face and full-face helmets. Open-face models ranged from Rs248 to 310, and full-face models were priced between Rs434 and 558. The most expensive helmet in the Studds line was priced at Rs1,200; however, sales of this model were small. Aerostar's models ranged in price from Rs100 to Rs500.

Studds produced seven models in the full-face design and five models in the open-face design. As each model was produced in several color schemes, over 120 designs and colors of bi-wheeler helmets were produced. Both full-face and open-face designs had achieved ISI, ECE22.03, DOT,

CSI, SNELL and ANSI certification. Among a similar range of products, Aerostar had only received ISI certification for two models.

Studds also produced helmets for other user groups. Sales of sports helmets, used in such activities as cycling, canoeing, horse-riding, skating and skateboarding, accounted for the remaining 30 per cent of revenues. All helmets in this line were manufactured to meet ANSI-Z-90 (a U.S. standard) specifications. Studds' adherence to stringent international quality control laws had enabled its bicycle helmets to receive quality approvals from the United States, Canada, Mexico, and all of western Europe. Receiving Canadian (CSA) approval was an important benchmark, as companies from only nine nations worldwide had achieved it.

India in 1995

In the 1990s, India was going through a resurgence. Policy reforms, designed by Dr. Manmohan Singh, the Finance Minister, and implemented by the government of P.V. Narasimha Rao in July 1991, had created a feeling of widespread optimism in the country. Despite initial high inflation and a February 1992 stock market scandal, early indications were that the economy had responded positively to economic liberalization. GDP growth increased from less than one per cent in 1991 to 1992, to a projected five per cent in 1994 to 1995, and six per cent in subsequent years. The dollar value of imports and exports grew by 25 per cent in this same period, while foreign direct investment tripled. In addition, numerous multinationals had established a presence in India by 1994. Many markets were opened to foreign competitors under the new policy guidelines. Automatic approval existed for the markets in which Studds competed, and in the transportation markets from which the demand for Studds' products was derived. The middle class, the main purchasers of motorcycles and scooters, was expected to reach close to 300 million people by the turn of the century.

Infrastructure was an area of developmental concern. While India possessed an extensive network of railways and roads (there were 1.97 million km of roads of which less than half were paved), the road network was still insufficient for the number of vehicles on the roads. Traffic tie-ups were frequent, and travel by road was complicated by the wide variance in modes of transportation. Motorized trucks, cars and bi-wheelers shared the nation's highways and urban roads with pedestrians and animal-drawn vehicles. On-time delivery of goods was hampered by road congestion.

Other conditions in India hindered firm efficiency. For example, government approvals were required at several stages in a joint venture set-up. Investment (both capital goods and monetary) by foreign partners in a joint venture had to be approved by the Secretary for Industrial Approvals of the Department of Industrial Development, Ministry of Industries. Joint venture agreements had to be approved by the Reserve Bank of India of the Government of India, and permission was required from the Reserve Bank to issue shares to the foreign joint venture participant.

Other regulations governed the remittance of royalties and dividends, and the repatriation of capital. Furthermore, land purchases for industrial use often had an unaccountable component. This informal aspect to the economy was, at times, a reality in doing business in India. While conditions such as these impeded the conduct of business in India, an overall optimism, reinforced by several years of strong economic growth, prevailed.

The Domestic Market

From its birth in the early 1970s, the helmet market in India had grown to an annual size of nearly one million helmets in the 1990s. In 1992, Studds was the market leader, and held a 36 per cent share. Aerostar, with a 12 per cent share, occupied the number two position. Aerostar, which entered the market in the 1980s, competed directly against Studds' premium product line. Adopting a strategy similar to that used by Studds against Steelbird, Aerostar priced its premium product 10 per cent less than Studds', and undercut Studds' prices at the low-end of the market as well. Steelbird, with a five per cent share, was the number three manufacturer. Vega, which sold about 10,000 helmets per year, led a host of 90 or more other manufacturers who divided the remaining portion of the market among themselves. Helmets from these small manufacturers were low-end models, often sold in temporary roadside stands by individual sellers, independent of any buildings.

A few of these smaller manufacturers infringed on Studds' brand name. These small manufacturers made helmets identical in appearance to the Studds line but at a much lower cost. The duplicates bore the Studds name and could not be distinguished from genuine Studds helmets. Duplicates retailed for Rs170, while Studds' cost of manufacture was greater than Rs210. Trademark infringement was not legal under Indian law; however, in the past when Studds had tried to prosecute violators of its trademark, the penalty for infringement was not high enough to justify the two year prosecution period.

The domestic market for helmets, a derived demand from bi-wheeler usage, grew steadily through the early 1990s (see Figure 1 below), as did the number of competitors. However, in recent years, Studds' domestic sales had been fairly stagnant. As a result, their market share had declined from its 36 per cent level in 1992, to 30 per cent in 1994. Regionally, Studds' sales were concentrated in the northern states of India. However, the final distribution of Studds' helmets was more even than the regional sales figures suggested. Wholesalers were concentrated in northern India, and helmets sold to these firms were distributed to all regions of India. Thus, Studds helmets were used throughout India.

Market Segmentation

While Studds helmets were popular across India, Studds' market share in individual markets varied dramatically. For example, in New Delhi, Studds had a market share of approximately 10

Figure 1   Motorcycle Demand in India

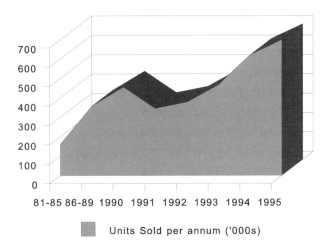

Units Sold per annum ('000s)

Note:
(i) Demand for 1995 is estimated.
(ii) Demand for mopeds was similar to that for motorcycles, while demand for scooters was double that for motorcycles.
Source: Government of India documents.

per cent; in Bombay, Studds commanded 75 per cent to 80 per cent of the market. Individual buyer behavior and helmet laws explained this trend.

Regions within India had the authority to create their own helmet laws. As a result, helmet use was mandatory in some regions and optional in others. Helmet laws were enacted and retracted frequently, as local governments changed. In 1994, only three cities, Delhi, Calcutta and Bangalore (with an aggregate population of approximately 30 million people, or 1/30 of India's population) had made helmet use compulsory. These three urban areas accounted for a large fraction of the bi-wheeler market.

Market Segmentation

Studds enjoyed its largest market share in regions which had optional helmet use. Motorcycle and scooter riders, who were safety conscious, were willing to pay for a premium product such as a Studds helmet. Other helmets were perceived not to offer the safety or style desired by voluntary wearers of helmets. In regions in which the rider was forced by law to wear a helmet, the sole criterion for helmet purchase was price. Safety, style and brand name were not important factors in these consumers' minds. As a result, Studds' largest market share was in regions in which helmet use was optional.

Similarly, for market development, Studds was not an advocate of compulsory helmet use. While Studds would gain a few sales should helmet use become mandatory across India, its market share would be eroded. The large increase in sales would be absorbed by low-price, unbranded helmet lines. The long term trend in India was towards the mandatory use of helmets, especially as national concern for health and safety increased.

High End versus Low End

Currently one in five bi-wheeler drivers wore a helmet voluntarily. Passengers were seldom observed to wear helmets. Even in regions in which helmet use was mandatory, only the driver was required to wear a helmet. Passengers were permitted to travel without a helmet, and at times, the number of riders on a bi-wheeler reached four or five, as a motorcycle or scooter often served as a family's main mode of transportation.

Internationalization

Export markets

In 1994, exports accounted for 20 per cent of the company's sales. Studds had exports to 35 countries in several regions of the world (see Figure 2). Its greatest presence was in South America, followed by South East Asia. Based on large populations and increasing bi-wheeler usage, particularly small motorcycles and scooters, tremendous potential existed in developing country markets. However, as Studds was still new to international markets, a market focus had not been determined.

The Studds group was the only Indian helmet company active in international markets. Studds began to consider foreign markets in 1990 because of a slack in the domestic market and a lot of growth in international markets. In 1991, when Studds decided to go international, the company elected to attend, with the assistance of the India Trade Promotion Organization (ITPO), the IFMA Cologne Motor Show at Milan. The show provided a high profile presence for Studds, as it was the premier trade show for motorcycle and motorcycle-related products.

In subsequent years, Studds tried to separate its display from other Indian manufacturers and ITPO. Associating with ITPO did not benefit Studds, and Madhu Khurana wished to distance Studds helmets from other Indian products which did not enjoy as good a reputation internationally. Studds helmets were equivalent in quality to leading international manufacturers, and following the first order from Mauritius, the helmets penetrated world markets rapidly and aggressively. From 1991-92 to 1993-94, export sales quadrupled.

Studds sold to most markets under its brand name. Only in Canada, where Studds helmets were sold under the CKX brand to snowmobilers, and Sri Lanka were Studds helmets not sold under its brand name. In Germany, helmets for the lower end of the market maintained the Studds brand name; helmets for the upper end of the market were custom-branded. In none of Studds' international markets were funds spent on marketing and advertising. As yet, Studds' international sales were too low to fund such expenditures. Larger companies, such as Arai, were actively involved in developing and maintaining their brands.

Figure 2   Studds' Export Markets

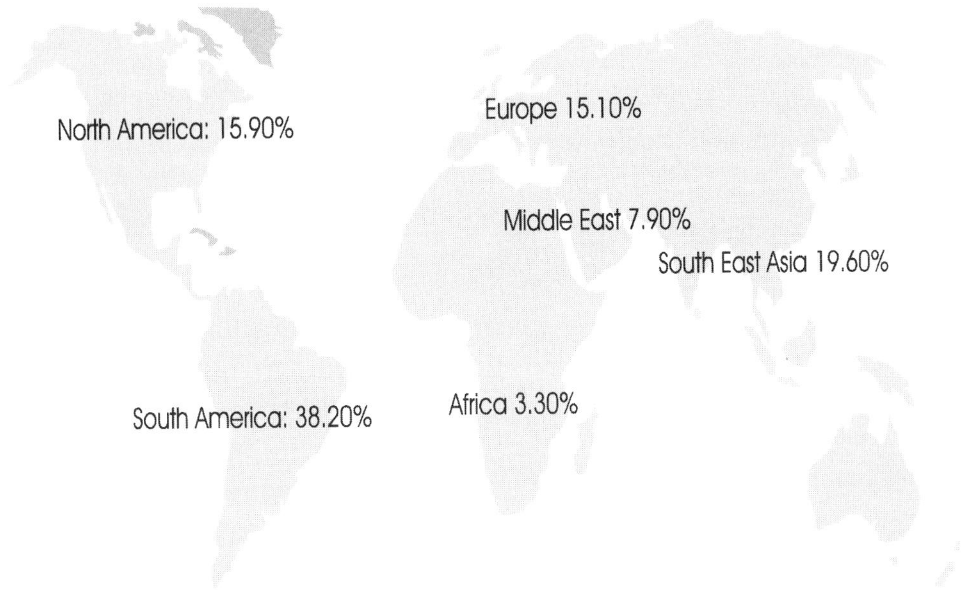

North America: 15.90%

Europe 15.10%

Middle East 7.90%

South East Asia 19.60%

South America: 38.20%

Africa 3.30%

Studds' international contacts were made at trade shows where it contacted distributors who would move the helmets to local retailers. Four or five distributors were sufficient to cover a region the size of the United States. The main competitors for Studds in most markets were companies from Taiwan and South Korea. Other India-based competition was non-existent. Studds held a considerable cost advantage over non-Indian competitors. Studds, operating with a 15 per cent to 20 per cent gross margin, sold open-face helmets for Rs248 to Rs310 and full-face helmets for Rs434 to Rs558. South Korean producers, the next lowest-priced producers, sold full-face models for Rs1,550 to Rs1,705. Labor costs, particularly in fiberglass models, accounted for Studds' cost advantage. Studds' cost advantage prompted one South Korean firm to offer Studds a subcontract on a North American order.

The Global Market

While export sales growth had been impressive, Studds helmets were still a small component of total world sales. The global market for motorcycle and bicycle helmets was estimated by Madhu Khurana to be approximately Rs20 billion and for sports helmets, Rs10 billion. Studds covered all three segments, with the strongest sales for motorcycle and bicycle helmets in British and South American markets. For bicycle helmets, Studds had identified Canada as a promising market. In the mid-1990s, helmets were expected to be made compulsory for all bicycle riders in Canada, creating a demand for two million helmets. Studds intended to garner five per cent of this market.

In international markets, firms from Italy and Japan were strongest, and they competed primarily in developed country markets. Italian companies held a 55 per cent to 60 per cent share in international markets, and the two main Japanese firms, a 15 per cent to 20 per cent share. Companies from Taiwan held a five to seven per cent share. The remainder was accounted for by a variety of firms from, for example, South Korea and India (Studds). The Studds Nolan Joint Venture was Studds= first equity venture with a foreign partner.

The Studds Nolan Joint Venture

During early 1994, the management of Studds decided to expand capacity in helmets and motorcycle accessories. To be competitive in international markets, Studds' management believed that the new facilities built in this expansion must incorporate the most modern manufacturing technology. For this reason and the desire to gain access to world markets, Studds decided to partner with one of the world's market leaders.

During March 1994, Studds identified the top ten helmet manufacturers in the world. Each of these manufacturers received a letter from Studds stating its intention to expand capacity and offering the opportunity for a joint venture. Serious responses were received from three companies, two from Italian companies and one from a German company. Figure 3 presents a financial comparison of these three companies.

Representatives from both Italian companies visited Studds in May 1994 and discussed, in depth, the possibility of a joint venture. In July 1994, a team of managers from Studds visited the two Italian manufacturers — Bieffe and Nolan — and, on the basis of its market leadership position and well-defined policies, selected Nolan as their joint venture partner. See Appendix A for a description of Nolan.

Figure 3   A Comparison Between Nolan, Bieffe and FIMEZ

	NOLAN		FIMEZ		BIEFFE	
	1991	1992	1991	1992	1991	1992
Sales	23.0	27.0	11.0	13.0	20.0	21.0
Net Income	1.0	0.8	0.1	(0.1)	0.2	0.1
Cash Flow	2.6	2.7	0.5	0.4	0.8	0.3
Number of Personnel	184.0	169.0	n/a	n/a	84.0	84.0
Debt vs Banks	6.8	6.3	1.7	3.3	7.2	6.7
Investments	1.1	1.4	0.7	0.8	0.2	(0.3)

Note: All monetary figures in US$ millions.
Source: Company documents.

Letter of Intent

The Studds group and the Nolan group of India signed a Letter of Intent on July 27, 1994, thereby agreeing to establish a joint helmet manufacturing unit in Faridabad, India (See Appendix B for a Summary of the Letter of Intent). Under the terms of the agreement, which were valid until September 1994, Studds Accessories was converted from a closely held to a widely held public limited company. Gadgets remained in the control of the Khurana brothers. The two groups had equal equity participation, with new manufacturing activities added to the existing trading activities of Studds Accessories. The name of Studds Accessories was changed to Studds Nolan Ltd.

While both partners had equal equity (Rs10 million) in the venture, each possessed only a 20 per cent share. The remaining 60 per cent was issued to the public. At the time of the agreement, the current paid-up capital of Studds Accessories was Rs2 million. Rs8 million more was soon contributed to bring the holdings of Studds to the requisite Rs10 million. Nolan invested Rs10 million in the form of cash and molds. The total equity of the venture was US$1,625,000.

The Joint Venture Agreement

In September 1994, representatives from Nolan visited Studds in India for a second time to work out a final joint venture agreement. During these meetings, most of the discussion centered on operational and control issues. Partner objectives for the joint venture received less attention. As the managers for Studds and Nolan continued to discuss issues related to the management of the joint venture, tension began to enter the relationship. Nolan, which had engaged a local Indian attorney for these negotiations, inserted new clauses into the legal agreements for the joint venture which were not included in the original Letter of Intent. Nolan, keen to proceed with the joint venture, gave Studds the option of framing the basic terms of the final joint venture agreement. The attorney for Studds framed a new agreement which was handed over to Nolan in November 1994.

At this point, both parties became very cautious about the legal aspects of the agreement. The intervention by the attorneys led to increased concern with the exact wording of the legal agreement. Managers from Studds and Nolan wanted to be sure that the agreement would fairly lay out the exact conditions under which the joint venture would be operated. In the words of one Studds manager,

> Representatives from Nolan and Studds were both very cautious about the legal aspects of the agreement. Both parties wanted to read between the lines in the agreement. The lawyers were helping to foster suspicion about the intention of every line written in the agreement.

Implementation

Studds' managers began to implement certain aspects of the agreement in late 1994. The first task was the land purchase. The total cost of the land exceeded the budgeted Rs7.2 million. The additional expenditures for the land were related to the informal economy in India. Some of the disbursements made by Studds were necessary to secure the land but were to parties that could not issue a receipt. Nolan became concerned about these payments, and felt that Studds was not being completely veracious in accounting for these expenditures. Other expenditures, too, had non-accountable components. Nolan's managers expressed a desire to manage more day-to-day operations, contrary to earlier agreements.

In the new agreements put forth by each partner, the offers were largely consistent in their treatment of technology transfer, the location and set-up of the venture, methods of payment, and the transference of molds and dies. However, some divergence emerged concerning the management and administration of the venture. The two sides could not resolve what were to be day-to-day concerns and what were to be long-term concerns.

Nolan's proposal listed 15 decisions that required the approval of the Board of Directors. Many of the decisions were related to strategic concerns; however, others related to operational issues and expenditures. Specifically, real estate property and machines exceeding Rs2 million in value could not be bought or sold without prior approval of the board of directors. Studds' proposal contained no such provision, though both proposals stated that all day-to-day operating expenses of the joint venture might be incurred by a director or official of the company, provided the expenditure fell within the approved budgets and guidelines.

The February 1995 Meeting

In February 1995, Studds' management team visited Nolan in Italy to work through existing concerns about the operation of the venture and to finalize the joint venture agreement. Neither partner felt confident of the other, and much of the discussion concerned the jurisdictional point for the joint venture agreement. Studds insisted on India as the jurisdictional point but Nolan was firm on London or Paris as the place for adjudication.

The meetings continued for three days, and the remaining faith that the parties had in each other continued to deteriorate. Mr. Khurana and others in the Studds management team began to feel that this joint venture could not be salvaged. They began considering breaking off the existing agreement. Doing so would delay Studds in its efforts to become a global leader in helmet manufacturing; however, Bieffe and other helmet manufacturers remained as potential partners for Studds should the agreement be broken off. Other courses of action, such as a go-alone internationalization, could also be taken by Studds. Mr. Khurana and his team evaluated these considerations as they decided on the immediate action to take in their meeting with Nolan.

Appendix A   Nolan — Company Profile

The companies which formed the Nolan Group (Nolan) produced protective helmets for motorcyclists, bicyclists, and other sports enthusiasts. Nolan, formed in the 1970s, began as a supplier of motorcycle and car accessories to a large multinational. In 20 years of operations the company's products were characterized by competitive pricing, high technical performance and consistent quality. Substantial innovations and product developments had improved the esthetic appearance and performance of the helmets, while consistently respecting the regulations and standards which governed safety products.

Nolan's marketing strengths had grown with its technical expertise. Nolan's trademark had increased in importance in principal markets, and was one of the most well-recognized across the world. A network of loyal distributors contributed to Nolan's success. The dealers comprising this network were specialized for sales in this market and adjusted their sales tactics to Nolan's product line changes. Recently, a new line of Nolan products had been developed, but had not yet reached the market. These new items were designed to increase protection to the face, and had excellent mechanical and optical qualities.

Investment supporting continued renovation and improvements in the product lines came to US$1.53 million in 1993. For 1994, investment was projected to exceed US$1.75 million. These investments, which accounted for 6.4 per cent of gross revenues, were for renovations in machinery and products alone. A further 3.6 per cent of sales was dedicated to ongoing product design and research. Nolan's performance is summarized below.

	1993 (Actual)	1994 (Projected)
Turnover	26.408	30.761
Cost of sales	16.584	19.187
Gross profit	9.824	11.574
Less depreciation	1.539	2.137
Less other operating expenses	5.465	6.322
Operating expense before interest	2.819	3.115
Net interest	(1.261)	(847.000)
Extraordinary items	(0.265)	(233.000)
Profit before taxes	1.294	2.035
Taxes	(0.515)	(1.018)
Accelerated depreciation	(0.285)	-
Net profit	0.493	1.017

Note: All amounts are in US$ millions.
Source: Company Documents.

Nolan's 1993 sales were divided between several markets. Exports were larger than domestic sales as depicted in the following table.

Subdivision of Sales	US$ Millions	
Helmets	24.521	
Optical area (visors)	1.555	
Subdivision of Helmet Sales		**% of Total Helmet Sales**
Domestic — Italy	4.832	19.710
Exports	19.689	80.290
Subdivision of Export Sales		
Europe	15.051	61.380
North America	2.487	10.140
Other countries	2.151	8.770
Total — 55 countries	19.689	

Source: Company Documents

Nolan's products were marketed domestically and in other developed countries using a common advertising strategy. Nolan used standard industry promotional vehicles such as advertising in specialty magazines and sponsoring race-car drivers and motorcycle riders. However, the company preferred to concentrate on the commercial end in its marketing strategy. It helped retailers display, promote, and demonstrate its products to the customer. Thus, the company's advertising was less aggressive than its competitors, since Nolan preferred to provide good service to its dealers and customers rather than pay for other, more glamorous, forms of advertising.

The joint venture with Studds would provide Nolan with the opportunity to expand capacity with little capital input. Also, Nolan would lower its cost of production significantly by producing helmets in India. A third but relatively minor benefit of partnering with Studds is the access Nolan would gain to the growing Indian market.

Appendix B   Letter of Intent

The factory of the venture was to be located in Faridabad, Haryana, six to seven kilometres from the present offices of Studds. The existing offices and sales staff of Studds Accessories were to be used for marketing activities. In the joint venture agreement, land for the factory building and measuring 6,000 m^3 was to be purchased by February 1995. The land price was estimated to be Rs1,000/m^2. With duties, brokerage fees and other set-up costs, the total cost to the company for the land was estimated to be Rs7.2 million.

Construction on the factory building was to begin in March 1995, following purchase of the land and receipt of approval from the relevant authorities. The factory building was proposed to consist of 25,000 square feet, with the cost at Rs6.25 million. Machinery installation was to occur in November, and production would start in December 1995 (see Exhibit 1, all Exhibits are located at the end of Appendix B). The commercial launch date for Studds Nolan helmets was to be January 1996. The figures in this agreement were considered realistic given Studds managers' familiarity with local operating conditions.

Management of the Joint Venture

Studds Nolan Limited was controlled by a board of directors which numbered five including the chairman. The chairman was from the Studds group, and Nolan and Studds both appointed two other directors. The chairman and one director of the Studds Group were the working directors and took care of day-to-day operations of the company.

The board of directors would meet quarterly to review the performance of the company. The Nolan directors would be reimbursed for travel to and from India for two of their trips each year. Employees, both skilled and unskilled, were locally available; thus all managers and factory staff were from India. The organization was structured in a form similar to that of Studds Accessories (see Exhibit 2).

Projections

Several detailed projections were made concerning production, prices, sales and revenues. Capacity estimates were based on a three-shift operating schedule, during which both full-face and open-face helmets were to be produced. Full-face helmets had a greater market value than open-face helmets; thus more of these would be produced (see Exhibit 3).

While close to 400,000 helmets could be produced at capacity, sales were estimated to be less than this amount during the first few years of operations, though early sales would exceed the break-even quantity of 92,000 helmets (see Exhibit 4). Helmets would be sold under the "Studds Nolan" brand name. If sales grew as projected in a market survey, 75 per cent of capacity would be utilized in 1998, the third year of the factory's operation. Most raw materials for production could be sourced locally, though anti-glare visors for the full-face helmets would be procured from Nolan or Korean suppliers depending on the price. The venture was expected to be profitable in its first year of operation (see Exhibit 5).

Exhibit 1   Machinery Equipment

Machinery:

600 Ton injection molding machine	Rs7.00 million
400 Ton injection molding machine	5.50 million
180 Ton injection molding machine	2.00 million
	14.50 million
Assembly equipment	0.50 million
Maintenance equipment	1.20 million
Sales tax and installation expenses	1.95 million
Total machinery and equipment cost:	18.15 million

Molds and dies:

Molds and dies imported	3.00 million
Custom duty (25 per cent)	0.75 million
Freight, insurance, etc.	0.40 million
Total molds and dies:	4.15 million

Generators and vehicles:

1 No. generator set 500 KVA	2.00 million
1 No. generator set 250 KVA	1.20 million
Vehicles	1.00 million
Total generators and vehicles:	4.20 million

Factory workers (annual costs):

Skilled labor (40 @ Rs3,500/month)	1.680 million
Unskilled labor (30 @ Rs2,700/month)	0.972 million
Total labor	2.652 million
Add: 35 per cent (other associated labor costs)	0.928 million
Total annual labor cost:	Rs3.580 million

Note: All industries installed generators because electrical supply was not consistent in India.
Source: for Exhibits 1 to 5: Company documents.

Exhibit 2   Studds Nolan Organizational Structure

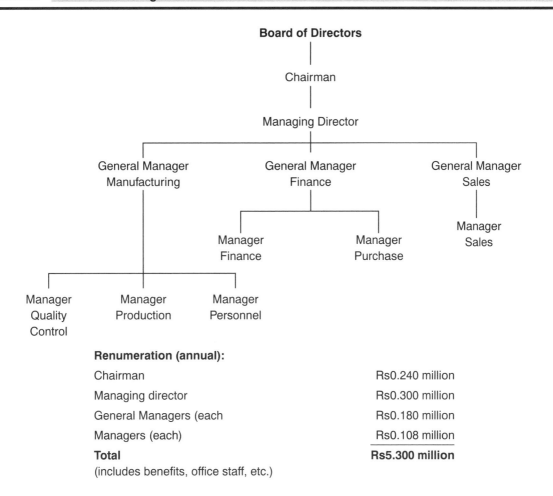

Renumeration (annual):

Chairman	Rs0.240 million
Managing director	Rs0.300 million
General Managers (each	Rs0.180 million
Managers (each)	Rs0.108 million
Total	**Rs5.300 million**

(includes benefits, office staff, etc.)

Exhibit 3   Capacities and Selling Prices of Products

Product	Capacity	Selling Price (RS/unit)
Full-face helmet	280,000	750
Open-face helmet	120,000	400
Sunpeaks, visors	120,000	70
Spare visors (full-face)	–	190

Exhibit 4   Sales Projections (Units)

Product	1995	1996	1997
Full-face helmet	168,000	196,000	210,000
Open-face helmet	72,000	84,000	90,000
Sunpeaks, visors	40,000	50,000	50,000
Spare visors (full-face)	30,000	40,000	50,000

Exhibit 5   Pro Forma Income Statement

	1995	1996	1997
Sales	163,300	191,700	206,500
Cost of sales	112,900	132,640	143,400
Gross profit	50,400	59,060	63,100
Depreciation	3,381	3,381	3,381
Operating expenses	23,800	27,785	31,137
Operating profit	23,219	27,894	28,582
Interest	5,425	5,600	5,200
Profit before tax	17,794	22,294	23,382
Taxation	4,046	6,230	7,106
Net profit	13,748	16,064	16,276
Dividend	9,400	9,400	9,400
Profit for general reserve	4,348	6,664	6,876
Return on capital	27%	29%	27%

TROJAN TECHNOLOGIES INC: THE CHINA OPPORTUNITY

In August 1999, Sarah Brown, senior market associate of Trojan Technologies of London, Ontario, reflected on the water shortages anticipated in developing countries as a result of their explosive economic growth. Trojan sold water disinfection equipment, and Sarah's job was to find new areas for growth. China was particularly intriguing because it had as much water as Canada but 40 times the population, and its economic boom would further stress current water resources. Given Trojan's high growth expectations, China offered an enormous opportunity. Sarah knew little of China: how decisions were made for water disinfection equipment, whether Trojan's patents would be protected, what level of resources would be required, etc.. Her task in new market development was to determine if Trojan should enter China, and if so, when, where and how. Ralph Brady, the vice president of New Business Development, wanted to see her recommendations within the month.

Trojan Technologies Inc: More Than "Light in a Pipe"

An Overview of Trojan

Located in London, Ontario, Canada, Trojan Technologies Inc. started with a staff of three in 1977. Its original technology was based on a pioneering patent on an ultraviolet (UV) water disinfection system. The idea was simple — often referred to as "light in a pipe" — but its implementation embodied complex engineering, science and technology. Banks of UV light

tubes were installed inside an open water channel constructed of either concrete or metal. As water flowed through the channel, the high-intensity UV light destroyed the DNA structures of the microorganisms in the water so the risk of disease would be eliminated.

There were two major applications of UV technology. One was to disinfect the wastewater discharged into receiving waters. Applications included primary, secondary and tertiary treatment for industrial, commercial and municipal waste treatment processes. The other was to disinfect incoming clean water. Applications included household drinking water supplies, municipal drinking water treatment plants, industrial product and process water requirements, and commercial applications (See Exhibit 1).

As UV technologies became more accepted as an environmentally responsible and cost-effective replacement for the widely used chemical disinfection methods, Trojan had posted an annual compound revenue growth rate of 27 per cent since 1989, and 36 per cent since 1994. In 1998, Trojan was a TSE 300 company, employing about 400 employees, with annual sales reaching almost $70 million. As a world leader in ultraviolet water disinfection technology and the world's largest supplier of ultraviolet disinfection systems for municipal wastewater applications, Trojan now had some 2,000 UV systems in operation around the world, treating in excess of six billion gallons of water per day.

In 1998, the company approved a five-year strategic plan, which projected a continued growth rate of at least 30 per cent for the following five years. By 2003, the annual sales were expected to reach over $300 million and total employment more than 1,000.

To achieve the goal, Trojan was actively looking for growth opportunities. Trojan decided to increase its investment in the clean water market. Currently, 95 per cent of Trojan's business was in the wastewater market. The clean water business' five per cent contribution was marginal. However, recent research results showed that UV could destroy giardia and crytosporidium in municipal drinking water supplies, which further enhanced its competitiveness in the clean water market. Giardia and crytosporidium are responsible for waterborne outbreaks causing diarrheal infections, and are resistant against chlorine.

In the same year, Trojan obtained the exclusive worldwide licence for an innovative photocatalytic technology used in air treatment applications. The Air 2000 system using the technology won the 1998 Environmental Technology Innovator Award in the U.S., and had similar features to Trojan's UV water systems, i.e., they were both more environmentally-positive and cost-effective substitutes for current treatment technologies.

Trojan was also looking to expand geographically, especially to new markets with legal regulations and standards regarding discharging water and clean water. One potential market being evaluated was Asia, especially the world's most populous country — China. Trojan made a breakthrough sale of a $4.5-million System UV4000™ water disinfection unit to Hong Kong in 1999, after a few smaller installations there. In the same year, Trojan shipped seven industrial clean water units to Mainland China through a Chinese-owned company in the U.S. Sales had also been made to Thailand, Indonesia, the Philippines, Taiwan and Korea.

The Product Market

Water disinfection was usually the last step in water treatment, following other physical, chemical or biological purification processes, killing the organisms, viruses, bacteria in the effluents from primary and secondary treatment. Three water disinfection methods were commonly known: ozone, chlorine, and UV. Chlorine was the most commonly used in the world, accounting for over 80 per cent of the market. Chlorine offered a residual disinfection effect that lasted after treatment point, and could prevent the growth of algae and slime in pipes and tanks, a feature that was important when the water supply and sewage systems were dated and leaking. However, chlorine could combine with the residual elements in the treated water and create new environmentally harmful and potentially carcinogenic compounds which often resulted in facilities installing dechlorination equipment to reduce chlorination by-products. Also, chlorine must be handled and transported cautiously as spills were toxic. Therefore, it was under considerable scrutiny in Europe and North America.

In contrast to the traditional chlorination method, UV technology had the advantage of being environmentally positive. It did not add anything to the water or change its chemistry, nor did it use dangerous additives or leave chemical residues harmful to plant and marine life. It was also more efficient, treating water instantly. Chlorination required contact time so large contact tanks needed to be constructed. The relative capital cost of UV and chlorine depended on the cost of labor and land, the size of the facility and the need for dechlorination equipment. Generally, operating and maintenance costs were lower for UV, offering a better net present value in the life of the equipment (see Exhibit 2). The major ongoing costs of UV units are the electric power consumption and lamp replacements. The UV units also required limited space for installation, which was important to large metropolitan areas, where land costs could be high. The Water Environment Research Foundation funded research in 1995 to compare UV and chlorination. The research confirmed the environmental and economic advantages of UV technology, and predicted that, as existing chlorine facilities concluded the end of their useful life, many would be replaced with UV systems.

For both the wastewater and clean water market, roughly four segments could be identified: (1) the municipal; (2) the industrial; (3) the commercial (dealing with the discharges from and the water supplies for office buildings, hotels, restaurants, shopping malls, etc.); (4) the residential. Trojan could supply products for all the four segments in both clean and wastewater markets. However, the municipal wastewater market was the most important revenue source for Trojan. A UV disinfection system typically accounted for about four per cent of the total cost of a municipal water treatment plant.

Trojan had about 80 per cent of the world's UV wastewater treatment market. Trojan's 1998 annual report estimated "that only 5% to 10% of municipal wastewater sites in North America use UV-based technology . . . (and) of the approximate 62,000 wastewater treatment facilities operating worldwide, only 2,500 currently utilize UV disinfection systems".

Trojan's UV units vary considerably in price. A small residential unit could range from $200 to $1,000. Commercial and industrial units could be as high as $100,000, while municipal units could cost several million dollars. The cost of the unit would depend on the volume and the quality of water (both in and out).

International Presence

Most of Trojan's sales were made through its 90-plus agents scattered around the world. The agents worked on commission. By leveraging their relationships with major project design and contractor companies in their territories, these agents could influence the type of disinfection technology that was used in the project. When the customer, such as the municipal government, made the decision, it was important that the customer be familiar with UV technology. In Hong Kong, for instance, Trojan initially sold a few small installations, which convinced the government officials to install a larger system because of the advantages of UV systems.

So far Trojan's development had been focused in North America and Europe. Because of the greater interest in and financial resources for environmental protection, this area accounted for 80 per cent of the world's total water treatment market, of which North America had about 55 per cent, and Western Europe about 24 per cent. Although industry experts estimated that the annual growth rate for these developed areas would slow down to less than five per cent in the coming years, replacement of chlorine systems would fuel growth in UV. However, as these markets matured, competition was escalating and profit margins thinning. Furthermore, technology regulations and customer preferences could change rapidly in these markets. In addition to their London, Ontario head office, Trojan had branch offices in The Hague, Netherlands, California, U.S.A., Australia and UK. In 1998, out of a total of 1,975 wastewater installations worldwide, 1,526 were in the U.S., 227 in Canada, 64 in Europe, 34 in South America, 82 in Asia, and 34 in Australia and New Zealand.

Human Resources

UV systems required very little maintenance. Usually one Trojan staff person was enough to help with the installation and the training of local staff. Trojan's London staff could often assist in maintenance of the units through verbal instructions. Only occasionally would on-site repair be required.

Currently, the company did not have personnel experienced with the Chinese water disinfection market and Chinese business practices. There were five engineers working in the R & D department, however, who were originally from Mainland China. None of them had a business or marketing background and none of them were in management positions.

Competitive Pressure

As the pioneering leader in ultraviolet water treatment technologies, Trojan had been able to thrive with the growing demand for the UV technology without facing much competition. However, the market had become increasingly competitive in the past two years. On June 29, 1999, the company announced lower than expected earnings for the fiscal year, citing competitive pressures, increased product development, and patent litigation as reasons behind the earnings disappointment. The next day its share price plummeted from $38.80 to $27.10. Trojan's main competitors in UV technology were Wedeco in Germany, and Infilco Degremont and Calgon Carbon in the U.S. To Trojan's knowledge, none had entered China. However, Trojan also faced competition from manufacturers of chlorine-based disinfection systems, where numerous companies existed. The most powerful players were the full-service water treatment companies, who could provide a complete set of services from consulting, to design, to installation and maintenance.

The company had responded to the competitive challenge with a series of strategic moves. One was to accelerate the development of next-generation technologies; the other was to launch a comprehensive cost engineering program. The strategic moves, together with the patent litigation discussed in detail below, would nevertheless incur increased costs for the short term.

Trojan had also made some significant investments recently. In 1998, Trojan acquired Sunwater Limited of U.K. and spent $2.8 million in purchasing a 39-acre property for future expansion. Additional capital expenditures were expected in support of company growth. In the same year, Trojan issued 700,000 common shares for gross proceeds of $21.7 million. In 1998, the net debt equity ratio stood at 0.53:1, compared to 0.20:1 in 1997.

Exhibits 3 and 4 provide the financial statements of Trojan Technologies Inc.

Intellectual Property Protection

Trojan was built on patented technologies. As a high-tech enterprise, Trojan spent heavily on research and development. The management believed that continued development of proprietary, state-of-the-art technologies were critical to maintaining a competitive edge in an increasingly competitive environment. However, direct and indirect imitation of its patented technologies would seriously hurt its business and damage the return on its investment in R&D.

The raw materials for the UV systems were concrete channels, metal reactors, pipes, UV lamps, and electronic components. Many of the components were made of stainless steel and manufactured in a Trojan subsidiary in London, Ontario. These parts were all standard and easily available. The single most important input were the patented ballasts. These circuits were designed for each unit and ensured superior effectiveness and reliability of the UV lamps. As well, Trojan offered unique knowledge by custom-designing each unit to the quality and volume of water at the site.

Trojan's management was constantly on the watch for any possible loss of intellectual property. In January 1999, Trojan initiated patent infringement action in the U.S., accusing Calgon Carbon Corporation, Calgon Carbon Canada, Inc. and the City of Hinesville, Georgia of infringing Trojan's U.S. Patent for a fluid purification device based on its System UV4000™ technology. The action intended to seek damages and an injunction against further infringement and also showed Trojan's determination to defend its patent rights in the world.

The China Opportunity

The Environmental Protection Market in China

China's economy had been growing at double-digit speed since its 1979 reforms. However, the development had come at the cost of the environment. By taxing environmental resources such as air, land and water, its economic growth was constrained. China's population was 1.2 billion and was expected to grow to 1.5 billion by 2020 at the current rate. Already, 60 million were without sufficient clean water for their needs. Arguably, the additional people would further tax water resources which would mean further deterioration of coastal and inland waters so that drinking water and water needed for industrial processes would become increasingly scarce. The failure of the government to respond quickly and responsibly could lead to devastating social and economic outcomes.

Recognizing the constraints imposed by a deteriorating environment on sustainable development, the Chinese government put environmental protection onto its agenda as a key issue. By the year 2000, an aggregate investment of US$34 billion, almost one per cent of China's GNP, was anticipated in order to control national pollution. The investment in environmental protection would continue well into the next century. Exhibit 5 presents the forecasted investments in environmental protection and demand for equipment in China from 2001 to 2010. The forecasted ten-year annual growth rate of the industry would be 23 per cent, way above the annual GNP growth. Priority in environmental protection for the next few years would go to four areas: development of urban sewage treatment systems; equipment to curb air pollution; solid waste disposal; and monitoring equipment.

Even though the size of the market was growing, corporate profits were not. While the annual output for the environmental protection industry increased by 721 per cent from 1988 to 1993, the average profit margin decreased from 22 per cent to 13 per cent, and to 8.5 per cent in 1997. The environmental protection industry in China was heavily concentrated in the densely populated coastal areas, due to the higher level of industrialization and commensurate pollution in these areas. The trend would most likely continue for the next decade, because these areas would remain financially better off and better endowed with advanced technologies and human resources in science and research. China had recently designated a few Environmental Industry Parks, encouraging foreign direct investments in the industry. Exhibit 6 identifies the output in the environmental protection industry by province for three years, i.e., 1988, 1993, 1997.

Water Resources and Water Treatment in China

The per capita water resource in China was only one-quarter of the world average. By 1997, about 400 of China's 668 cities were suffering from water shortages, of which more than 100 had serious water shortages and poor quality water supply. Underground water resources were overexploited. Ninety per cent of the urban water resources were seriously polluted; about 50 per cent of the drinking water supplies in major cities were below the national standard.

Water pollution resulted from two major sources: industrial wastewater and sewage water. Industrial wastewater could be effectively reduced through cleaner production processes. However, municipal wastewater would increase with the rise of living standards. The average per capita water usage in China had already increased from 162 litres in 1986 to 208 litres in 1996. The average percentage of municipal wastewater in the total wastewater discharge was around 40 per cent in China. However, in rich coastal cities like Shanghai and Guangzhou, the percentage was already close to 50 per cent and still on the rise.

About 82 per cent of China's wastewater was discharged into water bodies without any treatment, seriously contaminating the water resources of the country, and resulting in epidemic diseases and deteriorating aquatic life. The National Environmental Agency had required that by 2000, 74 per cent of the industrial wastewater and 25 per cent of the sewage water be treated before being discharged into receiving waters.

Therefore, one priority in water treatment in China had been the construction of urban water treatment plants. Urban water treatment facilities were growing in number faster than industrial wastewater facilities. Yet, of the 668 cities existing in 1997, only 123 cities had a total of 307 urban water treatment plants. Moreover, the majority of the country's 17,000 towns did not have any sewage and water treatment facilities. Therefore, the potential demand of the municipal segment would be significant in the coming years.

The Water Treatment Industry in China

In 1997, there were 2,558 manufacturers of the water treatment systems. More than 80 per cent of the companies were small enterprises with limited resources and low technological strength. Most of the domestic-made products were 10 to 20 years behind current world technology levels. Many were being made by village and township enterprises. Experts believed that 70 to 80 per cent of the domestic-made water treatment equipment were below acceptable international standards.

Water disinfecting equipment was among the products most in demand. However, the most widely used disinfection method was chlorination. Ultraviolet disinfection was a new idea to China. The cost of chlorination was roughly $200 per ton of water treated in China. One major cost of UV was electricity, which cost about $.10 per kilowatt hour in China.

A large proportion of the water treatment projects, especially the costly municipal water plants, received foreign funding. The environmental sector had absorbed more than US$3.3

billion in foreign funds by 1999. Foreign capital from various sources like the World Bank, the Asian Development Bank, United Nations Development Program, as well as bilateral government organizations and multi-lateral international organizations made up a substantial contribution to the environmental projects. The majority of the bilateral government loans made it clear that 60 per cent of the loan total must be used to purchase equipment from designated sources. Even when no such conditions were attached, foreign-made equipment was preferred for advanced technology and quality, or sometimes for other obscure considerations (e.g., foreign trips desired by the city officials). As a result, the municipal water treatment market was dominated by imported products, although the imports were usually three to six times more expensive than the domestic products. The U.S. Department of Commerce estimated that the percentage of imports of the total demand for wastewater treatment equipment had risen from 2.7 per cent in 1992 to 37.7 per cent in 1996. The government had, however, repeatedly called for the development of a domestic water treatment industry.

The project design market of water treatment plants was still dominated by domestic players. Since the engineering design market of China was not yet open to foreign competition, almost 98 per cent of the water treatment project design market in China was dominated by the "big eight institutes". The "big eight institutes" referred to the five institutes of civil engineering design affiliated to the Ministry of Construction and the institutes of civil engineering design in Beijing, Tianjing and Shanghai.

The Legal Environment and the Decision-Making Process

China's legal framework regarding environmental protection was quite advanced relative to other developing countries. Environmental policy had been written into the country's constitution since 1983, and the Environmental Protection Law was released in 1989. Standards for air, surface water, and noise had been established. The National Environmental Protection Agency (NEPA) was the leading government institution for developing policies, laws, and regulations related to environmental protection. Approximately 2,300 Environmental Protection Bureaus (EPBs) or Environmental Protection Offices (EPOs) existed at every level of local government, setting standards, monitoring the environment, conducting inspections, and issuing punishments for violations (usually in the form of fines). In addition, most EPBs and EPO's at the provincial level had in-house research institutes.

The legal framework for environmental protection in China was similar to that developed in the West. However, the implementation of the policies was considerably different. The levels of bureaucracy were deep and the project approval process lacked transparency. The involvement of numerous decision-makers made it difficult for firms to identify the person that had the power to make a binding decision.

The Municipal Segment

Theoretically, municipal governments had the power to determine what to do in building a water supply or treatment plant in their city. However, assistance in funding, foreign exchange, fuel, or transportation services might have to come from the central government, and therefore, approvals from higher levels were necessary. Large projects would always require feasibility studies submitted to both the Ministry of Construction and NEPA for approval. Frequently, contracts were awarded after a bidding process. However, the selection of the winning bid was not always based on business considerations. Personal contacts with the key people could influence the bidding process. The key decision-makers, however, varied from place to place.

In the coastal areas, different ways of building and maintaining water treatment facilities were being explored. Among them were long-term contracts, build-operate-transfer forms (in which a firm would build the facility, operate it and collect fees for a predetermined period before transferring it to the government), and turnkey projects (a foreign operator would build the project which would be turned over to the local authority for maintenance).

The Industrial and the Commercial Segments

The decision making for industrial and commercial facilities was decentralized. The government environmental agencies were in charge of stipulating standards, issuing permits, and conducting inspections. Although approvals from higher level authorities were always necessary, unless they had a vested interest, usually decisions made by the managers of the businesses would be honored. Contracts would be awarded through a bidding system. Again, the bidding processes were not transparent, and the final decision could be based on many non-business factors.

The Residential Segment

More than 90 per cent of urban families had access to running water, which was purified to some extent, but never clean enough for drinking. At home, people would boil water before they drank it. The demand for small, under the sink, household water purification products was weak, largely because of the lack of penetration of this type of equipment into the Chinese household market.

Urban real estate developers often installed sewage systems for residential buildings, and sometimes also installed sewage treatment facilities. The decisions for procuring suppliers lay with the developers, given the fact that all equipment was inspected and approved by environmental agencies.

Problems of the Chinese Environmental Market

The environmental protection market in China was not a well developed, orderly market with normal and healthy market competition. Problems abounded. Some issues were common to the whole Chinese market, which was in the painful process of changing from a command to a market economy.

First, there was an issue of local protectionism. Many local governments restricted products made outside their areas to protect their tax revenues. Some even required permissions for the sale of non-locally-made products. Second, corruption led to unfair competition. Bribery or abnormally high commissions were sometimes necessary to make sales. The bidding process was often not transparent, creating opportunities for corruption. Last but not least, there was a lack of respect and protection for intellectual property. Despite all the protection laws, violations of intellectual property happened with alarming frequency. It was not unusual for good products to not succeed because of competition from cheaper and inferior imitations. The water treatment market was no exception. One CEO of a Beijing water treatment company commented that one could not afford to go after all the imitators. However, he pointed out that quality, reputation and financial strength were still essential to stay in the market, especially the municipal water treatment market.

The Decision

There was little doubt that China offered enormous market potential and a strong need for water disinfection. Furthermore, selling environmental products in developing countries offered significant sustainable growth opportunities for Trojan. However, a number of issues complicated the decision so that Sarah was not sure if, when, how, and where Trojan should enter the Chinese market.

The contrast between the image outside of Sarah's window and her image of China was startling. As her gaze moved to the glass of crystal clear water on her desk, she recognized the enormous value of clean water and China should not be without it. The question was whether Trojan would be one of the companies that provided it.

Exhibit 1   Applications of Trojan's UV Systems

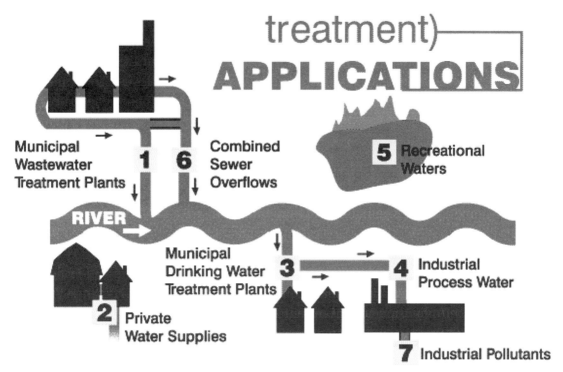

1. **Municipal Wastewater Treatment Plants**

   System UV4000 – 10 million gallons per day and up or 37,800 cubic meters per day and up

   System UV3000 – 1 million gallons per day to 30 million gallons per day or 3,780 cubic meters per day to 113,400 cubic meters per day.

2. **Private Water Supplies**

   Aqua UV Units - 2 to 12 gallons per minute or 5.5 to 45 liters per minute

3. **Municipal Drinking Water Treatment Plants**

   System UV8000 – 20 to 2000 gallons per minute or 75 to 7,500 liters per minute

4. **Industrial Process Water**

   System UV8000 – 20 to 2,000 gallons per minute or 75 to 7,500 liters per minute

5. **Recreational Waters**

6. **Combined Sewer Overflows**

   System UV4000 – 10 million gallons per day and up or 37,800 cubic meter's per day and up

7. **Industrial Pollutants**

   System UV3000 PTP - up to 1 million gallons per day or up to 3,780 cubic meters per day

   System UV3000 – 1 million gallons per day to 30 million gallons per day 3,780 cubic meters per day to 113,400 cubic meters per day

   AIR2000 - for remediation of contaminated air, soil and groundwater

Source: The company website of Trojan Technologies Inc., *http://www.trojanuv.com*, August 1999

Exhibit 2   Comparison of UV and Chlorination

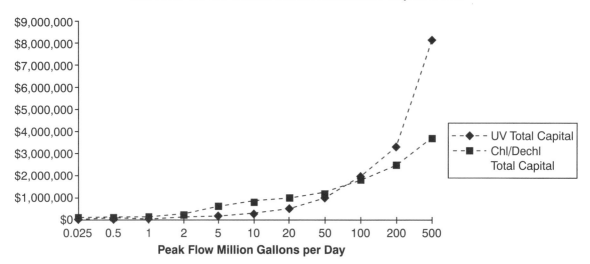

Ultraviolet vs. Gas Chlorination/Dechlorination Capital Costs

Legend:
- - - ◆ - - UV Total Capital
- - - ■ - - Chl/Dechl Total Capital

X-axis: Peak Flow Million Gallons per Day

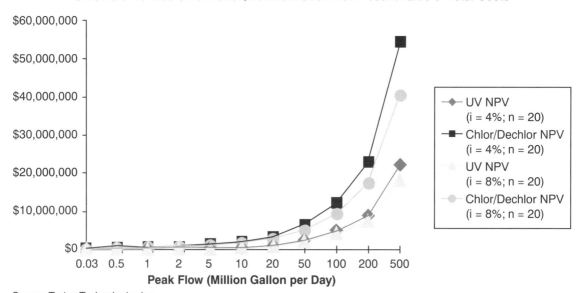

Ultraviolet vs. Gas Chlorination/Dechlorination Net Present Value of Total Costs

Legend:
- UV NPV (i = 4%; n = 20)
- Chlor/Dechlor NPV (i = 4%; n = 20)
- UV NPV (i = 8%; n = 20)
- Chlor/Dechlor NPV (i = 8%; n = 20)

X-axis: Peak Flow (Million Gallon per Day)

Source: Trojan Technologies Inc.

Exhibit 3   Consolidated Balance Sheets as at August 31 1998 (in CDN$000)

	1998 $	1997 $
ASSETS		
Current Assets		
Temporary investments	21,730	--
Accounts receivable	32,266	23,294
Accrued revenue on contracts in progress	18,965	5,618
Inventory	12,117	6,105
Prepaid expenses	320	254
Income taxes receivable	393	--
Total Current Assets	85,791	35,271
Investments in other companies	2,191	2,236
Capital Assets	16,367	12,866
Patents, trademarks and licence (net of accumulated amortization of $825,117 ($650,637 in 1997))	1,512	729
Goodwill (net of accumulated amortization of $25,231)	984	--
	106,845	51,102
LIABILITIES AND SHAREHOLDERS'EQUITY		
Current Liability		
Bank Indebtedness	23,296	6,308
Accounts payable and accrued charges	14,258	10,356
Income taxes payable	--	1,108
Deferred income taxes	2,224	1,300
Current portion of long-term debt	1,195	--
Total Current Liabilities	40,973	19,072
Long-term debt	6,407	--
Deferred income taxes	282	338
Shareholders' Equity		
Share capital	42,108	19,070
Retained earnings	17,075	12,622
	59,183	31,692
	106,845	51,102

Exhibit 4   Consolidated Statements of Income and Retained Earnings

	1998 $	1997 $
Sales	69,852	51,150
Cost of goods sold	40,586	30,156
Gross margin	29,266	20,994
EXPENSES		
Administrative and selling expenses	13,560	10,415
Research and development, net	3,318	3,184
Interest and bank charges	1,183	210
Amortization	1,807	982
	19,868	14,791
Operating income	9,398	6,203
Other income		
Interest income	51	248
Income from equity investment	935	698
Income before special charge and income taxes	10,384	7,149
Special charge	2,650	--
Income taxes	2,571	2,414
Net income	5,163	4,735
Retained earnings, beginning of year	12,623	7,888
Share issue costs, net of taxes	(712)	--
Retained earnings, end of year	17,074	12,623
Earnings per share		
Basic	0.67	0.62
Fully diluted	0.67	0.61

Exhibit 5 **Ten-year Forecast for the Chinese Environmental Market (2001 to 2010, US$ billions)**

Year	2001	2002	2003	2004	2005	2006	2007	2008	2009	2010	Total
Investment Amount	58.5	63.5	68.5	74.0	79.9	86.4	93.2	100.6	108.8	117.9	851.3
Market Demand	23.4	25.4	27.4	29.6	32.0	34.6	37.3	40.2	43.5	47.2	340.6

Exhibit 6 **Distribution of Chinese Environmental Industry (Annual Production Output, US$ billions)**

Year	Country Total	Eight Provinces, Municipalities with Highest Annual Production in Environmental Industry							
1988	3.8	Jiangsu	Liaoning	Shanghai	Shandong	Jilin	Hunan	Zhejiang	Beijing
		0.899	0.472	0.36	0.188	0.182	0.155	0.136	0.130
1993	31.2	Jiangsu	Zhejiang	Liaoning	Tianjing	Guangdong	Shanghai	Anhui	Hubei
		4.734	4.448	2.606	2.435	2.287	1.781	1.311	1.273
1997	52.17	Jiangsu	Zhejiang	Shandong	Tianjing	Guangdong	Shanghai	Sanxi	Henan
		9.755	7.263	3.914	2.848	2.845	2.425	2.21	2.16

case

10 BUNDY ASIA PACIFIC – CHINA STRATEGY

> The strategic concern is not about how risky it is to invest in China but how risky it is not to invest in China.
>
> Tony Martin, CEO of Bundy Asia Pacific.

In early 1996, Phil Stephenson, the Director of China for Bundy Asia Pacific (BAP), leaned back in front of his office window in Adelaide, Australia. He had been preoccupied with Bundy's business in China since his meeting that morning with Tony Martin. Martin had shown Phil the fax from Robin Thompson, the new marketing and product development director of Bundy International, BAP's U.K.-based parent company. Thompson had asked BAP about its strategy for the refrigeration business in China. This strategy would be part of Bundy's proposed global refrigeration strategy.

Bundy was a world-class fluid carrying system manufacturer serving the automobile and refrigeration industries. Bundy had entered the Chinese market by selling tubes to China nearly 20 years ago. It had established its first joint venture in China in 1987. However, Bundy had only achieved a 6.2 per cent market share in supplying the Chinese refrigeration industry, far from its goal of becoming the market leader. Bundy International recently had questioned whether BAP was realizing its full potential in the Chinese refrigeration market, as well as voicing its concern that Bundy's earnings were perceived to be too reliant on the cyclical automotive industry. Phil had been involved in Bundy's business in China since the very beginning. He had experienced the dramatic changes in China and Bundy's development there.

Richard Ivey School of Business
The University of Western Ontario

Jack Li, Nancy Wang and Steven Zuo prepared this case under the supervision of Professor Paul Beamish solely to provide material for class discussion. The authors do not intend to illustrate either effective or ineffective handling of a managerial situation. The authors may have disguised certain names and other identifying information to protect confidentiality. Ivey Management Services prohibits any form of reproduction, storage or transmittal without its written permission. This material is not covered under authorization from CanCopy or any reproduction rights organization.

Copyright © 1998, Ivey Management Services

Changing China

China had been undergoing economic reform for 20 years, creating an attractive environment for foreign investors. With its 1.2 billion population and large, fast-growing economy, China was viewed by many as the economic giant of the 21st century.

Until 1996, China had achieved a relatively stable political environment although it had done little towards political reform. Fears that the death of Deng Xiaoping, China's senior leader without portfolio, would result in widespread instability appeared to have abated. Instead, political stability depended more on economic growth, social security system development and Deng's successor, Jiang Zemin. Jiang had focused on strengthening control over the speed of economic development while risking increased unemployment and deteriorating governmental relationships. Employees in the less competitive state-owned enterprises (SOEs) counted on government subsidies for survival. Few people wished to see economic, social and political instability. The leadership also was committed to institutional, administrative and legal reforms. It intended to alter government's role from direct intervention to macroeconomic control. Overall, China was separating its economic development from its political reform and instability, similar to Singapore, Taiwan, South Korea, and even Japan.

Despite providing a huge consumption base, China's growing population had become the toughest challenge to the Chinese government. Birth control had been a high priority policy for many years, with some success in the eastern and major cities, but failing to some degree in middle and western China, especially in the rural areas.

Ironically, the most serious underlying issue of doing business in China lay in the shortage of qualified managers, sales people, marketers, quality control personnel, and to a lesser degree, engineers and technicians. The long history of a planned economy left few people over the age of 50 with an innovative mindset. The cultural revolution had simply disabled another generation from the age of 40 to the early 50s. Thanks to the 20-year reform, a well educated young generation with entrepreneurial spirit was available in the labor market and trainable for management positions. However, while a few foreign-invested enterprises (FIEs) were devoted to systematically training local people, the entire country produced only a few hundred MBA graduates each year from internationally accredited programs. The shortage was getting worse as China's economy galloped ahead. Therefore, there had been tough competition for the limited resource of qualified people, which resulted in poaching, job-hopping and a steady spiralling of pay packages.

In addition to the shortage of qualified people, China faced other difficulties, including limited financial resources, outdated technology and poor infrastructure conditions. To encourage development in certain areas first, China granted special status to five special economic zones, 14 open coastal cities, open coastal economic zones, high-technology development zones and other areas. In these regions, special incentives and privileges were accorded to foreign investors. These included: reduced corporate income tax rates; tax holidays; exemption from or reduction in withholding taxes for profits remitted overseas; exemption from or reduction in import and export taxes; lower land-use fees; simplified entry and exit procedures; and freedom of employment.

Due to the success in these areas, China had seen rapid economic growth for more than a decade. Under tight government control, its GDP growth dropped from an overheated 13.4 per cent in 1993 to 10.2 per cent in 1995, with forecasts of a further decrease to the more healthy level of nine per cent in 1996 and in the near future. In the meantime, China had successfully controlled its retail price inflation, which fell from 21.7 per cent in 1994 to 14.8 per cent in 1995 and was estimated to be eight per cent in 1996. Foreign exchange rates had also been effectively controlled due to the big increase in foreign reserves, up over $100 billion. Infrastructure had been well developed around these special areas, but still underdeveloped in other areas. Both the quantity and the quality of roads and transportation vehicles were still a barrier, or at least unfavourable, for efficient cross-country and even cross-region transportation in terms of timing, volume and costs. This limited the feasibility of some operations to cover country-wide markets.

To keep its growth sustainable, and to avoid unrest from unbalanced geographic development, the Chinese government recently had paid increasing attention to development in middle and western China. With the government shifting its focus from coastal cities in eastern China to middle and western China, many incentive policies also followed this pattern. For instance, on the expiration of the five-year tax holiday period (originally applicable only to a special area along the coastline), a further tax-rate reduction of 15 per cent to 30 per cent might be granted for an additional 10 years for projects located in economically underdeveloped areas. Recent statistics showed that growth in industrial value-added was 22.7 per cent in eastern China, and 24.5 per cent in middle and western China. This message was significant, indicating a successful shift of economic focus from eastern to middle and western China.

Refrigeration Market

A real Chinese refrigeration market emerged in the mid-1980s. It was expected to experience four phases in its development. Phase one — introduction of refrigeration into the Chinese market and rapid growth along coastline areas and major cities took place from the mid-1980s to the mid-1990s. In phase one, market sales reached 11 million refrigerators and three million freezers a year. In phase two the refrigerator market was expected to peak at 12 million units per year in 1997, and remain relatively stable until the year 2000, while the freezer market would have modest growth. The existing market was highly penetrated, but the replacement market was still in its infancy. Rural and mid-western areas were expected to grow at a slow rate due to consumers' limited purchasing power. Phase three would entail rapid growth of the total market, including an increasing replacement segment in the saturated market and growth in the rural area as well as in mid-western China, from 2000 to 2010. The market would mature with sales of about 30 million units of refrigerators and five million units of freezers a year. This estimate was quite conservative because it was based on the assumptions of a family size of four members and the country-wide success of birth control. The one-child policy and lifestyle change did create a smaller family size, but the size on average could be over four members due to a higher percentage of population in rural areas where it was still common for three generations to live in the same household. In this stage, the mid-western region would contribute to most of the market growth. In phase four the market would stay stable after 2010.

The Chinese refrigeration industry had been dominated by local manufacturers. Most major OEMs were concentrated in three areas along the coastline: Guangzhou, Shanghai and Qingdao, to serve the more developed areas in China (Exhibit 1). Over 40 per cent of refrigeration production capacity was concentrated in the Shanghai area. However, some refrigeration OEMs had started their strategic moves into middle and western China. After 10 years of overheating, this industry was facing high overcapacity with a current utilization rate of 69 per cent. According to the planning of each major OEM, total capacity would continue to grow and end up with a 62 per cent utilization rate in 2000. Market competition had consolidated 150 original players into several dozen, with the top 12 OEMs taking 85 per cent of the total market (Exhibits 2 and 3). It was predicted that further consolidation would sooner or later decrease the OEMs to about five giants. In the last year, global OEMs, such as Whirlpool, Siemens, Electrolux and Samsung, had entered the Chinese refrigeration market through joint ventures with medium-sized Chinese OEMs.

With respect to tube supply, refrigeration OEMs had always faced a tradeoff between quality and price. At the beginning, when few local suppliers could produce qualified tube, the emphasis was on quality. At that time, Bundy won the market because of its high quality. However, as some local products became acceptable, some OEMs favoured cheap local tubes with adequate quality. As the supplier base grew, however, refrigeration OEMs had become more and more demanding of both quality and price to sustain their competitiveness. This quality requirement had been accelerated by the introduction of CFC-free products, which required a much higher level of technical input for either the tube and system design or the process technology, depending on the refrigerants used. The OEMs had been tightening their sourcing price to shift the burden of their high costs caused by overcapacity and their low prices forced by tough competition. The change had been considered both an opportunity and a challenge to BAP and its local competitors.

The total refrigeration components market value in 1996 was estimated at RMB1.36 billion. The opportunity value for a steel tubing-maker and component-fabricator was RMB527 million. Exhibit 4 provides some basic analysis about the market value and BAP's share. The opportunity value consisted of tube components that used steel and other materials that were directly substitutable for steel tube. The opportunity market value for tube alone was about RMB349 million. An internal condenser needed around 25 meters of steel tube. The potential market would be 270 million meters of steel tube a year. This was the capacity of nine production lines of single-wall tube manufacture. This capacity excluded potential demand for other refrigeration parts, which could amount to over three lines.

Tubing Industry

In 1987, when BAP established its first joint venture in China, the company met almost no head-to-head competition with Chinese tube manufacturers. However, with the rapid growth of the refrigeration and automobile industries, dozens of local players emerged. Competitors could be divided into two tiers: tube-fabricators and commodity tube-makers. Some played both roles. All the commodity steel tube manufacturers, except BAP, were local players. The typical capital investment to set up a one-production-line tube plant was about RMB27 million. Exhibit 5 provides some detailed information about these tube-makers. Most local tube-makers encountered various quality issues. However, despite some OEMs that still imported tubes, local competitors were catching up and imports were decreasing drastically because of the high cost.

Fabricators consisted of refrigeration OEMs, who produced parts in-house, and component-makers. PLA No. 9511, Jiaonan, Xinxiang Kelong and Qingdao Haier were the key components suppliers in China. Like the tube-makers, nearly all the component-makers were private companies, so their financial data were not available. Capital investment required for fabrication capability could be from RMB7 million to RMB60 million, depending on the scope of business.

The refrigeration industry was aware of the benefits that could be gained from outsourcing non-core activities. In regions where the infrastructure was reliable and suppliers had a good quality record, manufacturers had already outsourced components. Outsourcing was mainly to improve product quality rather than achieve cost reductions, since the low labor rates made it difficult for suppliers to offer significant savings. However, there still existed a trace of the traditional organization concept of self-sufficiency or "small but complete units." It was difficult to forecast the increase in outsourcing given the complexity of the manufacturers' existing capability, low costs, the social burden of bearing the spare labor force and transportation difficulty. In 1995, outsourcing and in-house production were nearly even (Exhibit 6).

Bundy Asia Pacific

Structure

Bundy was a member of TI Group, a U.K.-based diversified multinational company engaged in three types of business: Bundy, Dowty Aerospace and John Crane. Bundy itself was a multinational, consisting of 73 plants in 27 countries with sales of £717.7 million and profit before interest and exceptional items of £73.5 million in 1995.

Bundy strengthened its market leader position through its focus on organic growth and the successful execution of its strategy to grow share in existing markets by introducing new products and continuing to increase the added-value of systems. The industry spread was approximately two-thirds automotive and one-third industrial, which was principally refrigeration. Bundy's current geographical spread was 45 per cent North America, 45 per cent Europe and 10 per cent

Rest of World. Bundy was continually focusing on the global refrigeration market. BAP, as a member of Bundy International, was a wholly owned subsidiary of Bundy.

BAP's headquarters were located in Adelaide, Australia. Four country directors and a finance director reported to the CEO of BAP, Tony Martin. A 1984 graduate of Ivey's MBA program, he became BAP's CEO in 1995. The Australia Division was responsible not only for its local production, marketing and sales, but also for BAP's administration function. There were three joint ventures under its China division: Hua Yan Bundy Tubing (HBT), Bundy South China (BSC) and Wuhan, a recently established joint venture to be focused on the automotive industry. All the general managers of the JVs were financially accountable to their own board of directors, which in turn were responsible to their local shareholders and BAP. According to the joint venture agreements, BAP also provided the operations with technology support. Since all the general managers of these joint ventures had been assigned from and by BAP, they also reported to Phil Stephenson, the Director of China. Exhibit 7 illustrates BAP's organizational structure.

In addition, TI had a representative office in Beijing, China. The current representative, Patrick Bontemps, also held the title of Director of China Program, BAP. He played a key role in liaison, marketing and business development for BAP. With respect to new projects, he could be deeply committed to project negotiations or just coordinate the business activities taking place in China.

Strategy

BAP aimed to be the leading manufacturer of fluid carrying systems, focusing on the market niche of supplying small-diameter steel tube and systems to refrigeration and automotive industries in the Asia Pacific area. BAP's industry spread had more emphasis on the automotive than the refrigeration industry. Geographically, the major existing markets it served were Australia and New Zealand, while the markets it pursued for organic growth were China and Korea. Because of the rapid growth of the Chinese refrigeration market, and the fact that refrigeration market potential was bigger than the automotive market from BAP management's perspective, BAP had committed primarily to the refrigeration industry in China. Except for BAP's subsidiaries in China, no other Bundy member could sell products into the Chinese market. Furthermore, the Chinese subsidiaries could ask for technological support from BAP or any other Bundy members all over the world. This worldwide technology support was limited to the existing technology BAP had invested in the subsidiaries. To sustain its competitive advantage, BAP would need to be able to continuously transfer its latest technology into its subsidiaries in China.

BAP's management believed that it had made efforts to sustain its competitive premises in China through:

1. offering its customers cost-effective products of world-competitive quality delivered on time;

2. adding value to its employees by supporting and motivating them in a good work environment;

3. ensuring profitable production of high quality steel tubing products, using technologically advanced equipment, operated by well trained, competent and highly skilled employees;

4. dedicating itself to continuous improvement through a data-based approach to quality assurance and performance measurement; and,

5. getting technological support from other Bundy units.

BAP had mainly focused on tube manufacture in China. But, to raise the added value, it had pursued certain levels of vertical integration. It was backward-integrated with the capability of copper-coated strip production, and forward-integrated with the capability of tube end fabrications. It had also started to produce some components of refrigeration systems and auto parts.

BAP's Business Development in China

Exporting Before 1987

BAP started to sell its tube into the Chinese market as early as the late 1970s when China commenced its economic reform. China had no import quotas, but China's foreign trade was regulated primarily through a system of import and export licensing. Foreign trade corporations, authorized by government to conduct import business, needed a general license to import commodities within their approved scope of business. State-owned enterprises and FIEs importing products from abroad were first required to obtain approval from the relevant government authorities. Import duty was assessed on the normal cost, insurance and freight (CIF) value, while export duty was assessed on the free-on-board (FOB) value. The redundant procedure and high duty rate made local customers' imports comparatively time-consuming and expensive. After learning about the Chinese market, and bringing the concept of Bundy Tube into China through exporting, BAP started to look for a higher level of opportunity to increase its commitment in the Chinese market in order to keep pace with market growth.

Bundy had never licensed its technology to any Chinese tube-maker. In the early days, when Bundy decided to invest in China, several major factors led Bundy away from licensing. One was the lack of qualified candidates in terms of quality control, reputation, qualified people and big customer base. Another was the question of intellectual property rights protection. Neither of the first two could justify licensing. As well, the top management of BAP preferred a deeper involvement than a licensing agreement, in accordance with their vision of potential business development in China. In addition, Bundy's success in other countries in Asia Pacific provided it with strong financial resources and some knowledge for a capital investment in China.

First Joint Venture, HBT, in 1987

In 1987, in northern China Bundy established its first joint venture, HBT, primarily as a tubing operation supplying the local refrigeration and automobile industries. This commitment made Bundy one of the earliest entrants into China from Australia. HBT was a 50:50 joint venture with two Chinese partners, Qinhuangdao Development Company (QDC), owned by the government of Qinhuangdao Economic and Technological Development Zone (ETDZ), and Central Iron & Steel Research Institute (CISRI), a state-owned academic institution in Beijing, with 30 per cent and 20 per cent of HBT shares, respectively. CISRI was considered to have the best tubing technology and the best technology staff in China. It could make the transferring process of Bundy's technology smoother and quicker from Bundy's point of view. CISRI might also add some value to the knowledge of the Chinese tubing industry. From the Chinese side, the involvement of CISRI might help the Chinese to digest the most advanced tubing technology. In fact, the operation and engineering managers of HBT came from CISRI. The QDC was brought in to ease the joint venture start-up and obtain continuous support from the local government. The 50:50 share split between the Chinese and foreign partners of HBT reflected the need for risk-sharing and the lack of experience among the partners at the early stage of economic reform.

HBT was located in the ETDZ of Qinhuangdao City, Hebei Province, along the coastline of northern China. Qinhuangdao was one of the 14 open coastal cities with ETDZ. When established, HBT was certified as a technologically advanced joint venture by the Ministry of Foreign Trade and Economic Cooperation. This status provided it with additional special treatment from the government in the designated area. For example, tax holidays allowed it to exempt its income tax for the first two profitable years and half of the regular tax rate for the next three years, and the amount of tax, which had been paid, would be refunded to the joint venture by the government if the joint venture reinvested its income in China for innovation or expansion. In addition, the joint venture might be granted a 50 per cent reduction of the usual income tax rate for the three years following the expiration of the initial tax exemption and reduction period.

HBT had two double-wall tube product lines and one single-wall tube product line, with the capacities of 5,000 tons (roughly 60 million meters, depending on the combination of tube sizes supplied) and 2,500 tons (30 million meters on average) a year, respectively. The product lines were imported from Australia. HBT also had a production line of copper-coated steel strip. HBT was capable of controlling its tube quality because of the Bundy tubing technology and because it used imported steel belt and its own copper-plating facility located on site. It was believed that HBT's tubes qualified for CFC-free refrigerators. HBT also had some tube-end fabrication and components production capabilities, such as bending machines.

Because of the rapid growth of the refrigeration and automotive industries in the late 1980s, coupled with Bundy Tube's quality reputation and almost no competition from the Chinese tubing industry, HBT made good profits in its initial years. HBT's presence and success gave rise to a broad awareness of the high quality of Bundy Tube and the advanced technology process required for production within both Chinese refrigeration and tubing industries. HBT's employees were still excited when they recalled those good years when there was always a waiting list for Bundy Tube.

The Second Joint Venture, BSC, in 1990

HBT's early success and the further rapid development of the Chinese refrigeration industry encouraged Bundy to set up the second joint venture, BSC, in southern China in 1990. The new facility started production in 1992. The Chinese market then was divided geographically by the Yangtze River into two segments according to Bundy's China strategy. HBT served the northern segment, while BSC covered the southern segment.

BAP held 80 per cent of the shares of BSC with CISRI and Lanshi Industrial and Trade Co. accounting for the other 20 per cent. There was no Chinese local government involved in the joint venture. CISRI was not as involved in the business as it had been in HBT. BSC's general managers were expatriates from Australia. The current general manager had a Chinese background.

BSC was located in Foshan City, Guangdong Province, the pilot area for the whole country's economic reform. Due to government special policies, the economy of Guangdong had exploded one or two years ahead of other regions. Its proximity to Hong Kong also helped its rapid economic development. A FIE in this area, Pearl River Delta, had enjoyed similar incentives to those in the open coastal cities since 1988. Some major refrigeration OEMs, such as Kelong, Hualing and Wanbao, were concentrated within Pearl River Delta, about 50 kilometers away from Foshan. However, BSC's other major customers in Shanghai and Zhejiang province were over 1,000 kilometers away.

BSC was smaller than HBT. It only had one double-wall tube product line with a capacity of 2,500 tons a year. Also, it had some tube-end fabrication and tube-bending machines for value-added tubing and components production.

Before BSC started its production, Bundy had enjoyed a steady growth and a good profit from its business in China. There seemed to be no doubt about Bundy's bright future for business development in China.

Issues Emerged in the First Half of the 1990s

In the early 1990s, a group of local competitors began to mature. The local players basically competed on low cost and proximity to customers, while Bundy competed on quality. On average, Bundy's price had been 10 per cent higher than that of local competitors. Bundy's higher price came from its greater costs: imported material, high quality criteria with a high rate of waste and expatriate cost. Mr. Bontemps, Director of China Program, BAP, commented on the high price:

We focus on differentiation with high quality in the market. We will not be competitive until the customers realize that tube quality is so important that it is worth paying a premium for better quality. This has happened in our auto industry.

However, because local competitors were catching up, Bundy did not commit to continuously introducing its latest technology and further investing in China for sustainable growth. The reason for the lack of commitment was the unresolved ownership issue at both levels of Bundy Asia Pacific and Bundy China. Bundy Asia Pacific Division was established by Bundy International of TI Group and Tubemaker of Australia (TA) with 40:60 shares, respectively. According to TI's policy, Bundy International would not invest or introduce the latest technology continuously into a project if it did not see an increase in TA's value because of TI's investment. HBT was falling into the same situation. In June 1995, TI successfully acquired 10 per cent of its shares from TA, and complete acquisition was also in negotiation. This event released Bundy International from the restrictions on its commitment to Bundy Asia Pacific's business development in China.

As the waiting list for Bundy tubes gradually disappeared, Bundy China's sales and profitability went down. As a matter of fact, unlike HBT, BSC did not enjoy major success when it opened. The poor sources of local raw materials and foreign exchange restrictions, which had been disguised by high prices in those good years, made the two operations more difficult and expensive. Severe credit restrictions on the availability of renminbi also had a negative impact on the business. Eventually, both of the joint ventures encountered a loss for the first time in 1994, and carried similar operating and financial performances forward into 1995. The two joint ventures together had projected sales of RMB85 million (including the auto market) for 1996. They would break even, but held only a 6.2 per cent share of total market value. Due to the decrease of sales, the equipment utilization rate had been as low as 50 per cent to 80 per cent of its former levels.

Internal Issues

To assess the major obstacles confronting Bundy China's growth, Phil carefully analysed several internal and external issues causing the slippage in sales in the last few years. Internally, the nature of the 50:50 share holding and the need for consensus on all major decisions had made the business of HBT difficult to manage efficiently. The difficulty mainly came from the partners' differences in objectives and systems. The difference in objectives between partners in China had been described as "in the same bed but different dreams." What QDC, the local government partner, wanted from HBT were local economic development, advanced technology transfer, capital infusion and local employment. CISRI was more interested in learning advanced technology and management skills, as well as generating some rapid returns. BAP, like most foreign investors, wished for market share and profitability. Moreover, although Chinese law allowed a joint venture to set up its system to fit its own needs and desires, neither of the two Chinese partners nor the Chinese employees could quickly adapt to a Western management system. The Chinese partners wanted to appreciate and learn the way in which BAP ran the business, but they found it difficult to break with their long-existing framework, particularly in a short period of time. Under these circumstances, the equally shared joint venture resulted in endless conflicts.

During the last nine years, Bundy had successively sent six employees to China as general managers of HBT. Other staff in its finance and engineering departments were sent over on a problem-solving basis. Bundy had also rotated its BSC general manager three times within four years. This helped BAP accumulate knowledge of doing business in China. However, the high turnover of management was perceived as contributing to the recent losses.

In general, it could take as long as a year for any foreign general manager to understand the new business environment, market, employees and methods by which the Chinese do business. The greatest challenge a foreign manager faced was the communication hurdle. This hurdle was created up by all the differences in language, culture and values, the separation of the foreign manager from Chinese managers and employees, and the lack of qualified local people who knew the Western way of doing business. In the Chinese employees' eyes, some of BAP's general managers never did break through the hurdle. The perceived failure isolated them from their subordinates, Chinese customers and competitors. As a result, they appeared to have become more ethnocentric and short- tempered. One general manager had been teased by Chinese employees for the attention he paid to those who didn't flush the toilet or who dropped cigarette butts. Under these circumstances, it was not realistic to expect a general manager to focus on strategic planning. Even though some expatriates eventually survived the culture shock, many were not psychologically far from departure for home.

Recent adverse profitability had also upset front-line laborers. Most of the current 200 employees had been in HBT for several years. Their compensation was slightly above the average level in Qinhuangdao ETDZ. Employees had been basically satisfied with the system and income during those good years. However, due to declining sales, front-line operators' piece-rate wages had been affected badly. Their income, between the best and worst scenarios, could drop from RMB2,000 to below RMB1,000 a month. To reduce cost, HBT had also exercised a downsizing in the last two years. Under usual circumstances most state-run companies with losses hardly ever laid off their employees. The downsizing seemed evidence of the old mindset that a joint venture would not provide its employees with job security. Together with the decrease in income, the downsizing had caused some morale issues among the remaining employees. As a result, some skilled operators voluntarily left HBT. An HBT employee commented: "If his job is not secure and his income has been decreased drastically, why should a skilled operator stay for loyalty?"

Moreover, there also seemed to be an incentive issue for HBT's sales force. The sales section consisted of four experienced salespersons, each of whom was assigned a region as his market. They were very skilled technologically (not very skilled commercially) and tended to work hard. However, some salespersons had complained about an unstable reward policy. When sales went down, management wanted to use commissions to stimulate the salespersons' commitment, and everyone agreed. But when commissions climbed with increased sales, salespersons usually made more money than other employees, on the same level, in other sections. Payment disparity was still not a fair concept to most Chinese employees, especially where employees had previously worked in state-run companies. It often caused trouble for management if the incentive system for the sales force was not changed. Currently, the sales force worked on a salary-based compensation system, which definitely did not motivate them.

External Issues

Like most companies, Bundy China had to give up some customers to reduce its "triangle debt" burden when its sales went down. Triangle debt was a chain of overdue debt or delayed accounts receivable involving other companies in the market chain and the related financial institutions. It resulted from a failure of some part of this chain to pay its due debt or accounts payable, but for various reasons the government did not allow it to go bankrupt. The payment delay might cause serious cash-flow problems to all the members in the value chain. It had been a country-wide issue for quite a while, and so far there had not been any effective solution. Consequently, a competitive firm had to have the financial strength to finance not only its formal capital investment and operating expenses, but also the triangle debt in order to keep its major customers afloat. In the tubing industry, payment was usually due when customers loaded their trucks with tubes. But, there were only a few good customers who were able or willing to pay the due bill. Some customers paid their bill one or two months later, while many others would delay the payment up to or over 100 days, if they ever paid it.

Furthermore, there was an increasing erosion of Bundy's intellectual property rights to its technology, and confusion about the brand name of Bundy Tube. After Bundy Tube had gained broad awareness, almost all local double-wall tube-makers informally claimed that they supplied Bundy Tube. Even the refrigeration OEMs used to refer to all double-wall tubes as Bundy Tubes. It was believed by Bundy people that some locally made production lines were simply an imitation of Bundy's technology. The confusion mainly came from the local players' ignorance of intellectual property rights. This attack had damaged Bundy Tube's reputation because of the poor quality of local tube. This issue had also attracted the attention of the Chinese Household Appliance Association. An article with the title "Bundy Tube is not a fast food," written as a warning to both tubing and refrigeration industries, was published in the *Chinese Household Electronic Appliance Newspaper* in 1994. But nobody knew whether the warning stopped the imitation or if it set a benchmark for local imitators. According to a recent market survey, nearly all double-wall tubes in the marketplace were perceived as Bundy Tube, and some major local tube-makers were gradually improving the quality of their products.

Strategic Concern in Early 1996

Bundy China's financial downturn in the last few years had sent Phil a clear signal that China had changed. To turn the current situation around and to lead Bundy China to further growth, BAP needed a strategic plan for a systematic investment in China, instead of a few relatively independent operations. After thinking through all the major issues that Bundy China encountered, Phil turned his attention to Bundy China's organizational structure.

Satellite System versus Concentrated Locations

Phil had always faced a trade-off between proximity to major customers and economies of scale for each operation location. To keep its high costs from further increases, and to reduce its exposure to the uncertainty of its major customers, Bundy China had made every effort to operate at high capacity in its existing concentrated locations. Therefore, Bundy China's long-distance relationship with some major customers, especially in the Shanghai area, remained an unresolved issue.

Proximity was important in China because it could allow a competitor to gain such advantages as close customer relationships, short lead times, and transportation cost reductions. A well-established relationship with customers was a prerequisite of successfully doing business in China. Business relationships in China required personal involvement and continuous contacts. If a customer said, for instance, "long time no see" to you, it could be a warning for you to check out whether your relationship with the customer was still as close as before. Not surprisingly, some competitors located themselves near major customers, and their general managers and technical staff even worked in the customers' plants day in and day out. There were also plenty of relationship-building activities involving both competitors and customers after regular work hours. It was very hard for a distant supplier to keep a close customer relationship with so many local competitors trying to cut in. "Long-distance relationships just don't work for a common-law marriage," commented an observer.

Due to miserably poor transportation conditions, refrigeration OEMs usually allowed two weeks as the lead time for tube supply, while their change-over time from one product to another needed only a couple of hours. In the refrigeration market, over 100 different sizes and styles existed. Most OEMs produced various refrigerators in response to changes in market demand, though they had annual and monthly plans. Short lead time was what they were looking for to reduce their inventory, and quick response to market change. In addition, shipping costs could be as much as 10 per cent of finished costs. A purchasing manager of a medium-sized refrigeration company complained that he spent RMB6 million on the transportation of tubes each year. Transportation issues were even more important as BAP increased its forward integration to components supply. The shaped tubes which occupied large spaces increased transportation costs and even made a long-distance components delivery unfeasible in some instances.

To cope with these problems, Phil was drafting a satellite structure for Bundy China, which was expected to balance proximity to major customers and economies of scale of each operation. Also, it would leave Bundy China's organizational structure with enough flexibility to respond to the rapid changes required by major customers. This structure would basically consist of three levels: headquarters, tubing operations and value-added fabrications. But this plan needed to be rationalized in details such as locations, sizes, modes and timing.

Representative Office versus Holding Company

A systematic investment in China would require an increased presence of Bundy China's headquarters in China. This greater presence might help Phil to set up a team that pulled together all existing and prospective management resources, inside and outside of China, to pursue a common objective, synergy of strategic moves and closer relationships with major customers. Currently, foreign companies were not permitted to establish branch offices in China. Therefore, Phil drew up some simple comparisons between a representative office and a holding company in China based on the data he had.

A representative office was easy to establish. To set up a representative office, a foreign company simply had a local Chinese organization sponsor its application and then undergo a formal registration process. However, representative offices could engage only in "non-direct operating activities," such as liaison work, consulting, market research, general information gathering, and sourcing and procurement of products and materials.

Unlike FIEs, all Chinese employees who worked in representative offices had to be hired and assigned to the offices by the Foreign Employment Services Corporation (FESCO) or some other approved labor service agent. The offices would pay FESCO for the cost of the personnel and FESCO, in turn, would pay the employees about 40 per cent to 50 per cent of that amount; FESCO retained the difference to cover employee benefits. Since the income the Chinese employees would take home was much lower than they expected, the offices were generally expected to provide additional payments to employees in various forms of subsidies.

In addition, Chinese governments imposed taxes on the offices based on their deemed gross revenue due to the clarification difficulty of business activities. The deemed gross revenue of a representative office was determined by applying a cost-plus formula based on 110 per cent of the representative office's operating expenses. If the net taxable income of the representative office could not be accurately determined, the local tax bureau might deem 10 per cent of the representative office's gross revenue as its taxable profit.

In general, if a foreign enterprise was interested in establishing manufacturing operations and a sales network in China for the local market, a Chinese holding company (CHC) seemed a good substitute for a representative office. Limited liability CHCs might be in the form of either wholly foreign-owned subsidiaries or Sino-foreign equity joint ventures. A CHC could play a much wider range of roles, such as country-wide strategic planning, marketing and sales, business development, technology co-ordination, information centre, financing support, management training and performance assessment.

As with all FIEs, CHCs might directly recruit their required staff and workers locally, with the assistance of the local department of labor and personnel. By law, it had the right to hire and dismiss staff and to determine its own personnel system. If workers were not available locally, it might recruit personnel from outside the region. It also might set its own wage levels, salary payment methods and systems of bonuses and allowances.

However, the Chinese authorities' intention was currently to restrict the establishment of CHCs to only those multinational companies with major investment plans in China. The rigid prerequisites for a foreigner to set up a CHC included either minimum net assets of US$400 million, with registered capital of over US$10 million already contributed to FIEs in China, and three or more future project proposals approved, or ownership of at least 10 FIEs that conducted production-oriented or infrastructure-related activities. The total capital contributed must be in excess of US$30 million. Upon approval, the foreign investor had to make a capital contribution of not less than US$30 million within two years from the date of the issuance of the business license. It seemed that BAP's existing subsidiaries in China did not qualify it to set up a CHC. But, the situation might be changed following systematic investment in China, especially rationalized with the development of both refrigeration and automotive industries.

Joint Ventures versus Other Modes

After entering into China, BAP's management team and supporting staff had a broad interface with its operations in China. It seemed clear to Phil that there was not much value the current Chinese partners could add to the business since BAP knew the Chinese market and so many employees were involved. It might be time for BAP to look for an opportunity to acquire some or all of HBT's shares from its Chinese partners. The acquisition could be justified by more management control, capital infusion, operating financial support and transfer of its latest technology into the subsidiaries. As the number of FIEs in the area were blooming, the local government became less interested in owning HBT's shares. The reduced cash flow of the last two years might give rise to a perfect time for the acquisition. However, Phil did not intend to ignore his relationship with local government. In China, a foreign investor was always facing a tradeoff between how much control he was willing to give up and how much support he wanted from local government. Phil questioned whether he should get rid of the local government partner though local governments, in general, were becoming more supportive in the eastern area. The further question in Phil's mind was what he should do if he set up some new plants in China, especially in the middle and western areas, which were about 10 years behind the eastern area.

Phil had been deeply involved in BAP's business development in China, including the start-up of the two joint ventures. Although he was located at the headquarters in Australia, he travelled frequently between China and Australia. It was time for him to think through the potential changes. Although some strategic movements had been considered and executed, he needed to systematically consider BAP's business development in China in terms of its market, structure, mode and timing, and come up with a new strategy for Bundy China. This would be due in two weeks.

Exhibit 1   Chinese Map with BAP's Joint Venture and its Major Customers

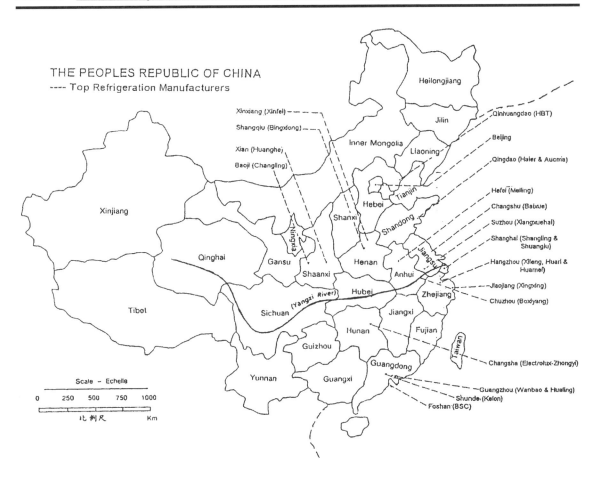

Exhibit 2   Refrigerator Manufacturers — Production Volume (000)

Name	Location	1995	1996 (estimate)
Kelon	Guangdong Province	1,222	1,500
Haier	Shandong	1,000	1,500
Shangling	Shanghai	853	1,000
Meiling	Anhui	754	900
Boxinyang (Yangzi)	Anhui	750	300
Xinfei	Henan	719	980
Changling	Shaanxi	626	750
Wanbao	Guangdong	569	700
Xileng	Zhejiang	505	630
Shuanglu	Shanghai	366	450
Hualing	Guangdong	350	400
Huari	Zhejiang	340	410
Subtotal		8,054	9,520
Others		1,546	1,480
Total		**9,600**	**11,000**

Exhibit 3   Freezer Manufacturers — Production Volume (000)

Name	Location	1995	1996 (estimate)
Aucma	Shandong	656	1,200
Xingxing	Zhejiang	333	400
Haier	Shandong	332	550
Baixue	Jiangsu	290	340
Xiangxuehai	Jiangsu	239	280
Bingxiong	Henan	180	300
Huamei	Zhejiang	176	210
Xileng	Zhejiang	171	205
Subtotal		2,377	3,485
Others		473	15
Total		2,850	3,500

Exhibit 4   Total Refrigeration System Market Values 1996 (000)

Total Market Value	RMB	US$
Refrigerators	958,192	119,774
Freezers	402,875	50,359
Total	1,361,067	170,133
Opportunity Value		
Evaporators	44,659	5,582
Condensers	382,746	47,843
Door Warmers	99,422	12,428
Total	526,827	65,853
In-house Production		
Evaporators	84,861	10,608
Condensers	136,342	17,043
Door Warmers	52,968	6,621
Total	274,171	34,271
Aluminum and Copper		
Evaporators	560,077	70,010
Market Share Analysis		
Opportunity/Available Market	38.70%	38.70%
In-house Production	20.10%	20.10%
Aluminum and Copper	41.10%	41.10%
Bundy China Market Share		
Sales	84,505	10,563
Market Share of Total Market Value	6.20%	6.20%
Market Share of Opportunity Value	16%	16%

Exhibit 5   A List of Major Tubing OEMs in China

NAME	TYPE OF TUBE	# OF EMPLOYEES	TECH SOURCES	CAPACITY (t/y)	MKT SEGMENT	OWNERSHIP*	LOCATION
Shashi	Double wall	300	Turkey	4,200	Refrigeration	State (PLA)	Hubei Province
Xian	Double wall	9,450**	Turkey	3,000	Refri. & Auto	State	Shaanxi
Nanjing	Double wall	3,450**	Italy	2,400	Auto	State	Jiangsu
Changchun	Double wall	100	Yanshan U.	4,000	Auto	J.V.	Jilin
Yanshan U.	Double wall	100	Yanshan U.	2,000	Auto	State	Hebei
Dandong	Double wall	100	Turkey	2,000	Refrigeration	J.V.	Liaoning
Qingdao	Double wall	500***	Turkey	2,400	Refrigeration	Collective	Shandong
Others							
Total				39,200			
Zhangjiagang	Single wall	200	U.S.	4,500	Refrigeration	J.V.	Jiangsu
Zhongshan	Single wall	N/A	U.S.	3,000	Refrigeration	J.V.	Huangdong
Pingdingshan	Single wall	N/A	Italy	3,000	Refrigeration	State	Hebei
Weifang	Single wall	300	U.S.	3,000	Refrigeration	J.V.	Shandong
Qingdao	Single wall	N/A	U.S.	3,000	Refrigeration	J.V.	Shandong
Rafter							
Others							
Total				31,500			

* Claimed by each manufacturer.
** Conglomerate.
*** For both components and commodity tubes.

Exhibit 6   The Ratio of Outsource and In-house Manufacture in the Chinese Refrigeration Industry – 1996

Manufacturer	# of Units Production	In-house	Outsource	Comments
Refrigerator				
Kelon	1,500	80%	20%	Plan to rapidly increase outsourcing
Haier	1,500	90%	10%	Maintaining In-house is a high priority
Shangling	1,000	50%	50%	No plans to change
Meiling	900	50%	50%	Mixed
Boxiyang (Yangtzi)	300	30%	70%	Unsure — although initially in-house
Xinfei	980	0%	100%	To continue
Changling	750	50%	50%	N/A
Wanbao	700	10%	90%	To continue
Xileng	600	20%	80%	Plan to decrease outsourcing — new evaporator factory
Shuanglu	560	20%	80%	Willing to totally outsource
Hualing	500	50%	50%	Unsure
Huari	410	50%	50%	N/A
Others	1,300	50%	50%	N/A
Total	**11,000**	**49%**	**51%**	
Freezer				
Aucma	1,200	55%	45%	To continue
Xingxing	400	50%	50%	N/A
Haier	550	100%	0%	In-house to remain
Others	1,350	N/A	N/A	N/A
Total	**3,500**	**N/A**	**N/A**	

Exhibit 7   Organizational Chart of Bundy Asia Pacific

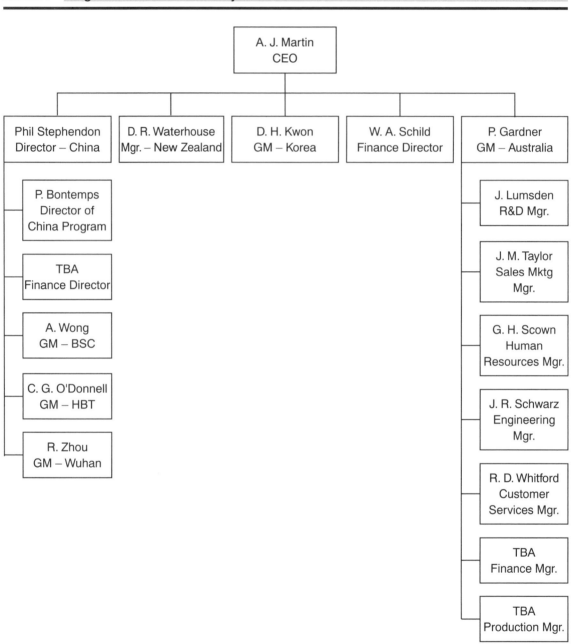

SAMSUNG CHINA: THE INTRODUCTION OF COLOR TV

In October 1995, Mr. Chung Yong,[1] President of Samsung China Headquarters (SCH), was spearheading a major drive to integrate various business units in China into a single Samsung. Prior to the establishment of SCH in 1995, business activities in China had been conducted separately by each of Samsung's business units, based on its own business strategies. Mr. Chung was considering a recent meeting with the SCH marketing director, Hyun Young-Koo, who was responsible for developing a marketing strategy for the entire China market. The topic at the meeting was the marketing strategy for color TVs, which had been chosen as the flagship product for the China market. However, they had not yet agreed on a basic market strategy for China. The immediate decision was on the market segment and product line that SCH should target. Should SCH cover all the market segments and product lines? Or should SCH focus on the low-end market segment with a limited line of products, just as Samsung Electronics had done when it entered the U.S. market? Or should SCH target the high-end market segment, as most Japanese electronics companies had done in the U.S. and China markets?

The Chinese Economic Environment in 1995

The Macro Environment

Although China had introduced many market-driven economic reforms, it was still primarily a centrally planned socialist economy. The most important lesson learned by foreign firms in

Richard Ivey School of Business
The University of Western Ontario

Chang-Bum Choi prepared this case under the supervision of Professors Paul Beamish and David Sharp solely to provide material for class discussion. The authors do not intend to illustrate either effective or ineffective handling of a managerial situation. The authors may have disguised certain names and other identifying information to protect confidentiality. Ivey Management Services prohibits any form of reproduction, storage or transmittal without its written permission. This material is not covered under authorization from CanCopy or any reproduction rights organization.

Copyright © 1998, Ivey Management Services

China was that there was a huge gap between the stated plans and the actual ability of the government to manage and control the economy. Therefore, a tremendous amount of economic interaction took place outside the government's formal economic plan. In China's computer industry, for example, factories stood idle when printed circuit boards failed to be delivered as promised. The reason was either that circuit boards were diverted to another facility through the so-called "back door" or that the circuit board factory received the wrong order. Furthermore, smuggling and piracy were major issues in China as well as the U.S.S.R. and other former Eastern Block nations.

Competition Among Governments: Self-Interest versus National Interest

There existed a high degree of competition among governments at both the central and local levels. This was due to a scarcity problem as well as the incomplete planning system. Governments tended to vie with one another to protect their already scarce resources. The self-interested competition among local governments caused another form of competition — "regional blockades." For example, one province or city might make an effort to utilize a foreign joint venture project as a means of expanding national market share. To counter what it called "market trespassing," government authorities in certain localities created various obstacles to block such competition. It was only after high level intervention from Beijing that the distribution channel would be opened up. Therefore, some MNEs targeting both the domestic market and the export market set up production bases in at least two places: typically, one in the south and the other in the north.

Difference in Emphasis on Economic Profitability versus Social Profitability

The Chinese government emphasized social profitability more than economic profitability when it evaluated the worthiness of a proposed project or the success of an existing project. The Chinese concept of social profitability referred to the benefits of a particular project in terms of "social factors" such as employment, the construction of a new building, the training of workers, the prestige or recognition that came from having a big, foreign-invested project located in one's province or city. These "soft" criteria could be a major source of confusion for foreign firms when determining whether or not a project would be attractive to their Chinese partner, because their socialist counterpart might be interested in something other than the basic ROI.

The Over-Employment Problem

Underlying the issue of social profitability was the fact that many socialist enterprises suffered from the problem of over-employment. Foreign managers visiting Chinese factories often commented on the huge number of workers that seemed to be present, but not engaged in any real productive activities. Many foreign firms entering into joint venture agreements with socialist firms had found themselves in the position of having to inherit a large number of workers and staff, of which perhaps only 50 per cent were needed to complete the production tasks at hand. While changes had been introduced to allow the streamlining of the work force, it was often politically difficult to release workers. Besides, China made it a compulsory rule to work only five days a week. The idea was that a five-day work week would make the company employ more workers.

The Micro Environment

The Chinese Color TV Industry

China was estimated to have an annual production capacity of 18 million color TV sets, with total output for 1995 hitting 16 million sets, including two million units exported to Europe, North America, Africa and Australia. The Chinese government judged that its current TV production capacity was sufficient to fulfill demand in both domestic and export markets. On the demand side, the Chinese color TV market was the second largest after the United States and the third largest after NAFTA and EU in unit sales. As such, it had been the principal battleground for the major international color TV manufacturers. Therefore, the Chinese color TV industry was quite heterogeneous in terms of the composition of its supplying firms which came from many different nations, notably Japan, the Netherlands, France and Germany. Exhibit 1 shows the market size of China, together with the other major markets.

Competition

Since the Chinese market was strategically important, competition in the color TV market was intense. In particular, Japanese firms stood out in the high-end market segment. Sony and Matsushita, with excellent brand recognition from high-income consumers, had a combined market share of about 75 per cent in the high-end market segment. Their combined sales in 1994 were estimated to be around 1.5 million units. The next group of firms, including Sharp, Sanyo, Toshiba, Mitsubishi, JVC, and Hitachi had also established significant market share. On the production side, Japanese firms had already set up 19 production bases all over China. As part of their strategy to increase sales in China, they were said to have plans to increase the production bases from 19 to 30. On average, Japanese color TV manufacturers produced 69 per cent of their production outside Japan. In the case of Sony, the overseas production ratio approached 90 per cent.

China had more than 20 indigenous firms which focused on the low-end market segment. Some of them were competitive enough to attack the medium-end market segment. Changhong, Konka, and Panda were the three major local TV manufacturers in the country, with a combined domestic market share of nearly 35 per cent. While Chinese firms were capable of competing with foreign firms in producing small and medium-sized sets, they were less competitive in large screen color TVs because of their low technology, insufficient capital, and lack of promotion. Furthermore, unlike the foreign firms which were notable for their global strategies, Chinese firms remained mostly national in the scope of their operations. Exhibit 2 shows the major Chinese firms and their product lines.

Market Size by Product Line

In the Chinese market, the small color TV (less than 17-inch) market was shrinking rapidly while the medium and large screen color TV markets were growing fast. As of 1995, the 18-inch, 20-inch and 21-inch sets made up the largest segments of the color TV market. Together the 20-inch and 21-inch screen sizes represented 60 per cent of the total in 1994. The second largest screen-size category was 18-inch which represented 23 per cent of sales. Most Chinese firms marketed only a few of the most popular sizes of television sets, such as 18-inch, 20-inch and 21-inch, because the large market size of these product lines facilitated the fast achievement of cost reduction not only through the experience curve but also through economies of scale. China's market size by product line was 29-inch — two per cent; 25-inch — 11 per cent; 21-inch — 36 per cent; 20-inch — 24 per cent; 18-inch — 23 per cent; 17-inch or less — four per cent.

Market Penetration Level

In 1994, China had 300 million households. The percentage of households with a color TV set was just 41 per cent. However, unlike the rural market, the urban market for color TV sets was nearing saturation. It was estimated that about 80 per cent of China's 80 million urban households already owned a color TV, whereas only 28 per cent of 220 million rural households owned color TV sets. Though replacement demand in urban markets still remained, it did not offset the decreasing market potential for these products. This situation implied that the market strategy of depending on a low- and medium-end urban market segment was not a viable long-term option. However, the overall market was still expanding at a rate of 10 per cent per year. The color TV market in China expanded rapidly from 12.6 million units in 1994 to 14 million units in 1995. In terms of unit sales, China's market size was one and half times as large as Japan's.

Consumer's Buying Power

McKinsey, the management consulting firm, determined that 60 million Chinese had per capita purchasing power exceeding US$1,000, an income level above which Chinese could start buying color TVs, washing machines and imported clothing. By 1992, average per capita income levels in five urban areas had already topped the US$1,000 threshold. These were Shenzhen with US$2,000, Shanghai with US$1,700, Guangzhou with US$1,500, Beijing with US$1,400, and Tianjin with US$1,100. Exhibit 3 shows the cities where per capita income in 1995 exceeded

Guangzhou's. Experts predicted that the list would grow to between 30 and 40 cities by the year 2000, and the number of Chinese above the US$1,000 threshold would hit 200 million.

Where were the Chinese getting all this money? First, many Chinese did not report all their income — they had more than the government knew about, thanks to a booming black market in labor, goods, services, and foreign exchange. Second, government housing subsidies meant that there were no mortgages in China. Hence, the amount of household income the Chinese spent on housing and utilities was between five and 10 per cent, compared with 20 to 40 per cent in other East and Southeast Asian countries. All this implies that the Chinese market had started to expand quickly in terms of high-end as well as low-end market segments.

First Mover Advantage

China was a market where the first mover enjoyed advantages over late comers. Consumers had a tendency to be loyal to a first mover's products. This meant that the first image of a product lasted long in the eyes of the consumer and that the first to enter the market could gain the largest market share. In China, there was a saying that "old friends are welcome," meaning that firms that came into the market early could be guaranteed that their initial "good will" would not be forgotten when other firms entered the market. The first mover advantage effect can be evidenced by the market competition between Pepsi and Coca-Cola in China; whichever firm had entered a city/province first, continued to have the dominant market share. In the color TV market, Japanese manufacturers that entered the China market first received the highest brand recognition from Chinese consumers. In particular, the Sony and Panasonic brands made up the largest market share in the high-end market segment.

Consumer Preferences

Consumers' color TV preferences in urban areas were different from those in rural areas. City dwellers were more concerned about brand names and the functionality of the products, while consumers in rural markets preferred color TVs with reasonable quality and lower prices. Consumers in rural areas preferred TVs with 21-inch and 19-inch screens which cost less than RMB3,000 (US$361). Local manufacturers with the brand name of Panda shipped 21-inch TVs at a price of RMB3,000, whereas Japanese brand TVs cost well over RMB4,000.

Protectionism

China was a highly protected market. Although the tariff for color TVs had decreased from 100 per cent to 60 per cent on average in 1995, it was still high. The tariffs for smaller than 15-inch, 17-inch or 18-inch, and more than 19-inch screen color TVs were 50 per cent, 60 per cent, and 65 per cent respectively. In late 1995, the Ministry of Foreign Trade and Economic Cooperation

(MOFTEC) announced that the tariff rates were scheduled to be lowered to 36 per cent on average in 1997 and that it would make continuous efforts to lower its import tariffs to 15 per cent, a level equal to that in most developing economies. Industry observers said that China strongly hoped to enter the World Trade Organization (WTO) which encouraged free trade among nations.

The TV Industry

Product Differentiation

The importance of product differentiation through brand name recognition posed another barrier against firms relying on low prices for their unknown branded products. In the TV set industry, a few established firms such as Sony, Matsushita, and Philips had succeeded in making their brand names (Sony, Panasonic and Philips, respectively) well entrenched in many national markets through their global coverage. They had made significant up-front investments not only in advertising, but also in after-sales service facilities and dealer networks to support the brand image and to move from the low-end to the high-end market segment.

Economies of Scale and Learning Effects

Cost competitiveness obtained through economies of scale and the learning effect was a critical competitive weapon. Given that economies of scale always led to cost advantages for large scale firms over small scale firms and that the learning effect did the same thing unless the smaller firms came up with advanced production technologies, economies of scale and the learning curve effect functioned as other entry barriers in the TV set industry. In particular, Japanese giants in the consumer electronics industry were famous for exploiting these advantages on a large scale.

Home Country (South Korea)

Realities of the 1990s

One of the most significant threats Korean firms were facing by the mid-1990s was that Korea's major advantages in labor costs had been deteriorating not only in relation to advanced countries, but more importantly, in relation to its immediate competitors such as the Southeast Asian countries. Wages, averaging $1,144 a month, were now among the highest in Asia outside Japan. Considering the entry into the color TV industry of firms from the Peoples' Republic of China, the relative position of Korean firms as low cost suppliers would be increasingly endangered. Furthermore, The World Competitiveness Report of 1994, an annual assessment of relative economic prowess by Swiss business school IMD and the World Economic Forum, ranked South Korea sixth among 15 newly industrializing economies — behind even Malaysia and Chile. The

South Korean economy was undergoing a fundamental restructuring. Moreover, the government, once so supportive of big business, had cut back on subsidies and export credits.

In short, Korean industries were no longer competitive in the low-end products. As an example, the market performance of Korean goods in the U.S. market, a representative global market, was poor. In particular, Korean goods were losing market share to Chinese goods. Korean share in the U.S. market declined from 3.7 per cent in 1990 to 2.6 per cent in 1996, whereas that of China went up from two per cent to 6.4 per cent in the same period. In order to make up for lost market share in low-end products and traditional industries, Korea had to catch up to developed countries in high-end products and in high-tech industries.

Market Liberalization

Another change in the home market was that the Korean domestic market witnessed new entries as it became more competitive. Thanks to deregulation of distribution channels in Korean markets, foreign firms were allowed to sell their products directly to consumers as of July 1993. Market entry barriers were supposed to be fully deregulated by 1996. By October 1995, foreign firms such as Sony, Matsushita, Sanyo, Sharp, Phillips, GE, Siemens, Whirlpool, and Laox were busy building their market competitiveness by developing distribution networks, professional sales forces, and after-sales services.

Existing firms would have to rely more on foreign business to compensate for potential losses in the domestic market. Samsung was facing increased competition in the home market as well as the global market.

Samsung's Experience in the United States

Samsung Electronics Co. actively started to penetrate the U.S. market when it first set up its overseas marketing subsidiary there in 1979. The market strategy for the United States was to focus on the low-end market segment, based on its home country-specific comparative advantage in low labor costs. The low-end segment had two merits. One was that it had a large demand base and the other was that the market entry barriers were low.

Samsung particularly selected only a few of the most popular sizes of television sets, such as 13-inch and 19-inch sets, because the large market size of these two products enabled it to achieve cost reduction through economies of scale and the experience curve. In the market, traditionally the 13-inch and 19-inch sets had comprised the largest segments of the color TV market. The 19-inch screen size represented 52 per cent of total sales in 1983. The second largest screen-size category was 13-inch which represented 19 per cent of sales.

Furthermore, the competition in the low-end market segment was low because Japanese firms were changing their focus from the low-end to the medium- and high-end market segment. Investing heavily in advertising, Japanese firms were emphasizing color TV sets with innovative features suited to high-income markets.

At the beginning of U.S. market penetration, Samsung adopted mostly a "buyer brand name" product policy. It was understandable that, given its unknown brand names, the only way to create a volume large enough to achieve economies of scale was to adopt a "buyer brand name" policy, especially for large retailers or OEMs. By doing so, Samsung could rely on foreign buyers for marketing and physical distribution functions through the latter's established marketing networks.

However, Samsung tried to build its own brand image at the same time as it adopted a "buyer brand name" policy. Samsung retained its own brands mostly for small to medium-size buyers, and used buyers' brands for mass retailers and OEM buyers. This dual branded-product policy was intended to reconcile both the short-term and long-term objectives of the firm. The short-term objective was high volume business initially to achieve the experience curve and economies of scale, and the long-term one was stable volume business with differentiated products through the establishment of its brand name.

In terms of production, it served the U.S. market by establishing a production subsidiary in 1984. According to the firm, the major reason was that the U.S. trade barrier, which it had thought to be temporary, turned out to be a more or less long-standing one, though not permanent. The clincher was the antidumping suit filed by a few U.S. domestic firms and labor unions in 1983. This charge, which would add extra costs in the form of antidumping duties if Korean firms were found guilty, would easily wipe out the already low margins of the export business. However, in anticipation of NAFTA, the assembly plant in New Jersey was moved to Tijuana, Mexico, in 1988. Samsung Electronics Mexicana (SAMEX) which had been expanded in 1992, produced 1.17 million color TVs in 1994. Exhibit 4 shows SEC's color TV production network in 1994.

In the U.S. market, Samsung Electronics grew to be one of the top 12 companies with approximately three per cent of market share in 1995 (see Exhibit 5). However, Samsung Electronics' operating profit was much smaller than that of Matsushita (Panasonic) with four per cent market share. The reason was that Samsung could not avoid intense competition in the low-end segment because products in that segment were not differentiated. However, Matsushita in the high-end market could avoid intense competition and so commanded a much higher price than Samsung, based on differentiating its products through brand name recognition (see Exhibit 6). Exhibit 7 shows Samsung's quality score in 1995 according to *Consumer Reports*. Samsung still seemed to pursue an aggressive pricing strategy.

In 1995, Samsung Electronics' total color TV production volume was six million units, 44 per cent of which were produced overseas. It had six overseas production bases: SAMEX (Mexico), SEH (Hungary), SEMUK (United Kingdom), SETAS (Turkey), TSE (Thailand), TTSEC (China). The largest production base was SAMEX in Mexico which produced 19 per cent of overseas production. TTSEC of China produced 70,000 units, most of which were 14-inch TV sets. TTSEC was originally intended as an export base. Besides six overseas production bases, four more production bases — SEDA (Brazil), SVEC (Vietnam), SEIL (India), and SESA (Spain) — were under construction.

Samsung Electronics, ranked 221st in Fortune's Global 500 in 1995, was the largest consumer electronics firm in Korea. It recorded US$21 billion in total sales in 1995, up 40 per cent from the 1994 figure of $14.6 billion. Net income grew to $3.2 billion in 1995 from $1.2 billion in 1994.

Samsung Electronics was organized into four divisions — semiconductors, telecommunication systems, multimedia, and home appliances. In terms of sales contribution, the largest division was the semiconductor division which accounted for 47.9 per cent of total sales in 1995, a big jump from 39.8 per cent in 1994. The semiconductor division made Samsung the second largest DRAM chip producer in the world. Home appliances was Samsung Electronics' second largest division. In 1996, the sales of the home appliances division grew by 13.3 per cent to 5,127 billion Korean won, thanks to a 31 per cent increase in TV sales in emerging markets.

Samsung's Market Participation in China

In 1985, when Chung first moved to Beijing to pioneer new businesses for the Samsung Group, his phone rarely rang. These days, he sat in a suite on the 15th floor of the Beijing Bright China Chang An Building and his phone rang constantly. "Now we have more than 13 projects all over China and the list is getting longer all the time," he said, motioning towards the maps on his wall (see Exhibit 8). More than 16 projects throughout China projected Samsung both as a major investor in China and as a multinational company with a global vision.

However, Samsung's active move into the Chinese market had really started only after Beijing and Seoul established diplomatic relations in 1992. Before 1992, the Chinese market was indirectly penetrated through Hong Kong because the Korean government strictly regulated business investment in China. As a result, Samsung's market presence was far behind that of the Japanese electronics companies. Furthermore, prior to the establishment of SCH in 1995, Samsung's focus was on investment in production facilities all over China rather than marketing its own products in China. That was because the Chinese government strongly encouraged foreign companies in China to focus on exports rather than the domestic market.

In 1995, Samsung established SCH in Beijing to coordinate the more than 16 operations, each of which had been separately managed by the various business units of the Samsung Group. SCH would be responsible for coordinating all development, production, logistics, and marketing in China, most of which had previously been done in Seoul. SCH would also formulate the overall marketing strategy for China, in place of separate plans from each business unit headquarters in Seoul. The establishment of SCH would enhance Samsung's insider image in China because it showed Samsung's commitment to the Chinese market. The SCH would also speed up the accumulation of local knowledge of the market which had been acquired by each business unit. In April 1995 when Lee Kun-Hee, chairman of Samsung (the largest non-Japanese conglomerate in Asia with US$54 billion in sales), visited Beijing, he announced that the Samsung Group would invest an additional US$4 billion in China by the year 2000. Exhibit 9 shows the relationship of SCH to other business units in the Samsung Group and Exhibit 10 shows the organization chart of SCH.

Options and Controversies

Mr. Chung, who was responsible for coordinating Samsung's business units in China, had proposed that Samsung introduce the high-end color TV first in order to position Samsung as a premium product producer. His argument for prioritizing a premium brand image was aligned with Samsung Group's recent commitment to its higher quality image. However, the idea had been met with skepticism from Samsung's Seoul headquarters. Many in Seoul questioned the idea of introducing a high-end product in a market with annual per capita income levels of US$353. China was stereotyped in Seoul as the land of "subsistence-level peasants, mystic sages on mountaintops, Chairman Mao's 'Little Red Book,' 89-year-old Deng Xiaoping and the events in Tiananmen Square."

Many in Samsung Electronics supported the low-end market strategy. It emphasized that the low-end market segment was still the largest market segment in China. It also pointed to the relatively faster growth in sales of small and medium-sized product lines. Moreover, it was argued that the Samsung brand could compete effectively with local TV manufacturers better than Japanese TV manufacturers. They asserted that these markets, where the largest demand existed, should be targeted.

Moreover, a premium-priced product would not sell in large volumes in the Chinese market, it was argued. Some of the Seoul-based people in Samsung Electronics, which was supposed to supply SCH with color TVs, were more interested in sales volume. Because Korean consumer electronics firms had invested in production capacities which far exceeded the domestic market size to realize scale economies, they had a high fixed cost. This led to a volume business-oriented strategy necessary to achieve break-even. In fact, the consumer electronics industry, including color TVs, was recognized as a global industry where scale economies in product development and manufacturing, rather than responsiveness to national market demands, were considered key success factors.

However, Mr. Chung thought that if Samsung did not establish a strong brand image in China, it would have to lower prices to offset the Japanese high brand image. In fact, Japanese firms that had a high quality brand reputation commanded a high price in both China and North America. Moreover, Japanese consumer electronics products which were produced in Southeast Asia were as competitive in terms of price as Korean consumer electronics products which were produced in Korea and Southeast Asia. Therefore, Mr. Chung thought, " if we do not build up a brand image equivalent to that of Japanese firms, we could not compete in China as well as in North America in the near future." Mr. Chung also thought that China was not going to stay in the low-end market even though the low-end market was currently the largest one. The product line Mr. Chung wanted to introduce to China was the latest 29-inch model which had recent success in Korea. Mr. Chung wanted to present to the people in Seoul a clear reason why Samsung China should start with high-end products rather than low-end products.

Exhibit 1   The Demand for Color TVs in Selected Markets (in millions)

1990		1995		2000	
United States	20.8	NAFTA	29.4	NAFTA	28.7
Canada	1.6				
Mexico	1.2				
Germany	5.6	EU	20.5	EEA	22.9
United Kingdom	3.3				
Italy	2.8				
France	2.7	China	14.0	China	21.0
Netherlands	0.8	Japan	10.1	Japan	10.3
Spain	2.0	CIS	4.8		
China	7.7	Brazil	3.8	MERCOSUR*	7.6
Japan	9.6	Korea	2.1		
CIS	6.5	India	1.4	CIS	6.0
Brazil	2.3	Indonesia	1.2	ASEAN	4.7
Korea	2.0	Thailand	1.2		
India	0.7	Argentina	1.1	Korea	2.5
Thailand	0.9			India	2.0
Australia	0.9			Australia	0.8
Taiwan	0.8				
Poland	1.0				

Source: JETRO, 1994
Note: MERCOSUR is common market in South America. Member countries are Brazil, Argentina, Paraguay, and Uruguay.

Exhibit 2   Major Chinese Color TV Manufacturers

Brand Name	Product Size(in inches)
1. Changhong	18, 20, 21, 25, 29
2. Xiongmao (Panda)	18, 20, 21, 25, 29
3. Konka	18, 21, 25
4. Haiyan (Petrel)	18, 20
5. Hongmei	18, 20
6. Kongque (Peacock)	18, 20
7. Jingfeng	18, 20
8. Kaige	18, 20
9. Feiyao	18, 21
10. Changcheng (Great Wall)	18, 21
11. Xihu	18
12. Jingxing	18, 21
13. Xinghai	18
14. Shanyuan	18
15. Huanghe (Yellow River)	18
16. Beijing	20, 21
17. Shangahi	20, 21
18. Mudan (Peony)	18, 20

Source: KORTA, 1995

Exhibit 3   Cities above 1995 Guangzhou Level in per Capita Income

*Estimated
Source: China Statistical Yearbook, 1995; McKinsey analysis

Exhibit 4 **Samsung Electronics' 1994 Color TV Production (thousands of units)**

	Suwon (Korea)	SAMEX (Mexico)	SEH (Hungary)	SEMUK (U.K.)	SETAS (Turkey)	TSE (Thai)	TTSEC (China)	Total
13-inch	1	219				264	15	499
14-inch	1,188	43	71	97	9	109	55	1,572
16-inch	96					8		104
19-inch	12	610						623
20-inch	1,480	48	80	398	32	46		2,083
21-inch	454	62	12	160	12	25		725
25-inch	53	99	2	36		1		190
26-inch	23	5						29
27-inch		70						70
28-inch	6			51				57
29-inch	69	8	1					78
31-inch		3						3
33-inch	2	3						5
Others	14							14
Total	3,397	1,172	165	742	53	453	70	6,051

Source: Company data

Exhibit 5   Color TV Market Share and Price Position in the United States

Company (Brand Name)	Market Share (1) (%)	Overall Price Position (2)
Thomson (RCA/GE)	21	72/65
North America Philips (Magnavox)	14	70
Zenith (Zenith)	13	75
Sony (Sony)	7	80
Sharp (Sharp)	6	69
Emerson (Emerson)	5	64
Sanyo Fisher (Sanyo)	5	69
Toshiba (Toshiba)	5	73
Matsushita (Panasonic/JVC)	4	72/73
Mitsubishi (Mitsubishi)	3	75
Samsung (Samsung)	3	67
LG (LG)	2	61
Others	12	

Note:
1. Market shares shown are based on 25.2 million units shipped in 1995.
2. Ratings are based on a scale of zero to 100.
3. According to 1996 report of U.S. Bureau of Census, population and households are 265 and 98 million, respectively.
Source: Robert Lanich, *Market Share Reporter — 1997*, Gale, New York, 1997. Gale Research Inc., Consumer Product and Manufacturer Ratings, Detroit, 1994.

Exhibit 6   Comparison of Advertising Expenses among Major Electronics Firms in the United States Market (1968 – 1994)

Brand	Cumulative Advertising Expenses (US$ million)
Sony	522
Matsushita (Panasonic)	413
Sharp	278
Samsung	27

Source: Media Watch

Exhibit 7   **The Comparison Between Quality and Price**

20-inch Color TV — 1995

Brand Name		Quality Index	Average Retail Price (US$)
Sharp	20-FM100	86	235
Zenith	SMS2049S	83	235
RCA	F20602SE	82	235
Zenith	SMS1935S	82	225
GE	20GT324	81	215
Samsung	**TTB-2012**	**80**	**210**
Sony	KV-20M10	79	290
Sanyo	AVM-2004	75	210
Zenith	SMS1917GS	70	210
Panasonic	CT-20R11	68	260
Emerson	TC1972A	59	185

27-inch Color TV — 1995

Brand Name		Quality Index	Average Retail Price (US$)
Panasonic	CT-27SF11	95	650
Samsung	**TXB2735**	**94**	**430**
Sony	KV-2756	93	740
Toshiba	CF27D50	93	555
JVC	AV-27BP5	90	615
Mitsubishi	CS-27303	89	635
Toshiba	CX27D60	89	630
RCA	F27701BK	87	605
Magnavox	TP2790 B101	86	565
RCA	F27701BK	86	535
Zenith	SM2789BT	85	620
Goldstar	GCT2754S	83	405
Sony	KV-27V10	82	615
Panasonic	CT-27S18	79	590
Sanyo	AVM-2754	79	380
GE	27GTR618	78	400
Zenith	S2773BT	75	520

Source: Consumer Reports, 1995

Exhibit 8   Samsung Business Group's Production Facilities in China

Business Unit of Samsung Group	Location	Equity Position	Products	Investment Startup	Operation Startup
Samsung Electronics Co., Ltd.	Huizhou	90%	Audio system	Aug. 1992	Jul. 1993
	Tianjin	50%	VCR	Feb. 1993	Jun. 1993
	Standing, Weihai	62%	Telecommunication switching system	Aug. 1993	Sep. 1993
	Guangdong	90%	Compact disk player	Sep. 1993	
	Tianjin	50%	CTV	Jun. 1994	Jan. 1995
	Suzhou	100%	Semiconductor assembly	Dec. 1994	Jul. 1996
	Suzhou complex	80%	Refrigerator Microwave Oven Washing Machine Air Conditioner	Jul. 1995	Sep. 1996
Samsung Aerospace Industries Co., Ltd.	Tianjin	55%	Camera	Feb. 1994	
Samsung Corning Co., Ltd.	Tianjin	100%	Head drum for VTR	Apr. 1992	
Samsung Electro-Mechanics Co., Ltd.	Tianjin	91%	Electronic components for TV	Dec. 1993	
	Tianjin	91%	Assembly metal	Dec. 1995	
	Guangdong	100%	Speaker, Deck, Keyboard.	Jul. 1992	
	Guangdong	100%	Assembly metal	Dec. 1995	

Source: Company data

Exhibit 9   Organization Chart of Samsung Business Group

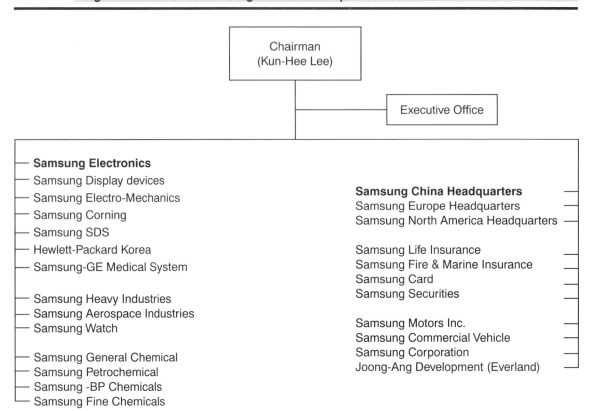

Source: Company data

Exhibit 10   Organization Chart of Samsung China Headquarters

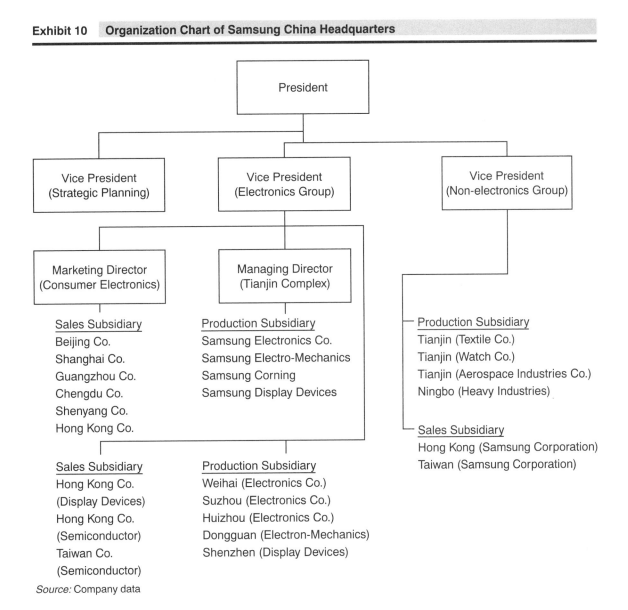

Source: Company data

Footnotes

[1] The name is written as it would be in Korean: family name first and first name last.

12 IPC CORPORATION, SINGAPORE

In the first week of December 1992, Patrick Ngiam,[1] Chairman and CEO of IPC Corporation, Singapore, was considering the company's strategy for the North American market. He had to give his final decision to the Board of Directors scheduled to meet that day. Leading among the options was a proposal to acquire a computer mail order business, Austin Computer Systems Ltd., based in Austin, Texas. An offer had to be finalized within that week. Patrick did not want to rule out the other option of developing IPC's own subsidiary in the United States. The board was also scheduled to review the company's plans to list the company on the Singapore Stock Exchange in the next six months.

Company History

IPC was incorporated on May 8, 1985 under the name of "Essex Electric Pte. Ltd." to manufacture and market personal computers (PCs). Patrick Ngiam, along with his brother Benjamin Ngiam, started the company soon after completing their degrees in Electrical Engineering at the University of Essex. IPC adopted its present name in March 1991, to symbolize "intelligent personal computers," and much later "integrated processors and communications." The company's initial focus was on manufacturing printed circuit boards for multinational companies. Later, it diversified into board assembly on a contract manufacturing basis. After researching the European markets, Essex introduced its own IPC line of PCs in 1985. Since the initial launch of its first IBM-

Richard Ivey School of Business
The University of Western Ontario

Charles Dhanaraj prepared this case under the supervision of Professors Paul Beamish and Chow Hou Wee solely to provide material for class discussion. The authors do not intend to illustrate either effective or ineffective handling of a managerial situation. The authors may have disguised certain names and other identifying information to protect confidentiality. National University of Singapore (NUS) has the right to reproduce and use this case for its educational purposes. Ivey Management Services prohibits any form of reproduction, storage or transmittal without its written permission. This material is not covered under authorization from CanCopy or any reproduction rights organization.

compatible PC, the IPC XT, the company had grown aggressively. An overview of the major milestones of IPC is shown in Exhibit 1.

The financial performance of the company was considered impressive, with a strong and steady growth in sales volume and profitability. Sales in 1992 were estimated at S$275 million and the profit after tax was estimated to be about S$42 million (See Exhibit 2).

Products

IPC's product lines were broadly grouped into three product groups: general purpose computers (GPC), consumer computing products (CCP) and application specific products (ASP). The GPC group comprised desktop PCs including the IPC Dynasty series, and sales of semi-knocked-down kits to other PC assemblers, both locally and abroad, who assembled and sold the PCs under their own private brands. The CCP group included the portable PCs (notebook and laptop computers) of which the IPC Porta series computers were the dominant products. The ASP group comprised primarily the point-of-sale (POS) terminals for chain stores, specialty stores, supermarkets, general retail stores, and the hospitality industry. Contract manufacturing of POS terminals for other overseas manufacturers was included under this category. Besides these product groups, the company also carried out trading and distribution of computer related components, parts and sub-systems of other manufacturers. The overall contribution of these product groups to the company's sales and profitability is shown in Exhibit 3.

Operations Management

IPC had close control over the management of its operations. Realizing that computer-related products had a relatively high rate of obsolescence compared with other durable goods, the company followed a policy of minimal inventory. IPC's strategic alliances with its vendors played an important role in the maintenance of its inventory policy. In order to have an optimal level of inventory of parts and components, IPC worked with vendors to replenish its stocks on a weekly basis for most of its high value items. IPC also implemented a well-managed system of coordinating its sales, purchasing and production functions whereby orders for high value items were made only when orders were received from its customers, in a manner similar to the "just-in-time" concept. The production department would then schedule its operations so that assembly could commence the moment the required parts and components were received from IPC's vendors. IPC salvaged obsolete stocks by selling them to less industrialized countries and sometimes converting them into service parts/components.

The Globalization Program

Since inception, the Ngiams had placed a strong emphasis on international markets rather than the domestic market. Singapore had a number of computer manufacturers: multinational companies such as IBM, Digital, Hewlett-Packard, and Compaq, as well as local companies such as GES (Datamini), and Aztech. There were also strong niche players such as Creative Technology which focused exclusively on the multimedia components (sound cards, etc.) market. Patrick recalled the beginning of the company:

> Singapore is a very small country and the domestic market is very small. We are not a protectionist country and the competition is very stiff. If you want to compete, you need economies of scale and the only way we could get that is to go beyond our local market. We need to go beyond Asia even. So we had to look to either the United States or Europe. We chose Europe to begin with.

> We knew right from the beginning that we had to have a broader market to survive. In the mid-1980s, Asia was not the most attractive market for the IT products. The market was fairly small, and the 'big boys' had a strong hold.

The European Market

IPC entered Europe first by appointing distributors in The Netherlands and Sweden in 1986. Later it appointed Systec S.A. as a distributor in France. With excellent progress in partnership, Systec S.A. was renamed IPC France. Plans were underway in 1992 to acquire 50 per cent of the French company and position IPC France as the European headquarters for IPC's products.

IPC introduced the IPC POS terminal and a new 386SX desktop PC to the European market in March 1989, and also started to mass produce the IPC POS terminals in April 1989. In describing the reason for IPC choosing Europe as the first market for these products, Patrick said:

> Europe, to a large extent, resembles Asia with a number of small countries each with its own language and culture and unique business environment. Most of the larger countries have 60 to 65 million people, large enough to create their own industry but not big enough when the industry is maturing. So you can go in and be profitable but you need to expand beyond any given market.

> The United States is a homogenous, consumer-oriented market, and highly competitive. So you need to have either a 'fantastic' product, no matter how small you are, to cater to a specific niche, or you need to have a sizable organization to compete. Our product at that time was just 'an alternative product' to IBM PC and so our advantage did not lie in going to the United States.

Acceptance of IPC's products continued to grow in Europe, and in October 1989, a survey conducted by Datapro and published in 01 Informatique, a French magazine, ranked IPC second among all commonly used PCs in France. Acceptance of IPC's products in Europe was given a further boost when IPC was placed in the No. 2 position, ahead of established brands such as Dell and Hewlett Packard, in terms of overall user satisfaction in a survey of approximately 1,800 French PC users, 65 per cent of whom were technical professionals. IPC was rated the highest in terms of price/performance ratio, and was rated highly for its before and after sales service, proving the effectiveness of IPC France as IPC's distributor in France.

To further expand and consolidate its distribution network in Europe, IPC set up a wholly owned subsidiary, IPC Austria, in June 1992 to cater to the Austrian and Central and East European markets. Essex Electric Holdings, B.V., the Netherlands also wholly owned, and its wholly owned subsidiary Essex Electric B.V., were set up in September 1992 to cater to the Dutch market. A 51 per cent owned joint-venture, IPC Czechoslovakia, was likewise set up in the Czech Republic in September 1992. European revenues went from S$17 million in 1988 to S$112 million in 1992. Patrick Ngiam, in commenting on IPC's success in the European market, noted:

> We entered Europe at the time when the Taiwanese were offering a lot of cheap products for they needed to get a critical mass for their PC industry. We believed we had a strong business concept and a clear strategy for gaining market leadership and we went around talking to a number of potential partners in Europe to build our business and we found partners who shared our vision for the long term. Unlike the short-term philosophy of our Taiwanese competitors we focused on cultivating the brand name. We were able to achieve a strong product differentiation which helped us to earn premium prices. We were able to invest the profits in manufacturing facilities to upgrade the quality even further. That has been our strategy all through and that probably was a reason for our success in the global market. Our partners liked to do business with us for they saw something of a unique value we were bringing to the market place.

Asia Pacific Market

IPC also prepared itself for aggressive growth in Asia after having successfully established itself in Europe. In June 1991, IPC Malaysia was incorporated as a wholly owned subsidiary of IPC Singapore to distribute IPC products in Malaysia. The lifetime warranty concept was introduced in Singapore to build up a high-quality image for IPC's products. Between December 1991 and January 1992, IPC also invested in three of its resellers in Singapore, the IPC Centres. In January 1992, IPC was awarded the 1991 Enterprise Award of the Business Times-DHL Singapore Business Awards for its success in penetrating overseas markets for computer products. IPC was awarded the Singapore Design Award 1992 at the Third International Design Forum for the IPC Porta-PC 386SLP3 notebook which was introduced later that year.

IPC decided to make a concerted effort to penetrate the Chinese market in 1991, and set up a Beijing representative office in 1992 and carried out an aggressive marketing campaign through a series of advertisements in several major Chinese newspapers and computer journals to promote its products. To further build IPC's name, a seminar was organized in Zhuhai in late 1992 for major resellers throughout the main cities of China, together with some of IPC's major vendors. The total Asia Pacific sales grew from S$12 million in 1988 to S$140 million in 1992.

The North American Market

IPC's initial entry into the North American market came when the company participated in the Comdex Fall '88 exhibition in the United States in October 1988, and launched the prototype of the IPC POS terminal. The IPC point-of-sale (POS) terminal utilized integrated open architecture which combined the transaction speed of electronic cash registers ("ECR") with the data processing capability of a computer. In April 1989, seeing the interest of the American consumers, IPC set up IPC America, a wholly-owned subsidiary located in Delaware. The small sales office employed three sales people and was mainly responsible for the sales and distribution of the POS terminals throughout the United States. Despite significant efforts, the North American sales were not as strong as expected (see Exhibit 4). Established brands such as NCR and AT&T had a strong hold on the POS market, and had superior products in the market.

Acquisition Opportunity and Corporate Objectives

Patrick, despite the strong growth in Asia and the success in Europe, continued to investigate opportunities for a significant presence in the United States. In 1990, he even suggested to his board that the company should seriously consider moving the company's headquarters to the United States. Despite an interest in the U.S. market, there was a lot of resistance to such a move from the board.

Board of Directors

IPC Corporation was a family-controlled company. The board of directors was fully made up of family members. Patrick Ngiam, 38 years old, was the central figure as the Chairman and Chief Executive Officer of the company, with his brother Benjamin Ngiam (36) supporting him closely in the marketing and operations area. Benjamin was also responsible for the day-to-day operations as the Managing Director of the company. Ms. Lauw Hui Kian, Patrick's spouse, was the Administration and Finance Director, and Patrick's two other younger brothers, Bernard (32) and Alfred (29), were in charge of the sales/marketing and engineering areas, respectively. With the company's rapid growth and increasing opportunities around the globe, the company decided to go for a public listing of 20 per cent of its equity in 1993.

The company was hoping to raise about S$150 million through the initial public offering, part of which would be used for financing the working capital requirements and the rest of which would be used for accelerating the company's growth through acquisitions. The overall mission of the company was to become a S$5 billion company by the year 2000 AD. The North American market was of great interest to the company. Patrick summarized his position as follows:

> The United States is a tough market to crack. But we look at it as a 'land of technology,' where many of the innovations originate. Being in the United States would help us to be at the leading edge in terms of technology. I wanted a direct link to what is happening.

Despite the tough competition and the large number of players, the market is also large and we want to take advantage of that. We really would like to have one third of our revenues come from the United States.

In the IT industry, it is never too late to enter a market. Maybe, you can be 'too early' an entry . . .

The U.S. market (including Canada) was indeed the largest market for PC sales (see Exhibit 5) and showed a continued growth. Many Asian companies were entering the U.S. market to enhance their product image as well as to take advantage of the large market and the latest technology.

Market Entry Options

After almost two years, just at the time when the company was reconsidering its options for the United States, it was informed of the availability of a computer mail-order business, Austin Computer Systems Ltd., in Austin, Texas. Austin Computer Systems Ltd. seemed to present the ideal fit with what Patrick had been looking for in an acquisition: a small company, with established technology, and distribution channels, and skilled manpower.

Some of the board members had suggested developing IPC's own subsidiary, either by using its existing unit, IPC America, or by starting a new venture in the Bay area (California) in the United States. With aggressive marketing such a unit could contribute substantially to the company's sales within three to five years. Patrick had gathered some information on the status of the PC industry in the United States, as well as the details of Austin.

The PC Industry in the United States

The PC industry had evolved rapidly since the invention of the microprocessor in the early 1970s. It was estimated that in 1992, about 35 per cent of U.S. households had a computer at home. The computer industry, which encompassed a broad range of activities, was approaching the US$300 billion mark or about five per cent of the GNP, and the estimates for the year 2000 were at US$700 billion. PC products comprising desktops, laptops and notebooks were about one-tenth of the total industry. High growth was the norm in the computer industry. Even though the overall industry was growing at 10 per cent per year, there were segments such as the workstation and notebook computer segments which were growing 50 to 100 per cent per year. Companies such as Compaq were pursuing aggressive strategies to outdo the industry leaders such as IBM. Most of the top global players in the industry were U.S. multinational companies (see Exhibit 6).

Mail Order Business

The mail-order business was a growing segment within the computer industry. In 1992, mail-order computers accounted for an estimated 14 per cent of the US$29 billion-a-year market for personal computers and peripherals in the United States (see Exhibit 7). According to a Chicago-based catalog consultant, computer suppliers led the mail-order business in sales growth. The attractions of mail order were quite powerful and primarily due to the price. Mail-order operators did not have the expense of running stores, and their huge volumes guaranteed some of the best prices from the component manufacturers on whom they relied. As a result, prices could run 30 per cent below the list price on store-marketed major brands. For customers of reputable dealers, helpful salespeople, fast deliveries, and a policy of hassle-free returns were as much a part of the attraction of mail order as low price. For example, Dell Computer Corp., one of the pioneers in the computer mail-order business, recorded US$546 million in sales in 1990 and also topped J.D. Power & Associates' first PC customer satisfaction survey in the same year.

Dell Computer Corp. symbolized the best of the mail-order business. Sales in 1992 were expected to be near US$2 billion. Earnings during the previous 12 quarters had never dipped below five per cent. Dell contended that the company had the most efficient and effective means of distributing and supporting PCs. Since Dell Computer sold almost all of its products directly, it could maintain lower prices by eliminating dealer and distributor profit margins. User problems were resolved over the telephone or through Xerox Corp., which was contracted to provide field service. Other leading competitors were Gateway, which was aggressively expanding in the mail-order business, and some small companies such as Austin Computer Systems Ltd., and Zeos International Inc.

Austin Computer Systems

Austin Computer Systems Ltd. (ACS) was one of the smaller companies in the mail order business but with a good reputation for customer service and brand recognition. The company was started by Robert Diwan in 1984, when he moved to the United States from Saudi Arabia. Diwan was born in Lebanon, and graduated from the American University of Beirut with a degree in business administration. Prior to starting Austin, Diwan was the financial controller of Midmac in Saudi Arabia.

Initially, the company focused on retailing personal computers as a reseller of IBM compatibles and peripherals. In 1987, when IBM introduced the PS model with a closed architecture, the market for add-ons slowed down. Diwan saw the phenomenal success of Dell in the mail-order business, and took to the direct channel, manufacturing PCs and selling them direct nationwide. From the beginning, Diwan focused on superior marketing to keep customers informed and also satisfied. Initial efforts were directed at a direct marketing campaign with magazine advertisements and an 800 number access. In 1988, ACS worked out a strategic agreement with General Electric for on-site service. Under the agreement, GE service units would provide the physical front to Austin's customers distributed throughout the United States. Diwan focused on customer service and offering technologically up-to-date products. Between 1989 and 1992, Austin received five "editor's choices?" from *PC Magazine*. Under Diwan's leadership, the company sales grew from US$2 million in 1984 to projected sales of US$65 million in 1992.

In 1989, Diwan started a subsidiary, Austin Applications, Inc., to focus on software development. Most of the software development efforts were addressed to the needs of ACS but Diwan saw that the software could be successfully marketed to other companies. By 1992, Austin Applications had developed software packages such as StoreKeeper, Contact Manager, Dental Keeper, Medical Keeper, and PC Tracker. While the copyright for StoreKeeper was registered, the rest had yet to be registered for copyrights. In 1990, Diwan started a subsidiary in England, Austin U.K. Ltd., which was to serve as a European hub to market the computers to Europe and Asia. The company had signed a number of distribution agreements with overseas suppliers in South America and the Middle East, as shown in Exhibit 8.

Advertising and Promotion

With an aggressive advertising campaign and timely product introductions, Austin had quickly captured local media attention. The customer base was slowly expanded to include small and medium businesses, and government clients. Advertising expenses were typically in the range of eight to 12 per cent of sales. Austin was ranked as one of the top 100 business markets in America by *Business Marketing* magazine in 1991 as well as 1992 (see Exhibit 9). The accumulated advertising expenses of the company over the past five years amounted to US$11.7 million. Austin participated regularly in the COMDEX/Fall trade shows, and other PC shows promoted by government and local bodies.

Customer Service

In addition to the promotion efforts, ACS also provided a number of pre-sales and post-sales services. ACS' PC-Tracking system let customers track the status of their order by permitting them to tap into ACS' production and shipping files via their own computers and a modem. Electronic bulletin boards for customers also became a standard channel for addressing customer queries, where round-the-clock customer support via telephone lines was not feasible. The sales divisions were organized to cater to specific industry segments, including Fortune 1000 companies; small-and-medium companies; individual end-users; retail outlets; federal and Texas state government and education bodies; value-added resellers; international interests; and networking. Austin had major corporate clients such as Exxon and Houston Light & Power which were based in Texas. It also sold a significant proportion of its PCs through mail-order by advertising in various U.S. computer magazines and had a widely dispersed customer base throughout the United States.

Manufacturing

Austin had a leased manufacturing facility and had the equipment to assemble and test desktops and notebooks. Most of the assembly was done manually and tested manually. Given the low volume at which it was operating, it did not want to invest in automation. A simple database of materials was used to control and monitor the materials flow. Often raw materials annual forecasts were provided by the product engineers and, based on the forecast, purchase orders were released. For most purchase orders (overseas), annual requirements were mandatory to get the supply of parts. When the forecast was not made properly, as was often the case, the company had to contend with a huge build-up of inventory.

The Problems at Austin

Austin's growth over the years was quite impressive but the profitability of the company was continuously being eroded. The stiff competition in the PC market put the low-volume players under extreme pressure. Compaq had stepped up its marketing campaign, introducing the Prolinea line, kick-starting a price war in 1992, and continuing to market aggressively. Dell was responding by introducing the Dimension line, offering a good price/performance ratio. Service demands from customers were going up and with the liberal provision in the sales agreements, the company had no control over the returns of defective products.

The company had problems with some of its vendors. Most of the components were procured from Taiwan and other parts of Asia. The delivery wait was over two months and the payment terms were often strict. Added to this, the company had to contend with quality problems in some of the components. In terms of key components such as microprocessor chips and memory, Austin, owing to its low volume, had very little power in negotiating with suppliers such as Intel for getting its computer chips. Large competitors like Compaq and Dell were able to strike much better procurement agreements with Intel, Microsoft and other vendors. Diwan believed that a merger with a bigger company was essential for survival.

Organization Structure

Robert Diwan was a hands-on manager and had a very simple management structure (shown in Exhibit 10). Mike Zamora, President of the company, had been with the company for a number of years and had the full confidence of Diwan. While Diwan focused on strategy and marketing, Mike focused on operations and accounting. Mike also had close contacts with the corporate customers and was a strength when it came to corporate accounts. The Director of Operations was generally responsible for manufacturing, purchasing, quality and shipping and reported to Mike. Rich Jacobson, an engineer by training, was in charge of the finances. In 1992, Austin had 185 employees. Personnel turnover was generally high in Austin, given the large number of high-technology companies within the region.

Diwan did not plan to quit the business scene but he was prepared to resign his executive positions to pave the way for new management. Indications were that he would not be willing to report to another CEO, if IPC decided to appoint one. If IPC decided to acquire ACS, Patrick had to resolve this management issue. With most of the Singapore managers actively involved in the initial public offering planned for 1993, Patrick did not see the possibility of any of the top managers being sent to the U.S. subsidiary.

David Scull

As Patrick was brooding over the alternatives, he remembered one of his American acquaintances whom he had met in one of the business conferences. David Judson Scull (40) was then working as Executive Director, Asia Pacific Sales, with Seagate Technology (Singapore) Pte. Ltd., an American disk-drive manufacturer with manufacturing operations in Singapore. Seagate was also one of the large multinational corporations in Singapore and had an excellent reputation for marketing and management. Between 1977 and 1983, Dave had worked in Indonesia with two different U.S. MNCs, as Logistics Manager, and in an Indonesian oil company as District Manager. Later he worked for another U.S. MNC in Malaysia and China as Manager of Operations until 1987, when he joined Seagate as Sales Manager, and was subsequently promoted to Executive Director.

Dave had shown an enthusiastic interest in joining IPC to further its American operations. Patrick considered this a good opportunity to get him to join IPC. He could assign him to head the U.S. operations, and give him a broad mandate to accomplish the company's goal of becoming a S$3 billion company by 1997, with one third of the revenues coming from the U.S. operations. Patrick sensed that Dave was very confident of accomplishing these goals. Dave could be hired under the IPC Corporation umbrella, and assigned as the Head of the U.S. operations, and he could be charged with the implementation of IPC's plans in the United States. One of the critical issues in such an arrangement was to decide how to design the compensation package for him.

Acquisition Decision

Patrick had to find a way to evaluate the fair market value of Austin. The company was privately held and managed by Diwan for all practical purposes. Patrick had met with Diwan just a week earlier where they had discussed the computer market in general and Austin's business in particular. The discussion also centered around the need to compete head on against Dell and Gateway.

IPC had received Austin's financial statements for the years 1990 and 1991 with projected figures for 1992 (Exhibits 11 and 12). The auditors' provision for future losses was very alarming. Evaluating the company in order to assess a fair market price was turning out to be a complex job. Diwan had mentioned that he had rejected an offer to sell the company for US$10 million in 1991. There were some indications that Diwan would be prepared to sell the company for US$5 million cash, given the difficulties he was facing in 1992. Although it seemed like a bargain, Patrick wondered if the acquisition of Austin was the best option to enter the North American market.

Exhibit 1   **IPC Corporation — Milestones 1985–1992**

Year	Major Events
1985	– Incorporated in Singapore as Essex Electric Ltd. Launched its first 8088 (XT) computer
1986	– First R&D department was set up in Singapore. – Entered the European market, appointing its first distributors in The Netherlands and Sweden.
1987	– Appointed Systec S.A. (currently known as IPC France) as distributor in France.
1988	– Launched the IPC Point-of-Sale terminal.
1989	– Launched its first portable PC, the IPC Portadesk 386SX. – Awarded pioneer status by the Economic Development Board (EDB) with a five-year tax-free holiday. (This was further extended by another three years in 1993 to December 31 1996.)
1990	– Incorporated IPC Europa GmbH in Germany. – Invested in a highly integrated and automated computer assembly and burn-in production facility at a cost of approximately S$1.1 million in October.
1991	– Introduced its first notebook and also its first RISC-based multi-processor server. – Change of corporate name to IPC Corporation (Pte.) Ltd., together with a change of a new IPC logo.
1992	– Set up IPC Austria GmbH to penetrate the Austrian, Central and East European market. – Established a China marketing office in Beijing to tap the Chinese market.Plans initiated for the public offering of the company.

Exhibit 2   **Financial Highlights 1988–1992 (all figures in thousands singapore dollars)[3]**

	1988	1989	1990[4]	1990a	1991	1992
Turnover	30,119	54,947	67,676	54,012	183,567	274,496
Operating Profit	246	922	6,412	6,988	14,381	42,573
Profit after tax & extraordinary items	174	860	6,390	6,953	13,028	41,526
Fixed Assets	195	849	1,160	2,041	3,492	11,124
Current Assets	6,626	9,637	15,706	18,456	25,554	99,852
Current Liabilities	6,468	9,125	9,135	10,040	13,879	53,069
Long-term Liabilities	31	179	220	505	188	115
Net Tangible Assets	322	1,182	7,972	14,929	27,458	49,384

Exhibit 3   IPC Corporation — Product Group Analysis (as % of total)

	1988	1989	1990	1990a	1991	1992
Sales Contribution						
GPC	100.0	100.0	86.6	83.2	82.6	76.0
CCP	–	–	0.2	1.4	2.9	8.9
ASP	–	–	13.2	15.4	10.4	8.9
Distribution	–	–	–	–	4.1	6.2
Profit Contribution						
GPC	100.0	100.0	60.0	68.5	55.9	69.3
CCP	–	–	0.2	1.1	4.3	8.5
ASP	–	–	39.8	30.4	38.8	21.2

Exhibit 4   Geographic Distribution of Sales (percentage of total sales)

	1988	1989	1990	1990a	1991	1992
Singapore	23.5	20.8	13.3	19.3	27.8	25.6
Other ASEAN countries	1.0	0.6	4.0	10.4	7.9	5.0
China, Hong Kong, Taiwan	3.6	1.9	2.3	0.4	12.1	16.3
Japan & Korea	–	–	0.4	0.8	0.5	0.8
Other Asia Pacific	11.7	17.6	5.5	4.2	3.6	1.9
France	25.2	31.5	30.3	25.6	13.9	25.9
Other European Countries	30.8	26.0	39.9	33.6	28.4	18.5
North America	0.1	0.5	1.7	3.2	2.2	3.2
Middle East	2.2	0.3	1.6	2.1	2.8	2.2
South Africa	1.9	0.8	1.0	0.4	0.8	0.6
Total	100.0	100.0	100.0	100.0	100.0	100.0

Exhibit 5   Worldwide PC Market (revenues in billions of US$)

Region	1991	1992	1993 (Expected)	AverageGrowth Rate (%)
Western Europe	17.517	18.872	17.999	2%
United States and Canada	26.666	28.262	32.502	10%
Japan	4.586	4.750	5.885	13%
Asia Pacific	4.573	5.219	7.052	24%
Rest of World	4.236	6.991	10.255	56%
Total	57.579	64.095	73.694	13%

Source: Dataquest

Exhibit 6   Top Ten Players in the Global Desktop PC Market (1991)

	Revenues (US$ billion)	Group Share (%)
IBM	5.25	29.2
Apple	4.38	24.4
NEC	2.04	11.4
Compaq	1.68	9.3
Olivetti	1.17	6.5
Groupe Bull	0.91	5.1
Commodore	0.74	4.1
Packard Bell	0.70	3.9
Tandy	0.58	3.2
Dell	0.40	2.2
DEC	0.12	0.7

Source: Dataquest

Exhibit 7   PC Sales by Channel Distribution in the United States

	1992	1995 (forecast)
Traditional resellers	47.0%	27.0%
Mass merchandisers	12.0	25.0
VARs/systems integrators	20.0	25.0
Mail-order /direct marketers	14.0	13.0
Computer Superstores	3.0	10.0

Source: Market Share Reporter

Exhibit 8   Austin Computer Systems, Inc. Overseas Distribution Agreements

Year Signed	Name of the company and Location	Type of Agreement	Remarks, if any
1991	Oman Computer Co., Oman	Exclusive	
1992	Desktop Equipment & Solutions, Lebanon	Exclusive	
1992	Riad Computer Center, Syria	Non-exclusive	
1992	Riad Computer Center, Jordan	Non-exclusive	
1992	G. Kallenos Infosystems Ltd., Cyprus	Exclusive	
1992	Compu Rent & Services, Egypt	Exclusive	
1991	Computer Data Networks, U.A.E.	Non-exclusive	Expired but can be renewed
1992	Computer Data Networks, Kuwait	Non-exclusive	Expired but can be renewed
1991	Procom S.R.L., Bolivia	Exclusive	
1992	Safari Co. Ltd., Saudi Arabia	Exclusive	Validity of contract currently being disputed due to payment problems
1991	Factum Sistemas S.A. de C.V., Mexico	Exclusive	

Exhibit 9   Marketing Expenses of Selected Firms in "Top 100" List

	1991 Ad Spending (US$ million)	1991 Ranking	1992 Ad Spending (US$ million)	1992 Ranking
AT&T Co.	35.486	1	39.318	4
Hewlett-Packard Co.	32.182	2	41.322	2
IBM Corp.	31,027	3	50.447	1
Dell Computer Corp.	18.318	10	19.943	13
Compaq Computer Corp.	14.512	13	26.563	9
Apple Computer Inc.	12.710	15	13.537	19
Gateway 2000	12.549	16	21.175	11
CompuAdd Corp.	8.519	30	10.092	29
Advanced Logic Research Inc.	5.096	58	3.233	92
Austin Computer System	4.417	69	3.654	81
Corel Systems Corp.	4.387	72	7.197	44
Advanced Micro Devices Inc.	3.695	89	5.112	61

Source: Business Marketing

Exhibit 10   Austin Computer Systems, Inc. Organization Structure (1992)

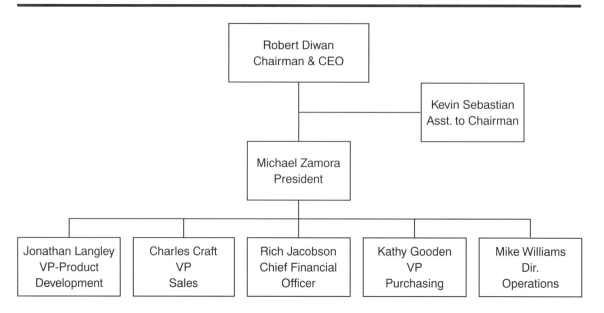

Exhibit 11   Austin Computer Systems, Inc. Consolidated Income Statement (figures in thousands US$)

	Dec. 31, 1990	Dec. 31, 1991	Dec. 31, 1992(Projected)
Product Sales	39,011	40,832	59,446[1]
Cost of Product Sales	29,380	29,995	46,981
Gross Profit	9,631	10,837	12,465
Selling & Admin Expenses	7,759	9,798	12,333
Other Income (expenses)			
Interest expense	(175)	(249)	(395)
Interest income	64	45	35
Credit line charges	(259)	(200)	(441)
Total other income (expenses)	370	(404)	(801)
Income (loss) before taxes	1,502	635	(669)
Income tax	0	26	0
Net income (loss) after tax	1,502	609	(669)
Net income (loss) after adjustment[2]	–	–	(3,200)

Notes:

1. Original product sales projection of US$65 million was adjusted downward based on past trends to include possible returns which are typical of a mail-order business.

2. Obsolete inventory may call for a write-off about US$1 to US$2 million. Given the nature of the computer industry, an exact analysis may be required before finalizing the exact value of the write-off. Some customers' bills have been outstanding. Up to US$1.2 million may have to be written off as bad debt. A conservative estimate of final adjusted loss is shown in the statement.

Exhibit 12   Austin Computer Systems, Inc. Consolidated Balance Sheet (figures in thousands US$)

	Dec. 31, 1990	Dec. 31, 1991	Dec. 31, 1992
Assets			
Current Assets:			
Cash and cash equivalents	969	653	568
Trade accounts receivable	3,470	4,767	5,055
Receivable from affiliates	395	745	747
Inventory	1,877	2,961	3,520
Other assets	79	379	169
Total current assets	6,790	9,506	10,059
Property and equipment	461	499	579
Others	8	8	13
Total Assets	7,259	10,013	10,651
Liabilities and Stockholders' Equity			
Current Liabilities:			
Accounts Payable	3,981	6,306	7,850
Accrued liabilities	2,502	1,281	2,792
Notes payable (N/P)	0	850	1,650
N/P to shareholder	40	406	405
Total current liabilities	6,523	8,843	12,697
Capital lease obligation	0	8	4
Total liabilities	6,523	8,851	12,701
Stockholders' equity:			
Common stock	26	26	26
Prior years' earnings	(51)	710	1,135
Dividends to shareholder	(740)	(185)	(50)
Current year earnings	1,502	610	(3,161)
Total stockholders' equity	736	1,161	(2,050)
Total liabilities and stockholders' equity	7,259	10,013	10,651

Footnotes

[1] The surname is pronounced "Niam."

[2] In the PC business, "editor's choice" had a lot of positive impact on customer perception of the quality and reliability of the product.

[3] Average exchange rates for Singapore Dollars (units per US$) were 2.00 in 1988, 1.94 in 1989, 1.90 in 1990, 1.74 in 1991 and 1.63 in 1992.

[4] The financial year changed from July-June to January-December in 1991. Figures for the six months ending on December 31, 1990 are given separately under column titled 1990a. This applies to Exhibits 2, 3, and 4.

PACIFIC CENTURY CYBERWORKS (A): CONNECTING TO THE WORLD[1]

> When people focus on only one piece of what we are they just don't get it. We are operators, but we are also a totally integrated Internet play, with an infrastructure side, a service platform and an incubator, all of which converge to make each other more valuable.[2]

In February 2000, Richard Li was considering the next phase of the implementation of Pacific Century CyberWorks' (PCCW) strategy. Singapore Telecommunication's (SingTel) estimated US$6 billion to US$9 billion bid for Cable & Wireless Hong Kong Telecom (HKT) had indicated HKT was in play. British investment house Warburg Dillon Read had brought HKT's availability to Mr. Li's attention and, with his usual speed, Mr. Li had begun pursuit. In response, SingTel sweetened its bid by US$1 billion and added STAR TV's media baron Rupert Murdoch's support. Li and PCCW had to respond to this new challenge quickly to continue its pursuit of HKT.

Pacific Century Cyberworks

Richard Li, the founder of PCCW, was the second son of Li Ka-shing, Hong Kong's best known multi-billionaire, with reputedly strong connections to China's political elite in Beijing. Richard Li bought a small telecommunications-equipment distributor in April 1999 (see Exhibit 1 for a summary of Li family holdings and Exhibit 2 for a profile of PCCW's management team) to found PCCW. Launched as a "backdoor" listing in Hong Kong in May 1999, PCCW was set to be the world's largest high-speed Internet access provider. By February 2000, the share price had

Richard Ivey School of Business
The University of Western Ontario

soared by more than 1,400 per cent, making PCCW the seventh-largest company in Hong Kong. Mr. Li's own net worth had risen to more than US$6.5 billion since PCCW's listing.

Li had two main strategies for PCCW. In the first, Li wanted to turn PCCW into a giant Internet venture capital fund. PCCW had spent US$600 million through its CyberWorks Ventures arm buying stakes in more than 30 Internet companies. Targets included software developers, content providers and other Internet infrastructure firms. Other Net powerhouses like Japan's Softbank Corp., controlled by Masayoshi Son, and the United States Internet conglomerate CMGI Inc. had pursued similar empire building strategies. PCCW's most lucrative investment so far had been a 3.4 per cent stake in CMGI, acquired in a share-swap deal valued at US$350 million. That stake was valued at US$910 million on February 1. In January, CMGI and PCCW formed a joint venture positioned to serve as a Hong Kong-based holding and management company for 18 of CMGI's U.S.-based Internet subsidiaries.

Li's other strategy was to provide hybrid Internet access and interactive television to millions of subscribers in India, China and Japan. PCCW had been using its flagship subsidiary, the Pacific Convergence Corp., to implement this strategy. Mr. Li planned to develop his Internet and television services in phases. PCCW planned to launch the first phase, the Network of the World (NOW) television channel, in mid-2000. Mr. Li intended to give the channel away through cable operators, defray the costs through prepaid advertising sales and then use the channel to promote PCCW's Internet service with more advertising.

The second phase was aimed at merging television programming with Internet content. The content would be accessible to subscribers through set-top boxes developed by Intel Corp., through an agreement with PCCW. The third phase would be based on a revenue-sharing plan with cable operators. Under this plan, PCCW worked with cable operators to upgrade their networks to permit two-way data access. The revenue model of this phase was that cable companies will charge their users higher fees of which PCCW received a piece. Together, these phases would help PCCW compete in the new Internet environment that was emerging in 2000 in Asia.

Internet Revolution: Broadband, Content, Vortals And Portals

In 1999 and 2000, a wave of mergers struck the Internet as companies explored various scopes for services. These mergers linked access providers — broadband, dial-up and wireless, with portals, such as Excite. Traditional media companies tried to move into the World Wide Web via merger. Disney had linked up with the portal Infoseek and NBC had done the same, but with the portal Snap. Other companies, like Microsoft and AOL-Netscape, were positioned to offer a full range of services from access, to portal services to content.

With the advent of broadband services and the potential for greater access speed, a new generation of Internet-based computing was arriving in 2000. Personal-computer users who were willing to pay for improved Internet services drove the Internet revolution. The services included fast broadband access that enabled much more content to be delivered to users with greater reliability and much greater speed.

Increased access speed and greater service reliability meant an explosion of new possibilities in content and internet-based entertainment. Excite, with its merger with @Home, had spearheaded the development of new portal, content and access services in the emerging broadband generation in the United States. The merged company, Excite@Home, served 72 million U.S. households. An executive at Excite@Home, the U.S.-based broadband Internet cable network operator that provided a model for PCCW, had his own thoughts about broadband potential in the Asian market.

> Maybe that doesn't fit what's happening in Asia. But we've found getting customers to pay anything to get interactive is very difficult; we've found them pretty unwilling to pay for even cable modems, let alone installation fees. I don't doubt that the cable upgrades CyberWorks wants to do can eventually be done. But getting a return on your investment, it seems like a big gamble and I think the valuations of such a project reflect the euphoria and insanity surrounding Asia's Internet craze.[3]

Pacific Century Cyberworks[4]

PCCW's core business activities involved technology related to the Internet and the delivery of broadband services and the provision of ISP-enabling services. PCCW's objective was to become a leader in Internet infrastructure, content and services. The company had developed three arms — Cyberworks Ventures, Cyberport and Pacific Convergence Corporation, to pursue this objective (Exhibit 3).

Cyberworks Ventures: Hotbed for Cyber Ventures in Asia

CyberWorks Ventures (CWV) was one of the three major subsidiaries of PCCW. It operated in the form of a venture capital fund. CWV's investment strategy was manifold. It aimed to foster rapid growth and industry leadership across PCCW's network and the Asian Internet economy; it sought to aggregate investee companies' technologies into turnkey servers operating system solutions that provided a one-stop-shop for businesses planning to migrate onto the Web; and it wanted to build the largest, most diverse network of Internet companies in Asia.

CWV's investments came in a number of forms – cash, advertising, inventory, a swap for equity in PCCW or a combination of these. CWV had invested across all the technology and infrastructure layers of the Internet economy. CWV also served to find complementary investment opportunities for Pacific Convergence Corporation's partner companies. Investee companies were often positioned to take advantage of Pacific Century Corporation's broadband network and benefit from its potentially massive customer base. In return, these companies offered an array of infrastructure services like World Wide Web hosting, World Wide Web consulting and design, systems integration and information technology management to other companies in which CWV had interests. By early 2000, PCCW had paid out or made the commitment to pay, in cash or other means, for acquisitions of strategic interests worth at least US$780 million.

CyberPort: Home to All Techs

Cyber-Port Limited, also a wholly owned subsidiary of PCCW, was formed to handle the multi-billion dollar Cyberport project, which PCCW had been awarded without tender from the Hong Kong, SAR government. Set to foster the development of Hong Kong as Asia's information, multimedia and telecommunications hub, Cyberport was a campus-style, multi-use environment. It covered a floor area of 540,000 square feet and it was situated on 26 hectares of reclaimed land at Telegraph Bay on the south-western coast of Hong Kong Island. It offered a low-density environment tailored to the requirements of a strategic cluster of leading-edge information technology and services companies and multimedia content creators. Cyberport offered a carefully planned mix of commercial, business, educational and recreational facilities. There were 15 anchor clients: Cisco, CMGI, Hewlett-Packard, Hikari Tsushin, Huawei, IBM, Legend, Microsoft, Oracle, Pacific Convergence Corporation, Portal Software, Silicon Graphics, Softbank, Sybase and Yahoo! Inc..

Pacific Convergence Corporation: Broadband Empire

Broadband was the equivalent of the killer ap for the year 2000. Broadband was about fast Internet connections. NOW, which was to be PCCW's flagship enterprise in broadband, would use a broadband connection that was about 20 times faster than standard dial-up connections. With broadband and NOW, the user could combine all mainstream media including telephone, video, e-mail and Internet into one interactive service through the same wire at home, in the office either or on a PC, TV or mobile phone.

Pacific Convergence Corporation (PCC), a subsidiary of Pacific Century CyberWorks, was positioned to become the leading global provider of broadband Internet services via NOW. NOW would be the first of its kind to provide converged Internet and digital video content service combining the unique capabilities of TV, the PC and the World Wide Web. The head of London-based PCC, Michael Johnson, who founded the satellite TV forerunner to Li's STAR TV venture, had his vision of broadband.

> We're dealing with a new medium and a new set of rules for telling stories. At their heart, the new stories will combine the TV world with the 3D focus driven by the computer-games world . . . . As the Internet gets faster, on-line material only gets more interesting and more emotive.[5]

Broadband started with deploying a satellite to cable head-end or telecom earth station infrastructure. This technology enabled the rapid establishment of contact and connectivity with local access operators across the AsiaSat III footprint. NOW would enable operators who adopted its system to provide full broadband Internet access to their consumers and enterprise customers. Content would be channelled through a number of "vortals" (Webspeak for vertical portal, a term that was supposed to suggest a portal like Yahoo! Inc., but focused on one subject), each covering a particular subject, such as sports, education, music and lifestyle. Content would be available in different formats via satellite through cable systems, dial-up ISP's, DSL and wireless devices — including WAP and 3G technologies. The NOW service would be rolled out first in English, and then in Chinese and Japanese.

Through NOW, PCC would offer eight Web channels targeting areas like entertainment, money, lifestyle, games and sports. Trans World International (TWI), the London-based programming division of International Management Group (IMG), was providing initial production services for NOW English-language programs and Web services. NOW had access to TWI's library of 100,000 hours of program materials and to the more than 5,000 hours of new program materials that TWI produced annually. In addition, PCC was negotiating for the Webcast rights of Wimbledon. It wanted to develop a deep interactive library of archive material and player profiles and interviews, in addition to the broadcast of live action. Finally, PCC had a 75,000 square-foot, fully digital studio and production centre in London. Three hundred producers and designers were working on the production of four hours of new content every day to fuel NOW's English-language offering. PCC planned to launch NOW in June 2000.

Among the different offerings of NOW, one vortal, called MP3TV, looked like regular TV. It was like MTV but it focused on downloadable MP3 songs by bands that were willing to give away their music on the Internet. There was also a plan for an agriculture portal that would provide infomercial-like videos on seeds and farm equipment. George Chan, a senior CyberWorks executive in charge of sales, had confidence in the potential of this agriculture portal.

> There are about 800 million people in China who are in farming or related industries. The NOW service can actually improve their profitability.[6]

Even with this wide variety of offerings, there was uncertainty about NOW's revenue model. PCC expected that most of NOW's revenue would first come from advertisements. Later, PCC expected that the fees collected from e-business services transacted through its sites and the subscription fees for its broadband connections would be its main sources of revenue.

Nevertheless, collecting payment for NOW's services would be a difficult task. China and India were the two huge markets for which PCC had high hopes. STAR TV had 3,500 cable operators in India. James Murdoch, son of Rupert Murdoch and STAR TV's chairman and chief executive, spoke on the task of collecting user fees.

> It's hard to do. It takes a lot of on-the-ground resources. A lot of people talk about it and underestimate the effort.[7]

In China, PCC appeared to be doing better. It already started testing its broadband service with 10 cable operators and had plans to offer full service by the end of 2000. However, it was facing several problems. First, China had to open its Internet market under the agreements made to join the World Trade Organization. Second, PCC had to lower the cost of operation of its broadband business in China. It wanted the price of its Intel designed broadband set-top boxes to drop to HK$300 a piece.

Aside from making services economical and collecting fees, luring mass consumers to broadband involved its own challenges, according to Simon Davies, executive director of the Cable and Satellite Broadcasting Association of Asia.

> If the broadband services don't provide significant added value to the existing services, the consumer is going to say: "Hang on, why should I pay?" The hype around broadband service has been pretty good but ask the consumer what he wants and he doesn't know.[8]

In fact, broadband had not yet entered the daily life of everyone. In Singapore, the world's first nation to provide universal broadband access, there were about one million Internet users, but just 35,000 broadband subscribers. In Hong Kong, HKT had 400,000 narrowband (regular Internet dial-up) subscribers but it just had 60,000 subscribers for its two-year-old broadband service. Even in the United States, just five percent of Internet users had broadband accounts in early 2000.

PCCW's Competition

In 2000, rival broadband companies were scrambling for market share in the lucrative broadband market. Several companies were competing for PCCW's anticipated core markets. Hong Kong-based I-Cable, Siti Cable in India, the Winstar Communications Inc. / KDD Corporation / Sumitomo Corporation joint venture in Japan and STAR TV were the biggest names already in this game. Almost daily, competition was becoming more and more intense, a process encouraged by continued deregulation of the telecommunication market in Asia. Hong Kong had issued 17 new licenses in January 2000 and Singapore awarded 66 in February 2000.

I-Cable Communications Limited[9]

The I-CABLE Group owned the second largest broadband network in Hong Kong and was the leading pay-TV system operator. Wharf (Holdings) Limited in Hong Kong was controlling shareholder with a 79.5 per cent stake. I-CABLE aimed to be Hong Kong's leading provider of integrated multimedia communications services.

I-CABLE Communications Limited, which was listed on both the Hong Kong Stock Exchange and Nasdaq in the United States on November 24, 1999, had a base of over 450,000 pay-TV subscribers by the end of 1999. This base accounted for 26 per cent of the total number of homes in Hong Kong with access to cable television. The Group had launched Internet access service through dial-up telephone modems that served over 140,000 subscribers in 1999. While I-CABLE had a network that could reach 1.7 million (or 98 per cent) homes in Hong Kong, to boost competitiveness, I-CABLE planned to replace microwave trunks with fibre trunks to bring its two-way broadband hybrid fibre coaxial (HFC) cable network into operation by 2001. With these in hand, the Group planned to leverage its broadband HFC cable network, local content production and repackaging, marketing and customer service capabilities to become a leading high-speed Internet access service provider in Hong Kong.

Siti Cable[10]

Siti Cable covered a customer base of 4.5 million homes in 43 cities in India. It had the largest Cable TV network in India with approximately 8,000 kilometres of cable. The networks of Siti Cable were typically state-of the art imported cables and network equipment that served 20,000 to 50,000 homes. Up to 45 TV channels were offered in these networks, which had a capacity of 69 channels. Siti Cable's networks were also capable of processing two-way communication. Siti Cable also had important access to content along with an exclusive and popular cable channel, Siti Channel. Further, Siti Channel had already acquired cable rights for more than 1,000 quality movies and was continuously acquiring the rights for new movies.

Like other media giants, Siti Cable was leveraging its strengths as a player in an entertainment service industry to transform the company into a powerhouse in the Internet business. It had plans to be a giant Internet Service Provider to provide Internet services on the cable. Upgrade plans to replace the existing networks with HFC networks were already in place. This network could carry data more than 1,000 times faster than the telephone company's twisted pair copper lines. Apart from speed, the cable-accessed Internet provided 24 hours of service without interfering with existing cable television or telephone service.

KDD Winstar Corporation

In January 1999, Winstar Communications Inc., KDD Corporation and Sumitomo Corporation announced the formation of a joint venture — KDD Winstar Coprporation — to pursue deployment of fixed wireless service in Japan, beginning in Tokyo in 1999. The aim of the joint venture was to build a broadband network capable of delivering high-speed data and information services in major Japanese markets. KDD Winstar Corporation would draw upon the different strengths of the trio of parents. Winstar had experience and technical expertise in providing high-speed local access to businesses over its own fixed wireless network. KDD had experience in the marketing and provision of telecommunications services throughout Japan. Sumitomo had the operational expertise as one of Japan's leading integrated trading companies. Upon securing spectrum rights, KDD Winstar Corporation would market its broadband service to businesses with high-speed data transmission needs.

STAR TV

STAR TV reached 300 million viewers in more than 50 Asian nations. It had 30 channels in seven languages and its Phoenix channel claimed to reach 45 million people in China. The channel, 45 per cent owned by STAR TV, was probably its biggest success to date. STAR TV had content rich programming, including the Channel V music-video network, Asia's answer to MTV, ESPN STAR Sports, a joint venture with ESPN, Fox News and STAR Movies. With its alliances, STAR TV's content was spread throughout Asia, including Hong Kong, where it had formed an alliance in November 1999 with HKT to package its content to Hong Kong homes.

Hong Kong Telecom[11]

Cable & Wireless Hong Kong Telecom (HKT), one of the largest telecommunications companies in Asia, was the leading provider of integrated communication services in Hong Kong (see Exhibit 4 for financial statements). HKT provided fixed and wireless voice services, data services and leased circuits, narrowband and broadband Internet access, interactive multimedia services, call centres, application provision and systems integration services. Each of these services was backed by a fully digital fibre-optic broadband network. It had 3.7 million fixed lines in Hong Kong, or more than one line for every two people.

HKT's flagship was its network infrastructure business. An optical fibre network, with over 444,000 kilometres of fibre contained in 6,120 kilometres of cable, was the backbone of its network infrastructure business. With investment of HK$20 billion in the world's largest Asynchronous Transfer Mode (ATM) broadband network using optical fibre-to-the-building and DSL technology, HKT rolled out Hong Kong's first ATM service. It covered 70 per cent of Hong Kong households. It had dedicated bandwidth for each individual user, meaning that the number of users did not affect the transmission speed. It had secure point-to-point connection between user and service provider, with a maximum bandwidth of 25 Mbps.

The revenue model for HKT's broadband business was based on the applications enabled by this technology. The bandwidth of the broadband allowed multimedia interactive applications and multiple services such as HKT's Interactive TV (iTV) service and its NETVIGATOR 1.5M Ultra Line broadband Internet access service. iTV enabled customers to enjoy a variety of entertainment programs, such as movies, music, karaoke, Channel [V] on demand, games magazines, finance information and news, children's favorites, interactive learning programs, fashion, documentaries, sports and leisure programs and other innovative services such as Home Shopping and Banking. The NETVIGATOR 1.5M Ultra Line broadband Internet access service was the only broadband Internet access in Hong Kong in 2000. It provided Internet access of a speed 30 times faster than normal 56K modems. Both private consumers and local businesses were customers for HKT's broadband services.

HKT also had international telecommunications facilities consisting of cable, radio and satellite-based systems. This aspect of HKT's business focused on capturing corporate customers, ISPs and other value-added service providers. HKT offered one-stop-shop facilities management services. It provided end-to-end managed network solutions, local and international Internet connectivity. Its data centres provided co-location and World Wide Web hosting services and e-commerce applications and services. Its local telecommunications services offered direct exchange lines for business and residential customers, public and private data network services, dial-up audio content services and a virtual private network and video conferencing services.

HKT provided mobile services. It owned three mobile brands: 1010, One2Free and 1+1, that served all local market segments. HKT operated the advanced digital GSM and D-AMPS mobile systems and offered packages of post-paid mobile services and pre-paid rechargeable stored value mobile SIM cards and also supplied mobile handsets. HKT's mobile services development strategy was to support access to advanced multimedia and e-commerce services through the adoption of 3G high-speed wireless data technologies. It had launched a series of value-added services based on Wireless Application Protocol (WAP) in December 1999.

The Merger

In January 2000, HKT was reorganized into seven core divisions, together with six business and two resources units. The restructuring announcement, together with the America Online-Time Warner merger, had sparked speculation that the British parent, Cable & Wireless PLC (C&W), was preparing the company for a sale. C&W was trying to get into the Internet business to counter erosion in its existing businesses from increased competition. In the same month, C&W moved closer to its goal of becoming the leading provider of Internet services to business customers by acquiring eight of Europe's top business Internet-service providers for US$500 million.

Speculation was fuelled by C&W's increased focus on information-technology services for business clients, while forgoing retail services, such as mobile telephone and television. HKT had been trying to build up its full-service telecommunication provider empire, expanding, at great expense, into consumer products such as the Internet and cable television. This divergence of strategy had led analysts to believe that a global telecommunication player would buy HKT.

Competition in Telecoms

Competition in Hong Kong's telecommunication market had become more intense than expected. In the same month that HKT reorganized into seven divisions, Hong Kong's Office of the Telecommunications Authority had awarded wireless fixed network telecommunications licenses to five companies, while 12 carriers had been granted licenses to operate external international facilities.

In this environment of deregulation, HKT, Hong Kong's fourth-largest company and Asia's 16th-biggest telecom company, reported its first-ever loss. This loss, which amounted to US$353 million, was for the six months to September 1999, after a write-off of US$907.7 million for obsolete equipment. Analysts estimated that HKT would make US$1.1 billion in the year to March 2000, which was down more than a third from fiscal 1998. After losing its monopoly on fixed lines in 1995 and on overseas calls in early 1999, the company no longer had an exclusive right to operate an international direct dial gateway. Together with nimble newcomers and mutating technologies HKT's mobile phone, Internet and other businesses were being undermined.

HKT was not the only Asian telecom giant adapting to deregulation, new competition and new technology. Japan's NTT, Korea Telecom, Singapore Telecom and Philippine Long Distance Telephone were each under pressure. However, HKT had to deal with a large number of deep-pocketed competitors that had made headway into its core businesses. HKT had 97 per cent of the fixed-line market and a 26 per cent share in mobile phones. International calls accounted for 70 per cent of revenues, but market share for international calls had fallen from 1,000 per cent in 1995 to 45 per cent in 2000, with forecasts for a 30 per cent share in 2000.

With four private fixed line operators and 11 mobile phone providers after years of gradual liberalization, Hong Kong was one of the most competitive telecom markets. Meanwhile, HKT had moved into new businesses such as video-on-demand. This service allowed consumers to download shows to their TV through phone lines. The service had 100,000 subscribers, which was short of the 250,000 target.

Enter SingTel

In November 1999, Singapore Telecommunications (SingTel) made an estimated US$6 billion bid for HKT. SingTel was positioned to be the new millennium's leading info-communications carrier of regional corporate data, wholesale, mobile, systems integration and Internet and e-commerce businesses in Asia-Pacific. However, like HKT, SingTel faced similar problems — increased competition, rapid deregulation pushed up to April 2000, declining margins and the need to outgrow dial-tone roots in a cyberspace world. In January 2000, HKT and SingTel both went public. The companies confirmed they were working on a merger.

With deregulation, regional players had to consolidate to bulk up to competition. Potential opponents included United States giant AT&T, which had applied for an international services license in Hong Kong and was considering moving into the Singapore market. GlobalOne, a joint venture of Deutsche Telekom, France Telecom and Sprint, which used SingTel's local networks to service its Singapore clients, was planning to use its own lines beginning in April 2000. Yong Yingi, the head of Singapore's new InfoComm Development Authority, drew a dynamic picture of the telecom market.

> We have been inundated with calls from leading telecom companies around the world who want to know how soon they can set up in Singapore.[12]

SingTel-HKT

If the merger went through, SingTel-HKT would have US$6.6 billion in total revenue, making it the fifth largest Asian telecom. The merged telecom giant would be positioned to serve Southeast

Asia and the Greater China region with a 60 per cent share of the lucrative market for multinational companies based in Asia, but outside Japan. The market capitalization of the company post-merger would be $55 billion.

A merged SingTel-HKT would have a cash pool of US$8 billion that could be used to fund acquisitions in international markets. Key among new markets was China. By investing in one of the world's fastest growing telecom markets, SingTel-HKT could better compete against behemoths like NTT, AT&T and MCI WorldCom. Deutsche Telecom had been trying to hook up its Asian cellular operations with SingTel, or a merged SingTel-HKT. Chua Sock Koong of SingTel summarized SingTel's strategy.

> Everybody else is looking excitedly at China to see how the Chinese market will be liberalized. Clearly, positioning in Hong Kong would be an advantage for investment in Greater China.[13]

Under the terms being discussed, the Singapore government, which owned 80 per cent of SingTel, would end up as the largest shareholder in SingTel-HKT. SingTel would own a 40 per cent stake and HKT would take a 20 per cent stake in the newly merged company. This arrangement was in line with SingTel's expansion policy. Its target was to have overseas investments account for 20 per cent of pre-tax profit by 2005, compared with 14 per cent for the six-month period that ended September 1999.

Enter PCCW

PCCW was a pioneer in combining Internet content and television programming, while coordinating satellite and cable delivery. However, there was much uncertainty about the ultimate success of its strategy. PCCW's key delivery tool, set-top boxes, were still in test markets. Much of the satellite technology on which Mr. Li was banking was three to four years away. For broadband Internet service and interactive television, PCCW had to upgrade cable networks in key target markets. Much of the cable in India and China was of inferior quality and would require extensive financial resources for upgrading. In the China market, the Chinese government had tight restrictions on content that would initially limit NOW to sports programming in English.

Perhaps most importantly, PCCW had to deal with the provision of content. STAR TV had teamed up with HKT to offer a range of pay television and Internet-related service across Asia that eventually might compete directly with Mr. Li. The competitive advantage that STAR TV had was its library of content, including Chinese-language programming supplied by Mr. Murdoch's television networks.

To PCCW's advantage, it was sitting on a pile of cash that amounted to US$1.3 billion (Exhibit 5) and a market valuation that had grown rapidly in the past several months (Exhibit 6). PCCW had earmarked US$200 million for start-up investment and as much as US$600 million for launching Internet and television business. Rajeev Gupta, a research analyst at Goldman Sachs (Asia), evaluated PCCW's prospects.

Compelling content is the key. When investors look for clues about the progress of the convergence project, they'll want to see a series of strategic acquisitions or alliances with excellent content partners. AOL had a market capitalization of US$169 billion and 20 million subscribers. Why couldn't CyberWorks Convergence move in that direction?[14]

In fact, PCCW was moving in the direction of HKT. After British investment house Warburg Dillon Read had brought HKT to Mr. Li's attention, Mr. Li, with his typical alacrity, had begun pursuit of HKT. On February 11, just three months after SingTel's bid for HKT, PCCW announced its interest in HKT (Exhibit 7). Two weeks later, PCCW sweetened its bid by arranging with a coalition of four banks for bridge financing of US$12 billion cash for HKT. Still hot in pursuit, SingTel responded in kind by adding US$1 billion to its bid, plus the support of STAR TV's Rupert Murdoch.

PCCW, which had already put more than US$10 billion on the table, had now seen SingTel up the stakes. Certainly, there were advantages to PCCW if it acquired HKT. Aside from HKT's US$2 billion in cash reserves, HKT owned Hong Kong's biggest fixed-line network, the second largest mobile phone business and the most popular Internet service. Further, its broadband telephone network covered 80 per cent of Hong Kong. Francis Yuen noted the appeal of HKT to PCCW. "We have no intention to dispose of specific assets of HKT. We want the long-term infrastructure …. for our company. It gels very well."[15]

While HKT seemed a good match for PCCW, the investment community was mixed in its appraisal of the proposed merger. Jay Chang, an analyst with Credit Suisse First Boston in Hong Kong, identified the potential acquisition as a huge vision fraught with risks. Most business analysts advocated a focused strategy for internet businesses. A Hong Kong fund manager summarized some of the uncertainty about PCCW. "They (PCCW) want to be all things to all people. But you get the feeling they are unwilling to commit to one strategy."[16]

Alexander Arena, Deputy Chairman of PCCW, responded.

Why march in with a narrow business plan when you have an open playing field? We (will) have the ability to carry internet traffic, host it at our data centres and have the local links to deliver it, so we can actually take a piece of the transaction along the way.[17]

For PCCW, the issue was whether HKT really was the appropriate vehicle, and if it could still be acquired at a price that would let PCCW realize its anticipated value.

Exhibit 1   The Li Empire in 1999

Cheung Kong (Holdings)

Business: Property development, investment holding

Chairman: Li Ka-shing

Vice-Chairman and MD: Victor Li Tzar-kuoi

1998 Sales: $1.52b.

1998 Net Profit: $1.22b.

Market Value: $30.5b.

Top Shareholder: Li Ka-shing (34.99%)

Cheung Kong Infrastructure

Business: Utilities, infrastructure

Chairman: Victor Li Tzar-kuoi

1998 Sales: $422m.

1998 Net Profit: $366m.

Market Value: $3.1b.

Top Shareholder: Hutchison (84.6%)

Pacific Century CyberWorks

Business: Broadband networks, Internet ventures

Chairman and CEO: Richard Li Tzar-kai

1998 Sales: $36.4m.

1998 Net Loss: ($8m.)

Market Value: $25.7b.

Top Shareholder: Pacific Century

Regional Developments and its affliliates (59.3%, controlled by Richard Li)

Hutchison Whampoa

Business: Ports, telecommunications, retail, investment

Chairman: Li Ka-shing

Deputy Chairman: Victor Li Tzar-kuoi

Deputy Chairman: Richard Li Tzar-kai

Sales: $6.59b.

Net Profit: $1.04b.

Market Value: $60.6b.

Top Shareholder: Cheung Kong (49.9%)

Hongkong Electric

Business: Electric power for Hong Kong Island

Executive Director: Victor Li Tzar-kuoi

Executive Director: Richard Li Tzar-kai

1998 Sales: $1.19b.

1998 Net Profit: $637m.

Market Value: $6.3b.

Top Shareholder: Cheung Kong Infra. (36.1%)

Tom.com

Business: Internet ventures

No sales, profits or Li family board members

Market Value: $2.8b.

Top Shareholders: Cheung Kong (32.29%), Hutchison (16.15%)

Source: Asiaweek, www.asiaweek.com., July 3, 2000.

Exhibit 2   Profile of the Management of PCCW

Richard Li

Age 33. Executive Chairman of PCCW, chairman and chief executive of the Pacific Century Group and chairman of Pacific Century Regional Developments Limited. Richard Li started STAR TV, Asia's first satellite-delivered cable service. In three years STAR TV had a subscriber base of 53 million Asian, Middle Eastern and European homes. Sold STAR TV in 1993 to Rupert Murdoch of News Corp. Capital received from sale was used to launch the Pacific Century Group in October 1993. Also a member of the Center for Strategic and International Studies' International Councillors Group in Washington, D.C., the World Economic Forum and the International Advisory Board of the Center for International Development at Harvard University. Educated at Stanford University.

Peter To

Age 52. Deputy chairman of PCCW and managing director and chief executive officer of Pacific Century Regional Developments Limited. Joined Pacific Century Group in September 1997. In charge of the overall strategy of the property development business of the company and the CyberPort Project. Twenty-seven years experience in the property development and investment business. Received a Certificate of Housing Management from the University of Hong Kong. Fellow of the Chartered Institute of Housing (UK) and Hong Kong Institute of Housing. Was managing director of the Hutchison Whampoa Property Group with responsibility for the development, marketing and management of all development and investment properties in the Hutchison Whampoa Property Group's portfolio.

Francis Yuen

Age 47. Deputy chairman of PCCW, deputy chairman of the Pacific Century Group, chairman of Pacific Century Insurance Holdings Limited and deputy chairman of Pacific Century Regional Developments Limited. Joined Pacific Century Group in 1996. From 1992 to 1994, was a member of the International Markets Advisory Board of NASDAQ in the United States. From 1988 to 1991, was chief executive of The Stock Exchange of Hong Kong Limited. Was a founding director of Hong Kong Securities Clearing Company Limited. In October 1986, was appointed as the managing director of Citicorp Scrimgeour Vickers Hong Kong Limited and was admitted to the firm's main board in London in 1987. Bachelor of Arts degree in Economics from the University of Chicago.

Source: Adapted from information in Pacific Century Cyberworks Web site. http://www.pcg-group.com/, July 28, 2000.

Exhibit 3   Pacific Century Group Organization Chart

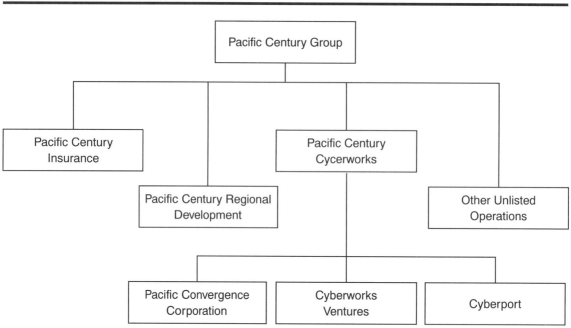

Source: Adapted from information in Pacific Century Group's Web site: http://www.pcg-group.com/pcg/index.html. July 28, 2000.

Exhibit 4   **Financial Information for Hong Kong Telecom 1997, 1998 and 1999 (dollar amounts in US$ millions)**

Income Statement	March 1999	March 1998	March 1997
Revenue	4,155.0	4,523.8	4,205.8
Cost of Goods Sold	800.0	705.7	557.2
Gross Profit	3,355.0	3,818.1	3,648.6
Gross Profit Margin	80.70%	84.40%	86.80%
SG&A Expense	1,837.0	2,107.4	2,073.2
Operating Income	1,518.0	1,710.7	1,575.4
Operating Margin	36.50%	37.80%	37.50%
Total Net Income	1,475.0	2,198.3	1,443.0
Net Profit Margin	35.50%	48.60%	34.30%
Diluted EPS ($)	1.24	1.86	1.25

Balance Sheet	March 1999	March 1998	March 1997
Cash	1,324.0	412.3	1,195.7
Net Receivables	548.0	487.3	470.5
Inventories	98.0	74.7	34.5
Total Current Assets	2,856.0	2,696.8	1,867.4
Total Assets	6,920.0	6,634.2	5,479.1
Short Term Debt	268.0	-	-
Total Current Liabilities	1,920.0	1,755.4	1,467.0
Long Term Debt	-	-	-
Total Liabilities	2,046.0	1,864.4	1,568.9
Total Equity	4,874.0	4,769.8	3,910.1
Shares Outstanding (mil)	1,195.9	1,190.9	1,169.3

Source: Hoover's Online-Business Network, http://www.hoovers.com/. July 24, 2000.

Exhibit 5   Financial Information for Pacific Century Cyberworks 1998 and 1999 (dollar amounts in US$ millions)

Income Statement	December 1999	December 1998
Revenue	19.6	36.8
Cost of Goods Sold	8.5	23.7
Gross Profit	11.0	13.1
Gross Profit Margin	56.40%	35.50%
SG&A Expense	48.5	19.3
Operating Income	(37.4)	(6.2)
Operating Margin	-	-
Total Net Income	44.6	(8)
Net Profit Margin	228.10%	-
Diluted EPS ($)	0.01	-

Balance Sheet	December 1999	December 1998
Cash	650.4	1.4
Net Receivables	39.1	11.2
Inventories	2.6	8.8
Total Current Assets	830.9	21.4
Total Assets	1,789.8	45.0
Short Term Debt	125.6	11.9
Total Current Liabilities	190.4	27.5
Long Term Debt	113.5	2.3
Total Liabilities	328.3	29.9
Total Equity	1,461.5	15.1
Shares Outstanding	-	-

Source: Hoover's Online-Business Network, http://www.hoovers.com/. July 24, 2000.

Exhibit 6   Stock Price Movements of PCCW, HKT and SINGTEL (1999–2000)

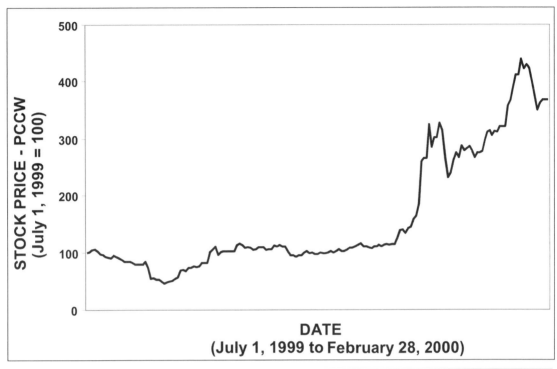

**DATE
(July 1, 1999 to February 28, 2000)**

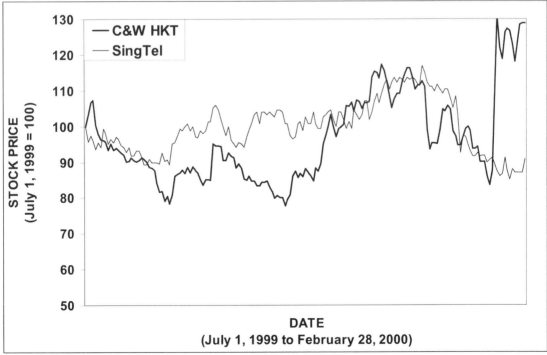

**DATE
(July 1, 1999 to February 28, 2000)**

Source: SEQUENCER on-line database.

Exhibit 7   A Merger at Internet Speed

Date	Development
November	• SingTel announced an estimated $6 billion bid for HKT
February 11	• PCCW announced its own bid for HKT
February 14	• Overnight, PCCW converted $1 billion of its stock into cash to impress HKT's parent, Cable & Wireless
February 16	• Hong Kong papers reported rumors that China had exerted indirect opposition to SingTel's bid and had favored the Li family to take control of HKT.
Week of February 22	• Upon Cable & Wireless's reluctance to accept stock, Li immediately arranged a loan of $13 billion from four banks.
February 29	• SingTel brought in Murdoch to sweeten its (undisclosed) offer by $1 billion
	• Murdoch had harbored ambitions to race into the India and China mass entertainment market via his cable television vehicle, STAR TV. To 2000, his ambitions had been spurned by the high level of regulation that existed in these two markets.

Source: "Generation Next," <u>Newsweek</u>, March 13, 2000.

Footnotes

[1] This case has been written on the basis of published sources only. Consequently, the interpretation and perspectives presented in this case are not necessarily those of Pacific Century CyberWorks or any of its employees.

[2] "Integrated Circuit: Pacific Century CyberWorks Casts Wide Net Over Asia," <u>Wall Street Journal</u>, February 1, 2000. Pacific Century Group's Web site http://www.pcg-group.com/pcg/index.html, July 3, 2000.

[3] Ibid.

[4] Material in this section is based on information found in Pacific Century CyberWork's Web site, http://www.pccw.com, July 22, 2000.

[5] "Broadband Buzz," <u>Far Eastern Economic Review</u>, May 11, 2000: 163(19), pp.34-36.

[6] Peter Stein and Michelle Levander, "Richard Li Makes a Bet on Future of Entertainment," <u>Wall Street Journal</u>, June 29, 2000: p. 1 and p. 6.

[7] Ibid.

[8] "Broadband Buzz," <u>Far Eastern Economic Review</u>, May 11, 2000: 163(19), pp.34-36.

[9] Material in this section is based on information found in I-Cable's Web site, http://www.i-cable.com, July 22, 2000.

[10] Material in this section is based on information found in Siti Cable's Web site, http://www.siticable.com, July 22, 2000.

[11] Material in this section is based on information found in Hong Kong Telecom's Web site, http://www.HKT.com/ , July 22, 2000.

[12] "Competition Calling," <u>Asiaweek</u>, February 4, 2000. Accessed at Asiaweek's Web site www.Asiaweek.com, July 3, 2000.

[13] "Asia's Telecom Market Enters a New Era," <u>Asian Wall Street Journal</u>, January 26, 2000, pp. 1-2.

[14] "Integrated Circuit: Pacific Century CyberWorks Casts Wide Net Over Asia," <u>Wall Street Journal</u>, February 1, 2000. Pacific Century Group's Web site http://www.pcg-group.com/pcg/index.html, July 3, 2000.

[15] "HKT Presents a Challenge for PCCW," <u>Asian Wall Street Journal</u>, March 6, 2000, p.1 and p.4.

[16] "Cyberworks's broad approach to the market brings an old economy feel to the internet'" <u>Wall Street Journal</u>, May 30, 2000: p. 15.

[17] Ibid.

14 MABUCHI MOTOR CO., LTD.

In September 1995, a full year had elapsed since Mabuchi Motor Co., Ltd., the world's most successful producer of small electric motors, had implemented a new management training program at one of its foreign operations in China. The program, called New Integrated Headquarters And Overseas Operations (NIHAO), was intended to improve the management skills of local managers in Mabuchi's foreign operations to enable the corporation to maintain its strategy of cost minimization and to allow continued aggressive production expansion. The Manager of Mabuchi's Internal Affairs Department, Nobukatsu Hirano, was responsible for the development and implementation of NIHAO.

A Brief History of Mabuchi Motor Co., Ltd. (see Exhibit 1 for an overview)

After founding Kansai Rika Kenkyusho, a scientific research institute, in 1946, Kenichi Mabuchi invented the world's first high performance horseshoe-shaped magnetic motor, a significant improvement over prior technology. In the coming years, this product was refined and experiments were undertaken to develop the process of mass production of these small motors.

In 1954, Kenichi and his brother, Takaichi Mabuchi, set up a workshop within a toy company to begin production of small electric motors under the name of Tokyo Science Industrial Co. for the Japanese toy industry. In an effort to diversify from the toy business and into emerging markets for small motors, the Mabuchi brothers established their own trading company in 1957 under the name of Mabuchi Shoji Co., Ltd.

Richard Ivey School of Business
The University of Western Ontario

Anthony Goerzen prepared this case under the supervision of Professor Paul W. Beamish solely to provide material for class discussion. The authors do not intend to illustrate either effective or ineffective handling of a managerial situation. The authors may have disguised certain names and other identifying information to protect confidentiality. Ivey Management Services prohibits any form of reproduction, storage or transmittal without its written permission. This material is not covered under authorization from CanCopy or any reproduction rights organization.

Copyright © 1998, Ivey Management Services

Their modest business continued to grow when, in 1964, Mabuchi established a production facility in Hong Kong despite the fact that the yen was very weak, trading at the time at ¥360:US$1. Subsequently, in 1969, a second offshore facility was constructed in Taiwan. These early investments in foreign production were rather unusual for a Japanese company; already by that time, most buyers considered goods produced in Asia outside of Japan to be of inferior quality. Nonetheless, by the end of the 1960s, Mabuchi had established sales offices in both Germany and the U.S. to manage its developing markets.

In the following decade, the markets for small motors grew significantly in Europe, the U.S., and Japan. Mabuchi was encouraged to continue its strategy of production expansion, establishing new plants in Taiwan in 1978 and 1979. By this time, many of the firms that had previously manufactured small motors had fallen away, leaving Mabuchi as the dominant world force commanding about 60 per cent of total international demand. Although Mabuchi's main customers were the Japanese manufacturers of audio and visual equipment (i.e., CD players, camcorders, VCRs, etc.), the company also had strong sales positions in Europe and in North America. As Japan's producers became dominant in the expanding world market for consumer electronic products, Mabuchi also enjoyed significant growth in sales and profitability. Throughout the period of 1970 to 1980, in fact, sales multiplied more than six-fold.

Throughout the 1980s, Mabuchi continued to expand production with a focus on China in order to take advantage of the low cost of Chinese labor. In 1986, Mabuchi constructed a firm in the southern Chinese city of Dongguang. It also expanded its production base by subcontracting its requirements on a commission basis to a collection of firms in the free trade zone near Shenzhen, Guangdong just over the border from Hong Kong. In 1987, Mabuchi made headlines in the popular press by establishing in Dalian, Liaoning the first Japanese wholly owned subsidiary in China. By 1988, Mabuchi relied on Chinese operations to supply over 40 per cent of its total output of small motors. Therefore, in an attempt to diversify from this reliance on China, Mabuchi added a fifth wholly owned production unit in 1989, this time in Malaysia. During this period, Mabuchi's main market remained the audio and visual equipment manufacturers but it was also enjoying strong growth in the automotive and precision tool markets. Just as the Malaysian plant reached full capacity in 1990, Mabuchi's consolidated sales totalled over ¥60 billion and net income reached a new high of nearly ¥7 billion.

From record highs in 1991 of net income (almost ¥10 billion) and earnings per share (¥230 per share), these indicators dropped in 1992 and 1993 due to the depreciating Japanese currency and high capital depreciation costs. In 1993, net income and EPS were 64 per cent and 57 per cent, respectively, of what they had been two years prior. Nonetheless, Mabuchi continued along its path of expansion, constructing a plant in 1993 in Wu Jiang, Jiangsu, China and following with another Chinese plant in the next year in Wangfandian, Liaoning. At this point, the share of Mabuchi's production that came from China exceeded 70 per cent. To diminish its reliance on Chinese output, Mabuchi began actively seeking another production base outside China as established markets continued to grow and new markets were being developed. By 1995, producing over one billion motors a year, Mabuchi's forecast for all markets was bullish and its overall demand figure was projected at double-digit growth. In the view of senior management, there was still a lot of potential to be developed in the small motor business.

The Electric Motor Industry

In the 1950s and 1960s, the main markets for small electric motors were toys and games including racing cars and model airplanes although, towards the end of this period, the audio and timepiece markets were beginning to emerge. In the 1970s, new applications for small electric motors were being found in household electronics such as blenders and shavers as well as other applications such as hand-held power tools including circular saws, hedge trimmers, and drills. Throughout the 1980s, the audio and visual markets for motors were very strong as consumer electronic goods firms successfully developed new markets for VCRs, cameras, and camcorders. At the same time, the market for small motors in the automotive industry began to expand rapidly when options such as power windows, power locks, and cruise control became standard features on new cars. By this time, the average car contained between 15 to 20 micro motors while many luxury cars contained three times that number. In the 1990s, with toys becoming more sophisticated (and, hence, requiring more motors), household electronics, audio, and visual equipment becoming increasingly common possessions of the average consumer, and automobiles becoming more automated, demand for motors continued to be great. At the same time, new markets for small motors emerged in such areas as personal computers, computer peripherals, and communication technology including pagers and cellular phones. The market for small electric motors had been very strong for many years and expectations were bullish for the foreseeable future.

Despite its strong worldwide position, Mabuchi was still not free to pick and choose its markets. Johnson Electric, also a well-established and successful family-owned business, was an aggressive competitor absorbing the 35 to 40 per cent balance of market share not occupied by Mabuchi. A Hong Kong company established in 1959, Johnson Electric had accumulated over HK$1.5 billion in sales and profits of HK$350 million. With over 90 per cent of its production capacity in technically sophisticated but low cost operations in southern China, Johnson Electric tried to take away any developing or established markets over which Mabuchi did not have firm control.

Mabuchi Management Style and Organizational Structure

Mabuchi's management philosophy was based on the assumption that all people are essentially the same, having similar needs and wants. Whether in an affluent developed country or faced with the struggles that are part of every day life in less developed economies, people have a common longing for security, peace, ease of living, and freedom from want. In Mabuchi's view, the small electric motor had the capacity to contribute to the fulfillment of these desires by freeing people from the demands and dangers that come with physical labor. It was also believed that the motor had the capacity to increase productivity to the point where these common goals were easier to achieve. This attempt to lift the activities of the firm out of the everyday and onto a higher plane was common for Japanese firms. Traditionally, Japanese firms had placed a greater emphasis than many of their western counterparts on finding ways to encourage employees to take on the organization's goals as their own.

In certain ways, Mabuchi was not a typical Japanese organization. Partial evidence of this can be found in the firm's early willingness to develop offshore production capability. However, Mabuchi's management style was, nonetheless, more or less characteristic of Japanese companies. There was a great respect for hierarchy and the lines of authority were very clear (see Exhibit 2). Throughout its history, Mabuchi's head office had always firmly controlled the activities of its subsidiaries setting standards for both product quality and work practices.

Mabuchi Corporate Strategy

The cornerstones of Mabuchi's strategy were the diversification of both production bases and markets, the maintenance of high quality standards, and the minimization of production costs. Since small motors had become a low technology item that could be easily reproduced by new or established competitors, Mabuchi also believed that, tactically, it was very important to move quickly once an opportunity emerged. In other words, quick response time to market opportunities could enhance competitive advantage by simply occupying the maximum amount of competitive space.

Diversification

Although a single product company, Mabuchi had always been concerned with diversification of both markets and production locations. In its earliest days, the company moved away from excessive dependence on the toy industry, stretching instead for other markets. By 1995, Mabuchi divided its markets for small motors into four basic segments: audio and visual equipment, automotive products, information and communication equipment, and home and industrial equipment. One of the significant benefits of its diversified market position was that, since the demand cycles of these market segments were not closely related, when one market slowed, others tended to pick up, thus smoothing the demand. The fact was, however, that in many years the demand from all segments was up at the same time.

Similarly, Mabuchi's ongoing effort was to maintain a diverse base of production facilities. While it might have been easier to locate all plants in China, where costs of labor were among the lowest in the Asian Pacific region, Mabuchi attempted to reduce its dependence on a single country by maintaining facilities in other locations such as Taiwan, Hong Kong, Malaysia; in addition, it was searching for another non-Chinese location in 1995. While this aspect of its market strategy may have been more difficult to implement, the company believed it added a measure of security to its long-term plans.

Quality

In the view of top management, one of the responsibilities of running a worldwide production network was to guarantee an identical level of high quality product no matter where that particular product came from. The primary method of maintaining quality control was to ensure that all operations adhered to the standards set by the head office Technical Center. As early as 1984, Mabuchi had established the Technical Center, relocated and refurbished in 1992, where new technologies were tested and new products were developed. In general, technical service and the management of the international network of subsidiaries were centrally located and, once a new product or work practice was devised, it was then introduced to Mabuchi affiliates as quickly as possible by head office personnel. The various plants were expected to attempt to implement as closely as possible the patterns and processes devised in corporate headquarters.

Cost Minimization

Mabuchi endeavoured to maximize its competitiveness by minimizing its costs of labor, making its work practices more efficient, reducing the variety of products offered, and streamlining its administration.

Cost of Labor

Since small electric motors were a labor-intensive product, one of the key competitive considerations was, of course, the relative cost of labor. It was this factor that led to the establishment of Mabuchi's first offshore production facility in Hong Kong in 1964 where, at the time, labor rates were low. By 1995, all of Mabuchi's production capability had been shifted outside of Japan to take advantage of the low cost labor available elsewhere. In fact, since labor rates in the 1990s in Taiwan and Hong Kong had become expensive relative to those available in other East Asian countries, Mabuchi was forced to begin realigning its production distribution away from these locations in order to stay cost competitive. Rather than abandoning these high cost facilities, however, the sites that were experiencing escalating costs of labor were made to change their focus, concentrating instead on higher value-added operations such as the fabrication and maintenance of production equipment for other plants.

Efficient Work Practices

Mabuchi's top management clearly believed that there was one best way to build small motors.

These methods were developed over years of experience with new methods being tested in the Technical Center. One of the many roles of expatriate managers was to ensure that the methods of production designed in Japan were mirrored in their foreign locations.

Reduction of the Variety of Products Offered

While many organizations worldwide had attempted to satisfy their increasingly demanding customers by offering tailor-made products, Mabuchi steadfastly resisted this trend. Senior management believed, instead, that customers cared more about price than selection. Although selling about four million motors a day, at least 70 per cent of total sales were made up of no more than 20 models. Further, about 55 per cent of total sales consisted of 10 models. In general, Mabuchi concentrated on producing as few models as possible in order to achieve greater speed of production and, hence, lower average costs.

Streamlining of Administration

In 1971, Mabuchi reorganized its administration of marketing and production to concentrate responsibility for these functions in the head office. Since then, Japanese personnel had always been in firm control over the activities of all subsidiaries. This initiative was originally an effort to reduce duplication of effort and inefficiency in management control. However, beginning in the early 1990s, the firm began to try to shift many of these responsibilities back to the individual subsidiaries. Given the rapid growth in production over the 1970s and 1980s, Mabuchi's centralized, multilingual organization had become cumbersome and difficult to manage for the head office administrative staff. Mabuchi management felt that their organization resembled a train where the head office was the locomotive, the only source of power, pulling the totally dependent subsidiaries behind. As a result, Mabuchi began to encourage subsidiary managers to communicate directly with their counterparts in other subsidiaries in an effort to attain greater corporate-wide administrative effectiveness and operational efficiency.

Strategic Initiatives at Mabuchi

In 1992, in the spirit of Kaizen (continuous improvement), Takaichi Mabuchi announced the formulation of the New Mabuchi 21 Steering Committee made up of a select group of 20 young (under 35 years) Mabuchi managers under the leadership of Executive Vice President Akira Ohnishi. This committee was charged with the task of examining and making recommendations on three key aspects of Mabuchi's business:

1. product quality
2. delivery lead time
3. costs of production

To address the product quality issue, the New Mabuchi 21 Steering Committee recommended implementing ISO 9000 standards at all plants. To reduce delivery lead-time, the Committee introduced the Coordinated Mabuchi Production and Sales System (COMPASS) program, a computer-based management information system designed to improve and quicken the transfer of information between departments and between subsidiaries. Finally, the Steering Committee determined that in order to decrease costs of production, the number of Japanese managers posted to foreign subsidiaries must be reduced.

The Plan to Develop a Training Program for Foreign Managers

In many East Asian countries, the cost of maintaining a Japanese expatriate (salary, travel allowances, accommodation, etc.) was 10 to 20 times that of a local manager. According to a major U.S.-based institution that focused on international human resource management, the all-inclusive cost of maintaining a senior-level Japanese manager in China was no less than US$400,000 annually and approximately US$325,000 for a mid-level Japanese manager. Even a lower level technician from Japan would cost at least US$175,000 annually including salary, bonus, and travel allowances. In 1995, Mabuchi had 84 expatriates in various locations abroad (see Exhibit 3). Notwithstanding the cost, there did not exist a large pool of local management talent that Mabuchi could draw on in its foreign locations; therefore, a program had to be implemented to train local personnel to enable them to achieve Mabuchi's standards of production efficiency and product quality.

Mabuchi's corporate strategy included aggressive plans to continue expansion of production to reduce the possibility of the emergence of new competition or, for that matter, the loss of developing markets to current competitors. Further, since Mabuchi's market position was based on a reputation for supplying high quality products on a timely basis, all established plants were required to continue to run at a steady state and new plants had to be brought on stream without major difficulties.

Therefore, in late 1992 it became the responsibility of Nobukatsu Hirano, Manager of Internal Affairs, to oversee the establishment of detailed plans to fulfill these important and related goals. Since Mabuchi had limited previous experience in developing corporate training programs for foreign personnel, Andersen Consulting was retained to assist in elaborating a detailed plan. Under the direction of Mr. Hirano, a team of five Mabuchi employees and two Andersen Consulting people worked out a plan they named the New Integrated Headquarters And Overseas Operations (NIHAO). It was decided that the Dalian plant would be the first to go through the NIHAO program.

A Review of NIHAO

Fundamentally, the training program was intended to reinforce the hierarchical notion of management control where each management level was expected to play a specified role. The standardization of management practice was emphasized where tasks were to be divided between management levels so that there was no overlap or omission of duties. Further, it was clearly spelled out that there should be no individual differences in tasks or procedures when comparing personnel in similar positions; in other words, Mabuchi saw little room for individual interests or capabilities when it came to the fulfillment of managerial tasks. Overall, management was seen as a generalist task that was suited to some people and not to others and, if an individual could not complete the tasks as per company policy, he or she should be reassigned to a more suitable, perhaps more specialized, task.

A second major element of the training program was the requirement for regular performance evaluation of all employees. The belief at Mabuchi was that, if an individual was not evaluated and challenged to improve, then morale would inevitably decline. All managers were, therefore, required to formally evaluate their subordinates twice a year. In actual practice, the subordinate was required to evaluate himself/herself and the manager was then required to review this self-criticism and formalize the process with a signature. Repeated unsatisfactory performance evaluations were expected to lead to demotion, whereas satisfactory evaluations usually resulted in significant bonuses. Regular workers and group leaders were often awarded bonuses of as much as 150 per cent of salary and higher level managers (i.e., factory and section managers) were commonly given bonuses of up to 300 per cent of regular salary.

While it was a common experience for foreign-owned companies to lose valuable employees once improved management skills made the individual more marketable, Mabuchi did not expect to encounter this problem. First of all, to reduce the attractiveness of other employers, the corporate policy was to pay at levels higher than the local average as well as to provide all benefits required by Chinese labor regulations. Further, Mabuchi believed it could offer the sort of upward mobility necessary to retain capable young managers. In fact, Mabuchi could point to the fact that the President of its Taiwanese subsidiary, a local manager from Taiwan, had even been appointed to the corporate board of directors in 1993. An explicit goal of the NIHAO training program was to allow local managers to take over key positions as their skills developed to sufficient levels.

The Implementation of NIHAO

With five different training manuals designed to address the concerns of each level of management (see Exhibit 4), a delegation of Mabuchi staff traveled to Dalian to commence the training program. In a series of seminars that were given in Japanese and then translated into Chinese, the sessions began with the upper levels of the hierarchy and then proceeded to include lower echelons on a level-by-level basis. After each session, a short test was administered to determine whether the main points were being grasped. In cases where test results were not satisfactory, remedial sessions were offered. Subsequent batteries of seminars were held to enhance and reinforce the understanding of the management trainees regarding the basic concepts of the division of labor and the responsibilities of management. These later sessions, however, were led by a

Mandarin-speaking Mabuchi employee and a Chinese Andersen Consulting employee to improve the level of comprehension.

In order to determine to what extent Mabuchi's management training program had an impact, Andersen Consulting was asked to conduct periodic follow-up tests. It was soon realized that the trainees in Dalian were having great difficulty in internalizing some of the essential aspects of Mabuchi's requirements of management, personnel management in particular. It seemed that the Chinese managers, regardless of prior experience, were either not capable of, or perhaps simply not accustomed to, controlling their subordinates. The clear division between subordinate and superior was not being manifested in actual practice. Mabuchi was convinced that it had hired the best managerial talent that Dalian had to offer — yet perhaps the prior exposure of these people to the methods of management in Chinese state-owned enterprises made them poorly suited to the demands of a capitalist enterprise.

Similarly, the performance evaluations were not being completed with the rigor required by Mabuchi where less than satisfactory performance was not being met with remedial action or demotion. Evaluations were a central component of Mabuchi's management incentive system; however, the Chinese were more sensitive to personal networks and were also accustomed to a more collective approach to compensation. For example, after a particular foreman had been awarded a performance bonus, the foreman's subordinates demanded a similar bonus in keeping with what had become a Chinese custom — when one person in a work group receives a reward, the entire group shares the benefit. However, this was not Mabuchi corporate policy and, in fact, went counter to the concept of isolating people for individual reward in order to encourage everyone to attempt to achieve their personal best. The discontented employees were eventually pacified when a subsidiary-wide raise was given, although the situation was not formally resolved.

The corporation's future plans for expansion hinged on its ability to move quickly into new markets, producing high quality micro motors efficiently. NIHAO was expected to play a central role in Mabuchi's process of organizational development.

Exhibit 1　Summary of Important Events in Mabuchi's History

1946	K. Mabuchi designed the world's first horseshoe-shaped magnetic motor
1954	Tokyo Science Industrial Co. is established to begin production
1957	Mabuchi Shoji Co. Ltd. is established to undertake export operations
1958	Mabuchi Industrial Co. is established
1964	Factory is constructed in Kowloon, Hong Kong
1965	Sales office is established in the U.S.
1966	Sales office is established in Germany
1969	Factory is constructed in Taipei, Taiwan
1978	Factory is constructed in Hukou, Hsinchu, Taiwan
1979	Factory is constructed in Kaohsiung, Taiwan
1984	Mabuchi stock is listed for public sale via the over-the-counter market
	Technical Center is established in Japan to centralize R&D activity
1986	Mabuchi becomes a member of the Tokyo Stock Exchange second section
	Factory is constructed in Dongguang, Guangdong, China
1987	A representative office is established in Singapore
	Factory is constructed in Dalian, China
1988	Mabuchi becomes a member of the Tokyo Stock Exchange first section
1989	Factory is constructed in Chemor, Perak, Malaysia
1992	New Technical Center is completed
	Sales office is established in China
1993	Factory is constructed in Wu Jiang, Jiangsu, China
1994	Factory is constructed in Wangfandian, Liaoning, China

Exhibit 2   Mabuchi Motor Co., Ltd. Organizational Structure

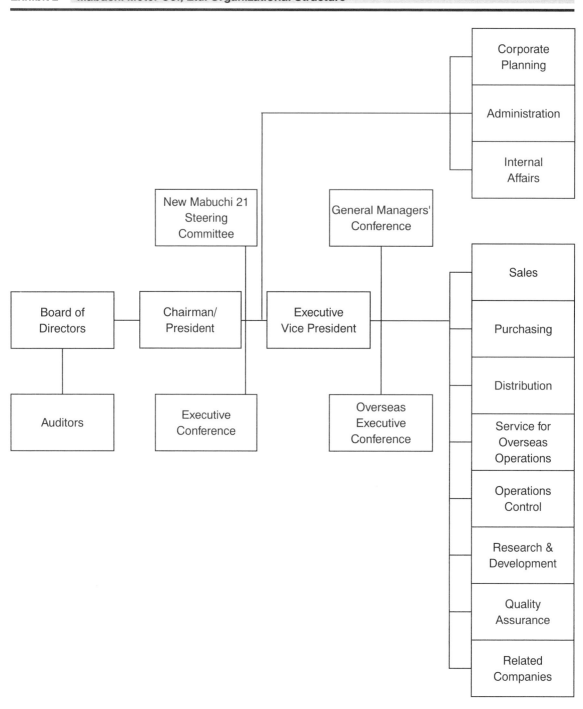

Exhibit 3   Mabuchi Motor Co., Ltd

Local Management/Expatriates Levels
(as of December, 1995)

Plant Location	Workers	Group Leaders	Foremen	Section Chiefs	Factory Managers	Managing Directors	Total Employed
Wangfandian	214	12/0	2/0	6/0	1/0	0/1	236
Guang Dong 1	5,407	288/0	58/0	5/5	0/1	0/1	5,765
Guang Dong 2	6,378	340/0	68/0	5/9	0/1	0/1	6,802
Guang Dong 3	4,877	260/0	52/0	14/4	0/1	0/1	5,209
Guang Dong 4	1,405	75/0	15/0	11/0	0/1	0/1	1,508
Guang Dong 5	6,947	370/0	74/0	5/9	0/1	0/1	7,407
Taipei	1,889	101/0	20/0	15/4	0/1	0/1	2,031
Hukou	1,716	92/0	18/0	9/10	0/1	0/1	1,847
Dalian	7,605	405/0	81/0	5/18	1/0	0/1	8,116
Chemor	3,848	205/0	41/0	9/3	0/1	0/1	4,108
Wu Jiang	1,942	104/0	21/0	11/2	0/1	0/1	2,082
Total	42,228	2,252/0	450/0	95/64	2/9	0/11	45,111

Exhibit 4   Mabuchi Motor Dalian Ltd. Organizational Structure Title (number of positions)

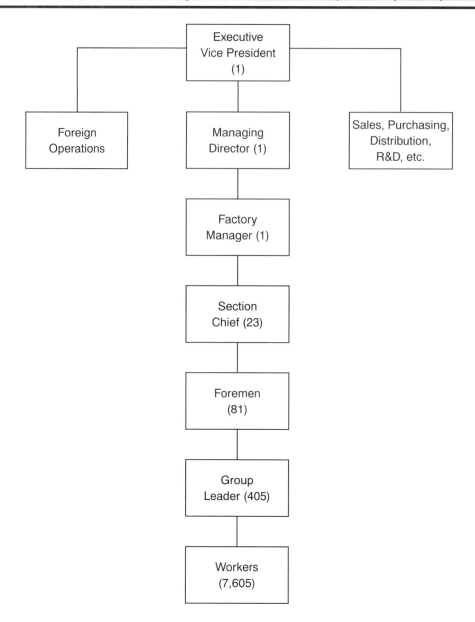

15 PHIL CHAN (A)

Saturday, September 26, 1998. "We're getting there!" thought Phil Chan as the Air France flight took off from Paris on its way to Lagos, Nigeria. Phil Chan was the Vice-President Marketing of Basic Software, a middle-sized Hong Kong-based software producer. He was going to Lagos to close a business deal that Allen Lee, the owner of Basic Software, had been negotiating in the preceding weeks. Phil had left his home in Hong Kong sixteen hours earlier and he looked forward to reaching his final destination.

Phil decided to review one more time the specifics of the deal, and the strategy that he would follow in the next day's meeting with his Nigerian partners. This was his first trip to Africa and he was somewhat uncertain about local business practices. Since he would be in Lagos for a short stay, he wanted everything to go smoothly.

The Deal

The deal required Basic Software to facilitate a financial transaction involving an international transfer of funds and would earn the company over $5 million, their 35 per cent share of the US$14.3 million deal. Allen Lee had been approached a month earlier by Tokunbo Jacobs with the business proposal (see Exhibit 1 for a copy of Mr. Jacobs' initial letter to Mr. Lee). Intrigued by the prospect, he entered into discussions with Mr. Jacobs. Mr. Lee was in the process of negotiating a sale in Bahrain on the Persian Gulf and thought that Africa could offer additional prospects for his company: "Business is all over the world for us. You have to adapt yourself to

Richard Ivey School of Business
The University of Western Ontario

the fact that conditions are different in other countries from how they are here. This is just part of living in today's world."

In response to his inquiries, he received further details on the deal (see the two faxes in Exhibit 2 and Exhibit 3) and decided to send Phil Chan to Nigeria to complete the negotiations with the Nigerians.

The Nigerian Context

Nigeria offered significant business opportunities (for a profile on Nigeria, see Exhibit 4). With 115 million people, Nigeria was the giant among Africa's 55 countries. Home to both Christians and Muslims, it possessed great assets. Nigeria's Gross Natural Product was the fifth largest on the African continent (in 1996 it amounted to US$28 billion). The country was endowed with significant resources. For example, Nigeria was among the world's largest producers of peanuts and rubber. It also produced important quantities of cotton, cocoa, yams, cassava, sorghum, corn and rice.

Nigeria was a producer and exporter of petroleum. Oil revenues were channeled towards the creation of an industrial base and the strengthening of the agricultural sector. Other important industries included mining (natural gas, coal) and processing (oil, palm, peanuts, cotton, petroleum).

Phil's Position

Phil Chan wondered how to approach the negotiations with the Nigerians and resolve a few issues which had not been addressed. He wanted the deal to go through without upsetting his partner. Phil had recently read a business publication which emphasized the need to be "skillful in the art of bargaining" when dealing with Nigerians (see Exhibit 5).

Phil and Allen had agreed on what should be obtained from the Nigerians. They believed that five per cent (i.e., $715,000) was more than sufficient to cover the contingencies associated with the completion of this deal. They wanted the contingency fund reduced from 10 per cent to five per cent and their share raised from 35 per cent to 40 per cent.

Phil's plan was to negotiate the financial commitments to be made by both sides prior to the release of funds in order to minimize Basic Software's exposure. To have a clear picture of the expenses to be incurred in the implementation of the deal and of the respective contributions expected from each side, he wanted to examine the pro-forma financial statements prepared by Mr. Tokunbo. His objective was to modify them to Basic Software's advantage.

In a phone conversation with Mr. Tokunbo, Phil had found that in order to do business with the Nigerian government and its agencies, it was necessary to be registered in the official list of pre-qualified suppliers. Various approvals and stamps were required in the registration process. The US$48,000 requested in the September 21st fax was for that purpose.

Phil also wanted to obtain a written commitment that all expenses and advances incurred by Basic Software would be reimbursed from the contingency fund including his travel and accommodation expenses that amounted to just over $5,000.

Phil brought with him all the documents requested by the Nigerian partners, including a power of attorney signed by Allen Lee which authorized him to conclude the deal on behalf of Basic Software.

As he closed the Nigerian file and put it back in his briefcase, Phil wondered how he should conduct the negotiations in order to achieve his objectives without jeopardizing the relationship.

Exhibit 1　　Initial Letter Sent by Tokunbo Jacobs to Allen Lee

---

26th August 1998

Tokunbo Jacobs

32 Falkar Street, Lagos, Nigeria

Tel. 234-1-874235, FAX 234-1-442157

TELEX *37854* RT NG

Dear Mr. President,

I am Mr. Tokunbo Jacobs, a staff of Nigerian National Petroleum Corporation (NNPC) and a member of the "Tenders Committee" of same corporation. I got your contact address through a close relation who is the corporate affairs manager of Nigerian Export Promotions Council. The transaction which is detailed below is being presented to you based on mutual trust and confidentiality.

After due consultation with other members of the Tender Committee, I have been specifically mandated to arrange with you the remittance of US$14.3M. being an over estimated sum resulting from contract executed by an expatriate contractor. The original value of this contract was purposely over inflated by us (Tender Committee) with the sum of $14.3M. Now that the firm have received their supposed payments accordingly and the projects commissioned, I want you to nominate an account into which this money will be paid for division between us and you.

Sharing terms are: 35% to you as the owner of the account into which the money will be paid, 55% to the officials of the three parastatals. 10% is set aside for contingencies. The big bosses of the three parastatals involved in this transaction namely: Nigerian National Petroleum Corporation (NNPC) Federal Ministry of Finance (FMF) and Central Bank of Nigeria (CBN) are aware and behind the deal.

Meanwhile, you are required to indicate your interest through my <u>FAX LINE</u> or <u>TELEX</u> or by <u>personal call</u>. Please in your reply include your personal telephone, fax and telex numbers for easy communications.

You can be rest assured that within few weeks of my receipt of your positive reply this amount will be remitted into your nominated account.

May I demand with the highest respect for the code of business morality and secrecy that under no circumstance should you circumvent or share with any uninvolved person the contents of this letter and other vital documents that may arise in the course of this noble transaction until it is accomplished.

I look forward to your pragmatic conformity to this mutual proposition.

Yours faithfully,

TOKUNBO JACOBS

The text of the letter is original. The address, phone, FAX and TELEX numbers have been disguised.

Exhibit 2 **September 12 Fax From Jacobs to Lee – 12 September 1998**

FROM: TOKUNBO JACOBS

ATTENTION: ALLEN LEE

Thanks for your fax of 9th September 1998 accepting to do this business with us. As you rightly mentioned there must be some responsibilities from your company to see this deal through. As a matter of fact you will be required to send to us some basic documents regarding your company to enable us process payment to your account.

These requirements are:

Two of your company's letter headed papers
Two of your company's proforma invoices
Bank particulars in which the said money will be transferred to:
the name of the bank, the account number, the telex number of the bank

On receipt of these above requirements the money will be remitted within twenty one working days.

Allen, I will suggest you visit us with the requirements to expedite this deal and to enable the officials involve in this transaction meet with you person to person for more confidence and to enable to meet who we are entrusting our money. Furthermore I want your personal home phone number for easy communications. Remember we will not hesitate to ask for your assistance financially if the need arises which will be duely deducted from the 10% set aside as contingencies during the process of this transaction. All request needed by you will be given proper attention.

Note: There is no risk whatsoever in this transaction putting into consideration our good home work and calibre of people involve in this deal.

Acknowledge receipt of this message through my fax number 442157.

Thanks and God bless.

TOKUNBO JACOBS

Exhibit 3   September 21 Fax From Jacobs To Lee

FAX: 21ST SEPTEMBER 1998

FROM: TOKUNBO JACOBS

ATTENTION: ALLEN LEE

Consequent to our telephone discussions, these are the required information. When you despatch those documents via DHL courier service, including your company's catalogues fax the air way bill number to me to enable me pick them up in earnest.

I want you to realize that there are some expenses which we cannot afford to ignore if this transaction <u>must</u> succeed highfreely. We will need US$48,000.00 in order to off-set these expenses. We therefore solicit you to assist us with the already set aside amount. As regards the account:

Beneficiary: Larry Olunitgo

Bank Name: National First Bank of Nigeria PLC
Broad Street, Branch Lagos
Nigeria

Account Number: 1554

Below is the format for the attorney:

The Governor of Central Bank of Nigeria
Tinubu Square Lagos

Dear Sir,

Letter of Authority

I wish to inform you that I Mr. Allen Lee, the president of Basic Software Company of

Hong Kong hereby authorize barrister Eze Bakoto to sign on my behalf for the release of the sum of US$14.3 million U.S. dollars being payment for contract completed in 1996 for N.N.P.C. This is due to my present indisposed condition.

I look forward to your anticipated co-operation.

Yours faithfully,

Allen Lee (President).

N.B.:   The about format should be typed on your company's letter-headed paper and should be included with the courier documents.

Exhibit 4   Nigerian File

1963   The establishment of the Republic of Nigeria.

1966   Military coup. The Biafran war begins, lasting two years and causing several million deaths of which approximately two million were Biafran.

1983   Military coup. Benral Buhari overturns President Shagari.

1984   Demonetization operations; bank notes are no longer in circulation and are replaced by a new currency.

1985   State coup. General Ibrahim Babangida replaces General Buhari.

1986   End of the flat exchange rate. Seventy per cent devaluation of the Naira and currency fluctuations.

1990   Unsuccessful state coup against President Babangida. 42 military shot after aborted state coup of April 22nd, 1990.

1991   Riots provoked by Shiite fundamentalists cause two hundred deaths.

1993   Civilian elections held. Results annulled by Babangida, who then steps down and gives power to an interim government.

1994   General Abacha overthrows government.Widespread strikes against regime of Abacha, who arrests union leaders.

1995   Dissident writer Sara-Wiwa hanged. International pressure on Abacha builds.

1996   National Election Commision of Nigeria names five political parties allowed to participate in future elections.

GNP per person: US$240 /1996,
   *United Nations
   Development Programs,
   The World Bank*

Educational attainment: 47%

Languages spoken: English and approximately 200 dialects

Area: 923,768 sq km

Agricultural land: 34%

Density: 117 persons/sq km

Average Annual Inflation Rate: 1990-1996 - 37.6%

Capital: Lagos - 10,000,000 inhabitants

Total External Debt: US$31,407 million

Exhibit 5   Doing Business in Nigeria

Greetings: In Nigeria, greetings are highly valued among the different ethnic groups. Refusing to greet another is a sign of disrespect. Due to the diversity of customs, cultures, and dialects that exist among the different ethnic groups in Nigeria, English is widely used in exchanging greetings throughout the country. Visitors are advised and encouraged to greet while in Nigeria. "Hello" is the most popular greeting. More formal greetings, such as "Good Morning", "Good Afternoon", and "Good Evening" are also appropriate. Avoid the use of casual or colloquial greetings and phrases such as "Hi" or "What's happening?" In addition, visitors are also encouraged to be courteous and cheerful when exchanging greetings. Do not be arrogant. Nigerians treat visitors with respect and, in return, expect to be treated with respect. Personal space between members of the same sex is much closer than in North America. This may cause discomfort to those not accustomed to conversing at close quarters.

Visiting: Nigerians try very hard to please their guests. Although Nigerians are generally not too concerned with time, they know about the western habit of punctuality and expect their western friends to arrive at the appointed time. Most Nigerians prefer "African time" to western punctuality. Nigerians treat their guests with congenial respect and expect their guests to respond in the same manner. Nigerians possess a rich heritage and hope for a bright future as a modern African nation, and thus can be offended by the "superior" attitude of some visitors.

Tipping: A dash (from the Portuguese word das, meaning "give") is a common Nigerian form of compensation in money, goods, or favours for services rendered. With the exception of services performed by waiters or bellhops, a "dash" is normally paid before the service is given. If the service offered is not desired, a firm refusal is usually necessary. The government is officially committed to discouraging certain kinds of "dash" that resemble bribery, such as payments for help in clearing customs, getting visas, or obtaining preferential treatment from government officials. But the custom is widespread and one has to be skillful in the art of "bargaining".

Personal Appearance: Dress varies according to the area and the culture. In the Muslim north, dress is very conservative for both men and women. Dress is more casual in the non-Muslim east and west. Shorts are not considered appropriate attire for Nigerian adults. For men, a shirt and tie are appropriate for formal and most other semi-formal occasions. Visitors will be most comfortable in cotton clothing — polyester is too warm. Traditional Nigerian men's dress is loose and comfortable. Although women in the cities and young girls often wear western dress, most women wear traditional long wraparound skirts, short-sleeved tops and head scarves. The fabric is renowned for its color and patterns.

Gestures: Nigeria is a multicultural nation and gestures differ from one ethnic group to another. Generally, pushing the palm of the hand forward with the fingers spread is a vulgar gesture and should be avoided. One should not point the sole of the foot at a person. Using the left hand in eating (unless left-handed) or in receiving something from someone has a bad connotation. The Yorubas (a large major ethnic group), in addition to the Ibibios and Igbos (two smaller, although major ethnic groups) will wink if they want their children to leave the room.

General Attitudes: Individual Nigerians are proud of the unique cultural heritage of their particular ethnic group. There is some ethnic tension, but continuing efforts are gradually unifying the nation. The Nigerians are striving to create a modern industrial society that is uniquely "African", and not "western". Because of negative connotations attached to the word "tribe", Nigerians avoid its use and "ethnic group" is often used in its place. Life in Nigeria moves at a relaxed pace with the exception of Lagos which can be very frenzied. People are generally not as time-conscious as in the west.

Language: English is the official language in Nigeria. However, because of the Nigerian mother tongue influence, spoken English may be difficult to understand. Pidgin English (broken English) is widely spoken by uneducated Nigerians, although even educated people widely use Pidgin English as a medium of informal conversation among themselves. Each of the over 250 ethnic groups also has its own distinct language. Hausa, Yoruba, and Ibo are widely spoken. Educated Nigerians usually are fluent in several languages.

Religion: In very general terms, Nigeria can be said to be divided between the Muslim North (47%) and the Christian South (34%), with a strong minority of traditional religions throughout the country (18%). However, it is important to note that both the Christians and the Muslims have strong missionary movements all over the whole country making the division of faiths into particular regions not exactly accurate. In addition, Nigerians may claim membership in a particular religion but may also incorporate traditional worship practices and beliefs into their daily life.

Family: Although the technical details of family structure vary from culture to culture, Nigerian families are generally male-dominated. The practice of polygamy is common throughout the country. The protected status of Muslim women in Nigeria is similar to other Muslim countries; however, most other Nigerian women enjoy a great degree of freedom by influencing family decisions and engaging in open trade at the market place, where the money they make is their own. Large families traditionally help share the workload at home. Nigerians pay deep respect to their elders. Children are trained to be quiet, respectful, and unassertive in their relations with adults. Marriage customs vary, but the payment of bridal wealth (money, property, or service traditionally given to the family of the bride by the husband) is common throughout the country.

<u>Social and Economic Levels:</u> Nigerians have the third highest average income in sub-Sahara Africa, but are still very poor by western standards. The average home consists of 1.4 rooms and more than three people per room. About 30% of the people live in absolute poverty. Nigeria once had the ninth lowest crime rate in the world, but without current statistics, it is difficult to determine the country's rank today.

<u>Business Schedules:</u> Most businesses are open from 8:00 AM to 12:30 PM, and then reopen from 2:00 to 4:30 PM. Government offices are open from 7:30 AM to 3:30 PM Monday through Friday. Many establishments and shops are also open on Saturdays with shorter hours. Every fourth Saturday is "Sanitation Day" (where no one is allowed on the street before 10:00 AM) and shops normally are not ready to receive business before noon. Sunday is the normal day of rest. Business appointments must be made in advance. Due to the poor telephone communication, business is often discussed on a person-to-person basis rather than via the telephone. Westerners are expected to be prompt, even though they may have to wait for some time after arriving.

Source: Canadian High Commission, Lagos

LIST OF COMPANY NAMES AND URLS

Company/Organization	URL for Company/Organization
ABS-CBN Foundation	www.abs-cbnfoundation.com
Acer	www.global.acer.com
Adcock Ingram	www.adcock.com.za
Airline Financial Support Services	www.airlinefinancial.com
ALi Corp.	www.ali.com.tw
Ambit	www.ambit.com.tw
American Apparel & Footwear Association	www.americanapparel.org
Andean Common Market (ANCOM)	www.comunidadandina.org
Anheuser-Busch	www.anheuser-busch.com
Arab League	www.arableagueonline.org
Asian Institute of Technology	www.ait.ac.th
Association of South East Asian Nations (ASEAN)	www.aseansec.org
AT Kearney	www.atkearney.com
Au Optronics	www.auo.com
Australia's wine industry	www.wineaustralia.com.au.
Australian College of Wine	www.nmit.vic.edu.au/acw
Avon Company	www.avon.com
Bangladesh Enterprise Institute	www.bei-bd.org
Bank of China	www.bank-of-china.com
Basel Convention	www.basel.int
Beijing Animal Production	—
Benpres Holdings Corp.	www.benpres-holdings.com
BenQ	www.benq.com
BHP Billiton	www.bhpbilliton.com
BP America Inc.	www.bp.com
BreadTalk	www.breadtalk.com
Budweiser Japan	www.budweiser.co.jp
Café de Coral Holdings	www.cafedecoral.com
Cámara Nacional De La Industria Del Vestido	www.canainvesyuc.com.mx
Cangtong Highway Co.	—
Caribbean Community and Common Market (CARICOM)	www.caricom.org
Carlsberg	www.carlsberg.com
Carrefour	www.carrefour.com

Carrefour in Dubai	www.carrefouruae.com
Carrefour in Japan	www.carrefour.co.jp
Cathay Pacific	www.cathaypacific.com
Central American Common Market (CACM)	www.sieca.org.gt
China Petroleum and Chemical Corporation (Sinopec)	www.sinopec.com.cn
Chrysler	www.chrysler.com
Chulalongkorn University	www.chula.ac.th
CITIC Pacific Ltd.	www.citicpacific.com
CNBC	www.moneycentral.msn.com
Comcast	www.comcast.com
Common Market for East and South Africa (COMESA)	www.comesa.int
Daewoo	www.daewoo.com
Daewoo Group	www.daewoo.com
Daewoo-FSO Motor	www.daewoo.com.pl/fso
Daimler	www.daimlerchrysler.com
Dairy Farm Group	www.dairyfarmgroup.com
Dana Corporation	www.dana.com
Dana's Spicer Driveshaft Group	www.spicerdriveshaft.com
Dankotuwa	www.dankotuwa.com
Dansk	www.dansk.com
DHL	www.dhl.com
Din Tai Fung	—
Dr Reddy's	www.drreddys.com
Economic Community of West African States (ECOWAS)	www.ecowas.int
Economist Intelligence Unit	www.eiu.com
Eli Lilly	www.lilly.com
Escorts Ltd.	www.escortsgroup.com
Eugenio Lopez Foundation	www.lopezmuseum.org.ph
Euromoney	www.euromoney.com
European Management Foundation	—
European Union (EU)	europa.eu.int
Executive planet website	www.executiveplanet.com/index2.jsp
Federation of Bangladesh Chamber of Commerce and Industry (FBCCI)	www.fbcci.org
Fernwood Porcelain	www.fernwoodporcelain.com
Foreign Investment and Foreign Trade Agency of Mongolia	www.investmongolia.com/index.htm
Formosa Chemicals & Fibre Corporation	www.fpcc.com.tw
Formosa Petrochemical Corporation.	—
Formosa Plastics Corporation	www.fpc.com.tw
Foster's	www.fostersbeer.com
Franklin's	www.franklins.net

Gamania	www.gamania.com
Global Commerce Initiative (GCI)	www.globalcommerceinitiative.org
Gulf Cooperation Council (GCC)	www.gcc-sg.org
Haier Group	www.haier.com
Haier Middle East Trading Co.	www.haiermideast.com
Haier – European Division	www.haiereurope.com
Harvey Norman	www.harveynorman.com.au
Headway Technologies	www.hdwy.com
Heineken Japan	www.heinekencorp.com
Hewitt Associates	www.hewittasia.com
Hewlett Packard	www.hp.com
Honda Motor Company	www.hondacorporate.com
Hong Kong Exporters' Association	www.exporters.org.hk
Hutchison Whampoa Ltd.	www.hutchison-whampoa.com
Hyundai	www.hyundai.com
IMD	www.imd.ch
Infosys	www.infosys.com
Infosys	www.infosys.com
International Labor Organization (ILO)	www.ilo.org
International Monetary Fund	www.imf.org
International Programme on the Elimination of Child Labour (IPEC)	www.ilo.org/childlabour
Japan Intercultural Consulting (JIC)	—
Jardine Matheson Ltd.	www.jardine.com
KFC	www.kfc.com
Kirin Breweries	www.kirin.com
Kobe Steel Ltd.	www.kobelco.co.jp
Kose	www.kose.com.jp
L'Oreal	www.loreal.com
Lanka Tile	www.lankatile.com
Lanka Wall	www.lankawall.com
Levi Strauss and Co.	www.levistrauss.com
LG (Lucky Goldstar)	www.lg.co.kr
LG Chemicals & Energy	www.lgchem.com
LG Electronics & Telecommunications	www.lge.com
LG Finance	www.iflgkorea.com
LG Services	www.lgicorp.com
Li & Fung	www.lifung.com
Lik Sang International Limited	www.lik-sang.com
Matsushita Electric Industries	www.mei.co.jp
McDonald's	www.mcdonalds.com
MIC Capital	www.miccapital.com

Ministry of Science, Technology and Environment of Vietnam	www.vista.gov.vn
Mitsubishi	www.mitsubishi.com
Mitsubishi Corporation	www.mitsubishicorp.com
Mitsubishi Motors	www.mitsubishi-motors.com
Mitsubishi Motors Australia, Ltd.	www.mitsubishi-motors.com.au
Mitsui & Co.	www.mitsui.co.jp
Mitsui Toatsu Chemicals Inc.	www.mitsui-chem.co.jp
MMC Sittipol Co. Ltd.	www.mitsubishi-motors.co.th
Monash University	www.buseco.monash.edu.au/units/Wine
Mongolian government	www.pmis.gov.mn/indexeng.php
MOS Food Services Inc.	www.mos.co.jp
Nan Ya Plastics Corporation	www.npc.com.tw
National Pharmaceutical Pricing Authority of India	nppaindia.nic.in/index1.html
NBC	www.nbc.com
NC Taiwan	www.nctaiwan.com
NCsoft	www.ncsoft.net
Neutrogena	www.neutrogena.com
New Asia Group	www.newasia.sh.cn
New Eastern Corp.	—
New World Development	www.nwd.com.hk
New Zealand wine industry	www.nzwine.com
Ngoc Linh	—
Nike	www.nike.com
Nintendo	www.nintendo.com
Nivea	www.nivea.com
North America Free Trade Agreement (NAFTA)	www.nafta-sec-alena.org
Organization of Arab Petroleum Exporting Countries (OAPEC)	www.oapecorg.org
Organization of the Petroleum Exporting Countries (OPEC)	www.oapecorg.org
Pacific Century CyberWorks Limited (PCCW)	www.pccw.com
Petro-CyberWorks Information Technology Company Limited (PCITC)	www.pcitc.com
Popular Holdings	www.popular.com.sg
Pro-Tec Coating Co.	—
PT Putra Staba Industrial	—
Ralph Lauren	www.rlhome.polo.com
Ranbaxy	www.ranbaxy.com
Samsung	www.samsung.com
Samsung Corning	www.samsungcorning.com
Samsung Electro-Mechanics	www.sem.samsung.com
Samsung Networks	www.samsungnetworks.com
Satyam	www.satyam.com

Schein Pharmaceutical	www.schien-rx.com
Seagrams	www.seagramscoolers.com
Shanghai Mitsui Plastics Compounds Ltd.	—
Shanghai New Asia Snack Co. (SNAS)	—
Shell	www.shell.com
Shop N Save	www.shopnsave.com.sg
SK Group	www.sk.com
Sony	www.sony.com
Sony America's Video Audio Integrated Operations (VAIO)	www.vaio.net
Southern African Development Community (SADC)	www.sadc.int
Southern Common Market (MERCOSUR)	www.mercosur.org.uy
Spanish division of Haier	www.haierspain.com
Spicer Axle ZPZP	www.spicerdriveshaft.com
Sri Lanka Apparel Exporters Association	www.srilanka-apparel.com
Sri Lankan Ceramics Industry	www.ceramics.lk
Sumitomo Corp.	www.sumitomocorp.co.jp
Swire Pacific	www.swirepacific.com
Tabcorp Holdings Ltd.	www.tabcorp.com
Tae Kwany Vina Industrial Co.	
Tata Consultancy Services	www.tcs.com
Tata Group	www.tata.com
TDK Corporation	www.tdk.co.jp
TDK Group	www.tdk.com
Thailand Ministry of Education	www.moe.go.th/English
The Gap	www.gap.com
Toray Industries	www.toray.co.jp
Trade Union Congress of the Philippines	www.tucp.org.ph
Transparency International	www.transparency.org
Tsingtao	www.tsingtaobeer.com
Uniform Code Council (UCC)	www.uc-council.org
United Nations Conference on Trade and Development (UNCTAD)	www.unctad.org
United States Steel Corp.	www.usx.com
Unocal	www.unocal.com
US division of Haier	www.haieramerica.com
US-based Dow Corning	www.dowcorning.com
Vietnamese Chamber of Commerce and Industry (VCCI)	www.vcci.com.vn
Vinataba	www.vinataba.com.vn
Voltas Ltd ACnR	www.voltasacnr.com
Voltas Ltd.	www.voltas.com
Wacker-Chemie	www.wacker.com
Wal-Mart	www.walmart.com

Wine MBA	www.winemba.com
Wistron	www.wistron.com
Woolworth	www.woolworth.de
World Bank	www.worldbank.org
World Economic Forum	www.weforum.org
World Trade Organization (WTO)	www.wto.org
Yamaha	www.yamaha.com

INDEX